THE
ENCYCLOPEDIA
OF
TALMUDIC
SAGES

THE ENCYCLOPEDIA OF TALMUDIC SAGES

Gershom Bader

translated
by Solomon Katz

Jason Aronson Inc.
Northvale, N.J.
London

First Jason Aronson Inc. softcover edition—1993

Copyright © 1988 by Jason Aronson Inc.

10 9 8 7 6 5 4 3 2

Library of Congress Cataloging-in-Publication Data

Bader, Gershom, 1868-1953.
   The encyclopedia of Talmudic sages.
   Translation of: Unzere gaystige riezen.

   Includes index.
   ISBN 0-87668-903-9 (hardcover)
   ISBN 1-56821-036-1 (softcover)
   1. Talmud—Biography. 2. Rabbis—Biography.
I. Title.
BM501.15.B3313 1988
296.1'2'00922

                                                                 87-33465

Manufactured in the United States of America. Jason Aronson Inc. offers books and cassettes. For information and catalog write to Jason Aronson Inc., 230 Livingston Street, Northvale, New Jersey 07647.

Contents

Foreword   ix

Part I Mishnah

1   Introduction   3
2   The Three Main Parties of the Talmudic
      Period   21
3   The Samaritans   34
4   Simon the Just   42
5   Antigonos of Socho   49
6   Jose ben Joezer and Jose ben Jochanan   53
7   Jochanan the High Priest   59
8   Joshua ben Perachiah and Nittai of Arbela   68
9   Jehudah ben Tabbai and Simeon ben
      Shetach   72
10   Shemaiah and Abtalion   79
11   The Men of Bathyra   85

12	Choni the Circle Drawer	89
13	Hillel	94
14	Shammai—Hillel's Colleague	107
15	Akabia ben Mahalalel	116
16	Rabban Gamaliel the Elder	121
17	Rabban Simeon ben Gamaliel	127
18	Rabbi Chanina, Deputy to the High Priest, and His Contemporaries	133
19	The Time of the Destruction of the Temple	138
20	Rabban Jochanan ben Zakkai	152
21	The Colleagues of Rabban Jochanan ben Zakkai	164
22	Rabbi Chanina ben Dosa	175
23	Rabban Gamaliel II of Jabneh	182
24	Rabbi Eliezer ben Hyrcanus	193
25	Rabbi Joshua ben Chananiah	205
26	Rabbi Eliezer of Modiin	217
27	Onkelos (Aquilas) the Proselyte	222
28	Rabbi Eleazar ben Azariah	228
29	Rabbi Ishmael ben Elisha	236
30	Rabbi Tarphon	246
31	Rabbi Jose of Galilee	251
32	Rabbi Akiba ben Joseph	257
33	The Ten Martyrs	280
34	Simeon ben Azai and Simeon ben Zoma	295
35	Elisha ben Avuyah—"Acher"	303
36	Rabban Simeon ben Gamaliel II	311
37	Rabbi Nathan of Babylonia	320
38	Rabbi Meir	328
39	Rabbi Jehudah bar Elai	341
40	Rabbi Jose ben Chalafta	347
41	Rabbi Simeon ben Yochai	352
42	Rabbi Eleazar ben Shamua and Rabbi Jochanan the Sandalmaker	362

43   Rabbi Nehemiah and Other Disciples of
        Rabbi Akiba   367
44   Rabbi Jehudah Hanasi   371
45   Contemporaries of Rabbi Jehudah Hanasi   394
46   Rabbi Chiya Rabbah bar Abba   404
47   Rabbi Simeon ben Chalafta   409
48   Levi ben Sisi   414

Part II   Jerusalem Talmud

49   Introduction   421
50   Life in Palestine During the Creation of the
        Jerusalem Talmud   430
51   Rabbi Jehudah N'siah I and His Successors   452
52   The Aggadah and Its Authors   469
53   Rabbi Jochanan, Compiler of the
        Jerusalem Talmud   481
54   Rabbi Simeon ben Lakish   499
55   Jehudah and Hezekiah, the Sons of Rabbi
        Chiya   510
56   Rabbi Jannai Rabbah   514
57   Rabbi Jonathan ben Eleazar   519
58   Rabbi Oshaiah Rabbah   524
59   Rabbi Chanina bar Chama   528
60   Rabbi Joshua ben Levi   535
61   Rabbi Shmuel bar Nachmani   546
62   Rabbi Simlai bar Abba   554
63   Rabbi Eleazar ben Pedat   559
64   Rabbi Avahu of Caesarea   566
65   Rabbi Chiya bar Abba Hacohen   574
66   Rabbi Ami and Rabbi Asi   578
67   Rabbi Yitzchak the Blacksmith   586
68   Rabbi Abba Kahana and Rabbi Chanina bar
        Papa   592
69   Rabbi Zeira   597

Part III Babylonian Talmud

70	Introduction	607
71	Rav, Abba Arecha	626
72	Shmuel Yarchina'ah of Nehardea	669
73	Mar Ukba the Exilarch	679
74	Rabbah bar Avuha	684
75	Rav Nachman bar Jacob	688
76	Rav Huna, Head of the Academy in Sura	694
77	Rav Chisda the Priest	700
78	Rav Jehudah bar Ezekiel	707
79	Rabbah bar Nachmani	715
80	Rav Joseph bar Chiya	722
81	Rabbah bar Rav Huna	725
82	Abayei bar Chailil	727
83	Rava bar Joseph bar Chama	734
84	Rav Nachman bar Isaac	740
85	Rav Papa	743
86	Rav Huna, the Son of Rav Joshua	746
87	Rav Chama of Nehardea	748
88	Rav Sheshet	752
89	Rav Ashi, Compiler of the Babylonian Talmud	757
90	Tavyomi Mar bar Rav Ashi	766
91	Ravina, the Final Compiler of the Babylonian Talmud	771
	Notes	775
	Index	847

Foreword

Great ideas may at times be deceptive. Swept away by eloquence and the sublimity of words, a student of intellectual history may make a leap into higher worlds of thought, secure and at peace in his or her own mind.

And yet, a gap often appears: There can be a jolting of sensibilities. As one reads the biographies of the great thinkers, one may be struck by a dissonance; the *lives* of the creators of ideas may not live up to the *ideas* they put forth. Indeed, I have often wondered why in university lecture halls ideas are given higher priority than the biographies of the idea-makers of philosophy, theology, psychology, mathematics, history, or economics.

I would say that, for a Jew, this is an uncomfortable posture, and it *should be* an uncomfortable one. Judaism strives to teach people how to *live* life decently and fairly, as a *mensch*, kind, compassionate, generous, dealing with others with a sense of justice and caring. Consequently, if the expounder of "The Great Idea" does not live up to that "Great Idea," we ought to be ill at ease and confused as to why human beings can achieve so much with the mind and fall so short in acting on those thoughts. That is why so many people admire such figures as Albert Einstein, Golda Meir, and Henrietta Szold. Einstein, acknowledged as the greatest physicist of modern times, was also a pursuer of peace and a lover of Zion. Realizing that his work in the world of science could have catastrophic consequences in an emerging nuclear age, he advocated extreme caution when dealing with the atom, urging humankind to use his insights not to obliterate civilization, but rather to create a better world for all. Golda Meir, builder of Israel *par excellence,* committed her life to bringing the dream of Israel into reality. And Henrietta Szold, while not setting out to change the face of medical care in the Middle East, in fact did so, living out her compassion and greatness of soul in the Holy Land. They all had great visions and pursued those visions with a vigor and forcefulness that were of heroic proportions.

This book expands our visions of the heroic and heroes. Gershom Bader offers to the English reader the lives of many of the heroes of the most fruitful intellectual seven centuries in Jewish history—the centuries of the Talmud, from around 200 B.C.E. to 500 C.E. The Talmud and the related texts of that period, the *midrashim,* present the ideas and lives of literally hundreds of people who pursued wisdom, always asking: How exactly does a Jew live life fully in the image of God, using the precious moments on earth to build a society based on justice, concern for others, and decency? The human mind and the development of human knowledge were servants to wisdom, to seeking out insights that would bring people to this glorious goal.

And that is why it is important to draw a distinction here between the terms *scholar* and *sage. Scholar,* which connotes someone well versed in a field of intellectual endeavor, a person who has mastered certain ideas and texts, carries no moral overtones. *Sage,* on the other hand, implies a person who has acquired wisdom (based on knowledge) and, in the Talmud's case, a certain kind of wisdom: Torah-wisdom, a wisdom that leads people to live a life of *mitzvot* and *menschlichkeit,* the life of the "fully human being." The people in Bader's book are sages. True, they are scholars; but beyond that, they are seekers of a unique wisdom, the Torah-wisdom already described.

For approximately seven hundred years, these scholar-sages spent long hours, days, months, years, in the Torah schools of Palestine and Babylonia, raising issues and working out a set of values that would represent the best that Judaism could offer. They grappled with such questions as: How does one treat the elderly? Why is stealing such a societally destructive crime? May a person open a shop down the block from an identical one, if it might possibly destroy the competition's livelihood? How does one raise a child to be fully conscious of his or her responsibilities to other individuals and to society at large?

These heroes of the Talmud labored at their task with love, digging into the Torah, learning it by heart, comparing and contrasting passages, expanding the words of the Holy Text to include contemporary issues. The fruits of their labor helped people to live under a foreign government, to retain integrity and Jewishness in the most oppressive time. We *know* from Elie Wiesel and others that, even in the death camps of the Nazi regime, people still studied Torah, so great was the influence of these talmudic heroes of centuries ago. The Bible, which was the primary text of the talmudic sages, was expanded over the talmudic centuries and became the Babylonian Talmud (twenty volumes with commentaries), the Jerusalem Talmud (seven volumes with commentaries), and perhaps forty or fifty miscellaneous texts in the various books of *midrash.*

What Gershom Bader has done is to concentrate his vision on the lives and thoughts of a number of these specific individuals. Trained in European yeshivas, he was eminently equipped to categorize and organize this material, to present a compendium that would not only fascinate us, but also move us to admire these sages and to change our lives to be more like theirs.

And yet, this still does not capture the importance of Bader's work. His book is, after all, a study of the *lives* of the talmudic rabbis (and some non-rabbis), more so than a study of their *thoughts.* We see how the talmudic sages lived their own lives in relation to their words and ideas. The sages were not perfect. On the contrary, what strikes the student of Talmud is that they were very human, neither separate nor distant from the common people of the Jewish congregation of those days. They did not live isolated from the people, and some, in fact, earned their livings in the most menial ways: as woodcutters, blacksmiths, peddlers. They knew the strains and tensions of everyday life and the realities of raising a family, making a living, being fair in business disputes, as well as the larger issues of relating to the Roman government, or bringing the people to spiritual and physical recovery after the destruction of the Temple in 70 C.E. and the crushing of the Bar Kochba revolt a mere sixty-five years later.

When we study *The Encyclopedia of Talmudic Sages*, we should seek out not only the sages' lofty ideals and spiritual principles, their aspirations to have people be good creations of the Almighty and decent human beings. We should also examine how the talmudic masters embodied these same high principles in their daily living. *Were* they the same human beings they said human beings *ought to be?* And if they did not measure up fully to that image, did they then endeavor throughout their lives to reach that goal of humanity and *menschlichkeit?*

In the late twentieth century, media-soaked as people are, many of us have no heroes. Others choose heroes from the world of politics, sports, pop music, wealth, only because these "heroes" are famous. It would do well for all of us to focus on Bader's study, turning its pages again and again, in order to find other kinds of heroes, admirable people with whom we can identify and to whom we can cling in our minds and deeds. By studying this volume, we can add depth and breadth, warmth and wisdom to our own days and years as we strive to achieve meaning as individuals and members of the larger society, participants in the flow of Jewish history.

Danny Siegel

PART I

MISHNAH

1

INTRODUCTION

THE HISTORY OF A PEOPLE is primarily constructed out of the biographies of those individuals whose activities characterize the specific nature of the progress and development of the national forces, both internal and external.

No prominent person can be entirely detached from his environment. It makes little difference whether such a person influenced the environment in which he lived or whether his individuality was conditioned by it, for this type of influence is mutual and complementary. Just as the individual presents a picture of his environment in miniature, an environment presents a composite photograph of its component individual parts.

Every person develops in a different manner; neither does this development follow an unbroken path from beginning to end. On the contrary, life follows some very devious ways, and the chronicler must find a suitable approach for each complex historical situation in order not to go astray.

"World history is the history of heroes" is the claim of a German philosopher. This rule also applies to Jewish history, with this difference: our heroes are generally "spiritual heroes," master navigators of the deep and stormy literary sea, and commanders on the battlefields of the Torah.

Especially heroic were the struggles of our spiritual heroes at the time we lost our political independence and were becoming accustomed to the role of a wandering people that is forced to live in a foreign environment but that still insists on retaining its own mode of life.

World history is motivated by an eternal force that flows in an endless labyrinth of channels and is given form and direction by the leading spirits of each generation. It is therefore necessary, first of all, to observe the ways of the leading spirits rather than the events that transpire.

The historical development of a people contains no accidents. Every event has its cause and reason, which are results of previous events. It is therefore important to bear in mind that a matter-of-fact relation of events is not as significant as the understanding of the spirit and the logical necessity of such an event. We must also remember that ever since we lost our homeland, the spirit of our people has found its expression in ideas and theories.

The Talmud in the form that it was taught in Babylonia (and therefore called the Babylonian Talmud) as well as in the form in which it was expounded in Palestine (and therefore called the Jerusalem Talmud), is recognized as the exclusive creation of the Jewish spirit to which the Gentile world can lay no claim.

As far as the Bible is concerned, Jews are confronted with various accusations. The enemies of Jewry find it undignified to admit that the Jews are the creators of the greatest spiritual treasure that the civilized world possesses. Therefore, they claim that the Bible is not specifically Jewish. The liberal legislation of the Pentateuch and the noble ideals of the prophets, they say, have been borrowed from neighboring peoples. When they do recognize the greatness of the Bible, they give equal credit to other peoples.

The style of the Bible is today the possession of all civilized peoples and has become a fructifying element in every language; but the Talmud cannot be taken away from us and the honor of being the creators of this great work will remain with us forever.

Seven centuries passed from the time of Simon the Just, the last of the members of the Great Synagogue or Great Assembly, when the oral law became popular among the masses of the people until the conclusion of the Talmud. On the foundations of the Torah there was erected an imposing structure—an eternal monument to Jewish spirit as it developed in those seven centuries. This development began immediately after the conclusion of the Bible, when the Jews lived on the soil of Palestine for the second time and continued even in Babylonia, where they sought refuge and found freedom and happiness for many years. It lasted in Babylonia until they had to flee the sword.

Seven centuries is a long time in the life of any nation, even in the life of such an old nation as the Jewish one. For no matter how conservative our historical evaluation, it would be impossible to assume that no changes occurred during seven centuries. As among other nations, so also among the Jews there appeared new ideas and new concepts during these centuries. In the course of the years, these new ideas developed and spread, only to disappear later on and to be supplanted by others. This is especially true when we consider that we are dealing with a time when the political conditions of the nation changed radically. At times the Jews lived freely in their own land, and at other times they were involved in wars; at times they were exiled from their own country, and at other times they prospered in other lands.

It may also be stated with certainty that in all Jewish history there never was a period so characterized by unusual events as were the seven centuries during which the Talmud was created. The sources of information concerning that period are very meager, and every historian must fall back on his imagination in order to complete the picture that was handed down to us.

If one wants to establish the facts concerning events that took place at that time from the information contained in

Talmudic literature, he must bear in mind that these books were not written with the aim of presenting history. The compilers were, therefore, not careful to present exact dates or precise information regarding the people of whom they wrote. History is generally embellished with many legends, and even the personalities of the heroes are not definite.

For our purpose, the event that occurred may be of paramount importance, but the authors stressed a personality; in other cases, we may be interested in a personality whereas they stressed the event. It is also necessary to remember that the original text of the books regarding historic events and names of persons was not strictly adhered to. Therefore, there exist in the Talmud numerous versions of a tale pertaining to people and events. Thus, we read a story regarding a certain Talmudic personality, but another version of it may vary by one word and change the sense of the event to have involved another person or to have occurred in a different manner.

Such variations could easily creep into the Talmud when the copyists made an error in transcribing a name or when they sought to shorten their work and employed abbreviations that can be interpreted in numerous ways. These errors are not important in establishing a law. It makes but little difference if the name of the person who rendered the deciding opinion regarding a law was misspelled. But where we are concerned with establishing historical facts, such errors are very confusing.

The basis for the Talmud was provided by the *sofrim*. These were the copyists of the Torah who were at the same time teachers explaining the sayings of the Torah to the people. The original text of many laws was not very clear and could not be understood unless they were interpreted. But the interpretations of the *sofrim* became accepted, and on the foundation of their explanations there grew an organization of seers and elders that came to be called The Men of the Great Synagogue.

The Great Synagogue acted as a Supreme Court in deciding all religious matters, and it was presided over by the High Priest. The Great Synagogue began in the time of the last prophets (Haggai, Zachariah, Malachi) when the people, under

the leadership of Ezra and Nehemiah, signed a written covenant to observe the laws of Judaism. It ended with Simon the
Just.

At first it was prohibited to put the interpretations of the
sofrim in writing, and they were transmitted orally. Later it
became obvious that they would be forgotten, and so the
Scribes began to write down all the traditional interpretations
to the commandments of the Torah. These interpretations were
considered laws that God orally conveyed to Moses from
Mount Sinai. But before this was done, the Bible was canonized
in twenty-four books so that no one should try to add any of
the traditional interpretations to its text.

Even today it is difficult to establish with certainty the time
of the duration of the Great Synagogue. Of the history of the
Second Temple we lack the chronicles of the events of a period
covering about 200 years (from the time of Alexander the Great
until the reign of Antiochus). All we know is that it was a time
of turbulent political changes and that control of Palestine
changed hands several times. It is believed that these were the
years of the Great Synagogue.

Ezra the Cohen and Scribe was the greatest scholar of the
Torah at that time. When he observed that the Jews did not
faithfully follow the commandments, he tore his clothes, gave
himself over to fasting, and grew melancholy. Later there
arrived Nehemiah ben Chachaliah, the cup bearer of
Artaxerxes, and together they introduced regulations which
later became laws. Their first move was to nullify all mixed
marriages and to expel the non-Jewish wives together with
their children. They were strict in preserving the purity of the
race in spite of the fact that the richest and most prominent
Jews, not excluding the family of the High Priest, had intermarried with non-Jews.

The main achievement of the Great Synagogue was in
purifying the Jewish faith from imitation of other peoples'
customs, which the Jews at that time freely copied. In order to
prevent a return to idol worship, as had occurred in the time of
the First Temple, the Great Synagogue prohibited the erection
of altars for offering sacrifices outside of Jerusalem. Instead

they established prayers by means of which a person could praise his Creator in a few heart-felt words without having to resort to the blood of a sacrificed animal to attain nearness to God. The Talmud indirectly refers to this achievement when it states that the Great Synagogue killed the "Tempter" of idol worship. Of equal importance were the regulations of the Great Synagogue regarding interfamily marriages of which the Talmud says that "they captured the 'Tempter' of love and blinded his eyes."[1]

In addition the Great Synagogue established the correct form of every word in the Bible. They introduced the custom of having all the inhabitants of the villages surrounding Jerusalem meet every Monday and Thursday to hear the reading of a chapter of the Torah. In Jerusalem itself the whole weekly portion was read every Saturday. They established a new calendar so that the count of years should begin with *Tishri* instead of *Nisan,* and that the day of the blowing of the ram's horn, the first day of *Tishri,* should be the New Year.

Many of the old institutions of the Temple were dispensed with. Thus no *Cherubim* were made for the second Temple because when Nebuchadnezzar's soldiers destroyed the first Temple they carried out the *Cherubim* and exhibited them as the Jewish God. The Jubilee was also done away with; since it was prohibited to hold Jewish slaves it was no longer necessary to observe a Jubilee to free such slaves. The *urim* and *tummim* were also done away with, although the High Priest retained all of the other vestments.

The Great Synagogue also appointed judges in all places where Jews resided so that everyone could find justice according to the laws of the Torah. They determined the content of *tefillin* and *mezuzot* on the door posts and tightened all prohibitions, even forbidding many things that were previously permitted. This was done to prevent laxity in the observance of all prohibitions. The commandment of the Torah "an eye for an eye" they interpreted to mean that monetary compensation should be granted to the victim for the damage caused him instead of the literal meaning that is implied in Leviticus 24: 2.

The necessity for preserving the oral law from getting lost

was especially keenly felt about the interpretations of the commandments. When sacrifices were done away with and prayers took their place, it was necessary to codify the laws pertaining to prayers as well as to elucidate those laws which were not clearly explained in the Torah. In addition there was the constant change in the concepts of the people going on over a period of seven centuries. When the Jews returned to Palestine from the Babylonian exile they were primarily tillers of the soil and shepherds. Later there arose a class of wage workers, merchants, and artisans. This necessitated new interpretations of the laws to conform with the development of the times.

Out of all these interpretations there developed a wide literature whose content is the pride of the Jewish nation. This includes sixty tractates of the Talmud in two different texts as well as *Tosefta, Safra, Sifri, Mekhilta* together with hundreds of various *midrashim*.

This whole literature is divided into *halakhah* and *aggadah*. The *halakhah* includes the injunctions of the law. The *aggadah*, on the other hand, introduces a living spirit into the dry legal commandments; it enriches the law with poetic softness and lends to it characteristic beauty. The *halakhah* teaches how to observe the Sabbath and the feast days, how to make a *Sukkah*, and what four kinds of plants are to be used on *Sukkot*. The *aggadah* explains the spiritual value of the Sabbath as well as the significance of the other feast days and their attendant customs. Both the *halakhah* and the *aggadah* are basic foundations of the oral law and are of equal worth to the development of Judaism.

Concerning the *aggadah* it is also worth remarking that it is of special significance for another reason. It deals continually with the concepts of justice even as it is concerned with the attributes of godliness. It relates many historical events, and cites scientific and medical knowledge as well as proverbs and axiomatic truths of life that accumulated among the Jews in the course of those seven centuries.

In the *halakhah* we find those religious injunctions that a Jew must follow, as well as the code of just relationships between man and man. These two types of law the Talmud refers to as prohibitions and laws. The expounders of these two types of law are divided into two classes. One carries greater authority in religious matters and the other in matters pertaining to human relationship.

The scholars endeavored to define the boundaries of the "fence around the Torah," which the members of the Great Synagogue ordered to be erected insofar as this pertained to the religious regulations. But some of these limitations were considered too extreme by the later scholars, and the *tannaim* who created the *Mishnah* ruled that "whoever attempts to interpret a law more severely than is accepted must prove his source of authority."[2] Afterward it was said that "anyone who attempts to abide by the restrictions of the school of Shammai and the school of Hillel is like a foolish man who walks in the darkness"[3] and Rabbi Chiya warned against attaching more importance to the "fence around the Torah" than to the essence of the Torah itself.[4]

It was for this reason that the scholars objected to having the people assume obligations to perform deeds that the law did not impose upon them, and they said that whoever does something that is not made obligatory by law may be called a simpleton.[5] One of the *amoraim* expressed this attitude in the following words: "Are there not enough prohibitions in the Torah already that one should seek to establish still other prohibitions?"[6] Although some of the scholars were strict in the enforcement of certain rabbinical commandments, even stricter than in their interpretations of the commandments of the Torah,[7] the general tendency was nevertheless to lighten the burden of the observance of the laws.

This "fence around the Torah," which the scholars erected, was very timely because the masses of the people were not acquainted with the precepts of the law. From these preventive measures there later developed numerous and various laws as, for instance, the restrictions pertaining to regulations concerning marriage, of which it was said that they are like a garden watchman—if a man watches his garden from the outside he protects it completely.

Very much concerned with the sanctity of morals and the purity of people's lives, the scholars ruled that a man might not remain alone with a strange woman in an unfrequented place. However, there are indications that this prohibition is derived from a much earlier period.[8] In addition to the prohibitions of adultery which are listed in the Torah (Leviticus 18), the scholars also prohibited marriage between twenty-six different degrees of relatives.[9]

Since the Sabbath was not properly observed in previous generations until the days of Ezra and Nehemiah, the people were warned to observe this day and to sanctify it by means of the restriction of its regulations in order to avoid false interpretations as to what may be done on that day and to prevent people from performing work that is not allowed. At this time the exact meaning of the word *melakhah* (*work*) was defined in order that everyone should know what work is permissible on the Sabbath. The scholars enumerated thirty-nine major types of work which are forbidden on the Sabbath and the performance of which is punishable by death or by flogging. Among these are the following: sowing, plowing, reaping, hauling grain from the field, threshing, baking and cooking, lighting or putting out a fire, hunting, slaughtering, cultivating fields, writing and erasing, building and wrecking, sewing and tearing, carrying objects from a house to the street and vice versa.[10]

In addition to these occupations they forbade many other activities, that do not properly speaking constitute work, but that introduce a weekday atmosphere such as, climbing a tree, riding on an animal, swimming, judging, buying and selling, getting married and similar pursuits. All of these activities may not be performed on the Sabbath in order to insure complete rest and are also forbidden on feast days.[11]

Out of concern for the sanctity of the Sabbath, the scholars prohibited the carrying into the street of such objects as are used in the performance of weekday labor. In order to safeguard the Sabbath, they ruled that it is to be observed from sunset on Friday until the stars appear on Saturday. At the same time they introduced the custom of pronouncing the *Kiddush* (sanctification) and *Havdalah* (separation) over a glass of wine at the beginning and at the departure of the Sabbath.[12]

There also was appointed a man who was to give the signal with a *shofar* (ram's horn) for everyone to stop working. The first blowing of the shofar was a signal to the laborers in the fields to cease working; the second blast of the shofar was a signal to the merchants and artisans in the city to put away their work; the third blast was a signal to stop all work in one's house. The shofar was blown once more as a sign that the Sabbath had begun.[13]

Particular effort was exerted by the scholars to remove the disabilities and difficulties that surrounded deserted wives. This need was very keenly felt at that time due to the fact that many men had to leave their homes in search of a livelihood. The highways were then unsafe, and many of these men lost their lives or were captured and sold as slaves after which they were never heard of again and the status of their wives remained indefinite.[14] Similarly, an attempt was made to facilitate the procedure of buying land in Palestine from non-Jews. It was ruled that such a bill of sale might be drawn up even on the Sabbath. In the Talmud we find a query in this matter: "How can one write such a contract on Saturday? How would that be possible?" The answer given to this question was that it is permissible to have such a contract drawn up on the Sabbath by a non-Jew, while other activities may not be performed on the Sabbath even through the agency of a non-Jew.[15]

It was also accepted as a rule that just as it is forbidden to declare the impure to be pure even so it is forbidden to declare the pure to be impure.[16] Rabbi Nechunia ben Hakanah therefore constantly prayed to be preserved from declaring the pure to be impure, and the impure to be pure[17] and whenever the scholars prohibited certain actions to be performed or pleasures to be enjoyed, they carefully determined beforehand whether the people could abide by these restrictions.[18] It is therefore interesting to note that they applied the rule of the "greater power of leniency" only in religious questions. Only in such questions did the school of Hillel decide in favor of leniency and the law remained according to the decisions of the school of Hillel.[19]

But their attitude was different whenever the law involved relations between people. In such a case our scholars studied the problem in all its implications and always considered it on its own merits in an attempt to avoid the severity of the rule that claimed that "the law must penetrate mountains." They believed that Jerusalem was destroyed because its people insisted on enforcing the letter of the law and did not practice mercy outside of the law.[20]

The scholars therefore maintained that the aim of the Torah was not to impose stringent legislation but to encourage the practice of kindness among people. They said that whenever a man aids his neighbor with money or by means of other good deeds, but he does so only out of a feeling of duty, then such deeds are not acceptable to God because they lack love and generosity.[21] Similarly, they believed that even the study of the Torah is worthless when it is not accompanied by kindness to other people.[22]

Harmony between husband and wife they held to be the very foundation of family life and they said: "Whoever loves his wife even as he loves himself and respects her more than he respects himself and leads his children in the proper ways and loves his neighbors and welcomes his relatives, such a man fulfills the wishes of God."[23] The scholars also instructed that man should not be partial in his love for his children and should show no favoritism in the division of the inheritance even in order to compensate a good son at the expense of a wicked one.[24]

As an example of the fear of God, the scholars extolled Job and they cited Abraham as an example of the love of God. Both of these were ready to overlook their own comfort and dignity in order to be of use to others. Therefore, a man must permit himself to be insulted rather than to insult others; if a man is slandered he should not reply in kind; he must fulfill the commandments out of love and he should rejoice in his suffering.[25] Similarly a man must permit himself to be persecuted without persecuting others.[26]

In addition to the above virtues, the Talmud defined the ideal person as a scholar, *talmid hakham*, who strives only for the Torah and whose innermost wish is to attain a high degree of morality in his relations with God and man. But who is to be considered a *talmid hakham*? The Talmud says that a *talmid hakham* is a person who can answer a question of law whenever he is asked. Others maintain that a *talmid hakham* is one who disregards his own interests and devotes himself to godly matters solely.[27]

Such *talmidei hakhamim* (scholars) must always endeavor to set an example for others with their behavior as well as by their exterior appearance. A scholar must not allow his clothes to be soiled and must keep himself as attractive as a girl.[28] He must also maintain better manners than others while eating, sitting down, standing up, and walking about the street.[29]

Various commandments of the Torah were observed by Jews even before the Torah was handed down. After they received the Torah it was only necessary to define and to strengthen these long since accepted commandments. When the Talmud states that Abraham observed all the commandments including *Eruv Tavshilin*,[30] it expresses a profound idea that most of the laws which the scholars read into the Torah were operative among Jews for a long time preceding the giving of the Torah.

It is not necessary here to describe what *tefillin* (phylacteries) are. But it is interesting to note that the Mishnah makes no mention of the laws pertaining to phylacteries, nor of their appearance and how they should be made. Likewise it makes no mention of the benedictions that have to be pronounced over the phylacteries. It is therefore safe to assume that all of these laws were well known during the time that the Mishnah was created. But later scholars feared that the laws and customs pertaining to phylacteries might be forgotten and they therefore had them written down.

The phylacteries contain four passages of the Bible that refer to the deliverance from Egypt, and mention is also made of the injunction that "these words shall be a sign upon your arm and a decoration between the eyes." For the concept of decoration, the text employs the Hebrew word *totafot*. The scholars tried to explain this word to prove that phylacteries must contain four passages. Using the fact that the word *totafot*, which appears three times, is written once in abbreviated form without the letter *vav* and twice with the letter *vav* they tried to conclude from this that all four passages must be included in the phylacteries. At a later date Rabbi Akiba, who always forced the texts to prove his contentions, tried to deduce the same conclusion in a different manner. He explained the word *totafot* to mean four on the basis of two ancient tongues.[31]

The word *totafot* is also mentioned once in the Mishnah and is meant to be a forehead piece. Interpreters declare it to be a decoration worn instead of phylacteries. In the Talmud the word *totafot* is used once and is synonymous with phylacteries.[32]

Long before the Torah was handed down it was the accepted custom among all nations that priests, as well as all other people who deal with religious matters, should wear religious emblems to distinguish them as men who are devoted to godly service. In later years, this custom of distinguishing between people according to their office was also transferred to social and political life. Leaders of the army and officials thus carried special insignia to mark them as servants of the government. In similar manner Jews adopted phylacteries to symbolize that their bearers are in the service of God.

It is therefore essential to know that even though the commandment to wear phylacteries is not expressly stated in the Torah and is only sanctioned by tradition, and despite the fact that it is possible to interpret the word *totafot* differently, there is nevertheless not the slightest doubt that the law of wearing phylacteries was in effect among Jews at all times. As additional proof of this we may adduce the fact told by Rabbi Azariah of the Adomim that when Ptolemy, the king of Egypt, sent messengers to Jerusalem to learn about the Jewish religion, the High Priest Eleazar explained to them the custom of wearing phylacteries.

There is a dispute in the Talmud whether phylacteries should be worn on Saturday. Rabbi Akiba is of the opinion that since phylacteries are worn as a reminder of the deliverance from Egypt, it is not necessary to wear them on those days that serve, in themselves, as reminders of this event, such as the

Sabbath and the feast days. The question as to whether they should be worn at night he answers in the affirmative.[33]

Women, slaves, and children are not obliged to wear phylacteries.[34] The Talmud derives this conclusion from the well-known rule that women are exempt from all those positive commandments that depend on a definite time.[35] It is characteristic that on another occasion the Talmud questions the authority of this rule and finds substantiation for it in the law of phylacteries. "Since phylacteries are obligatory only during a definite time and women are exempt from this commandment, it follows that women are exempt from any commandment that is obligatory only during a definite time."[36] This logical conclusion regarding the exemption of women from the law of phylacteries thus proceeds in two directions. On the one hand it liberates women from this law, and then it proceeds to liberate them from all laws that have the common time characteristic with it.

Phylacteries, as was explained before, are an emblem which indicates that those who wear them are devoted to God solely and do not recognize any other authority. But women, according to the concepts of that time, were the property of their husbands, and a married woman was as obedient as a slave and was not the mistress of her actions. For this reason women could not wear phylacteries. It is told, however, that Michal the daughter of Kushi (in the opinion of some she is identified with Michal the daughter of Saul) did wear phylacteries.[37] This conclusion is derived from the fact that Michal the daughter of Saul once spoke sharply to King David (II Samuel 6). There is also the case of one other woman, whose name remains unknown, who wrote the phylacteries for her husband.[38]

Slaves were considered in the same category as women in the matter of phylacteries. Since *tefillin* contain the statement that God is the only lord of the world, it was impossible for a person who recognized the overlordship of a human being to wear them. Mention is made, however, of one Tabbai, a slave of Rabbi Gamaliel, who wore phylacteries.[39]

The opinions of the scholars regarding God were highly

original when compared to the prevailing concepts of that time. These opinions differed from those of the nations among whom the Jews lived. Greek culture had attained a high level of perfection, but the Greeks still clung to polytheism. The same was true of the Romans, the Parthians, and the Persians. In later years the Christians tried to prove that the trinity was a direct continuation of the Jewish faith. One is therefore astounded by the fortitude of our scholars and their success in the struggle against attempts to introduce competing deities.

The representation of God in a corporeal form, such as the sayings: the hand of God, the mouth of God, the foot of God, the back of God, the scholars explained by the need to describe Him in a manner that should be understandable according to human concepts. At the same time they expressly stated that under no circumstance must these concepts be understood literally that God possesses a hand, a foot, or a mouth.[40]

The scholars then began to refer to God with names whose aim was to elevate the idea of God above human concepts. They referred to Him with the word *Shekhinah* which means that grace that emanates from the godly majesty. At times they called Him *Gevurah,* in an attempt to convey the idea that He represents strength. Similarly they used the name *Makom* (place) because He is present everywhere, and *Shamayim* (heaven) after the name of His residence. It is also characteristic that these names were not invented by the scholars but were current long before that.

The creation of the world they explained as creation ex nihilo. The central aim of creation was man, who was made in the image of God, whose face turns heavenward and who stands upright on his feet. Man possesses a soul and a free will to do as he chooses. Speaking of man, they considered the Jews to be the chosen people; within the Jewish people the pious and righteous man was the one elect.[41]

The idea of God's unity our scholars held to be of the highest importance. They considered it to be a privilege for the Jews to recognize God as the only creator and to be recognized by Him as the chosen people.[42] Jews also took an oath not to change their God.[43] The reason why man was created on

Friday before sunset, after all else was created, they explained as a lesson in modesty to man that he should not attempt to set himself up as a partner to God in the work of creation.[44]

Thus it was stated in the name of God: "I am first and I have no father, I am also last and I have no brother, there is no God outside of me because I have no son."[45] Similarly they taught that God is one and eternal, without body and unchangeable. God said to Moses: "I shall be where I shall be," which was interpreted to mean: "I have been long before, I am now, and I shall be the same in all time to come."[46]

When studying the Torah one must aim to observe its commandments. Observation of the commandments is also conditioned by faith in Him who gave the commandments. The Jew was also enjoined to do all things for the sake of God and not merely out of feeling of duty or because he was persuaded that these things must be done.

Faith imposes the obligation to accept the authority of the "kingdom of heaven," and it includes the duty of thanking God on all occasions for the favors as well as for the hardships; one must also submit to the guidance of God and believe that whatever He does is ultimately for the best. It is necessary to serve Him out of love and to endeavor to make others love Him. In doing so man's behavior will become akin to that of God; even as God practices compassion and mercy so also must man strive to attain these virtues.

Before the reciting of prayers was introduced it was customary to offer sacrifices. The offering of sacrifices was not a brutal murderous procedure but aimed at the purification of a man's thoughts.[47] After the Temple was destroyed it only remained possible to take a vow of abstinence (Nazarite), to refrain from drinking wine or cutting one's hair or to observe a fast day and thus inflict suffering on one's self through abstaining from all food and drink.

Most important of all is charity that one contributes with money or by means of personal effort on behalf of another person. Charity is founded in love of one person for another, which Hillel expressed as a rule of the Torah: "Do not unto others what you would not have done unto yourself."

When observing this rule one is led to the practice of true justice, mercy, and compassion toward all living things including animals.

Another desirable trait is the preaching of moral truths to others. A Jew is under obligation to preach until the person being corrected becomes angry and shouts and is ready to curse and to beat the moralist.[48] This trait acts as a safeguard against gossip, hatred and envy; it leads one to seek peace and friendship with others and eliminates the desire to cause harm to others.

One must also believe that God sees all the actions of man; that He knows the needs of the whole world and helps everyone; He particularly aids the Jews because of their justice and their faith in His mercy.

God's messengers are the angels, the prophets, and the just men. The piety of a just man may lead him to the "holy spirit," and such a man can achieve great things for Jews through prayer. Repentance similarly safeguards people from evil.[49]

But the most beautiful element of the faith is the belief in compensation and punishment. After his death, man is compensated for his good deeds and punished for his evil doing; children of good parents are credited with the deeds of their forefathers. And even as the individual meets with justice after death so also does the group. For the nation this assumes the form of the coming of Messiah and the coming to life of the dead. Of these matters the scholars spoke briefly when they referred to the "wars of Gog and Magog," the "pains of Messiah," the return of the "kingdom of David," the "future that is to come" and others. All of these were to compensate the nation for the suffering it has had to endure.

In the course of the generations there arose at times groups or individuals who questioned the validity of the "oral law" and asked: "Of what use are these interpretations of the scholars? Have they ever permitted the eating of a raven or forbidden the eating of a dove?"[50] But none of these opposed the moral views of the scholars, for even the opponents of the oral law understood that it is possible to condemn certain interpretations of the Torah, but that the moral teachings are so important and of such a humanitarian character that one cannot oppose them.

The measures of God's justice are mercy and truth. This is also the meaning of the verse, "Your justice is like the mountains of God; your verdict like a deep abyss," for if His justice were not like the highest mountains, who would be able to withstand his verdicts?[51]

When God sits in judgment over man, He does not consider man's previous deeds nor his possible future deeds but only the actions of the moment of trial.[52] But God is strict with just men and punishes them for every little transgression.[53]

From among all the nations—the scholars believed—God chose the Jews as his beloved children.[54] The Jews are likened to oil; just as oil gives light even so are the Jews the light of the world.[55] Because God loves the Jews he called them his firstborn children.[56] It is therefore a great virtue to sanctify His name. The Torah was given in order that God's name be sanctified throughout the world. Whenever there exists the danger that God's name will be profaned, one must do all in his power to prevent it.[56]

Nevertheless, the scholars were willing to grant that there is a possibility that the Torah is not the only means to vanquish passion in man, for one must also possess piety. A man who knows the Torah but possesses no piety was likened to a manager of a palace who was given only the inner but not the outer keys to the palace.[58]

2

THE THREE MAIN PARTIES OF THE TALMUDIC PERIOD

THE PHARISEES

FOLLOWING CLOSELY UPON THE VICTORY of the Hasmoneans over the Greek armies and their Jewish protégés, there began a dispute over the interpretation of the commandments of the Pentateuch concerning which many of the scholars held varying opinions. These disputes were frequently so serious that they constituted a threat to the existence of the nation.

Out of these disputes there emerged three main tendencies that eventually crystallized into three different parties: the Pharisees, the Sadducees, and the Essenes.

In general it is impossible to grasp the spirit of the Talmud and to understand clearly the teachings of its authors if one is not knowledgable about the tendencies of these parties. It is also necessary to know that nearly all of the authors of the Talmud were Pharisees and that their spirit impressed its stamp on the Talmud, although it also contains numerous aphorisms by people who frequently joked at the expense of the Pharisees.

It is worth noting that the Pharisees were active in

establishing regulations over the conduct of Judaism that would serve as a defensive wall around the Torah. To this end many laws of the Torah were made more severe and others assumed a form that to the casual observer seemed to deviate from the original text. These interpretations were generally based on traditions which in turn had to be substantiated by the Torah. These different opinions were sharply disputed until the people were divided into the above mentioned three parties which afterward attacked each other.

Many of the Pharisees practiced such extreme piety that they renounced all earthly pleasures and by their actions and customs they set themselves apart from the rest of the population. On the other hand, there were many people who refused to recognize any interpretation of the law that, to them, seemed to be in disagreement with its literal meaning. These people particularly objected to the restrictions of the oral law. They allied themselves with those who fought against the laws based on tradition. The opponents of the Pharisees argued that the devotion of the Pharisees to the interpretations goes to such extremes of unreasoning belief that were their leaders to tell them that right is left and vice versa, they would unquestioningly obey the advice of their teachers.

The opponents of the Pharisees numbered in their midst rich and politically influential Jews who felt that their attempts to attain closer spiritual relations with the neighboring peoples were hindered by the activities of the Pharisees. They particularly opposed the Pharisees because of the latter's devotion to faith and because of their lack of concern for the other problems of life. The Pharisees, on the other hand, held these views because of their conviction that man can achieve nothing without God's consent and that every attempt that runs counter to God's will is doomed to fail.

Separated from all other people by their manner of observing Jewish customs, the Pharisees considered the other Jews as idol worshippers with whom no pious man should have any contact. Their very name indicated that they were a class apart in their behavior. (The Hebrew word *perushim* means people separated or isolated.) They were especially severe in their observance of the laws pertaining to cleanliness and the paying of the tithe to the Priests and Levites. They believed that forbidden foods as well as grains from which no tithe was given to the priests were impure. The Pharisees were also careful to observe all the dietary rules of cleanliness, even when they ate ordinary food and not that of sacrifices.

As a pious precaution, many Pharisees abstained from dealing with the so-called *amei aratzim* (people of the soil). A Pharisee would not eat at the same table with an *am ha'aretz* out of suspicion that the latter may not have contributed his share to the Priests and Levites. Neither would a Pharisee buy from or sell to an *am ha'aretz*, nor invite one to his house, nor go visiting into the house of an *am ha'aretz*.

The name *am ha'aretz* was at that time applied primarily to tillers of the soil. Although agricultural work, as such, was highly regarded by the scholars, many of them openly confessed their dislike for the *am ha'aretz*, the man of the soil. Certain historians try to interpret this attitude as an indication that the tillers of the soil were not racially pure and freely intermarried with their gentile neighbors. In the Talmud there are widely diverging opinions as to which people should be classified as *am ha'aretz*. Some would have it that an *am ha'aretz* is a person who does not contribute the tithe from the fruit of his land. Rabbi Eliezer held that an *am ha'aretz* is one who does not recite the *shema* morning and evening. Rabbi Joshua said an *am ha'aretz* is one who does not wear phylacteries. Ben Azai said it is one who does not wear fringes. Rabbi Nathan said it is one who has no *mezuzah* on his door; Rabbi Nathan, the son of Joseph, said it is one who does not raise his children in the knowledge of the Torah. Others contended that even if a person studied much himself but did not serve other scholars, he deserves to be called an *am ha'aretz*.[1]

The Pharisees disdained an *am ha'aretz*. From other sources in the Talmud we know that the *am ha'aretz* hated scholars.

Concerning the meaning of the word *Pharisees* it was noted above that it indicates people who separated themselves from all others by their behavior. Others would have it that the name derives from the fact that they devoted themselves to interpreting the law as they saw fit in order to adapt the religious commandments to the needs of the times. Since the Pharisees deeply understood the spirit of the Torah, they gave up the search for pleasure in life even as they avoided pride or any action that might seem immoral. They practiced brotherly love toward one another, and each individual sought with all his might to avoid temptation.

The Pharisees were organized as a society, and every member was addressed as "Friend." This was not a closed organization and it did not limit its membership. Any person could join if he promised, in the presence of three members, to observe the rules of the organization that concentrated on cleanliness and ablutions. It is interesting to note that in accepting a new member no distinction was made between a scholar and an uneducated person. Both were considered of equal worth, and any person who was willing to assume the burdens of Pharisaism could join the society.

As soon as a person became a member of the Pharisee society, he undertook to serve God with his whole life. Such a person had to believe that God's eye is all-seeing and that He observes all man's acts in order to judge every injustice. Since man possesses a free will to do as he chooses, he is held responsible for every act and he will have to account for his deeds before his Creator. The Pharisees also believed that God sometimes issues decrees governing nations or all of humanity and that such decrees may seem unreasonable to the victims. But such decrees are certainly just since God is just to the individual as well as to a group. If it appears that reward for good deeds or punishment for wrong doing is delayed, then one must remember that there is a reckoning after death, or later yet, when the dead will be resurrected, the deserving ones to eternal life and the evil ones to everlasting shame and suffering.

The Pharisees were very careful in their judgment of people and events. This is clearly seen from their verdicts involving physical punishment. They also treated everyone modestly; they received people kindly and tried to do good deeds to others, insofar as they could, at times even going beyond the limits of their strength. They were, therefore, deeply loved by the people and enjoyed their fullest confidence.

But what frequently happens to many high-minded people also happened to the Pharisees. In spite of their good qualities, many people doubted the purity of their motives and they were suspected of doing many things in order to deceive their neighbors.

A specially strong hatred toward the Pharisees is evidenced in the New Testament. As a result of this the term *Pharisee* is now a derogatory term in world literature and has become synonymous with a hypocrite. In other Christian writings the Pharisees are pictured as people who outwardly abstain from earthly pleasures but lead immoral lives. They are said to refuse to eat honey from impure bees, but do not abstain from pork. They are accused of fasting in order to atone for their sins against God even while they plan to deceive their neighbors.

It is probably true that among such a large group as the Pharisees, there must have been a number of individuals who were dishonest in their convictions. But it is also certain that the majority was honest, or they could not have maintained the leadership of the nation in those times.

It was already stated that some scholars ridiculed the Pharisees. They portrayed seven different types, none of whom was presented in a favorable light. The seven types were: (1) one who is pious as Shechem, the son of Chamor, who was circumcised in order to obtain Dinah; (2) one who goes about with bowed head and hardly dares to raise his feet off the ground in order to display his modesty; (3) one who beats his head against a wall or goes about with closed eyes so as not to look at women; (4) one who goes about with twisted neck and head bowed like a hammer; (5) one who would persuade people that he has already done everything and challenges them to point out something he has not yet done; (6) one who does good deeds out of love for the reward which they bring; (7) one who obeys the law out of fear of the punishment disobedience will bring.[2]

THE SADDUCEES

The Sadducees were the second largest party among the Jews during the creation of the Talmud, and they were separated from the Pharisees by a wide spiritual gulf. It is believed that the principles that were accepted among the Sadducees originated in the misconceptions of Zadok and Boetus (pupils of Antigonos of Socho). Other historians hold a different opinion. Those claim that the Sadducees were descendants or disciples of the Zadok family which was a part of the priestly aristocracy and produced numerous high priests in the course of several centuries. When, in later years, the Hasmoneans triumphed over the Greeks, they also took over the high priests' office. Thus ousted from power, the descendants of Zadok were forced into a status of opposition to the majority of Jewish leadership.

The first source of friction between Sadducees and Pharisees was thus purely political and only at a later date did it develop into an acute religious dispute. There is also no reason to doubt the talmudic tradition that the Sadducees were the followers of Zadok and Boetus and at the same time to accept the theory of the historians that they were the descendants of the house of Zadok who allied themselves with these followers in undermining the foundations of Jewish traditions.

But it would be incorrect to maintain that the Sadducees completely rejected the traditional interpretations of the law. They too held to numerous traditions and many of their interpretations of the religious law were substantially the same as those of the Pharisees. They had their own *Book of Decrees* which expounded their explanations of the commandments of the Torah and, in spite of their desire to resemble the other nations in behavior, they also observed some customs that tended to set them apart from the Gentiles.

The customs of the Sadducees, at any rate, were better adapted to the religious beliefs of the rich and the aristocracy that governed the land. But the greater the number of rich men who joined the Sadducees, the stronger became the concentration of the masses around the Pharisees and the abyss between the two grew from day to day.

The primary difference between the Sadducees and the Pharisees was that the Sadducees rejected the oral law accepted by the Pharisees. They maintained that only the written law of the Torah was binding upon men. In rejecting the traditions of the Pharisees, they refused to believe in the resurrection of the dead, which is not explicitly promised in the Torah. They ridiculed the Pharisees for the latter's belief in the immortality of the soul and in a life after death and made fun of the notion that the souls of the pious will rest under the throne of glory. Another subject of their humor was the Pharisees' readiness to endure suffering in the hope of being rewarded in the life to come.

The development of this party proceeded favorably because of the response its ideas found among aristocratic and government circles that usually had the power to suppress opposition by force. There is also much justification for the view that the party of the Sadducees prospered due to the discomfiture of the Hellenists after the triumph of the Maccabees.

A major source of difference was the Pharisees' belief that even though a man may possess a free will to do either good or evil, according to his inclination, nevertheless God controls him in everything and is the ruler of his thoughts. The Sadducees maintained that God does not interfere with man's behavior and that no reward or punishment awaits one after death. Reward or punishment, they argued, is inherent in the deed itself.

Twelve points involving disputed interpretation of ritual and law were contested by the Sadducees who claimed that: (1) the date of the Feast of Weeks should always fall upon a Sunday; (2) The daily sacrifice is to be provided by the individual and not by the community; (3) Frankincense burned on the Day of Atonement should be kindled by the High Priest before entering the Holy of Holies; (4) the ashes of the Red Heifer sacrifice should be gathered by a man who underwent purification the same day according to Numbers 19: 9. (5) The Sadducees burned only a small share of their meal offerings and ate the rest. (6) The commandment "an eye for an eye" they interpreted literally, so that if one crippled another, he himself should be crippled in like manner. (7) In the case of a false witness whose evidence causes the defendant to be punished, the false witness was to receive the same punishment. If the judgment brought about a death sentence, the false witness was not to receive his punishment until after the defendant was executed. (8) The law that only male offspring were to share the inheritance of their father was interpreted to mean that, if the heir was an only son and he died leaving only daughters, then his sisters as well as his daughters shared the inheritance. (9) The Sadducees held that a man was responsible for damage done by his slave just as he was liable for damage done by his livestock since the slave, possessing intelligence, might have caused the damage on orders of his owner. (10) They held a utensil to be unclean if from it a liquid was poured into an unclean utensil, thus making the liquid unclean. (11) They literally adhered to the procedure prescribed for a childless widow whose dead husband's brother refused to marry her, holding it necessary that she spit in his face whereas the Pharisees held that she only need spit on the ground before him. (12) They also held to the literal meanings of the injunction in Deuteronomy 22:17, regarding disputed virginity, whereas the Pharisees gave it a broader interpretation.

There were also six traditional customs, which had no sanction in the Pentateuch, that the Pharisees observed and the Sadducees rejected: (1) One was the pouring of water on the altar on the night following the first day of Sukkot. All night water was drawn from the river Shiloah to the accompaniment of music and singing and was poured on the altar. The Sadducees ridiculed this custom as of Greek origin, but the Pharisees were devoted to it. Once, when a Sadducee priest poured the water on his feet instead of the altar, the angered populace showered him with their *etrogim* and he killed them. (2) The procession round the altar with willow branches was rejected by the Sadducees. When the seventh day of the Feast of Tabernacles occurred on Saturday, as was then possible due to the inaccuracies of the calendar, the Sadducees held that the custom of beating the willow branches did not supersede the Sabbath, contrary to the custom of the Pharisees. (3) They were opposed to the Pharisee custom of washing hands after reading the Bible. (4) They opposed the inclusion of the phrase "according to the law of Moses and Israel" in divorce certificates. Since these certificates bore the name and the year of the reign of the king, the Sadducees thought it would show disrespect for Moses to have his name appear alongside that of the king. (5) They denied the validity of Nehemiah's injunction against carrying objects from one household to another on the Sabbath. (6) They refused to recognize the new restrictions with which the Pharisees embellished the laws pertaining to purification of women.

But in spite of the opposition of the Sadducees to the teachings of the Pharisees and in spite of having the support of the rich and the officials, they were not strong enough to withstand the pressure of the population which was mostly on the side of the Pharisees and ready to defend its convictions with its life.

Many customs were introduced by the Pharisees purely out of spite for the Sadducees. They endeavored to impress the people that under no circumstances must they act according to the dictates of the Sadducees even when these were nearly accurate. The Pharisees established the date of the Feast of Weeks on the sixth day of *Sivan* which, according to their calculations, was the date of the giving of the Torah. In the prayers to be recited on that day they included the words "the time our Torah was given" in order to strengthen the conviction that this feast was celebrated in commemoration of the giving of the Torah and not as a celebration of the bringing of the first fruits.

THE ESSENES

The third significant party in Jewish life of that time were the Essenes. This party left no permanent imprint on Jewish life, and even at its zenith did not occupy a prominent place. From the Pharisees have evolved the Jews of the present day whose customs and beliefs are based on the talmudic interpretations of the Torah. From the Sadducees in later times evolved the sect of the Karaites, who represent the same mode of thinking. Of the Essenes we can only say that the early Christians conducted themselves along similar lines.

The development of the Essenes began in the early years of the Hasmoneans, and they are derived from the Hasidim of that time who fought against the Syrian Greeks under the banner of Judah Maccabee and his brothers. They were those who would rather undergo martyrdom than do anything that might make them suspect of imitating the Greeks. However, many became dissatisfied with the situation even as it existed after the victory of the Maccabees. To them the behavior of the Hasmoneans was not sufficiently Jewish. They fled the cities and sought refuge in the mountains, where they lived in an unusual manner apart from everyone else and awaited a change in the direction of Jewish ideas.

The meaning of the name Essenes is not entirely clear. Josephus called them Essenes; in Hebrew they are referred to as *Essiim*. Some historians claim it means modest, others say it means shy. Another version interprets the name as "healers" because the Essenes devoted themselves to healing the sick. The Talmud refers to them as "morning baptists" due to their habit of performing long morning ablutions. They were sometimes called pious fools and the Talmud defines a pious fool as a person who would not rescue a drowning woman for fear of touching her.

The conduct of the Essenes was not always the same, and in the course of time it changed although the basic principles remained constant. They avoided impurity of the body because of their belief that an impure body harbors an impure soul. Because of the fear of an impure soul, the Essenes refused to marry. They considered woman as the source of immorality and discord. However, they later realized that celibacy would diminish their society. Some of their members decided to marry in order to bring children into the world. The rest stubbornly clung to the original principle and remained unmarried their entire lifetime.

The Essenes did not follow any employment at first since

they believed that all work soils the body. When they suffered a shortage of food because no outsider would provide for their needs, they refused to steal, and since there were not enough fruit trees and wild grasses to subsist on, they decided that work is permissible and engaged in agriculture.

Some customs of the Essenes remained unchanged. When a person was sworn into their society, he had to promise never to take an oath again, even if it was to tell the truth and his very life depended on taking the oath. They also believed that by means of their special customs they could become imbued with the holy spirit and be able to foresee the future. They had their special books, which they successfully guarded from the eyes of strangers even as they avoided coming into contact with people holding other beliefs. Some of them devoted themselves to healing the sick with various grasses and herbs; others did their healing with the aid of incantations and prayers to the angels in charge of cures whose names they knew. Instead of bringing sacrifices, the Essenes offered prayers which generally began with praise to the Creator of light who "daily repeats the miracles of Genesis."

The Essenes never consumed food or drink that was not absolutely essential for the maintenance of life. They ate no meat and drank no wine and did not seek any pleasure in life. On the contrary, they hardened their bodies and gloried in suffering. Slavery they considered shameful because all men are brothers, and as long as a man can serve himself he has no right to allow himself to be served by others. Every member of their society received what he needed free. They avoided anger and their word was sacred. They respected each other and even refrained from spitting in the presence of another person.

There were neither poor nor rich among the Essenes, for every person who joined them had to give all of his possessions to the society. Young and old all wore similar linen clothing that they guarded as carefully as they guarded their bodies, against dirt, for they held cleanliness to be a decoration for a human being. Nevertheless, they did not don any new garment as long as the old one could still be used.

They observed all the minutest regulations pertaining to

Sabbath until it became practically a fast day for them. Since cooking was prohibited, they ate nothing but dry bread, and would not take any object into their hands; none of them even rose from their places on this day.

Many customs the Pharisee scholars introduced into Jewish life were meant to be a protest against the Essenes. Since the Essenes did not eat meat or drink wine and narrowly circumscribed their actions on the Sabbath, the Pharisee scholars expressly commanded that people should joyfully celebrate the Sabbath with meat and wine. The Pharisees also permitted the carrying of certain objects from one place to another (within the same household). When the Essenes became more strict and prohibited the lifting of any object on the Sabbath, the scholars relented and permitted the touching of any vessel that was a bodily necessity or convenience, with the exception of tools used in everyday labor. When the Essenes refused to marry, the Pharisees declared that any person who does not marry can be compared to a murderer who diminishes the stature of the Jewish people and drives the spirit of God from its confines. Since the Essenes healed the sick with incantations, the Pharisees announced that whoever attempted to perform a cure by means of an incantation would lose his share in the life to come.

The Essenes customarily rose before dawn and bathed in cold water both summer and winter. They then put on newly washed clothes and, without uttering a word, began their collective praise to the Creator. When the sun rose, each one went to his work, which lasted five hours. After work they gathered again, removed their work clothes and bathed anew; they put on different clothes and entered their meeting house where no outsider was allowed. There they ate their bread and greens, each one maintaining silence, convinced that they were performing a necessary act in sustaining the body that God had given them and that must therefore be guarded. After the meal the oldest gave praise to God for His great mercy. Then they removed the clothes they wore when eating, put on their work garments and returned to work until nightfall. At sunset the procedure was repeated; they bathed and again changed clothes for the evening repast.

When a newcomer desired to join the Essenes, he was not so readily accepted. The candidate was put on probation for a year to test his self-control and his ability to observe all the regulations of the society. Then he was given a white shirt, a cloak, and a small ax, and was put to work together with the rest. When, at the end of the year, the person proved that his conduct was consistent, he was allowed to perform his ablutions together with the others. However, he still was not permitted to partake of food with the rest for an additional two years. Only if he was found worthy at the end of that time to join the society, was he allowed to eat with the rest, and the secrets of the society were confided to him. Before the candidate had his first meal together with the other members, he had to take an oath that he would love and fear God above all else and with his whole soul, that he would love other people more than himself, and that he would be kind to all creatures. He had to promise not to deceive anyone even if the greatest fortune were at stake; he promised to help the oppressed, not to be haughty toward other people, to love truth and hate falsehood with his whole heart, and above all, to divulge none of the secrets of the society to any person.

Only after he had thus sworn did the candidate become a full-fledged member of the Essene society, to whom all secrets were entrusted with the assurance that he would not desecrate his oath by revealing them to others.

3

THE SAMARITANS

IN DESCRIBING THE EVENTS in the lives of the authors of the Talmud, reference will be made to the Samaritans and their various attitudes to political development in Palestine. It is important to pause to explain who these people were.

It is stated on historical grounds that the Samaritans are a mixture of a small remnant of the Ten Tribes whose kingdom in Samaria was destroyed by King Sargon of Assyria (722 B.C.E.). This king exiled over 27,000 inhabitants of the Samaritan population to Habor, the river Gozan, Halach, and the cities of Media, and in their place he settled people from Babylonia, Kuta, Ava, Hamath, and Sfarvaim. The remaining people of the Ten Tribes mixed with the newly settled peoples, and as a result of this union there developed in time the so-called Samaritans.

The Samaritans constituted a considerable population during the existence of the Second Temple and for some time after its destruction. Later they assimilated with other Jewish sects to some extent, and the majority of them disappeared entirely.

Whenever the Samaritans are referred to in the Talmud or in the Midrashim, they are called Kutim. The probable reason for this was that the people of Kuta constituted the most important element among the settlers whom the king of Assyria colonized in Samaria in place of the exiled Israelites. According to the Bible, these people did not observe the Jewish laws and did not believe in God during their first years in Samaria. As a punishment their dwellings were attacked by lions who killed many of them. The king of Assyria was then informed that the people whom he had settled in the cities of Samaria in the place of the exiled Israelites did not know the laws of the God who rules there and, in his anger, God had set upon them many lions to devour them. The king of Assyria thereupon commanded to have one of the exiled priests sent there to teach the people the laws of the God of Samaria.

One of the priests came and settled in Beth El, and he taught the inhabitants to fear the God of Israel. From that time on the inhabitants continued to worship their old idols, but they also erected an altar for the offering of sacrifices to the Jewish God. Since these people were converted to belief in the Jewish God because of their fear of the lions, they were called "Lions' Converts."

It is also necessary to keep in mind that insofar as the people of the Ten Tribes were descendants of the tribe of Ephraim, they harbored a deep-seated hatred for the tribe of Judah, dating back to the time of the Judges, when the people of Ephraim were warlike, loved to rule and constantly quarreled with the other tribes. From the tribe of Ephraim descended Jeroboam, who rebelled against King Solomon and at a later date detached the kingdom of Israel from the kingdom of the House of David.

One hundred thirty-three years passed from the time of the exile of the Ten Tribes until the destruction of the first Temple. The land of Samaria underwent many changes during these years. Assyria ceased to exist and its nations came under the rule of another people. Even before the destruction of Samaria, there was a spiritual kinship between Jerusalem and Samaria, as is indicated by some of the prophets. We may also assume that this relationship between Jerusalem and Samaria continued to exist and was strengthened when the Samaritans saw that the God of Judah saved Jerusalem from the Assyrians, a feat which their idols had failed to accomplish.

It is probable that many Samaritans went to Judea at that time and joined the kingdom of Judah. There are also indications that the king of Judah had some control over Samaria at certain times. Thus we read in Kings 2: 23 that King Josiah destroyed the high places in Beth El and in the cities of Samaria. There also exists the possibility that only a small part of the Samaritans denied the sacredness of Jerusalem even before the destruction of the first Temple. Thus it is told that after the death of Gedaliah ben Achikam there came eighty men from Shechem, from Shiloh, and from Samaria with offerings and incense in their hands to sacrifice in the Temple, for they did not know that it had been destroyed.

It is not quite clear what took place among the Samaritans during the 133 years from the exile of Samaria until the destruction of the First Temple, nor later, in the time of the Babylonian captivity. One thing we do know is that when the Jews returned to Palestine from Babylonia under the reign of Cyrus, king of Persia, and the Samaritans heard that they were planning to build a new temple, they approached Zerubabel and the other leaders of the people and said: "We will gladly participate in your work, for we serve the same God that you do and to him we have offered our sacrifices since the time of Esaradon, king of Assyria, who brought us here."

The Samaritans are there called "the enemies of Judah and Benjamin," which may serve as proof that the relations between the Samaritans and the Jews at that time were of a hostile nature. The Jews suspected evil intentions on the part of the Samaritans and refused their assistance. According to Josephus Flavius, the Jews replied: "Why should you help us when you too will be able to use our Temple, for our Temple will be a house of prayer for all nations."

This refusal to accept the cooperation of the Samaritans revived the old feud between the tribe of Ephraim and the people of Judah. The Samaritans erected their own temple on Mount Gerizim. It is told that when Nehemiah came to Jerusalem and found that the son of the High Priest Jojada ben Eliashiv was a son-in-law of Sanbalat the Horonite, who hindered the building of the Temple through false reports to the Persian government, he expelled him from Jerusalem.

Josephus offers a somewhat different account. He relates that Menasheh, the brother of the High Priest Jojada, married the daughter of Sanbalat the Samaritan. Nehemiah commanded him to send away his wife even as he had everyone send away their non-Jewish wives. When Menasheh refused to do so, he was driven out from among the Jews. He thereupon went to his father-in-law Sanbalat who built a temple on Mount Gerizim for him, where an altar to offer sacrifices had already existed for some time, and he appointed him priest of the temple. Josephus continues to relate that many other men of Judea flocked to Samaria because they refused to send away their foreign wives, and there they abolished the regulations of Ezra the Scribe. They did other things in order to sanctify Mount Gerizim and even falsified the text of the Torah as suited their purposes.

Ezra the Scribe regulated the form of the Hebrew script at that time. Historians differ as to the reasons for this. However, we may safely assume that prior to this the Jews used the old Phoenician script, which is now used only by the Samaritans, and not the square Assyrian alphabet which we have today. The broad masses of the people were illiterate, and the Phoenician letters were difficult to learn. Another motive of Ezra in selecting the Assyrian script was to establish a dividing wall between the Jews and the Samaritans. This choice of an alphabet was approved and carried through by the Great Synagogue.

According to Josephus, Sanbalat built the Samaritan temple on Mount Gerizim with the consent of Alexander the Great. This consent was granted as a reward for the assistance the Samaritans had extended to him in his war against Tyre.

But according to the Talmud the Samaritan temple no longer existed in the days of Alexander the Great. However, there is an obvious contradiction in the talmudic legend confusing two events that transpired at widely separated periods, namely, the journey of Simon the Just and other Jewish leaders to meet Alexander the Great, who intended to destroy Jerusalem, and the destruction of the Samaritan temple by the High Priest Jochanan.

The Talmud relates: The twenty-fifth day of Tevet is the

day of Mount Gerizim on which no eulogies must be delivered. On this day the Kutim (Samaritans) tried to obtain permission from Alexander the Great to destroy God's house, and he readily granted this request. When the news was related to Simon the Just, he put on his priestly vestments and taking the best men from among the Jews, he put torches in their hands and thus they walked all night to meet the king.

The Jews went on one side and the Samaritans on the other side until dawn. When morning came and the king saw the Jews, he asked his followers: "Who are these?" His people replied: "These are the Jews who revolted against you." By this they meant to remind the king that the Jews had refused to open the gates of Jerusalem for him before he conquered the Persians.

When they arrived in Antipatris the sun rose, and when the king saw Simon the Just, he descended from his carriage and bowed to him. Then the king asked the Jews: "What is the purpose of your coming?"

They replied: "Is it possible that idol worshippers can persuade you to destroy a house in which prayers are offered for you and your kingdom?"

"Who would have done that?" the king asked.

"These Kutim who stand before you," the Jews replied.

"I give them into your hands," the king answered to this.

The Jews seized the Kutim and pierced the soles of their feet. They then tied them to their horses and dragged them over the thorns until they came to Mount Gerizim. When they reached Mount Gerizim, they plowed it and sowed it with lentils even as the Kutim had planned to do with the house of our God.

Later, this day was set aside as a day of feasting.[1]

With the construction of the Samaritan temple on Mount Gerizim near the city of Shechem, located in the very center of Palestine, Sanbalat hoped that it would soon become the religious center for all those for whom the road to Jerusalem is too long. In selecting Mount Gerizim he believed he was doing the best thing possible because it was there that God's blessing was pronounced on those who follow his commandments.

In later years the priests of the temple on Mount Gerizim attempted to persuade the people that the Torah was handed down from Mount Gerizim and not from Mount Sinai as the Jews claimed. To lend strength to this contention, the text of the Torah was falsified, but this attempt did not succeed and the claim was later dropped.

From that time the struggle between the Jews and Samaritans gained in intensity. Often it was a struggle of ideas, each side claiming that the truth was on its side. On other occasions it took the form of bloody wars lasting for centuries. The mutual hatred between the contending sides was so strong that even in times of relative peace it was considered a good deed to kill a member of the opposing side. Every time the Jews were attacked by enemies, the Samaritans made common cause with these enemies, with two notable exceptions: the destruction of the Second Temple and the siege of Betar.

How deeply rooted this hatred between the Jews and Samaritans was we can see best from the writings of Josephus. However, he might have been prejudiced against them because in his time they fought on the side of the Jews against the Romans. But this hatred of the two peoples is also mentioned earlier in the books of the Maccabees and Ben Sira says of them that he was "disgusted with the shameful people who dwell in Shekhem."

When the Hasmoneans warred against the Greeks, Josephus relates, the Samaritans allied themselves with the enemies of the Jews and, at the time that religious Jews were tortured and persecuted by the Greeks, the Samaritans wrote to Antiochus Epiphanes: "We are not Jews and we do not recognize the Jewish God. If to this day we observe the Jewish Sabbath and other Jewish feast days, we do so not of our own choice but through compulsion. If the king disapproves of our going in the ways of the Jews and our worshipping their God, we will return to the Gods of our forefathers, and we will dedicate our temple to Zeus."

After the victory of the Hasmoneans, the Samaritans joined with the nations about Palestine and sought to incite them to war against the Jews. Their hatred of the Jews was very

great. It was for this reason that Jochanan Hyrcanus conducted
a war of annihilation against them and destroyed their temple
two hundred years after it was founded.

He was followed by his two sons, who, although they
fought amongst themselves, were united in their hatred of the
Samaritans. When they conquered the city of Samaria, they
leveled it and plowed up the site of the temple. The inhabitants
fled the city to save their lives. Only much later, when
Jerusalem was occupied by the Romans under Pompey, did the
Samaritans return to their dwellings.

The religious relations between the Jews and Samaritans
varied with the times. Since the Samaritans resided among
Jews for hundreds of years, legislation concerning them did not
always follow the same system. At times they were considered
as idol worshippers, and it was told that their temple contained
an image resembling a dove that they worshipped. On other
occasions some of the talmudic scholars maintained that the
Samaritans should be considered Jews.

It was thus only natural that the Samaritans, too, should
invent all kinds of stories about the Jews. Their main contention was that *they* were the real Jews and that only they
observed all the commandments of the Torah. In order to prove
that the Jews did not properly observe the laws of purity, they
did the following: In order to desecrate the Temple on a certain
Passover when the Jews were gathered in Jerusalem, they
placed the bones of a dead person with the wood that was kept
near the altar. But this action did not have the effect the
Samaritans had anticipated. After the bones were removed the
scholars declared the Temple to be pure again and argued that
such bones do not have the power to desecrate the Temple.
Since no one knows where the bones of those drowned during
the flood are nor those of the victims of Nebuchadnezzar, who
destroyed the First Temple, it is entirely possible that some of
those bones are interred near the Temple. Nevertheless, they
said, no one would claim that the Temple is desecrated because
of such bones.

At other times the Samaritans tried to spite the Jews.
When the latter lit fires on the mountains to announce to
far-away residents that a new month was beginning, the

Samaritans sometimes put out these fires in order to cause erroneous celebration of the feast days.

At the time of the destruction of the Second Temple, the Samaritans were the allies of the Jews in their struggle against the Romans. The Romans did not distinguish between Jews and Samaritans and the same was true in the wars of Bar Kochba.

After the destruction of the Second Temple, the Samaritans remained in their city, and their shrine continued to exist. However, about 150 years later, they revolted against the Romans. The emperor Septimus Severus vanquished them, destroyed the city of Samaria, and killed its inhabitants. The same thing happened when the Romans warred against the Persians and the Samaritans helped the Persians.

The opinions of the talmudic scholars concerning the Samaritans were not always the same. The great disputes occurred when both Samaritan and Jewish temples existed at the same time. Later, the opinion prevailed that the Samaritans were true converts and according to Rabbi Simeon ben Gamaliel, a Samaritan was the equal of a Jew in every respect.

Sharply opposed to this idea were the opinions of Rabbi Eliezer who said that "one who eats the bread of a Samaritan is like one who eats pork."[2] Other scholars were milder in their attitude and permitted partaking of Samaritan food.[3]

4

SIMON THE JUST

THE FEW DECADES THAT THE JEWS spent in Babylonia, from the exile of Jehoyachin, king of Judea until their return under Cyrus king of Persia, deeply influenced their spiritual development insofar as the outward manifestations of the Jewish religion were concerned. It was from the Babylonians that they learned to identify angels by name. In all the books of the Bible preceding the book of Daniel, angels are not named. According to the story of the Torah and the Prophets, angels were created by God's wish to perform a definite mission. When that mission was completed, the angel would vanish without a name even as he had appeared without a name.

Only after their return from Babylonian captivity did the Jews begin to name the angels according to their function. Raphael became the angel of healing. Gabriel was the angel of strength and victory, and Michael became the defender of the Jewish people.

In order to obtain a clearer understanding of the political situation, we must remember that from the return of the exiles until the breakdown of the Persian empire comparative political stability prevailed. The Jews gathered internal strength and fortified the foundations of their religious and national life. But we do not know the name of any person of that period who could be said to have been the leader of the people.

Leadership was concentrated in the hands of the High Priest and the group known as *sofrim* (scribes) who copied the holy writings. The people stayed within their modest boundaries and diligently devoted themselves to the rebuilding of their homes and lands, seemingly indifferent to whom they paid their taxes or who ruled the land. Nothing unusual occurred at this time.

Only much later, in the days of Artaxerxes III (362–338 B. C.E.) did trouble begin when the Egyptians tried to liberate themselves from the yoke of the Persians. The Persian armies marched into Palestine on their way to Egypt. The Egyptians, too, did not wait until their land was invaded and proceeded to meet them. Both armies met in Palestine and there the battle was fought.

The Jews were thus forced to provide for both armies. Each of the contending sides tried to gain their support, but they remained neutral in this conflict. The war ended with the withdrawal of Persia from Egypt, and Palestine became the apple of discord between the two powers, each of whom desired to possess it for strategic reasons.

Meanwhile, the Persian nation sank into a spiritual decline. When the Persians conquered Babylonia and other Asiatic lands they found the inhabitants worshipping various gods of fertility and indulging in immorality as a form of piety. Artaxerxes III introduced this type of worship into all the lands of his domain. The new form of worship strained the loyalty of the Jews toward the Persians because it ran contrary to all their concepts of religion. As the king devoted himself to the new cult, he refrained from active participation in matters of state and entrusted the conduct of the government to his officials. One of these officials was put in charge of Jerusalem. Another official, named Bagases, assassinated the king and his whole household and assumed the throne.

It was to this ruler that Joshua, son of the High Priest Jojada, appealed to have himself appointed High Priest after the death of his father, instead of his older brother Jochanan,

who was the legitimate heir. When Jojada died, Joshua attempted to claim his office and was killed within the Temple by
Jochanan. On hearing this, the governor hastened to Jerusalem
to avenge Joshua and utilized the opportunity to plunder the
Temple. (Jochanan went unpunished.) In addition he imposed
upon the Jews a fine of fifty golden drachmas, to be paid daily,
and he entered the Holy of Holies and stripped it of all
valuables.

Seven years later saw the beginning of the wars of
Alexander the Great, king of Macedonia, in which he conquered all the domains of the Persians. Some of these battles
were also fought on Palestinian soil. The prophet Daniel
described those wars as he foresaw them in his dream: ". . .
The four winds of the heaven strove upon the great sea. And
four great beasts, different one from another, came up out of
the sea. The first was like a lioness and had the wings of an
eagle; I beheld till her wings were plucked off and she was
lifted up from the earth, and stood upon her feet as a man, and
the heart of a man was given to her. And behold another beast
like a bear stood up on one side and it had three ribs in its
mouth between its teeth. . . . After this I beheld another like a
tiger which had on its back four wings of a fowl and also four
heads. . . . After this I saw in the night visions and behold, a
fourth beast dreadful and terrible and exceedingly strong and it
had great iron teeth; it devoured and broke in pieces and
stamped the residue with its feet" (Daniel 7).

The High Priest at that time was Simon the Just who was
a direct descendant of the High Priest Joshua, the first after the
return from the Babylonian captivity. The personality of Simon
the Just is veiled in legend, and it is difficult to establish the
exact years of his life. The generally accepted date of his death
is about 310 B.C.E. Some historians claim he lived at a later date.
But it is certain that he was the last of the Great Synagogue and
that this institution was abolished in his time.

Of all the teachings of Simon the Just, there remains the
one statement he must have repeated on numerous occasions.
"Upon three things the world rests: the law, worship, and the
showing of kindness."[1]

Simon the Just was High Priest for forty years according to the Talmud. These were years when Palestine went through terrible difficulties. As in the days of the first Temple, the country became the battlefield for many nations. These events became so commonplace that they were not even properly recorded. But the Jews of the surrounding countries (Babylonia, Persia, Egypt) lived under more favorable circumstances, and they refrained from coming to Jerusalem. With the weakening of the attachment to Jerusalem, they strove to establish spiritual centers within the countries of their residence. One competing Temple, the temple of the Samaritans, already existed on Mount Gerizim. It had for its High Priest Menasheh, the son-in-law of Sanbalat the Horonite, whom Nehemiah had expelled from Jerusalem.

Many wonders are said to have occurred in the Temple in Jerusalem during the High Priesthood of Simon the Just. Some of these are described in the Talmud.[2]

During the service of the Day of Atonement, two he-goats were placed near the High Priest, one on his right and one on his left. Lots were cast to determine which one would be sacrificed as a sin offering and which one would be sent to Azazel in the desert, and each time the lot of being the sin offering fell to the goat on the right side of the priest.

The second wonder was the changing of the red string. A red string was tied around the neck of the goat being sent to Azazel. After the goat was thrown from the top of the precipice and it was cut to pieces in the fall, the red string remaining in the hands of the messenger turned white. This was a sign that the sins of the people were forgiven.

The third was the wonder of the burning western light. Since the menorah in the Temple was situated between the north and south, its lamps were always lit from west to east. But in spite of the fact that the westernmost lamp was lit first, it continued burning even when the oil in the other lamps was already consumed.

The fourth wonder was that of the altar fire. The fire on the altar increased of itself. Only two pieces of wood were added at sundown and the fire never went out.

Another wonder was that of the sheaf. A blessing rested on the sheaves which were given to the priests and on the holy loaves. Every priest received no more than the size of an olive, and of that he ate his fill and there was still some left over.

As a protest against those Jews who indulged in extravagant living there appeared Nazarites who abstained from wine and vowed not to cut their hair. Of these Simon the Just disapproved because he considered it a sin to renounce pleasures which God created for the benefit of people. He made only one exception to this rule and of this he tells himself:

"There once came to me a man who had beautiful curly hair and he wanted to cut his hair because he ended the period of being a Nazarite. I asked him, "My son, what made you decide to cut off your beautiful hair?" And the man answered me, "I am a shepherd for my father. Once, when I went to the spring to draw water for the cattle, I looked at my image in the water and I was tempted to be proud of my beautiful appearance and thus to lose my life through sin. So I said to myself, 'Wicked man, you are proud of something which is not yours, and you will, at any rate, turn to forms. I therefore swore to cut off this hair in honor of the Almighty.' "

Simon the Just kissed the Nazarite on the head and said to him: "May there be many like you in Israel."

Two Red Heifers were sacrificed in the days of Simon the Just. The Red Heifer offering was the sacrifice of a cow without even two black hairs. The animal also had to be without fault and must never have been put to work. Such an animal was therefore very rare, and it was considered a miracle that two such were found during the forty years of his priesthood. In spite of the fact that sometimes as high a price as sixty measures of gold were paid for such an animal, there were only nine such heifers sacrificed during the existence of both Temples. Legend says that the tenth will not be found until the coming of the Messiah.

Tradition tells us that Alexander the Great wanted to destroy Jerusalem. He was then conducting a war against Syria and Phoenicia and he wanted the Jews of Palestine to help him. The Jews informed him that they could not do so because they had sworn loyalty to King Darius the Mede. Hearing this, Alexander announced to his soldiers that he would take revenge. When the Jews heard that Alexander was marching on Jerusalem with a great army, they were stricken with fear. The High Priest Simon the Just together with all the priests and elders went to greet him.

Simon the Just was dressed in the priestly vestments he wore when going into the Holy of Holies on the Day of Atonement. As soon as Alexander saw him he descended from his chariot and bowed to him.

The commanders of his troops asked Alexander why the conqueror of so many lands, who had placed his foot on the necks of so many kings, had bowed before a Jew whom he previously threatened to destroy. Alexander answered that every night preceding a victory he had seen an old man in his dream who resembled the Jewish High Priest. He therefore refused to do him any harm and believed that being kind to him would bring him luck in the coming wars.[3]

Simon the Just then led Alexander into the Temple. Alexander liked the Temple and asked that a stone image of himself be placed near the altar. Simon the Just answered that this was impossible because the Jewish faith does not allow images in the Temple. But he promised to immortalize the memory of Alexander's kindness in another manner. He had all the boys who were born that year named Alexander. The king liked this idea even better than having his statue near the altar.

The Samaritans then came before Alexander to complain against the Jews. They attempted to prove that their temple on Mount Gerizim was the true Jewish temple. Alexander asked them to debate the question with the Jews of Jerusalem in his presence. The spokesman of the Jews was one Gabiha ben Pasisa who, with his sensible arguments, destroyed the claims of the Samaritans. When Alexander acknowledged the Jews to be the victors of the debate, the Samaritans fled.

Numerous customs still in force were introduced at that time. Among them were the *Kiddush* and *Havdalah*, the blessings over wine on Friday eve and Saturday night, and the regulation that even the poorest person must drink no less than four glasses of wine at the *seder* on Passover eve. With the consent of the Great Court in Jerusalem, the blessings over food were established. The reading of the *Haftarah* was introduced for Saturdays and feast days. Since the Samaritans did not acknowledge the sanctity of the Prophets, an appropriate chapter from the Prophets was selected to be read each week.

The Temple in Jerusalem was then in existence about two hundred years and naturally the structure was weakening. Simon the Just had the building repaired and had verandas built around it. Jerusalem suffered a chronic shortage of water and much water was also required for the Temple service. The priests had to perform ablutions several times a day and even an ordinary person had to bathe before entering the precincts of the Temple. Simon the Just had a well dug under the ground near the Temple from which an aqueduct was later built to bring sufficient water to the city through copper pipes.

Immediately after the Day of Atonement of the year in which he died, Simon the Just announced that he would die. When he was asked how he knew this, he said that on every Day of Atonement, when he entered the Holy of Holies to perform the service, he saw an old man dressed in white who used to leave the Holy of Holies together with him. That year the old man was dressed in black and did not leave the Holy of Holies with him. It happened just as he predicted. Seven days after *Sukkot* he became ill and died.

Simon the Just was survived by two sons, Shimei and Onias, of whom Onias was the wiser and more capable. Simon the Just wanted Onias to succeed him to the High Priesthood. But Shimei intrigued among the people against the will of his father and caused them to believe that a man such as Simon the Just would not want his younger son to take precedence over the older. Disappointed, Onias left for Alexandria where a large Jewish community of over a million people existed. There he established a competing temple (the house of Onias) with an altar for the offering of sacrifices to the God of Israel even as the Samaritans had done in their Temple on Mount Gerizim.

5

ANTIGONOS
OF SOCHO

SIMON THE JUST WAS THE LAST of the generation to
consider that knowledge of the Torah and its interpretations
was the exclusive privilege of the priests. He had numerous
disciples among whom were many non-priests. Antigonos of
Socho was one of the latter, and he came to occupy the position
of Simon the Just in the continuation of scholastic development.

There is even some doubt as to whether Antigonos was
the direct successor of Simon the Just or whether he really lived
some generations later. But since history does not mention any
intermediate person between the two, we can rely on the
Mishnah[1] that Antigonos received his knowledge directly from
Simon the Just.

The Greek name Antigonos is characteristic of the time.
We have already described how the name Alexander came to
be accepted among Jews and it is possible that the name
Antigonos was popularized in a similar manner. One of the
Greek governors of Palestine, Antigonos by name, showed
kindness to the Jews, and out of gratitude to him they decided
to immortalize his name. However, it is more logical to assume
that the Hellenist movement which sought to bring the Jews

closer to Greek customs was already in vogue at that time, for we find many other Greek names in popular use such as Aristobul and Boetus. Even the Great Court in Jerusalem was known by the Greek name *Synhedrion* (*Sanhedrin*) and this name was later sanctified through popular use. During the time of Antigonos a crisis in Jewish thought developed. It is probable that the spirit of philosophic doubt became prevalent in the country and, unknowingly, Antigonos contributed to its spread.

He frequently used to say: "When you serve God, be not like servants who serve the master with the expectation of receiving gifts, but rather be like servants who serve the master without expecting gifts, and the fear of Heaven will be upon you." Two of his pupils, Zadok and Boetus, who heard his words said: "What can be the meaning of these words? Can a person expect that his servant work for him all day without receiving compensation? We must conclude that our teacher would not say so if he believed in a life to come and the resurrection of the dead."

Zadok and Boetus thereupon founded a new mode of living and organized a new party which came to be known as Sadducees or Boetusians. This party began to imitate the extravagant mode of living of the Greeks under the following pretext: Why should a person deny himself the pleasures of life, if he can await nothing after death? In time this party evolved new forms of observing Judaism different from those of the majority of the people. They clung to the literal meaning of the Torah commandments as against the traditions of the scholars. For that reason they denied the resurrection of the dead and also the theory of compensation and punishment in a life to come. They ridiculed the belief of the masses that a new redemption would be brought by a Messiah since the conditions then prevailing could not be the culmination of the dreams of the prophets.

Jews very particularly observed all regulations pertaining to the "uncleanliness of the dead." At death, a person ceased to exist for his family and friends and the body was given over to strangers for burial. The Sadducees considered this procedure disrespectful toward one's parents, since one could not be sure what was done with the bodies. In rejecting the traditions they insisted that the commandment "an eye for an eye" should be interpreted literally and not, as the talmudic scholars claimed, that monetary compensation was sufficient.

Antigonos lived in a time of constant wars between the kings of Egypt and Syria. Palestine was frequently the battleground of the warring armies and it was impossible to maintain order and to assure the security of life. Plunderers invaded the land from outside and the population was further impoverished by domestic banditry. Learning was on the decline. In a time of changes it was necessary to modify the Torah to adapt it to the needs of the day, but there was no one capable of doing this. As a result, the people neglected their studies and Judaism was being forgotten. For nearly a hundred years the people lived in ignorance and spiritual poverty until circumstances changed and the throne of Syria was occupied by a king who interfered with the religious life of the Jews and undertook to destroy the entire Jewish religion.

Alexander the Great followed the principle of religious tolerance toward the peoples of his empire. This principle was adhered to by his followers. Any deviation from the religious observances on the part of the Jews occurred as a result of their own neglect. This condition lasted until Antiochus Epiphanes of Syria attempted to impose his religion on all the peoples of his kingdom. Among the Jews, this attempt led to the revolt of the Hasmoneans and started a new epoch in Jewish history.

The belief that God protects the Jewish nation and will punish its enemies was deeply rooted among the people. They believed that the historical events chronicled in the Torah were not related simply as historical events, but that their aim was to teach people to understand the rules according to which the world was governed. This was held to be the intention of Moses in describing the war with Amalek so that coming generations might know how to deal with the Amalekites who warred against the Jews in their wanderings in the desert after their first liberation.

Considerable attention was also given to the Hebrew

language. Upon returning from Babylonia, the people spoke a mixture of the neighboring languages as well as Hebrew. Later the Syrian Greek language predominated. The court of the Hasmoneans then commanded that Hebrew should be the spoken language. This ancient language had lost some of the power of its expression, but it developed again until it could be used to express all concepts. In the new development and revival of the Hebrew language, both Aramaic and Greek were borrowed from extensively for certain new expressions.

6

JOSE BEN JOEZER
AND
JOSE BEN JOCHANAN

FOLLOWING ANTIGONOS OF SOCHO, a new period in Jewish history characterized by dual leadership began. This period lasted for about five generations and was called the time of the "pairs" because two men simultaneously led and governed the people. One of the two was generally the Nasi (chief) and the other was called the *Av Beit Din,* the father of the court.

At first these "pairs" were in complete agreement on all fundamental issues and differed only on minor religious questions. Later these disagreements increased and reached the point of severe disputes which engendered dangerous bitterness.

In all there were five such pairs: (1) Jose ben Joezer of Zeredah and Jose ben Jochanan of Jerusalem; (2) Joshua ben Perachia and Nittai of Arbela; (3) Jehudah ben Tabbai and Simeon ben Shetach; (4) Shemaiah and Abtalion; (5) Hillel and Shammai. The reverence with which the teachings of these leaders were considered is illustrated by the statement of one of their followers, Nachum Halavlar (the Scribe): "I received a tradition from Rabbi Miasha, who received it from his father, who heard it from the "pairs" who received it from the Prophets as a law handed down to Moses from Mount Sinai."[1] This saying indicates the mood of the people who believed that every word of the "pairs" was a law handed down to Moses from Mount Sinai.

The first pair lived in the days of the High Priest Alkimos who allied himself with the Greeks against the Jews under the reign of Demetrius Soter (about 300 B.C.E.). This High Priest met with considerable opposition from the pious elements who objected to his treacherous actions and attempted to lead the people along the true paths.

Jewish history has known such dual leadership even before the time of Jose ben Joezer and Jose ben Jochanan. Thus we find Jehoshaphat, the fourth king of Judea after Solomon, appointing two leaders to conduct the government. The priest Amariah, was the authority of the word of God and the other, Zachariah ben Ishmael, was the lord of the king's commands. After the return from the Babylonian captivity, there ruled Zerubabel as the secular leader and Jeshua ben Jozadak as High Priest. Still later the government was shared by Ezra and Nehemiah. Despite this dual leadership and the rarity of two leaders cooperating amicably, no disputes arose between the first "Pair" except in the matter of one ritual question on which Jose ben Joezer and Jose ben Jochanan could not agree. This question was also disputed by the later "pairs." It involved the problem of placing one's hands on a sacrifice on a feast day.

The Bible enjoined a person to "place his hand" on the sacrifice which he brought and this was interpreted to mean that he was to assist in the slaughtering of the animal. Since this procedure involved a considerable effort, it was held by some that a person should not do so on the Sabbath or on a feast day. Others maintained that the restrictions of the Sabbath are not operative in the Temple, and the individual must therefore assist in the slaughtering of the sacrifice if it is to be offered according to the law.

The procedure of the "placing of hands" was as follows. The animal to be sacrificed was placed on the north side of the slaughterhouse and faced west. The person bringing the animal stood on the east facing west. Then he placed his hands between the horns of the animal and confessed the sins for the atonement of which he had brought the sacrifice. Those who prohibited this procedure of placing of hands on a feast day believed that it involved an effort and was therefore unnecessary; the others considered the whole procedure and the confession as sanctifying the sacrifice and permitted this effort in the Temple.

The problem for the Jews living outside Palestine who sent their sacrifices to Jerusalem was of paramount importance in the discussion of this question. The decision involved the acceptance of the sacrifice without the presence of the penitent. Those who permitted the offering of a sacrifice on a feast day without the presence of the owner feared that any undue severity might tend to encourage those Jews living outside of Palestine to erect altars wherever they lived and thus to compete with the Temple in Jerusalem; they feared that it might even lead to idolatry. Those who opposed this leniency were motivated by opposition to the Sadducees who tried to make the regulations of conduct on the Sabbath or a feast day so severe as to be impossible of observance.

Two other decrees were introduced by Jose ben Joezer and Jose ben Jochanan. They declared all countries surrounding Palestine impure and where no Jew may live. One who does live in any of these lands must perform numerous ablutions and rites of purification before he may enter Palestine. This decree was apparently aimed to limit the dispersion of Jews among the neighboring nations, that was assuming large proportions due to the persecutions by the Greek government. The decree caused great hardships to those who refused to submit to the laws of the Palestine administration attempting to eradicate Judaism. The second decree promulgated by them declared all glass vessels made by non-Jews to be impure even as earthen dishes were.

It is worth mentioning that both of these decrees were done away with in time even by observant Jews settled in gentile lands in later years. And glass vessels in later times were considered pure after being rinsed in water. Jose ben Joezer also introduced three rules which lightened the burden of the laws. During years of famine, when the people could not identify the four types of locust which the Bible permits to be used as food, he sanctioned the use of a locust that had invaded the country from Babylonia. He permitted people to use the water and blood of the sacrificial slaughterhouse for household purposes and as garden fertilizer. He also declared that only the person who comes in direct contact with a dead body or an impure object is impure but such a person does not convey the impurity to other people. This declaration was of special significance due to the preparations then going on for a rebellion against the Greeks who persecuted the Jewish faith. Many were reluctant to go to war out of fear of contamination through contact with people who touched dead bodies. It was for this reason that Jose ben Joezer declared that only the first person directly touching a corpse is impure.

Jose ben Joezer is credited with the following moral saying: "Let thy house be a place of meeting for the wise and dust thyself with the dust of their feet and drink their words with thirst."[2] These words were directed against the government that aimed to separate the people from their teachers; anyone who converted his home into a place of instruction risked his very life if he was caught.

Of Jose ben Jochanan's life we know little. Of his teachings there remains the following saying: "Let thy house be opened wide and let the poor be like thy household and talk not much with a woman, not even with thy own wife."[3]

This statement, too, was aimed against the attempts of the government to introduce the morals of the Greeks and their lack of hospitality toward strangers and the poor. Since the Greeks worshipped goddesses, Jose ben Jochanan feared that people might come to deify woman through sexual motives and therefore sought to keep the sexes apart.

Jose ben Joezer was referred to as the "zealot of the priesthood." The death of both Joses marked the end of the Encyclopedists who directed the nation in all spheres of life. The Talmud also states that from the death of Moses until the death of Jose ben Joezer, the pursuit of study was as high as during the lifetime of Moses.

How Jose ben Jochanan died we do not know, but Jose ben Joezer died at the hands of Greek soldiers. He was condemned to be crucified because of his anti-government activities, and his last words testify to his noble spirit and to the strength of his faith.

The High Priest Alkimos was related to Jose ben Joezer. In his endeavor to gain the favor of the rulers, Alkimos ordered the destruction of all pious Jews who refused to submit to the Greek religion. At his behest, sixty Jews were caught and sentenced to death; among them was Jose ben Joezer. As they were being led to execution, Alkimos again tried to persuade his relative to submit to the government and save his life.

The following conversation between them was handed down through the generations:

"Look," said the High Priest, "at the wealth and great honor I possess because I obey the orders of the government. Also observe the misfortune you have brought upon yourself so that you have to die the death of a criminal."

To this Jose quietly replied: "If those who anger God live as well as you do, you can readily imagine how good will be the share of those who do his will."

Alkimos said further: "Can you show me another person who obeyed God's will more than you did?"

To which Jose replied: "If those who do God's will end as I do, what a terrible end must await those who anger him with their evil deeds."

These words made a deep impression on the High Priest and, according to the Midrash (*Bereshit Rabbah*) he thereupon committed suicide. Others claim that he died of a stroke. (Josephus, *Maccabees*).

Jose ben Joezer and Jose ben Jochanan were designated as "Ashkolot," (literally: clusters) because they united many virtues within themselves. Great as their scholarship was, they also excelled in moral behavior. When they passed away, the people declared that with their death all virtue had departed.[4]

It is also related that Jose ben Joezer had a son who was not capable and did not follow in the footsteps of his father. Jose therefore gave all his possessions for communal purposes.[5]

It was a time of unrest and wars between the kings of

Egypt and Syria, and Palestine was the battleground of the
contending armies. In this turmoil little attention was paid to
learning and ignorance prevailed. The general tendency was to
imitate the customs of the Gentiles, and the idea was current
that Jews should assimilate with the ruling Greek nation.
Among the first Greek customs to become popular were
athletics and public tournaments. Many Jews were persuaded
that their national welfare would be enhanced by training in
the various sports and gladiatorial exercises. There might have
been little objection to these sports were it not for the Greek
custom of engaging in them while altogether nude. It happened that when Jewish young men engaged in these exercises, they were ashamed of being circumcised and in various
ways tried to graft foreskins so as not to be recognized as Jews.

In time such manifestations of assimilation became secondary, and, as the party of the "Friends of the Greeks"
expanded through the richer elements of the population, they
attempted to modify the service in the Temple to resemble
more nearly the form of worship of the Greek temples.

Pious Jews considered such deeds as the peak of immorality and they rallied as a group and came to be known as
"Assembly of the Pious" or "Congregation of the Just" in order
to separate themselves still further from those whom they
considered to be Jews no longer.

There thus developed a great hatred between the two
contending parties. The friends of the Greeks were denounced
as "traitors to the covenant," "dregs of the people" and
"profaners of the holy covenant." The assimilationist elements
considered the pious people to be fools who observe strange
ceremonies that hinder a closer understanding between Jews
and Greeks, and before very long, the friends of the Greeks
called on the government to come to their assistance in their
struggle against the pious Jews.

7

JOCHANAN
THE HIGH PRIEST

Days of terror and tribulation beset the Jewish faith. Jerusalem was occupied by Syrian-Greek troops. The image of Zeus was installed in the Temple and swine were offered on the holy altar of the God of Israel. There was also no lack of Jewish traitors who assisted the enemy in his work, and it seemed that the last hour had struck for the Jewish religion. Pious Jews sought safety in the mountains and caves of Judea, hidden from the eyes of strangers. There they observed the laws of Judaism and avoided desecrating the Sabbath; there, too, they inducted the new born children into the Jewish faith.

In the town of Modiin, not far from Lud, there gathered a group of the faithful. One of the priests, Mattathias ben Jochanan of the Hasmonean family, who could trace his descent from the priest Jojariv, erected an altar to the God of Israel. When the representative of the government heard this, he sent an officer with a detachment of soldiers to investigate the situation. The Greek officer called Mattathias and commanded him to sacrifice a pig on the altar. To this Mattathias replied: "Were all the people of the king's domains to worship your god and were all the Jews to join them in this worship, I and my sons would still not deviate from the ways of my

59

forefathers and I will not serve any other God but the only living God in Heaven."

When one of the Jews approached the altar to fulfill the command of the officer, Mattathias stabbed and killed him. As the Greek officer tried to attack Mattathias, he and his soldiers were set upon by the surrounding people and were slaughtered.

Everyone realized that this act of rebellion would be followed by the revenge of the government and that they were facing a choice between struggle and annihilation. This deed of Mattathias, therefore, acted as a call to battle and a long and bitter war ensued. The Greeks could bring onto the field of battle many more well-equipped soldiers than the Jews could. The Jews therefore feared to face them in open battle and conducted a guerrilla form of warfare. Judah Macabbee, the son of Mattathias, fell in one of these battles and he was succeeded by his brother Jochanan who led the Jewish forces to victory in several engagements. With the consent of the king, Jochanan assumed the high priesthood which he held for a short time until he was betrayed to the enemy and killed. Simeon, the youngest son of Mattathias, then assumed the leadership of the people and also successfully completed the war of liberation.

The religious leadership of the nation rested then not in the hands of individuals or of a "pair" but was vested in a *Beit Din* (a court of at least five people and sometimes more). This body came to be known in the Talmud as the Court of the Hasmoneans but history does not record the names of any of the members of this court.

It is probable that this court did not exist before the rule of Jonathan, son of Mattathias. When Jonathan sent letters to the Lacedemonians to renew the alliance against the Syrians, we find these letters signed by men of the Great Council. When Simeon became Nasi, we read that this position was given to him by the Elders and the Heads of the People. These men apparently were the members of the Court of the Hasmoneans.

This court worked to erect an impenetrable wall between Jews and non-Jews. All the previous laws of the Torah pertaining to relations with other peoples were interpreted in the severest possible manner. They also instituted difficult regulations in all matters pertaining to uncleanness; all of these decrees later came to be known as the laws of the Hasmonean court.

It was this court that established the annual feast of eight days to commemorate the miracles that transpired during the war with the Greeks. This feast came to be called Chanukah, (dedication) because it was originally celebrated to rededicate the altar which the Greeks profaned with unclean sacrifices. Although many feast days to commemorate various triumphs of the Macabbees were in vogue at that time, only Chanukah with its lights and singing of praise continued to be celebrated throughout the years and was sanctioned by the Hasmonean court.

In addition to the new regulations, the ultrapious voluntarily assumed many other restrictions. Prayers that were introduced by the Great Synagogue were already in common use, but before beginning to recite them it became customary to devote a few minutes to spiritual communion with "the father in heaven." This spiritual communion they would not interrupt under any circumstances were even a king to drive by or were a snake to wind itself about the foot of the supplicant. Disregarding all perils, the ultrapious were ready to face any danger if only it would enable them to observe the laws of the Torah. The observance of the Sabbath was held in special esteem so that even the killing of a poisonous snake on that day was considered to be sinful. At first they even refused to fight their enemies on the Sabbath and history records one case during the lifetime of Mattathias when one thousand Jews were burned to death in a cave to which the Greek soldiers set fire because they did not want to desecrate the Sabbath by putting out the fire. After this occurrence Mattathias instructed all his followers to desecrate the Sabbath, if necessary, when fighting the enemy.

But the observance of the Sabbath was not the only law which they obeyed in its minutest details. They cleared the roads used by travelers of all thorns, glass and other hindrances lest some person stumble and be injured due to another's negligence. These they buried deep in the ground so that not even a ploughshare might turn them up.

After the triumph of the Hasmoneans, the people felt free and joyous and on feast days they all gathered together, both those who previously sinned as well as those who never departed from the faith, and joined in a common chorus. The past sinners would begin their song with the words, "Praised be he who never sinned" and the chorus responded "He who sinned shall be forgiven." Then those who felt free of wrong-doing intoned, "Praised be my youth which did not bring shame on my old age" and the sinners of the past joined with, "Praised be my old age which atones for the transgressions of my youth."

The court of the Hasmoneans was systematically strict in the enforcement of those laws that did not cause any loss to the people, but practiced leniency where the legislation was becoming intolerably severe, as in the cases of the Nazarites and the Passover offering. These lenient or strict interpretations were based on new studies of the text of the Bible to whose every letter great significance was being ascribed. The scholars of that time also began to ponder the events of Jewish history and attempted to explain the causes of the great suffering Jews had to endure. They came to the conclusion that all injury inflicted on the Jews invariably is avenged on the evildoers. Thus Amalek tried to destroy them and he was wiped off the face of the earth. Pharaoh enslaved the Jews and caused their children to be cast into the river, and as a result the Egyptians were drowned in the sea. This, they reasoned, must be the fate of every nation which does harm to the Jews; to be repaid with the same measure.

Simeon, the son of Mattathias the Hasmonean, was assassinated in a treacherous fashion by his son-in-law Ptolemy ben Chabub who occupied the post of tax collector in the district of Shechem. Feeling secure after his triumph over the Greeks, Simeon frequently accepted the invitations of his son-in-law to visit him together with his family. It was on one of these visits that he was murdered by Ptolemy who was secretly negotiating with the Greek rulers to have himself appointed governor of the country after the death of Simeon. But Ptolemy's hopes proved to be in vain. The king of Syria did not fulfill his promise, and Simeon's son Jochanan succeeded his father. Jochanan united within himself both the religious and the secular authority over the people as prince and High Priest.

Historically, Jochanan is known as John Hyrcanus or Hyrcanus I to distinguish him from King Hyrcanus III, the grandfather of Queen Miriam the Hasmonean. In the Talmud he is called Jochanan the High Priest. The surname Hyrcanus came from his conquest of the fortress Hyrcania.

After Ptolemy murdered Jochanan's father he held his mother as hostage for fear of reprisals from Jochanan. When Jochanan stormed Ptolemy's fortress and it seemed that it might fall, Ptolemy led his mother-in-law to the wall of the castle and there he tortured her in sight of her son. Jochanan was ready to withdraw in order to spare his mother any more suffering, but she exhorted him in the name of his father not to be affected by her injuries and to exert every effort to take the fortress. But the stronghold was well fortified and he could not conquer it. Seeking for an excuse to retreat without shame, Jochanan declared that the new year, which was just then beginning, was a sabbatical year during which no wars might be waged. Ptolemy murdered his mother-in-law and fled after which he was never heard of again.

Shortly after this event Jochanan was again involved in war with the Greeks who, under their new king Antiochus Sedetis, attempted to regain control of the country. They advanced on Jerusalem with a great army but they could not take it. The power of the Greeks was broken, and they feared the intervention of Rome that was bound by treaty to assist the Jews. After much fighting a new peace was declared and under its terms the Jews had to pay 500 measures of silver and to deliver a number of young men from the noble families as hostages. In time the relations with the Syrian Greek kingdom improved to such an extent that Jochanan even sent military assistance to their king in his wars against the Parthians.

Jochanan was engaged in many protracted wars until he finally succeeded in completely freeing his country. With the

aid of gold treasure that he found in the tombs of the kings of
Judea, he hired a mercenary army and marched on the
Idumeans. To them he offered the choice of accepting the
Jewish faith or being exiled. The Idumeans preferred to accept
the Jewish religion rather than be driven out of their homes.
Jochanan then attacked Samaria and he destroyed it together
with the Samaritan temple which was the greatest hindrance to
the existence of the Temple in Jerusalem.

As a result of these conquests, it became necessary to
introduce new regulations to fit the newly created conditions.
Among the conquered cities there were some which were
previously a part of Syria and as such were considered unclean,
where no Jew might live. These cities were now considered a
part of Palestine and were subject to all the laws pertaining to
tithes, the sabbatical year, the bringing of the first fruits, the
pilgrimage to Jerusalem, and the offering of sacrifices. The rule
was established that if one buys a field in Syria it is as if he
bought a field in a suburb of Jerusalem, and all the newly
conquered cities which could be reached without passing
through foreign territory were considered to be the equals of
the holy Palestine towns. In this manner Jochanan extended
the boundaries of Palestine to include Syria in the possession of
the Jews, even as he did with the cities of Idumea.

Some of the regulations relating to the bond of Syria with
Palestine were changed at a later date. It soon became evident
that the Idumeans who were converted by force did not add to
the well-being of the Jewish people. But the sincerity of the
intentions of Jochanan was appreciated by all and even though,
in later years, he came in conflict with the scholars, the Talmud
nevertheless credits him for his good intentions.

Other religious innovations were directed against the
Samaritans (Kutim) who mingled with the other Jews after the
destruction of their temple, but in their hearts still bore a great
hatred toward them. This hatred caused uneasiness and the
Samaritans were mistrusted; their adherence to the Jewish
people was questioned even though they seemed to observe
some customs even more strictly than did the Jews. It was then
forbidden to partake of a Samaritan's food and eating the bread

of a Samaritan was considered the same as eating pork.

Among his other innovations, the High Priest Jochanan also did away with reciting the dedication which was prescribed for all men who brought the tithe. He sent out messengers throughout the cities of Palestine to see whether the tithes were properly contributed. These messengers reported to him that the Palestine farmers gave only the "large tithe," the exact amount of which was never established; they therefore offered only between 2 and 3 percent. When Jochanan heard this he ordered that whoever bought grain or fruit from a farmer (*am ha'aretz*) should produce tithes, and he was obliged to offer the necessary amount even though the seller assured him that the tithes were already given. It was for this reason that he abolished the confession during the offering of tithes; out of fear that a falsehood might be uttered before God, if a person should say that he gave the proper tithes.

The difficulties with the giving of tithes began during the days of Ezra. Since not all the Levites wanted to return to Palestine from Babylonia, Ezra fined those who refused to return by taking away their rights to the tithe. It thus became impossible to include the words "and I gave it to the Levite" which are contained in the Biblical text of the confession of the tithes. Others thought that since the tithes were frequently collected by force it would not be true to confess that the tithes were "given." The High Priest Jochanan also realized that the conditions affecting the tithes changed radically. During the days of the first Temple, Palestine was divided among the tribes and the Levites did not possess any lands; they were thus entitled to the tithes. But in his time conditions were different, and the tithes weighed heavily on the farmers who had to pay taxes in addition to the three different kinds of tithes (first tithe, second tithe, tithe for the poor). Realizing the injustice of this condition and being powerless to abolish the commandment of the Torah, he introduced a new system. He appointed overseers to see that the farmers obeyed the law and to take the tithes, by force if necessary. But when a person bought produce from a farmer he did not have to inquire where tithes were given but had to consider his purchase as *Demai*, doubtful produce, from which the buyer had to give the tithes.

Until the time of Jochanan it was customary to work in Jerusalem in the period between the first and last day of a holiday and the pounding of hammers was heard throughout the city. Jochanan considered this a profanation of the holy city and he forbade it. When in later years it was altogether forbidden to work with hammers in Jerusalem, the new regulation was based on Jochanan's ordinance.

He also did away with the singing of Psalm 48 by the Levites during the service. Verse 24 of this Psalm reads "Awake, why do you slumber, Lord." It came to be chanted at a time when the Jews were sorely pressed on all sides while the other nations lived in peace. But Jochanan held that it is disrespectful to ask God to awake from slumber. He also changed the procedure of offering sacrifices. Previously, it was customary to make an incision between the horns of the animal with a sharp knife in order that the blood might blind it and make it easier to bind. Jochanan said that this practice was equivalent to crippling the sacrifice as the cut might pierce the animal's brain and thus make it unfit for sacrifice. He ordered that a ring be made to be placed on the neck of the animal and thus facilitate its binding.

In the observance of the commandments of the Torah, Jochanan always sided with the Pharisees. But once, during the closing years of his life, the Pharisees incurred his anger and he forsook them to take the part of the Sadducees. It happened during a feast which he gave after one of his victories, that, flushed with wine he challenged the assembled to mention any evil which they knew of him. One of the guests, Eleazar ben Poirah, whom the Talmud calls "a wicked and hard-hearted scoffer," said to Jochanan: "The Pharisees are displeased with you." When Jochanan inquired for the cause of the displeasure, there rose an old man Jehudah ben Gadidiah and said: "Enough that you have the crown of royalty; leave the crown of the priesthood for a pious descendant of Aaron, for you are the son of a woman who was held in captivity." (He was referring to the fact that Jochanan's mother was held captive among the Gentiles which may have cast some doubt on his parentage.) Very much concerned, Jochanan had the whole matter investigated and when the statement was not substantiated, Jehudah ben Gadidiah was tried by the Sanhedrin and sentenced to be flogged.

But Jochanan was not satisifed with this punishment and the Sadducees further incited him to believe that all the Pharisees thought as Jehudah ben Gadidiah did. When Jochanan tried to justify the verdict of the Sanhedrin on the grounds that the Torah commands a slanderer be flogged, Eleazar ben Poirah said: "True, this is the law for one who slanders an ordinary person, but in this case where a king and high priest was slandered, the Sanhedrin should have acted differently."

Jochanan allowed himself to be persuaded. He removed all the Pharisees from the Sanhedrin and filled their places with Sadducees. The new Sanhedrin immediately tried Jehudah ben Gadidiah a second time and condemned him to death together with a number of other Pharisees. From that time on Jochanan remained an adherent of the Sadducees.

8

JOSHUA BEN PERACHIAH
AND
NITTAI OF ARBELA

THE PERIOD OF THE SPIRITUAL ACTIVITY of the
High Priest Jochanan also marked the rise of another "pair" of
spiritual leaders. Sympathizing at that time with the Pharisees,
Jochanan recognized the necessity of bringing to the forefront
of religious life the two most outstanding scholars, one of
whom was to serve as Nasi of the Sanhedrin, and the other was
to be head of the Supreme Court, even as in the days of Jose
ben Joezer and Jose ben Jochanan. He accordingly appointed
Joshua ben Perachiah as Nasi and Nittai of Arbela to head the
Supreme Court.

Whatever innovations were introduced by these scholars
were credited to Jochanan because, as political and religious
leader of the nation, he had sufficient authority to enforce
them. But when Jochanan transferred his allegiance to the
Sadducees after the Sanhedrin sentenced Jehudah ben
Gadidiah simply to be flogged for slandering him, he removed
all the Pharisees from the Sanhedrin and abolished all their
legislation. Joshua ben Perachiah feared to remain in the
country and fled to Egypt where, it may be assumed, he was
joined by Nittai of Arbela.

From Egypt Joshua ben Perachiah wrote to the Jews of
Palestine that wheat shipped from Alexandria should be considered unclean because he believed it was being contaminated

by unclean hands in the irrigation and fertilization processes in practice in Egypt. This restriction was based on the text of the Torah (Leviticus: 11). Others explained his prohibition of the use of Alexandrian wheat on the grounds that by using irrigation and other artificial methods to encourage plant growth, humans interfered with natural laws and attempted to improve the natural course of development as it was ordained by God.

However, the leaders in Jerusalem refused to abide by his prohibition and said that even though he might consider it unclean, all other Jews considered it fit for consumption.[1]

It is regrettable that no mention is made of Joshua ben Perachiah's relation to the Temple of Onias in Alexandria. It is possible that he did not openly condemn the Temple of Onias because it was held in great reverence by the Jews of Egypt, but secretly he must have been opposed to it. He was too deeply attached to Jerusalem and to its temple to reconcile himself to the idea that Jews could have another temple outside of Jerusalem. He therefore tried to create the impression that whatever came out of Egypt was impure, both the grain that was shipped out as well as the sacrifices that were offered there.

The manner in which Onias, the son of Simon the Just, left Jerusalem and erected the Temple of Onias to compete with the temple in Jerusalem was related in a previous chapter. It is characteristic that the scholars had no definite attitude toward this temple. They were convinced that it was built for sacred purposes and therefore stated that "The Temple of Onias is not a house of idolatry."[2]

But in spite of the official sanction they gave to this temple, they never wholeheartedly approved of it. The priests of the Temple of Onias were equal to the priests of *bamot* (high places for offering sacrifices) built for sacred and not idolatrous purposes. This type of *bamah* was forbidden during the time that the Temple existed, but a *bamah* erected by an individual for sacred purposes was permitted. Therefore, they looked on the temple of Onias as a private *bamah* built for sacred purposes.

The *Mishnah* established a rule that whoever vowed to

bring a burnt offering to the Temple of Onias must offer this sacrifice in the Temple in Jerusalem, but if the person sacrificed the burnt offering in the Temple of Onias he had fulfilled his vow. Josephus relates that during the civil war between the Princes Hyrcanus and Aristobulus, when the Jews of the various cities of Palestine could not go to Jerusalem to sacrifice the Paschal lamb, they went to the temple of Onias to bring this offering.

It is interesting to note the contradictions that characterize Josephus's writings on the Temple of Onias. On one occasion he states that when Onias built this temple, he persuaded the king of Egypt that such a temple would serve to keep alive the hatred of the Jews toward Antiochus for having destroyed the Temple in Jerusalem. Several pages further, Josephus maintains that by building this temple, Onias sought to avenge himself for the wrong he believed perpetrated by the Jews of Jerusalem.

Of the teachings of Joshua ben Perachiah there has come down to us one noble maxim: "Make thee a teacher and win thee a friend and judge every man favorably."[3]

The political and social conditions in Palestine were such that if a person wanted to remain true to the traditions of his people he needed a teacher and a guide whom he might emulate or a friend to correct any error in his ways. Joshua ben Perachiah especially believed in judging people fairly. Forced to flee Jerusalem and seek refuge in Alexandria, he never spoke evil of the high priest Jochanan who was responsible for his exile.

But Nittai of Arbela held a more pessimistic point of view. He stated: "Keep far from an evil neighbor and do not consort with the wicked, and do not despair in time of punishment." This pessimism of Nittai of Arbela, ending on a hopeful note, was an outgrowth of his life experiences. It is probable that he was friendly to the Sadducees in his youth and realized later the dangers inherent in such friendship, but he did not despair of the situation and never gave up hoping that times would change for the better.

In time, conditions did change in Jerusalem. The High Priest Jochanan died, and in his will appointed his wife queen, and his son Aristobulus High Priest. But Aristobulus seized the royal crown. When was chided by his mother for not adhering to his father's will, he imprisoned her together with three of his younger brothers. In prison, the queen died of starvation.

A disagreement between Aristobulus and his brother Antigonos, leader of the army, led to the assassination of Antigonos. Aristobulus died a short time later and was succeeded by his widow Salome who then freed Jochanan's third son, Alexander Jannai. Alexander married her, even though as High Priest he was forbidden to marry a widow, and together they reigned over the land.

Queen Salome was friendly to the Pharisees and she appointed her brother Simeon ben Shetach religious head. Simeon immediately invited Joshua ben Perachiah to return from Egypt. Joshua hastened to Jerusalem, but whether he resumed his previous position remains unknown.

It is related that Joshua ben Perachiah once came into conflict with one of his disciples named Jeshu. (Some would have it that Jeshu was really Jesus, but this is altogether impossible since Jesus lived during the latter part of the reign of Herod when Joshua ben Perachiah would have been 160 years old.) Once, when Joshua lived in Egypt, he was kindly treated by the proprietress of his inn. Joshua praised her to his disciples and said: "See what a beautiful woman she is." Jeshu said: "Rabbi, she is not beautiful for her eyes are almond-shaped." Thereupon Joshua said to him: "Wicked man, are you concerned with such trifles?" and he drove him away. Jeshu returned numerous times to reconcile with his master but Joshua paid no attention to him. Once he came while Joshua was in the midst of reciting the *Shema* and was ready to forgive him. Joshua motioned to him with his hand to wait until he completed the prayer. The disciple misunderstood the gesture and believed he was being driven away. He left and began to devote himself to magic. Joshua went to his house to tell him that he would be forgiven if he repented, but was told that it was too late.

9

JEHUDAH BEN TABBAI
AND
SIMEON BEN SHETACH

JEHUDAH BEN TABBAI and Simeon ben Shetach were the third of the "pairs" in the series of dual leadership. It is not clear who was Nasi of the Sanhedrin and who was head of the court. The name of Jehudah ben Tabbai is listed first whenever they are mentioned together and one might conclude that he was the Nasi. However, there is an opinion that Simeon ben Shetach was Nasi and Jehudah ben Tabbai was head of the court.[1]

They lived in an unsettled period. The Sadducees were strongly entrenched in the government of Judea and the struggle with them was difficult and protracted. After the death of the High Priest Jochanan, the throne was assumed by his son Aristobulus and shortly after *his* death, it was ascended by his widow who married his brother Alexander Jannai. This marked the beginning of a new epoch for the Pharisees. The new king, (always referred to as Jannai), was too preoccupied with matters of state to devote himself to the religious problems of the country during the first years of his reign. He left these matters to the queen who referred them to her brother Simeon ben Shetach. Simeon could not free the country of the Sadducee leadership all at once but instead proceeded gradually. At first he was the only Pharisee in the Sanhedrin. He made it a practice to challenge the decisions of the Sanhedrin and to demand that such decisions be authenticated by the text of the Torah. Such proof had to be produced in the presence of the king and queen and he used those opportunities to point out that the Sadducees did not interpret the Torah correctly. One by one he managed to remove the Sadducees from the Sanhedrin and to replace them with Pharisees.

The conflict between the Sadducees and the Pharisees thus reached a breaking point. The majority of the religious decisions which Simeon ben Shetach sponsored were largely in protest against the opinions of the Sadducees whose influence on Jewish life he tried to eradicate.

Alexander Jannai spent most of his time in extensive wars that threatened the freedom of the country. When, upon his return from a victorious war, he realized that the Pharisees had gained the upper hand in the religious life of the land, he decided to humble them. During the festival of *Sukkot*, as he was standing near the altar and preparing to pour water upon it (a custom much in favor with the Pharisees) he poured the water on his feet instead. Greatly enraged, the populace threw their etrogim at the king and called him insulting names. The king evidently expected this reaction from the people for he had previously stationed a number of mercenaries outside the temple. When the disturbance began, the soldiers were called in and a terrible slaughter ensued. Eight hundred Pharisees, who escaped from the temple, were also executed.

Many prominent Pharisees then fled from Jerusalem. Some of them sought refuge in Egypt, where they were welcomed with open arms, while others hid in the mountains and caves of Judea. Among those who hid there was Simeon ben Shetach who realized that his sister, the queen, could defend him no longer.

Jehudah ben Tabbai found shelter in Egypt. It is related that just as Simeon ben Shetach recalled Joshua ben Perachiah during the first years of the reign of Alexander Jannai, he similarly recalled Jehudah ben Tabbai at a later date. In his letter recalling Joshua ben Perachiah, Simeon wrote: "From me, the holy city Jerusalem to you, my sister Alexandria. My master resides within you while I am deserted." When Simeon invited Jehudah ben Tabbai he wrote: "From the great city of Jerusalem to the small Alexandria! How long will my bridegroom reside with you while I am sorrowing for him?"

How Simeon ben Shetach returned to Jerusalem from his hiding place is related thus: Alexander Jannai was entertaining foreign guests and when they were merry with food and drink one of them said: "We remember that a few years ago you had an old man here who entertained us with wise maxims. Where is he now? Will you call him here?" Jannai looked toward the queen and after he promised her that no harm would befall him, Simeon was recalled.

For a short time the persecution of the Pharisees ceased. The king desired to reconcile the people, and he sent messengers to inquire what he should do to regain their devotion. But the people would not hear of reconciliation and answered that only the death of the king would eradicate the memory of the bloodshed. Some of the Pharisees were not satisfied with this reply and allied themselves with a foreign ruler to oust Alexander Jannai. This still further enraged Jannai against the Pharisees and when the foreign invader was defeated he executed a great number of Pharisees.

This last act of revenge stilled the king's anger against the Pharisees and he persecuted them no more. On the contrary, he became convinced that in order to possess the throne securely, a Jewish sovereign could have no subjects more loyal than the Pharisees. On his death bed, he admonished the queen to fear neither the Pharisees nor the Sadducees but to beware only of those who pretend to be Pharisees and commit the acts of Zimri while they demand the reward of Pinchas.[2]

Jannai died at the age of 49 after a reign of twenty-seven years. Before he died he appointed the queen to rule the country and asked her to keep his death secret as long as possible. She fulfilled his wish and appointed their son, Hyrcanus, High Priest.

Simeon ben Shetach returned as head of the Sanhedrin (or the court) and directed all his energies to the struggles with the Sadducees whose teachings he was determined to eradicate.

He introduced the law of the "dissenting elder" that imposed the death sentence on any member of the Sanhedrin who opposed a majority in interpreting the law, even if the dissenter held a more severe interpretation or attempted to add to the laws enjoined by the Torah.

Nothing is known of the activities of Jehudah ben Tabbai during this time. He is mentioned only once as having permitted the execution of a false witness whose testimony (had it been accepted) would have caused the defendant to be put to death. The Pharisees held that in such a case the false witness should be executed even though the defendant was not put to death. The Sadducees, on the other hand, maintained that as long as the defendant was not put to death the false witness, too, should not be executed. It was also acceptable to sentence both witnesses of the prosecution.

After Jehudah ben Tabbai sentenced a single perjured witness to death, Simeon ben Shetach told him he had shed the blood of an innocent man because the testimony of two witnesses was required to condemn the defendant. One false witness could, under no circumstance, cause a death sentence to be passed. Jehudah ben Tabbai realized his error and thenceforth refused to pass any sentence in the absence of Simeon ben Shetach. He frequently visited the grave of the executed witness and wept bitterly. It was said that whoever heard Jehudah ben Tabbai weep thought that he heard the weeping of the slain man.[3]

The following maxim of Jehudah ben Tabbai has come down to us: "Do not make yourself as one of the advocates. When the suitors are before you let them be as wrongdoers in your sight, and when they have departed let them be as innocent men in your estimation, seeing they have accepted the sentence."

Simeon ben Shetach used to say: "Examine thoroughly the witnesses and be careful in your words lest through them they may learn to lie."

Jehudah ben Tabbai was noted for his modesty. To illustrate the harm success may bring to a person he recounted: "If someone had told me before I attained greatness that I would succeed, I would have become his enemy for life. Now that I have attained greatness, were someone to tell me that I might lose it, I would be ready to pour boiling water on him."[4]

There is a story related of the sojourn of Jehudah ben Tabbai in Egypt that is very similar to the one told about Joshua ben Perachiah. Praising the generosity of the proprietress of his inn, he said to his disciples: "Do you remember the proprietress who treated me so generously?" To this one of his pupils remarked: "Rabbi, she had diseased eyes." Jehudah ben Tabbai said to him: "With one statement you have commited two wrongs. You suspected me of considering the beauty of that woman, and I also see that you carefully looked at her face while I only beheld her good deeds."[5]

Witchcraft was commonly believed in Palestine at that time and many people fell under the influence of so-called witches who undermined their religious beliefs. Although Simeon ben Shetach did not place any faith in the power of "witches," he nevertheless realized that they were a pernicious influence and led many to immorality. Therefore he had eighty "witches" captured and hanged on the same day. Ordinarily he would not have permitted so many women to be executed on the same day even, though the Bible commands that witches be· put to death. But he defended his action on the grounds that the condition of the country required that this plague that was devouring the people like a contagious disease had to be stopped.[6]

Among the executed "witches" were many whose relatives sought to avenge their deaths. These bribed false witnesses to testify that the son of Simeon ben Shetach had committed a crime that was punishable by death. The Sanhedrin, after hearing the testimony, condemned the young man to death. But as he was being led to execution, the witnesses confessed their perjury. Simeon wanted to accept their recantation, but his son said to him: "If you would have the teachings of the Pharisees accepted without question, then you must not permit witnesses to repudiate their testimony. You must accept this as my fate to become the means for the attainment of your ends."[7]

Simeon's son was concerned lest it should become impossible to punish false witnesses, if they were given the right to repudiate their previous testimony. Whether Simeon made other attempts to save his son and whether he was successful remains unknown.

Another time, it is told, Simeon saw a man with a knife in his hand pursuing another man into a ruin. Simeon followed him inside where he saw blood upon the knife and the other man wounded and expiring in agony. Simeon addressed the murderer: "Wicked man, it is clear who murdered this man, but you are lucky that I can do nothing to you for the Torah says that two witnesses are required to condemn a criminal, while I am the only one who witnessed the crime."[8]

That the relations between Simeon ben Shetach and King Jannai were never cordial even when they were together is amply illustrated by numerous stories concerning the two men. Once, it is told, a man was killed by the king's slave. (Probably one of his mercenaries.) The Sanhedrin informed Jannai of the crime and the king sent the slave to face judgment by the court. But the court demanded that the king appear since in the eyes of the law a slave was like any other livestock for which its owner is responsible. When Jannai appeared before the Sanhedrin he sat down and Simeon ben Shetach said to him: "King Jannai, stand on your feet, not to honor us but to honor the Creator of the universe." To this Jannai replied: "I will stand only if your colleagues also demand it." But all the members of the Sanhedrin remained silent. Simeon turned to his right and saw them lower their eyes; he turned to his left and he met the same sight. Simeon said: "Let him who can read your thoughts punish you for your thoughts at this moment."[9] Since that time, the law stated that a king could not judge nor could he be judged; he was not to be called as a witness nor was anyone to bear testimony against him.[10]

One of the important regulations instituted by Simeon ben Shetach concerned the *ketubbah* (marriage certificate) of a woman. Until that time women had no right over the property of their husbands. The husband gave to the father of the bride a sum mentioned in the *ketubbah*. When a man wanted to divorce his wife he told her: "Go and take the money of the *ketubbah* from your father. Simeon ben Shetach ruled that the husband should retain the sum specified in the *ketubbah*. In this manner the wife became a partner to all his possessions which served as her guarantee. Indirectly it also made it more difficult to obtain a divorce.[11]

Simeon ben Shetach also ruled that every father must engage a teacher for his children. Previously it was customary for a parent who wanted his son to acquire knowledge to send him to the academies of the great scholars; otherwise the children grew up in ignorance and came in contact with religious training only on the rare occasions when they visited Jerusalem.[12]

Simeon ben Shetach lived in poverty most of his life. During the time he was in hiding to save himself from the wrath of his royal brother-in-law, he could not use his scholarship to gain a livelihood and became a flax merchant. Once he bought a donkey from an Ishmaelite. When he brought his donkey home, his disciples found a diamond in a little bag tied around the animal's neck. They said to their teacher: "God's blessing has made you rich." But Simeon answered: "I bought only the animal but not the diamond." When he returned the diamond to the Ishmaelite, the latter exclaimed: "Praised be the God of Simeon ben Shetach."[13]

10

SHEMAIAH AND ABTALION

SHEMAIAH AND ABTALION SUCCEEDED Jehudah ben Tabbai and Simeon ben Shetach to leadership in Jewish life. Shemaiah became Nasi of the Sanhedrin and Abtalion became head of the court.

Of their descent it is told that they were children or grandchildren of proselytes. But despite the fact that the position of the descendants of proselytes, even to the tenth generation, was not very favorable, they achieved the highest honors which Jews of that time could hope to attain. It is also necessary to remember that Shemaiah and Abtalion lived before the treason of the Idumeans and proselytes were therefore not viewed with suspicion.

We also do not know who chose these two scholars for their positions and whether their election was peacefully accomplished. It is possible that the king of Judea, who surrounded himself with mercenaries to protect himself from his subjects, purposely chose descendants of proselytes to head the Sanhedrin in the hope that they would side with the Sadducees. However, if that was his intention he was mistaken, for although Shemaiah and Abtalion were peaceful people who did not meddle in politics, they faithfully clung to the Pharisees and did not make the least change in the system of interpreting the commandments of the Torah as was established by previous scholars.

Shemaiah and Abtalion were influential during one of the unhappiest periods in Jewish history. Before her death, Salome, the widow of Alexander Jannai, relinquished the throne to her son Jochanan Hyrcanus who was a peaceful retiring man. Jochanan's brother, Aristobulus, did not approve of the arrangement and began a war against his brother that ended in a compromise. Aristobulus became king and Jochanan Hyrcanus assumed the High Priesthood. This arrangement might have proved to be lasting were it not for Antipater, a friend of Hyrcanus, who was a descendant of the forced Idumean converts, brought into the Jewish fold by Hyrcanus's grandfather. Antipater sought to create discord between the two rulers. He tried to persuade Aristobulus that his brother was planning to regain the throne. But Aristobulus paid no heed to his accusation, although there was some justification in it since Hyrcanus was the older of the two brothers and thus the rightful heir to the throne. Failing in this attempt, Antipater told Hyrcanus that Aristobulus wanted to be rid of him in order to unite the throne and the High Priest's office in his person.[1]

Antipater suggested that it would be easier to carry on a war against his brother from outside the city and advised Hyrcanus to leave Jerusalem. Hyrcanus accepted the advice and together with a host of followers left the city. Hyrcanus established an alliance with a neighboring Arab king who was told that Aristobulus wished to annex his land, and he was promised considerable compensation for his aid in the forthcoming war against Aristobulus.

Reinforced by the Arab king, Hyrcanus besieged Jerusalem. This siege, however, was only against the king and not against the people, and the besiegers agreed to permit the daily sacrifice to be offered at the temple. Every day the priests within the city lowered a sum of money from the wall of the city and the besiegers hoisted up the animals required for the sacrifice.

One of the besiegers, a man who spoke Greek, told the

soldiers to hoist up pigs instead of the usual animals, because it would be impossible to take the city as long as the daily sacrifices were properly conducted. It is unknown where they obtained pigs in Palestine, but this act shocked the whole populace who fantastically embellished the consequences of this horrible mockery. It was told that when the pigs stuck their nails (?) into the walls of Jerusalem, the whole countryside shook for four hundred miles. A tornado accompanied by an earthquake swept the land. Darkness covered the land during midday and in one moment all the grain on the fields surrounding Jerusalem wilted. When it was later necessary to bring the *Omer*, the first ripened sheaf, none was found near Jerusalem and it was necessary to bring one from a long distance.

The Sadducees had lost most of their influence by that time and when the inhabitants of the countryside about Jerusalem had to bring the Paschal lamb but could not enter the city, they went to offer this sacrifice in the Temple of Onias in Alexandria.

Jerusalem continued to withstand the siege. The besiegers could not take the fortress by storm and the besieged would not surrender. Both contending brothers then appealed to the Roman general Pompey, who happened to be near Palestine, to arbitrate between them. Pompey arrived in Jerusalem with a large army. He removed Aristobulus, executed many of his followers, and appointed Hyrcanus High Priest with the title of Ethnarch, ruler of the land and representative of Rome. To impress upon Hyrcanus still further that he was not an independent ruler, Pompey appointed Antipater his assistant in the secular government. Antipater thus became virtual ruler of the country and Hyrcanus had to be satisfied with the High Priesthood and the official title of Ethnarch.

After the death of Aristobulus, his two sons Alexander and Antigonos continued the struggle against Hyrcanus to regain the country. They formed an alliance with the Persians and with their aid Antigonos, the younger son of Aristobulus, succeeded in defeating Hyrcanus and he led him as a captive to Babylonia. Antigonos maintained himself in Jerusalem for three years. At the end of that time, Herod, the son of

Antipater, appeared with a large Roman army. Antigonos was overthrown as a rebel against the Romans and the throne was occupied by Herod who recalled Hyrcanus to the High Priesthood.

These wars lasted for more than thirty years and caused endless suffering, but scholarship and the learning of the Torah did not cease. For a short time, the Sanhedrin were divided into five groups according to the division of Palestine under five governors. By means of this division the Romans attempted to weaken the power of the Sanhedrin; but the attempt failed and the Sanhedrin were again reunited in Jerusalem under the leadership of Shemaiah and Abtalion.

There is a legend that Shemaiah and Abtalion were descendants of Sancherib, king of Assyria. They did not interfere with the political affairs of the country, and it is possible that as descendants of converts they did not feel keenly the national humiliation the Jews had to withstand in their own country. As long as they were permitted to observe the Torah according to the interpretations of the Pharisees, and the temple was not disturbed, they were not greatly concerned with the political storms agitating the land.

Two maxims of Shemaiah and Abtalion have come down to us. These sayings are not entirely clear and require some elucidation. Shemaiah said: "Love work and hate mastery and do not mingle with the officials." Abtalion said: "Wise men, take heed of your words lest you incur the guilt that is punished by exile; you shall be exiled to a place of evil water, and the disciples who come after you will drink and die, and the name of Heaven will be profaned."

It is evident that both sayings referred to the events of the time. All those who sought to rule met with misfortune, and many of the scholars had to seek refuge in Egypt where their disciples absorbed many new ideas opposed to those current in Palestine.

Shemaiah and Abtalion sought to limit the number of students in their academy and instituted an admission fee for some reason that has never been definitely established. Everyone had to pay a half-penny to the gate keeper. This sum was considered quite large for at that time a person had to work half a day to earn it.

Since the downfall of Aristobulus, small detachments of his army roamed in the Galilee and conducted guerrilla warfare against the Syrians and Romans. Herod tracked them down with great cruelty until he finally captured their leader, Hezekiah, and killed him together with some of his men. The populace was enraged against Herod and, with the consent of Hyrcanus, he was summoned to appear for trial before the Sanhedrin. Herod appeared, not as a defendant, but as a great commander dressed in purple and armed with a sword. He was surrounded by a large number of armed warriors, ready to attack anyone who should attempt to touch him. The Sanhedrin was displeased but out of fear its members maintained silence. Shemaiah warned them not to spare the defendant, for if they showed fear, Herod would convict them at some future time. Encouraged by Shemaiah's words, they began to question Herod and the witnesses. However, when Hyrcanus saw that the Sanhedrin might convict Herod, he suggested postponing the sentence until the following day. Herod fled from Jerusalem the same night.

Later, when Herod became virtual ruler of the country, he remembered that the scholars dared to bring him to trial and he persecuted them. Many of them were killed, but he spared Shemaiah and Abtalion. He was deeply impressed by Shemaiah's courageous stand at that trial, and he also feared to touch the most prominent elders of the nation. And so he waited until they all died natural deaths.

All the wrongs which the Hasmoneans ever committed against their people, their persecution of the Pharisees, their civil wars, their immorality, and imitation of Greek morals, all of these were visited upon the Hasmonean family and upon the people during that terrible time when they suffered the yoke of Herod. For Herod, the people had no other appellation than the "Idumean slave." Secretly the people admitted that they deserved this punishment, because they had permitted the

House of David to decline and allowed priests to become rulers.

Shemaiah and Abtalion exhibited their courage on still another occasion. Once, when the High Priest was returning home after the Day of Atonement service accompanied by all the people, he met Shemaiah and Abtalion. The people thereupon left the High Priest and followed Shemaiah and Abtalion. Although he was angered, the High Priest said nothing. When Shemaiah and Abtalion later came to greet him he said: "Let the children of the Gentiles go in peace." This hint at their non-Jewish origin evoked the following response from Shemaiah and Abtalion: "Let the children of the Gentiles come in peace, for they do the deeds of Aaron who was a lover of peace, but let the son of Aaron not come in peace, for he does not follow in the ways of Aaron."[2]

11

THE MEN
OF BATHYRA

HEROD, THE SON OF ANTIPATER, and one of the
Idumean proselytes, seized the government of the country. His
every move was drowned in Jewish blood for he annihilated all
the scholars of that time. He was especially vengeful toward
those who had any relation to the royal Hasmonean family. He
spared Shemaiah and Abtalion, the two representatives of the
Sanhedrin. Because of their advanced age he considered it wise
to wait until they died and not many years passed before both
of them died a natural death.

When the two leaders died, and who passed away first,
we do not know. But we do know that for a considerable time
after their deaths scholarship went into decline. The people
were preoccupied with the desperate political situation and
whenever the Talmud refers to those days, it hints that it was
a period when the Torah was forgotten by the people. The one
virtue that characterized the time was that those who were
ignorant revered those who were learned. In later years the
situation changed to such an extent that people were ashamed
of scholarship, and the ignorant *am ha'aretz* was reckoned
higher than a scholar.

In the place of Shemaiah and Abtalion there came two
men who are known only through their city of origin. The

Talmud calls them the men of Bathyra. No mention is made of their descent but they probably were not related or they could not have both been members of the Sanhedrin. Bathyra, from where they came, was located in northeastern Palestine near Mount Hermon. It was founded as a fortress against the attacks of robber bands who roved near the borders.

The Torah was largely forgotten by the people, but we may assume that here and there scholars were still to be found outside of Jerusalem. When Herod had to choose new leaders for the Sanhedrin, he sought them among the scholars of the outlying districts, convinced that men of the provinces would be loyal to him and do his bidding.

The men of Bathyra—it must be noted—were pious, God-fearing and modest, and endeavored with all their might to preserve the Jewish faith. They did not deviate from any of the ways of the Pharisees. Only once were they in doubt about the observance of a religious law. It happened that Passover eve fell on a Saturday and they did not know whether the sacrifice of the Paschal lamb superseded the Sabbath and should be offered as on a weekday or whether the sacrifice should not be offered at all.

They spent a long time seeking a solution but they could not find one, neither was there anyone in Jerusalem who could inform them. They were ready to declare that since an ordinary feast day offering does not supersede the Sabbath, neither does the Paschal lamb offering. Then a man came to them and said that in Jerusalem there lived Hillel of Babylon who had studied with Shemaiah and Abtalion, and he would certainly know whether the sacrifice of the Paschal lamb supersedes the Sabbath. Hillel was summoned before them and declared that the offering of the Paschal lamb *does* supersede the Sabbath. The men of Bathyra did not want to accept his opinion until he assured them that he had received this law from Shemaiah and Abtalion. When they heard this they finally believed him and, being honestly ashamed of their ignorance, withdrew from their positions, declaring that they were not worthy to retain them.

In later years numerous versions of this event developed.

The great modesty of the men of Bathyra was frequently recalled and many a man remarked: "I could do everything but not what the men of Bathyra did."

Meanwhile Herod continued his bloody rule of the land. In his war against Jerusalem, with Roman aid he wiped out all male descendants of the Hasmoneans. Later, attempting to gain the confidence of the people, he married the Hasmonean Princess Miriam, the daughter of Alexander, who was the son of Aristobulus and the grandson of King Alexander Jannai. On her mother's side Miriam was a grand daughter of King Hyrcanus. At the same time that Herod was becoming firmly entrenched in the country and was annihilating the Hasmonean dynasty, Hyrcanus remained in Babylonia. The Babylonian Jews loyally promised to defend him all his life. But Herod was dissatisfied with this state of affairs and by various wiles succeeded in bringing Hyrcanus back to Palestine. Soon after his return, Herod had one of Hyrcanus's ears cut off in order to make him unfit for the priesthood. But even a disfigured Hasmonean seemed too dangerous to Herod and he accused him of allying himself with the enemies of the country. He allowed Hyrcanus, who had once saved Herod from the Sanhedrin, to be sentenced to death despite the fact that he was 81 years old.

Herod then chose Chanamel as High Priest. It was rumored that Chanamel was a descendant of Onias, the son of Simeon the Just, and Herod hoped to use him for his own political ambitions. But Herod was soon forced by circumstances to appoint as High Priest the only remaining Hasmonean, Aristobulus, his wife's brother. He allowed Aristobulus to conduct the service in the Temple once and then invited him to visit Jericho with him. While they were bathing in the Jordan, Aristobulus was drowned by one of Herod's servants. Chanamel was reinstated to the high priesthood for a short time.

As whim dictated, Herod changed High Priests very frequently. When some of the ambitious priests realized that the high priesthood was no longer an office to be inherited, they outdid one another in the sums they were ready to pay for the office. The people called these priests by various nicknames because the office changed hands nearly every year and frequently a high priest did not last even that long.

We must keep in mind, however, that no matter how barbarous the behavior of Herod, he never tried to undermine the Jewish religion. Whenever he acted against the laws of the faith, he did so because he felt that the religious commandments interfered with his political ambitions.

No one, not even the nearest friends of the king, was certain of his life. In previous years the Sadducees had tried to do away with the Torah, and some of the Hasmoneans helped in their effort. But Herod did not try to interfere with the laws. He did not care whether Judaism developed along the lines laid out by the Pharisees, nor would he have minded if the Sadducees had their way. But he annihilated anyone he suspected of opposition, and in those days annihilation was an easy matter. One command of Herod was sufficient to lead hundreds of men to execution. He thus did away with the Hasmoneans, and later he executed his beloved wife, his mother-in-law, and his own sons. Not facetiously was it said in Rome that only a pig was safe in Herod's house, because since he was a Jew he would not kill it.

12

CHONI THE CIRCLE DRAWER

CHONI THE CIRCLE DRAWER, was one of the saintliest of the *tannaim*. Of all his ethical maxims there remains only one that states: "If a man does not enjoy the society of his fellows it is as if he were dead." Nothing remains of his interpretations of the Torah commandments, although it is said of him that his penetrating reasoning resolved all the doubts of the other scholars.

The name of Choni is surrounded with wonderful legends whenever it is mentioned in the Talmud. His every move was accompanied by miracles, and he was described as one to whom God refused no request.

The name Choni was not rare in those days and probably was an abbreviated form of Chonio or Chunia. But the appellation of circle drawer is unique in history and does not appear again in connection with any other name that has come down through the ages. The exact meaning of this appellation (in Hebrew: *Hamagel*) has not been determined. According to the book of geneology he was called Hamagel because he came from a city named Megilo. Others maintain that he received this name because, according to legend, he once slept for seventy years and they interpreted Hamagel to mean—one who has rested on the way. But the most common explanation is based on the legend that he once drew a circle about himself and took an oath not to stir out of it until God fulfilled his wish.

Once—so relates a *mishnah* in *Taanit*—there was a protracted drought in the country. According to some there had been no rain for three years. It was already the twentieth day of *Adar* when everyone was expecting the late rains that mature the grain, but not the smallest cloud appeared. Trees and grass withered, and the people feared that famine would come. They came to Choni, the circle drawer, to request that he pray to God for rain. Because of Choni's great piety, everyone was convinced that his appeal for rain would not be denied by God, and a request from him would be considered as a command.

Choni said to the people: "Take the Passover ovens into your houses that they may not be dampened by the rain." (Ovens that were dampened were not considered fit for Passover use and Choni felt certain that his prayer for rain would be answered.)

Choni prayed for a long time but still there was no rain. He thereupon drew a circle about himself and said to God: "Creator of the world! Your children have turned to me to pray for rain because they think that I am acceptable in your sight. I swear by your great name that I will not stir from here until you will have mercy on your children."

Small drops of rain began to fall. Choni's disciples then said: "God has permitted these few drops to fall so that you may not break your oath." Choni addressed God again: "Not for these few drops have I prayed. I prayed for a rain that should fill the wells with water." As he finished speaking a heavy rain storm began to descend and every drop of water was large enough to fill a barrel. His disciples again appealed to Choni: "God is sending down a rain that will flood the world." Choni again appealed to God: "Not for this have I prayed. I prayed for rain that should bring blessing to the fields."

Then an ordinary rain began to fall until all wells were filled and the streets of Jerusalem were flooded. Some of the residents of those streets sought refuge on the Temple mountain, while others came to Choni with a new request, that just as he had prayed for rain and it was granted, even so should he now pray for the rain to cease. Choni asked them to see if the wanderer's stone was already covered with water, for as long as that stone was not submerged he could not ask that the rain cease. (The wanderer's stone was a place where all lost articles were redeemed by their owners upon identification.)

Later, that the rain might cease, they brought an ox to be sacrificed to God. Choni placed both hands on the offering and said: "Thy people Israel whom you have redeemed from Egypt cannot bear too great a bounty even as they cannot bear too great a punishment. When you were displeased with them, they could not withstand your anger and besought me to intervene on their behalf. Now that you have bestowed upon them too much generosity, this they cannot bear either. Therefore, Creator of the world, I beg you to consider the rain that fell so far, sufficient and to permit the world to breathe freely again."

Immediately a strong wind arose and dispersed the clouds. The sun shone warm and the people scattered over the fields to gather mushrooms.

This is said to have occurred during the lifetime of Simeon ben Shetach who was greatly angered that Choni almost forced God to change his will in order to please one pious man. Simeon ben Shetach sent a message to Choni saying: "If you were not Choni I would have you excommunicated, but I can do nothing to you because you are to God as a petulant child and he fulfills your wishes even as a father fulfills the wishes of his favorite son."[1]

Josephus relates that Choni was killed in the war between the brothers Hyrcanus and Aristobulus. Hyrcanus was then besieging Jerusalem, while Aristobulus fortified himself in the temple on Mount Moriah. One day Choni was captured by the soldiers of Hyrcanus and brought to their camp. They asked him to pray to God to help them defeat Aristobulus. Choni thereupon recited the following prayer: "Creator of the world! Have mercy on both contending sides, for on one side are your priests and on the other side are your children. I pray that you shall not heed the curses of one upon the other." This prayer so enraged the soldiers of Hyrcanus that they killed him.

But the Talmud has woven another legend about the last days of Choni. It was said that Choni grieved because he could not comprehend the meaning of the verse "When God returned the captivity of Zion we were as dreamers." He repeatedly asked: "Is it possible for a person to sleep for seventy years and have the same dream?"

Once, as he was out walking, he saw a man planting a carob tree and asked: "How long does one wait until this tree bears fruit?" The man replied: "It takes seventy years." Choni asked him: "Are you certain that you will live another seventy years?" But the man replied: "The whole world is like a carob tree. My forefathers planted for me, and I am planting the tree for my children."

Choni sat down to weave baskets and a deep sleep descended upon him. A crag of a mountain extended to cover him and to hide him from the eyes of passersby. He slept there for seventy years.

When he awoke, he saw a man picking the fruit of the tree that was planted when he fell asleep. Choni asked him: "Are you the man who planted the tree?" The man replied: "I am not he. The man who planted the tree was my grandfather." Choni realized that he had slept for seventy years and he went to his home to inquire for Choni. There he was told that both Choni and his son were no longer living.

He said to the people, "I am Choni," but they would not believe him. He then went to the academy where he heard the scholars repeat his interpretations of the Torah saying, "I wish we had a man like Choni today who could elucidate all the hard questions." He said to them, "I am Choni," but they would not believe him either, and did not accord him the proper respect. This pained Choni very much and he used to repeat: "A man who does not enjoy the society of his fellows is as if he were dead."

According to another talmudic version, Choni lived during the last days of the First Temple and he slept through all the years of the Babylonian captivity. He awoke from his sleep when the Jews began to return from Babylonia. Of the Choni who prayed for rain, the Jerusalem Talmud claims that he was the grandson of the first Choni.

The Jerusalem Talmud continues to relate of the Choni who slept for seventy years, that when he awoke he asked what was going on in the world, and his hearers wondered that he did not know that the Temple was destroyed and was being rebuilt. They would not believe him when he claimed to be Choni. But since he persisted, the people said to him: "If you are Choni you have to prove it. We have heard that when the real Choni entered the Temple the whole house became suffused with light. We want to see you do likewise." Choni entered the temple and immediately a light spread throughout the building. He then said: "When God returned the captivity of Zion, we were as dreamers."

13

HILLEL

KING HEROD INAUGURATED HIS REIGN with the
slaughter of all the outstanding scholars in the country. He
destroyed them, just as he had annihilated the Hasmonean
dynasty, out of conviction that they would challenge his right
to the throne. He knew that the scholars secretly called him the
"Idumean slave" and because he was married to a Hasmonean
princess, in order to establish a Herodian-Hasmonean dynasty,
they ruled that whoever pretends to be of Hasmonean descent
is a slave.

But since Herod could not, under any circumstances,
abolish the Torah, he had to recognize the religious authority of
the Sanhedrin. His first attempt was to appoint the men of
Bathyra to head the Sanhedrin but they resigned in favor of
Hillel of Babylonia. Herod was thus forced by circumstances to
recognize the significance of Hillel and to tolerate his control of
the religious life even as he previously was forced to spare the
aged Shemaiah and Abtalion.

The appellation "Babylonian" clearly indicates that Hillel
was born in Babylonia; in order to differentiate him from other
scholars who were named Hillel, he was also called Hillel the
Old.

When Hillel came to Palestine, he was in his late thirties

94

and already possessed much knowledge. He came to the country in order to clarify for himself three religious questions of which he was in doubt. These were: (1) Whether a man who underwent purification had to be declared pure by a priest or whether the procedure of purification was sufficient. (2) The disagreement between two texts of the Bible, one of which says that the Paschal offering is to be made from sheep and cattle and the other states that the offering is to be selected from sheep and goats. (3) The contradiction between two texts, one of which enjoins that *matzot* be eaten for six days and the other that they should be eaten for seven days.[1]

He sought clarification of these questions from Shemaiah and Abtalion and was ready to return to Babylonia, where he lived in favorable circumstances. He had one brother who was a merchant and other relatives who undoubtedly also aided him. But his great desire for learning delayed his return, and as time went by it still seemed to him that he did not know enough. He thus became estranged from his native country where Jews lived in peace, and he was not frightened by the discord and political revolutions that agitated Palestine.

The Babylonian Jews of that time were pious and God-fearing people who observed all the regulations of Judaism insofar as that could be done outside of Palestine. They were especially strict in their observance of the Sabbath to its minutest details and they sent their *shekalim* and sacrifices to Jerusalem. But there were few colleges for the study of Torah and the Babylonian Jews were therefore held in contempt by the Palestinian Jews because their ignorance. In addition both Babylonian and Palestinian Jews believed that only in Palestine could the religious regulations be correctly interpreted and any regulation that did not have the sanction of the Great Court of Jerusalem was not accepted by the people.

While studying with Shemaiah and Abtalion, Hillel lived in straitened circumstances and earned his livelihood from hard labor. Altogether he earned but a small coin a day, half of which he spent for himself and his household and the other half he gave to the gatekeeper of the academy. But one day he did not earn any money. Neither he nor his family ate on that day but, being anxious to hear the discourse of Shemaiah and Abtalion and not having the money to pay the gatekeeper, Hillel climbed onto the roof of the academy and lay near the chimney where he could hear the discussion inside. All night he lay on the roof. This was in the month of *Tevet* in midwinter, and all that night it snowed and the snow covered his whole body to a great height.

On the following morning the academy seemed darker than usual. The skylight was covered with snow, but when the people looked closer they saw the body of a man under the snow. They immediately went up and removed the snow and recognized the man as Hillel. They washed him and anointed his body with oil and warmed him before the fire. Although such work is prohibited on the Sabbath, the scholars declared that a man like Hillel deserved that the Sabbath be desecrated for his sake.[2]

All this time Hillel did not reveal his great knowledge. Besides Shemaiah and Abtalion no one knew him intimately, neither did he confide in anyone as to whether he and his household were in need.

After the death of Shemaiah and Abtalion he apparently returned to Babylonia but frequently visited Jerusalem whenever any doubt arose in his mind. Mostly he came before the feast days in observance of the commandment to make a pilgrimage to Jerusalem, but he always kept in the background. Once, on the eve of Passover, which occurred on a Saturday, the men of Bathyra, who were the religious authorities, were in doubt whether the Paschal lamb offering should supersede the Sabbath or whether it should not be offered at all because of it. One of their pupils rose and said: "There is in Jerusalem a man from Babylonia who studied under Shemaiah and Abtalion; he will certainly know the law." But the men of Bathyra nodded their heads as if to say: "What can one learn from a Babylonian?"

Nevertheless, they summoned Hillel and asked him what should be done. Hillel said: "Are you concerned about the Paschal lamb only when there are many other sacrifices offered on the Sabbath?" He expounded the rules of the Torah all day to prove that the Paschal lamb offering supersedes the Sabbath. Still they would not listen to him until he said that he had received the law from Shemaiah and Abtalion.

They then asked him: "What should be done if the people do not bring the slaughtering knives? For even if the offering of the sacrifice supersedes the Sabbath, it is still prohibited to carry any object on that day." Hillel then replied: "I do not remember what Shemaiah and Abtalion taught in this matter but I am certain that the people will know the law, for whenever there is any doubt what to do one should observe the custom of the people and decide the law accordingly."

On the following day, Passover eve, it happened just as Hillel predicted. The people brought their sacrifices and had the slaughtering knives hidden in the wool of the lambs and between the horns of the goats. When Hillel saw this, he remembered that Shemaiah and Abtalion had instructed that it should be done so.[3]

Hillel was the first of the authors of the Mishnah who insisted that the object of religion is to enforce the fulfillment of the duties of one man toward another and that all practical commandments are a means to this end. Therefore he established the principle of brotherly love as the main condition for all the commandments of the Torah. Once, when a Gentile wanted to adopt Judaism on the one condition, that he be taught the whole Torah in the time that he could remain standing on one foot, Hillel gave him only one rule: "Do not unto thy neighbor that which you would not have him do unto you. This is the whole Jewish law. All else are but commentaries on their commandments which you will know when you study them."[4]

Hillel was very gentle in his relations with other people and suffered their capricious behavior without anger. He particularly insisted on showing friendship to the poor. Not only did he provide them with necessities but also with luxuries they were previously unused to. Once he provided a poor man with a horse and a slave to run before him, as was the custom. However, when he could not obtain a slave, he ran before the man himself for three miles.[5]

Hillel's modesty and unusual patience gained wide renown and many interesting stories were told of futile attempts
to make him angry. After the person who wanted to learn the
whole of Jewish law while standing on one foot, there appeared before Hillel a heathen who was ready to embrace
Judaism on condition that he be made high priest. Hillel
answered both satisfactorily and converted them.

Probably the most interesting story concerns a man who
wagered a large sum of money on angering Hillel. The man ran
to Hillel's house on a Friday, just at the time that Hillel was
bathing in preparation for the Sabbath. In a loud voice he
shouted: "Hillel, who is Hillel and where is he?" Hillel
wrapped himself in a cloak and came out saying: "I am Hillel.
What do you want, my son?"

"I want to ask you a question," the man said.

"Ask," Hillel replied, "and whatever I know I will tell
you."

"I want to know," the man said, "why the Babylonians
have round heads."

"You have asked a correct question," Hillel answered. "It
is because the Babylonians do not have skilled midwives; the
heads of the newborn children become rounded in their
hands."

A moment later the man again shouted: "Hillel, where is
Hillel?"

Again Hillel came out and said: "I am Hillel. What do you
want, my son?"

"Can you tell me," the man asked, "why the eyes of the
people of Tadmor are weak?"

"You have asked well," Hillel said. "It is because Tadmor
is located in a sandy region and dust gets into people's eyes."

Once more the man shouted: "Hillel, where is Hillel?"

Hillel wrapped himself and came out saying: "Here I am,
what do you want, my son?"

"I want to know," the man said, "why the feet of the
Africans are so wide."

"It is a good question," Hillel said, "it is a result of their
going barefoot in swampy land."

Thereupon the man said: "I wish to ask you other questions but I fear that you will be angry."

"You may ask as many questions as you want and I shall answer them to the best of my knowledge," Hillel said.

"Are you the Hillel who is a Nasi among Jews?" the man exclaimed.

"I am he," Hillel replied.

"Then I wish the Jews that there should be no more like you," the man said.

"Why do you wish them this?" Hillel asked.

"Because through you I have lost a large sum of money. I wagered that I could make you angry, and now I do not know what to do to anger you."

To this Hillel replied, "Even if you were to lose twice that sum, you still could not anger me."[6]

Hillel served as Nasi from 30 B.C.E. to 10 C.E. In the prevailing political situation of the country it was significant that Hillel was a descendant of King David. (His mother was descended from Shefatiah, the son of David.) The people considered him a scion of the royal house of David and accorded him appropriate honors. While everyone looked upon Herod as a tyrant whose only aim was to collect taxes for the foreign rulers and to protect the borders of the land, they revered Hillel as a religious leader and obeyed his every word. It was then that the benediction of the House of David, ending with the words, "He raises a ray of hope," was introduced into the daily prayers (*Shemoneh Esrei*), and it is possible that the people looked upon Hillel's exalted position as a beginning of the restoration of the House of David. This was also the cause for the introduction of still another benediction, to be recited on Saturday after the reading of the Prophets, that begin with the words: "Gladden us, oh Lord, with the prophet Elijah, your servant, and with the kingdom of David, your anointed" and ended with: "On his throne a stranger shall not sit nor shall others inherit his honor."

From Hillel were descended three generations of Nesiim who governed religious life for one hundred years. For the external world, Herod and his successors were the sovereigns of the country, but the internal life of the nation, concentrated around the faith, was guided by Hillel's heirs.

Doubtlessly Herod knew of the honor being accorded to Hillel and that he was looked upon as a successor of David. But in his political sagacity he realized that Hillel would constitute a real danger only if he claimed to be a descendant of the Hasmoneans.

In later generations Hillel's importance was compared with that of Ezra. It was said that Ezra renewed the Torah after it was forgotten by the people, and similarly Hillel came out of Babylonia to teach the Torah, neglected after the deaths of Shemaiah and Abtalion.

The Talmud relates: Eighty of the most important men of the generation were pupils of Hillel. Thirty of these were worthy enough to have the *Shekhinah* rest upon them even as it rested upon Moses. Another thirty were deserving enough to have the sun stop in its course for their sake even as it did for Joshua ben Nun. The remaining twenty were intermediate men and among them was Jonathan ben Uziel of whom it was said that his enthusiasm for studying the Torah was so great that were a bird to fly by him when he was expounding the law it would have been burnt by the flames of his enthusiasm.[7]

Aside from his humility and patience Hillel was also noted for being satisfied with his lot and he was in the habit of saying: "Blessed be God for this day." He was never worried over what the following day might bring and taught the members of his household to feel likewise. Once, as he was approaching his house, he heard shouts coming from that direction and he said to his disciples who were accompanying him: "I am certain that these quarrelsome shouts do not come from my home."[8]

In his moral teachings he frequently used picturesque language and employed short epigrammatic maxims. It is difficult at times to know his exact meaning, since these maxims can be interpreted in various ways. But this does not diminish their moral worth since, no matter how one interprets them, they still express elevated moral teachings and are an honor for the whole people who could produce a personality like Hillel in such difficult times.

One of his maxims stated: "Wherever my heart loves, there my feet lead me; if you will come to me then will I also come to you, but if you do not come to me neither can I come to you." This maxim has been interpreted in many ways and many people found in it that which they sought.

Nearly every day as he left his pupils, he was in the habit of saying that he was going to entertain a guest. Once they asked him: "Do you have a guest at home every day?" and he replied: "Our soul is only a guest with us; today it is here and tomorrow it may leave us."[9]

But when Hillel spoke of entertaining a guest, he did not have in mind only food and drink. Although he never underestimated these he said that it is a great virtue to preserve God's image in man in the same purity as it was created. But he particularly insisted that man is obliged to perfect his spiritual self, for if a man does not do so himself no one will do it for him. To this he added that one man for himself counts for little and he must also have the assistance of others, and he stressed the importance of the present moment in one's life, for if not now, when?

Hillel firmly believed that there was no unjust suffering and even when it seemed that divine justice was wrong, one must bear in mind that all one's deeds are reckoned and that one receives his punishment at the hands of another sinful creature. Once he saw a head floating upon the water. It was a time of many murders; Herod frequently had many people executed and had their bodies thrown into the water. Hillel believed that if those people had not deserved it, God would not have permitted their being killed but, at the same time, he was convinced that the murderers would also meet their punishment. He therefore addressed the floating head: "You drowned others and therefore you were drowned; but in the end your assassins will also be drowned."[10]

Hillel placed learning in the very center of the scheme of life and he said that whoever refuses to study deserves to be condemned to death. Also, he insisted that one must not say "I will study when I have time," for it is possible that one will never find the time. Study, he maintained, also leads to fear of

God and he who is ignorant cannot be pious. But a person who devotes himself to learning in order to gain a great name for himself is certain to lose his name.

With all the power at his command Hillel strove to popularize the Torah. He said: "When others gather, you must spread; but when others spread, you must gather." Seeing that the people did not understand him he explained his words in this manner: "When you see a generation that loves the Torah, then you must spread your knowledge among them; but if you see a generation that does not love the Torah then you must hide your knowledge within yourself."[11]

In his exposition of the law Hillel was tolerant toward his opponents. This was contrary to the custom of the scholars of that generation who did not tolerate any divergence of opinion and sharply reacted to differing interpretations. Hillel expressed his opinions peacefully and when he tried to prove the truth of his statements he did so in a calm manner. He said that man must love peace and search for it. When one attains the state of love for his fellow man he brings other people closer to the Torah.

Although Hillel was devoted to the traditions of the "oral law," he did not attack those who doubted them. He never drove the doubters from himself, as others did, but merely sought to convince them that it was impossible to observe the written law without recognizing the validity of the oral law. Once a heathen came to him saying that he wanted to embrace Judaism on condition that he learn the written law only. Hillel accepted him and then he showed him that it was impossible to study anything without accepting the opinions of one's teacher. The proselyte understood that since he had to believe Hillel, he also had to accept Hillel's belief that the written law cannot be explained without the aid of the oral law.

The scholars preceding Hillel opposed the Sadducees violently but achieved little. Even Simeon ben Shetach, who opposed the Sadducees with the force of the government, could not prevail against them. But Hillel's method of peaceful argumentation served its purpose. He said of them: "There were many sinners among the Jews who were brought close to the study of the Torah and in time they became pious and just men."

So far as we know, Hillel was the first of the *tannaim* to establish a system of expounding the laws of the Torah that was based on rules of logic or "measures according to which the Torah was expounded," as they were called in the Talmud. There were seven rules defined by Hillel.

We may assume that Hillel did not invent these seven rules (or measures) without a definite foundation. These rules were in use before his day. But when Hillel analyzed those methods of interpreting the texts of the Torah used by his predecessors, he discovered that their interpretations and expositions followed a definite system of logical rules.

Hillel established seven rules, but his successors increased the number of these rules. Rabbi Ishmael defined thirteen; Rabbi Eliezer, the son of Rabbi Jose of Galilee identified as many as thirty-two rules.

Hillel's seven rules of logic for interpreting the Torah are: (1) *Kal vachomer* — argument from minor to major and vice versa. (2) *Gezeirah shavah* — argument by analogy. (3) *Binyan av* — a standard passage serving as a basis for interpretation. (4) *K elal ufrat* — general and particular limitation of the general by the particular and vice versa. (5) *Sh enei ketuvim* — standard from two passages — a decision involving two laws having a common characteristic is applied to other laws having the same characteristics. (6) *Ke yotzei bo mimakom acher* — like that in another place — explanation of one passage according to another of similar content. (7) *Davar halameid mi'inyano* — definition from context.[12]

Hillel employed these rules of logic for the first time in his argumentation with the men of Bathyra. Later these rules continued to be used by other scholars in the same manner.

Hillel's first rule — *Kal vachomer* — argument from minor to major and vice versa — implies that the accepted interpretation of a law of minor importance may be applied to a law of major importance when the latter is in doubt: This rule is generally applied in order to establish a more severe interpretation of a doubtful law. Sometimes, however, it may also be used to limit the restrictions of a doubtful commandment.

According to our scholars there exist ten examples of *Kal vachomer* in the case of Joseph's brothers when they were accused of stealing the beaker from Joseph's house. They said: "The silver we had found in our sacks we returned to you from the land of Canaan; how then shall we steal silver or gold from the house of your lord." Their reasoning implied that if they took the greater trouble to return silver from the distant land of Canaan they would not stoop to steal from his house. A statement of Moses serves as a second example of a *Kal vachomer*. Moses said: "Even when I am with you today you disobey God, what will you do after my death?"

When Hillel stood before the men of Bathyra discussing whether the offering of the Paschal lamb supersedes the Sabbath he argued as follows: "If the daily sacrifice, the nonoffering of which is not punishable by death, supersedes the Sabbath; the Paschal lamb, the nonoffering of which *is* punishable by death, certainly supersedes the Sabbath."

Hillel's second rule—argument by analogy—employs the comparison of the text of one law to the text of another in order to apply the interpretation of the first to the latter. But the Talmud states that a person may use this rule only to substantiate an interpretation but not to abolish one.

An example of argument by analogy occurs when the Talmud tries to establish that the commandment "an eye for an eye" is not to be taken literally although the biblical text states, "If one shall cripple his neighbor, as he did so shall be done to him." The Talmud argues that in another case involving a man whose ox gored his neighbor's ox, the Bible enjoins that the man shall "pay an ox for an ox." From this the Talmud deduces that "an eye for an eye" also implies that monetary compensation shall be given to the victim.[13]

The Jerusalem Talmud indicates how broadly the "argument by analogy" may be employed by stating: "Whenever the text of the law is not clear, that law may be substantiated from other texts."

Hillel also employed this rule in his argumentation before the men of Bathyra. He said: "The commandment to offer the daily sacrifice employs the word *bemo'ado* (in its appointed time), so does the commandment to offer the Paschal lamb. Since the daily sacrifice supersedes the Sabbath, we must conclude that the Paschal lamb offering does so as well."

The rule *gezeirah shavah* could also be called the rule of comparison and the Talmud does say that it is possible to "compare and to derive an argument by analogy." But the rule of comparison later became differentiated from argument by analogy.

The *gezeirah shavah* was derived from the Torah which compares differing circumstances in order to cast light from one onto the other. Thus, in the case of the rape of an engaged girl that took place outside the city, the girl is not to be punished for it because it is assumed that she called for help but no one came to her assistance. The case is compared to that of a person being murdered.

The third rule of Hillel—*binyan av*—concerns a subject whose text is expressed in a general manner, and from this text decisions are deduced concerning other subjects not mentioned in the Torah.

The name *binyan av* means "paternal structure" because the expounder is like a father and the pupils are like children. This appellation also indicates that his rule is like a building in which one large stone is supported by numerous smaller ones.

Whenever we find subjects in the Torah, similar to one another in content or in some other characteristic that is clearly defined in one instance but is not definite in another, we interpret all doubtful texts according to the clearly established one and we compare this one to a father whose influence extends over a wide range of texts and binds them into a family unit.

The fourth rule—*k elal ufrat*—involves a general law whose specialized interpretations explain the doubtful phases of its generality.

As was already stated, one of the causes of Hillel's coming to Palestine was his desire to ascertain whether a man who underwent purification required the statement of a priest to establish that fact, or whether the purification procedure was sufficient in itself. Hillel came to the conclusion that since in the case of the cure of a *netek* the Bible states "he is clean," and this is a generalization (statement is later followed by the words "the priest shall purify him," a specification) it is impossible to understand the generalization without the specification. The specific therefore elucidates the general, that the man is not clean until he is so declared by the priest.

The fifth rule is *sh enei ketuvim*. This concerns two contradictory texts such as those affecting the offering of the Paschal lamb. One of them states "and you shall slaughter the Pesach to your God, sheep and cattle," while another text says "from the sheep and from the goats you shall take it." Therefore Hillel did not know which animal should be offered for the Passover sacrifice until he elucidated this matter with the aid of a third text that states "take for yourself sheep for your families and slaughter the Pesach." He explained it to mean sheep for the special Passover sacrifice, and sheep and cattle for the general feast-day offering.

Similar to this was Hillel's explanation of another set of contradictory texts about which he was confused and had come to Palestine to seek elucidation. One text that says "six days you shall eat *matzot*" is contradicted by another stating "seven days you shall eat *matzot*." He interpreted it to mean that one must eat *matzot* made out of the new grain (garnered after the Omer) for six days and on the seventh day one should eat *matzot* made out of old grain.

The sixth rule—*k eyotzei bo mimakom acher*—involves the explanation of a word in the text of one law by another law which may be entirely unrelated.

The seventh rule—*davar halameid mi'inyano*—governs the interpretation of a doubtful part of one subject from the text of the same subject.

14

SHAMMAI–
HILLEL'S COLLEAGUE

AFTER HILLEL BECAME NASI, Menachem was chosen to head the court. Very little is known about Menachem, but the Talmud relates that he, together with eighty pairs of his disciples, left the temple after they received gifts from the king and, donning royal attire, they entered the king's service.[1]

What impelled Menachem to take this step is also a mystery. Some scholars hold that he was forced to do so against his own will. Josephus tells us that Menachem at first belonged to the Essenes, and when Herod was still young, predicted that he would become king. When this prediction came true, Herod remembered him and treated him graciously.

If this account is true, then it is possible that Herod persuaded Menachem that his life and career would be safer if he left the temple and engaged in royal service. Menachem was convinced and was succeeded by Shammai. It is also unknown how long Menachem collaborated with Hillel; but this relationship must have been of short duration since he left no impression and no words of his are mentioned anywhere.

The Talmud characterized Shammai as an angry man in contradistinction to Hillel who was noted for his modesty and patience.

Every non-Jew who wanted to embrace Judaism on certain

conditions, and whom Hillel *did* convert, had first visited Shammai. But Shammai became angered with them because of the conditions they imposed, and in one case the dispute actually developed into a physical struggle. But this tendency to anger on Shammai's part must not be interpreted as a sign of an evil nature, for whenever he realized his opponent was right, he gladly conceded it. Shammai once had a dispute with Jonathan ben Uziel, a disciple of Hillel, who did not spare Shammai in the course of the debate. When Shammai became convinced of the justice of Jonathan's arguments, he conceded his defeat and complained only of the insults his opponent had heaped upon him.

The best indication of Shammai's character is shown in his advice that every man should be received in a friendly manner. But some historians interpret this as an attempt to rid others of that weakness from which he could not free himself.

Shammai studied under Shemaiah and Abtalion together with Hillel. But it appears that he headed an academy soon after the death of Shemaiah and Abtalion and before Hillel started an academy of his own. Whenever the two academies (the House of Shammai and the House of Hillel) are mentioned in the Talmud, the House of Shammai is usually listed first.

Shammai was very extreme in his piety. He held the Sabbath to be the most important day of the week, in anticipation of which, every Jew must prepare even as one would prepare for the reception of a prince. Beginning on Sunday, he would therefore search for the best things and reserve them for the Sabbath. He never permitted good food to be served at his table on a weekday unless he had better food prepared for the Sabbath.

It was accepted at that time that children should not fast on the Day of Atonement. It was customary for fathers to wash one hand on that day to offer food to their children. But Shammai refused to do this because of the prohibition against washing on the Day of Atonement and permitted his small child to fast. When other scholars realized that the child's life was in danger, they forced Shammai to feed the child with both hands. It also happened that Shammai's daughter-in-law gave birth to a son on *Sukkot*. Shammai thereupon removed the roof of the house and covered the balcony overhanging the mother's bed with green branches so that the newborn son might not be outside of a *sukkah*.

It is apparent from Shammai's behavior that he was careful to observe all the minutiae of the commandments. It is also evident that he did not interfere with the political situation in the country and devoted himself solely to the interpretation of the laws, in which he was seldom in agreement with Hillel. Hillel sought broader vistas in his exposition while Shammai clung to the literal meaning of the text even in those cases where logic indicated that it should be interpreted otherwise. Hillel sought the causes underlying the laws and critically analyzed previous interpretations before he arrived at his own conclusions.

In time these differences between the disciples of Hillel and Shammai increased, and it seemed as if there were two Torahs instead of one, for the claims of one school were invariably contradicted by the other. This opposition reached such a state that on one occasion all the people were prohibited from leaving the academy on pain of death until a decision was made on whether Hillel or Shammai was the correct exponent of the law. "This day," the Talmud states, "was as difficult as the day on which the golden calf was made." The Talmud makes no mention of the results of that day. However, on another occasion it relates that after many years of dispute a "voice" announced that both contending sides were correct but that Hillel's teaching was according to the law. It is told that one of the later *tannaim* (Rabbi Tarphon) repeated the *Shema* in the manner prescribed by Shammai and soon after he was beset by robbers. The scholars thereupon told him that he deserved that danger because he had deviated from the law of Hillel.

Most of the differences of opinion between the two schools centered about the laws pertaining to sacrifices, tithes, and the rules of purity. Some sharp clashes also arose in problems of marriage where one school permitted and the other school prohibited. It might have been expected that differences of opinion on this subject would lead to accusations of illegitimate birth. But this was not the case since both schools were tolerant toward each other and their disciples intermarried freely.

But in spite of Shammai's strictness he nevertheless had the interests of the people at heart. Whenever he realized that it was impossible to enforce a certain stricture he overlooked it and waited for a more favorable time to introduce it.

The laws pertaining to the sabbatical year were frequently ignored at that time. While no one sowed his fields during that year, in accord with the literal meaning of the Torah, many people, nevertheless, permitted themselves to plow their fields in anticipation of next year's planting, because the law does not explicitly prohibit plowing. This procedure was similar to that of preparing food on a holy day for consumption on a weekday and many people expected Shammai to prohibit it. But Shammai said: "If the times were to permit, I would decree against the sowing of fields that were plowed during the Sabbatical year."

From these words, it is evident that the reason he refrained from issuing such a decree was that Herod did not allow interference with the farmers because of the income which he derived from them. Were it in his power, Herod would have abolished the sabbatical year, but he feared to tamper with a law that was commanded by the Torah. He limited himself to forcing the scholars to issue such decrees regarding the cultivation of fields during the sabbatical year as would least interfere with the work.

One of the main differences between Hillel and Shammai involved the question of *semikhah*, the placing of hands on a sacrifice. The Torah commands a man "to rest his hand" on the sacrifice he offers, and this was interpreted to mean that the penitent must participate in the slaughtering of the sacrifice. Since such a procedure involves a considerable effort, a dispute arose as to whether one has to do so on feast days and on the Sabbath. One school absolved the penitent from this procedure while the other maintained that without it the sacrifice was not valid.

Shammai and Hillel founded two schools of interpreting the Torah according to which they decided all religious problems. While basing themselves on the same texts and on the same traditions they had inherited from Shemaiah and Abtalion, they nevertheless arrived at contradictory conclusions in nearly every case.

Up to the time of Hillel and Shammai all disputes were decided along party lines. The opposing sides—the Sadducees and the Pharisees—held differing points of view and everyone could readily understand the origin of the disputes. With Hillel and Shammai, the disputes assumed an inner-party nature. This was a new phenomenon since both of them belonged to the Pharisees in whose ranks peace prevailed until that time. Only in the matter of *semikhah* was there any difference of opinion; complete unity was the rule in all other questions. It is surprising therefore that the disputes between Hillel and Shammai developed in such intensity until the abyss between them became ever greater and more ominous.

Hillel, as was related previously, had eighty disciples. Thirty of these were deserving to have the *Shekhinah* rest upon them even as it rested on Moses. Thirty deserved to have the sun stop in its course for their sake, just as it did for Joshua. Twenty were intermediate men. The least of Hillel's disciples was Rabbi Jochanan ben Zakkai of whom it was said that "he was familiar with all the nooks of the Torah, the *Mishnah*, the *Gemara*, the *halakhot* and *aggadot* and the minutest interpretations of the Torah and of the *sofrim*. He understood all the mysteries of *Gematria* (numerical evaluation), the language of the angels and of the evil spirits, the language of the palm trees as well as many fables of apes and foxes. When the Talmud lists the praises of the disciples of Hillel it is to show what a learned man the greatest of them must have been if the least of them, Rabbi Jochanan ben Zakkai, was so well versed.

The names of two of Shammai's outstanding disciples have come down through history, and of them it is told that, in spite of their training in the school of Shammai, they believed that all laws should be observed according to Hillel's interpretation. One of these was Rabbi Jochanan of Hauran and the other was Baba ben Buta.

Baba ben Buta was blinded by Herod during the latter's

extermination of the sages. Herod later repented and asked Baba ben Buta, what he could do to atone for his misdeed. Baba ben Buta is described as being a pious man who daily offered a sacrifice to atone for any possible sin he may have committed.

In connection with Baba ben Buta, a story is told of a man from Babylon who settled in Jerusalem and married there. But the language of the Babylon Jews was different from that of the Palestinian Jews, despite the fact that they all spoke an Aramaic dialect, and this man's wife could therefore not understand what he was saying. Once he commanded her to bring him "two butsinis," (watermelons) and she brought two candles instead. (The word meant watermelons in Babylonian and candles in the Palestinian dialects.) Angered at her misunderstanding, the man commanded his wife to "break them on the doorstep." This was a customary remark in Babylonia, when one was brought something he did not want. The woman believed she was told to break the candles on Baba's head and did so. ("Resha de'baba" means the head of the door and also the head of Baba.) Baba was not angered and merely asked her why she had done that. The woman told him that she had been commanded to do so by her husband, whereupon Baba said to her: "Because you obeyed the will of your husband, God will give you two sons who will be like Baba ben Buta."

The differences of opinion between the House of Shammai and the House of Hillel lasted until the destruction of the Temple. After its destruction the House of Shammai practically disappeared. According to the Talmud this dispute continued until the days of Rabbi Gamaliel of Jabneh who was five generations removed from Hillel.[2] He convoked all the scholars of his time to Jabneh, and there they decided by vote whether the opinions of Shammai's school or those of Hillel's school should be enforced. The debate lasted three years until a *bat Kol* (a divine voice) announced that the opinions of both schools are from God, but that the law is according to Hillel.

The disciples of Hillel's school endeavored to lighten the burden of the law in imitation of the ways of Hillel who was the personification of modesty and kindliness. In many instances they sought to find better ways for man to follow. It was customary at that time to dance before the bride during the wedding and to praise her virtues in order that the bridegroom might appreciate her qualities. Hillel insisted that a bride should be praised for her beauty even when she was not beautiful, in the same manner that one praises an article another has bought even when one realizes that it was not a good buy.

The school of Hillel paid particular attention to the moral and spiritual consequences of every law. The law of that time said that a girl who was married before she was of age could not reject her husband after she became of age. But the school of Hillel maintained that if the girl was an orphan and was married off by her mother or brother, she could reject the husband that was chosen for her before she was old enough to choose for herself.

Similarly in the matter of *Yibum*, in the case of a man who dies childless, the man's brother has to marry the widow. If he refuses to do so he has to grant her *Halitzah*. In such a case the widow had no choice. The school of Hillel tried to modify this law to allow for cases where the widow refused to marry her deceased husband's brother. They ruled that if the woman claims to have taken a vow during her husband's lifetime never to have any dealings with her husband's brother, then the court must force him to release her from his claim, although legally the argument remains that he refuses to marry her. If the widow took such a vow after her husband's death, then the court should request the brother of the dead man to forgo his right and to grant *Halitzah* to the woman.

The school of Hillel modified the law permitting divorce in a similar fashion. The school of Shammai allowed divorce only on the grounds of the wife's infidelity. Any other complaint of the husband about his wife's physical or spiritual unfitness was considered insufficient grounds for divorce. The school of Shammai held the bond of matrimony to be sanctified by divine powers, and no human agency could break that bond except by express command of the Torah. But the school of Hillel maintained that the morals of society and the happiness of humanity would be improved if man were allowed to divorce his wife for any undesirable traits he found in her.

The school of Shammai never deviated from the literal meaning of the text of a commandment, while the school of Hillel always studied the possible intentions of the text first, and only later did they issue their edict according to reason and for the betterment of humanity. In sum, Shammai's group always decreed the law in its severest interpretation while Hillel's school tended to lighten the burden whenever possible.

The political situation of the Jews of Palestine was very difficult. The country was in constant turmoil due to foreign and civil wars. But the greatest calamity occurred when the country lost its independence and became a Roman province under the rule of a governor who could dictate the material as well as the spiritual life of the country. There developed a party of patriots who openly or secretly opposed Rome. This party declared in its program that God is the sole ruler of the Jews and they said: "Woe to the nation that chooses a man to rule over it."

Historians claim that this party consisted primarily of the followers of the school of Shammai. The followers of Hillel were also dissatisfied with the political situation, but they did not believe in revolutionary propaganda and attacked the enemy through laws against those people who aided the Romans in collecting taxes from the Jews. They held that it is difficult for *gabbaim* (treasurers) and *mohesim* (tax collectors) to repent their sins because they are robbers and it was forbidden to receive any contribution from them for charitable purposes. Despite all this, the followers of Hillel accepted their fate realizing that there was no force that could avail against Rome.

The attitude of Shammai's followers was entirely different as they openly opposed the Romans. At a gathering held in the house of Chananiah ben Hezekiah eighteen political questions were debated and the opinions of Shammai's followers prevailed. But these decisions were never written down, and in later years it became impossible to determine what they were.

We must bear in mind that the followers of Shammai were

revolutionaries, and this meeting probably took place during the days of Agrippa I when the patriots were preparing for a struggle with Rome. Fearing a Roman attack, the meeting was arranged so that it should be possible to claim that it was not a political meeting but merely a gathering to discuss religious questions.

15

AKABIA BEN MAHALALEL

NUMEROUS INDICATIONS IN THE TALMUD suggest that during the lifetime of Hillel and Shammai there were other spiritual leaders who followed individual methods in interpreting the Torah and who did not identify themselves with either Hillel or Shammai. Some of these are mentioned by name on a number of unimportant occasions, but others did not even attain this recognition.

Akabia ben Mahalalel was one of the scholars who developed an individual method of exposition. We have only a vague knowledge of his life and activities. One report states that he was excommunicated without naming the sin for which he was thus punished. But there is an immediate contradiction declaring that whoever invented such a slanderous rumor about such a saintly man deserves severe punishment.[1]

Considering all the references to Akabia ben Mahalalel in the Talmud, one must conclude that he was an unusual man gifted by nature with great perseverance. The nation was then engaged in a great struggle to preserve its independence against outside enemies and was rent by an internal conflict over the observance of the Torah. Akabia ben Mahalalel succeeded in remaining above the inner and outer struggles and in maintaining his neutrality toward the contending sides.

So far as we know, Akabia ben Mahalalel held no official position. In religious questions he contributed his opinion on only four subjects that occur so rarely that a century may pass before such problems present themselves again. Since his point of view differed from that of the other scholars, and he expressed his opinions with a certain disrespect for the leaders of the previous generation, he was excommunicated.

The original source of the four laws on which Akabia ben Mahalalel held dissenting views we find in *Mishnah*. One dealt with special cases of leprosy, another concerned a woman who has an issue of blood, the third dealt with the wool shed by a clean firstborn animal that was crippled, and the fourth concerned a woman who was a proselyte or a freed woman suspected of infidelity.

The first two laws come under the category of legislation pertaining to cleanliness and impurity and their interpretation involves medical considerations. We will, however, devote a few words to the third and fourth laws.

The firstborn of a clean animal had to be sacrificed in Jerusalem according to the prescribed custom for minor holy offerings *kedoshim kalim*. As long as such an animal lived, one was not allowed to put it to work, nor to shear its wool. In case such an animal became crippled, it had to be slaughtered and given to a priest. The wool could not be utilized after it was slaughtered. But Akabia ruled that the priest was entitled to that wool which the animal shed while it was still alive, while the other scholars disagreed with him.

The fourth law about which Akabia held a dissenting opinion concerned a *sotah* (a woman who is suspected by her husband of infidelity). The prescribed procedure in such a case was for the husband to bring the wife together with an offering of barley meal to the priest. The priest took a clay vessel filled with pure water and placed some earth from the temple in it; he then wrote the verses of the Torah pertaining to a *sotah* on a piece of paper and read them to the woman after which he washed the ink from the paper with the water and gave it to the woman to drink. If the water caused the woman no harm, it was proof that she was innocent.

Akabia held that this procedure need not be applied to a *sotah* who was a proselyte or a freed servant. In attempting to dissuade him, the scholars cited the case of Shemaiah and Abtalion who gave the water to a *sotah* who was a freed servant. Akabia retorted that "they gave it to one like them-selves."

The exact meaning of Akabia's words is not clear. (The Hebrew word *dugma* means similar.) They are interpreted to indicate that Akabia believed that Shemaiah and Abtalion did not give the woman the prescribed water to drink, nor did they write the prescribed passage. They merely attempted to influ-ence her psychologically in order to obtain the truth. But some scholars thought these words to be a slurring reference to the origin of Shemaiah and Abtalion and they placed him under a ban. When Akabia died the people stoned his casket.[2]

But the statement of Rabbi Jehudah, elsewhere referred to as Rabbi Jehudah of Bathyra, is immediately quoted to the effect that one must not believe that a just man like Akabia could have been put under the ban, nor could he have slandered the names of Shemaiah and Abtalion in the case of the freed servant. Whoever assumes that Akabia was excom-municated is deserving of punishment. Rabbi Jehudah main-tains that the matter of the excommunication crept in through an error and involved another person, Eleazar ben Chanoch who was put under the ban because he ignored the command-ment of "washing hands" in the belief that this commandment was not implied in the Torah.

The respect in which Akabia was held by the Jews can be seen from the fact that he was offered the position of the head of the Court, if he would recall his decisions in the matter of the four previously mentioned laws. But Akabia answered: "I would rather be called a fool all the days of my life than be wicked in the eyes of God for one hour, or that people should point at me and say that I betrayed my convictions in order to obtain an office."

These four laws concerned subjects so rare that a court may have had no occasion to pass on them throughout its existence. We also find that later scholars held the same opinions as did Akabia.

We must also bear in mind that immorality was very widespread in Judea at that time and the whole procedure of the trial of a woman suspected of infidelity was done away with. The biblical text, "the woman shall be a curse within her people," was interpreted to apply only in case the people led moral lives.[3] There is therefore some doubt whether Akabia passed on these questions or whether his decisions caused any serious opposition.

Before Akabia died he instructed his son not to observe these four laws according to his interpretation.

His son asked him: "Why then did you not recall your decisions?" Akabia answered: "I have heard them adopted by a majority and my opponents heard their views adopted by a majority. For this reason I clung to the law as I heard it, and they observed it as they received it. But you heard the decisions from me, who am but one, and from my opponents who are many. It is therefore better that you give up the opinions of the individual and abide by the opinions of the majority."

On this occasion Akabia's son also asked his father to instruct his colleagues to treat him better, but Akabia answered that he would not speak to them about this matter. His son then asked him: "Have you found any evil in me?" The father answered: "I have seen no evil in you but I believe that intercession will not help you. Your own deeds will make you beloved among people and your own deeds will make them stay away from you."

The editor of the *Mishnah* in *Pirkei Avot* cites the following maxim in the name of Akabia ben Mahalalel: "Keep in view three things and you will not come to sin." Expounders interpreted these to be that a man should refrain from pride and sinful desires. Akabia stated further, "Know whence you came, whither you go, and before whom you have to give strict account. Consider how you came into the world, remember that you are bound for a place of dust and worms, and that you will have to give account before the King of kings, the Holy One blest be He."

In a somewhat different form we find this passage quoted in *Avot Derabi Natan*: "Akabia ben Mahalalel said: 'He who ponders the following four subjects will sin no more. Think of whence you come, whither you are going, what will become of you, and who will be your judge. Whence you came? From a place of darkness. Whither you are going? To a place of darkness. What will become of you? Dust and worms. Who will be your judge? The King of kings, the Holy One blest be He.' "

Some people claim that the request to Akabia to recall his four opinions did not refer to the described decisions concerning cleanliness and impurity, the wool of a firstborn crippled animal, and a *sotah* who was a proselyte, but rather to those four maxims which he held that a man must take to heart in order to be saved from sin. These teachings placed Akabia in the category of one who spreads ideas that are dangerous to the world. By having people think constantly of death and of the sufferings in their grave, their desire to live is undermined.

It was then that he was called upon to revoke the four maxims that deprived people of the desire to live so that he might be appointed head of the court. However, it is difficult to explain how a man who was under the ban for following an original system of interpreting the law could be considered a desirable candidate to head the Court.

But this explanation is not based on fact, for it seems evident that Akabia *was* excommunicated, despite the denial of Rabbi Jehudah ben Bathyra. In the Talmud we find a passage of a later date which seriously poses the question of why Akabia was not executed, as was the law regarding a "dissenting elder," if he really ridiculed Shemaiah and Abtalion. The answer given to this question was that Akabia's words regarding a *sotah* who was also a freed woman had only a theoretical implication and were not meant to be taken as a law to be practiced.[4]

The time of Akabia's life has not been definitely established. It is certain that he lived after the death of Shammai in whose stead he was to be appointed as head of the court. When Akabia refused this office, it was thenceforth abolished.

16

RABBAN GAMALIEL THE ELDER

HILLEL WAS SUCCEEDED AS NASI of the Sanhedrin by his son Simeon. The office of Nasi assumed added importance after the office of Head of the Court was abolished, and the Nasi became the sole ruler in all religious questions.

But it seems that Simeon did not live very long. He is only mentioned in the Talmud as Hillel's successor and no teaching of his has been recorded. When Simeon died his son Gamaliel was elected Nasi. Gamaliel came to be known as Rabban Gamaliel the Elder and he was the first one to be titled *Rabban*.

The title "Elder" was conferred upon Gamaliel because he was the first scholar of that name. The title Rabban (our teacher) was conferred on him because he was the only Head of the Sanhedrin. At that time the custom of *Semikhat Ze'keinim*, (ordination of the elders) was introduced, during which the Nasi or his representative ordained one of the disciples by placing his hand on his head. This procedure conferred upon the disciple the title Rabbi and the right to judge in all disputes except those involving life and death which were then the prerogative of the Roman government.

Most of the time that Rabban Gamaliel served as Nasi was unfavorable for the Jews; only one short period of improvement intervened. These were the last years preceding the destruction of the Temple, and the country was in a state of constant crisis. Officially the land was a province of the Roman empire and was ruled by the iron hand of a Roman governor. Even the slightest disobedience to the governor's will was punishable by death.

In those days Christianity began to spread in the country. The Apostle Paul (Saul of Tarsus) claims to have been a disciple of Rabban Gamaliel. If this claim is justified, then the trial of Jesus must have taken place during those years.

During that time, too, the Sanhedrin left the stone chamber in the Temple and moved to Chanut, a place in Jerusalem outside the Temple. The cause of the transfer of the Sanhedrin probably lay in the realization that the political situation of the country was rapidly approaching a crisis. If the Temple could not withstand the enemy, it aimed to save the Sanhedrin at least.

Almost at the same time, the throne of Rome was held by the mad Caligula who demanded that all the nations of the empire accord him divine worship. He also commanded the Jews of Palestine to place his image in the temple.

This command was received on the eve of the festival of *Sukkot* when Jews from the whole country were gathered in Jerusalem for the festivities. Their joy immediately turned to mourning and everyone felt certain that the royal decree would not be fulfilled, for the whole nation would rise against the attempt to desecrate their sanctuary. It was obvious that such a rebellion against the emperor's command would cost tens of thousands of lives.

One of the scholars addressed the people saying: "Let not the festivities of this day be disturbed. God in Heaven will save us from Caligula's decree even as he delivered us from other such decrees in the past."

His prediction came true and before this decree could be enforced, Caligula was slain. With the death of the emperor, the decree was abolished. Another political factor was influential in this case, although its influence was exerted secretly.

The Jewish prince Agrippa, son of the executed prince Aristobulus, who was the son of Miriam the Hasmonean, was educated in Rome where he had been very friendly with Caligula. He once exclaimed that he wished Emperor Tiberius was dead so that Caligula could ascend the throne. When this remark was reported to Tiberius, Agrippa was imprisoned. A short time later Tiberius died, and Caligula freed Agrippa. In spite of the intrigues of his sister, who was also a grandchild of Miriam the Hasmonean, Agrippa was made ruler over several districts in the old Jewish kingdom. In addition to this, Caligula offered to fulfill any wish of Agrippa's that lay in his power. Agrippa asked that the decree to have his image installed in the temple be revoked. Although Caligula was displeased by this request, he agreed to postpone this event, and in the meantime he was assassinated.

After Caligula's death, Agrippa used his influence with the Roman senate to have Claudius named emperor, and Claudius, in gratitude, named Agrippa king over the whole land of Judea. Agrippa's seven-year rule marked a bright period in the life of the Jews of Palestine.

In contradistinction to his predecessors, without requesting any royal privileges, Agrippa strove to observe all the laws of the Torah in the same manner as they were observed by the common people. Despite this many were dissatisfied with the king. The behavior of previous kings was fresh in the memory of the people, and many Jews felt that it would be better if there were no king.

One of the scholars told the king that he was not worthy to cross the threshold of the temple because he built a theater in Caesarea according to Roman custom. Agrippa did not punish the man but had him taken to Caesarea to convince him that the performances were not against the Jewish faith. The king was also accused of not being a full-blooded Jew, since his grandfather (Herod) was an Idumean convert, and of not being raised in the Jewish faith.

Once when Agrippa was standing on the platform in the Temple during the festival of *Sukkot* and was reading the king's portion of the Torah (Deut. 17), he reached the verse "you shall not make a stranger who is not your brother king over you." He then remembered their accusation that he was not a pure Jew and he began to weep. The scholars felt a great pity for their weeping king and they said to him: "Fear not King Agrippa, you are our brother."[1]

King Agrippa was very much attached to Rabban Gamaliel. He obeyed his advice in all religious matters and Rabban Gamaliel was his guest on all festive occasions.

Many of the king's regulations were aimed to make peace between the Jews and non-Jews. The Roman administration attracted many non-Jews to Palestine, and these considered themselves privileged citizens because they enjoyed the direct protection of Rome. The Jews, on the other hand, believed themselves to be the more privileged since they were natives of the land. Agrippa endeavored to establish friendly relations between the two groups and in this Rabban Gamaliel aided him. It was then that they permitted the non-Jewish poor to glean the fields together with the Jewish poor, and they ruled that it was obligatory to give charity to Gentile and Jewish poor alike. Similar rites were prescribed for the dead of both peoples.[2]

Agrippa reigned for seven years. In spite of his attempt to gain the favor of Rome, he secretly sympathized with all those who dreamed of freedom from the Roman yoke. During the last days of his life, he tried to ascertain the number of men the Jews could raise for an army. He convoked all the Jews of the country to Jerusalem for a census that was made by means of the Paschal offerings they had brought. The High Priest hid a part of every offering, and the number was found to be 600,000. This was proof that there were 600,000 families in Palestine aside from those who could not come to Jerusalem because they were impure or because of the distance. Since every family consisted of an average of ten people, it was accounted that the Jewish population of the country numbered over 6,000,000 people.[3]

During the same period Agrippa went to Caesarea to a theater performance, and while in the theater began to suffer great pain. He was immediately taken to his palace where he soon died at the age of fifty-four.

Rabban Gamaliel died soon after. With his death, the

scholars said, there departed the glory of the Torah and all justice and purity passed away.

Of the innovations of Rabban Gamaliel, there were some of great importance for his time. He introduced a new procedure for taking testimony regarding the beginning of a new month. When it was necessary to hear such testimony on a Sabbath, the witnesses were kept in a *Beth Yazek* and, they were not permitted to leave because of the Biblical prohibition that "no man shall leave his place." Rabban Gamaliel amended this law to permit one to walk 2,000 ells in every direction from where one was. He permitted a similar liberty for midwives on their way to women in labor, in case of fire, attack by a foreign army, and flood.[4]

Up to that time two witnesses were required to testify to the death of a man, before the widow was permitted to remarry. But since cases of violent death had increased as a result of Roman executions as well as through murder on the highways, Rabban Gamaliel ruled that just as one witness was sufficient to validate a marriage, even so the testimony of only one witness to the death of a man should be sufficient to permit the widow to remarry.[5]

Aside from these innovations Rabban Gamaliel introduced other rules pertaining to divorce and other important occasions in the lives of the people. In all of these regulations he aimed to lighten the burden of the laws. Only in those laws pertaining to cleanliness was he more severe than his predecessors. He also introduced various customs that placed the Nasi in a privileged position compared with that of the common people.[6]

Rabban Gamaliel was a person of delicate health. He was not strong enough to stand during his studies, as was then customary, and he permitted sitting during study for teacher as well as for pupils.[7] Although he was rich, he commanded his followers that he be buried in a plain linen shroud; this was contrary to the custom of the rich of that time. And so the custom of luxurious burial for important people fell into disuse.[8]

The following saying of Rabban Gamaliel characterizes his

opinion of his disciples: "There are as many types of disciples as there are varieties of fish; there are unclean fish, clean fish, fish from the Jordan, and fish from the great sea. A disciple who comes from poor parents and who, although he has studied Torah, *Mishnah, Halakhah* and *Aggadah*, has no native intelligence is like an unclean fish. A disciple who comes from wealthy parents, has studied Torah, *Mishnah, Halakhah* and *Aggadah*, and also has native intelligence is like a clean fish. One who has studied Torah and *Mishnah* and can also expound *Halakhah* and *Aggadah* but is not intelligent enough to solve problems that are put before him is like a fish from the Jordan. But like a fish from the great sea is a disciple who has studied Torah and *Mishnah* and can also expound *Halakhah* and *Aggadah* and can solve all problems put to him."

From Rabban Gamaliel we discover, for the first time, why the Sanhedrin declared some years to contain thirteen months. In a letter sent to the Jews of Palestine and neighboring countries, he said: "The time of Pesach is drawing nigh but there is no sign of spring and we will have not lambs for the Passover offering, nor young pigeons to be sacrificed by women who have given birth, nor will there be new barley for the offering of the sheaf.[9]

It also seems certain that the great academy of Jerusalem was transferred to Jabneh during the time of Rabban Gamaliel. It remained in Jabneh for many years after the destruction of the Temple with the permission of the Roman government.

17

RABBAN SIMEON BEN GAMALIEL

WITH THE DEATH OF KING AGRIPPA the political situation in Palestine took a turn for the worse. The Roman governors oppressed the people until life became unbearable. Meantime Rabban Gamaliel the Elder died, and he was succeeded by his son Rabban Simeon ben Gamaliel who found himself in a very difficult position throughout his stay as Nasi. He would have liked to continue the tradition of his forefather Hillel as a seeker after peace, but it became impossible to witness the barbarities of the Roman rulers and to maintain one's peace and even less so to attempt to pacify the people.

The party of the zealots grew from day to day and a life and death struggle against the Romans developed. The Nasi could no longer maintain the position of neutral bystander. The political situation demanded that he declare himself in sympathy with one or the other of the contending sides. At first Simeon came out against the zealots and their bloody struggle but realizing later the justice of their cause, he joined the patriots and personally participated in many of their warlike endeavors.

Rabban Simeon ben Gamaliel became Nasi seventeen or eighteen years before the destruction of the Temple. The great gathering of scholars that took place in the home of Chananiah ben Hezekiah, mentioned before, took place in his time. Fearing the Romans would attack the gathering, they prepared a number of religious questions to be clarified, in order to be able to say that this was not a political meeting but only a religious disputation.

In his religious conduct, Rabban Simeon ben Gamaliel observed his family tradition of making the laws of the Torah as easy as possible to observe. He evinced a certain tolerance toward the Sadducees who, since the days of Simeon ben Shetach, were looked upon as non-Jews by the Pharisees. He also believed that the religious burden imposed upon the people should not be greater than they were willing to accept.

Had Rabban Simeon ben Gamaliel lived in another period, his spiritual development might have followed a different line. Raised in luxury and reverence, he was certain to become an enthusiast of beauty, and it is hard to evaluate how much of the "beauty of Japheth" he might have introduced into the "tents of Shem." Thus it is told that he once saw a beautiful gentile woman and, although it was the accepted custom among Jews not to express admiration for the beauty of a gentile, he could not restrain his wonder and exclaimed: "God, how wonderful is your creation."[1]

He sometimes performed gymnastic feats that no one could imitate. During the *Simhat Beit Hashoeva*, the festive ceremony of the pouring of water, he threw into the air and caught again eight burning torches, without their touching one another in the air or in his hands. When he bowed during prayer he leaned on two fingers, kissed the ground, and rose again without any assistance.

A characteristic expression of his beliefs we find in *Pirkei Avot* where he says: "All my days I have spent among the scholars, and I have not found anything better than silence; study is not the chief thing but action, and whoever speaks much causes sin."[2]

To gain a better understanding of his words we must bear in mind that among the Jews outside of Palestine, such as in Alexandria, the opinion was current that the study of the Torah had only a theoretical value, since it deals with the theories and not with the practical observance of the laws. But it is probable that he aimed to make the people understand that the struggle against the Romans must be carried on in a more practical manner with less discussion and more actual struggle.

Meanwhile the struggle against Rome became more intense. The Romans brought blood and fire into the land, and the Jews adopted the same means. The peace-loving elements of the population were annihilated. Some were killed by the Romans and others lost their lives at the hands of the patriots. Bloody clashes also occurred with non-Jews and the Idumeans, who had largely given up the Jewish faith they embraced five generations earlier and joined forces with the enemy. The Samaritans (Kutim) now also showed their violent hatred of the Jews.

The one-time converts and friends of the Jews sought to benefit from the Roman-Jewish struggle, and their attempts still further increased Jewish suffering. The struggle was bitter and each group sought the total annihilation of the Jewish people to which the latter responded in kind.

The wealthier Jews sided with the Romans. They had no occasion to feel the slavery, and the anger of the governors seldom descended upon them. The Roman administration had treated them gently and granted them numerous privileges as tax collectors to induce them to get the maximum out of the impoverished population. But these wealthy elements had no understanding of their class privileges. Many of them devoted themselves to the study of Torah, observed all the laws and honestly contributed their tithes. Still others were characterized by their love for money and that led to violent mutual hatred among them.[3]

The Sanhedrin lost most of its authority, since it lost the power to pass sentence in matters affecting life and death. The people lost its fear of them and felt free to disregard their commands. Immorality and excesses became prevalent even in Jerusalem. People from low social strata were elevated to high position and former notables lost their influence. The wealthy spent their money on excess food and drink and immoral practices saying: "Why save for the morrow? Man should afford himself all possible pleasures for if he will not spend his wealth, the Romans will take it away from him."

Robber bands spread throughout the land and it meant certain death to travel the highways without military escort. Jews and non-Jews were members of these bands and they attacked travelers irrespective of their nationality. Only armed caravans and large Roman detachments could offer them any resistance.

An organized band calling themselves Sicarii sprang up at this time. They used small daggers that they conveniently hid under their robes. They mingled among the people of Jerusalem and listened to the conversations, and whenever anyone expressed an opinion favorable to the Romans, he would be stabbed while the assailant easily made his escape.

The most difficult task was to preserve peace during the Passover. Jews came to the city from all over the country to celebrate the feast day, and among the pilgrims also came many thieves and robbers. The crowds congregated in the streets in an attempt to see and to be seen. The Roman governor of the city was empowered to maintain order and he stationed soldiers about the Temple. On one occasion one of the soldiers committed a nuisance against the wall of the Temple and the enraged crowd fell upon him and killed him. When the other soldiers attempted to save him, the crowd attacked them as well and the governor had to call the whole army to subdue the disorders. The narrow streets of Jerusalem, crowded with 1,500,000 pilgrims, became a field of slaughter and about 10,000 Jews lost their lives in one day.

On another occasion Jews attacked the slaves of the governor who were carrying gold and food for the soldiers; they killed the slaves and robbed them of all their possessions. The governor then ordered the destruction of all villages around Jerusalem. This command was carried out and the soldiers killed all whom they encountered. During one of these clashes, a Roman soldier seized a scroll of the Torah and trampled it in the dust and then burned it exclaiming that he had trampled and burned the Jewish God. For this act he paid with his life to the enraged mob, but as a result hundreds of other Jews lost their lives.

The Samaritans also rose against the Jews. Their temple on Mount Gerizim had been destroyed a long time before and the majority observed Judaism very scrupulously. But the age-old hatred against the Jews continued to burn within them. When the people of Galilee wanted to make a pilgrimage to Jerusalem, they had to pass through the Samaritan villages. On the way they were attacked and slaughtered. This act was followed by a reprisal on the part of the inhabitants of Jerusalem who killed every Samaritan they could find and burned their villages. Then the Roman governor stepped in to punish the avengers and executed several thousand Jews.

Meanwhile Claudius died and was succeeded by Nero. He granted some powers to the Jewish Prince Agrippa, son of the benevolent King Agrippa who had lived in the time of Rabban Gamaliel the Elder. But the rule of Agrippa II was limited to part of the Galilee including the city of Tiberias and to twenty-four villages on the eastern bank of the Jordan. Agrippa had the power to appoint the high priest and he used this right extensively. The office of the high priesthood could be purchased, and whenever a new candidate offered more for the position, he was immediately appointed and the previous high priest was deposed. Money was the only consideration, and the candidate did not even have to be a descendant of Aaron.

Only one high priest of that time, Ishmael ben Phabi, is mentioned by name, but even he was not held in esteem. The broad masses of the people had no reverence for any high priest at that time, and of Ishmael ben Phabi it was told that he cruelly oppressed the people through his servants.

The people commonly believed that the high priests employed magic to rid themselves of one another. A poet of that time composed a verse with a list of injustices the people suffered from their high priests. It reads: "Woe is me from the house of Boetus and woe from their course; woe is me from the house of Kathros and woe from their pen; woe is me from the house of Ishmael and woe from their fist. All of them are high priests, their sons are tax collectors, their sons-in-law are overseers of the temple, and their slaves beat the people with rods."[4]

When Rabban Simeon ben Gamaliel came to the conclusion that the struggle against the Romans was justified and that as Nasi of the Sanhedrin he had to stand in the forefront of the revolt, he sharply condemned the activities of Josephus (Joseph ben Gurion Hacohen) who was entrusted with the leadership of the revolt in Galilee. From the first moment Rabban Simeon ben Gamaliel believed that Josephus was not a capable military leader, and he also suspected that Josephus would surrender to the Romans on the first occasion. Josephus himself relates this distrust but says nothing against his opponent.

It is entirely reasonable to suppose that a man such as Rabban Simeon ben Gamaliel did not die a natural death during this revolutionary period, and many believed that he was killed. Other historians claim that he was not killed by the Romans, but that he fell at the hands of the "patriots" who doubted his devotion to the revolutionary cause. *Megillat Taanit* only mentions the day of his death, 25 *Sivan*, and that he was killed together with the High Priest Rabbi Ishmael ben Elisha.

18

RABBI CHANINA, DEPUTY TO THE HIGH PRIEST, AND HIS CONTEMPORARIES

DESPITE THE FACT THAT JUDEA was convulsed by the last agonies of political death throughout the fifty years preceding the destruction of the temple, and in spite of the brutal yoke of the Roman Empire that did not allow the Jews to breathe freely, the study of the Torah nevertheless did not decrease during these years of crisis. The enemy spread terror and thousands of patriots gave up their lives, but within their homes the people devoted themselves to study and ignored the dangers which beset them.

The Romans did not realize then how the study of Torah might influence and encourage the patriotism of the nation. Therefore it did not occur to them to hinder the pursuit of learning. Only after the destruction of the Temple did it dawn on them that the Jews find strength and consolation in the Torah. Before the destruction, the Roman political leaders were convinced that the Temple was the only stimulus to Jewish rebellion, and the same belief was held by the Jewish sympathizers of Rome. The Roman Empire, therefore, concentrated all its efforts against the Temple and not against learning.

Aside from the Nasi and his followers there were tens of other scholars who delved into the Torah and they exerted a great influence on the life of the people. Among the most important of these scholars was Rabbi Chanina (sometimes referred to as Chahaniah), deputy of the High Priest.

The title *Sgan* (deputy) is the equivalent of overseer. The deputies were assistants of the High Priest and overseers and superintendents of the Temple who were ready to help the High Priest whenever necessary.

Deputies were appointed for a long period of time and they maintained their office even while High Priests were being changed. There were usually several deputies at the same time, but only one of them was prepared to act as assistant to the High Priest. If for any reason something happened to the High Priest, preventing him from continuing the service, the deputy stood ready to take his place. But as long as the High Priest could perform his duty, the deputy merely stood beside him and was not allowed to do any of his work.[1]

Rabbi Chanina was one of the outstanding scholars during the last years of the Second Temple. When the patriotic movement first became active, Chanina identified himself with the peaceful elements of the nation who openly condemned the patriots. He said then that people should pray for the welfare of the government, for were it not for fear of government people would swallow each other alive.[2] On another occasion he praised peace highly and compared it in importance to the work of creation.[3]

But later, when the conduct of the Romans became more murderous, Chanina joined the patriots together with the Nasi, Rabban Simeon ben Gamaliel. He openly criticized the wealthy Jews who had abandoned the rule of God for the rule of man, for "whosoever considers the words of the Torah is absolved from the fear of the sword, from hunger, from evil desires and from the rule of man as the Torah says: 'Because you have not served God joyfully and wholeheartedly when you had enough of everything, you will have to serve the enemies, that God will send upon you, in hunger and in thirst, naked and abandoned by everyone.' Such a man will want a piece of barley bread and will not find it, but at the same time he will be forced to give his enemy good bread and fat meats; he will thirst for a drop of vinegar or beer and will not find it, but his enemies will demand the best of wines and he will be forced to supply it to them; he will want a cloak of wool or flax and will have none, but his enemies will demand of him the best of silks, and he will have to give it to them. Thus he will remain forsaken by all, without a candle, without a knife and a table, and without even a pinch of salt."[4]

It is told that Rabbi Chanina inaugurated special privileges for his office even as Rabban Simeon ben Gamaliel did. As long as the Temple was in existence, he was the highest authority in all matters pertaining to sacrifices. Frequently he supported his opinions by citing the customary procedure of his father, and the customs of his father were based on family traditions.

He was particularly interested in preserving the detailed memory of all the customs of the service in the Temple. Believing that the Temple would soon be rebuilt, he wanted to be sure that the customs in the new Temple would not differ from those in the old one.[5]

Chanina, deputy of the priests, influenced Jewish life in other ways aside from temple service procedure. In his time in a village near Jerusalem there lived a man who lent money. This man was in the habit of writing the loan note himself, and the borrower merely signed the note or attested to his signature by a witness. Rabbi Chanina declared these notes to be valid, although the accepted law of the time stated that the borrower must write the note himself. Chanina believed that as long as the signatures of the witnesses were authentic, it did not matter who wrote the note.

He also stated that during his performance of the service various miracles had occurred. One of them concerned the menorah that was lit once a year on Rosh Hashanah but continued to burn throughout the year.[6]

Because of the mourning for the Temple, Chanina held that as long as it was in ruins no one should bathe on Tisha B'Av, not even a person who must perform an ablution, but in this he was contradicted by other scholars.[7]

The name of Chanina is not mentioned among the martyrs but the opinion prevails that he was executed and the date of his death is said to be 25 *Sivan*, the same as that of Simeon ben

Gamaliel and Rabbi Ishmael ben Elisha. This does not mean, however, that he was killed before the destruction of the temple, for it is known that he indeed survived it. It merely indicates that the date of his death coincided with that of the two martyrs.

At about the same time there lived two *tannaim* whom the Jerusalem Talmud refers to as the "judges of robberies" and the Babylonian Talmud calls the "judges of decrees." This contradiction, however, is easily explained by the difference in pronunciation in the two countries.

It was the duty of these judges to settle various disputes and to punish those whom they found guilty of robbery. They also considered cases of damages and the infliction of minor wounds. These judges were generally elected by the community who also paid their fees in order to avoid their being bribed by one or another of the contending parties. Their verdict was final, and they had the authority to enforce it.

There were many such judges, for Jerusalem alone had 394 courts, each of which had 25 judges, according to the Talmud. But the *Mishnah* names only two judges whose decisions served as a basis for future verdicts. These two were Admon ben Gadai and Chanan ben Avi Shalom.

The rule that these judges followed in arriving at a decision was to consider the specific circumstances of the place and time. We must also remember that of all the sentences passed by these judges, not one involved actual robbery. They concerned financial disputes, and the judges gave their verdict according to the dictates of reason. Later scholars used these decisions as a basis for passing sentence.

Admon ben Gadai passed seven sentences, four of which became a basis for future law, although they were based on reason and not on texts of the Torah. Chanan ben Avi Shalom contributed two decisions in the same spirit.[8]

Mention should also be made of Joshua ben Gamala who was elected High Priest several years before the destruction of the Temple. This office he obtained through bribery because he was not descended from priests and had married a widow.

Martha, the daughter of Boetus, married Joshua and in order to obtain the office of High Priest for him, she sent a bagful of gold to King Agrippa II.[9]

Joshua ben Gamala was very rich and he spent much money to beautify the Temple and increase its vessels. It is told that he had a golden vessel made for the purpose of casting the lot to determine which of the two sacrifices was to be offered in the Temple and which was to be sent to Azazel.[10]

During the last rebellion Joshua ben Gamala opposed the patriots and the war with Rome. Agrippa soon removed him from office, as was his custom with High Priests, and Joshua remained a member of the Sanhedrin. When large numbers of Idumeans came from Galilee to Jerusalem to seek refuge from the Romans, Joshua ben Gamala together with the High Priest Anan strongly opposed their admission into the city. But the majority of the inhabitants opposed them, and when the Idumeans were finally admitted, they attacked Joshua ben Gamala and the High Priest Anan and killed them.

Despite the fact that Joshua ben Gamala bought the office of High Priest, the Talmud mentions his name favorably, because he ruled that there must be teachers in every city in Judea to instruct the children so that the Torah might not be forgotten.[11]

19

THE TIME
OF THE DESTRUCTION
OF THE TEMPLE

From THE PREVIOUS CHAPTERS we get a clear picture of the political situation of the country and its inhabitants, as well as of the means employed by the enemy to oppress them. But the internal life of the Jewish home was not greatly affected by the war raging outside its walls. All those laws and customs governing the life of the people were already strongly established to the smallest detail; the regulations concerning the daily prayers, the observance of the Sabbath, and the holy days were clearly defined. The same was true regarding family organization, permissible and prohibited marriages, financial disputes among Jews, as well as the punishment of offenses against the public order. There were also well-established dietary regulations and rules of cleanliness. All customs regarding offerings to the priests and the obligations toward the poor were defined. Even questions pertaining to the offering of sacrifices, that many scholars no longer considered as the most important foundation of the Jewish faith, and the laws affecting life and death, that had been taken out of the jurisdiction of the Jewish courts, were codified in great detail together with their traditions and forms. But all of this legislation was not yet written down and the people had to guard it in their memory for use in future interpretations of the law.

We may say definitely that the whole "oral law" as we have it today was already completed by that time. Such disputes as arose over interpretation came about as a result of the law not being written and contained only in the memory of the students.

In the observance of everyday customs everyone had his own traditions and these varied only slightly. But the regulations regarding cleanliness and the laws pertaining to the offering of sacrifices, that were no longer practiced, were increasingly disputed as time went on. Many of the regulations pertaining to sacrifices were forgotten soon after their offering was discontinued, and it frequently occurred that a later scholar who never witnessed the service in the Temple had to correct an older scholar who had witnessed the service but whose recollections were vague.

A rule was therefore adopted that whenever one expressed an opinion about a practice no longer observed, such an opinion had only a theoretical significance as to the desirable form of the observance, but it did not serve as proof that this had *actually* been the form when the practice was observed in the past.

Laws affecting civil disputes involving monetary matters attained a high level of development. This was especially the case in the matter of offering proof in numerous forms, depending on the nature of the case; at times it was necessary to bring witnesses, at other times an oath, a written document or other proof of possession was required.

Usually two witnesses were required in such law suits. They they had to be men of high moral standards and their testimony had to coincide. For this reason no *am ha'aretz* was eligible to be a witness, nor a person who might be suspected of falsifying his testimony out of fear of one of the litigants, or through irresponsible levity. Women, children, cripples (blind and deaf) and fools who cannot judge what they see were also ruled out as witnesses. Similarly relatives of the litigants were rejected, and in case both witnesses were related only one of them was allowed to testify. Persons known as "wicked," gamblers, pigeon thieves, and usurers were ruled out because they were already considered robbers who deprived people of their money. The same was true of persons who dealt in fruit of the sabbatical year or who were suspected of robbery. Among those also not qualified to testify were tax collectors for the Roman government, shepherds who grazed their herds in strangers' fields, and people suspected of having a personal interest in the case.

There were cases when the court had to be satisfied with the testimony of only one witness. Thus, the testimony of one witness to the death of a person was sufficient to free the widow to remarry. In other cases where the plaintiff could produce only one witness, the defendant could swear to his innocence and thus invalidate the testimony. Similar to this was the case of a woman who came before the court in times of peace and declared that her husband was dead. If she was known to have lived happily with him, her testimony was accepted as valid, in spite of the fact that women were not allowed to testify, and despite the rule that no one might testify on his own behalf.

When hearing a witness, the court had to impress upon him the possible significance of his words and to cross-question him minutely. If the witnesses contradicted each other, the testimony of both was ruled out. If they recanted their testimony, they were considered false witnesses, and the punishment that was to be meted out to the defendant was imposed upon them. In some cases it was possible to convict a defendant on the basis of testimony of witnesses who had not seen the crime themselves but who had heard of it from the defendant. But there were also limitations; for example, a man could not be convicted on his own confession even though such a confession was worth the testimony of a hundred witnesses, for no man could make himself out to be wicked.

An oath was exacted when there were no witnesses or when only one witness appeared against the defendant. Similarly, watchmen who disclaimed responsibility for damages to property in their charge had to take an oath. This was also the case when a defendant admitted part of his guilt, or one who denied guilt and was confronted by one witness. There were also cases when the plaintiff had to take an oath. These included workmen who claimed they had not been paid, the victim of a robbery where the defendant pleaded not guilty, and the case of a man suspected of falsehood but against whom there were no witnesses.

The best proof in a lawsuit was a written document attesting to a loan, an engagement, a marriage, or a divorce. Other documents recognized were contracts of sale or purchase, wills affecting inheritance, certificates of gift, receipts, mortgages, evaluation of property during the division of an inheritance, certificates of alimony to a deserted wife or children, written declaration of a married minor rejecting her husband, statements of arbitration, and numerous others. Sometimes an oath was required in addition to the written documents, whenever the signatures were doubtful.

Circumstantial evidence was highly regarded. Property in possession of a person was considered to be his own, and any claim to it had to be proved by the claimant.

People were at that time imbued with a strong desire to fortify and define their faith and it is remarkable that, in spite of the unfavorable political position of the Jews, Judaism nevertheless gained adherents, and many neighboring peoples came closer to it. It may be assumed that the period was one of spiritual crisis among the heathen nations. Tiring of their idols, many people confusedly speculated that the forces of nature were not gods but part of an invisible power that governs the forces of nature. When they heard that Jews worshipped such an invisible God, many came to Judea to acquaint themselves with the worshippers of this God.

It was characteristic that the seekers after a new truth belonged mainly to the upper educated strata of their nations. Adiabene, a small buffer state on the banks of the Tigris, was then ruled by Queen Helene. This queen was married to her brother Izates, and after his death she visited Jerusalem. Deeply impressed by what she saw and especially by the religious ceremonials of the Temple, she was converted and adopted Judaism. Later her son, Izates II, also joined the faith.

It is probable that some of the Jewish scholars of that time were not too happy over the new converts. It seems certain that the strict regulations against proselytes and the sharp expressions against them in the Talmud such as, "proselytes are as difficult for Jews as a swelling," all date from this period. The troubles Jews had withstood from the Samaritans and the Idumeans, taught them to be careful in admitting new converts.

Most of the proselytes of that time were women. Conversion was more difficult for men and fewer of them adopted Judaism. When King Izates II decided to become a Jew, one of the scholars taught him the precepts of Judaism and told him rather than arouse the anger of his countrymen he must not undergo circumcision; it would be sufficient if he recognized the principles of the Jewish religion and the overlordship of an invisible God. But Izates was later circumcised, when he realized that without this rite he was deprived of the rights of a Jew.

Many highly placed persons strove toward the Jewish faith. They were intrigued by the high moral teachings of the Jewish religion, although they did not highly regard the Jew as a person. It therefore seems certain that were the political situation of the Jewish nation more favorable, all the surrounding nations would have embraced Judaism.

It is also remarkable that some of the scholars of that time were not overly concerned with the continued existence of the Temple. Many events transpired then were not recorded, and those that history did note express a definite tendency of thought. And it seems certain that some scholars considered the development of the Torah more important than the maintenance of the Temple. They probably reasoned that were the Temple to be destroyed it could be rebuilt in more auspicious times, but if the Torah were neglected it might spell the doom of the Jewish nation.

It is also evident that some scholars did not attach much importance to the offering of sacrifices, while others carefully pondered the minutest details of the Temple service. This, however, took place after the Temple was destroyed and it was only after this that its significance as a central national force dawned upon people. Only then did those who considered the

Temple to be of minor importance in the Jewish religion grasp its importance. Revolutionary sentiment died down after the rebels were slaughtered or led captive to Rome to fight with wild beasts in its arenas. A new concept of the significance of sacrifices was then gained. It was now understood that when the text says that sacrifices are offered as "pleasing odors" it was not meant that God enjoys the odor of burnt flesh, but rather that He is satisfied to see men do His will. When it was no longer possible to offer sacrifices, some scholars held that fasts and self-inflicted suffering are considered by God to be worthier than burnt offerings, while others maintained that prayer was of greater importance than sacrifices.

While the revolution was raging throughout the land the Temple service was conducted as usual. At the same time, many scholars sought to escape from the revolution-torn city, and they established a new sanctuary for the study of the Torah in Jabneh.

The Romans did not yet persecute the study of the Torah, for in those days they did not see any danger in the Torah to the unity of the Roman empire. They paid no attention to scholarly pursuits as long as the Jews regularly paid their taxes. It also seems certain that the Romans would not have destroyed the Temple were it not for their allies among the Jews who constantly reminded them that as long as the Temple remained in existence Jews would never submit to Roman rule, and no matter how they were persecuted they would continue to revolt.

Among the friends of the Romans who constantly insisted that the Temple must be destroyed because its continued existence gave encouragement to the embattled Jews, were the Jewish king, Agrippa II, and his sister Berenice. Berenice was not noted for modesty in her personal life, and she became the mistress of Titus, commander of the Roman army in Judea.

The relations between Titus and Berenice are described in the Talmud by: "He held a harlot by the hand and entered the Holy of Holies."[1] Just as the Talmud never referred to Herod except as "the Idumean slave" so also did they refer to Berenice as a "harlot."

Historical legend relates that Titus commanded his soldiers not to harm the Temple. But Agrippa and Berenice
refused to obey him in this matter and hinted to the soldiers
that they would never subdue the revolt as long as the Temple
remained intact. Berenice is said to have climbed on the
shoulders of a Roman soldier and with her own hand to have
thrown the burning torch that set fire to the Temple. When
Titus heard the Temple was burning, he ran to help put out the
fire, but the flames had already enveloped the whole building.

It is obvious that there is no sin against historical truth if
one doesn't believe this legend. It was originated by Josephus
who is not entirely trustworthy when chronicling the role of
Titus and King Agrippa in the destruction of the Temple.

The revolt lasted many years. It was not concentrated in
one locality but flared up in different sections of the country
until it assumed a general nature, and on a certain day the
priests refused to offer the daily sacrifice for the welfare of the
Roman emperor, and also rejected sacrifices offered by non-
Jews who lived in Judea.

Friends of the Roman government immediately informed
them of the new rebel tactics. When Roman soldiers were
dispatched to enforce the offering of the sacrifice for the welfare
of the emperor and to force the acceptance of the sacrificial
offerings of the non-Jews, the patriots occupied the Temple and
killed many of the soldiers who were stationed in Jerusalem
and its vicinity.

This action caused great confusion among the Jews because it was unauthorized, and many prominent persons in
Jerusalem publicly expressed their displeasure. For their expression of loyalty to the Romans, the zealots executed many of
them as well as numerous others whom they suspected of
secret sympathy with the Romans.

Later, others declared that since the deed could not be
undone, it was necessary to wait for the reaction of Rome,
meanwhile fortifying the cities in anticipation of the coming of
the enemy.

There lived in Jerusalem then three wealthy men who
belonged to aristocratic families who could trace their descent

as far back as King Saul and Moses. They were Nakdimon ben Gurion, Ben Kalba Savua, and Ben Tzizit Hakeset. These three undertook to supply the city with wheat and barley, wine and oil, as well as salt and wood, for the duration of the siege of Jerusalem even were to last many years.

But the zealots were eager to come out in open struggle against the Romans, and they felt sure that they were strong enough for the contest. They feared that the presence of large supplies of food during the forthcoming siege might induce the people to stay within the walls and discourage them from attacking the enemy outside the gates. Angry with the offer of the wealthy men, in the dark of night they burned the store rooms filled with grain. A great famine then followed, such as the city had never experienced before.

The Roman governor meanwhile incited the Greek population of Caesarea against their Jewish neighbors. When news of this clash became known, the Jewish inhabitants of Jerusalem attacked the Greeks as well as other non-Jews within the city. This mutual enmity quickly enveloped the whole country, and whenever Jew and non-Jew met, a battle ensued in which the weaker side was given no mercy.

These clashes spread to Acco, Haifa, Ashkelon, and other cities and also affected the Jews of Alexandria who until this time had lived in peace. When the news reached Alexandria, the Greek population began to attack the Jews and, meeting with resistance, they started a war of annihilation against them. The leader of the Greeks was a Jewish apostate, Tiberius Alexander.

The chronicles of these violent events speak of tens of thousands of people being killed. While it is possible that some of these figures are exaggerated, there remains no doubt that large numbers perished and the horrors of the situation were not exaggerated.

When the Romans finally decided to suppress the Jewish insurrection, their army was put under the command of Galus. With him was the Jewish King Agrippa who acted as his guide and who instructed the soldiery to kill all whom they met.

Meanwhile the disturbances within Jerusalem gained in

intensity from day to day and a violent struggle raged between those who wanted peace and the militants who demanded war. Outside the cities, the Jewish warriors showed feats of prodigious valor that terrified the Romans to such an extent that many of them deserted their camp and joined the Jews in the struggle for liberation.

The story in the Talmud about the disputes between the school of Shammai (who wanted war) and the school of Hillel (who wanted peace) that says that "a sword was placed within the Temple, and it was announced that one might enter, but he might not leave until a decision was arrived at"[2] is interpreted by some historians to refer to these times. On another occasion it is told that "the disciples of Shammai stood at the foot of the wall armed with swords and spears and they beat the disciples of Hillel."[3]

Others campaigned for war by means of the written word. In order to arouse the people against their insufferable troubles, the *Megillat Taanit* was written, citing all the inflictions the Jews had withstood throughout their existence. Still others wrote *Megillat Bet Chashmonai*, the story of the Hasmonean family, that told of the causes of the Hasmonean revolt in order to remind the people of the great miracles that transpired when a small handful of valiant Jews undertook the struggle against the mighty Greeks. All of this was aimed to encourage the rebels in the belief that God would certainly aid them against the Romans even though their military forces were small.

The greatest error the leaders of the war against Rome committed was when they appointed Josephus to head the war in Galilee. In his history of the war, Josephus relates the tricks and intrigues he resorted to in his fight against the insurrection until the destruction of the Temple. He then received an appointment from the Roman emperor, and out of gratitude to Rome he assumed the surname Flavius which was also the name of the Emperor Vespasian and his son Titus.

To save the situation, the Romans dispatched a horde of 600,000 armed men under the leadership of Vespasian against the Jewish rebels. Vespasian, noted for his victories over the Germans, proceeded to storm the fortresses outside Jerusalem in an attempt to cut that city off from all avenues of escape. He was always successful in using traitors who informed him of the weaknesses of the various cities and how they might best be taken. His conduct lacked all the ethics of combat, and whenever he occupied a city, after promising to spare its inhabitants, he invariably broke his promise and brutally slaughtered them.

The Jews fought with indescribable heroism but they were everywhere betrayed and the Romans took one city after another. Jerusalem alone remained steadfast and would not surrender, but it was afflicted by another difficulty. Tens of thousands of refugees from the surrounding towns fled into the city and attempted to dictate the activities of its inhabitants. A large portion of the Jerusalem population would have been glad to end the insurrection in any way possible, but the zealots considered them traitors and once a man was stamped with the suspicion of treason he could easily be killed.

The internal conflicts of the Jerusalem Jews as well as the famine that broke out after the food supplies were burned were a great encouragement to Vespasian who saw in them a sign that the gods were favoring him. Secure in the belief that Rome would triumph in the end, he was satisfied to watch the Jews aid him in his work.

Vespasian then entrusted the conduct of the war to his son Titus who maintained friendly relations with King Agrippa II, with Josephus, and was also on intimate terms with Princess Berenice. They instructed him what means to employ and, knowing the city was without food, pointed out how he could also cut off its water supply. When these attempts brought no results, Titus announced to the besieged that he would provide food and drink to all those who would come out to him and that he would also permit them to return to the city.

Many of the besieged were deceived by these promises, and as could be expected, Titus did not keep his promise. Some of the deserters were given salty food but no water; others were crucified in front of the fortress in full view of the besieged; still others had their arms cut off, and so were returned to the city.

But in spite of the siege, the Temple service continued

until the 17th day of *Tamuz*. Throughout long months, the inhabitants had had nothing to eat, but the daily sacrifice was offered until the last lamb was gone and not even a handful of flour was left in the city. Thus the sacrifice ended and the fire on the altar was extinguished.

With the aid of famine and plagues, internal conflict and other suffering reached such a stage that the people were forced to become cannibalistic, and the Romans conquered Jerusalem. But even when the Romans were already within the gates of the city, the Jews continued to fight valiantly until they saw the Temple in flames and only then did they lose their courage.

No one believed that God would permit His Temple to be destroyed, and when this finally did happen, everyone within the city, men and women, young and old, were crazed with despair. Thousands cast themselves into the fire while others fell on their own swords.

The burning of the Temple marked a spiritual crisis in Jewish life. Life now centered about the Torah and Jerusalem was superseded by Jabneh.

After four years of bloody warfare Jerusalem lay devastated, the Temple destroyed, the best people were killed or sold as slaves into the copper and lead mines. The young men of the aristocratic families were forced to run after the triumphal chariot of Titus carrying the Temple vessels that became Roman booty, and after the celebration of the triumph they had to face each other as well as wild animals in battles staged in the Roman arenas for the pleasure of the populace.

These spectacles were visited by the ex-King Agrippa, his sister Berenice, and Josephus who later described those wars in a tone of praise for Vespasian.

Jabneh had developed into an important city during the revolt, preceding the destruction of the Temple. Its population was so large that the city had provided 40,000 men for the war; it may therefore be reckoned that its population was about 200,000. When the Romans spared the city, they hardly knew the strength inherent in the Torah and how dangerous for them it might become.

It seems certain that many of the scholars left Jerusalem before the destruction of the Temple because they refused to participate in the revolt. They settled in Jabneh that was apparently not affected by the tumult of war. When Rabban Jochanan ben Zakkai visited the Emperor Vespasian in his camp, he found favor in his eyes and Vespasian asked him to make a request. Rabban Jochanan did not ask that Jerusalem or the Temple be spared, but he requested that Jabneh and its scholars be saved. This clearly indicates that Jabneh was already the home of a large number of scholars.

Jabneh then became the center of Judaism—a new Jerusalem without a Temple or sacrifices. A new Sanhedrin was organized and assumed the rights of the previous Sanhedrin of Jerusalem to regulate Jewish life according to the interpretations of the Torah. The scholars of Jabneh were of no less stature than those of Jerusalem. They would not have been chosen had they not been men of great religious and secular learning. They were also masters of the languages of the neighboring peoples, so as to be able to try cases between Jews and non-Jews without having to resort to outside experts and interpreters.

The scholars of Jabneh gathered in a place called "the vineyard of Jabneh." The meaning of this name is not entirely clear and some claim that it refers to their manner of being seated in rows just as vines are planted in a vineyard.[4] In Jabneh the decision was finally made that in all disputes between the school of Shammai and the school of Hillel, the law should be practiced according to the school of Hillel. This decision was arrived at as a result of a *bat kol*[5] to announce that the opinions of the school of Shammai are also from God but that only the opinions of the school of Hillel should be put into practice.[6]

When the people saw that sacrifices were no longer offered, they fell into great despair. Many of them could not understand the value of the prayers that were substituted for the sacrifices, and the weaker ones joined the various religious sects that sought a new god outside of the Jewish faith. It was then that the *tanna* Shmuel Hakatan established the prayer against the disbelievers (*birkat haminim*) cursing all those who depart from the Jewish faith to be taken from among the living.

Many laws were codified in Jabneh and special attention was paid to determining the first of the month and the feast days. This calendar was also valid for the Jews of Rome, Greece, Egypt, and Babylon.

Jabneh thus became a place of refuge for fugitives from the strife in Jerusalem. While the tumult of war still resounded and the hearts of people bled at the sight of the dead and wounded and the sound of Roman cheers, this group of scholars forged the essence of the Jewish nation. It was not difficult for them to find what they sought. They realized that the Torah was the only hope for continued national existence, and their work could not be hindered by strangers nor by all the legions of Rome. While the enemy could kill people, destroy the Temple, and lay waste the land, he could not annihilate the spirit of the nation.

After a short time a court having the same powers as the court in Jerusalem was also founded in Jabneh. The text of the Bible stating "if a thing shall be hidden from you in a judgment between blood and blood, or between one claim and another, or between one damage and another in a dispute within your gates, you shall arise and go to the place which the Lord God will choose" (Deut. 17:8) they interpreted to mean that the court gives authority to the place where it is located, and not the place to the court. It was therefore concluded that Jabneh might also be such a place.

Jabneh came to be considered the equal of Jerusalem in the matter of some customs such as the blowing of the *shofar* (ram's horn) on *Rosh Hashanah* when the first day of the year falls on a Sabbath. It had been previously prohibited to blow the *shofar* on the Sabbath outside of Jerusalem where no sacrifices were offered.

It is related that the introduction of this custom in Jabneh met with some difficulties. Prominent opponents of this measure, such as the men of Bathyra whose ancestors once headed the Sanhedrin in Jerusalem, could not agree that Jabneh should be considered the equal of Jerusalem in sanctity, and that the blowing of the *shofar* on a Sabbath should be permitted within it. They wanted to debate the matter with Rabban Jochanan ben Zakkai, but he said: "Let us first blow the *shofar* and then we shall debate the issue." When they wanted to debate the question after this was done, he said: "Now that the sound of the *shofar* has been heard in Jabneh, it is useless to debate the matter."

Until then, it was customary for the head of the Court to announce the beginning of the new month, but in Jabneh it was ruled that any member of the court might announce it even in the absence of the head of the court.

The basis for these new innovations was that with the destruction of the Temple, the needs of the people had changed in accordance with the new political situation. The great changes brought about by those events eliminated the original purpose of many of the customs, and they had to be changed according to the new state of affairs. It is characteristic of the people that they adapted themselves rapidly to the changed circumstances and looked at the present and toward the near future instead of to the past.

As the people devoted themselves to the observance of the commandments according to the traditions of oral law, they gained the necessary strength to rise above the gloom of the present and to concentrate their thoughts on spiritual matters. Their first activity was to gather all the traditions and put them in writing. Seeing that many old customs were being forgotten and that even some scholars, who were active in the academy, sometimes forgot what they had seen, they began to collect in book form all the traditional customs and laws, including those that were no longer practiced after the destruction of the Temple.

20

RABBAN JOCHANAN BEN ZAKKAI

RABBAN JOCHANAN BEN ZAKKAI PLAYED the most important role in the great spiritual crisis that took place during the time of the destruction of the Temple. Since he was known to favor peace with the Romans, the zealots kept him under constant surveillance but, by trickery he succeeded in escaping the city, together with two of his best disciples (Rabbi Eliezer and Rabbi Joshua) and in persuading the Romans to spare the city of Jabneh and its scholars, in order to permit the perpetuation of the customs of Judaism according to the regulations of the Torah.

The event is described in the Talmud thus:

Abba Sikra, a nephew of Rabban Jochanan ben Zakkai, was a leader among the zealots. One day Rabban Jochanan summoned him to appear before him secretly. When Abba Sikra arrived, Rabban Jochanan asked him: "How much longer will you permit the people to die of hunger before you surrender to the Romans?"

Abba Sikra replied: "What can I do? Were I to mention peace to my comrades I would be killed."

"Then advise me how I can leave the city. Perhaps I shall be able to bring some salvation for myself and for others," Rabban Jochanan said.

To this Abba Sikra answered: "Pretend that you are sick and have people come to visit you. Afterward, have it announced that you died, but permit only your disciples to attend to the funeral and to carry your body out of the city, for strangers may become aware that they are carrying a living body."

The advice of Abba Sikra was followed to the letter and when the pallbearers approached the gate of the city, the guards wanted to pierce the body to make sure that it was really dead. But Abba Sikra said to them: "Do not so, for if the Romans hear of it they will say 'The Jews have stabbed their Rabbi.' " The guards then wanted to throw the body from the litter and Abba Sikra again intervened saying, "Do not so, for if the Romans hear of it they will say 'The Jews have thrown the body of their Rabbi on the ground.' "

Upon finding himself outside the city, Rabban Jochanan ben Zakkai went at once to the Roman camp to see Vespasian, who was then conducting the siege of Jerusalem. After he gained his confidence with wise words, and because Vespasian knew of his favorable attitude toward peace with the Romans, Vespasian asked him to request whatever he liked. Rabban Jochanan asked for three things: His first request was to spare Jabneh and its scholars; the second request was to spare the family of Rabban Gamaliel the Elder; the third request was to provide a doctor for Rabbi Zadok who had spent forty years in fasting and prayer to God to spare the Temple.

The Talmud remarks that sometimes God deprives the wise of their intelligence, for on this occasion Rabban Jochanan ben Zakkai should have asked the Romans to end the siege. But the same paragraph criticizing Rabban Jochanan also defends him by saying that he refrained from speaking about the siege for fear of gaining nothing if he asked for too much.[1]

The manner in which Rabban Jochanan ben Zakkai came before Vespasian is related in a somewhat different manner in the Midrash.[2]

According to this version, the name of Rabban Jochanan's nephew was Ben Batiach, and it further states that when the zealots of Jerusalem burned the food stores given by the three wealthiest men of the city to tide them over the period of the siege, Rabban Jochanan ben Zakkai wept in anguish. It was immediately reported to Ben Batiach that his uncle cried out "Woe" (Vai). Ben Batiach summoned his uncle and asked him: "Why did you cry out 'Woe'?" But Rabban Jochanan replied: "I did not cry out 'Woe' but 'Wah.' " (Wah was an exclamation of joy.)

Ben Batiach further queried, "Why were you so glad?" To this Rabban Jochanan replied, "I was glad that you burned all the food supplies, for as long as there is food in the city you will not succeed in getting the people to participate in the war."

Three days later Rabban Jochanan ben Zakkai was walking in the street and he saw people boiling straw and drinking the broth. He then remarked that if people who boil straw to drink the broth attempt an insurrection against Vespasian and his army, it was best to leave the place.

He then sent a message to Ben Batiach saying: "Allow me to leave the city." But Ben Batiach answered, "We have an agreement to permit no living person to leave the city."

According to Midrash *Eikhah*, Rabban Jochanan ben Zakkai *did* request Vespasian to end the siege but Vespasian is said to have answered: "The Romans have made me emperor in order to destroy this land, but you may take out of the city all the friends you wish to save from death."

According to another legend, Rabban Jochanan ben Zakkai once saw the daughter of Nakdimon ben Gurion, who was one of the three wealthy men who provided the city with food before the zealots burned their food stores, picking barley from beneath the horses' hooves. He then exclaimed: "When Jews do the will of God, no nation on earth can rule over them; but when they ignore the will of God, He hands them over to a lower nation. Not only that, He even hands them over to its horses."

Avot Derabi Natan relates the manner of Jochanan's leaving Jerusalem in a much simpler form. According to this source Rabban Jochanan simulated death and succeeded with the aid of his disciples in escaping (only without his nephew being involved in it).

The origin and descent of Rabban Jochanan ben Zakkai remains unknown. For three generations the house of Hillel ruled the religious life of the Jews, and the people obeyed it because they considered it to be an offshoot of the royal house of David. Suddenly an outsider appeared, who was held to be the least of Hillel's disciples, and the whole people followed him. Many years before the destruction of the temple, people flocked from near and far to hear him expound the Torah. It was for this reason that Rabban Jochanan ben Zakkai considered himself a representative of the nation and it was as such that he spoke to Vespasian.

In those days he habitually sat in the shadow of the Temple and expounded the Torah all day long before an audience too numerous to be accommodated by the Temple. The wall of the Temple was one hundred ells high and it cast a broad shadow where many could find protection from the sun. Rabban Jochanan concerned himself little with the brutal oppression of the Romans or with the terrible disputes that rent the Jewish parties. This was also his attitude years later when after the destruction of the Temple he taught in Jabneh and refrained from commenting on the political situation. His teachings were devoted to peace, and even during the days of the sharpest struggle he was not afraid to speak of the necessity for peace with Rome.

Rabban Jochanan ben Zakkai was a pupil of Hillel. Since he survived the destruction of Jerusalem and was later active in Jabneh, there seems to be no exaggeration in the tradition that claims he lived to be 120 years old. It may also be said of him what was said of Moses that "his eyes were not dimmed nor did his freshness leave him."

Hillel himself recognized the worth of Rabban Jochanan ben Zakkai. When Hillel became sick, his disciples came to visit him before his death, but Rabban Jochanan remained standing outside the door. "Where is the small Jochanan?" Hillel asked, and he then predicted that when Jochanan grew up he would be "a father in wisdom and a father for future generations."

It is told that even long before the destruction, Rabban Jochanan ben Zakkai understood that the Jews would not be able to withstand the Romans and that the Temple would be destroyed. A legend relates that forty years before its destruction, the gates of the Temple began to open by themselves as if ready to receive the enemy. Rabban Jochanan is said to have scolded them for their fear saying: "Everyone knows that you will be destroyed, but you do not have to open your gates to make the entrance of the enemy easier."

Even before the Temple was destroyed, Rabban Jochanan found himself in Arav (near Sepphoris) where he spent eighteen years, but in all this time he reached only two verdicts. He concluded that the place was not adapted to the study of the Torah and said that since Galilee hates the Torah it would in the end revert to being a region of robbers.[3]

With his great intelligence Rabban Jochanan grasped the whole Torah including all its interpretations, laws, and legends; his every word was carefully weighed, and he did not engage in idle conversation. He never walked four ells without phylacteries or without speaking of the Torah. On the street he had a friendly greeting for Jew and non-Jew alike. He was the first to come to the academy and the last to leave it, nor was he ever seen sitting idly or asleep, but he always was engaged in study. He allowed no one to open the door of the academy for his disciples, but he opened the door himself for every one and led each one to his place. He never said that it was time to go home except on the eve of Passover, in order to slaughter the Paschal offering, and on the eve of the Day of Atonement in order to prepare for the fast.

Of his master, Rabban Jochanan ben Zakkai said: "If all the heavens were parchments, and all the trees were quills, and all the seas were ink, it would still be impossible to write down even a part of what I learned from my teacher. And all this," he would add, "is only as much as a fly might absorb when plunging into the great sea."

But Rabban Jochanan did not consider his great learning to be a virtue deserving of praise. He was in the habit of saying: "If you have learned much, do not be proud of it. It was for this purpose that you were born." He also said: "Whoever possesses wisdom without fear (of God) is like a craftsman without tools."

He believed that the Torah protects from death, and when all the male offspring of a certain priestly family of his day died at the age of eighteen years, he declared that they must be descendants of Eli, upon whom rested the curse of early death for all men. If, however, they had devoted themselves to the Torah then its virtue would have protected them from the curse.

It is characteristic of Rabban Jochanan that he was not deeply influenced by the destruction of the Temple. A legend relates that when he learned of its destruction, he tore his clothes but when he heard his disciple Rabbi Joshua mourn: "Woe to us, the place that has brought forgiveness for the transgressions of the Jews had been destroyed," Rabban Jochanan replied: "Do not be grieved for we have another means to attain forgiveness of our sins and that is through charity."[4]

The great crisis, wrought by the destruction of the Temple in Jewish life, met with a different response between the two diametrically opposed elements within the nation. One group could not reconcile itself to the destruction; the essence of their faith was centered in the Temple, and when that was burned they became obsessed with the idea that the whole nation was destroyed along with it. Unable to adapt themselves to the new circumstances, they renounced their lives or joined some of the outlandish religious growths that cropped up in profusion.

But there was another group that secretly nurtured its sorrow. These even felt certain that God would not allow the Temple to remain desolate for long, and they drew encouragement from the historical fact that the Babylonian captivity had lasted only seventy years. They fervently believed that the prophets' predictions regarding the future of Jerusalem and the renewal of the Temple would certainly be fulfilled. But until a new Tempie should be erected, they introduced customs to take the place of the sacrifices; they devoted themselves to pondering the sanctity of the Jewish nation and delved deeply into the Torah and its interpretations.

Meanwhile death and destruction stalked the land. Not satisfied with the desolation of the land and the blood they had shed, the Romans daily introduced new laws to humiliate the

Jews. Knowing that the Jews had taxed themselves a half shekel per person for the maintenance of the Temple, the Romans levied a tax of fifteen *shekalim* on every person for the expense of their temple of Jupiter who "helped them triumph over their enemies."

When the reports of the valor of the Jews in the war became known, and the world realized that without the aid of Jewish traitors mighty Rome with its iron legions could not have conquered the small land of Judea, the Roman rulers hired scribes to belittle the bravery of the Jewish warriors and to make them appear as ordinary robber bands who could have been annihilated by a single Roman battalion were it not that the "kind" Titus sought to spare the land, but his patience exhausted, he decided to show the rebels the might of Rome.

Rabban Jochanan ben Zakkai wanted to establish the custom of pilgrimages to Jabneh to take the place of the previous pilgrimages to Jerusalem. He partly succeeded in this. Many people did come from far and near to celebrate the feast days there, especially those Jews who lived outside of Judea who came to learn the law regarding matters of which they were in doubt. But the majority of the people continued to observe their feast days in the desolate Jerusalem on the site of the burned Temple that had lost none of its sanctity in their eyes.

Rabban Jochanan succeeded in concentrating the priests about himself in Jabneh so they might wait there until called to the rebuilding of a new Temple. In the meantime he instructed the people to observe the commandments of the tithes, and the priests had to observe all the laws of cleanliness and to eat their tithes in purity even as they did when the Temple was in existence.

Even as he had done in Jerusalem, Rabban Jochanan ben Zakkai now continued to search for the basic explanation of all the laws, and in this he was highly successful. Every commandment of the Torah he explained in wise and convincing words. Only in the matter of the prohibition of the flesh of pigs and of wearing *shatnez* (cloth woven out of wool and flax), the commandments of *halitzah* and *yibum* (the marriage of a childless widow to her husband's brother), the laws of the purification of lepers, the scapegoat sent to Azazel on the Day of Atonement and the sacrifice of the red heifer, these he did not attempt to rationalize. These were all laws of such a fundamental nature, he was wont to say, that they should not be debated.

A Hebrew slave who refused freedom at the end of six years of servitude had the lobe of his ear pierced, Rabban Jochanan explained, because the ear heard the words of God uttered from Mount Sinai that "all Jews are my servants." He who has exchanged the rule of God for the rule of man is deserving that his ear be pierced as a sign of eternal shame.

Once his disciples asked Rabban Jochanan why no iron might be used in the construction of an altar. To this he replied that since swords are a symbol of punishment and are made out of iron, while the altar is a symbol of forgiveness, it is necessary to keep these two opposing symbols apart. And if the inanimate stones of the altar that cannot speak or think, must not be cut with iron because they cause peace to be made between Jews and their Father in Heaven, one must therefore consider how much more honor is due a person who makes peace between man and wife, between one city and another, between one nation and another, or between one family and another.

In spite of the fact that the Temple was burned and Jerusalem destroyed, the Jews did not consider themselves as exiles as long as they remained on their own soil. But all those Jews who lived in Babylonia and other lands were considered to be in captivity, since Nebuchadnezzar had exiled them. Rabban Jochanan was once asked by his disciples why God caused most of the Jews to be exiled to Babylonia, and he answered that they were like a woman who sins against her husband and is sent by him to her father's home. God exiled the Jews to Babylonia when they sinned against him, because that is the land Abraham came from.

There is an opinion that Rabban Jochanan ben Zakkai was a priest and that he officiated in the Temple service together with the other priests. Thus it is told that his disciples asked him about some custom pertaining to sacrifices, but when he answered they were dissatisfied with his reply and proved to him that he did not remember the procedure in the Temple on certain occasions. Rabban Jochanan said: "You are right. I have forgotten what I did myself." When he was still in Jerusalem he came into conflict with the High Priest, whom he threatened with revenge, but this High Priest died before Jochanan's plan of vengeance was carried out.

Rabban Jochanan also objected, while still in Jerusalem, to the procedure of stunning the animals brought as sacrifices in order to facilitate their slaughter. He claimed that such a procedure crippled the animal and caused unclean flesh to be offered on the altar.

It is obvious that while the Romans ruled over the lives and the possessions of the Jews in a barbaric fashion, the morals of Jewish women could not remain in their former purity. The royal house of Agrippa II as well as that of his sister Berenice, and some of the priests of that time could hardly serve as an example of morality for Jewish women. Rabban Jochanan ben Zakkai realized that Jewish family life was being wrecked by this immorality. He then abolished the procedure of taking a *sotah* before a priest and the administering of the water, since it would have to be applied to the majority of women of Judea if it remained in force.

Rabban Jochanan ben Zakkai frequently debated the commandments of the Torah with non-Jews. Despite the fact that the Jews had lost the war and that the Romans hired scribes to slander them, this was a time when numerous gentile scholars were deeply interested in the Torah and were anxious to discuss its commandments with Jews. They were amazed at the stubbornness with which this small people clung to its faith.

Rabban Jochanan engaged in similar disputations with the Sadducees. Although these no longer existed as a separate party, there were still men in prominent positions who conducted themselves according to the teachings of the Sadducees. Rabban Jochanan liked to debate with them and attempted to prove that they were not Jews.

But his attitude was entirely different when disputing with a Gentile. When a Gentile asked whether there would ever come a day when Jews and Gentiles would be happy together, Rabban Jochanan answered that it would have to be a rainy day.

Later his disciples asked him whether God approved of charitable deeds of Gentiles, because the verse "the kindness of nations is a sin" was then commonly interpreted to mean that even good deeds of Gentiles are sinful. Rabban Jochanan said that the real meaning of the verse is different from the accepted one, and that it intends to convey the idea that just as a sin offering brings forgiveness for Jews even so do charitable deeds compensate for the sins of Gentiles.

Rabban Jochanan ben Zakkai devoted himself to the mysteries of the creation of the world and to the Divine Chariot of Ezekiel's prophecy. A legend relates that he was once riding on a donkey while his best pupil, Rabbi Eleazar ben Arach, was walking behind him. Rabbi Eleazar said: "Let us now study a chapter on the construction of the Chariot." But Rabban Jochanan said that one must not discuss this subject with only one pupil unless he understands everything himself without explanation from his teacher. To this Rabbi Eleazar answered: "Then let me expound the construction of the Chariot, and you will see whether I understand it without an explanation of my teacher."

Rabban Jochanan ben Zakkai descended from his donkey and wrapping himself in his robe, they sat down on a rock under an olive tree. After he heard the pupil's exposition he kissed him on the head and said: "Blessed be the God of Israel who granted to Father Abraham a son who understands so much and who expounds so nicely for the glory of his Father in Heaven."

Of the great number of his pupils five were particularly noteworthy and Rabban Jochanan praised each of them for his virtues. The names of the five were: R. Eliezer ben Hyrcanus, R. Joshua ben Chananiah, R. Jose Hacohen, R. Simeon ben Nathanel, and R. Eleazar ben Arach. Of these Rabban Jochanan said that R. Eliezer ben Hyrcanus was like a lime pit that does not lose a single drop of water; of R. Joshua ben Chananiah he said, happy is the mother who gave birth to such a son; of R.

Jose Hacohen he said that he was pious; R. Simeon ben
Nathanel avoided sin, and R. Eleazar ben Arach was like a
spring that wells up ever stronger.

Of them Rabban Jochanan said further: "If the wisdom of
all Jewish scholars were to be placed on one side of the scale
and the wisdom of R. Eliezer ben Hyrcanus on the other side,
then his wisdom would outweigh that of all the others." At a
later date he was said to have declared: "If the wisdom of all the
Jewish scholars together with that of R. Eliezer ben Hyrcanus
were to be placed on one side of the scale, and the wisdom of
R. Eleazar ben Arach were to be placed on the other side, then
his would outweigh that of all the others."

There seems to have been no limit to the reverence the
disciples of Rabban Jochanan accorded him. They referred to
him in no other terms than "the light of Israel," "the right
pillar" and "the strong hammer." They said of him that he was
the only teacher of kindness and peace who realized the worth
of human freedom, for he sharply opposed slavishness in man.
Rabban Jochanan also admired all good qualities in man
irrespective of what nation that man belonged to. When he
taught the necessity of loving God, he instructed that He
should be loved as a child loves its father and not as a slave
loves his lord.

When Rabban Jochanan ben Zakkai left Jerusalem he
established his academy in Jabneh, but his private residence
was in Barur Chail, and there he was followed by his disciples.
It seems that when Rabban Gamaliel II (the son of Rabban
Simeon ben Gamaliel who was killed before the destruction of
the Temple) grew of age, and Rabban Jochanan realized that he
was fit to follow his father in the leadership of Jewish life, he
resigned as Nasi. He gave this office to Rabban Gamaliel and he
settled in Barur Chail. But even there he was followed by many
people who did not leave him until the day of his death.

As the days of Rabban Jochanan neared their end, he
regretted his coming death. When his disciples came to visit, he
wept in their presence. They asked: "Rabbi, why do you
weep?" and he replied, "When a man has to appear for trial
before a king whose rule is only temporary, whose kindness is

passing, and whose anger does not last, he is seized by terror; how much more understandable is the terror that seizes one who is to be tried by the King of kings, whose rule is eternal, whose anger is everlasting, and whose kindness endures forever."

21

THE COLLEAGUES
OF RABBAN JOCHANAN
BEN ZAKKAI

NUMEROUS PROMINENT SCHOLARS SURVIVED the suffering of the destruction in Jerusalem together with Rabban Jochanan ben Zakkai. Some of them escaped the city at an earlier or later date and together they settled in Jabneh.

One of these scholars, the closest to Rabban Jochanan, was Rabbi Zadok ben Eleazar. This was the same Rabbi Zadok for whose healing Rabban Jochanan asked the services of a doctor. Just as Rabban Jochanan visualized the destruction of the Temple forty years before it occurred, so did Rabbi Zadok fast every day for forty years that the Temple might not be destroyed.

It is told that when Rabban Jochanan presented Rabbi Zadok to Vespasian in the Roman camp outside Jerusalem he showed more reverence to Rabbi Zadok than he did to Vespasian. When Vespasian noted this he asked, "What distinction has this man?" and Rabban Jochanan replied: "I can assure you that had there been another one like him, you could not have triumphed over our people even if you had brought twice as many soldiers as you did."

Vespasian further asked, "Wherein lies his strength?" and Rabban Jochanan answered, "For forty years he neither ate nor drank anything more than the juice of one fig every night, and after this he taught a host of disciples all day. Therefore you can realize that had there been another like him, God would have had to spare our city for the sake of two such holy men."

It is further told that once when Rabbi Zadok was a priest in the temple, he saw two young priests hurrying to the service. In their haste they tried to overtake each other, and when the nimbler one gained the lead he was stabbed by the one that trailed behind. Rabbi Zadok then called out: "Hear me oh, Jews. Here you see the body of a slain man and you all have learned that when a murdered man is found and it is not known by whom he was killed, it is necessary to behead a calf and over it the elders of the city must declare that they are innocent of the blood that was shed, that their hand was not in the crime, nor have they seen it committed. Now the question arises whether the city or the temple has to bring this case, for I alone saw the crime, and the law states that one witness is insufficient to condemn a man to death. According to the law it would seem therefore that the identity of the murderer has not been established, and it is necessary for the elders to declare their innocence. Now the question of whether the city or the temple has to bring this offering, for neither one of the two can conscientiously say 'our hands did not shed this blood'; both the city and the people are guilty and the blood of the murdered man is a blot on both."

Speaking in this vein he aroused all those gathered until they shed tears. When the father of the murdered man later declared that the victim was not killed outright and the dagger with which he was stabbed was therefore not unclean from coming in contact with a dead body, and he thus established that it was unnecessary to bring a sacrifice, because the victim had atoned with his blood for the sins of the city, all those gathered rushed at the murderer and in an instant he was annihilated so that nothing remained of him.

It was told of Rabbi Zadok that R. Gamaliel ben R. Simeon (commonly referred to as Rabban Gamaliel of Jabneh, who was also Nasi after the death of Rabban Jochanan ben Zakkai) once gave a feast in his house for the scholars. Rabban Gamaliel waited on his guests himself and with his own hand he filled their beakers. He handed the first beaker of wine to Rabbi Eliezer ben Hyrcanus, but Rabbi Eliezer refused it, not wishing to be waited on by Rabban Gamaliel. Rabban Gamaliel then handed the same beaker to Rabbi Joshua ben Chananiah who accepted it.

Rabbi Eliezer then exclaimed: "How can one tolerate that Rabban Gamaliel should stand and wait on us while we are sitting down?" but Rabbi Joshua answered: "One greater than Rabban Gamaliel did the same. Our father Abraham was the greatest man of his generation; nevertheless, he waited on his guests and served them. Even though his guests were angels, Abraham did not at first know it but thought they were Arabs. I therefore see no wrong in Rabban Gamaliel serving the students of the Torah."

Rabbi Zadok then arose from his place and said: "How much longer will you remain indifferent to the honor of God while you devote yourself to the honor due to man? God causes the winds to blow and the rain to fall, he fructifies the earth and provides for every creature according to its needs. All this he does not only for the just but also for the wicked and the idolaters. Is it not more than right that scholars like you should be served by Rabban Gamaliel himself?"

Sometime later Rabbi Zadok saw the ruins of the Temple and turning his eyes heavenward said: "Creator of the world, You have done well. You have destroyed Your city, You have burned Your temple, and You remain calm as if You were not concerned." That same night Rabbi Zadok had a dream. In his dream he saw God mourning over the ruins of the Temple while the angels wept bitterly. He was then convinced that God mourned the destruction just as the people did.

When the leaders of the people realized that the laws and customs of Judaism were being forgotten, they called all the scholars together on a certain day, and each of them recounted the laws and traditions as he remembered them. Rabbi Zadok testified in every case of doubtful law and his words were accepted as law.[1]

The Talmud quotes the opinions of Rabbi Zadok a number of times in substantiation of laws. A maxim of his regarding the worth of the Torah, that later became popular among scholars, is also quoted. Rabbi Zadok used to say: "You must not make the Torah as a crown to magnify yourself nor as a spade wherewith to dig."

Rabbi Zadok had a son, Rabbi Eleazar, who was prominent during the decade preceding the destruction of the Temple. His son devoted himself to commerce mostly, and he received the title of Rabbi, although he did not found an academy. When Rabbi Zadok was cured after his long fast through the intercession of Rabban Jochanan ben Zakkai with Vespasian, his son said to him: "Give your healers their reward in this world that they may make no demands upon you in the world to come." Instead of paying them with gold, Rabbi Zadok taught them to calculate on their fingers and also the rules of the calculation of weights.[2]

Rabbi Eleazar also quoted his father as saying: "To what may one compare a just man in this world? One may compare him to a tree growing in a clean place but whose branches extend over an unclean place. If those branches are cut off, the tree and its roots continue to remain clean. Even so does God bring affliction on just men so they may be worthy of the pleasures of the world to come.

Rabbi Zachariah ben Hakatzav was another colleague of Rabban Jochanan ben Zakkai. His name is mentioned in connection with a situation that throws some light on the moral and social relationships of that time.

A woman who is held captive by the Gentiles in order to obtain a ransom may continue to live with her husband after she is released. A woman who is captured with the intention of being killed is forbidden to live with her husband after she is released, for we are justified in assuming that she submitted to the Gentiles in order to save her life. If a city has been occupied by an army, the wives of all the priests may not continue to live with their husbands unless they bring witnesses to testify to their purity; even if the witnesses are slaves or women servants their testimony is trustworthy. Untrustworthy is one's own testimony, for one may not testify on his own behalf. Then

Rabbi Zachariah said: "I swear by the sanctity of the Temple that as long as the soldiers were in Jerusalem I did not let my wife out of my sight." But the other scholars told him that no one might be trusted when testifying on his own behalf.[3]

He was thus given a theoretical answer without being told what to do and the outcome of the case remains unknown. From other instances in the Talmud we learn that Rabbi Zachariah always sought to be lenient in such circumstances. Thus we find another case[4] of a young girl who was held hostage among the Gentiles of Ashkelon. When she returned from her captivity her family disowned her. There then appeared witnesses who testified that the girl was not violated while in captivity, but the members of her family refused to believe their testimony. Then the scholars said to them: "If you believe that the girl was held captive then you must accept the testimony of the witnesses; if you refuse to believe them, then you have no grounds to believe that she was captive."

Rabbi Zachariah's name also appears on other occasions. Once the scholars were trying to determine a case of the inheritance of a daughter who had no brothers. In relation to this case the Talmud states that the law was established according to the opinion of Rabbi Zachariah.

Among the colleagues of Rabban Jochanan ben Zakkai there was also Rabbi Nechunia (or Jochanan) ben Gudgada. He was a Levite in the Temple and was in charge of the gates. He was a very pious man, and even after the Temple no longer existed he continued to observe all the regulations pertaining to purity scrupulously. In the performance of his office he was very severe and while still gatekeeper he said that any Levite who becomes confused during the singing at the service deserves to be put to death. When Rabbi Joshua ben Chananiah once wanted to aid him in closing the Temple gates, he refused the assistance for the same reasons.

The opinions of Rabbi Nechunia ben Gudgada, that he expressed at the time that all the scholars were questioned regarding the traditions of the laws, are interesting and characteristic of the times. He declared that a deaf girl who was given in marriage by her father might be divorced by her husband. Until that time it was accepted that a deaf woman might be divorced, but the case was not clear if the woman was given in marriage by her father. Until then it was also the accepted rule that if a man stole wood and used it in the construction of a building, that the building be destroyed and the wood returned to its owner.[5] But Rabbi Nechunia ruled that it was only necessary to pay the value of the article that was stolen. Similarly he ruled that a person who sacrifices a stolen animal as a sin offering has discharged his duty as long as it remains unknown that the animal was stolen.

One of the most outstanding contemporaries of Rabban Jochanan ben Zakkai was Rabbi Nechunia ben Hakanah. Long before the destruction of the Temple he was recognized as the leader of his own academy that remained a separate school and was not under the jurisdiction of Rabban Jochanan ben Zakkai.

It is told that whenever Rabbi Nechunia went to his academy and returned home from it, he would repeat a prayer whose contents have become immortalized and serves as an example for later generations. When asked about his prayer he said: "When I go to the academy I pray to God to save me from error; that I should have no occasion to be angered at my comrades, nor that they should have to be angered with me. I pray that in my teachings I should not declare the clean to be unclean and the unclean to be clean, and that I should not be put to shame either in this world or in the world to come. When I leave the academy I thank the Creator for all that happened to me during the day; especially do I thank Him for this that it is my share to sit in a house of learning and not among the sinful, the idle, and the scornful, for my way leads to eternal life and their way leads to hell."

Rabbi Nechunia ben Hakanah was already an old man during the time of Rabban Jochanan ben Zakkai. When his disciples asked him what he had done to deserve to be rewarded with long life he answered them: "I never sought to gain honor through the shame of another; I also never went to sleep until I knew that there was no person harboring ill will against me, and I was never stingy with my money."

Although Rabbi Nechunia headed an academy of his own the most friendly relations always existed between him and Rabban Jochanan ben Zakkai. This was clearly illustrated at the time when Rabban Jochanan ben Zakkai expounded to his disciples the meaning of the Biblical verse "Justice exalteth a people but the disgrace of nations is a sin" (Proverbs 14:34). Everyone was asked to express his opinion of the meaning of the verse. At the request of Rabban Jochanan, Rabbi Nechunia also stated his interpretation and Rabban Jochanan said to his pupils: "I favor the opinion of Rabbi Nechunia more than my own and more than the opinions you rendered."

A maxim of Rabbi Nechunia that he frequently repeated was characteristic of the man. He was wont to say: "Whoever assumes the yoke of the Torah is relieved of the yoke of government and of the yoke of worldly occupations." From this saying we may conclude that he was wealthy and not worried about finding a livelihood; however, there is no documentary substantiation for such an opinion.

Of all his numerous decisions in matters pertaining to law, there remains only one rule about the laws affecting the Day of Atonement. "Just as one who desecrates the Sabbath has forfeited his life but is free from payment, even so does one who desecrates the Day of Atonement forfeit his life but is free from payment."[6] This statement is interpreted by some to mean, that a person who has done work on the Sabbath is to be condemned to death, but such a person no longer has to observe the Sabbath and is not to be punished for any further violations of the Sabbath. Similarly one is to be punished for the desecration of the Day of Atonement, but until such punishment is meted out the offender is no longer bound by the regulations of the day. Another interpretation of his statement is that a person who has forfeited his life for desecrating the Sabbath does not in addition have to offer a sacrifice for the atonement of his sin; similarly, one who desecrated the Day of Atonement does not have to offer such a sacrifice, even though the punishment for his transgression is in the hands of God.

Rabbi Ishmael ben Elisha, the pupil of Rabbi Nechunia, learned much from his teacher. Pondering the mysteries of life, he cited numerous sayings of his master especially in respect to the interpretation of various texts. He thus proved the power of repentance by the example of Pharaoh. Pharaoh asked Moses, "Who is God that I should listen to his voice?" but later, when he was being engulfed by the waters of the sea he realized that the God of Moses was the true God and in order to gain favor in His eyes he cried out, "Who is like you among the gods, oh Lord!" God, therefore, saved him from the sea and he later became king of Nineveh. When the prophet Jonah came to Nineveh to announce the word of God, Pharaoh already understood that he spoke in the name of the God of Moses, who may not be resisted. He arose from his throne and rent his clothes; he put on sackcloth and ashes and commanded his people to fast in order to appease the anger of God.

Rabbi Dosa ben Harkinas was another contemporary of Rabban Jochanan. The mention made of him in both the Babylonian and Jerusalem Talmud indicates that he played an important role in codifying the *halakhah*. Ordinarily he was inclined to lenience where other scholars advocated severity. He frequently argued against the opinions of Rabban Jochanan ben Zakkai, Akabia ben Mahalalel, and Rabbi Chanina, deputy of the High Priest, and his opinions touched on all matters of Jewish life.

The respect in which he was held by the other scholars can be seen from the fact that when old age and failing eyesight made it impossible for him to come to the academy, the scholars came to his home to discuss the various laws. Being a rich man, the Talmud relates, he seated his guests on couches of gold. The attitude then toward learning is evident in the story of Rabbi Dosa who told that the mother of Rabbi Joshua ben Chananiah was in the habit of bringing her infant son to the synagogue in order that he might absorb the words of the Torah.[7]

A maxim of Rabbi Dosa concerning the proper conduct for men has been immortalized by the people. It said: Morning sleep, midday wine, children's talk, and spending time with the vulgar drive a man from the world.

The most interesting of the scholars of that time was undoubtedly Rabbi Nachum of Gimso. He was a native of Gimso located east of Lud. This town is mentioned in II Chronicles as having been conquered by the Philistines during the reign of King Ahaz. Since Nachum was in the habit of saying "All is for the best" (*gam zu letovah*) on every occasion, the name of his native town assumed a double significance, and the appellation "the man of Gimso" may have referred to his native town or to his oft-used maxim.

None of his teachings have come down to us, although it is mentioned proudly that he was Rabbi Akiba's teacher.[8] However, his whole life is described as a continuous series of miracles that happened to him, and because of his worth these also affected the whole people.

It is told that even when the worst befell him, he would say "All is for the best."[9] Once, when the emperor was angry and threatened new decrees, the Jews decided to appease him with a gift. But there was no one whom they could send, for the messenger was in danger of losing his life in case the emperor refused the gift. They therefore decided to send it with Nachum of Gimso, feeling certain that if he were the bearer of the gift it would be accepted, and he would succeed in gaining the desired concessions.

The Jews of his city then filled a box with diamonds and pearls for the emperor. On his way, Nachum stopped overnight at an inn which harbored thieves. The thieves removed the diamonds and pearls and filled the box with sand. When Nachum saw this he was not afraid but said, "It is for the best," for he felt certain that God would so order it that the king would accept the sand instead of the diamonds.

Thus he proceeded on his way until he arrived in the royal city, and when it was discovered that the gift was ordinary sand there was great anger against the Jews, for it seemed as if they were mocking the emperor.

But then the prophet Elijah appeared in the guise of a courier and he calmed the assembly by saying: "I think the Jews have sent a very valuable gift to the emperor, for the sand in this box is the same sand used by Abraham who shot it from his bow at the four kings of the host of Kedarlaomer when they captured Lot." It so happened that the emperor was then engaged in a war with a neighboring country that he could not conquer. The sand in Nachum's box was therefore tried on the enemy, and its effects were so marvelous that the enemy was immediately subdued. When the emperor realized the value of the sand he decided to be kind to the Jews. The box was filled with diamonds and pearls from the emperor's treasury and Nachum was sent back in great honor.

On his return trip he again lodged in the same inn and everyone marveled that he was still alive. He told them all that had occurred and also of the marvellous nature of the sand.

The people immediately filled large boxes with the same sand and took these to the emperor. They told the emperor that Nachum was carrying diamonds and pearls as a gift for him but these were stolen and sand from their house was substituted instead.

The emperor commanded that this be investigated and when it was proved that the sand they brought did not possess the same virtues as Nachum's sand they were accused of trying to deceive the king and sentenced to death.

It is also told that in his old age Nachum became blind and lost the use of his arms and legs. He lay in an old shack that was about to collapse. The shack was also infested with vermin and the bedposts had been placed in bowls of water to prevent the vermin from climbing up. Once his pupils wanted to remove his bed from the house, but he requested that they remove the furnishings first, for they were certain that as long as he remained in the house it would not collapse. They did as he asked and as soon as they had carried him out on his bed, the house collapsed.

His disciples thereupon asked: "Is it possible that a just man like you should suffer such a bitter end?"

To this Nachum replied: "Children, I have well deserved it. Once, as I was going to the house of my father-in-law, leading three donkeys loaded with food and drink, a poor man came to me and asked that I should give him food. But I replied: "Wait until I unload the donkey." But before I had time to unload the donkey, the poor man fell dead from hunger. It was then that I cursed myself that my eyes that had no pity should become blind, and that all my limbs that did not hasten to feed the poor should become crippled."

22

RABBI CHANINA
BEN DOSA

From what we know of the material circumstances of Rabban Jochanan and his contemporaries we may assume that the poorest of them all was Rabbi Chanina ben Dosa. But he was also the most pious, and the miracles that are said to have occurred to him transcend even the wondrous adventures of Nachum of Gimso. It was commonly believed that Chanina's whole generation lived only through his grace.

Rabbi Chanina knew poverty long before the destruction of the Temple. He lived in the town of Arav in Galilee and was a stone cutter. This was hard work but it did not suffice to feed Rabbi Chanina with bread, and he had to content himself with a measure of carobs from one Sabbath till the next.[1]

Rabbi Chanina was a disciple of Rabban Jochanan ben Zakkai who also lived in Arav for some time. He did not head any academy and no legal decisions are quoted in his name, but he was held to be a great saint by all and whenever people were in trouble they came to Rabbi Chanina and asked that he pray for them, for everyone believed that his word carried great weight with the Lord.

He was also exemplary in his conduct before God and man and he frequently said: "All those whose fear of sin comes before his wisdom, their wisdom endures; all those whose deeds are more than their wisdom, their wisdom endures; all who please mankind with their deeds also please God."[2]

In his town Rabbi Chanina saw many people leaving for their pilgrimage to Jerusalem, carrying gifts for the Temple and he was grieved that whenever he went to Jerusalem he went empty-handed, for he had nothing to bring. But once, while at his work, he saw a beautiful large stone that was fit to lie before the Temple so that pilgrims who come there for the feast days might rest on it. He took this stone, polished it smooth, and vowed to bring it as a gift to the Temple.

But since he could not carry the stone from Arav to Jerusalem alone, he decided to hire five men who would be needed to carry it to the city. But these men asked for one hundred *selaim*. He would gladly have paid this sum and even more, but since he had not even a single coin he said to them: "Where shall I take one hundred *selaim* when I do not possess even half that sum? But if you will help me carry the stone without compensation, you may have whatever reward is due to me for this good deed."

The men then went away and left the stone on the ground. But God could no longer look at the sorrow of Rabbi Chanina and he sent him five other men who asked for only five *selaim* for transporting the stone. They agreed to do so on condition that Rabbi Chanina should help them carry it. Rabbi Chanina believed he would be able to borrow the five *selaim* to pay the laborers as soon as he arrived in Jerusalem, and he agreed to the price. But the work did not last long, for as soon as Rabbi Chanina lifted the stone, they all found themselves in Jerusalem. When he looked for the men in order to pay them, they had vanished and he could no longer find them.[3]

Rabbi Chanina's wife was said to have never complained about their poverty and bore all the suffering quietly. Only once did she lose patience and said to her husband: "How long must we suffer in poverty? Ask the Heavenly One to give you something now on account of what will come to you in the world to come."

Rabbi Chanina heeded her words and prayed to God. A

hand then appeared that gave him a golden table leg. In his dream that night he saw how all the just men sit in Paradise around golden tables with three legs. Only he and his wife sit at a table with only two legs. He awoke very much disturbed and asked his wife: "Would you rather see all other just men in the world to come at whole tables while we sit by a broken one?"

He therefore prayed to God that the gift be taken back and the same hand appeared and took it. The friends of Rabbi Chanina considered the second marvel to be even greater than the first.

Rabbi Chanina's wife had a neighbor who derided her for her poverty, and because of this neighbor she was in the habit of lighting a fire in the oven every Friday. Although she had nothing to cook or bake, she wanted the neighbor to see smoke rising from the chimney and to believe that nothing was lacking for the Sabbath. But this neighbor understood the trick and she once came to Rabbi Chanina's house to show his wife that she was not fooled. As she knocked at the door, Rabbi Chanina's wife opened it, but before the neighbor could enter she ran and hid in the attic so as not to meet her. When the neighbor came in, she saw the oven full of bread and the barrel filled with dough, and she called Rabbi Chanina's wife to come and take the bread out of the oven before it burned.

Still another story is related about Rabbi Chanina's wife. It is said that Rabbi Jochanan once traveled by ship and he saw floating in the water a basket decorated with pearls and diamonds and surrounded by all kinds of rare fish. A man jumped into the water to retrieve the basket, but a fish came and tried to bite off his legs. The people on the boat poured vinegar on the fish until it swam away, and then a voice from heaven was heard saying: "What do you want with this basket? It belongs to the wife of Rabbi Chanina ben Dosa, and in the world to come she will weave decorations from it for the prayer shawls of the just men."[4]

It has already been told that in time of calamity everyone turned to Rabbi Chanina. Thus it happened that the daughter of Nechunia the well-digger once fell into a well that her father had dug. People at once ran to Rabbi Chanina for his advice on how to raise the girl from the well.

Rabbi Chanina at once declared that this event would have a happy ending and then said: "Go home. She is out of the well." The people asked him: "How do you know? Are you a seer?" But Rabbi Chanina said: "I am not a seer but I feel certain that since the just man Nechunia occupied himself with digging wells so that pilgrims to Jerusalem might have water to drink, God will not permit a child of so just a man to be drowned in one of her father's wells."[5]

It was because of such events that people's faith in the efficacy of Rabbi Chanina's prayers increased. They came to him to pray for the sick and while he prayed everyone could see that he was so deeply immersed in it that had a snake wound itself about his feet, he would not have been aware of it. He also immediately foretold the result of his prayer and whether the sick would recover. When he was asked how he could tell the outcome of his prayer, he said: "When I utter the prayer smoothly, I know it was accepted, but if I have difficulty in praying, then I know that it was rejected."

The son of the Nasi, Rabban Gamaliel, once fell sick and the Nasi sent two of his outstanding disciples to Rabbi Chanina to ask him to pray for the sick person. Rabbi Chanina ascended the roof of his house to be nearer to God while praying. When he descended, he told the messengers: "You may now go home for the patient no longer has a fever." The messengers noted the words of Rabbi Chanina and the exact moment at which they were uttered. When they informed Rabban Gamaliel, he told them that everything had happened exactly as Rabbi Chanina said.

Another time, the son of Rabban Jochanan ben Zakkai was sick and Rabban Jochanan sent a message to Rabbi Chanina saying: "Chanina, my son, pray to God that my son shall live." Rabbi Chanina bowed his head between his knees and prayed a long time until he suddenly declared that Rabban Jochanan's son would certainly survive. When Rabban Jochanan thanked him for his effort, he also explained to his wife that had *he* prayed to God himself, even with his head between his knees all day, he would have achieved nothing. Rabban Jochanan's wife then asked: "Is Chanina more acceptable to God then you are?" But Rabban Jochanan answered: "He may not be more acceptable in the eyes of God, but he is as a servant in the palace of a king, who is closer to the king than all others. I am as a minister of the king who sometimes has to withstand the king's anger, and to whom the king may refuse to grant favors."[6]

Among the wondrous legends about Rabbi Chanina, it is told that once while he was traveling, a sudden rain began to descend and he was hindered in his journey. He turned his face heavenward and said: "Creator of the world! The whole world is enjoying the rain, only *I* am suffering from it." The rain immediately ceased and when Rabbi Chanina arrived home there was a drought. His conscience plagued him that the rain that the earth needed so much, had ceased and he further addressed God: "The whole world is now suffering and only I am glad," and the rain began to descend again.[7]

Of Rabbi Chanina's unusual honesty it is told that a man once passed and left a few hens on his doorstep. Rabbi Chanina then told his wife: "Since the hens are not yours you may not use their eggs." His wife then sold the eggs and with the money she saved, she bought some goats. When the owner of the hens came to claim them, Rabbi Chanina also gave him the goats.

Both before and after the Temple was destroyed, Rabbi Chanina scrupulously set aside the tithes from all food that came to his table. As he was once eating, all the food suddenly vanished. His wife explained that she had borrowed that day's food from a neighbor who probably had not set aside the tithes. Rabbi Chanina decided to set aside the tithes and the food reappeared on the table.[8]

His observance of the tithes was so extreme that even his donkey could tell whether the hay placed before it had been tithed. Once the donkey was stolen and when the thieves placed hay before it, it refused to eat. Realizing that if they kept the donkey it would starve to death, they released it and it ran back to Rabbi Chanina.[9]

It is further related there was a poisonous scorpion in a certain place that bit people and they died from its venom. This was told to Rabbi Chanina who said: "Come, show me where this scorpion hides." He was taken to the place and put his foot over the hole. The scorpion came to bite him and while doing so it died. Rabbi Chanina then carried the scorpion around the academy saying: "Now you can see that not the scorpion kills a person but his sins." Seeing this the people said: "Woe to him who meets a scorpion and woe to the scorpion who meets Rabbi Chanina ben Dosa."

Similarly it is told that Rabbi Chanina once met the queen of evil spirits, Igeret bat Machlat, who goes about accompanied by 180,000 destroying angels to harm people. Igeret said to Rabbi Chanina, "Had I not been warned from heaven not to touch you because of your knowledge of the Torah, I would now do you harm." Rabbi Chanina said: "If it is true that I am so important to Heaven, then I command you never to go again where people live." But she entreated him that he should not drive her out of human habitation completely, and he allowed her two nights (Wednesday and Saturday nights) every week when she might have power over people.

Once on a Friday, Rabbi Chanina noticed that his daughter was sitting sorrowful and depressed. He asked her, "What happened, my daughter, that you are so sorrowful?" and she replied, "By mistake I filled the Sabbath lamp with vinegar instead of oil." But Rabbi Chanina comforted her saying, "Why do you worry? God who commanded oil to burn can also cause vinegar to give light."

It is related that the vinegar burned all day Saturday and lasted until the *Havdalah* was lit from it.

When Rabbi Chanina was about to die he raised his hands to God and said: "Dear God, you know that all my life I never made the least use of your beautiful world." . . . After his death it was said in his praise that he never uttered a falsehood. He was also the last of the people who despised words and preferred deeds, and with his death the chain of piety was broken.

Of the importance of charity, it was later told that he held an opinion differing from that of other scholars of his generation and he said: "There is no better charity to save people from Gehenna than the Torah itself."[10]

23

RABBAN GAMALIEL II OF JABNEH

W HEN–ACCORDING TO TRADITION–Rabban Jochanan ben Zakkai died at the age of 120 years, he was
succeeded as Nasi of the Sanhedrin by Rabban Gamaliel, the
son of Rabban Simeon who was killed during the rebellion
against Rome, and grandson of Rabban Gamaliel the Elder.
Rabban Gamaliel the Elder was a grandson of Hillel. Rabban
Gamaliel II was thus the fifth descendant in the line of Hillel.

As a descendant of Hillel, Rabban Gamaliel was looked up
to as a scion of the royal house of David, and as long as one
such remained, no one doubted his right to the office of Nasi.
But his assumption of this office was probably delayed because
at the time his father was killed, Rabban Gamaliel was a young
and sickly child and could not be entrusted with such a
responsible office. Assumption of the position of Nasi was also
subject to the approval of the government, and therefore some
time elapsed before the Roman authorities were ready to
consent to the appointment of a Nasi whose father had lost his
life in a revolution.

Throughout the time that Rabban Gamaliel was Nasi, the
Sanhedrin was maintained in Jabneh with a membership of
seventy-two,[1] and although Rabban Gamaliel traveled extensively and issued his decisions in many places, he always

stressed that Jabneh must remain the focal point of Jewish life. Rabban Jochanan ben Zakkai previously strove to attain the same end. But it is interesting to note that the relations between Rabban Gamaliel and some of the outstanding disciples of Rabban Jochanan ben Zakkai were frequently strained. One of these disciples, Rabbi Eleazar ben Arach, was persuaded by his wife to leave Jabneh. He expected that a great number of scholars would follow him because of his prominence. It is told of him that when he expounded the mysteries of the Divine Chariot before his master, a fiery cloud descended from heaven and hid both of them from the eyes of the passersby, and a host of angels descended to hear his exposition. But in spite of all the reverence that these legends seem to indicate was accorded him, Eleazar ben Arach was later forgotten and no one was concerned with him.

While other scholars of that time attempted to set up academies in various cities of Palestine in an endeavor to spread the knowledge of the Torah throughout the land, Rabban Gamaliel sought to concentrate all of these efforts in Jabneh. He met considerable difficulties in attaining this aim and he was compelled to resort to forceful methods and a stubborn insistence on his decisions. These in turn frequently served to alienate him from the sympathies of the followers of Rabban Jochanan ben Zakkai. He would then go on protracted trips to places far and near to investigate the life of the Jews, their economic welfare, and their religious life. He was thus frequently to be seen in Jericho, in Acco, or in Kezib and wherever he went he spoke on all matters of Jewish life.

Of his relations with other people, it is told that he was very careful not to cause anyone the slightest suffering. When he discovered how many rules one must observe and that it was almost impossible to avoid conflict with friends and neighbors, he wept. In general he was very kind and prone to tears. When a neighboring woman lost her only son, and her weeping was heard for many nights, Rabban Gamaliel could not restrain his commiseration and wept until his eye lashes were soft.[2]

But in the execution of his duties as Nasi, he showed not

the least weakness. Here he ruled with a strong hand and was ready to crush all opposition by excommunicating or driving out the opponent without considering the position or his relationship to the antagonist. Rabban Gamaliel wanted his decisions to be final and he did not permit any decisions to be made without his consent. He therefore ordered an investigation of the opinions of all his pupils and whenever it was discovered that one secretly dissented, he was not permitted to enter the academy.

Rabban Gamaliel owned much land and other property, but he did not have time to devote to its management and therefore he rented these out to tenants. If a tenant lacked the money to buy seed, Rabban Gamaliel lent him the money or the seed to be repaid after the harvest. And if the price of the seed was lower at harvest time than it was when the seed was lent, he asked to be repaid at the harvest price; similarly if the price went up, he asked for the lower price at the time the seed was lent. Although the law did not require such treatment of tenants, he did this in order to prevent suspicion that he was profiting from his tenants.

Being a wealthy man, Rabban Gamaliel also owned numerous slaves whom he treated kindly according to the regulations of the Torah. He was particularly attached to his slave Tabbai, who, he boasted, was a scholar of no mean ability. When Tabbai died, Rabban Gamaliel mourned for him as for a member of his own family.

Of his relationship to Tabbai, it is told that Rabban Gamaliel wanted to free him but could find no cause for doing so. When he accidentally blinded Tabbai in one eye, Rabban Gamaliel was overjoyed, for this would give him an opportunity to free the slave according to the Torah's rule. But Rabbi Joshua informed him that he could not do so because there were no witnesses to the accident.[3]

Rabban Gamaliel was also versed in mathematics and astronomy. To derive practical benefits from this knowledge he had a telescope made with which he could discern objects at a distance of 2,000 ells both on land and on sea. In his house he had numerous drawings of the moon and when ignorant witnesses came to announce the new moon, they could point to the picture most nearly resembling what they saw.

Rabban Gamaliel served the people as Nasi for over thirty years and although he was strict in the conduct of his office, he was wont to say that his position was not that of a ruler but of a servant. He labored faithfully and with devotion for the preservation of Judaism. His period in office coincided with a difficult time for Jews. New decrees against the Jews were issued daily by the Romans, and Rabban Gamaliel constantly had to intercede to ameliorate the effects of these decrees.

As already mentioned, Rabban Gamaliel spared no opponent in his capacity as Nasi. When Rabbi Eliezer tried to establish a law according to the school of Shammai, he was excommunicated by Rabban Gamaliel despite the fact that he was his brother-in-law. The scholars of the academy sharply criticized Rabban Gamaliel for banning so brilliant a man as Rabbi Eliezer. Sometime later Rabban Gamaliel was travelling by ship to visit distant Jewish settlements. The ship encountered tremendous waves that threatened to capsize it and Rabban Gamaliel understood this to be a punishment for the ban he had imposed on Rabbi Eliezer. He then raised his hands to heaven and said: "God knows that I have done so not for the sake of my honor, nor for the honor of my household, but solely for the honor of God and in order to prevent disputes among Jews." When he finished speaking, the sea at once became calm and he arrived safely at his destination.

One of the chief opponents of Rabban Gamaliel was Rabbi Joshua ben Chananiah. Rabbi Joshua was known as a gentle peace-loving man. He was always dissatisfied with the innovations of Rabban Gamaliel, but he was powerless to contradict them because of his great poverty. Rabbi Joshua gained his livelihood from making needles.

At that time a definitely established calendar did not yet exist. Every month messengers were sent out to observe the appearance of the new moon and even though the scholars could calculate the exact moment of the appearance of the moon, it was prohibited to decide the day of the new month without the testimony of witnesses who saw the new moon.

On the basis of such testimony Rabban Gamaliel once determined the day of the new year and of all the other holidays of
the month of *Tishri*. But even as the witnesses were testifying
to having observed the new moon, Rabbi Joshua felt convinced
that their testimony was false for according to all calculations it
was impossible for the new moon to have appeared. Gathering
courage, Rabbi Joshua told the Nasi that he was wrong in
setting the date of the holidays on the basis of such testimony.
This opinion was also supported by other scholars, but Rabban
Gamaliel was adamant and refused to alter his decision. He
turned to Rabbi Joshua and said: "If you have another calculation of the holidays, then I command you to appear before me
carrying your cane and wallet in your hand and your bag on
your shoulders on the day you consider to be the right Day of
Atonement."

Rabbi Joshua was greatly grieved when he heard this, for
he was convinced that he was right, and that it was only
because of his poverty that the Nasi imposed upon him. Those
of the scholars who agreed with him felt likewise. Nevertheless
they advised him to do as he was bid for "everyone must obey
the Nasi and whatever he says must be considered the law."
The text of the Torah enjoining the observance of the holidays
they interpreted in such a manner as to prove that the court
may decide on the exact day. They argued furthermore that if
one allowed himself to criticize the decision of the Nasi he
would also criticize the decisions of all the courts since the
times of Moses.

Rabbi Joshua was thus persuaded by his comrades, and on
the day that according to his calculation was the Day of
Atonement, he came to Jabneh carrying his cane, his wallet,
and his bag. When Rabban Gamaliel saw him coming he was
overjoyed, he kissed him on the head and said to him: "Come
in peace, my teacher and my pupil—my teacher in learnedness
and my pupil in obedience."

But in spite of the apparent reconciliation, since this event
a feeling of bitterness rankled the heart of Rabbi Joshua. He
believed that he was humiliated because of his poverty. This
occurrence also engendered an unspoken bitterness among

other members of the Sanhedrin who resented the arbitrary behavior of their Nasi. But they stifled their opposition until another dispute arose between Rabban Gamaliel and Rabbi Joshua.

One of the pupils came to ask whether the reciting the evening prayer (*Maariv*) was obligatory or voluntary. Rabbi Joshua told him that it was voluntary and one could do as he chose. The same pupil then asked this question of Rabban Gamaliel who decided that reciting the *Maariv* was obligatory. The pupil then asked: "How is it that Rabbi Joshua declared it to be voluntary?" and Rabban Gamaliel answered: "Wait until all the scholars come to the academy and we will discuss this matter."

When all the scholars gathered Rabban Gamaliel declared, "I have ordained that reciting the evening prayer is obligatory"; saying this he asked those assembled, "Is anyone opposed to this decision?"

"No one is opposed," Rabbi Joshua answered. Upon hearing this Rabban Gamaliel said, "Joshua, stand up and a witness will testify that you have ordered otherwise before."

Rabbi Joshua obeyed and arose; he stood for a long time before Rabban Gamaliel told him to return to his place. The other scholars could no longer tolerate the overbearing attitude of the Nasi; there was an uproar of protest against his conduct and the impeachment of Rabban Gamaliel was taken to a vote.[4]

When this became known, hundreds of others whom Rabban Gamaliel had previously expelled from the academy appeared, and it was necessary to add 300 benches in the academy. Afterward they began to choose another Nasi instead of Rabban Gamaliel. When the qualifications of all the candidates were considered it became apparent that Rabbi Joshua could not succeed Rabban Gamaliel because the whole commotion arose on his account. Rabbi Eliezer ben Hyrcanus would have been a likely candidate, but he was an angry person and a follower of the school of Shammai. Rabbi Akiba could not be considered because he was not descended from aristocracy; no one knew his origin and it was rumored that he was descended from proselytes. All eyes therefore turned to

Rabbi Eleazar ben Azariah, who was the equal of Rabban
Gamaliel in scholarship; he was also a descendant of an
aristocratic priestly family, he possessed great wealth and was
recognized by the Roman rulers.

Rabban Gamaliel remained impeached for only a short
time and was reinstated a few days later. The sudden outburst
of the scholars against his severe conduct produced such a
change in him that everyone was moved to pity. When the
scholars saw that the aristocratically reared Rabban Gamaliel
bowed without complaint to the will of the people (although
losing his post as president) and that he did not break with the
academy, but immediately adapted himself to his new status
and took his place among other pupils as an equal, they
realized that they were overhasty and immediately considered
a reconciliation.

Only then was it realized what noble traits Rabban
Gamaliel possessed. He was terribly humiliated; no one even
thought of sparing the honor of the Nasi's family that derived
through Hillel from King David. Only a day before everyone
bowed before him, and suddenly the same people turned
against him. Nevertheless, he accepted the verdict of the
people and did not absent himself from the academy for even
one hour. He fully realized that his situation was a very difficult
one, for all his previous decisions would be reconsidered and
all his past disciples would attempt to prove them wrong.

But instead of dwelling on what had happened to him, he
considered his behavior toward others and realized that he had
conducted himself too severely. He then went to Rabbi Joshua
to ask his forgiveness. When he saw the darkened walls of the
low narrow house where Rabbi Joshua lived, he said, "From
the walls of your house one can tell your occupation." Believing
that this was said to slight him, Rabbi Joshua answered, "Woe
to the generation that has a leader like you, for you have no
understanding for the suffering of the scholars and you do not
know how they gain their livelihood."

Rabban Gamaliel said to him, "Now that I came to you,
forgive me! Do so for the sake of the honor of my family."

Rabbi Joshua was deeply touched at these words and they

were reconciled. Then Rabbi Akiba said to Rabbi Joshua: "We did all this for your sake; tomorrow let us both go to visit Rabban Gamaliel."

When the newly elected Nasi, Rabbi Eleazar ben Azariah, heard this, he declared that he wanted to accompany them to inform Rabban Gamaliel of his readiness to resign.

Rabban Gamaliel thus returned to his office and Rabbi Eleazar ben Azariah was made head of the court. They divided their duties among themselves. Rabban Gamaliel expounded the law on two Sabbaths in succession and Rabbi Eleazar expounded on the third Sabbath. It seems that from that time Rabban Gamaliel interested himself more with the occupations of his pupils. When Rabbi Joshua told him that two of his disciples, Rabbi Eleazar Chisma and Rabbi Jochanan ben Gudgada, could calculate the number of drops of water in the sea but could not afford bread to eat or a garment to wear, Rabban Gamaliel wanted to give them positions in the academy so that they might earn their livelihood. For some reason they refused these positions.

Peace was thus reestablished in the academy of Jabneh and Rabban Gamaliel remained Nasi until his death. His later conduct also indicates that he relaxed some of his severity and if he treated someone more harshly than the occasion deserved, it evoked no protest. In the meantime the decrees of Rome became more severe, and Rabban Gamaliel was frequently compelled to journey to Rome to intercede for the Jews and to effect the revocation of some decree or, at least, to ameliorate its effects. He was often accompanied by some of his comrades on these trips and he was invariably successful in the accomplishment of his mission. His aristocratic bearing and his fluent Greek gained him the confidence of the court and of the highest officials of the empire.[5]

In his travels he often visited Jerusalem and once when he saw a fox on the site of the Holy of Holies he wept bitterly. This was reported to the Roman authorities who considered it a sign of disloyalty and wanted to have him killed. But a Roman friend of Rabban Gamaliel came to the gate of the academy and announced: "The man with the prominent nose is sought."

Rabban Gamaliel understood the hint and remained in hiding for some time until a new government came to power.

When Rabban Gamaliel was impeached as Nasi, a special investigation into all the innovations he had introduced into Jewish life began. The scholars gathered testimony from all people who had seen or heard the customs of previous generations. On that day many rules on matters that were previously in dispute were adopted. In some matters the followers of the school of Hillel decided according to the opinion of the school of Shammai; other laws were given an entirely new interpretation. But no law previously in dispute was left in doubt.

Two of the laws discussed that day throw light on the scholars' opinions and on their ability to adapt to changed conditions. There is a text in the Torah that says "an Ammonite or a Moabite may not come in the congregation of the Lord." But these two nations were no longer in existence at that time, and those still called by these names were derived from other nations who settled in those lands during the wars and the migration of nations.

On the day that Rabban Gamaliel was impeached one of the pupils, Jehudah the Ammonite proselyte, arose and asked: "What about me? May I mingle with the Jews?" Rabban Gamaliel said that he must not, but Rabbi Joshua ruled to the contrary. When Rabban Gamaliel insisted on the literal meaning of the text, Rabbi Joshua asked: "Have the Ammonites and Moabites of old remained in their lands? Has not Sancherib confused the nations of the earth a long time ago?"

The explanation of Rabbi Joshua was accepted by all scholars and they permitted Jehudah, the Ammonite proselyte, to consider himself a Jew.

Another question concerned the inclusion of the Song of Songs and of Ecclesiastes in the Scriptures. The followers of the school of Shammai particularly objected to Ecclesiastes on the ground that the reader may misunderstand its words and may think that it has no religious message. Later Rabbi Akiba declared that there were no differences of opinion regarding the Song of Songs, for "all eternity is worth less than the day on which the Song of Songs was given to the Jews," but the argument centered solely on Ecclesiastes.[6]

An important regulation of Rabban Gamaliel related to the sabbatical year. According to a previous rule it was prohibited to cultivate the fields even on the sixth year immediately after *shavuot*. Rabban Gamaliel removed this restriction and permitted cultivation until the New Year. He also stabilized the prayers at three times a day. The exact order of the prayers, then accepted as taking the place of sacrifices, was determined in his academy. With the aid of two disciples, Simeon of Pakula and Shmuel Hakatan, the order of *Shemoneh Esrei* was determined, and it was ruled to be the duty of every Jew to recite these three times daily.

The benediction of God as the "Builder of Jerusalem" was introduced into the blessings pronounced after eating. Rabban Gamaliel also tried to determine the blessings to be pronounced over various kinds of food and, although his comrades did not agree with all of his definitions, he consistently clung to his opinions.

The Roman government seemed to realize at that time that it would not subdue the Jewish people unless it could control its spirit. The government then sent two educated Gentiles, who were to pretend conversion, to study the Torah with Rabban Gamaliel. The two arrived in Jabneh and studied everything. After they learned what they needed, they declared that they were satisfied with the whole Torah except the rule that it is permissible to derive benefit from robbing a Gentile. Rabban Gamaliel then ruled to prohibit this, for in so doing one dishonors the Jewish name.[7] Worthy of mention is also Rabban Gamaliel's regulation that every Jew must explain to his household the significance of *Pesach*, matzah, and the bitter herbs, else he has not fulfilled the duties of the day.

Rabban Gamaliel also introduced a regulation regarding the Samaritans (referred to as Kutim in the Talmud) whom the scholars tried to isolate from the Jews. After he assumed office Rabban Gamaliel sought to amend the laws against the Kutim believing that it was possible to bring them closer to other Jews. In the war against Rome, the Kutim sided with the Jews and fought side by side with them, unlike the Idumeans who betrayed the Jews and frequently allied themselves with the enemy. The Kutim were therefore looked upon more favorably, and although it was previously said that "whoever eats the bread of a Kuti is like one who eats the flesh of a pig," Rabban Gamaliel declared that a divorce obtained through a Kuti's testimony was valid. He also considered grains bought from Kutim to be *demai* in the same manner as were grains bought from an *am ha'aretz.*[8]

Later Rabban Gamaliel visited the cities of the Kutim and realized they were not true proselytes and far from Judaism. He then declared that their produce is *vadai* (certainly untithed) from which tithes must be offered. He also prohibited Jews to eat meat of their slaughtering.

Rabban Gamaliel strongly praised people who have a trade. Seeing that many Jews would have to leave the soil and turn to trades because of the political situation, he said: "Whoever possesses a trade is certain of his existence, even as one is certain of a vineyard surrounded by a fence."

Rabban Gamaliel and Rabbi Joshua were reconciled but nothing is known of the outcome of his dispute with his brother-in-law, Rabbi Eliezer ben Hyrcanus. We know of the excommunication but no mention is made of a reconciliation. The stories of the journeys of Rabban Gamaliel frequently mention Rabbi Eliezer as a companion. While this may indicate a reconciliation, there is also another legend that says that the wife of Rabbi Eliezer, the sister of Rabban Gamaliel, prohibited her husband from bowing at *tachnun.* She feared that in doing so he would avenge himself on her brother. But once she forgot to observe him at prayer and he bowed at *tachnun.* When she realized this she cried out that he had killed her brother and in the same instant Rabban Gamaliel died. He was mourned by the whole people who called him "father" and his wife "mother."

24

RABBI ELIEZER
BEN HYRCANUS

F ROM WHAT WAS RELATED in the previous chapter it
can be seen that Rabbi Eliezer was a man of firm convictions
from which he would not deviate in the least. This tenacity
caused him much trouble and brought him into conflict with
the Nasi despite of the family relationship existing between
them. He also disagreed with his comrades at the academy in
Jabneh from which he was removed. Later he left Jabneh for
Lud where he led an academy of his own founding and he
could no longer return to the meetings of the Sanhedrin.

Rabbi Eliezer was a follower of the school of Shammai in
his convictions. He was therefore called *Shamuti*. Since all the
other scholars including the Nasi were adherents of the school
of Hillel, Rabbi Eliezer was practically ostracized socially. When
the question of whether it was permissible to use a winding
oven (*tanur shel achnai*) was discussed, Rabbi Eliezer said it was
while all the others said it was not. On that day no decision of
Rabbi Eliezer was adopted, but he refused to reconsider his
opinion and it is told that many miraculous events then took
place upholding Rabbi Eliezer's views. A carob tree became
uprooted and was flung a distance of one hundred ells from
where it grew; a brook suddenly changed the direction of its
current; the walls of the academy began to lean and a *bat kol*

was heard from heaven declaring the correctness of Rabbi Eliezer's views.[1]

But Rabbi Joshua ben Chananiah firmly opposed Rabbi Eliezer and he said that no attention need be paid to the wondrous events. Regarding the *bat kol* he declared that the Torah was given for observance on earth and Heaven had no right to interfere in disputes that take place on earth.

Then the scholars burned all those articles that Rabbi Eliezer declared to be clean, and they voted on a punishment to be inflicted on Rabbi Eliezer for his stubbornness. It was decided that all the scholars should have no dealings with him, and Rabbi Akiba was chosen to inform him of the sentence. Rabbi Akiba donned a black garment and sat at a distance of four ells from Rabbi Eliezer. When Rabbi Eliezer asked him: "Why is this day different from all other days?" Rabbi Akiba answered: "Rabbi, I think that your comrades have abandoned you."

Upon hearing this, Rabbi Eliezer tore his garments, sat on the ground, and wept bitterly. It was said that the sorrow of Rabbi Eliezer was so great that all objects upon which his gaze fell immediately wilted.[2]

Among the disciples of Rabban Jochanan ben Zakkai, Rabbi Eliezer ranked highest and his master said of him that he was like a well lined with lime that does not lose a single drop of water. He also said that if all the scholars were placed on one side of the scale and Rabbi Eliezer on the other side, he would outweigh them all in wisdom. He also adopted the good qualities of his master of whom it was said that he never indulged in idle talk, never walked even a distance of four ells without phylacteries and without studying the Torah, and he was the first to arrive at the academy and the last to leave. Although Rabbi Eliezer conducted his own academy even before the destruction of Jerusalem, he never proclaimed opinions that he had not heard from his master. When such questions arose he usually replied that he did not know the answer although he knew the accepted regulations very well.[3] In this relation he frequently said that whoever debates the decisions of his master or pronounces opinions he has not heard from his master causes the *Shekhinah* to depart from the Jewish people.[4]

Rabbi Eliezer was a brother-in-law to Rabban Gamaliel. He married the Nasi's sister, the learned Ima Salim, of whom it is told that she confounded the injustice of a gentile judge with her wisdom. But despite this relationship, Rabbi Eliezer frequently was in conflict with the Nasi and with his colleagues. All of them opposed to him and the harmony of the academy was disrupted.

Rabbi Eliezer was sometimes referred to as Rabbi Eliezer the Great, but wherever reference is made to Rabbi Eliezer, with no other title, he is the person referred to. Among his disciples was Rabbi Akiba who, even after he attained the greatest position of leadership, never refrained from mentioning that he was Rabbi Eliezer's pupil. Rabbi Eliezer was also versed in the languages of the neighboring peoples and several times he accompanied Rabban Gamaliel on the latter's trips to Rome to plead the cause of the Jews.

Of the manner in which Rabbi Eliezer turned to learning it is told that his father was a wealthy man who owned many fields. Father and sons devoted themselves to the cultivation of the land and all of them were rude people, *amei aratzim*, who could not even recite the *Shema*. When he was over twenty years old, Rabbi Eliezer suddenly decided to leave the fields and turn to study. He told his plan to his father and old Hyrcanus laughed at him saying: "Now you wish to study? Now it is time for you to take a wife and to beget children, and raise them in the knowledge of the Torah." But Rabbi Eliezer would not hear of this and decided to leave his father's house at the earliest opportunity. When a cow with which he was plowing broke a leg, he was afraid of his father's punishment and fled to Jerusalem to Rabban Jochanan ben Zakkai.

In Jerusalem he declared his wish to study, but to all questions put to him he could give no answer. Out of pity Rabban Jochanan ben Zakkai permitted him to come to his academy even though he was so ignorant. But great was the astonishment of all when they saw his rapid progress. Having fled from his father's house empty-handed, Rabbi Eliezer had no money to buy food. In his great hunger he began to eat earth and this caused his breath to be foul. Rabban Jochanan then questioned him regarding his origin and why he had fled from his father's house. When Rabbi Eliezer told him all, Rabban Jochanan provided him with food, and seeing his great desire to learn he befriended him. Within three years Rabbi Eliezer became the outstanding pupil of Rabban Jochanan ben Zakkai.

Rabbi Eliezer's father meanwhile met with difficulties and lost all his possessions. Regaining them after some time, he learned that Rabbi Eliezer was studying in Jerusalem. Hyrcanus was then an old man and his sons said to him: "See what your son Eliezer did for you. When you were in difficulty he left you and went to Jerusalem to live in luxury, but when the inheritance is divided he will take his share together with the rest of us. Even if you write a will disowning him, it will not be heeded, for his master, Rabban Jochanan ben Zakkai, will rule in his favor."

To this Hyrcanus replied: "Do not be afraid, my children, for I will go to Jerusalem and on a Sabbath I will publicly declare that my son Eliezer will not share in my possessions."

When Hyrcanus arrived in Jerusalem and Rabban Jochanan ben Zakkai heard of it, he commanded that he be honored for his son's sake and that he be seated among the greatest of the nation; he also commanded Rabbi Eliezer to expound the Torah on that Sabbath.

Old Hyrcanus was surprised to see his son, who had been an *am ha'aretz*, expound before the Nasi and all the scholars. His face glowed with pleasure and he was astonished when he saw Rabban Jochanan ben Zakkai kiss Rabbi Eliezer on the head and heard him say: "Happy are the holy fathers Abraham, Isaac, and Jacob that one such as this was descended from them."[5]

After the lecture Rabbi Eliezer saw his father standing among the assembled. He ran to him and said: "How could I expound the Torah while my father was standing." Hyrcanus then mounted a bench and declared: "Be it known that I came to Jerusalem with the special intention of disowning my son Eliezer and disinheriting him after my death. But now that I see how all the scholars revere him, in my will I will assign him a portion double that of his brothers." To this Rabbi Eliezer replied that he never prayed for fields or for silver and gold but only for knowledge of the Torah and he therefore refused to take a greater share of the inheritance than his brothers would receive.[6]

Rabbi Eliezer had a stubborn and harsh disposition as befits one who would follow Shammai. He did not allow his pupils to express their opinions of the law in his presence. When one of them once did so, Rabbi Eliezer remarked to his wife: "I will not be surprised if this person does not survive a year." And in fact that person died within the year. Rabbi Eliezer's wife then asked him: "Are you a prophet that you could foretell his death?" He replied, "I am not a prophet nor am I the son of a prophet, but I have received it from my teacher that one who pronounces sentence in the presence of his master has forfeited his life."[7]

When Rabbi Eliezer was sick he was visited by Rabbi Akiba and his colleagues. Rabbi Eliezer sat in his garden bower and his visitors sat at a distance of four ells. He asked them: "Why have you come?" and they replied: "We have come to learn from you."

"Then why did you never come to me before?" he asked them, and they replied, "We never had the time." "Seeing that you never found the time to visit me until now," he continued, "I would not be surprised if you met with violent deaths."

Rabbi Akiba then asked him, "I too?" and Rabbi Eliezer answered: "Your death will be more cruel than theirs."

From this one can see that he never forgave any slight to his self-respect, nor did he ever go out of his way to show kindness.

It is told that once Rabbi Eliezer approached the *amud* (the cantor's pulpit) to pray for rain and although he pronounced twenty-four blessings there was no rain. Later Rabbi Akiba rose and merely said: "Our Father, our king. We have no other king but You. Our Father, our king, do for Your own sake and have mercy on us." Rain immediately began to fall. The scholars were displeased at this and a *bat kol* from heaven was heard saying: "Rabbi Akiba is not greater than Rabbi

Eliezer, but Rabbi Akiba practices forgiveness and Rabbi Eliezer does not."[8]

Of Rabbi Eliezer's moral maxims there remain the following: "Let the honor of your friend be as dear to you as your own; be not quick to anger and repent a day before your death; warm yourself at the fire of the wise and beware of their glowing coal lest you be scorched, for their bite is the bite of a fox and their sting is the sting of a scorpion, their hiss is the hiss of a serpent and all their words are like coals of fire."[9]

When the disciples of Rabbi Eliezer visited him during his sickness, they begged him to tell them what to do in order to deserve the life of the world to come. He instructed them to "be careful of the honor of your associates and do not allow your children to ponder the logic of events,[10] but raise them in the presence of scholars. When you pray, remember before whom you stand. By virtue of all these deeds you will gain eternal life."[11]

Later he raised his hands to heaven and said: "I have learned much from my masters and also from others, but with all my learning, I have received from my masters' knowledge no more than a dog who licks water from the sea, and my pupils have taken from me as much as a pen absorbs when it is dipped in ink."

As soon as he died Rabbi Joshua ben Chananiah arose and declared: "Now the vow is rescinded." Since the scholars vowed during the dispute with Rabbi Eliezer not to approach him within a distance of four ells, after his death they considered this vow no longer valid.

From this statement one may conclude that Rabbi Eliezer was not excommunicated, but was merely isolated from other scholars, else he would not have been allowed to conduct a separate academy, and the pupils of that academy would not have ranked with those of Jabneh. When Rabban Gamaliel died, Rabbi Eliezer sent all the pupils of his academy in Lud to Jabneh to participate in the funeral and the mourning.

When Rabbi Akiba heard of the death of Rabbi Eliezer, he came all the way from Caesarea to Lud to attend the funeral; on his way he flogged himself and when he arrived his whole body was bleeding. Later Rabbi Joshua ben Chananiah came to the academy of Rabbi Eliezer and found there a stone on which Rabbi Eliezer sat while he taught. Seeing this stone Rabbi Joshua kissed it and said: "This stone is like Mount Sinai and he who sat on it can be compared to the Ark of the Covenant."[12]

Idolatry presented a very serious problem at that time. Since the Temple was destroyed and sacrifices done away with, there were many Jews who felt God had abandoned His people, and they turned to other gods. Rabbi Eliezer furiously fought against these deserters and he believed that it was necessary to uproot this evil. If a book of the Torah is found in a house of idol worshipping, he ruled that such a book must be burned, since it is against the law to throw it away and because it was contaminated it could no longer be used.

Although Rabbi Eliezer was away from Jabneh for many years, there are many decisions of law quoted in his name as well as many legends about him. He was also praised as possessing the same qualities ascribed to his teacher Rabban Jochanan ben Zakkai. During the sickness that preceded his death, he was visited by four of the elders of the people: Rabbi Tarphon, Rabbi Joshua ben Chananiah, Rabbi Eleazar ben Azariah, and Rabbi Akiba.

Rabbi Tarphon said: "You were better for the Jews than rain." Rabbi Joshua said: "You were better for the Jews than sun." Rabbi Eleazar ben Azariah said: "You were better for the Jews than parents are for their children." When Rabbi Akiba was ready to speak, Rabbi Eliezer cupped his ear and said: "Let us hear what Rabbi Akiba has to say of me." But Rabbi Akiba said: "The dearest thing on earth is suffering."

Then came Rabbi Eliezer's disciples and he said: "A great wrath has descended upon the world." All the disciples began to weep, only Rabbi Akiba smiled. The disciples said: "Is it possible to refrain from weeping when one sees the Torah in suffering?" But Rabbi Akiba answered: "That is the reason why I laugh. Were my master not to suffer, it would seem that he has received the reward for his good deeds in this world. But since he suffers, I am convinced that the reward for his

good deeds is awaiting him and that he will receive it in the
other world."

Rabbi Eliezer was especially famous for the exactness of
his knowledge he received from his teacher. He often said that
a person must study every subject with his pupil four times
even as was done by the Jews when they were in the desert. All
Jews learned from the Elders, and the Elders learned from
Aaron, and Aaron learned from Moses, and Moses learned the
Torah from God. Study of the Torah is of such importance that
one must not abstain from it at any time. Even the holidays
must be devoted to this end, for only an *am ha'aretz* devotes his
holidays to earthly pleasures, but a scholar must continue his
studies. When one indulges in food and drink on a feast day it
is only that he may have more strength to devote to the Torah.

Of the significance of Rabbi Eliezer's learning, Elisha ben
Avuyah once told that on the day of his own *brit milah,* his
father prepared a feast and invited all the outstanding people of
that time including Rabbi Eliezer and Rabbi Joshua. After the
food and drink, those gathered sang various songs and played
a game of alphabet. One would recite a verse of the Bible
beginning with an *alef* and another immediately followed with
a verse beginning with a *bet.* Rabbi Eliezer then said to Rabbi
Joshua: "While these people devote themselves to their affairs
let us devote ourselves to ours." They began to discuss various
interpretations of the Torah, and they derived as much joy from
it as if the Torah had just been handed down from Mount Sinai.
A cloud of fire then descended from heaven and surrounded
them. Elisha's father said to them: "What are you doing?
Would you burn my house?" but they replied, "We devoted
ourselves to finding new interpretations to the Torah that was
given in fire." Then Avuyah said: "If the power of the Torah is
so great I shall devote my son to it when he grows to be of age."

Rabbi Eliezer held original ideas regarding the value of
prayer. "Whoever prays at well-defined times and according to
a determined form," he used to say, "his prayer is only a habit
and does not derive from his heart." Contrary to Rabban
Gamaliel, he did not recognize the necessity of reciting the
shemoneh esrei and he composed a shorter prayer. When one of

the pupils once prayed the shorter prayers before the pulpit his colleagues laughed at him, but Rabbi Eliezer said: "Abbreviated as his prayer is, it is not as short as the prayer Moses uttered for the cure of his sister that consisted of only five words." Another time a pupil recited a long version of the prayers and he was ridiculed for their length, but Rabbi Eliezer said: "His prayers are no longer than those of Moses who prayed for forty days." Then he continued: "There is a time for abbreviating one's prayers and a time for extending them. The important thing is to recite the prayer according to the need of the time."

Speaking on the same subject on another occasion, he gave his interpretation of the words God spoke to Moses: "Why do you pray to me? Tell the Jews they should advance." According to Rabbi Eliezer, God meant to say: "My children are in trouble. The sea has cut off their escape and the enemy is overtaking them. At such a time one must think of a means of salvation and not devote himself to prayer. Therefore tell the Jews to advance in spite of all obstacles."

Like all his contemporaries, Rabbi Eliezer deeply mourned the destruction of Jerusalem and the Temple which he had witnessed. He said: "Our forefathers permitted the roof of our sanctuary to be taken away, while we allowed the walls to be razed. Every generation that does not see the temple rebuilt is like a generation that participates in its destruction." He also said that three times every night God sits in mourning and roars like a lion over the ruins of the Temple exclaiming: "Woe is me that I have destroyed my house and have exiled my children."

At that time there prevailed a strong proselyting mood among the nations surrounding Palestine. Despite the fact that the Jews had lost all political significance, many Gentiles felt drawn toward the Jewish faith, intrigued by the stubbornness with which the Jews clung to it. Not a ray of light illuminated Jewish life and proselytes were being discouraged. Before one was admitted to the fold he would be asked: "Do you not know that Jews are persecuted everywhere? It is also very difficult to observe Judaism, especially for one who is not used to its rigors." But there were many Gentiles who were not discour-

aged and even among the highest classes of Rome there were
some who embraced Judaism. It became necessary therefore to
devise new regulations for the new Jews. Before the temple
was destroyed, Gentiles who undertook to observe the "seven
commandments of the sons of Noah" were allowed to live in
Judea and they were called "permanent proselytes." But after
the destruction, only those who undertook to observe Judaism
in all its details were accepted as proselytes. The Roman
historian Tacitus ridiculed the proselytes saying: "It is impossible to comprehend what happened to many prominent
Romans that they suddenly became filled with Jewish thoughts
and agreed to have their flesh cut and to deny the gods of their
forefathers." The Emperor Domitian then issued severe laws
against those Gentiles who embraced Judaism; and the Roman
satirist Juvenal used his sharp wit against those who taught
their children belief in a God who is all spirit, whom no one has
seen, who is not strong enough to protect his people, and who
is concerned only that people should observe the Sabbath and
should not eat pork.

One of these proselytes was a rich Roman matron named
Bloria, who was well versed in the Scriptures and frequently
addressed questions to Rabban Gamaliel and to his disciples.
Another proselyte was Aquilas (Onkelos), a scion of the
imperial family who translated the Torah into Greek because
the Septuagint version had by then been falsified. Rabbi Eliezer
and Rabbi Joshua approved this translation, and an Aramaic
version of it, the *Targum Onkelos* still exists.

But despite such outstanding examples, Rabbi Eliezer did
not approve of all proselytes and he maintained that there
always existed a possibility that a proselyte would return to the
Gentiles. When Rabbi Eliezer saw the suffering the proselytes
had to undergo at the hands of the Romans, he said: "Why is
it that proselytes of this day are persecuted and have to suffer
so much? This is probably because they do not show love for
Judaism but only possess an unexplained fear."

When Rabbi Eliezer declared that a man must repent a day
before his death, his disciples asked: "How can one know what

day he will die on?" "That was exactly my intention," Rabbi Eliezer answered, "one should repent every day for fear that he will die on the morrow."

Rabbi Eliezer considered a sword, a lance, and a bow as decorations which a man may keep when going about on the Sabbath. He opposed teaching the Torah to girls and declared that whoever teaches the Torah to his daughter is like one who teaches his daughter foolish things. Wild beasts, he said, should be killed wherever met. This was opposed to the opinion of other scholars who believed that a wild beast should be killed only if it has done some harm. He also said that whoever eats the bread of a Gentile is like one who eats the flesh of a pig.

Rabbi Eliezer always elaborated on the events related in the Torah and with poetic imagination embellished these events with wonders even greater than those described in the Torah. Of the ten plagues that were visited on Egypt according to the Torah, before the deliverance of the Jews, Rabbi Jose of Galilee said that they prove that the Egyptians were afflicted with fifty plagues when pursuing the Jews to the sea. He bases it on the verse of the Torah that says that the ten plagues were a "finger of God," but when at the sea "the Jews saw the great hand of God," it means that if one finger caused ten plagues, the hand of God must have caused fifty. But Rabbi Eliezer was still unsatisfied and he discovered a text that proved that every plague consisted of four; he therefore concluded that the Egyptians were afflicted with forty plagues in Egypt and with as many as two hundred plagues by the sea.

He also said that the miraculous events that transpired by the sea were so great that even women slaves saw more than Ezekiel and all the other prophets. Moses' song of praise, "This is my God and I shall glorify Him," he considered as proof that everyone saw God.

Rabbi Eliezer said that when the manna fell, it remained suspended two ells above the ground and the Jews picked it from the air and not from the ground. Before it fell, Rabbi Eliezer said, a north wind arose and cleansed the desert of sand; a rain then descended to wash the earth; after the rain a dew fell and spread like a cloth and on it the *mannah* descended.

Regarding the events at Mount Sinai the Torah says that "all Jews saw." Rabbi Eliezer declared this to indicate that there was no blind person among all the people. When it is said later that "everyone answered in unison," he interpreted this to signify that there was no mute person among all the people; from the declaration of the Jews that they will do and hear as they are told, he concluded that there was no deaf person among them, and the verse that says that all the people stood at the foot of the mountain he interpreted as meaning that there was not a lame one among them.

Rabbi Eliezer held the Sabbath in great esteem. He declared that whoever observes the Sabbath according to all its regulations will be spared three types of punishment—such a person will be spared the sufferings of the coming of the Messiah, the wars of Gog and Magog, and the great Day of Judgment.

Concerning the duty to honor one's father, Rabbi Eliezer related the story of a Gentile named Dama ben Nathina who owned a diamond worth 600,000 *shekalim* that he wanted to sell for the *efod* of the High Priest. But when the priests came to buy it, Dama's father was asleep and the key to the box with the diamond was under his pillow. Dama refused to wake his father even though this caused him a great loss. On another occasion Rabbi Eliezer said that the honor due to one's father must be so unbounded that even were one to see his father throw a bag of gold into the sea, he must not question his action.

25

RABBI JOSHUA BEN CHANANIAH

WHENEVER THE OUTSTANDING DISCIPLES of Rabban Jochanan ben Zakkai were enumerated, Rabbi Joshua ben Chananiah was accorded second place. Rabban Jochanan himself referred to him as "the triple thread" because he combined within himself the virtues of Torah, wisdom, and fear of God. On another occasion Rabban Jochanan is said to have exclaimed: "Happy is the mother who gives birth to such a son." Rabbi Joshua's mother well deserved this praise, for even before his birth she frequented the academies in order to influence the future of the child with the spirit of the Torah. When Rabbi Joshua was still an infant, she brought him in his cradle to the academy so that he might absorb the words of the Torah.[1]

Rabbi Joshua began his activities while the Temple was still in existence, and he served as a Levite among the singers. Years later he described the festival of the drawing of water then celebrated on the night after the first day of *Sukkot*, and during which no one slept because of the numerous ceremonies. On the morning of the first day of *Sukkot*, everyone arose early to offer the daily morning sacrifice, then the Levites sang a hymn after which it was time to offer the special holiday sacrifice. Following this everyone went to the academy and then home to partake of the holiday repast. But before that could be consumed it was time again for the *Minhah* offering, and then began the festivities of the drawing of water with rejoicing and dancing until the early hours of the morning when it was time again for the morning sacrifice. Those who became exceedingly tired would lean on someone's shoulder and nap while standing up.[2]

Rabbi Joshua was not favored with an attractive appearance[3] but he was gifted with great talent for study, and his teacher found him worthy enough to confide the greatest mysteries of the Torah. Legend relates that Rabbi Joshua went on a journey one hot summer day with his comrade Rabbi Jose Hacohen. On the way Rabbi Joshua began to expound the mysteries of the Divine Chariot and the sky suddenly became overcast with clouds, a rainbow appeared, and angels gathered to hear his lecture even as people gather for a wedding.

When Rabbi Jose related this to Rabban Jochanan ben Zakkai, the latter exclaimed: "Happy are you and happy are the mothers that bore you. My eyes rejoice to see this. In my dreams I see us all sitting on Mount Sinai and a voice is calling to us to go further, where we will find great palaces, and magnificent rugs will be spread before our feet, and we shall take our place in the front rows among those who sit before the *Shekhinah*."[4]

Together with Rabbi Eliezer ben Hyrcanus, Rabbi Joshua aided his master Rabban Jochanan ben Zakkai to flee from Jerusalem before its destruction, and he then followed him wherever he went. He is always mentioned as second to Rabbi Eliezer, although he was a pupil of Rabban Jochanan before Rabbi Eliezer arrived. And when Rabban Jochanan invited Rabbi Eliezer to eat, he said that he had eaten with Rabbi Joshua.

Like his master Rabbi Joshua did not greatly mourn the destruction of Jerusalem. The Talmud relates[5] that many Jews renounced the eating of flesh and the drinking of wine after the destruction. Rabbi Eliezer asked them: "My children, why do you abstain from flesh and wine?" and the people answered:

"How can we eat when flesh is no longer offered on the altar, and how can we drink wine when wine is poured no more on the altar."

To this Rabbi Joshua replied: "You are quite right, my children. But if we should do as you say, then we must also give up eating bread that is made of flour, for flour is no longer offered on the altar; and if you will say that one can do without flour by eating fruit, then must we also give up eating fruit, for the offering of the first fruit to the priest has been done away with; we should also give up drinking water because it is no longer poured over the altar."

The people then remained silent not knowing what to answer and Rabbi Joshua continued: "If I were to say that we should not mourn at all, that would be impossible, but one must not surrender himself entirely to sorrow. It is necessary to mourn in such a manner that everyone should be able to bear it, and that mourning should not interfere with people's lives."

Very few legal decisions are quoted in the name of Rabbi Joshua ben Chananiah and whenever he did give a legal opinion, he credited it to Rabban Jochanan ben Zakkai or to some other teacher. He was frequently in opposition to Rabbi Eliezer ben Hyrcanus, but despite these differences of opinion they were close friends for many years until the great dispute regarding the "winding oven" separated them.

Rabbi Joshua visited Rome and Alexandria several times, together with Rabban Gamaliel and other scholars, on behalf of the Jewish people. It seems that he was favored by the Gentile scholars and rulers who disputed with him regarding Judaism. His wisdom was also appreciated and the emperor once asked him to tell him what dream he had had that night. Knowing that the emperor was planning a war with the Persians, Rabbi Joshua said: "In your dream you saw the Persians dragging you into captivity; they forced you to do hard labor and they beat you with a golden rod." The emperor may not have had such a dream the previous night, but after he brooded over this all day he may have had such a dream the following night.[6]

Another time the emperor asked him why Sabbath foods have such a pleasing aroma. Rabbi Joshua said to him: "We have a herb called Sabbath; this herb we mix with food and it improves its flavor." "Will you not give me some of these herbs," the emperor asked, but Rabbi Joshua replied: "Whoever does not observe the Sabbath will get no benefit from these herbs."[7]

Like Rabban Gamaliel and other scholars, Rabbi Joshua also knew the languages of the neighboring peoples, and for this reason he was frequently chosen to represent the Jews before the rulers. Once it became necessary to gain the intercession of a matron who was influential among the Roman rulers. The scholars then asked: "Who will go to that matron?" and Rabbi Joshua volunteered.

He went, accompanied by several of his disciples, and when they approached within a distance of four ells of the house, Rabbi Joshua removed his phylacteries and entering the house, closed the door behind himself and his disciples remained outside. When he emerged, he bathed and went to finish the studies for that day.

Thinking that his disciples might suspect him of some evil he asked: "When you saw me remove the phylacteries before entering the house, what did you think?" and they replied: "We thought, that you did not want to bring a holy object into an unclean place." "And what did you think when you saw me close the door and leave you outside?" he further asked. His disciples replied: "We thought that you wished to discuss some political question." "And when you saw me bathe after I left the house, what did you think?" he asked, and they answered him: "We thought you bathed because of the possibility that while speaking to her a particle of her saliva may have fallen on your clothes." Then Rabbi Joshua said to them: "I swear to you that I did all these things even for the same reasons that you thought."[8]

The emperor once said to Rabbi Joshua: "It is written in the Torah that God is just and that he rewards each one according to his deeds. Then why are there so many blind, deaf, and lame people who suffer without cause because they were born crippled before they had an opportunity to sin?" And Rabbi Joshua answered him: "God knows what he does and if he creates a person with some disability, it is a sign that such a man is wicked and is therefore punished in advance for his sins." "But how can this be proved?" the emperor asked. "Give me," Rabbi Joshua said, "two of your men as witnesses and a thousand golden coins and I will prove to you that what I say is true." The emperor then gave him what he asked and Rabbi Joshua went together with the two men to a person who was born blind and he said to him: "The emperor commanded that I be put to death, and I have a thousand golden coins I want you to keep for me. If I am killed the money will be yours, but if my life is spared then you will return it to me." The blind man answered: "It shall be even as you say."

Then Rabbi Joshua gave the money to the man and three months later he returned together with the witnesses and said to him: "The emperor has spared my life and now I want you to return the money I gave you to hold for me." But the blind man answered: "What money have you given me? I know of none."

Rabbi Joshua appeared to be angry and he brought the man before the emperor for trial, but even there the blind man denied that he had received money, and when the witnesses testified against him he claimed that they were false witnesses. Then Rabbi Joshua said to him: "Woe to you, blind man, that you will in no way have any use of the money, for I have seen your wife entertaining another man, saying that as soon as the emperor puts you to death she will spend the money together with him."

Upon hearing this the blind man immediately ran home and brought the money and placed it before the emperor. Rabbi Joshua then said to him: "Now you can see that our God was just when he made this man blind, for even in his blindness he is a criminal; how much more so would he have been if he could see."[9]

As mentioned before, Rabbi Joshua did not possess a pleasing appearance but he was very wise, and the king's daughter, who admired knowledge, enjoyed discussing matters with him. Unable to restrain herself, she once said to him: "Is it possible that such wisdom should be contained in such an

ungainly vessel?" Rabbi Joshua said to her: "Why is it that your
father, who is an emperor, keeps his wine in a clay vessel as do
all other people? Why does he not keep it in a silver or golden
vessel?" The princess inquired of her father and he explained to
her that good wine would soon spoil in a silver or golden
vessel. She then understood what Rabbi Joshua meant to tell
her.

Rabbi Joshua's debates with the emperor are frequently
mentioned in various *midrashim* and the name of the emperor is
given as Hadrian, who later permitted the rebuilding of the
temple. According to the *Midrash*, the permission was obtained
by Rabbi Joshua.

It is told that the emperor once said to Rabbi Joshua: "I am
greater than your master Moses, for he is dead but I am alive."
To this Rabbi Joshua responded: "Can you decree that people
should not light fires in their houses for three consecutive
days?" "Yes, I can do so," the emperor answered and he
immediately issued such a decree. That same evening the
emperor and Rabbi Joshua went out of the gates of the palace
for a stroll and they saw smoke issuing from a chimney. Rabbi
Joshua said to him: "Look, even while you live, your commandments are ignored, while our teacher Moses commanded
many centuries ago that no fire be lit on the Sabbath and to this
day no Jew will make a fire on Sabbath."[10]

At that time disputes frequently occurred in Bei Avidan.[11]
The aim of these was to dissuade Jews from their faith. Rabbi
Joshua attended these a number of times but later he stopped
going. When the emperor once came to the debating place and
did not find Rabbi Joshua there, he later asked him why he was
absent. In his usual allegorical fashion Rabbi Joshua answered
him: "My mountain is already covered with snow and the foot
of the mountain is bedecked with ice. My dogs no longer bark,
nor do my grindstones turn, and when I walk it seems as if I
search for that which I have not lost." With these words Rabbi
Joshua implied that he feels his age; his head is white as snow,
and his beard and moustache are grey as ice; his voice is hoarse
and he has difficulty in speaking; his teeth can no longer chew,
and when he walks he is bent as if in search of something.

Hadrian, who later became relentless in his persecution of the Jews, had agreed to allow the restoration of the Temple. This permission is said to have been obtained by Rabbi Joshua ben Chananiah. But the emperor later changed his mind and rescinded his permission. Some historians maintain that the intervention of the Samaritans was responsible for this but others advance different reasons. The rescinding of the permission almost caused a new uprising, but Rabbi Joshua calmed the enraged mob with an allegoric tale.

"The lion," he related, "once almost choked when a bone became lodged in his throat. He announced throughout the land that whoever removed the bone would be richly rewarded. The stork came, and with its long bill extracted the bone. When the stork demanded its reward the lion said: 'You want reward? Is it not enough for you that you have been inside the lion's mouth and have come out alive?'"

Hearing this story the people understood its moral and their rebellious mood was calmed.

From what we know of the activities of Rabbi Joshua ben Chananiah, we may conclude that he made friends easily; he reserved his decisions and based them on a desire for peace; he was ready to compromise with other scholars in order to avoid disputes. Speaking of the disputes between the opposing schools of Hillel and Shammai, he said that these were being carried too far and were like "filling a barrel full of oil and then pouring water into it to spoil the oil."

Following the death of Rabban Gamaliel, Rabbi Joshua apparently became the spiritual leader of the people. It is possible that because of his poverty he was not chosen Nasi, but since he headed his own academy in Pekiin, and the Nasi of Jabneh was dead, we may conclude that his importance was then of the highest.

Politically the period was one of commotion. This was the time of Trajan (Trachinus in the Talmud and Midrash) and Hadrian (Adrianus in the Talmud and Midrash) to whose name was always attached the curse *shehik tamya* (may his dead bones be ground). This period was therefore marked by constant decrees against the Jews, and it was necessary to intercede continually in order to counteract their effects and also to keep a vigilant eye on what was going on among the Jews among whom rebellious feeling arose as a result of these decrees.

As long as Rabbi Eliezer ben Hyrcanus lived, his superiority was recognized by Rabbi Joshua as well as by other scholars. But differences of opinion existed regarding the interpretation of various texts dealing with metaphysical matters or the explanation of certain events in the history of the people, as well as regarding future events during the advent of the Messiah, and concerning the creation of the world and whether that took place in the month of *Nissan* or *Tishri*.

The belief was then accepted that every Jew is entitled to a share in the world to come and in the resurrection to follow the great Day of Judgment that will occur during the next redemption of the Jewish people. This belief grew out of the observation that fulfillment of some commandments, that were to be rewarded with long life, often entailed the immediate death of the observant.

Thus the Torah commands that "If you find on your way a nest of birds on a tree or on the ground containing birds or eggs, you shall not take the mother with her offspring but you shall send the mother away, and the offspring you may take for yourself in order that you may live long years" (Deut. 27:6–7). The same reward is also held out for the fulfillment of the commandment of honoring one's father and mother: "Your years will be long and your portion will be good" (Deut. 8:16).

But it once occurred that a father said to his son: "Go to the pigeon roost and bring me some young doves." The son did as his father asked, and he also sent away the mother bird, but on his way back he slipped and was killed. Then many people asked: "How could God do this since he promised in the Torah that these two commandments were to be rewarded with long life?" It was then explained that the reward was to be given in the future life and the text was interpreted to mean, "you shall enjoy this world which is perfect without pain and you shall live long years in the world which is eternal."[10]

The belief that all Jews have a share in the world to come or in the resurrection, Rabbi Eliezer interpreted to exclude non-Jews. Non-Jews, he said, were not even to be called for the Day of Judgment. But Rabbi Joshua maintained that the just men among the Gentiles would have a share in the world to come. According to Rabbi Eliezer, the people of Sodom, the generation of desert wanderers, and the congregation of Korah were to be excluded from the resurrection and from the Day of Judgment, but Rabbi Joshua was more generous to these sinners and although he conceded that they were ruled out from the world to come, claimed that they would be called to Judgment Day.

A saying of Rabbi Joshua that he frequently repeated stated that an evil eye, an evil thought, and hatred of mankind drive a man out of the world. He particularly believed in the importance of peaceful relations between people and he also said that "a pious fool, a clever, wicked man, an abstaining woman, and the plague of Pharisaism—these four types spoil the world." It was asked, what is a pious fool? The answer was that a pious fool is one who sees a woman drowning and would not save her for fear of touching her body. A pious fool is also one who sees a child drowning and does not save it because he has not yet removed his phylacteries. An abstaining woman was defined as one who renounces her husband and the joys of the world; the plague of Pharisaism was explained to mean those Pharisees who strike their heads against a wall to show their piety.

When Hadrian permitted the restoration of the Temple human bones were found where the wood room of the Temple used to be and some scholars wanted to declare all Jerusalem unclean. But Rabbi Joshua said: "It would be a shame for us to declare our sanctuary unclean. What if dead bones were found? Can anyone tell where the victims of the flood came to rest? Or those slaughtered by Nebuchadnezzar? Or the bodies of those killed in all the wars that took place to this day? The sanctity of the Land of Israel has been declared for all times and even when Jews are in exile, it cannot be profaned by dead bones."[13]

The frequent debates of Rabbi Joshua with the emperor and the philosophers (one group of philosophers is referred to in the Talmud as the Elders of Athens) are embellished by all sorts of legends. Nevertheless they hold an important religious significance. The Elders of Athens, it is told, once asked Rabbi Joshua: "Where is the middle of the world?" Pointing to the place where he stood, Rabbi Joshua declared it to be the middle of the world, and when they asked him how he knew this, he told them to take a line and measure the distance to convince themselves. Attempting to confuse him the Elders said: "We have a well in the desert and we want you to bring it into the city." But Rabbi Joshua said: "For that I need a rope of bran, for only such a rope can be used for moving wells."

Again they said to him: "We have a torn mill and we want you to patch it," but he answered that for this a thread of sand was needed. The Elders then asked him: "What should one use to cut a labyrinth of knives?" and he replied: "The horn of a donkey." Once two eggs were brought to Rabbi Joshua and he was asked which egg was laid by a white hen and which by a black one. Another time the Elders asked: "When a bird dies, where does its soul leave it?" and Rabbi Joshua replied: "The soul leaves through the same place it entered at birth." And when they asked: "Is there a case of something being brought into a house with great effort and the effort causes damage?" he said, "When you bring a rug into the house and in doing so you break the door."

To the debates between Rabbi Joshua and Hadrian the following may be added. Hadrian said: 'You say that God creates new angels every day to praise him and after they finish their praise they go away. I would like to know where they go." And Rabbi Joshua answered, "They go where they were created. They go to the River of Fire that flows day and night even as the Jordan flows day and night, and this River of Fire comes from the perspiration of the sacred animals that carry the throne of Glory."

Then Hadrian said: "I have noticed that God's name is mentioned in the first five of the Ten Commandments but it does not occur in the other five. How can you explain that?" Rabbi Joshua retorted: "Why is it, that wherever one looks he sees your statue, but in those places where a person goes to relieve himself he does not find your statue?" The emperor answered, "It is not fitting to place my image in unclean places." "Neither is it fitting to mention God's name together with murderers, adulterers, thieves, false witnesses, and other sinners who are the refuse of humanity," Rabbi Joshua replied.

Once Hadrian said to Rabbi Joshua: "I would believe in your God if you would only show him to me that I might know Him better." "I can do that easily," Rabbi Joshua said. "If you would see my God I will show him to you." He then led the emperor outside on a hot summer day and told him to look at the sun, but the latter declared that he could not do so, for the sun blinds his eyes. Then Rabbi Joshua said, "If you cannot look at the face of the least servant of God, how can you expect to see Him?"[14]

Brilliant as were the retorts of Rabbi Joshua to the emperor and to the philosophers of Athens, he admitted that he was confounded—not by the emperor or a gentile philosopher—but by a woman, a small boy, and a little girl.

Of how he was confounded by a woman Rabbi Joshua related: "Once I was lodging in an inn and the proprietress gave me beans to eat. I ate them all the first day and likewise on the second day. On the third day she put so much salt into the beans that I could not eat them. When she asked me why I didn't eat I answered that I had already eaten. But the woman said to me: 'If it is true, that you already ate, you would not have eaten the bread. There must be another reason for your not eating. You probably remembered that yesterday and the day before, you left no *peah*[15] from your food and you undoubtedly know that the scholars ruled that it is not necessary to offer *peah* from the pot but from the plate.' "

"A little girl confounded me," Joshua continued to relate, "when I was once going on my way and I had to cross a field. The little girl asked me: 'Rabbi, is not this a field that you allow yourself to walk on it?' But I said, it is a worn road. She said to me, 'If this be a worn road, then wicked people like you have made it so.' "

"A small boy confounded me," Rabbi Joshua told, "when I was going on my way and I came to a place where the road separated. I asked the boy which way I should go to arrive at the city and he replied, 'One way is shorter but longer; the other way is longer but shorter.' I followed the road the boy said was shorter but longer. When I approached the city I came to a place of gardens that I could not cross and I had to retrace my steps to follow the other road, which the boy said was longer but shorter."

With the death of Rabbi Joshua there ceased "wise counsel and good thoughts." Rabbi Joshua was always victorious in his disputes with the opponents of the Jewish faith, and as he was dying the scholars said to each other: "Who will lead our disputes now that Rabbi Joshua is leaving us?"[16]

26

RABBI ELIEZER
OF MODIIN

DURING THE DECADE FOLLOWING the destruction of the Temple and until the uprising of Bar Kochba, there lived in Palestine the *tanna* Rabbi Eliezer who exerted a considerable influence. His name is extensively associated with the legends of that time.[1]

Rabbi Eliezer was a native of the town of Modiin, which was also the birthplace of Mattathias the Hasmonean. According to legend he died as a result of being kicked by Bar Kochba, when the latter was told that Rabbi Eliezer sided with the Romans. The period was marked by revolutionary unrest not only among the Jews, but also among all the Asiatic nations dominated by Rome. National liberation movements were afoot everywhere. In an attempt to gain the confidence of the Jews and their assistance against the other nations, Hadrian permitted the restoration of the Temple. The historical occurrences of that time are not entirely clear. One thing is certain, since it appears in all historical records, that after a revolutionary clash with the Romans, Hadrian came to new terms with the Jews and that the outstanding condition of this peace was the permission to rebuild the temple.

But this permission was later rescinded when he abandoned his friendly attitude toward the Jews. By means of various legal amendments, the previous edict allowing the restoration of the Temple was nullified. The first move was to order the selection of a new site for the Temple; later an alteration of the dimensions, to differ from those of the old Temple, was ordered and the smallest possible number of Jews were to be employed in the reconstruction. When all the imperial caprices were finally complied with and work began, flames appeared from underground and frightened the laborers away. This phenomenon, caused by an accumulation of gases in the ruins, was interpreted as a sign that God was against the work.

The conduct of the emperor enraged the populace and the rebellious sentiments seething beneath the surface broke out in open revolt. Rabbi Joshua ben Chananiah restrained the revolutionary outburst for a time, but when Rabbi Akiba became the spokesman for the revolt, it burst into full force under the leadership of Simeon ben Kochba of Kezib.

It remains uncertain whether any other scholar besides Rabbi Akiba joined Bar Kochba, but we do know that Rabbi Eliezer of Modiin, who was an uncle of Bar Kochba, opposed the rebellion of the Jews. As long as the war of rebellion lasted, Rabbi Eliezer fasted and prayed that God should save the remnant of the Jews from extermination. Since everyone was convinced of the invincibility of the Romans, Rabbi Eliezer refused to sanction the warlike efforts of his nephew. This was interpreted as indicating sympathy with the Romans, and in an outburst of anger Bar Kochba kicked Rabbi Eliezer who died instantly from the blow.

The details of this occurrence relate that Rabbi Eliezer was standing deeply immersed in prayer, when a Samaritan came up to him and whispered something in his ear, but Rabbi Eliezer did not even notice his presence. This was reported to Bar Kochba who questioned Rabbi Eliezer regarding the subject of his conversation with the Samaritan, but Rabbi Eliezer did not know what to answer.[2] When the Samaritan was caught and questioned he admitted that he had spoken regarding the surrender of the city to the Romans.

Rabbi Eliezer of Modiin was a pupil and a friend of Rabban

Gamaliel II. It seems probable that he also conducted an academy of his own, but since he was an authority on the *Aggadah*, he was frequently invited to Jabneh to offer his interpretations. Rabban Gamaliel was in the habit of hearing the opinions of all the scholars and then would remark: "We must still hear from the man of Modiin."[3] The others were displeased at this and once remarked to Rabbi Eliezer: "How long will you continue to heap words on us?"

Devoting himself largely to preaching, he said that the meaning of *Aggadah* was the same as "flowing," for the legendary interpretations of the historical events and the texts of the Scriptures flow into one's consciousness like water. When he preached, his words caressed the ears of the listeners with a gentle grace that aroused the noblest feelings and he stimulated the fantasy of his listeners with poetic imagery.

An often-repeated maxim of Rabbi Eliezer said: "He who profanes the Sabbath desecrates the festivals, and shames his associate in public, and breaks the covenant of our father Abraham, and misinterprets the Torah, even though he possesses Torah and does good deeds, he has no share in the world to come."

This maxim characterizes his trend of thought and was probably also meant as a condemnation of the various sects of that time who profaned the Sabbath, desecrated the festivals, broke the covenant of Abraham, and falsely interpreted the Torah. Like most of his contemporaries, Rabbi Eliezer also considered the observance of the Sabbath as the most important element of the Jewish faith. "He who does not observe the Sabbath has no portion in the world to come," Rabbi Eliezer said, "but if the Jews were to observe the Sabbath as it should be observed, God would bestow upon them the following six gifts: the land of Israel, the world to come, a new world order, the reestablishment of the kingdom of David, the priesthood, and the Levites."

The developing sects among the Jews at that time began to criticize the Hebrew script. As previously described, the Jews had two types of script, the square Assyrian and the Phoenician used by the Samaritans. In the attempt to isolate the Samaritans from the Jews, Ezra the Scribe selected the Assyrian script to be used exclusively by the Jews. The opponents of the Torah then began to criticize this script saying that it was derived from a foreign nation. Rabbi Eliezer declared that the square Assyrian script was the original script of the Torah, and he based his statement on texts from the Torah and from the *Megillat Esther*.[4]

Rabbi Eliezer was opposed to Bar Kochba's uprising because it seemed to him to be altogether too natural. He awaited a redemption characterized by miracles, and he held that one must hope for it but must not attempt to hasten such a redemption violently. When he was asked about the prophecy that Jerusalem would become the gathering place of all the nations, how it would be possible for one city to contain all the nations, he explained that God would command the city to extend its boundaries to include all people.

Rabbi Eliezer's trend of thoughts was illustrated by his saying that the book and the sword were handed down from heaven at the same time. God said: "If you observe the Torah, you will be spared from the sword, but if you will not observe its commandments you shall be destroyed by the sword." Rabbi Eliezer frequently debated the meaning of various texts of the Torah with Rabbi Joshua ben Chananiah, and he loved to find hidden meaning whenever the wording of a text was unusual, or there was a superfluous word, or some word was lacking. Rabbi Joshua, on the contrary, sought the simple meaning of texts and attempted to find a rational explanation.

Rabbi Eliezer searched for secrets and mysteries in order to create fantastic embellishments for historical events. Even the miracles that were related he found insufficient and attempted to magnify them as in the case of the *manna* that he declared heaped up to a height of sixty ells.[5]

Other events he saw in a poetic light. When God gave the Torah to the Jews, he said, all the kings shuddered in their palaces. The thunder and the lightning on Mount Sinai confused them and the blast from the *shofar*, which the angels sounded, nearly deafened them. They then gathered around Balaam asking: "Is this not a repetition of the flood?" But Balaam answered: "Foolish people. God swore to Noah long ago never again to bring a flood." "Possibly He meant that He would never cause a flood of water to devastate the earth, but He may bring a flood of fire?" they questioned. Balaam reassured them, "He will bring no flood either of fire or water. The commotion you witness today is due to the fact that God is this day giving the Torah to Israel."[6]

He also said that whenever Jews depend on intercession based on the merits of their forefathers, who are beloved of God, they will be aided and will be victorious over their enemies. This idea he employed in explaining the events of the wars with Amalek as well as the supplying meat to the Jews in the desert. By means of these additions to the miraculous events, he sought to encourage people and to strengthen them in the face of the vicissitudes of dispersion. This policy he continued even when his colleagues disagreed with him.

27

ONKELOS
(OR AQUILAS)
THE PROSELYTE

It HAS BEEN POINTED OUT numerous times that even while the Jews were in a state of political subjection, while their land was devastated and the enemy triumphed and believed that their God has forsaken them, even then there were many people of high estate who gave up their careers and joined the Jews as proselytes. One of these was Onkelos, the son of Kalonymos, or Aquilas, as he is referred to in some places, who was closely related to the Emperor Hadrian.[1]

The story of how Onkelos (Aquilas) turned to Judaism is related in the following manner: Onkelos was the nephew of Emperor Hadrian and wanted to become a proselyte because he greatly approved of the Jewish faith. (Others say that he was brought to this conviction by a Jewish girl.) But he feared his uncle and once he said to him: "I would gladly engage in commerce." Hadrian replied, "If you lack money, my treasury is always at your disposal." But Aquilas continued, "I want to journey throughout the world and to meet many men; therefore I want your advice as to what merchandise I should take." To this Hadrian replied: "If you see merchandise fallen in price, deal in it, for it will surely rise again and you will gain thereby."

Onkelos then went to Palestine and began to study with

Rabbi Eliezer ben Hyrcanus and Rabbi Joshua ben Chananiah. Sometime later he returned to Hadrian and his uncle asked: "Why is your face so changed? It is obvious that you have suffered losses; or has someone done you harm?" Onkelos answered, "Neither."

Then Hadrian said, "You are my kin and I am pained at your poor appearance," and Onkelos declared, "I have learned the Jewish Torah and I have become a Jew."

Greatly shocked Hadrian exclaimed, "Who permitted you to do so?" Onkelos answered, "You told me to do so. When I asked your advice as to what merchandise I should trade in, you told me to get all merchandise that is depreciated, for it would surely rise in value again. I searched among all nations for a people which had fallen lower than the Jews but I found none. I therefore bethought myself that they are sure to rise to new heights again."

This conversation was witnessed by one of the emperor's ministers who praised Aquilas's step. Angered at this, the emperor struck his minister. Shamed, the minister leaped from the roof of his house and killed himself.

Hadrian persisted in trying to find the cause of Aquilas-Onkelos's conversion until the latter told him, "I wanted to know the Jewish Torah." "But you could have learned it without embracing Judaism," the emperor countered. Aquilas-Onkelos replied that a non-Jew can never comprehend the Torah.[2]

There are several versions regarding the conversion. One of them relates that when the emperor heard of it, he sent a few soldiers to bring Aquilas back to Rome, but Aquilas explained a number of Torah verses to them and they too were converted. The emperor then sent other soldiers to bring him back and commanded them not to engage in any discussion with him. When the soldiers took Aquilas-Onkelos and were ready to leave, he said to them: "Let me tell you one thing: among people it is customary that the one of lesser rank lights the way for those of higher rank, but my God is the greatest and still he lights the way that people may see where to go." Upon hearing

this, these soldiers too were converted. The emperor then sent
soldiers for the third time and commanded them neither to
speak nor to listen to anything Onkelos might tell them. As
they were emerging from the house with him, he placed his
hand on the *mezuzah* and said to them: "See the difference
between a human ruler and the great God of Israel. A human
ruler stays within his house and his guards stay at the gate, but
here the people stay inside the house, while the king stays at
the door to guard them." Hearing this these soldiers also were
converted and the emperor sent no more soldiers to bring
Onkelos back.[3]

When Onkelos spoke to the Roman soldiers, or on other
occasions compared the ways of God to the deeds of human
rule, it was entirely in accord with the concepts of that time.
The emperor was then looked up to as divine. Instead of
drawing a parallel between an idol, that the king worshipped,
and God, as the author of the Psalms did, it became customary
at that time to compare the conduct of a human ruler with that
of God.

Still another version of the story of Onkelos' conversion
relates that Onkelos bar Kalonymos was a nephew of Titus (or
of Hadrian as the Gaon of Vilna claims) and wanted to embrace
Judaism. With the aid of witchcraft he had Titus raised from his
grave and asked him: "Which is the worthiest people on
earth?" Titus replied, "The Jews are." Onkelos then asked,
"What would happen if I were to join them?" and Titus said,
"Their teachings are too great and it is impossible to observe
them. If you want to gain greatness there is no better way than
by oppressing the Jews."[4]

The *midrash* relates[5] that before Onkelos converted he
came before Rabbi Eliezer ben Hyrcanus and asked him: "Do
you think it is worthwhile for a person to embrace Judaism if
God offers the proselyte only divine love and bread to eat and
a garment to wear?" Rabbi Eliezer was greatly angered by this
question and answered: "Is it not enough for a proselyte that
he receives that for which our father Jacob prayed. To him God
offers it as a gift, is not that enough?" But this answer did not

satisfy Onkelos and he asked the same question of Rabbi Joshua ben Chananiah. Rabbi Joshua responded kindly saying: "The bread that God offers to the proselyte is not ordinary bread but the Torah. And when it is said that God will give the proselyte a garment to wear, no ordinary garment is meant but the *tallit* of wisdom. If the proselyte is worthy enough to learn the Torah, he deserves the *tallit* of a scholar and he may marry his daughter to a priest, and her sons may become High Priests." Later the scholars said that if Rabbi Joshua had not spoken so kindly to Onkelos he probably would have returned to the Gentiles.

In later years it was told of Onkelos that when he praised the virtues of God, he said that even at the creation of the world God showed his way was different from that of human rulers. A human ruler generally allows his goodness to be praised before he has achieved anything, and before he has established courts or built public baths. His name is mentioned before his deeds. But of God, the deeds are mentioned first and only then follows the praise.

According to the Christian church fathers, Onkelos was an adherent of Christianity first, and Hadrian sent him as the government representative to Jerusalem where new decrees were issued almost daily. At first the Jews were permitted to restore the temple; later it was commanded to convert the city to pagan purposes, and its name was changed to Aelia Capitolina in honor of the Roman god Jupiter. But since Onkelos devoted himself to astrology, which the Christians considered sinful, he was disowned by them and he turned to Judaism.

For those Jews who lived in Greek-speaking countries and did not know Hebrew but who wanted to acquaint themselves with the content of the Torah, there then existed a Greek translation of the Bible known as the *Septuaginta* or the translation of the seventy. But by that time this translation was considerably falsified, and it included incorrect interpretations of various Biblical texts. Onkelos-Aquilas undertook to make a new translation and he accomplished it with the consent of Rabbi Eliezer ben Hyrcanus and Rabbi Joshua ben Chananiah. They later characterized it as an introduction of the beauty of Japheth (Greece) into the tents of Shem.

According to the Jerusalem Talmud, Aquilas was a colleague or a pupil of Rabbi Akiba, and he is said to have sanctioned the new translation of the Bible into Greek. Onkelos's translation of the Bible became accepted among all the scholars, and the Jerusalem Talmud quotes tens of words as Onkelos translated them in order to establish the meaning of various verses. It is also told that in recognition of his authority in explaining the Bible, Hadrian consulted Onkelos in elucidating a certain text.[6]

Today we possess an Aramaic version of Onkelos's Greek translation (*Targum Onkelos*) that has become sanctified almost to the same degree as the Hebrew Bible text. When the Christian church father Hieronymus later translated the Bible into Latin he extensively used Onkelos's Greek translation. Commenting on it he said that it was a poor translation because "the translator slavishly followed the Hebrew text and translated literally without taking into consideration the Greek language and its syntax." The Jews adopted the translation of Onkelos, Hieronymus said, and some Jewish communities that used Greek as the spoken language read Onkelos's translation on the Sabbath instead of the Hebrew text of the Torah or they read both versions.

Onkelos's conversion apparently occurred after the destruction of Jerusalem during the time that Rabban Gamaliel II was Nasi, for Onkelos is frequently mentioned together with Rabban Gamaliel. Thus it is told that they were both in Ashkelon and Rabban Gamaliel performed his ablutions in an ordinary bath house. But since Ashkelon was considered to be outside the boundaries of the land of Israel, Onkelos considered an ordinary bath house there to be unclean and he bathed in the sea instead.[7]

When Rabban Gamaliel died, the Talmud relates that Onkelos burned sixty pounds of incense at the funeral, as was customary during the funeral of a king. When he was asked by the scholars why he did so, he replied, "In my eyes Rabban Gamaliel was more important than a hundred Roman kings."

Aquilas-Onkelos was very pious and although the temple no longer existed, he observed all the regulations of cleanliness pious Jews observed when the temple was still in existence. When Aquilas-Onkelos inherited his father's wealth he refused to derive any benefit from the gold and silver idols and cast them into the Dead Sea.[8]

28

RABBI ELEAZAR BEN AZARIAH

FROM WHAT WAS SAID in previous chapters, it can be seen that the material position of the Jews continually deteriorated due to political circumstances. The Roman officials oppressed and persecuted the population to the limit of their ability. Property was stolen and any opposition was considered as treason against the state and punishable by death. There was no authority from whom to seek redress. The way to Rome was long and difficult, and by the time one decree was rescinded another was issued, and negotiations had to start again to have its effects ameliorated, or a new governor would be appointed who would start his reign with a wave of persecution.

The country sank into deep poverty. For this reason much was said of the wealth of Rabbi Eleazar ben Azariah, and it was said that the tithe only of newborn cattle that he offered amounted to twelve thousand calves a year. Others said that whoever sees Rabbi Eleazar in his dream is to take it as a sign of coming wealth, and when Rabbi Eleazar ben Azariah died it was said that wealth departed from the learned.

The primary source of Rabbi Eleazar's wealth was the inheritance he received at his father's death, but he also engaged in commercial enterprises and traded in wine and oil despite the prohibition of the scholars against trading with the necessities of life in Palestine. It was said of Rabbi Eleazar that he was charitable and whenever he found a person who was willing to study but did not possess the means for his sustenance, he supported him. But in spite of his charities Rabbi Eleazar said that no person should give away more than one-fifth of his possessions for charity.

During the dispute with Rabban Gamaliel II, described before, Rabbi Eleazar ben Azariah was chosen Nasi. The reason why he was chosen from among other candidates who may have been better qualified for the office was because it was believed that he would easily relinquish the office in case of a reconciliation with Rabban Gamaliel. Additionally he was also respected because of his great wealth and his aristocratic origin. Rabban Gamaliel was a descendant of Hillel the Old, five generations removed, who was a scion of the House of David. Rabbi Eleazar ben Azariah was a tenth generation direct descendant of Ezra the Scribe.

When Rabbi Eleazar ben Azariah was chosen Nasi, he was still a very young man—according to tradition he was only 17 or 18 years old. Feeling grieved because of his youth and afraid that people would not respect him because of it, he arose one morning to find that eighteen rows of gray hair had appeared overnight. (According to the Jerusalem Talmud Rabbi Eleazar was really 70 years old when he exclaimed "I am like a man of 70.") But it is certain that despite his youth Rabbi Eleazar was well versed in *Halakha*. His learning he probably gained from his father who was a scholar of such renown that even his brother was always referred to as Simeon, the brother of Azariah.

In praise of Rabbi Eleazar ben Azariah, he was likened to a "basket full of incense" and to a dealer in perfumes who comes to a city and everybody gathers around him asking: "Have you good oils? Have you essence of roses?" and they find that he has all of these. And so the scholars came to Rabbi Eleazar and whatever they sought they found with him. If they asked a question about the Torah he answered from the Torah;

if he was asked about the *Mishnah* he answered from the
Mishnah; the same with exposition, law or legend. He knew
them all and possessed all knowledge.

In later years Rabbi Eleazar ben Azariah was often found
in the company of Rabban Gamaliel. They travelled together
with other scholars in the interests of the people. Although he
was no longer Nasi, he accompanied the leaders of Jabneh
whenever he was asked to do so, and for this reason it was said
that a generation that can boast of a Rabbi Eleazar ben Azariah
should not be considered an orphaned generation.

Rabbi Eleazar ben Azariah especially excelled in exposition. He was careful not to break up the text into its component
words and letters but clung to the realistic interpretation of the
verses. He compared the Torah to a plant: just as a plant grows
even so do the words of the Torah. When he noticed that the
people were losing their confidence and respect for the scholars
because of the differences of opinion that prevailed and that
whenever one of them declared a thing to be clean some one
else would declare it to be unclean, he said: Whenever scholars
differ in the interpretation of the Torah and seemingly contradict each other, for one says clean and the other unclean, one
prohibits while the other permits, it must not be concluded that
there is any doubt about these questions, for all these opinions
are derived from the same Torah. It is necessary to listen closely
and with open heart to try to understand all that is said by
those who declare a thing to be clean as well as by those who
declare it to be unclean, by those who permit as well as by
those who prohibit.[1]

It is told that Rabbi Akiba often tried to draw Rabbi Eleazar
ben Azariah to his own method of exposition, but Rabbi Eleazar
said: "Akiba, what have you to do with *Aggadah*? Finish your
speech and return to pondering the laws pertaining to
plagues." On another occasion Rabbi Eleazar said to Rabbi
Akiba: "Even if you were to speak to me all day I would not be
persuaded." Altogether different were the relations between
Rabbi Eleazar ben Azariah and Rabbi Eliezer of Modiin who
exerted a great influence on his method of exposition. Rabbi
Eleazar ben Azariah even adopted some of the latter's sayings

such as, "Whoever profanes the festivals is like one who worships idols."

Of the teachings of Rabbi Eleazar ben Azariah, particular significance should be attached to his maxims that lay down a practical foundation for man's moral and religious obligations. He said, "All those sins which a man commits against God are forgiven on the Day of Atonement, but sins which are committed by man against man are not forgiven on the Day of Atonement until the man who was sinned against forgives his malefactor."

"He who listens to gossip or gossips about others," Rabbi Eleazar said, "may be compared to a person who bears false witness against his neighbor and should be severely condemned." And commenting on the Biblical injunction to reprimand a person who had committed some wrong, Rabbi Eleazar ben Azariah said: "I doubt if there exists a man today who knows how to reprimand his neighbor properly." Regarding God's prohibition of the eating of the flesh of a pig, Rabbi Eleazar ben Azariah said, "One must not say, 'I am disgusted with it and therefore I cannot eat it,' but one should rather say, 'I would gladly eat it but my Father in heaven has forbidden me.' "

God rewards every good deed even when the doer had his personal benefit in mind. Thus the Egyptians kept the Jews in Egypt for their own benefit, nevertheless God commanded that no Egyptian be put to shame, for we were permitted to live in their land. We must therefore forget the hard labor with which the Egyptians oppressed the Jews and must only remember their generosity in allowing us to live in their country.

It was natural for Rabbi Eleazar ben Azariah to highly value the observance of the Sabbath; nevertheless he said that whenever human life is at stake the Sabbath may be disregarded. Speaking of the significance of the commandments, he concluded that the commandments were like the roots of a tree while the study of the Torah could be compared to its branches. He said: "One whose wisdom is greater than his deeds, what is he like? He is like a tree whose branches are many and whose roots are few and the wind comes and uproots it and turns it on its face. But one whose deeds exceed his wisdom, what is he like? He is like a tree whose branches are few and its roots are many and even though all the winds that are in the world come and blow upon it, they stir it not from its place."

There are few statements of Rabbi Eleazar ben Azariah regarding the Jews as a nation, but one expression is characteristic of his outlook. Pertaining to this subject he said: "It is written in the Torah, "You have this day chosen me as your God and I have chosen you as my people." By this God meant to say, 'You have given me one title and I have granted you one title. Even as you believe that I am the only God in the world so do I believe that you are one people in the world. God is one for his people Israel and Israel is the only people of God.' "

An important question under discussion at that time was the commandment of *Yibum* and *Halitzah*. The Torah commanded that if a man dies childless, it is the duty of his brother to marry the widow. If the brother refuses to do so he must grant the widow *Halitzah*. There then arose the question what to do in case the widow refused to marry her deceased husband's brother. Rabbi Eleazar ben Azariah ruled that if the brother has some defect that would make him socially undesirable he may be forced to grant *Halitzah* to the widow instead of marrying her.

When it was once remarked that a Sanhedrin that issues a death sentence once in seven years should be designated as a "bloody" Sanhedrin, Rabbi Eleazar ben Azariah added that even if a death sentence is issued once in seventy years it is a murderous deed.

The last days of Rabbi Eleazar ben Azariah marked the beginning of the great rebellion. The scholars left Jabneh and the academy was disbanded. Rabbi Eleazar went to Sepphoris and the Sanhedrin moved to Usha. The Talmud relates[2] how the Sanhedrin wandered from Jabneh to Usha and then back to Jabneh. Later it left Jabneh a second time for Usha and thence to Shefarom and other places. Rashi attempts to explain these wanderings by saying that the Sanhedrin followed wherever the Nasi or his son settled. When other historians accepted this explanation they became confused about the sequence of events. What is more likely is that the Sanhedrin left Jabneh due to the persecution of the Roman government and not in order to follow the Nasi. At that time the Jews had no Nasi. Rabban Gamaliel II was dead and the people feared to elect a new Nasi because the Romans disapproved of this office whose holders were looked up to as scions of the royal House of David and were therefore accorded royal honors. The people looked upon the Nasi as a Jewish king who was being interfered with by the Gentile rulers. At the time that the Sanhedrin moved to Usha, it may be assumed that the Roman government had already come to the conclusion that they would never subdue the Jews as long as they observed the Torah. This also seems to be the reason why the Romans allowed every other people to cling to its god as long as they paid their taxes to the government, while at the same time they undertook to annihilate the Jewish people through the suppression of the Torah.

As already stated, we cannot now determine the exact years of the wanderings of the Sanhedrin and whether it visited Usha twice or the repetition was merely an error of the copyists. It is also unknown whether the sessions of the Sanhedrin in Usha were officially sanctioned or whether they took place secretly. Usha was a city in Galilee situated between Acco and Safed. During the constant revolutionary struggles of that time, it is possible that the Roman government had no control over this city or that the military governor overlooked the actions of the Jews. This supposition may explain the transfer of the Sanhedrin from Jabneh to Usha.

It is certain that no cases affecting life were discussed there. But it was necessary to introduce various new rules necessitated by the times. Life continued in its development and the moral and material circumstances of the time required new regulations. It therefore became imperative to meet in order to determine various innovations.

Regarding the convocation at Usha, it is told that a call was sent out to all the elders of Galilee that "whoever is learned should come to teach others, and whoever is not learned should come to learn." Great numbers of people responded to this call and when the time came for them to depart they said: "This place received us in such a friendly manner, why should we leave it empty?" They therefore honored Rabbi Jehudah bar Elai who was a native of the city with an office although he was not the greatest of the scholars but because "the place adds to the honor of the man."

The people who gathered in Usha are referred to in the Talmud as the "wanderers to Usha" because they had lived elsewhere. In bidding farewell to the scholars who returned to their homes Rabbi Jehudah bar Elai said, "May God reward you for your effort in coming here, for one had to come ten miles, another twenty; one came a distance of thirty miles and another forty in order to hear the words of the Torah."[3]

Here are some of the most important regulations adopted by the Sanhedrin in Usha as characteristic of those times.

1) Since every man must provide for his children when they are small and cannot earn their own bread, it was decided that every father must provide for his son until the age of thirteen and for his daughter until the age of twelve. Because of the persecutions of the government, many men were forced to flee their homes. This regulation—the responsibility of the father toward his children—was a hint that one may not leave his family, and if one is forced to save his life by flight he must first provide for his wife and children.

2) If a man wills his property to his children, the heirs must support the father and mother as long as they live, and also the small children who were not included in the will. Until that time, any person who distributed his property to his heirs during his lifetime lost all rights to it and had to depend on the generosity of his heirs for his support.

3) Due to the great need that prevailed among the people, there were some individuals who denied themselves all worldly pleasures and distributed all their possessions to the poor. The assembly at Usha ruled that even one who is used to giving much for charity must not give more than one-fifth of his possessions and after that not more than one-fifth of his annual income.

4) It was ruled that a father should deal kindly with his son until the age of 12. If, after the age of 12, the son refuses to obey his father, the latter was entitled to chastise him with a whip or to refuse him food.

5) If a woman brought to her husband *nikhsei malug* (property belonging to the wife exclusively but the fruits of which the husband could enjoy) and then she sold this property during the lifetime of her husband, the husband was entitled to claim the property after his wife's death.

6) The law of possession was also defined at this gathering (*hazakah*). Just as an ox who gored three times was to be legally considered a dangerous beast and its owner was to be punished according to the law, thus also, if a man held an article for three years, he gained the right of ownership.

29

RABBI ISHMAEL
BEN ELISHA

ON THE HISTORIC DAY THAT the scholars of Jabneh revolted against Rabban Gamaliel and elected Rabbi Eleazar ben Azariah as Nasi, among those gathered was Rabbi Ishmael ben Elisha who participated in the discussions and the decisions of that day.

While still a child he was arrested by the Romans, but it is unknown for what transgression. Also unknown are the circumstances of his death. His name is therefore frequently confused with that of his grandfather who was known as Ishmael the High Priest and who was killed before the destruction of the Temple together with Rabban Gamaliel the Elder.

The story of how Rabbi Joshua ben Chananiah ransomed Rabbi Ishmael from captivity is told in the following manner. Rabbi Joshua ben Chananiah was visiting a certain large Roman city in the cause of his people, and he was told that within the prison there was a beautiful black-eyed, curly-headed Jewish boy who was held captive and was to be sold to some degenerate lascivious Roman. Rabbi Joshua ben Chananiah approached the prison to speak with the boy and he began with a verse from Isaiah (42:24): "Who gave Jacob to the looters and Israel to robbers?" The boy responded with the second half of the verse, "It is God, against whom we have sinned, refusing to follow in his ways and obey his teachings."

When Rabbi Joshua heard this he remarked: "I feel certain that this boy will grow to be a teacher in Israel. I therefore swear that I will not move from here until I have ransomed this boy for whatever money may be asked." Rabbi Joshua did ransom the boy from captivity and before long he became a teacher among the Jews. This was Rabbi Ishmael ben Elisha.[1]

In later years Rabbi Ishmael was a pupil of Rabbi Joshua ben Chananiah, Rabbi Eliezer ben Hyrcanus, and Rabbi Nechunia ben Hakanah. All the scholars came to call him "brother" and when he debated the interpretation of some text with Rabbi Eliezer ben Hyrcanus, the latter said to him: "Brother Ishmael, you can uproot mountains with your wisdom."

Rabbi Ishmael showed the greatest reverence for his teachers. Only with Rabbi Akiba did he differ occasionally in the interpretation of Biblical texts. Rabbi Ishmael followed his own system in expounding the Scriptures and he often said: "The Torah used the language of ordinary people." He therefore maintained that no particular significance need be ascribed to seemingly superfluous words occurring in the Scriptures. Rabbi Akiba, on the other hand, counted the letters of every word and sought hidden meaning in the slightest dot.

Rabbi Ishmael held to a definite system in his studies, and like Hillel the Old, he also established thirteen rules according to which the Torah is to be explained.

Rabbi Ishmael ben Elisha was descended from a priestly family and the legends refer to him as High Priest although he lived after the destruction of the Temple when there could be no high priests. When Rabbi Ishmael said: "I swear by the vestments of my father and by the golden headpiece between his eyes"[2] he probably referred to his grandfather, for we find numerous occasions where grandfathers are called "father."

The permanent residence of Rabbi Ishmael was in the village of Aziz in southern Palestine. From there he frequently came to Jabneh to participate in the deliberations of the

Sanhedrin. This custom he also followed after the Sanhedrin moved to Usha. When he was asked about his ancestral home, he said that it was desolate, for the people of his town settled monetary disputes before one judge only and they also tended sheep in the Land of Israel which was then prohibited.[3]

On the occasion of the death of his sons, the greatest scholars of the time (R. Tarphon, R. Jose of Galilee, R. Eleazar ben Azariah and R. Akiba) came to console him. Before entering the house, Rabbi Tarphon warned them to be careful of every word they said, for Rabbi Ishmael was renowned for his scholarship and it was necessary to speak carefully to him. As they came in, Rabbi Ishmael greeted them with the following words: "When a man sins, he is overcome with sorrow and must disturb his superiors."

Data regarding the death of Rabbi Ishmael is extremely confused. There is a legend that (Rabbi) Ishmael the High Priest was one of the Ten Martyrs. He is considered to be identical with Rabbi Ishmael ben Elisha. But one must bear in mind that none of the High Priests were ever called Rabbi. It seems that the grandson's title of Rabbi was ascribed to his grandfather and the martyrdom of the grandfather was ascribed to the grandson.

The Talmud relates that once, when Ishmael the High Priest was performing the service in the Temple on the Day of Atonement, he went into the Holy of Holies and there he beheld the face of God.[4] On another occasion he is said to have been revealed mysteries by Suriel, the Angel before the face of God.[5] It therefore seems certain that these legends deal with the grandfather of Rabbi Ishmael ben Elisha. It was previously related that during the reign of Agrippa II a pious High Priest, Ishmael ben Phabi officiated and later complained to the Roman authorities about the king. Some historians maintain that Ishmael ben Phabi was the grandfather of Rabbi Ishmael ben Elisha. This, however, is hardly plausible since Ishmael ben Phabi died a natural death and did not suffer martyrdom.[6]

The High Priesthood, that some legends ascribe to Rabbi Ishmael ben Elisha, may be explained by the fact that he was considered worthy of occupying the office of his grandfather.

Since everybody then looked forward to a speedy restoration of the Temple, it was probably said that Rabbi Ishmael ben Elisha was the outstanding claimant to the office and thus they came to call him "High Priest."

It is told that when Rabbi Ishmael and Rabbi Simeon (not designated more clearly) were led to execution, Rabbi Simeon said to Rabbi Ishmael: "Rabbi, my heart quivers with fear, for I do not know for what sins I am being executed." Rabbi Ishmael answered him: "Did never a man come to you to ask a question or to settle a dispute and you made him wait until you finished drinking your water, or lacing your shoe or wrapping your shawl about yourself? By doing so you have transgressed against the commandment of the Torah (punishable by death) not to cause suffering to a widow or an orphan regardless of whether the suffering was great or small."[7]

The same story is related in a similar form but with a clearer designation of the names of the participants:[8] When Rabban Simeon ben Gamaliel was being led to execution, he thought of his past deeds and exclaimed: "Woe to us, that we are led to execution as if we were the greatest criminals who deserve death." Rabbi Ishmael ben Elisha answered him, "Possibly it is so because poor men waited at your door and were not admitted while you ate," but Rabban Simeon ben Gamaliel replied, "I swear by Heaven that I never acted so. On the contrary, whenever I ate I had guards posted outside to bring in all the poor people who should happen to pass that they too may eat with me and praise God."

As they approached the place of execution, each one of them begged of the guard to be executed first. Rabbi Ishmael said: "I am a Priest, the son of High Priests and I must not see my comrade killed." Rabban Simeon said, "I am a Nasi, the son of a Nasi. Do not let me see the death of my friend."

If Rabbi Ishmael was executed together with Rabban Simeon ben Gamaliel, then this could have happened only before the destruction of the Temple and he could have been no other than the grandfather of Rabbi Ishmael ben Elisha. But in other places it is said that Rabbi Ishmael ben Elisha also suffered martyrdom, and it is told that when Rabbi Akiba heard of his death, he rent his garments and exclaimed to his disciples: "We must now prepare for calamity."[9] The Talmud also says[10] that whoever sees Rabbi Ishmael in his dream must expect some calamity to befall him.

A maxim of Rabbi Ishmael ben Elisha was: "Be submissive to the ruler, patient under oppression and receive everyone with cheerfulness.[11] It is also known that in any dispute between man and wife Rabbi Ishmael took the part of the wife. He used to say: "Jewish daughters are beautiful but poverty destroys their beauty." At his death it was said that Jewish women should bewail his passing even as King David did when mourning the death of Saul.

Rabbi Ishmael always heeded the simple meaning of the Biblical texts. When he debated this question with Rabbi Eliezer ben Hyrcanus, he exclaimed: "As I see it, you would have the simple meaning of each verse preceded by your exposition of it."

Rabbi Ishmael also established the rule that there is no prior and no latter in the Torah. The chapters of the Torah were not written according to the chronological order of the events, and when some statement is repeated, this repetition must be considered a sign that a new meaning is intended. The legal regulations, he believed, must be in accord with the text, and in case of contradiction between the accepted law and the text of the Torah, the law must be made to conform with the Torah. Only in three instances did he recognize the validity of laws at variance with the Bible.

In Deuteronomy (12:3) God tells Moses and Aaron that each Jew should take a lamb for the Paschal offering. Rabbi Ishmael asked: "Is it possible that both heard the words of God and that both spoke to the Jewish people?" But he explained it to mean that when Moses spoke, Aaron listened attentively to what he had to say, and it was considered as if both heard the words of God.

In case an ox gores a man and kills him, it is possible that if the animal was known to be dangerous and the owner has been warned, he would therefore have to forfeit his life together with the beast. Nevertheless, the Bible offers the owner of the animal an opportunity to redeem himself by paying a sum of money (Exodus 21:30). Of such a case Rabbi Ishmael said: "Here we may see the great mercy of the Creator who permits a man to redeem himself from a well-earned punishment with money."

If a man owned a Jewish slave and freed him at the end of six years, the Torah commanded that the slave should not be sent away empty-handed, but that he should be given gifts from the herd, the threshing floor, and the wine cellar (Deut. 15:14). Rabbi Ishmael said, "Come and see how great is the mercy of the Creator who says to a man, 'If a Jewish slave has worked for you and you send him away empty-handed, he will have to beg from door to door, or he will be forced to sell himself into slavery again. It is better that you give him some of that with which God has blessed you so that he should not have to beg or sell himself to another master.' "

Mourning for the destroyed Temple occupied a central place in the thoughts of Rabbi Ishmael even as it did with all his colleagues. He said: "Since the Temple is destroyed, it were better not to eat flesh nor to drink wine, but such a decree could not be complied with. It is the same with marriage. So long as Rome rules the Jews with severe decrees and does not allow us to observe all the commandments of the Torah, it were better that no Jew should marry and bring children into the world. But in doing so the seed of Abraham would be annihilated."

As was stated before, no certain information exists concerning the death of Rabbi Ishmael ben Elisha, and there is also no substantiation for the legend relating that a son and a daughter of Rabbi Ishmael the High Priest were sold into slavery to two Roman nobles who attempted to marry them to each other.[12] Whether this event happened to Ishmael the High Priest and contemporary of Rabban Simeon ben Gamaliel the Elder, or it occurred to the children of Rabbi Ishmael ben Elisha, the pupil of Rabbi Joshua ben Chananiah and friend of Rabbi Akiba remains unknown.

Worthy of mention is the Talmudic legend[13] concerning the death of Rabbi Ishmael the High Priest. Because of his great beauty Rabbi Ishmael was loved by the emperor's daughter, and at his execution she begged that his head be given to her. She later removed the skin from the head and had it preserved. It was also said that once every seventy years a man of Rome was chosen, and the head of Rabbi Ishmael was placed on him; sometimes the king himself tried on the skin of Rabbi Ishmael's face or placed his head upon himself.

From all these legends it can be understood that the political situation during the lifetime of Rabbi Ishmael was a sad one and became worse as time went on. The Sanhedrin could no longer meet even in Usha and the academy of Rabbi Ishmael ben Elisha became the center of Jewish spiritual life. Whatever was discussed in that academy later became immortalized in many sayings and decisions of the pupils of Rabbi Ishmael who repeated his moral and legal teachings during his lifetime and after his death.

The location of the academy has not been determined but apparently it was situated in a region over which the Roman government had no control. The Roman rulers had by that time discovered that in order to rule Palestine they must suppress the Jewish religion. It was now prohibited to observe the Jewish faith and maintaining an academy was punishable by death. A law was also promulgated that if any scholar ordains (*semikhah*) a pupil, both the teacher and the pupil were to be executed.

Of the legal and moral teachings of the school of Rabbi Ishmael, some possess permanent ethical value and may be used as examples for all times. Other decisions of the school mirror the political and social conditions of the land. These are some examples: "Whoever lives for forty years without suffering should take it as a sign that he has received his share of peace and should be satisfied,"[14] or, "One may add a measure of ground salt to a basket of grain without being guilty of deception, if together they are sold for the price of grain, because the grain is thereby saved from worms."[15] The same may be said of the opinion: that in time of danger it is permissible to write a bill of divorce and to hand it to the woman, even though the writer does not know the man.[16] Commenting on this opinion Rashi says that it refers to cases such as that of a man who fell into a well and shouted that whoever hears his voice should write a bill of divorce. In such a case one may believe that the man is the person he claims to be, or the opportunity might be lost and his wife remain an *agunah* for life.

One can well imagine that the Jews suffered at that time from spies and false reports carried by people against each other. The school of Rabbi Ishmael ruled therefore that spreading slanderous tales is a sin of the same magnitude as worshipping idols, immorality, or bloodshed.[17]

Other significant teachings of Rabbi Ishmael's school were:

If you see a scholar committing a sin at night, you should not think of it the following day, for he has probably repented. Nor must you doubt it, for he has certainly repented. This rule, however, applied only to corporeal sins. Where money was involved, it was necessary to ascertain that the money had been returned.[18]

He who wishes to be unclean, may remain so; he who wishes to become clean must be aided. One who sells kerosene and spices may be taken as an example. If a customer desires kerosene, he tells him, "Please go and fill the container yourself." But when a customer comes to buy spices, he says to him, "Let us measure it together that we may both enjoy its fragrance."[19]

When God was angry at the sin of the spies, he relented after Moses' prayer and said "I have forgiven according to your words" (Num. 14:20). This means that when the Gentiles learn of it they will say: "Happy is the pupil whose teacher agrees with his words."[20]

God's words are like fire and like a hammer that crushes rocks (Jer. 23:19). Just as a hammer crushes a rock into many pieces even so can God's word be explained in seventy languages.[21]

In order to use clean language, the Scriptures used six words instead of one as in the case of (I Sam. 20:26). Man must learn from it to form his language in the same manner.[22]

Four times a year God sits in judgment over the world: On

Passover He judges the fate of the grain harvest; on *Shavuot* He judges the fate of the fruit of the trees; on *Sukkot* the amount of rain during the coming year is determined. Man is judged on *Rosh Hashanah* and his sentence is signed on the Day of Atonement.[23]

In the conduct of the world, it is law that the innocent may atone for the guilty, but the guilty may not atone for the guilty.[24]

If two people engage in a fight, the Bible says that he who beats his friend shall heal the victim (Ex. 21:20). This indicates that it is permissible to engage in healing the sick.[25]

If you are accosted by the *yetzer hara* (evil desire) drag it into the school. If it is hard as a rock, it will be ground; if it is strong as iron, it will be crushed.[26]

How do we know that the *Shekhinah* is omnipresent? It is said, "When the angel that spoke to you went out, another angel came to meet him" (Zechar. 2:7). Since it does not say that the other angel left after the first one, but that he came to meet him, we may conclude that the *Shekhinah* is present everywhere.[27]

God commanded that during the offering of the burnt sacrifice the priest must wear one garment while burning it and another when carrying out the ashes (Lev. 7:4). This verse means to teach us proper conduct. The garments that one wears while preparing food for his master must not be worn while filling his beaker.[28]

When the Bible commands man to be generous to the poor in order to gain the blessing of God, it uses the word *biglal* (Deut. 15:10). This word shows us that fortune is like a wheel constantly turning. One day fortune smiles on you, the next day on another.[29] (There is a play on words here. *Biglal* means "in order that"; *gilgal* means "a wheel.")

Why is the lobe of one's ear soft while the rest of the ear is hard? So that he may stuff his ear with the lobe when he hears something unworthy.[30]

Whoever gives from his possessions for charitable purposes is saved from Gehenna. It is like the case of two sheep that have to cross a stream, one of which is shorn while the other is not. The shorn sheep wades through the water while the unshorn remains behind.[31]

In the case of a day laborer, the Bible says: "You shall give him his wage the same day before the sun sets, for he is a poor man" (Deut. 24:15). But there is no difference whether the wage of a man, an animal, or the rent for borrowed vessels is concerned. All must be paid for on the same day and their wage must not be held overnight.[32]

When the Bible says, "a man or a woman who commit a sin" (Num. 5:7) it intends to show that in the eyes of the Torah, a woman is punishable for her sins the same as a man.[33]

At noon Friday the *shofar* was blown six times as a sign that the Sabbath was beginning. At the first blast of the *shofar*, all men ceased working in the fields. Then they all came from near and far and gathered before the gates of the city so that they might enter it together. The stores were still open, but the bolts for the doors were held in readiness. After the second blast of the *shofar* it was necessary to lock the stores, but the pots still remained in the ovens. The *shofar* was blown a third time, after which all pots were removed from the ovens and candles were lit. After that the people waited the period of time it takes to bake a small fish, or to place the bread in the oven, and then three blasts of the *shofar* were blown at once and the Sabbath began.[34]

30

RABBI TARPHON

A REMARKABLE AND UNUSUAL personality of that time was Rabbi Tarphon. The name Tarphon is derived from the Greek Tryphon. He is mentioned once by that name in the Jerusalem Talmud. The period of his influence and activity extended from the destruction of the Temple until the destruction of Betar.

Rabbi Tarphon was descended from a priestly family and he told that once while pronouncing the benediction together with the other Priests, he bent close to the High Priest in order to hear him pronounce the express name of God, and was seized by a great terror.[1]

On another occasion, when the question was discussed of whether the singers in the Temple must be without fault even as the Priests were required to be, Rabbi Tarphon swore that he remembered his mother's brother, who was lame but nevertheless blew a trumpet in the Temple while the Levites sang. Rabbi Akiba asked him whether it was not a special festive occasion when such a thing would be permitted. Rabbi Tarphon replied: "It is as you say. It is remarkable that I witnessed it but forgot the nature of the occasion, while you were not there yet you know what happened."[2]

What happened to Rabbi Tarphon at the time of the

destruction and how he escaped the city is unknown. Later he settled in Lud and often came to Jabneh to participate in the sessions of the Sanhedrin. He was also present on the memorable day when Rabban Gamaliel was impeached. But he did not figure as a candidate for the office of Nasi despite his wealth, and his great scholarship that was so extensive that whenever he sat with other scholars and someone came to ask a question, he was the first to express an opinion.

As a scholar he was called "the father of Israel,"[3] and every time a dispute arose regarding some law he was very severe in his expressions. He frequently invoked old traditions with an oath that "if it is not as he says, then may he lose his children." When, after such an oath, Rabbi Akiba said to him: "I think that you have heard wrong," Rabbi Tarphon conceded his mistake and said: "Akiba, whoever departs from you is like one who departs from life." Whenever Rabbi Akiba met someone who did not show proper respect for Rabbi Tarphon, he was ready to punish him severely. Thus it is told that one of the pupils, Jehudah ben Nehemiah, once asked Rabbi Tarphon a difficult question that he could not answer. Rabbi Akiba said to that pupil, "Your face is joyous that you have asked the old man something he could not answer. I will not be surprised if you do not live long."

The legend further relates that this occurred sometime before Passover, and when the scholars gathered again on *Shavuot,* Jehudah ben Nehemiah no longer lived.

But we must not conclude that Rabbi Tarphon's inability to answer questions happened frequently, for his learnedness was likened to a heap of nuts.[4] The meaning of this simile is explained[5] in this manner—just as several other nuts roll from the heap when one nut is taken away, so also did Rabbi Tarphon respond to questions; he immediately adduced proof from the Scriptures, the *Midrash,* the *Mishnah* as well as from *Halakhah* and *Aggadah.*

Although the Temple was no longer in existence, Rabbi Tarphon continued to gather tithes from all those who would offer them. Rabban Gamaliel once met him in the morning and asked why he was absent from the academy on the previous day. Rabbi Tarphon replied that he was occupied with the "service." Greatly surprised, Rabban Gamaliel said: "Your words make me wonder for you say that you were engaged in service, but I do not know of any service that had to be performed on that day." To this Rabbi Tarphon answered, "The eating of tithes by a Priest in a city in the Land of Israel is like performing the service in the Temple."

When Rabbi Tarphon accepted tithes, he did so not out of poverty, for he was a wealthy man. He evidently followed the custom in order to give people an opportunity to fulfill the commandment of offering tithes; he never distinguished among the givers and accepted tithes from all. Nevertheless he was not greedy and generally returned the sums he received for a *pidyon haben* in his capacity of a "Cohen."[6] To aid the people during a time of famine, he exercised his priestly prerogative and married three hundred women (!) in order that they might partake of the tithes as wives of a Priest.[7] In telling this story the Jerusalem Talmud employs the word *he'erim* to indicate that he tricked the law.

In public Rabbi Tarphon always conducted himself modestly, so that no one should recognize him outside the academy and so that he should derive no benefits because of his knowledge of the Torah. Only once did he reveal his identity in order to escape a beating. As he was trying to take some fruit from his own vineyard, the watchman caught him and was going to beat him. Rabbi Tarphon exclaimed: "Woe to Tarphon that he is caught as a thief." The watchman then recognized and released him and since then Rabbi Tarphon was wont to say, "Woe is me that I have made use of the crown of the Torah."

Constant differences of opinion regarding interpretations of the commandments existed between Rabbi Tarphon and Rabbi Akiba, but this did not mar the great friendship by which they were bound. Rabbi Tarphon once gave Rabbi Akiba a sum of money to buy a field in order that they should have a permanent income and be able to devote themselves to the Torah exclusively. Rabbi Akiba took the money and distributed it to poor scholars.

This story is related in two versions. According to one

version[8] Rabbi Akiba said to Rabbi Tarphon: "If you wish, I will buy you a village or two." Rabbi Akiba took this money and distributed it to the poor. Sometime later Rabbi Tarphon met Rabbi Akiba and said: "Where are the villages that you were to buy for me?" Rabbi Akiba took him by the hand and led him to the academy where he had distributed the money.

The other version relates[9] that Rabbi Tarphon gave Rabbi Akiba six hundred measures of silver and asked him to buy a field from which they might both derive an income and be able to devote themselves to study. Rabbi Akiba distributed the whole sum to the scribes and the students of the academy. Some time later Rabbi Tarphon asked, "Have you bought the field of which I told you?" When Rabbi Akiba said that he had bought the field, Rabbi Tarphon asked if he could see it and Rabbi Akiba showed him the scribes and students to whom he had given the money.

Characteristic of Rabbi Tarphon's outlook was the occasion when he sat together with other Elders in Lud and they discussed the question of what is of greater importance, study or the fulfillment of the commandments. Rabbi Tarphon said that observance of the commandments was of greater importance. Rabbi Akiba maintained that study is more important, and the other scholars concurred with the opinion of Rabbi Akiba, for "learning leads one to the observance of the commandments."

The opinion, that observance of the commandments is of the highest importance, is also expressed in other statements of Rabbi Tarphon who compared the relationship of man to his Creator with the relationship existing between a laborer and his employer. For instance, one of his maxims states: "The day is short and the work is great and the laborers are sluggish, the wages are high and the master is urgent." He also said, "It is not incumbent upon you to finish the work, nor are you free to avoid it. If you have learned much Torah you will be well rewarded, and your master is trustworthy that he will pay your wages."[10]

Of the observance of the commandments, Rabbi Tarphon was led to speak of work in general. He said that God did not permit the *Shekhinah* to rest among the Jews until they had completed the building of the tabernacle. He also said that a man may die from idleness.

Rabbi Tarphon generally embellished his speech with expressions from the Torah which in his mouth assumed a new significance. Wishing to express approval, he exclaimed *kaftor vaferach* (a button and a bloom); to show disapproval he said, "my son shall not go with you" as an indication that he did not care to indulge in dispute or to openly express his disagreement.

A bitter struggle was then being waged against the early Christians who were Jews, and Rabbi Tarphon who was their severest opponent. He engaged in disputes with them in an attempt to dissuade them from their beliefs. This fact is also mentioned in the writings of the Christian patriarch, the martyr Justinus. Rabbi Tarphon then said: "May I lose my children if I would not burn their books, together with the mention of God that is made in them, if I could only obtain them."

It has been remarked that Rabbi Tarphon frequently exclaimed, "May I lose my children if this is not thus and so." He did lose some of his children and his wife also died. Remaining a widower and the father of children, he chose his wife's sister for a bride, and after the wedding he said to her: "Go feed the children of your deceased sister."

It is also necessary to note the great respect in which Rabbi Tarphon held his mother. It is said that she once lost a shoe and descended barefoot to search for it. Rabbi Tarphon placed his hand under her foot that she might not hurt herself while stepping on the bare ground.

It is to be assumed that Rabbi Tarphon lived more than seventy years. Traditions vary regarding his death. Some maintain that he was one of the Ten Martyrs, while others deny it.[11]

To the nature of Rabbi Tarphon's character, it should be added that despite his angry disposition he nevertheless said that if he were a member of the Sanhedrin at the time when it had the right to condemn people to death, there would not have been a single death sentence passed.

31

RABBI JOSE OF GALILEE

T HE DISTRICT OF GALILEE IN northern Palestine was inhabited by non-Jews throughout the period of the existence of the First Temple. Only in later years, during the time of the Second Temple, did Jewish settlements begin to extend into Galilee as the density of the population in the rest of the land increased. The emigrants who left the cities of Judea to settle in Galilee were mostly people poor in economic and spiritual resources, and there developed in Galilee a native type of *amei aratzim*. When these men of Galilee visited Jerusalem and later Jabneh, or some other city where the Sanhedrin resided, they were ridiculed for their childish naïveté and frequently called "Galilean fools." The inhabitants of Galilee were also easily recognized by their manner of speech and by their uncouth behavior, and the opinion was commonly held that Galileans were fools incapable of learning, and that it was a waste of effort to attempt to change them.

Then there suddenly arose a Galilean scholar, Rabbi Jose of Galilee, who came to be ranked with the highest from his very first appearance. It occurred during a discussion regarding the rules governing the eating of the flesh of a first born animal that Rabbi Jose arose from among the disciples and proved that the two leaders of the academy—Rabbi Tarphon and Rabbi

Akiba—were mistaken. One can readily imagine the surprise of all those gathered when they heard the Galilean present many proofs on behalf of his contention and they saw his firmness of conviction.[1] When Rabbi Ishmael ben Elisha heard the arguments of the Galilean, he asked that Rabbi Akiba be told that he was in error and that the law was as the Galilean said.

Since that day Rabbi Jose remained among the scholars of Jabneh and he was accorded greater honors from day to day. Everybody respected him. His opinions generally conflicted with those of Rabbi Akiba and although he considered him to be his teacher he once remarked, "Were you to argue all day, I would not accept your opinion."[2] Another time he interrupted Rabbi Akiba during a lecture and said: "How much longer will you speak of the *shekhinah* as one speaks of an everyday subject?"[3]

Later it was said that Rabbi Jose of Galilee "gathers every crumb of Torah wherever he can, even from the least of the disciples, even as God chose Mount Sinai, the smallest of the mountains, from which to hand down the Torah to the Jews."[4]

Regarding the scholarship of Rabbi Jose, it may be said that he succeeded in discerning that which others failed to see. Gentle as he was in his conduct, he nevertheless was severe to all those who tried to turn the Jews away from God and he said: "If someone tries to prove to you that his god is the right one, you must not believe him even if he were to stop the sun in the middle of the sky."[5]

Some historians maintain that Rabbi Jose was well advanced in age when he came to Jabneh from Galilee, and that he was already renowned at that time for his scholarship. They believe that, since Galilee was affected less than other sections of Palestine at the beginning of the revolt preceding the destruction, it probably became a place of refuge for the peace-loving elements among the Jews who fled there to escape the vengeance of the rebels. Among the refugees was the wealthy Azariah, the father of Rabbi Eleazar, who sent his son to study with Rabbi Jose.

Rabbi Jose was widely known for his piety and the belief was widespread that were a drought to occur and were Rabbi

Jose to pray for rain, he would undoubtedly obtain from God whatever he requested. It was also known that Rabbi Jose was unhappy in his domestic life. The wife of Rabbi Jose, who was also his niece, was a wicked woman. She frequently shamed him in the presence of his pupils and when they asked their master why he did not divorce her, he answered that he could not do so because he did not possess enough money to pay her enormous *ketubbah* (dower-rights).

Rabbi Jose once returned home from the academy accompanied by his pupil, Rabbi Eleazar ben Azariah. His wife paid no attention to him nor to his guest, and when he asked her whether she had any food prepared she replied angrily: "There is some boiled grass in the pot." Rabbi Jose uncovered the pot and found in it the flesh of fattened hens. Together with his pupil he partook of the repast. Rabbi Eleazar ben Azariah then asked: "She said that there was only boiled grass in the pot when it contained the flesh of hens. Why should she deceive you so?" Rabbi Jose replied: "Very probably a miracle occurred. She put grass into the pot, just as she told me, but the grass turned into the flesh of fattened hens."

After the meal was finished Rabbi Eleazar ben Azariah said, "Rabbi, send this woman away from your house. She does not know how to appreciate your worth." But Rabbi Jose said, "She has a large *ketubbah* and I have no money to pay it." Rabbi Eleazar answered, "We, your pupils, will provide the money to pay her *ketubbah* and send her away." Rabbi Jose then did as his pupils advised him.

The woman then married the night watchman of the city who, soon after, lost all his possessions and also became blind. He was forced to give up his position as watchman, and his wife had to lead him from house to house to beg for alms for their sustenance. But whenever she came to the street where Rabbi Jose lived, she passed it by. Her husband then asked her why she did not lead him through the street of Rabbi Jose the Galilean, for he had heard that Rabbi Jose was very charitable, and she replied: "I was divorced by him and I could not bear to go into his house to beg for alms."

But one day the watchman and his wife had made the

rounds of the whole city and received no money. She then entered the street where Rabbi Jose lived but she skipped his house. When the blind man noticed this, he began to beat her with his cane. Rabbi Jose heard her cries and when he realized their condition, he lodged them both in one of his houses and provided them with sustenance all the days of their lives.[6]

Especially interesting are the commentaries of Rabbi Jose on the commandments of the Torah. Sometimes he sought to lighten the burden of the commandments while at other times he tried to make them even more severe. The law concerning a "disobedient son" (*ben sorer u'moreh*) the other scholars interpreted so that it would have made it impossible to condemn him to death. Since a "disobedient son" could not be condemned unless he was also a "glutton," they declared that he could not be considered as such until he consumed a pound of meat, half-boiled and half-raw, at one gulp and at the same time drank half-a-quart of the best Italian wine at one sip. His gluttonous feast had to be made in the company of immoral youths and was to be bought with money stolen by the "disobedient son" from his father. In addition, they ruled that the "disobedient son" had to be at least thirteen years and one day of age (but not much older than that), for then he could no longer be considered a "son" dependent on his father. The culprit must have had both a father and a mother who were required to be of the same opinion and appearance, for both had to lead him to court and had to present the same complaints against him.

But Rabbi Jose believed that the essence of the sin of a "disobedient son" was gluttony and he believed that such a culprit deserved the death sentence because of his possible future. Engaging in such gluttony, a "disobedient son" was sure to waste his father's wealth and to turn to stealing in order to satisfy his habits. He therefore believed that the Torah preferred his death while still innocent rather than his execution after committing crimes.[7]

Rabbi Jose followed in the footsteps of Rabbi Akiba in the matter of expounding every saying of the Torah that might have seemed to be superfluous. Thus he explained the verse "but my Sabbaths you shall observe" (Ex. 31:13) to indicate that certain labors may be performed on the Sabbath, such as work in the Temple or in order to save a human life. This interpretation he based on the word *akh* in the Hebrew text.[8]

In the case of many other commandments Rabbi Jose sought to lighten the burden of their observance. He ruled that no *bikurim* (offering of first fruits) need be brought from the lands east of the Jordan because it was not characterized as a land of milk and honey.[9] He established the rule that so long as a person is engaged in the observance of one commandment he is absolved from observing any other commandments at the same time.[10] The verse, "Before an old man you shall rise," (Lev. 19:32) he explained to mean that only a scholarly person is to be accorded that honor.[11]

He also expressed opinions that were not accepted. He declared, for instance, that the prohibition against deriving any benefit from leavened bread during the Passover is not effective on all the seven days of the holiday. Leavened bread, which was held over the Passover, he suggested, could certainly be used.[12] In Rabbi Jose's native city people were in the habit of eating meat of fowl with milk, and Rabbi Jose attempted to justify this on the ground that birds do not yield milk and the prohibition, "you should not boil a kid in its mother's milk," therefore did not apply to fowl.[13]

Some Biblical descriptions of historical events, such as the exodus from Egypt and the giving of the Torah, Rabbi Jose raised to great poetic heights. Expounding the verse, "why do you skip on wrinkled hills," (Psalms 68:17) he said: "When God was ready to give the Torah from Mount Sinai, the other mountains skipped about in confusion. They argued among themselves and each one claimed the honor of having God give the Torah to the Jews from its top."

In describing the rending of the sea before the Jews, Rabbi Jose said that when the Jews jumped into the sea even before the waters parted before them, Mount Moriah was torn from its place, and the altar upon which Isaac was to have been sacrificed hastened to the sea. Only when the image of Isaac lying bound on the altar and Abraham standing over him with his slaughtering knife could be seen did the sea part its waters, for only because of the merit of Abraham's offering of Isaac was the sea rent for the Jews.

And when the Jews emerged on the other side of the sea and they began to chant songs of praise, even the children in their mothers' arms turned their faces heavenward and sang and the babies left their mothers' breast and also sang.[14]

No mention is made of the death of Rabbi Jose of Galilee. It is possible that at the inception of Bar Kochba's revolt, he returned to Galilee and there he died.

32

RABBI AKIBA
BEN JOSEPH

THE HIGHEST PLACE OF HONOR among all our national heroes undoubtedly belongs to Rabbi Akiba ben Joseph. Like the lives of all historically outstanding personalities, Rabbi Akiba's life history is also surrounded with legends that shed a heavenly glow over his origin and personal development.

Rabbi Akiba's father was a proselyte, or the son of a proselyte, and he traced his descent from Sisera, the field commander of Jabin, the king of Hazor. In his youth Rabbi Akiba was a shepherd in the service of the wealthy Kalba Savua.

Kalba Savua (sometimes referred to as Ben Kalba Savua) was one of the wealthiest men in Jerusalem before its destruction and he was renowned for his charities. During the war against the Romans, he undertook to supply the inhabitants of Jerusalem with food for the duration of the siege of the city. Different opinions exist regarding the meaning of his name. Some explain it to indicate that he was a descendant of Kaleb ben Jephuneh while others say that he obtained it because of his generosity—if a poor man came to his house hungry as a dog, he left it satisfied. But there is the much simpler explana-

257

tion that the name Kalba Savua meant a "storeroom filled with grain."

Rachel, the daughter of Kalba Savua, loved Akiba and promised to become his wife if he would agree to devote himself to learning. It is told that Akiba was then already close to forty years of age, and he did not even know the alphabet. He had a son, by a previous wife, who was also an uneducated man. The love of Kalba Savua's daughter was variously interpreted. Some said that it was but the whim of a rich man's spoiled daughter who became infatuated with a shepherd. Others reasoned that the shepherd must have possessed such noble traits as would captivate even so noble a lady as the daughter of Kalba Savua.

When Kalba Savua heard of this he disowned his daughter and vowed to disinherit her.[1]

It is necessary to mention that when Rachel asked Akiba to devote himself to learning, he at first doubted the wisdom of her request. At that time he felt a considerable disdain for scholars and also doubted his own capabilities of learning. But one day he happened to see how falling drops of water had, in time, hollowed out a stone, and he said to himself: "If water, which is soft, could hollow out the hard stone, the words of the Torah, which are hard, will certainly make an impression on my soft heart."

Together with his son he went to a teacher and began his studies. But after he finished studying the Torah, history makes no more mention of the development of his son but continues to tell of Rabbi Akiba alone. For many years he was a disciple of Nachum of Gimso, then he turned to Rabbi Eliezer ben Hyrcanus and Rabbi Joshua ben Chananiah to learn the ways of the oral law. Rabbi Eliezer paid not the slightest attention to him, allowing him only to audit his expositions but otherwise ignoring him. Rabbi Joshua, on the other hand, treated him seriously, for he appreciated his great desire to learn.

For a long time Rabbi Akiba sat at the feet of Rabbi Eliezer and Rabbi Joshua. In later life he told that he served them both, did whatever they commanded him to do, and even kneaded the dough for their bread. From this we may conclude how difficult Rabbi Akiba's circumstances were. He was a poor man and his father-in-law would not aid him in the least. He gained his livelihood by gathering a bundle of wood every day, half of which he sold, and from the other half he made faggots to light the house while he studied. His neighbors then complained that the smoke from the faggots inconvenienced them at night, and they advised him to sell all the wood and to buy oil instead.[2]

When, despite his work, there still was not enough food in the house, his wife Rachel cut off her beautiful braids and sold them to enable her husband to devote more time to studying the Torah.[3]

For thirteen years Rabbi Akiba studied with Rabbi Eliezer ben Hyrcanus and the latter never deigned to ask an opinion of him, until one day Rabbi Akiba began to ask questions of his master who could find no answer to them. Rabbi Joshua then addressed Rabbi Eliezer with the following verse, "Is not this the people that you have disdained? Go and contend with them," by which he meant to say that here was one whom Rabbi Eliezer constantly ignored and who now posed questions that could not be answered.[4]

Another description of those events relates that after an absence of twelve years, Rabbi Akiba returned to his native city accompanied by 12,000 disciples. Listening to what was going on within his house once, he heard his wife arguing with a neighbor who asked her, "How much longer will you lead the life of a widow?" and she replied that if she were sure that her husband was devoting himself to learning she would gladly wait another twelve years.[5] Upon hearing this Rabbi Akiba returned to his studies for another twelve years and then returned accompanied by 24,000 thousand disciples.

One can easily imagine what the poor woman felt when she saw her husband surrounded by so many thousands of disciples. As she made her way through the throngs and fell at his feet, Rabbi Akiba's disciples wanted to push her away, but he said to them: "Leave her be. That which I possess today and from which you all benefit I acquired only because of her."

When Kalba Savua heard that one of the outstanding Jewish scholars had arrived, he came to him so that he might absolve him of his vow regarding his daughter. At that time Kalba Savua repented having allowed his daughter to suffer hunger for twenty-four years. Rabbi Akiba made himself known to his father-in-law. They were reconciled and Kalba Savua gave him half of his wealth.

The Talmud relates that Rabbi Akiba had golden and silver tables in his house and that he ascended his bed on golden steps. As a reward for his wife who had cut off and sold her hair to help him, he bought the most expensive adornments, one was an image of Jerusalem engraved in gold that she wore on her head in place of the hair she had cut off. But such ornaments were not allowed to be worn by married women because of the mourning for the destroyed Temple. The wife of Rabban Gamaliel the Nasi envied the wife of Rabbi Akiba and told her husband. But Rabban Gamaliel said, "If you had done for your husband what she did for hers, I would buy you an ornament just like it."[6]

As might have been expected, Rabbi Eliezer was dissatisfied with the appearance of a new star in the firmament of Jewish learning, for it was obvious that he would tread new paths. Rabbi Eliezer clung strictly and without question to the traditional interpretations of the Torah. Rabbi Akiba, on the other hand, evolved a new method. He believed that the oral law was not a predetermined matter without spirit and incapable of further development that was not adduced from the text and the letters of the Torah.

The Torah as we have it, Rabbi Akiba said, is complete and there is nothing lacking or superfluous in it. In its entirety it is all content without embellishment; it contains no artistic descriptions and no useless words. Every letter and every dot possesses some special significance.

Wherever there occurs a repetition of a word it probably serves to indicate a special meaning. Even the connecting words and articles such as "if," "the," "but," and "also" are subject to interpretation. When it seems that there is a superfluous word in the Torah, it is only because the person cannot grasp its meaning with his limited intelligence. Even the word *leimor,* which occurs frequently in the Bible has its significance and could be expounded. The article *et* in the verse "you shall fear the Lord your God" he explained to indicate that man must fear both God and his Torah. Another time he modified his explanation to mean that man must fear God and the scholars.

Until that time scholars considered only the content of the law and not its form. The oral law was not classified according to content and it was necessary to study much and to possess a tremendous memory in order to retain the rulings of all the scholars. Rabbi Akiba began to classify each law according to its content, and he laid the foundation for the compilation of the *Mishnah* which was finally written down and edited many years later.

Regarding the significance of Rabbi Akiba's interpretations of the Torah a legend[7] exists that relates that when Moses ascended heaven to receive the Torah he saw God attaching little crowns to the letters of the Torah. Moses said to God: "Lord of the world! What prevents you from giving the Torah without these crowns?" and God answered: "Some day after many generations there will arise a man Akiba ben Joseph who will derive many laws from every little dash and it is for his sake that I prepare these little crowns." Moses then said, "Will you show him to me? I would gladly look upon him." God commanded Moses to look among the scholars sitting on the eighth bench and he saw there a man and he heard him expound to his disciples, but he did not understand a word of what was being said although he heard the man conclude, "This I received as law to Moses from Mount Sinai."

Then Moses said, "Lord of the world! You have such a great man and You give the Torah through me?" and God replied, "It is My will." Moses thereupon said, "You have shown me the man, now reveal to me his end," and God answered, "Turn backwards and you will see." Moses looked and saw the body of Rabbi Akiba being torn to pieces.

A similar legend is also related in the Talmud that God revealed to Adam the record of all the coming generations that will descend from him together with their scholars and their leaders, and He also showed him the generation of Rabbi Akiba. Adam greatly enjoyed this knowledge but was saddened at the sight of the death that awaited Rabbi Akiba. He attempted to obtain an easier death for him, but his request was denied.[8]

Rabbi Akiba headed an academy in Bnei Brak located southeast of Jaffa. He frequently came to the sessions of the Sanhedrin in Jabneh and no important law was ever adopted without his participation. Once he arrived late for a session at the academy and remained sitting outside. It was then said that "the Torah is outside" and no decisions were adopted until he came in.

Attempting to describe the work of Rabbi Akiba, the scholars said that he was like a man who goes through the streets with a basket in his hand and picks up whatever he can find. If he finds wheat he puts it in his basket; if he finds barley he picks it up; the same with beans and lentils. Rabbi Akiba did the same when he sought to introduce order into the laws.[9]

It is claimed that Rabbi Akiba was versed in the various sciences such as medicine and astronomy. He also spoke many languages and on several occasions he accompanied Rabban Gamaliel on the latter's trips to Rome in the cause of the Jewish people. When Rufus (or Tyranos Rufus as he is called in the Talmud) was governor of Palestine, he frequently debated with Rabbi Akiba many matters pertaining to the Jewish faith and the Torah. And when the Roman government began to suppress the observance of the Torah, Rabbi Akiba could easily counteract these decrees with the help of Rufus.

One of the brightest phases of Rabbi Akiba's life, perhaps the outstanding event, was his participation in Bar Kochba's revolt. Some historians claim that Rabbi Akiba was one of the leaders of the revolt, but this is probably an exaggeration as are the statements of others that Rabbi Akiba merely preached about Bar Kochba but took no active part in the revolt.

Rabbi Akiba was already too old to take his place in the foremost ranks of the revolution. But his 24,000 disciples, who probably did join Bar Kochba's forces, died according to legend between Passover and *Lag B' Omer*. Rabbi Akiba's trip throughout the cities of Palestine and also to those beyond the frontier in order to establish which year is to be *ibur* (a year containing thirteen months that occurs thrice every eight years according to the lunar calendar) was probably undertaken as a journey of agitation for the cause of the revolution. The same may be said with a large degree of certainty regarding the *seder* in Bnei Brak where the most prominent Jewish leaders were assembled in Rabbi Akiba's house.

It is regrettable that the records of this revolt are so meager. The description of the destruction of the Temple includes some accounts of the destruction of Betar, and it is very difficult to separate them. Definitive descriptions of Bar Kochba's activities are found only in the Jerusalem Talmud[10] and in the *Midrash Eikhah Rabati*. But these are also difficult to sort out and mixed with terrifying legends. In addition a description of Bar Kochba's revolutionary wars exists in the writings of the Roman historian, Dio Cassius, who described the Jewish hero in a horrible way. It thus becomes necessary to glean the events from various other occurrences of that time and leave the rest to the imagination.

When Rabbi Akiba saw Bar Kochba in all his glory, he is said to have exclaimed, "This is the king, the Messiah." He invoked the verse from the prophet (Haggai 2:21) that foretold that God would cause the heaven and the earth and the sea and the dry land to quake and that He would destroy the thrones of the Gentile kingdoms; their strength would be made as naught and their chariots and horses would be overthrown so that one would be slain by the sword of the other. Rabbi Akiba thus exerted a profound influence on the people. Hosts of people arrived daily to pledge their allegiance to Bar Kochba, for they all believed the words of Rabbi Akiba that Bar Kochba was the long-awaited Messiah and that he would bring about the redemption of his people.

Because of his belief in Bar Kochba, Rabbi Akiba allowed himself to be insulted by an obscure colleague, Rabbi Jochanan ben Toratha, who said to him: "Akiba, grass will grow out of your cheek bones and the Messiah will still not have arrived."

To explain the reason behind Bar Kochba's immediate

popularity, Talmudic sources relate that when the Roman soldiers hurled stones with their machines at the walls of the Jewish cities, Bar Kochba ascended the walls and catching the stones between his knees, hurled them back at the enemy killing a few of them with each stone. Dio Cassius, on the other hand, relates that Bar Kochba would light a flaxen faggot and hold it in his mouth to convince his followers that he was a fire eater.

Today we know definitely that the political situation of that time was intolerable. The Temple was destroyed and the Jewish state had not existed for sixty years. Only a handful of the older generation who remembered the Temple still survived, but its memory lived in the heart of the people and everyone dreamed of its restoration. The Temple hill had been transformed into a Roman soldiers' camp and the Jews were in a worse position than slaves in their own country. The Roman governor of Palestine was the murderous despot Tyranos Rufus and he persecuted them relentlessly and ridiculed their suffering. As the conditions became unbearable, the Jews thought constantly of liberation and whenever they gathered they would ask each other: "Will the Roman legions always keep their foot upon the neck of Judea? How much longer will the Roman eagle sink its claws into the living body of the Jewish people?"

Bar Kochba then undertook to organize a Jewish army of hundreds of thousands of men with the consent of Rabbi Akiba, and he succeeded in maintaining his revolt for three and a half years. Talmudic sources estimate the number of Bar Kochba's soldiers at 400,000. Dio Cassius relates that the number was 580,000 or nearly 200,000 more than the Talmudic figure. People streamed in from all sides and even the Samaritans, the traditional enemies of the Jews, forgot their hatred and joined the Jews in the struggle against Rome. Numerous neighboring people also joined the uprising in the hope that the liberation of Judea would also bring freedom from the Roman yoke for them.

Wishing to test the bravery of his soldiers, Bar Kochba commanded each of them to cut off, or with his own teeth, to bite off one of his fingers. But the scholars sent the following message to Bar Kochba, "Why do you cause your people to cripple themselves?" Bar Kochba replied by asking, "What other method shall I use to test their bravery?" And he was advised to command each soldier to uproot a cedar of Lebanon with his bare hands while riding by on a horse. Bar Kochba subsequently had 220,000 soldiers each missing a finger and another 200,000 who uprooted trees bare-handed while riding by on a horse.

Sometime after this experiment, Bar Kochba is said to have addressed the following words to God: "Since You have forsaken us and are longer with us in our wars, we ask that You should not interfere. We do not require Your aid but only ask that You should not aid our enemies."

One can see that the recorded descriptions of that war are very meager and at times contradictory. Nearly all the scholars of that time, with the exception of Rabbi Akiba, did not support the revolution and when it ended in failure, they condemned Bar Kochba. Of Rabbi Akiba's description of Bar Kochba as "a star arisen from Jacob," they declared that he should not have used the word *kokhav* (a star) but rather the word *kozeiv* (a deceiver).

The revolt was mounted during the famous *seder* night mentioned in the *Haggadah*. Several *tannaim* met in the home of Rabbi Akiba in Bnei Brak, where he headed a large academy with many thousands of students, to discuss the miracles of the departure from Egypt, because it was necessary to come to a final decision regarding the burning question of that day—the impatience of the younger Jewish generation and their spirit of rebellion against Roman tyranny.

The Roman authorities knew the mood of the people and attempted to suppress it. Informers mingled with the Jewish young men and every suspicious remark was reported to the Romans. Akiba and his guests therefore feared to openly discuss the problem of Roman oppression and they spent the whole night discussing the "exodus from Egypt" and the great number of plagues that were visited on Pharaoh, to the number of 250, for they considered ten plagues insufficient in view of the suffering of the Jews. They also sought to console themselves with the hope that God would punish the enemies of his people as they deserved.

This "debate" lasted all night while crowds of impatient people stood outside and waited for the decision of the scholars. In the light of the Passover moon, this group of men who came to celebrate the *seder* in the home of Rabbi Akiba telling each other of the wondrous valor of Bar Kochba, must have seemed strange indeed. But meanwhile the hours passed. As the moon paled and the horizon became suffused with crimson, the pupils of Rabbi Akiba began to look into the house where the scholars sat, still debating the "departure from Egypt." The people realized the danger of the situation, for Roman soldiers might arrive at any moment and inquire why the *seder* was lasting so long. Their patience finally exhausted, they opened the doors and shouted, "Our teachers, the time for the morning *Shema* has arrived," hinting that it was time to end the debate.

This exclamation put an end to the discussion. The impatience of the younger men triumphed over the weariness of the old. A ray of light penetrated the house and the scholars together with their disciples began to chant the old hymn of revenge, "Pour out Thy wrath upon the nations that have not known You."

The echo of the chant resounded from the hills of Judea. Like one man the people arose from Gilead to Bashan to cast off the yoke of the Romans. Young men armed themselves and the blacksmiths forged swords out of scythes.

The Roman legions stationed in Palestine were too weak to withstand the army of Bar Kochba, and the governor, Rufus, was forced to withdraw from the fortresses. Dio Cassius relates that the Jews immediately occupied fifty fortified cities and 985 open towns and villages. The Romans then withdrew from Judea, Samaria, and Galilee and the Jews took over the government.

When the first reports of the revolt were brought to Hadrian, he ridiculed them; but when other messengers arrived one after another reporting the defeat of the Roman legions and the danger that the revolt might spread to other provinces of the Roman empire in Asia, Hadrian became concerned and dispatched still other legions. But the reinforcements could achieve nothing.

The victories of the Jews inspired the belief within them that they had regained their national freedom. Many Jews, who had previously denied their origin and adopted heathen faiths to escape persecution, returned to the religion of their forefathers. Bar Kochba wanted to immortalize Judea's liberation and he had coins minted in honor of the victory with the Hebrew inscription (in Samaritan alphabet) "to the liberty of Israel" (*leheirut yisrael*).

It is not known whether Bar Kochba occupied Jerusalem or whether he planned to restore the Temple. There are grounds to believe that he was willing to forgo Jerusalem, and that he planned to move the boundaries of the land of Israel toward Galilee because of the condescending attitude and the ridicule with which the inhabitants of Jerusalem treated the people of Galilee. It is even told that the people of Betar celebrated with lighted torches the day that Jerusalem was destroyed."[11]

With deep concern Hadrian heard of the spread of the revolt and the failure of all the forces that he sent against it. The Jews were victorious in over fifty encounters with the Romans and the commanders whom Hadrian had sent returned to Rome defeated and shamed.

Hadrian then recalled his greatest military commander, Julius Severus, who was then engaged in a war in the British isles and placed him in command of the war in Palestine. Despite the bravery of Severus and his troops who outnumbered the Jews two or three to one, he did not venture to meet the Jews in open conflict after the experience of his predecessors, and he waited for an opportunity to employ his strategy of small attacks. This type of warfare wearied the Jewish soldiers. The Samaritans, who fought alongside the Jews at first, betrayed their allies. Severus persisted in attacking the Jewish forces on several sides at one time in order to force them to concentrate their armies in one place where he could finally engage them in a decisive struggle.

This strategy forced the Jews to concentrate in the fortress of Betar which Severus then besieged. The inhabitants of Tiberias and Sepphoris also deserted the cause of Bar Kochba and joined the Romans. An unusual drought affected the land at that time and deprived the people of water. But all of these circumstances proved of no avail until Severus bribed the treasonable Samaritans. Bar Kochba was wary of the Samaritans and probably guessed that their loyalty was doubtful. But since the Samaritans could enter and leave the fortress freely they had an opportunity to show the Romans the secret entrances and their treason succeeded.

The immediate cause of the fall of Betar as given by the Talmud was the blow that Bar Kochba struck against Rabbi Eliezer of Modiin resulting in his instantaneous death. Throughout the siege of Betar, Rabbi Eliezer of Modiin shielded the city with his piety and everyone was convinced that the fortress would not fall as long as he lived. As Rabbi Eliezer was standing deeply immersed in prayer, a Samaritan came up and whispered something to him which he could not hear. This was related to Bar Kochba who questioned the Samaritan as to the secret he had whispered to Rabbi Eliezer. The Samaritan replied: "If I will not tell you what I said to Rabbi Eliezer, you will kill me; if I do, Emperor Hadrian will have me executed." Bar Kochba guessed that Rabbi Eliezer was negotiating peace with the Romans and he therefore delivered the blow that caused his death. But this resulted in a moral defeat for Bar Kochba. The people within the fortress lost their war spirit and the Samaritans found it a relatively easy task to bring in the Romans.

The horror of the Roman occupation of Betar is described in the story that their horses waded in blood and that the river that flows around Betar was two-thirds full of blood. The blood of the victims flowed in a mighty stream to the Mediterranean Sea and in its onrush swept over tremendous obstacles.

Severus was anxious to capture Bar Kochba alive in order to lead him in triumphal entry into Rome just as Titus did with the heroes of Jerusalem after the destruction of the Temple.

When he failed in this he promised a great reward to whomever would bring him the body of Bar Kochba. A Samaritan brought Bar Kochba's head and claimed that he had killed him. But Severus commanded him to bring the body of Bar Kochba, for he did not believe that the Samaritan could have killed the Jewish hero. When the body of Bar Kochba was discovered, a snake was found coiled around it and Severus declared: "I knew that only God could kill such a man, for no man could avail against him."

After the destruction of Betar, Hadrian undertook to annihilate the whole Jewish people and wherever one was met he was put to death. If the person captured was of some importance he was tortured first and the tortures increased in brutality in proportion to the importance of the captive. Rabbi Akiba was one of the first victims. While still alive, his body was cut with iron flails. When the angels in heaven saw this they wept bitterly and their tears fell into the great sea and caused it to boil, and the whole world was shaken by their voices as they asked God: "Is this Your reward to a man who observed Your Torah?"

When Rabbi Akiba had only begun his career the aged Rabbi Dosa ben Harkinas said of him that "his name resounds from one end of the world to the other." Rabbi Tarphon similarly said to him, "Whoever departs from you is like one who departs from life." When Rabbi Akiba was dead, all the scholars agreed that "the arms of the Torah were severed and the springs of wisdom were sealed."

Rabbi Akiba often said, "Whatever God does, man must believe that it will end well. Whatever happens has been foreseen from above, but man nevertheless possesses a free will to control his actions. The world should be judged according to its virtues and whatever one receives in this world is but a small share of the reward which is to come. If one sees a wicked man who is happy, he may be sure that his end will be evil."[12]

If people are satisfied with a person, Rabbi Akiba said, it must be taken as a sign that God is also pleased with him, and if a person displeases his fellow men, it is a sign that he also displeases God. If one is satisfied with his possessions, it is a good sign for him, but if one is displeased with his possessions, it is a bad omen.

Rabbi Akiba laid down and taught his son seven rules of conduct. (1) Do not reside on the busiest street of the city if you wish to study undisturbed. (2) Do not reside in a city whose rulers are scholars, for they will be busy with their studies and will not devote themselves to the needs of the city. (3) Do not enter your house, and not especially your friend's house, suddenly, for its occupants may be engaged in some action you should not see. (4) Do not go about barefoot in the streets, for it is unseemly. (5) It is better to rise and to dine early during the summer on account of the heat and during the winter because of the cold. (6) It is better to set your Sabbath table as poorly as on a weekday rather than to ask for human aid. (7) Always endeavor to gain the friendship of men who are successful in their enterprises. [13]

Although Rabbi Akiba instructed his son not to go about barefoot, it happened that on one of his trips to Rome to intercede for the Jews he walked about the city without boots. He was met by one of the emperor's eunuchs who said to him, "You are a teacher among the Jews and I will tell you three things: If a man rides on a horse he is a king; if he rides on an ass, he is a free citizen; if he wears boots, he is an ordinary man. But one who possesses none of these would be better off dead." To this Rabbi Akiba replied. "Three things you have told me, and I will say three things to you: The ornament on a man's face is a beard; the joy of a man's heart is a wife, and the gift of God are children. Woe to the man who possesses none of these." [14]

During all of his lectures Rabbi Akiba moralized his listeners in an inspiring fashion and his sayings were repeated in every Jewish home, and every man tried to regulate his life according to Rabbi Akiba's moral precepts. In one such lecture he formulated six rules for his audience: (1) Do not associate with the scornful that you may not copy their deeds. (2) Do not partake of food with an ignorant priest lest he give the tithes to eat and you will be guilty of benefiting from the "holies." (3) Do not indulge in too many vows, for you may not be able to fulfill them and you will be guilty of breaking your oath. (4) Refrain from eating at all feasts, for some day you may have to depend on charity. (5) Refrain from actions the sinfulness of which you doubt and you will be preserved from certain sin. (6) Avoid leaving the Land of Israel, for it may lead you to idolatry.[15]

On another occasion Rabbi Akiba said: "For their three good habits I love the Medians: (1) When they cut meat, they do so on a table. (2) When they kiss each other, they kiss the hand. (3) When they have to confer with each other, they go out into the fields.[16]

The Talmud relates that when Rabbi Akiba was imprisoned[17] Rabbi Simeon ben Yochai came to visit him and said: "Rabbi, teach me." But Rabbi Akiba refused and Rabbi Simeon said, "If you will not teach me I will tell this to my father Yochai, and he will report you to the government."[18] Rabbi Akiba replied, "Much as the calf is willing to feed, the cow is even more anxious to feed it," and Rabbi Simeon responded, "If feeding is dangerous, the calf is in greater peril."

Rabbi Akiba then told him five rules of life: (1) If you wish to hang yourself, you must do so on a high tree (meaning that if one wishes to quote someone he should quote the words of a great man). (2) When you teach your son, teach him from a correct book that he should not become accustomed to errors. (3) Do not use a pot that others have already used (meaning that one should not marry a woman who was possessed by another man). (4) Observing a commandment, when one is certain of it, is like lending money on a field that bears fruit. (5) Observing a commandment with a clean body is like marrying a woman and begetting children.

Whoever takes even a cent from charity when he does not need it—Rabbi Akiba said—will certainly need charity before he dies. Whoever wraps his eyes or his arms and legs with rags in order to deceive people and to beg for alms will certainly become a cripple. One who throws bread upon the ground or scatters money in anger will be forced to depend on charity before he dies. He who tears his clothes or breaks a dish in anger should be considered as one who worships idols.[19]

Lending money for interest was always considered by the scholars to be a great sin. In defining interest Rabbi Akiba said that even an extra greeting may be considered as such. For example, when a person who never greeted another begins to greet him after he borrowed money from him, such a greeting is equivalent to interest.[20]

Rabbi Akiba believed that the Jewish people proved the greatness of God. When He redeemed them from captivity, He did so for His own benefit, for He redeemed Himself together with them. Wherever the Jews are in exile the *Shekhinah* is with them, and when they leave exile it is as if God had been redeemed as well. God also obtained a "bargain" in choosing the Jews as his people, because other peoples praise their gods when they prosper and curse them when their fortunes change; but the Jews praise God always, when they prosper and also when they are in difficulties.

He also compared the Jewish people to a bird; just as a bird depends on its wings to carry it, so also do Jews follow the teachings of their elders. He believed that even the poorest Jew could consider himself an aristocrat because of his descent from Abraham, Isaac, and Jacob.[21]

The highest phase of Jewish life is the Torah. This gift of God to the Jews deserves that people should sacrifice their lives for it. When Hadrian imposed the death penalty on anyone who devoted himself to its study, Rabbi Akiba gathered his disciples wherever he could to continue their studies. The people then asked him: "Are you not afraid of the government?" and he answered them with a fable:

A fox went near a river and saw the fish scurrying around in great fear. The fox said to them, "What do you fear and from whom are you fleeing?" and the fish replied, "We flee the nets that men have spread for us." The fox then said, "It would be better if you came out on dry land and we could live together just as my forefathers once lived together with your forefathers." But the fish answered, "Aren't you supposed to be the wisest of the animals? You are not the wisest but the most cunning. If we are afraid of being caught here in the water, where we live, how much more should we be afraid on dry land where we would die?"

Rabbi Akiba finished his fable by saying: "The same is true of our learning. If we are in danger of being caught when we are engaged in the study of the holy Torah, how much greater would the danger be if we should cease to devote ourselves to it."[22]

Terrible as the conditions were at that time, Rabbi Akiba did not give up hoping that the Jewish kingdom would be restored. This hope was so great that despite the might of Rome and the ruin of Jerusalem, when Tyranos Rufus ordered the site of the Temple to be plowed up at the command of Hadrian, he still believed in the happy future of his people. When other scholars mourned the destruction, Rabbi Akiba smiled, for in his imagination he visualized the future splendor of Israel's land of which he was convinced.

As related previously, the Roman governor, Tyranos Rufus, frequently debated questions of faith with Rabbi Akiba. Informed about the Jewish scriptures, he loved to debate those matters which seemed contradictory to him. He thus once asked Rabbi Akiba, "If your God loves the poor, why does he not feed them?" Rabbi Akiba answered: "He does so to provide us an opportunity to show charity and to save ourselves from Gehenna." "On the contrary, I believe that He condemns you to Gehenna," Rufus replied. "Take as an example a king who is angered by his slave and has him put into prison, and he commands that none of the servants should give the slave anything to eat or drink. If the king should hear that the slave was fed, would he not be displeased?"

But Rabbi Akiba replied: "Let us consider this example in a somewhat different version. A king was angry with his son and he had him put in prison, and he commanded that none should give food or drink to his son. Then there came a servant and offered the prince food and drink. Would not the king give beautiful gifts to the servant, when he heard of his deed?"[23]

The verse "you shall drink water from your well" Rabbi

Akiba explained to mean that the development of learning is based on a simple understanding of what one hears from others. Just as one can draw water from any side of the well without diminishing the water in the well, so also do students come to their teacher, but they do not diminish their teacher's knowledge any more than one who inhales the fragrance of an *etrog*, or one who lights his candle by the flame of another candle. But a scholar must remember that if he had disciples in his youth, he must also have disciples in his old age for one can never know which disciples will cling to their studies and which will abandon them.

The worth of a scholar may also be likened to a golden vessel. When a golden vessel breaks it can be mended and made whole again; when a scholar forgets his learning he can win it back again.[24] But a man must never be proud of his learning, and one who prides himself on his knowledge of the Torah may be likened to a carcass that lies on the road and every passerby holds his nose to avoid the smell.[25]

Much was said of Rabbi Akiba's modesty which could serve as a model for all generations. When his son died Rabbi Akiba said the following words over his grave: "Jews have gathered here not because of my learning, for greater scholars than myself have come; they also did not come because of my riches, for there are men present richer than myself. The men of the South know me and they have come to the funeral, but the men of Galilee, how should they know me? There exist many Akibas like myself, but they all came in honor of the Torah and to fulfill a commandment. This realization would console me were my sorrow sevenfold as great."[26]

Of all the books of the Bible, Rabbi Akiba loved the Song of Songs most, and he said that "the whole world is worth less than the day on which the Song of Songs was given to the Jews,"[27] and "If God had not given the Torah, the Jewish people could conduct their spiritual world with the aid of the Song of Songs." Rabbi Akiba was one of the first who visualized in the Song of Songs a description of the love of God for the congregation of Israel. Among the people who will lose their share in the life to come, he listed those who attempt to transform the Song of Songs into an everyday tavern song.[28]

Rabbi Eliezer ben Hyrcanus once arose during a fast day to pray for rain. He recited twenty-four benedictions and still no rain descended. Rabbi Akiba then approached the pulpit and exclaimed: "Our father, our king, we have no other ruler but you. Our father, our king, do for your own sake and have mercy upon us." Immediately rain began to fall. Those assembled were disappointed that God had answered the prayer of the pupil instead of the prayer of the teacher, but Rabbi Akiba calmed them with a fable: "There was once a king who had two daughters, one of whom was a quiet person while the other was loud in her demands. The king commanded his servants to grant at once whatsoever the insistent daughter demanded. But the quiet daughter never received what she wanted, for she asked for it humbly, and the king also loved to hear her suppliant voice."

Rabbi Akiba was condemned to death immediately after the fall of Betar. At that time he had already been imprisoned for some time either as a hostage or he had been captured during a raid on one of those gatherings where one could be arrested only for saying that Jews should not obey Roman decrees regarding the Jewish faith, or that one should sacrifice his life for his beliefs.

When Rabbi Akiba was in prison, a number of important problems arose that could not be decided before hearing his opinion. Since no one was allowed to visit Rabbi Akiba, the Talmud relates that the scholars once sent Rabbi Jochanan the Sandalmaker, a disciple of Rabbi Akiba, dressed as a peddler with a bundle of merchandise on his back. Rabbi Jochanan walked by the prison where Rabbi Akiba was held and he called out: "Needles, who'll buy needles? Hooks, who'll buy hooks? And what is the law regarding a *Halitzah* who has no witnesses?" Rabbi Akiba stuck his head out between the bars of his cell and called out, "Do you have any spindles? Yes, it is legal."[29]

The reasons for this question dated back to the case of a

man in prison who granted *Halitzah* to the wife of his deceased brother, not in the presence of a court and without witnesses, for none were allowed into his cell, and the people who accompanied the woman had to remain outside the prison and could not see what went on within.

On another occasion the decision of Rabbi Akiba was required in a case of a *m'anenet* (a woman who refuses to live with her husband to whom she was married before she reached maturity). It was then necessary to hire a person for forty dinars who would steal into the prison to ask Rabbi Akiba's opinion.[30]

Rabbi Akiba was imprisoned for a long time and during his incarceration he determined three consecutive leap years. This may indicate that he declared three successive years as leap years or—as is the opinion of some commentators—that he determined the three following leap years that were to be approved by the court, although it was forbidden at that time to establish leap years in advance.[31]

Although Rabbi Akiba was closely guarded while in prison, he was sometimes allowed some liberties. He was probably closely watched so that he could not continue to teach his disciples but he was allowed to have Rabbi Joshua Hagarsi to serve him and he stayed with him until the last minute.

It is told that Rabbi Joshua Hagarsi always brought water to Rabbi Akiba for his daily use. But once the prison overseer met him while he was carrying the water and was displeased, for it seemed to him that too much water was being brought for the use of one prisoner. He thereupon remarked, "Why do you bring so much water to your teacher? Are you trying to undermine the prison?" and saying this he poured out half the water.

Rabbi Akiba feared that if he drank some of it, there would not be enough water left to wash his hands, and he would thus disobey the commandment to wash one's hands. He therefore decided to suffer thirst rather than forgo the commandment of washing one's hands before a meal. The scholars afterward commented on this and said that if he was so observant while in prison one could easily imagine his conduct when he was at liberty.[32]

Finally the day of Rabbi Akiba's trial by Tyranos Rufus came. This was a day of terror for all Jews. Rabbi Joshua Hagarsi prayed to God for Rabbi Akiba until the sentence was passed, and as he stood immersed in prayer a cloud overcast the sky. Rabbi Joshua remembered the verse of Lamentations (3:44) and he addressed the following words to God: "You have covered yourself with a cloud that my prayer should not reach You and that You should not hear my appeal."[32]

After a terrible judgment Tyranos Rufus condemned Rabbi Akiba to the most horrifying death. Ordinarily the Romans condemned their victims to be crucified; the prisoner would then be nailed to a wooden cross where he would hang until he died. Rabbi Akiba was condemned to be flayed alive with iron combs.

As Rabbi Akiba was being led to execution, it was morning and time to recite the *Shema*. Even as his flesh was being torn he did not allow this to interfere with his reciting the *Shema*. The execution was public and was witnessed by the whole population. When Rabbi Akiba's disciples saw the suffering of their teacher they asked: "Maybe it is enough?" implying that perhaps it was time to pay more attention to the suffering of the body instead of the suffering of the soul. But he replied to them: "All the days of my life I have regretted that I had no opportunity to show my love for God in the manner the Bible commands, that one must love God with his whole soul, even if He were to take that soul away. Now that I have an opportunity to fulfill this commandment shall I not do so?" And in reciting the *Shema* he prolonged the word *echad* until he expired.[34]

The Jerusalem Talmud[35] relates the events at the execution in a slightly different manner. It tells that Tyranos Rufus was personally present at the execution and when he saw Rabbi Akiba recite the *Shema* with a smile upon his lips he asked him: "Are you a sorcerer that you laugh at your suffering or are you doing so to hurt me?" Rabbi Akiba answered: "May you die. I am not a sorcerer nor am I insensible to my suffering, nor is it my wish to pain you with my smile. But we were commanded to love our God with our whole hearts, our whole souls, and all our possessions. Until this day I have shown my love for God with my heart and my possessions. But this day I have an opportunity to show my love of God with my soul. I am therefore happy that I have attained this moment."

But the Roman governor was not satisfied that this execution would permanently insure the death of Rabbi Akiba, and so he commanded that the dead body be cut into pieces.[36]

Another legend describes the death of Rabbi Akiba in an idyllic manner. It relates that on the eve of a holiday, Rabbi Joshua Hagarsi, who was always with Rabbi Akiba, went to his home. But before he reached his house, he found the prophet Elijah waiting at the door who told him that Rabbi Akiba had just died in prison. They immediately hastened to the prison and they found the door of Rabbi Akiba's cell wide open. They placed the body of Rabbi Akiba on the couch and they departed. That night they returned and carried the body to Caesarea and there they buried it in a cave.

An interesting legend exists regarding the relationship between Rabbi Akiba and the wife of Tyranos Rufus. It relates that Tyranos Rufus was always dejected after his arguments with Rabbi Akiba, for the latter always triumphed over him in the presence of the emperor. After one such debate the wife of Tyranos Rufus asked: "Why are you so dejected?" and he replied, "This Rabbi Akiba always confuses me with his discourses and I can never conquer him." The woman then said, "The God of the Jews hates immorality. If you will allow me, I will cause Rabbi Akiba to sin and he will lose his militant spirit." "Do as you understand," Tyranos Rufus said to her.

The woman then adorned herself and came to Rabbi Akiba. She tried with all her wiles to cause him to sin. But when Rabbi Akiba looked at her, he spat, then he laughed, and then he wept. The woman asked him, "What is the meaning of these things you are doing?" and he replied, "Two things I can explain to you but the third I cannot tell you. I spat because I recalled the process whereby a person is brought into the world. I wept because I thought of your beauty that will end by rotting in the ground."

And why did he laugh? The legend concludes that he laughed because he foresaw with the aid of the *Ruah Hakodesh* that she would convert and that he would marry her. But this he refused to tell her.[36]

Although learning was forbidden, Rabbi Akiba found frequent opportunities to teach even when he was in prison. It may also be assumed that the six rules he gave to his son were formulated in prison.

In addition some maxims of Rabbi Akiba exist that bear the stamp of having originated in prison. Thus he said that five types of sinners can never be forgiven: (1) One who repents too much. (2) One who sins too often. (3) One who sins when others are pious. (4) One who sins with the intention of repenting. (5) One who causes the desecration of the name of God by his sins.[38]

Another time he poetically interpreted the verse of the Song of Songs "How is your lover different from other lovers?" as a question that the gentile nations might ask the Jewish people. How is your God different from other gods that you allow yourself to be killed for his sake? Such heroic people as you are could easily come and mingle with us. But the congregation of Israel replies: "My lover is clear and radiant, he is higher than ten thousand."[39]

It is interesting to recall of Rabbi Akiba's death that Rabbi Eliezer ben Hyrcanus once foretold he would meet a violent death. During an argument concerning the preparation of sacrifices for slaughter on the Sabbath, Rabbi Eliezer became annoyed at Rabbi Akiba's numerous questions, and he said angrily: "You have contradicted me in matters of slaughter and you will meet your death in slaughter."[40]

33

THE TEN MARTYRS

LEGEND RECORDS THAT ABOUT the time of the destruction of Betar, or immediately after that event, the Roman governor of Palestine had ten of the most prominent Jewish leaders executed in a most barbarous fashion.

Emperor Hadrian—so relates *Midrash Eikhah Rabbati*—then undertook to wipe the Jewish people from the face of the earth, and he was assisted in this plan by his governor, Tyranos Rufus, who also served as executioner. It was the habit of the emperor, or one of his representatives, to sit at the gate of the city and capture any passing Jew who would then be executed.

While doing so, the Romans made merry over the fate of the unfortunate Jews. If a Jew greeted a Roman, he would be addressed by: "How dare you, a Jew, greet me? You are probably trying to deceive me with your greeting while you curse me in your heart. You deserve to be put to death." But if the Jew did not greet the Roman, he would be addressed in this way: "There goes a Jew who shows no respect for his emperor; he therefore deserves to be put to death."

It seems probable that thousands of Jews lost their lives in this manner. This is evident from the Talmud[1] that cites a statement of the scholars to the effect that a man who loses his life because he is a Jew becomes sanctified and no one else may equal him in merit.

Although the martyrs numbered in the thousands, legend conferred a special holiness on ten of them. This legend mentions the names of the Ten Martyrs and it has been established historically that these were executed by the Romans although they did not all die at the same time.

The story of the Ten Martyrs is retold twice each year; once during the recitation of the Laments on the ninth day of Ab and the second time during the afternoon service of the Day of Atonement.

The author of this Lament as well as the author of the other prayer followed the events as they are related in the *Midrashim* where the names of the martyrs are listed in two different versions.

These men were executed—the legend continues to relate—when they were reading the Torah to the emperor and came to the law stating that a person who steals a man and enslaves him, is to be put to death (Ex. 21:16). The emperor then said: "Where are your forefathers, the sons of Jacob, who sold their brother into slavery? If I had them here I would immediately have them put to death. But since they are not here you will have to atone for their crime."

The emperor then allowed them three days to prepare themselves for execution. Rabbi Ishmael ben Elisha said to his comrades: "If you have taken upon yourself part of the sin, I will pronounce the *Shem Hameforash* (the express name of God) and by its power I will ascend to heaven to ascertain whether this decree is the will of God. If God willed it, we will bow to his will, otherwise I will try to undo the decree of the emperor with the power of God's name."

The other scholars answered, "Do whatever you can and we will assume our share of responsibility for the sin."

After he pronounced the *Shem Hameforash*, a strong wind arose and carried Rabbi Ishmael to heaven. There he met the angel Metateron whom he asked about the decree and the angel said to him, "I have heard it announced that ten of the greatest Jewish scholars are to lose their lives at the hands of the Roman government." Rabbi Ishmael descended and found his comrades engaged in prayer and fasting. They then began to discuss the laws pertaining to Passover. A messenger of the emperor arrived who asked in amazement: "You know that you have been condemned to death, and yet you have the patience to engage in learned discussions?"

Thus the *Midrash,* and the authors of the lament and the mentioned prayer, describe the events of the martyrdom that did away with ten of the noblest Jewish men. But the Talmud states that they died at widely separated intervals. This is also evident from the Book of Lineage (*Yuhasin*) that explicitly states that one must not be misled to believe that the Ten Martyrs were executed at the same time, for Rabbi Akiba lost his life sixty years later, and the other scholars suffered martyrdom at a still later date.

According to Talmudic sources[2] the first death sentence was pronounced upon Rabbi Simeon ben Gamaliel and Rabbi Ishmael ben Elisha. When Rabbi Ishmael was informed of the sentence he wept bitterly and Rabbi Simeon said, "You should be happy that two steps from here you will be taken to the bosom of the saints. Why do you weep?" Rabbi Ishmael answered, "I do not weep because I have to die, but because we are to be led to execution like common murderers."

When the news of their death was revealed to Rabbi Akiba and to Rabbi Jehudah ben Baba they said, "All Jews must realize that if good times were in the offing, these two, Rabbi Simeon and Rabbi Ishmael, would be among the first to benefit from them. But the Creator knows that terrible punishment is about to be visited upon the world and He therefore removed them from the earth."

When Rabbi Akiba was killed, the news was carried to Rabbi Jehudah ben Baba and to Rabbi Chanina ben Teradion. They rent their garments and donned sackcloth and said: "Hearken to us, brethren. Rabbi Akiba was killed not because he committed robbery, nor because he neglected God's Torah. This is a sign that evil times are about to come. We may therefore expect that before long there will not be a place in the Land of Israel that will not be strewn with human bodies."

Rabbi Jehudah ben Baba, another of the Ten Martyrs, lost his life during the period of the decree against ordination. He was a pupil of Shmuel (*Hakatan*) the Younger, and later he was a colleague of Rabbi Akiba in Jabneh who frequently debated the regulations of Jewish life with him.[3] When the persecution was in full force, he ruled that weddings were legal even when performed in the presence of one witness. When testimony was taken regarding the various Jewish customs, he related that on one occasion in Jerusalem, a rooster was condemned to be stoned to death for killing a child in its crib by piercing its head with its beak. He was renowned for his piety and all Talmudic stories that begin with the words, "It once occurred to a pious man" refer to Rabbi Jehudah ben Baba; only in a few exceptional cases do these refer to Rabbi Jehudah bar Elai.[4]

It is further told of Rabbi Jehudah ben Baba that all his actions were motivated by piety and that when he died no one could remember any sinful deed committed by him except that he had kept a goat in his house, which was forbidden by the scholars of Palestine because goats habitually graze in strangers' fields. The reason he kept a goat was that he suffered from severe coughing and the doctors advised him to drink goat's milk while it was still warm. To prevent his goat from entering strangers' fields, he always kept it tied to the bed post. Nevertheless, the scholars refused to enter his house when he was sick because of the "robber" that he housed.[5]

At that time the government issued a decree forbidding the ordination of pupils and anyone who issued or received such ordination was to forfeit his life, and the city where such ordination was conferred was to be razed to the ground. Rabbi Jehudah ben Baba then took his place between two mountains, between the cities of Usha and Shefarom, in order to ordain his disciples. He reasoned that if he were to be caught there, no city would suffer through his deed. There one day he ordained five or six of his pupils. Suddenly they noticed soldiers approaching and Rabbi Jehudah said to his pupils, "Children, flee from here." "But what will happen to you?" they asked him. He answered, "I will lie down on the ground and pretend death."

When the soldiers approached they saw what they thought to be a dead body lying on the ground. Wishing to assure themselves that he was really dead, they pierced his body with three hundred javelins until it was riddled like a sieve.[6]

Such seems to have been the death of Rabbi Jehudah ben Baba. It is also more than certain that some of his pupils were captured and killed.

Among the Ten Martyrs there were also men like Rabbi Yeshebab the Scribe, and Rabbi Hutzpit the Interpreter, who did not head academies but were officials of the court in Jabneh. They succeeded in hiding for some time in Sepphoris but were captured finally. Rabbi Yeshebab copied books of the Torah and recorded the proceedings of the court. He was a pupil of Rabbi Akiba and later became his colleague, and together they discussed various legal matters. The poverty of Palestine's Jews was very great at that time and many people distributed the greater part of their possessions, despite the warning of Rabban Gamaliel that one should not give away more than one-fifth of his possessions.[7]

According to another source, it was not Rabban Gamaliel but Rabbi Akiba who advised Rabbi Yeshebab to distribute no more than one-fifth of his possessions.[8] This suggestion was enacted as a law by the Sanhedrin in Usha.[9]

Of Rabbi Hutzpit we know that he was interpreter for the Sanhedrin in Jabneh. It was also his duty to explain the Torah to the uneducated men and the women. One legal opinion of his is cited in the question of *Prozbol*.[10]

Before the Roman executioner killed Rabbi Hutzpit, he cut out his tongue and threw it away. Later dogs were seen carrying the tongue and the scholars mourned that "The tongue that poured forth pearls lay in the dust."[11]

Among the martyrs of that time were also the brothers Pappus and Julianus. Even though they are not listed among the Ten Martyrs, they are mentioned in connection with Rabbi Akiba.[12]

According to the Talmud, Pappus and Julianus were executed by Tyranos Rufus in the city of Lodakia for this reason. When a princess of the imperial family was found murdered, the Jews were held to be responsible and the Roman governor commanded that all the Jewish inhabitants of that city be killed. The two brothers appeared before the governor and assumed all blame for the murder of the princess. They thus saved the Jewish community from annihilation.

Another version describes the death of the two brothers in this manner. The emperor said to them: "If you belong to the same people as Mishael, Chananiah, and Azariah, then God will save you from my hands." But the brothers replied, "Mishael, Chananiah, and Azariah were pious men and Nebuchadnezzar was a worthy king. Because of their merit a miracle occurred. But you are an ordinary wicked man and we are guilty. If you do not kill us, there will be others to do so. But if you kill us, God will avenge our blood upon you."[13]

From the complicated tangle of legends surrounding these men, we may conclude that Pappus ben Jehudah believed in maintaining peaceful relations with Rome. When he saw Rabbi Akiba publicly teaching the Torah to his disciples, despite government prohibition, he rebuked him. But when he was himself later arrested for some transgression and sentenced to death, he said to Rabbi Akiba, "Happy are you Rabbi Akiba that you were captured while teaching God's Torah, but woe to Pappus that he was captured because of some foolish deed."[14]

When the Roman government disbanded the central academy of the Sanhedrin in Jabneh, executing many of the scholars in Lud, and forcing the remaining ones to flee to Usha, there sprang up a number of academies in numerous towns that were difficult of access and where a measure of safety from the Romans existed. It was characteristic of these academies that every one knew of their existence despite the fact that any contact with them was punishable by death. Like Rabbi Akiba who insisted on continuing his teaching openly, Rabbi Chanina ben Teradion also scorned all danger and continued his educational work.

He often said that if two people are together and do not engage in "words of the Torah" it is a gathering of the scornful, but whenever two occupy themselves with the Torah, the *shekhinah* rests upon them. Even when a person is alone he should devote himself to study and God will reward him.[15]

But it is important to remember that it was almost impossible for a person to study alone. Aside from the Scriptures there were no written books, and even the possession by one person of a book of the Scriptures was very rare. All study was done orally; one man read a verse from the book and offered his interpretation; the others questioned him or offered their own commentaries.

In the early years of his career Rabbi Chanina ben Teradion studied together with Rabbi Jose ben Kisma, but it appears that Rabbi Jose departed when the situation became too dangerous and when learning of the Torah was declared to be an "offense" punishable by death. When Rabbi Jose fell sick before his death, he was visited by Rabbi Chanina and he chided the latter for his daring in endangering his life because of his teachings. Rabbi Jose said, "God handed the government to the Romans. They destroyed His house, burned His temple, slaughtered the pious, the best men of our people, and now I hear that you gather disciples and teach them from the book of the Torah you keep hidden in your bosom. Would it not be better for you to consider how all this will end?"

To this Rabbi Chanina replied, "God in heaven will have mercy!"

Rabbi Jose further said, "I speak to you logically and you answer about the mercy of heaven. I should not be surprised if you are captured with the book of the Torah in your possession."[16]

This attitude of Rabbi Jose, his readiness to bow before the might of the Romans, was probably known to the authorities.

He was highly regarded by the governor of Caesarea and when he died, Roman officials attended the funeral and mourned over his grave. Returning from the funeral, the Romans saw Rabbi Chanina ben Teradion with a book of the Torah expounding to his disciples who were seated about him. He was immediately brought to trial and condemned to be burned. His wife was also condemned to death and his daughter was sent away to a house of ill-repute.

Together with Rabbi Chanina, the Romans also captured his friend, Rabbi Eleazar ben Parta who had to face charges on five different infractions of the law. When they met, Rabbi Eleazar said, "Woe is me that I was caught while breaking five different laws." But Rabbi Chanina said to him, "You are a happy man indeed that you were arrested for five transgressions, and you will certainly be saved from all of them. Your salvation is more certain because you devoted yourself to learning as well as to charitable deeds while I engaged only in learning."

During his trial Rabbi Chanina bluntly declared that he was "fulfilling the command of God." He was then wrapped in the book of the Torah that he had kept in his bosom, he was surrounded with bundles of thin branches, and these were set afire. To prolong his agony the Romans placed moist wool over his heart.

The execution had to be witnessed by his daughter and his disciples, and his daughter exclaimed, "Woe is me, father, that I see you suffering like this." Rabbi Chanina said, "If I were to burn alone, my suffering would be very great. But since I am being burned together with a book of the Torah, I am certain that He who will punish the burning of the book will also avenge my death."

Rabbi Chanina's disciples then asked him, "Rabbi, what do you see?" and he answered, "I see the parchment burning but the letters on it are flying upward." His disciples cried, "Open your mouth and let the fire enter and you will die sooner," but he answered, "I do not wish to hasten my death by my own act."

Hearing this, the executioner who lit the fire asked Rabbi Chanina, "Rabbi, if I increase the fire that you may die sooner, will you lead me into the world to come?"

Rabbi Chanina assured him that he would do so, and the executioner removed the wool from over his heart and Rabbi Chanina at once expired.[17]

Rabbi Eleazar ben Parta, a kindly and scholarly man, was captured together with Rabbi Chanina. Of Rabbi Chanina it was said that he was very just in matters of charity but that he was always calculated and gave no more than his share. On one occasion only, did the sums he set aside for charity and for a Purim feast become mixed, and so he distributed the whole sum to the poor. This he mentioned afterward as an innovation.

Whether Rabbi Eleazar ben Parta was saved from a martyr's death remains unknown. If he was, then it was probably due to his leanings toward peace with Rome, as was also the attitude of Rabbi Jose ben Kisma. The legends regarding his defense against the accusations of the Romans indicate that in itself it would have been insufficient to save him from the bloodthirsty Romans. He was accused of devoting himself to learning and also of participating in the activities of the various robber bands infesting the land at that time. To these accusations he replied: "If you suspect me of devoting myself to the book, you cannot accuse me of using the sword, and if you accuse me of using the sword, you cannot suspect me of engaging in the study of the book. Since one is not true, the other also must be false."

"If you did not engage in the study of the book," the judges asked, "why do people call you Rabbi?"

"They call me Rabbi," Rabbi Eleazar replied, "because I am the teacher of the weavers."

Wishing to test his knowledge of weaving, the judges commanded that a piece of woven cloth be brought, and he was told to point out the warp and the woof. At that moment a miracle occurred and a drone alighted on a thread of the warp while a bee descended on a thread of the woof. Rabbi Eleazar understood the significance of the insects' action and he convinced the Romans of his knowledge of weaving.

"Why were you absent from the meetings of Bei Avidan?" the judges continued to ask, and Rabbi Eleazar replied that being an old man he was afraid of being crushed in the melee. The judges at first refused to accept this reason but another miracle occurred, and on the same day an old man was crushed at the meeting of Bei Avidan.[18]

"And why did you liberate your slave?" the judge further queried. But Rabbi Eleazar denied this. One of the witnesses was ready to testify against him when the prophet Elijah appeared in the guise of a Roman official and said, "Since miracles have already occurred to substantiate his statements, it is probable that another miracle will occur."

In justification of the severe punishment meted out to Rabbi Chanina ben Teradion—Rabbi Chanina was burned, his wife was killed, and his daughter was sent away to a house of shame—the scholars later declared that he deserved it because of his sins. Rabbi Chanina frequently employed the *shem hameforash*. His wife heard him pronounce it, but never warned him to refrain, while his daughter once passed by a group of Roman officials and heard them praise her graceful bearing; she was then filled with pride and her fate in later life was a punishment for this pride.

A second daughter of Rabbi Chanina became the wife of Rabbi Meir and she too met with much suffering because of her original convictions about women. It is also noteworthy that once, when the scholars were debating a legal matter, a son and daughter of Rabbi Chanina participated in the discussions. At that time Rabbi Jehudah ben Baba said that Rabbi Chanina's daughter showed a better understanding of the law than her brother did.

Rabbi Chanina's son joined a band of brigands during his father's lifetime. After the collapse of Bar Kochba's revolt, the remaining Jewish soldiers organized themselves into bands to conduct guerrilla warfare against the Romans, and they also looted and murdered wherever they could. The Romans applied all their efforts to rid the land of these bands and Rabbi

Chanina's son was caught. They promised to spare his life if he would disclose secret information regarding the band. He did so and his comrades later killed him and stuffed his mouth with mud. Three days later his body was found and it was placed in a casket for burial. Out of respect for his parents the people were going to mourn him, but Rabbi Chanina would not allow it.[19]

As previously mentioned Rabbi Jose ben Kisma was an adherent of the movement for peace with the Romans. He was convinced nevertheless that in the end the Romans would be driven out of Palestine by the Persians after they had conquered Babylonia. He instructed his disciples to bury him in a very deep grave because "the time will come when there will not be a single palm tree in the Land of Israel but a Persian horse will be tied to it, and there will not be a single casket in the land that a Median horse will not feed from."

His disciples then asked him when the Messiah would come. At first he refused to tell them but when they insisted, he said, "When the gate will be destroyed and rebuilt anew. Then it will be destroyed again, and before it is rebuilt again, the Messiah will come."[20]

Rabbi Jose did not explain which gate he was referring to and his statement was variously interpreted. *Yalkut Hamachiri* says that it refers to the gate of Tiberias; Rashi, on the other hand, claimed that it referred to the gate of Rome.

Further light is shed on the character of Rabbi Jose ben Kisma by the following story. It is told that a very wealthy man asked Rabbi Jose to settle in his city and he promised to reward him with much gold and silver and precious stones, but Rabbi Jose replied that were he to be offered all the gold and silver and precious stones of the world he would not reside anywhere except in a place of learning.[21]

Rabbi Eleazar ben Parta, who was captured together with Rabbi Chanina ben Teradion, left one law on the subject of a woman who is the wife of a *cohen* and who is informed that her husband was travelling on a ship that was lost or that he was facing trial and in danger of losing his life. The question was whether such a woman was entitled to eat of the tithes offered to a priest. Rabbi Eleazar ruled that she was entitled to benefit from the tithes because the possibility existed that her husband might still escape alive.

It seems probable that Rabbi Eleazar ben Parta was a pupil of Rabbi Eliezer of Modiin and a colleague of the scholars at Jabneh with whom he debated the interpretations of the laws. He said that since the destruction, the rains in Palestine had become lighter and less fruitful and that all of Palestine's natural phenomena had changed; either there is too much or too little rain; sometimes it falls on time and at other times it is delayed. "When rain falls on time, what may it be compared to? It may be compared to a slave whose master gives him his pay on Sunday and he can bake his dough and eat his bread on time. But when rain does not fall on time what may it be compared to? It may be compared to a slave whose master gives him his pay at the end of the week; he cannot properly bake his dough or eat his bread on time."[22]

Rabbi Eleazar said that gossip is severely punished. This is obvious from the punishment God meted out to the spies who Moses sent to see Palestine who slandered only trees and rocks upon their return. How much greater would be the punishment of one who slanders his neighbor.[23]

Another martyr was Chanina (or Chananiah) ben Chachinai, a disciple and a friend of the outstanding scholars of the time. It seems that he never received *semikhah* (ordination) to teach others in an academy of his own. His opinions, however, were held in great esteem and they were considered on numerous occasions when the laws were being determined.[24] Occasionally he is referred to as Rabbi, but this seems to be an error of the copyists who could not imagine that the *Mishnah* or Talmud should quote a man who was not ordained. His name is mentioned among the scholars who were said to know "seventy languages" and also in connection with other prominent men who did not possess the title of Rabbi such as Simeon ben Azai, Simeon ben Zoma, and Hanan the Egyptian.[25] One of his opinions that was cited concerned the weight of the stone circle that Joshua erected in Gilgal after the Jews crossed the Jordan.[26]

His mode of thought is illustrated by a maxim he frequently repeated: "He who wakes at night, and he who walks alone by the way, and he who makes his heart empty for idle thoughts is guilty against himself."[27] Also interesting is his interpretation of the Biblical verse regarding a man who denies his friend. He said that a man who denies the words of his friend does so because he denies God.[28]

Chanina studied for some time, together with other scholars, in the academy of Rabbi Tarphon. Later he became a disciple of Rabbi Akiba who found him worthy to discuss the mysteries of the Torah with him.[29] On one occasion he argued against the viewpoint of Rabbi Akiba.[30]

Chanina attended the academy of Rabbi Akiba at Bnei Brak together with Rabbi Simeon ben Yochai.[31] They remained there about twelve or thirteen years. Throughout these years Rabbi Simeon received messages from his home and he was informed of what went on there, but Chanina never sent any message home and seemed not to be concerned about what happened there. One day he received a message from his wife: "Your daughter is ready to be wed and you must return at once to give her in marriage."

Chanina received permission from his master to return home. During all these years the city and its buildings had changed and he did not know where to find the house where his family lived. He sat down near the city well to await someone who could direct him. He then heard some girls addressing another girl, "Chanina's daughter, fill your jar with water and go home."

He followed this girl until he reached the house. When his wife saw him she fainted from great excitement. Chanina then stopped to pray and he asked God, "Is this Your reward for the poor woman who waited for me so many years?" Realizing the justice of Chanina's prayer, God hearkened to it and the woman revived.

Chanina's wife was well known for her kindliness. At that

time the scholars interpreted the verse of the Bible "I will make a help against him" to mean that if a man is deserving, his wife is a help, but if he is not deserving she is against him. Rabbi Joshua ben Nehemiah amplified this interpretation and said that if a man is deserving he has a wife like Chanina ben Chachinai's wife, but if he is not deserving he gets a wife like the wife of Rabbi Jose of Galilee.

Still another martyr of that time was Rabbi Jehudah the Baker. Whether he was really a baker, as his name would seem to indicate, remains unknown. He was very close to Rabbi Akiba and knew his life history. His word was therefore accepted in correcting an error regarding the dispute of Rabbi Akiba with Rabban Gamaliel.

While trying to establish the day of the new month, Rabbi Akiba once delayed the testimony of people from his city. Rabban Gamaliel then sent a message to Rabbi Akiba saying, "If you prevent the majority from fulfilling a commandment, you cause them to sin and you deserve to be ostracized." The people believed that Rabbi Akiba was excommunicated but Rabbi Jehudah the Baker declared that it was not so and that Rabbi Akiba was only removed as representative of the city of Geder, a position he then held.[32]

The legend regarding the tongue of Rabbi Hutzpit the Interpreter, which the Romans are said to have cut out and thrown to the dogs is given in the Jerusalem Talmud[33] as referring to Rabbi Jehudah the Baker, for it is said that it was Rabbi Jehudah who was thus tortured. There also exists a *midrash* that relates that when Rabbi Jehudah the Baker was led to execution there came a man named Guphia who offered his life in place of Rabbi Jehudah. The Romans accepted the substitute, but Rabbi Jehudah was later indicted on another charge of violating Roman law and he was again condemned to death.

The name of Rabbi Eleazar Harsena is also listed among the Ten Martyrs and some historians identify him with Rabbi Eleazar ben Harsom who was said to be the owner of a thousand cities

on land and a thousand ships at sea. From the wealth Rabbi
Eleazar is said to have inherited from his father, he derived no
benefit. He would take only one sack of flour to bake the bread
he needed. He wandered from one city to another and visited
the academies. When he returned to his house and wanted to
enter, his own slaves did not know him and suspecting that he
was a thief, they beat him.

Another version declares Rabbi Eleazar ben Harsom to
have been high priest for eleven years.[34] This legend, however,
must refer to a person other than the martyr. Also no high
priest by that name is mentioned by Josephus in his list of high
priests. We may therefore assume that the legend refers to a
person regarding whom all information had been lost and his
name is therefore confused with other historical personalities.

34

SIMEON BEN AZAI
AND
SIMEON BEN ZOMA

THE TALMUD RELATES THAT FOUR of the most outstanding scholars entered *pardes*—the garden of knowledge—and with the power of their reason they sought to discover the causes underlying man's life and the mysteries of God.[1]

The affliction of the Jews were then indescribable. The Roman government endeavored with all its might to erase all trace of the Jewish faith. Since the Temple was destroyed, Judaism could only survive through the observance of such laws as had no direct relation to the Temple. The government therefore demanded the death sentence for the observance of Sabbath, for studying the Torah, or for the circumcision of male children. If a person openly renounced Judaism, he joined the Romans, or some other nationality, and was granted Roman citizenship which insured his security.

Four of the outstanding scholars therefore attempted to discover the reason why God inflicted this suffering upon the Jews. These four were: Simeon ben Azai, Simeon ben Zoma, Elisha ben Avuyah, and Rabbi Akiba. Ben Azai soon died from too much pondering; Ben Zoma lost his reason; Elisha ben Avuyah "cut down the plants," believing that God abandoned the Jews he said, "Of what avail is the Torah and why should we suffer to observe it?" He then abandoned the faith and became *Acher*, a stranger, an open enemy of the Torah, and of those who clung to it. Only Rabbi Akiba suffered no harm and emerged unchanged from this venture. Rabbi Akiba's strong spirit mocked death and the very moment that Romans were tearing his flesh with iron flails, gave him the strength to declare that he was happy to be able to show his love of God even at the price of his life, this spirit penetrated the mysteries of *pardes* without suffering any injury.

Simeon ben Azai, who died after pondering the mysteries, and Simeon ben Zoma who lost his reason, were members of Rabbi Akiba's academy and were recognized as prominent disciples whose opinions were frequently sought.[2] They were considered capable of heading separate academies although they were not confirmed[3] and special honor was accorded to Ben Azai. Although unordained, he was at times called Rabbi[4] and when he differed with Rabbi Akiba his opinion is mentioned first at least on one occasion.[5] At other times Rabbi Akiba retracted his opinions in favor of those of Ben Azai[6] and once Ben Azai vanquished Rabbi Akiba in a debate to the complete satisfaction of the other scholars.[7]

At first Ben Azai studied with Rabbi Tarphon[8] then with Rabbi Joshua ben Chananiah and later he became a disciple and friend of Rabbi Akiba.[9] He then had many opportunities to inform Rabbi Akiba of the legal opinions of Rabbi Joshua.[10] But his adoration of Rabbi Akiba was so great that he once said that in his eyes "all the scholars taken together are of no more worth than the shell of garlic, except Rabbi Akiba," to whom he referred as "the man with the bald head".[11] This contempt for the scholars of his time was expressed by Ben Azai, who on another occasion warned against underestimating any person and believing anything to be impossible.[12]

Ben Azai engaged in his scholastic work in Tiberias. He was famous for his unusual diligence and after his death it was said that all diligence had departed.[13] His great devotion to learning led him to become estranged from his wife[14] who was the daughter of Rabbi Akiba. Like her mother, she also sent her husband to an academy.[15] When Ben Azai once declared that "he who does not strive to bring children into the world may be compared to a murderer," the people said to him "You preach well but you do not practice your own principles." Ben Azai then answered, "I cannot help it. My heart yearns for the Torah and the world will have to recreate itself without me."[16]

At the time of his death, Ben Azai was still a young man. From the descriptions that we have of his life it is evident that his diligence, his renunciation of the joys of life, and his piety contributed to his early death. His piety was known far and wide, and people believed that "he who sees Ben Azai in his dream may expect to become pious."[17]

Another opinion exists that Ben Azai met with a violent death and that he was one of the first victims of Hadrian, but there is no historical substantiation for this point of view.

Ben Azai's legal opinions are frequently quoted in the *Mishnah* as in the case of the "red heifer" (*parah adumah*) and also his belief that the Song of Songs and Ecclesiastes are sacred.[18] In this particular instance the discussion ends with the following words: "They agreed and decided according to the words of Ben Azai." In the question of the advisability of teaching one's daughters, Ben Azai was of the opinion that every father should teach the Torah to his daughter.[19] He also expressed an opinion regarding the time of the offering of tithes from cattle.[20]

Ben Azai's philosophy of life is expressed in some of his teachings that rank with the most highly civilized ethical precepts. "Every man whose understanding is clouded by his knowledge," he said, "should be approved of; but it is a bad sign for a man if his knowledge is clouded by his understanding."[21]

His favorite maxim stated, "Be swift to fulfill a minor commandment even as you would an important one and flee from every transgression. For the reward of a commandment is a commandment and the reward of transgression is transgression.[22] A more ample version of this maxim is given in *Avot Derabi Natan*: "If you have fulfilled a commandment

without regret you will be led to fulfilling other commandments; but if you have committed a transgression without
regretting it, you will be led to commit other transgressions."

"The observance of God's commandments," he said,
"requires a strong will. Thus we are commanded not to eat
blood and the Bible says 'Be strong not to eat the blood.' Even
though this is an easy commandment to fulfill we must be
strong; how much stronger must we be to fulfill other commandments."

He also said, "When does God show the just men the
reward that He has prepared for them? When they are near
death."[23]

Another time he advised: "When you seek a place to sit,
choose one a few steps lower than what you think you deserve.
For it is better that you be told to go up rather than to
descend."[24] The most important element of the Jewish faith is
the Torah. Of this Ben Azai said: "Whoever allows himself to
be humiliated for the honor of the Torah, will be honored in the
end, and he who degrades himself for the sake of the words of
the Torah will be elevated in the end."[25]

Ben Azai expressed numerous interesting opinions regarding various omens accompanying death, according to
which it was possible to judge the life of the patient. It is a good
omen for a man to die with a clear conscience and without
regretting his life. Other good signs are if wise men are pleased
with one; or when the patient dies with his face turned upward
and looking at the people surrounding him, and when his face
becomes suffused with color.[26]

Once when the people asked Ben Azai to expound the
Lamentations, he said: "The Lamentations begin with the word
Eikhah and it should be explained according to its letters. The
aleph indicates that the Jews were exiled when they denied their
only God; the *yud* shows that they abandoned the ten commandments; the *chaf* proves that they did not fulfill the
commandment of circumcision that was given twenty generations after the creation of the world; the *heh* shows that they
denied the five books of the Torah."[27] (Use is here made of the

substitution of Hebrew letters for numbers: *aleph*, 1; *chaf*, 20; *yud*, 10; *heh*, 5.)

Legend relates that when Ben Azai was expounding, he was surrounded by tongues of flame. The people thought that he was explaining the mysteries of the Divine Chariot, but it was only an ordinary exposition of the Torah. He then explained that the tongues of fire were caused by joy of the Torah that remains as new as on the day it was given from Mount Sinai. Since the Torah was handed down in fire, it is always accompanied by fire.[28]

Aside from his underestimation of his colleagues, Ben Azai scorned those scholars who were not interested in gaining learning but merely wished to test their teachers. Of such people he said, "It is easier to conquer the whole world than to sit in front of people who wrap themselves in their shawls and whose faces one cannot see."[29]

In his method of exposition Ben Azai followed in the footsteps of Rabbi Akiba. At times he amplified the words of Rabbi Akiba with his own interpretation. Thus Rabbi Akiba said that it was because of the merit of the Jews that God spoke to Moses. Ben Azai expanded this statement to indicate that God spoke to all other prophets and not only to Moses because of the merit of the Jews. Another time he modified Rabbi Akiba's explanation of the duty to serve God with one's whole soul in a manner that would prove that man must be ready to give his soul for the privilege of observing God's commandments.[30]

Ben Azai believed in moralizing people with a view to improving them. When he was asked: "How far must one go in his moralizing, until the person preached to is ready to fight or to curse?" he answered that it was enough if such a person began to scold.[31]

Simeon ben Zoma was another one of the four who entered the Garden of Knowledge in an attempt to determine the ways of heaven and earth and to fathom what was before the world was created and what will be after the world will cease to be.

Together with Ben Azai he was a pupil of Rabbi Joshua ben Chananiah and later they both joined the academy of Rabbi Akiba who treated them as comrades and disciples. At the same time that Ben Azai met with an untimely death as a result of his attempt to fathom problems that human reason cannot conceive, Ben Zoma went out of his mind and died soon after. Despite the fact that he was not ordained, Ben Zoma is twice referred to as Rabbi in the Talmud[32] and he was listed among those disciples who attended the Sanhedrin and whose opinions were sought in discussing the laws.[33] He was also prominent as a preacher, and at his death it was said that good preaching had ceased.[34] The high esteem in which his education was held by the people may be gauged from the popular belief that a person who sees Ben Zoma in his dream may surely expect an increase in wisdom.[35]

Very few of his scriptural interpretations have come down to us, but those that have indicate a brilliant mind made somewhat eccentric from too much pondering. The *Midrash* cites[36] that when the verse "And God made the sky" was being discussed, Ben Zoma severely questioned its implication that God had to make the sky instead of creating it by pronouncing the word. The scholars frequently turned to him for advice and his opinion was taken as that of an authority.[37] When the question of the offerings to be brought by a Nazarite was being debated, Ben Zoma differed with his teacher Rabbi Joshua and *his* opinion was established as the law.[38]

When Rabbi Eleazar ben Azariah was elected Nasi, he declared that he could never convince his colleagues of the necessity of reciting during the evening *Shema* the chapter on *Tzitzit*, that mentions the deliverance from Egypt, until Ben Zoma proved it from the biblical verse "And you shall remember the day of your deliverance from Egypt all the days of your life" by concluding that the word "all" implies the obligation to mention the deliverance at night as well as during the day. But Ben Zoma could not understand the saying of the scholars that the deliverance from Egypt would have to be mentioned even after the coming of the Messiah until they derived their conclusion from the same word.[39]

The favorite maxim of Ben Zoma stated, "Who is wise? He who learns from every man! Who is strong? He who conquers his passions! Who is rich? He who is satisfied with his portion! Who is honored? He who honors others!"[40] *Avot Derabi Natan* adds the following to this maxim: "Who is a most modest man? He who is as modest as Moses! One who controls his passions may be compared to a man who conquers a city full of warriors."

It is related that Rabbi Joshua ben Chananiah once walked on the military highway, and he met Ben Zoma who was so preoccupied with his thoughts that he did not even notice his teacher and did not greet him. Rabbi Joshua stopped Ben Zoma and asked him: "Whence do you come and whither are you going, Ben Zoma?" And he replied: "I was contemplating the upper and the lower waters and I have discovered that the space between them is no more than the breadth of three fingers."[41]

When Rabbi Joshua heard his words he remarked to his pupils, "You see, Ben Zoma still stands outside." A short time after that Ben Zoma died.[42]

Another time Ben Zoma saw a great concourse of people and he said, "Praised be God who probes all mysteries and who created so many people, no two of which have like faces nor like opinions, and He nevertheless knows what transpires in the heart of each of them; and all these He created to serve me."

Ben Zoma also marveled at human progress and said: "Let us consider how much effort Adam had to exert before he could eat a piece of bread. He had to plow the field and sow the seed and harvest the grain, then bind and thresh and winnow and select the grains. After that he ground the wheat and sifted the flour and kneaded the dough and baked it and only then could he eat bread; but I rise in the morning and find it all prepared and ready for my use."

Speaking in the same vein he also said: "Let us consider the efforts of Adam before he had a garment to wear. He had to shear the wool or reap the flax, then he had to comb the wool or beat the flax, and after that he had to spin and weave it, and only then could he wear a garment; but I rise in the morning and find it ready for my use. All the artisans of the world diligently toil to prepare all these for my satisfaction."

Another time he said: "When a respectable person goes visiting, what does he say? May the name of my host be praised for the effort which he exerted on my behalf. How many wines and cakes and other good things he prepared for my sake. But when an ungrateful man goes visiting, what does he say? Whatever the host did, he did for his own wife and children. For how much did I consume? Only one slice of bread and one piece of cake and one glass of wine.[43]

Some commentators explain this saying of Ben Zoma as illustrating the attitudes of various types of people to God who prepared everything for the benefit of humanity. Some are willing to thank Him, while others say that no thanks need be given because God wanted to have people on the earth and He therefore had to provide for all their needs even as He provides for all the other creatures.

35

ELISHA BEN AVUYAH– "ACHER"

Elisha ben Avuyah was the third member of the group of four who penetrated the *pardes* of knowledge. Because of his unusual ideas regarding Judaism, which were held to be harmful to the faith, he came to be called "Acher"—the one who is different—and it was said that his delving into the mysteries of the faith confused him to such a degree that he finally came to oppose it. In the idiom of that day, it was said that he "cut down the plants."

When Elisha was still a student at the academy, everyone believed that he had no other interests outside the Torah, but he read Greek poetry, and books of philosophy filled his pockets. Years later, when the Roman government sought to suppress the Torah and forced the Jews to break its commandments, Elisha advised the Romans which labors a Jew may perform on the Sabbath without incurring a sin.

The "unclean" books that Elisha read are referred to in the Talmud as "books of the erroneous" and "books of the heretics." Because of the severe persecutions, the faith of many weakened and they turned to these sects. It would seem that Elisha hovered between the two, but the spark of Judaism continued to burn within him. He had absorbed too much of the Torah to be able to break away from it entirely.

It is difficult at this day to define the teachings of the
Gnostics. They pondered the mysteries of the Godhead and
employed both rationalism as well as mysticism in their attempt to solve the problem. An important question for them
was the determination of the material from which God created
the world. Recognizing that the world was motivated by
various forces, they concluded that God in heaven had no
control over events on earth. At first they believed that the
world was created out of a definite material that they could not
describe, and they also believed that forces existed that were
not subject to the control of God, and that angels participated
in the government of the world. Later they altogether denied
the existence of a God who rules the world.

These doubters were considered harmful to the Jewish
faith and they were persecuted and expelled from Jewish
society. They then joined other sects, but were also expelled
from them. These confused speculations brought Elisha to a
state of extreme pessimism and depression and he was
haunted by a voice from heaven which seemed to announce:
"Repent, all lost children, except Acher, for whom there is no
repentance."

Elisha believed that people suffer for the sins of their
parents, and he declared that when he was still a child his
father sinned in vowing to make a scholar out of his son, not in
order to fulfill the commandment of studying the Torah but out
of pride. He was also oppressed by the weight of the sin of his
mother who happened to pass by a house of idol worshippers
when she was pregnant, and inhaled the odors of the unclean
sacrifices.

Concerning his origin, Elisha told that his father was one
of the wealthiest men in Jerusalem. On the day of Elisha's
circumcision, his father prepared a great feast and invited all
the prominent men of the city, among whom were the two
greatest scholars of the day, Rabbi Eliezer ben Hyrcanus and
Rabbi Joshua ben Chananiah. When the guests turned to idle
conversation after the feast, Rabbi Eliezer said to Rabbi Joshua,
"Let them speak of that which interests them while we will go
to another room and discuss matters of the Torah." When they

began to discuss the Torah, a cloud of fire descended from heaven and enveloped them. Seeing this Avuyah said to them, "Do you wish to burn my house?" But they replied, "God forbid! We do not play with fire but are only discussing the Torah." Avuyah then said, "If the power of the Torah is so great, then I vow that if my son will live to reach manhood I will consecrate him to the Torah."

The Talmud relates that the name Acher by which Elisha was called was not given to him by the scholars but by a harlot. It is told that a decision was adopted in heaven that since Elisha embraced an "evil culture" and lost his share in the world to come, he was to be allowed to enjoy the pleasures of this world to the full. Elisha once encountered a harlot on the street and asked her to go with him, but she said, "Are you not Elisha ben Avuyah whose name is renowned throughout the world?" He tried to prove that he was another person and, it being a Sabbath day, he pulled a radish from a field and offered it to her. The woman then remarked, "If you do so, you must be someone else" (*acher*—a different one). Since that time the name Acher clung to Elisha.

But despite Elisha's heresies, he did not cease to study the Torah. Some even claim that he revered it to his dying day and praised those who fulfilled its commandments. Some of his sayings have been immortalized, but it seems probable that the scholars refrained from acknowledging his authorship in many instances and even refused to quote them as having been stated by Acher. His statements generally dealt with secular and human problems. In only one instance is his name mentioned in connection with a regulation regarding mourning.[1]

Elisha was the teacher of Rabbi Meir, who was also a disciple of Rabbi Akiba and who was held in great esteem by his colleagues. The name of Rabbi Meir is frequently mentioned as the author of many opinions; but whenever it was suspected that Rabbi Meir's statements were based on the opinions of his teacher Elisha, such statement were referred to as "others say" (*acheirim omrim*).

Legends surround all of Elisha's accomplishments from his childhood until the day of his death. Thus it was told that he sought to uproot the Torah and went from one academy to another driving out the pupils and handing over the teachers to be executed by the government. He then used to say, "Why waste the time of innocent children with such things? Would it not be better if they were taught to be masons or carpenters, hunters or tailors?"

Another legend tells that when Elisha entered *pardes*, he saw the angel Metateron whose duty it is to write down all the good deeds of the Jews once every day and he asked: "How is it that we have learned that none ever sit in heaven for no weariness exists there, but I saw the angel sitting when he recorded the deeds of the Jews. Is it possible that there are two kinds of forces which guide the world?"

The angel was then scourged with sixty fiery lashes to prove to Elisha that he had no more rights than the others. It was then asked, "Why should the angel have been punished?" The answer was given that the angel should have risen when he saw Elisha. But despite the punishment, the angel was allowed the privilege of erasing all of Elisha's good deeds from the book of records.

It is probable that Elisha headed an academy before he was overcome by doubts and of his pupils only Rabbi Meir attained prominence. Rabbi Meir said that he considered Elisha as one does a pomegranate—he ate the heart of the fruit and threw away the skin. Rabbi Meir sought every opportunity to listen to Elisha in an attempt to learn something new from him. Once on a Sabbath, Rabbi Meir was sitting with his pupils in the academy when he was informed that Elisha was riding by. Rabbi Meir went out to hear what Elisha had to say, but Elisha continued riding on his horse and Rabbi Meir followed him. When they approached the limit which one is allowed to walk on the Sabbath, Elisha said, "Turn back Meir, for you may go no farther. By the walk of my horse I recognize that we have reached the limit of the distance one may walk on the Sabbath."

Rabbi Meir then said, "Will you not return also?" but Elisha answered, "I told you long ago that once I heard a voice declare that all strayed children may repent except Acher."

Rabbi Meir insisted that they return to the academy. Elisha asked the first boy whom they met, what he had learned on that day and the boy replied, "There is no peace for the wicked, says God" (Isa. 48:22). They then approached another academy, and Elisha again asked the first boy they met what he had learned and the boy answered, "Even though you wash in much chalk and use much soap the stain of your sin will remain" (Jer. 2:22). They thus made the rounds of thirteen academies and in every instance the children recited verses that were bad omens. Finally they approached the fourteenth academy and the boy said that he had learned the verse, "To the wicked, God says, Why do you speak of my laws?" (Ps. 50:16). The boy stammered while reciting and it seemed to Elisha that the boy said "Elisha" instead of *rasha* (wicked). Elisha became very angry and some say that he drew a dagger and killed the boy, while others claim that he merely said, "If I had a dagger I would kill you now."

Another time Elisha is said to have asked Rabbi Meir for his interpretation of the verse, "One against another, God made them" (Eccles. 7:14). Rabbi Meir said that whatever God created, He also created its opposite. He created high mountains and low hills; He created the seas and the rivers. Elisha then remarked, "Rabbi Akiba explained this verse otherwise. He said that God created just men and wicked men; He created a Paradise and a Gehenna. Every Jew may therefore choose between two shares, one in Paradise and one in Gehenna. If he is a just man he takes his own and his neighbor's share in Paradise; if he is a wicked man he takes his own and his neighbor's share in Gehenna.

Elisha also asked Rabbi Meir's explanation of the verse, "She may not be valued in gold or in glass, and vessels of pure gold are not her equal" (Job 28:17). Rabbi Meir declared that the verse refers to the Torah that cannot be valued in gold but is broken as easily as glass. Elisha said, "Not so did your teacher Rabbi Akiba say. He said that just as golden and glass vessels may be mended after they are broken, even so may a sinful scholar be made whole again."

"Will you not repent now?" Rabbi Meir asked. But Elisha

answered, "I am lost, for I heard a voice say that all may repent except Acher."

The Talmud further relates that when Elisha died, it was said in heaven that he can neither be judged nor can he have a share in the world to come. He could not be judged because he devoted himself to the Torah and he lost his share in the world to come because of his sins. Rabbi Meir said that it was better that he be judged that he may afterward regain his share in the world to come. "When I die," Rabbi Meir said, "you will see smoke coming out of Elisha's grave for I will certainly bring him to judgment because of his knowledge of the Torah." Afterward Rabbi Meir also told that when Elisha was nearing death he wept because of his sins and it seemed that he repented in his heart.

After Elisha's death his daughter (the Jerusalem Talmud says his daughters) came to Rabbi Jehudah the Nasi to ask for bread. Rabbi Jehudah asked her who she was and she said, "I am the daughter of Elisha." Rabbi Jehudah wondered that such a wicked man had children who remained Jews, but the daughter pleaded, "Remember his Torah and overlook his deeds." Fire then descended from heaven and enveloped Rabbi Jehudah. Rabbi Jehudah wept and said, "If this happens to those who dishonor the Torah, how much more can happen to those who glory in it?"

Some historians maintain that one of the reasons for Elisha's abandonment of Judaism was his great envy of Rabbi Akiba. Elisha felt humiliated that a man of unknown origin who began his studies in his later years should be elevated to such a high position by the people. He then said, "He who learns as a youth may be compared to one writing with ink on new paper, but when one begins his studies after he is old it may be compared to writing on erased paper."[2] This is more exactly expressed in *Avot Derabi Natan*: "He who studies in his youth absorbs the words of the Torah into his blood and they come clearly out of his mouth; but he who studies when he is old does not absorb the words of the Torah into his blood and they come indistinctly out of his mouth."

From Rabbi Akiba's statements we may conclude that he was an enemy of Elisha. Rabbi Akiba opposed Greek philosophy and said that whoever studies it loses his share in the world to come. Since Elisha devoted himself to Greek writings, we may assume that Rabbi Akiba's words were directed at him.

Elisha seems to have had no sympathy with the movement of rebellion against Rome. When the Roman government began to persecute the students of the Torah, Elisha maintained, as did many other scholars, that one must not endanger his life for it.

A Talmudic legend traces the beginning of Elisha's doubts to his having seen a man climb a tree to remove a nest containing both fledglings and the mother bird. Although this was against the commandment of the Torah, nothing happened to the man. The following day he saw another man removing a nest with fledglings but he chased the mother bird away, as the Torah commanded. Although the fulfillment of this commandment is to be rewarded by long life, the man was bitten by a snake when he descended from the tree and he died immediately. Elisha then asked, "Where is the long life that was promised to the man?" Others said that he began to doubt when he saw the tongue of Rabbi Jeduhah the Baker (or of Rabbi Hutzpit the Interpreter) dragged around by dogs. Elisha then came to the conclusion that there was no reward for just men, and he also lost his belief in the resurrection of the dead.

It has already been noted that there probably exist numerous opinions of Elisha whose authorship is not acknowledged. But *Avot Derabi Natan* contains a chapter devoted to Elisha's sayings and to his opinions regarding men of great learning who also commit good deeds and men who only possess great learning. There Elisha says that a man of learning and of good deeds may be compared to a structure built on a foundation of stone while the walls are made of bricks; even the greatest flood cannot undermine such a structure. But a man who possesses much learning but has done no good deeds may be compared to a structure with a foundation of bricks and walls of stone. Such a structure is easily undermined.

Another statement of Elisha in the same book well characterizes the man. He said: "A man may study for twenty years
and forget all his knowledge in two years, so that he would not
know to differentiate between the clean and the unclean and he
would begin to confuse the opinions of one scholar with those
of another until he finally would have to remain silent."

It thus becomes obvious that Elisha was a man of contradictions. At times he honored the Torah and was a friend of the
scholars. On other occasions he was an enemy of the Torah and
aided the Roman government in persecuting the scholars. He
was always full of regrets and contemplated repentance, but he
was deeply convinced that he was beyond repentance because
of his many sins.

Elisha's greatest crime was his treason to his people and
aiding the enemy at a time of persecution against the Jews. His
intentions might not have been treasonable, and it is possible
that he honestly believed that bowing to the will of the Romans
was the best policy. But history has proved this opinion to be
false and the attempts to placate the Romans ended in catas-
trophe. It is therefore no wonder that Elisha was condemned.

36

RABBAN SIMEON BEN GAMALIEL II

ALL THE DECREES and the false accusations leveled against the Jews by the Roman government in its attempt to eradicate their feeling of national solidarity and to make impossible their observance of the Torah, proved unsuccessful. At the very moment that the oppression of their faith seemed to become intolerable, the Jews discovered that in neighboring Babylonia they would freely be able to maintain their faith and live openly as Jews. Babylonia was then ruled by the Parthians who had withstood all efforts of the Romans to subjugate them, and all the might of the Roman Empire could not penetrate their borders.[1]

Hadrian who was responsible for much of the suffering inflicted upon the Jews died and was succeeded by Antoninus Pius, who immediately lightened the burden of the Palestinian Jews. A rebellion of the non-Jewish population of Palestine that was supported by the Parthians occurred at that time. Wishing to placate the Jews and to prevent their participation in the uprising, Antoninus Pius ordered that they should be treated more kindly.

The news of the improved political position of the Palestinian Jews rapidly reached Babylonia and many of the exiles, together with a great number of the scholars who had fled Palestine, began to return. Among these repatriates was Rabban Simeon, the son of Rabban Gamaliel of Jabneh. Upon his return he was elected Nasi as Rabban Simeon ben Gamaliel II.

Rabban Simeon ben Gamaliel II was a sixth generation descendant of Hillel and he was considered a worthy successor of his forefathers. During the time of the Bar Kochba rebellion and the persecutions that followed, Rabban Simeon remained in hiding and no one heard of him; but when the Romans later permitted the reorganization of the Sanhedrin they had no objection to the election of Rabban Simeon as Nasi.

The newly reorganized Sanhedrin settled in Usha instead of Jabneh. Among the repatriates who also returned was Rabbi Nathan the Babylonian, the son of the Exilarch of that country, and he was appointed head of the court. Rabbi Meir, the disciple of Elisha ben Avuyah, received the title of *hakham* and was the third leader of the Sanhedrin.

But Rabban Simeon ben Gamaliel was not elected Nasi merely because he was a descendant of Hillel. His elevation to this post was primarily due to his personal qualifications. The scholars knew him well from the time when he was a young man in his father's house. At that time he strictly observed the commandment to honor one's father and in spite of the fact that Rabban Gamaliel owned many slaves, Rabban Simeon diligently sought to serve him. He frequently complained that "no matter how much I serve my father it is not even a hundredth part of that which Esau did for his father Isaac."[2]

As long as he was Nasi, Rabban Simeon sought to enhance the ceremony of that office. He once conceived the idea of doing away with the equality of the three leaders of the Sanhedrin which was the rule until that time. He then issued a regulation that when the Nasi entered the academy, everyone was to rise and remain standing until the Nasi commanded them to be seated. When the head of the court entered, the people on both sides were to form two lines and remain standing until he was seated; when the *hakham* entered everyone was to retain his position, whether seated or standing, until he took his seat.[3]

This regulation was issued on a day when neither Rabbi Nathan nor Rabbi Meir were in the academy. When they came on the following day, they considered this regulation an attempt to diminish their authority in the eyes of the people. They were both greatly angered and Rabbi Meir declared that by issuing this regulation, the Nasi had broken a long standing custom that a man may only be advanced in sacred authority but not demoted. They decided to repay the Nasi in kind and since they were considered to be better-informed in matters of law than the Nasi was, they determined to confront him with questions he would be unable to answer. In thus exposing the Nasi's inadequate learning, they hoped to have him deposed even as his father was once deposed.

Rabbi Nathan and Rabbi Meir decided to ask the Nasi to expound the regulations pertaining to the stems of fruit and their bearing on the cleanliness of the fruit. They expected to be able to confuse him very easily in these matters. But one of the Nasi's devoted adherents heard of the plan and thought that such questions and pilpulistic reasoning might bring shame on the Nasi. He therefore began to walk back and forth in front of the Nasi until he attracted his attention. He then told the Nasi of the plot, and Rabban Simeon prepared himself for all possible questions. To make doubly sure, he did not allow Rabbi Nathan and Rabbi Meir to enter the academy on that day. They then sent in their questions in writing from the outside and Rabban Simeon sought to answer them as best he could. Whenever he was in doubt regarding some matter, the two on the outside sent in their answers.

Seeing this game Rabbi Jose ben Chalafta said to the Nasi: "The Torah remains outside while we sit calmly within." Rabban Simeon permitted the two expelled scholars to return, but he ruled that all laws to be enacted according to their opinions from that day on should not be quoted in their names. This ruling was adopted and all the laws determined by Rabbi Nathan were prefaced by "some say" (*yesh omrim*) while those of Rabbi Meir were quoted as "others say" (*acheirim omrim*).

Some time later both Rabbi Nathan and Rabbi Meir beheld a dream where they were told to reconcile themselves with the

Nasi. Rabbi Nathan obeyed the dream; he bowed before the will of the Nasi and submitted to punishment, but Rabbi Meir refused to submit and he declared that all dreams were vain. The Nasi brought the matter before the scholars and they decided to excommunicate Rabbi Meir. When the Nasi heard of it he sent word to the scholars warning them not to take this unjust step and also that he would not recognize the excommunication.[4]

In the end Rabbi Meir had to leave Palestine and he settled in a city of Asia Minor, where he remained until his death. Before his death he sent a message to Palestine saying: "Your Messiah (!) died on strange soil." He also requested that he be buried on the shore of the sea that touches Palestine so that it should be the same as if he was buried in that country.[5]

In his exposition Rabban Simeon followed his own method. He taught his disciples only those laws sanctioned by the great court and avoided all those that were in doubt, or concerning which there were differences of opinion that had not yet been discussed with the consent of the majority of the scholars. Whenever people came to him for trial in money matters, he ruled that the custom of the country and common sense must determine the judgment, even when scholars arrived at conclusions different from the text of the Bible. Rabban Simeon also tried to raise the prestige of the court and said that the judge's decision must be considered as law.

In his father's house there were many scholars who studied Greek, and Rabban Simeon declared that it was permissible to write a book of the Torah in that language.[6] At another time he declared that it was possible to make a correct translation of the Torah only into the Greek language.[7] He was also versed in the natural sciences and in horticulture,[8] and he was acquainted with the sciences of anatomy and medicine. When he was consulted regarding problems of marital life or concerning laws that forbid or allow certain actions, he always paid more attention to the intent of the action rather than to its superficial aspect.

Rabban Simeon sided with the weak against the strong and he supported the rights of women in the laws of the *ketubbah*. He demanded justice for Gentile slaves and declared that people are commanded to redeem slaves just as they are obliged to ransom free men who had been kidnapped.[9] He supported capital punishment for murderers in order to prevent the increase of murderers among Jews. This conviction he held against the opinion of many scholars who were opposed to capital punishment.[10]

Tolerant toward people of other faiths, Rabban Simeon said that a Gentile who appears before a Jewish court should be judged according to Jewish law.[11] Documents of indebtedness signed by non-Jews he held to be valid, and in opposition to the conviction of other scholars he maintained that Samaritans were to be considered as Jews in all matters, for every commandment the Samaritans undertook to observe they observed more scrupulously than the Jews.[12]

Rabban Simeon said that the world is based on three concepts: truth, justice, and peace.[13] In his lectures he stressed the value of peace and declared that numerous passages of the Torah use ambiguous language out of a desire for peace.[14] On another occasion he declared that "he who makes peace in his own home is like one who makes peace among all Jews.[15]

Rabban Simeon was raised in royal splendor in his father's house and for this reason he frequently complained that Jewish life had lost its former elegance, and that even nature had changed in Palestine in comparison with earlier days. In bygone days God had shown his love for Israel and sometimes even changed the course of natural events for their sake.[16] But since the destruction of the Temple, the dew no longer caused the plants to grow and the fruit had lost its taste.[17]

All the religious innovations his father had introduced in Jabneh, such as the lighting of candles in honor of the Sabbath, Rabban Simeon sought to establish in Usha. In this attempt, however, he met with little success. He often recounted the memories of early days in his father's house, when the Temple was still in existence. He would gladly have introduced in Usha all those earlier customs were it not for the opposition he met from other scholars.

He also endeavored to strengthen the office of Nasi with

an eye to establishing the rule of the dynasty. Since he was the sixth Nasi descended from Hillel, he believed that a scion of the dynasty was entitled to the office of Nasi even if he were not the greatest in his generation, and that it was inconceivable for a member of another family to occupy the post. These efforts of his were especially strengthened by the remembrance that when his grandfather Rabban Simeon ben Gamaliel the Elder was killed by the Romans, he was not immediately succeeded by his son. When the son was later elected Nasi, he was later deposed for a short time. After the death of Rabban Gamaliel of Jabneh, the office was not at once conferred upon the rightful heir and other candidates were tested first. He was especially impelled by the desire to avoid any future repetition of what had happened to his father and what had almost happened to himself—that a sudden opposition to the actions or the opinions of the Nasi should make it possible to have him deposed.

With a special poignancy Rabban Simeon used to tell of the time before the Temple was destroyed. His father had seen the Temple when he was still a child and repeated his memories to Rabban Simeon. He told that Jews had no holidays happier than the fifteenth day of *Av* and the Day of Atonement when all the girls paraded through the streets dressed in white garments some of which they had borrowed from one another in order not to shame those who had no white garments. Afterward they danced in the vineyards and called upon the young men who came to watch and to choose the most beautiful or the wisest as their brides.[18]

He told of the Jerusalem custom of receiving guests. The host would offer them the use of his home and would himself remain outdoors overnight.[19] He also told of the river Shiloah whose waters welled-out through an opening no larger than a copper coin. When the king commanded the mouth of the river be widened, the quantity of water decreased; the king therefore ordered that the original opening be used again and the water continued to flow as heretofore. Rabban Simeon also declared that there was no organ in the Temple because it had interfered with the harmony of the singers, although the instrument is in itself pleasing to the ear.[20]

Rabban Simeon ben Gamaliel recounted these stories because he wanted to maintain the patriotic fervor of the people for Jerusalem, and because he was convinced that the city would regain its old splendor even in his day. He believed that when the Jews were liberated from the Roman yoke, Jerusalem would become a center for all surrounding nations and that people would flock there to learn the true faith. Because of his devotion to Jerusalem he stressed the significance of *Tisha b'Ab* and declared that one who breaks the fast of *Tisha b'Ab* is like one who eats on the Day of Atonement.[21]

For although the government persisted in its persecutions, the people seemed to have become accustomed to them, and as long as the existence of the Sanhedrin was permitted the people did not complain too much of the other forms of oppression. This is evident from the saying of Rabban Simeon that "our forefathers could not endure even a little suffering but we who suffer for so many generations have more cause to lose our patience.[22] Another time he said: "We have learned to love our sufferings but were we to write them down, we would not have enough strength."[23]

Some people once approached Rabban Simeon and attempted to persuade him that it would be well for the Jews to aid the Egyptians in their attempt to overthrow the Romans, and Rabban Simeon said to them, "If we look at the wealthy and wicked government we can see that all its regiments are always occupied both day and night, but when we look at Egypt we see its soldiers always idle. How then can we hope to be victorious with their help?"[24]

From the previously described behavior of Rabban Simeon one may get the impression that he was a proud man. Such a conclusion, however, would be far from the truth for Rabban Simeon was renowned for his modesty. In the performance of his duties as Nasi he dictated his will and brooked no opposition, but in private life there could be found no other man as modest as he was. When, in his capacity of Nasi, he determined a leap year (*ibur*), he wrote to all the Jewish communities informing them that he had consulted no one and made the decision himself—as against the custom of his father who wrote

that he made the decision with the advice of his colleagues. But
of his personal modesty an anecdote is related of a man who
vowed not to touch his wife until she had spit in the face of the
Nasi. The woman did so and Rabban Simeon did not scold her.
When Rabban Simeon's son complained to him that he had
been insulted by Rabbi Eleazar ben Simeon, he said to him,
"My son, pay no attention to it for Rabbi Eleazar is a lion, the
son of a lion, but you are only a lion, the son of a fox."[25]

In addition to those sayings of Rabban Simeon, the
following maxims are characteristic of his trend of thought:

"Every commandment the Jews joyfully accepted from
Mount Sinai they continue to observe with joy and no amount
of persecution will avail against them.[26]

"One may profane the Sabbath for the sake of a living,
day-old-child, but one may not profane the Sabbath for the
sake of a dead King David.[27]

"When a man sells his daughter or a book of the Torah in
order to satisfy his hunger, such a sale will never bring him
luck.[28]

"It is not necessary to erect monuments to just men, for
their words are their memorials.[29]

"It might have been necessary to pass a law forbidding the
eating of meat and the drinking of wine since the Temple was
destroyed; but such a law could not be enforced and it is
therefore unnecessary to enact it. Ever since the government
decreed that no one must engage in study of the Torah, it
would have been necessary to enact a law that people should
not marry and have children. The necessity for teaching the
Torah to children would then no longer exist. But one must not
think of doing so, and the Jews must be allowed to do as they
wish, and they will certainly find the right way to save
themselves from the decrees.[30]

"If a man vows not to eat meat, he may still eat the head
and the feet of an animal, for these parts are not considered as
meat and he who eats them is not considered a man.[31]

"He who studies the Torah in his youth is like a young
man who marries a virgin and both possess their youthful
ardor; she turns to him with love and he embraces her; but he
who began to study the Torah in his old age may be compared

to an old man who married a virgin; she lovingly caresses him but he avoids her.[32]

"A student who abandons the Torah may be compared to a bird that cannot find its nest and is sure to fall to the ground when it is weary of its wanderings."[33]

It has been mentioned before that many Jews settled in neighboring countries to escape the persecution of the Romans. Rabban Simeon ben Gamaliel strove to preserve the significance of Palestine as the center of Jewish faith in the minds of the exiles and to prevent the establishment of another new religious center similar to the Temple of Onias in Alexandria. In this effort he was eminently successful.

37

RABBI NATHAN
OF BABYLONIA

THE CITY OF USHA WAS CHOSEN as the seat of the Sanhedrin after that body was reorganized with permission of the Roman emperor Antoninus Pius, who ascended the throne some time after the destruction of Betar. When Rome was almost successful in eradicating Judaism from Palestine, a new center of Jewish spiritual life in Babylonia developed, that was not subject to Roman rule. The city of Nehardea occupied a particularly prominent place in the life of the Jews, because it was the seat of the Exilarch who represented the Babylonian Jews and who was granted special privileges by the Parthian government. Before Nehardea attained its importance, there was a large Jewish settlement in Netsivin that was closer to Palestine, but Hadrian's legions reached this city, laid it waste, and slaughtered its inhabitants. Among those who saved their lives there was Rabbi Jehudah ben Bathyra II who later organized an academy. But he did not succeed in concentrating a large number of people about his academy, because everyone sought to settle farther into the interior of Babylonia in order to be safe from Roman attacks. It was then that another scholar Chananiah (or Hanna) the nephew of Rabbi Joshua ben Chananiah, selected Nehardea as his residence and there established a large academy.

When it became known in Babylonia that all religious activity in Palestine was being suppressed, Chananiah undertook to establish a Supreme Court. Convinced that the main duties of the court since the destruction of the Temple consisted in determining leap years and establishing dates for the festivals, he believed that these functions could just as well be fulfilled in Babylonia. But this situation was considered by the Palestinian scholars as an attempt to undermine their authority. The Nasi, Rabban Simeon ben Gamaliel, especially objected to self-established authorities outside of Palestine and he sent two special messengers to Babylonia to attempt to change matters.

The mission to Babylonia is described in two differing versions.[1]

It is told that the Nasi entrusted three letters to the messengers he sent to Chananiah in Babylonia and he commanded them to deliver these letters one at a time. The first letter contained "greetings to the worthy holiness of Chananiah." When the messengers were asked what their motive was in coming to Babylonia, they said they had come to study. Chananiah then presented them to his colleagues and said, "These are renowned men whose forefathers conducted the service in the Temple."

The messengers then paid close attention to the expositions of Chananiah and attempted to prove to him that he was in error regarding various laws. Greatly angered Chananiah wanted to denounce them, but now they showed him the Nasi's second letter informing him that "the kids he had left in Palestine had meanwhile grown up and developed sharp horns."

Chananiah wanted to denounce the messengers from Palestine as swindlers but they said to him, "Since you believed our words before, you cannot now denounce us." At the same time they also gave him the Nasi's third letter where Chananiah was commanded not to assume the right of establishing the new years or determining the holidays. Chananiah objected that he had a right to do whatever he thought was best for the people, and he also cited that Rabbi Akiba once determined a leap year when he was outside the boundaries of Palestine.

"Do not compare yourself with Rabbi Akiba," the messengers answered, "for none could compare with him even in Palestine."

"Neither did I leave in Palestine anyone that could compare with me," Chananiah retorted.

The messengers then drew his attention to the contents of the second letter that reminded him that the small people he had left in Palestine had grown in stature and they commanded him, "If you will obey and depart from your ways all will be well, otherwise you will be driven out from the community of Israel, and you can choose a place for an altar and sacrifices and music even as the Jews of Alexandria once did."

When the messengers realized that Chananiah was still unwilling to submit, one of them ascended to read the Torah on a day that Chananiah had declared to be a feast day, but he changed the text to read, "These are the holidays of Chananiah." The congregation immediately corrected him that he should read "These are the holidays of God." The messenger replied, "It is true that in our books it is written 'These are the holidays of God,' but here one should substitute the name of Chananiah because he determines the holidays as he chooses and not as God commanded."

Then the second messenger arose and recited a verse "Out of Babylon shall come the Torah"; the congregation corrected him to say "Out of Zion." The messenger replied: "In our books it is written 'Out of Zion,' but judging by your conduct you may write 'Out of Babylon' in your books."

All the people gathered began to weep and were ready to obey the words of the messengers from Palestine, but Chananiah still refused to submit. He went to Rabbi Jehudah ben Bathyra of Netsivin to ask his advice. Rabbi Jehudah suggested that he submit because the Great Court of Palestine was the only body with authority to regulate the religious life of the people both within as well as outside of Palestine.

It is also related of Chananiah that he frequently travelled from Palestine to Babylonia but he was always grieved to leave the country. Once he was accompanied by Rabbi Jehudah ben Bathyra, Rabbi Matia ben Harash and Rabbi Jonathan. When they reached the boundary of Palestine and bethought themselves of the land they were leaving, they rent their garments and wept. Grieved at the thought of leaving the Land of Israel, they abandoned all thoughts of personal safety that awaited them in Babylonia and returned to Palestine.[2]

Chananiah was a pupil of his uncle at Jabneh and later he mingled among the greatest men of his generation. When he fell sick, he was visited by the most outstanding people, but because of his frequent departures from Palestine and his attempt to rebel against the scholars of Palestine he was never ordained. Two or three times he is referred to in the Talmud as Rabbi, but this appears to be an error of the copyists. His legal opinions are not quoted in the *Mishnah* but they frequently appear in the *Beraita*.[3]

Chananiah visited Babylonia several times returning always to Palestine, but after his clash with the messengers of the Nasi, he remained in Babylonia permanently.

The reason Rabbi Joshua ben Chananiah sent his nephew, Chananiah, to Babylonia is said to have been due, not so much to the danger threatening all scholars of Palestine as to the fact that the *minim* (the Jewish Christians) cast a spell on him and he forgot what day it was and came riding to the academy on the Sabbath. Wishing to save him from this spell, his uncle sent him away to Babylonia.

The Jews of Babylonia lived in security and peace while the Jews of Palestine were being sorely oppressed. Even after the emperor Antoninus Pius alleviated their prosecutions and granted them freedom to observe all the customs of the Jewish faith, the situation of Palestine Jewry still could not compare with that of the Jews of Babylon who enjoyed autonomy in their religious life under the leadership of an Exilarch. But these differences did not deter many Jews from returning to Palestine as soon as they heard of the improved situation in that country, for everyone believed that in Babylonia he was removed from God and that God's grace rested only in Palestine.

During the time that Rabban Simeon ben Gamaliel was

Nasi in Palestine, Rabbi Nathan of Babylonia came to settle in that country, and the Sanhedrin at Usha elected him head of the court soon after his arrival. Rabbi Nathan was the son of the Exilarch as is evident from the remark of Rabban Simeon ben Gamaliel who said to him: "Now that you are head of the court because of your father's silver girdle (the official symbol of the rank of the Exilarch) you should not strive to become Nasi." [4]

Some believe that Rabbi Nathan had visited Palestine before he was elected head of the court, and that he was a pupil of Rabbi Ishmael ben Elisha, Rabbi Eliezer ben Hyrcanus, and other scholars whom he later mentioned. But when the persecutions increased, he left the country and travelled through many lands until the political situation improved when Antoninus Pius ascended the throne.

He told that on one of his journeys there was brought before him a weak child of a woman whose two previous children had died as a result of circumcision. He looked at the child and seeing that his skin was red suggested that circumcision be postponed until the blood was diffused throughout his body.

During these journeys he kept informed on what transpired in Palestine, and he was filled with great reverence for the Palestinian Jews who sacrificed their lives for the observance of the Torah. He related that walking in the street, one could see Roman soldiers leading a Jew to execution, and when the man was asked what he had done to deserve the punishment he said that he had circumcised his son; another man would be executed for studying the Torah. Further, one could see a man being led to crucifixion and when asked what he had done, he said "I have eaten *matzah* on Passover" or one could see a man being scourged for taking up the *lulav*.[5]

The editing of the *Mishnah* into books and tractates was begun during the lifetime of Rabbi Nathan, but his role in this labor is unknown and there are only two references in the Talmud to the existence of a *Mishnah* of Rabbi Nathan.[6] According to another source, the *Mishnah* was completed by the Nasi Rabbi Jehudah and by Rabbi Nathan.[7] Rabbi Nathan did leave a book of social, ethical, and religious maxims very similar to the book of Avot and this book is called *Avot Derabi Natan*. In the opinion of some, the book *Mekhilta* was collated by the pupils of Rabbi Nathan from the sayings of their teacher who quoted the lectures of his master Rabbi Ishmael.

Rabbi Nathan's system of exposition was to trace every law to the original text and to remove all contradictions. His legal opinions are quoted in the Talmud and are always very penetrating.[8]

After the death of Rabban Simeon ben Gamaliel, Rabbi Nathan continued as head of the court of the Sanhedrin during the administration of Rabbi Jehudah, despite the fact that he was frequently in conflict with him. The Nasi Rabbi Jehudah declared that: "I was once childish and brazenly opposed Rabbi Nathan of Babylonia."[9]

Characteristic of Rabbi Nathan's trend of thought are the following social, ethical, and religious maxims based on the text of the Torah. The verse: "You shall not wrong or oppress a stranger, for you were strangers in the land of Egypt" (Ex. 22:20). Rabbi Nathan interpreted that to mean "a man should never accuse others of the fault from which he is suffering."[10]

The Menorah was constructed so that the three lights on either side were inclined toward the central light. This indicates that the one in the center is always the most important one.[11]

Rabbi Nathan opposed vows and he said: "For the sin of making a vow and not fulfilling it, a man is punished by the death of his wife.[12] Another time he said, "He who makes a vow is like one who builds a *bamah* (an altar outside of the temple) and the sin of one who fulfills his vow is like the sin of a man who offers sacrifices on a *bamah*.[13]

A man who accepts a bribe to pass an unjust sentence will not die before one of the following three calamities befall him: he will lose his reason, he will become dependent on human charity, or the vision of his eyes will be diminished.[14]

Another saying of Rabbi Nathan gives a clear picture of the conditions of that time: "It is a good omen for a man to receive his punishment immediately after his death by: not being buried, not being mourned, having his body devoured by animals, or by having his body exposed to the rain. All these indicate that the man received his due punishment immediately after his death.[15]

We have remarked before that Rabbi Nathan travelled through many countries and it was then that he observed the nature of the various nations which he characterized in the following manner:

(1) Nine-tenths of the harlotry in the world is concentrated in Alexandria, and the remaining tenth is spread over the rest of the world.

(2) Nine-tenths of the wealth of the world is in Rome, and the remaining tenth is scattered throughout the rest of the world.

(3) Nine-tenths of the poverty in the world is concentrated in Lud and the remaining tenth is distributed throughout the rest of the world.

(4) Nine-tenths of the witchcraft in the world is in Egypt and the remaining tenth in all the other countries.

(5) Nine-tenths of the foolishness in the world is possessed by the Ishmaelites and one-tenth by all other peoples.

(6) Nine-tenths of the filth in the world is possessed by the Persians and the remaining tenth by all other peoples.

(7) The land of Media possesses nine-tenths of the beauty in the world and all the other countries possess but one-tenth.

(8) Nine-tenths of the ugliness in the world is in the East (?) and one-tenth in all other countries.

(9) The Chaldeans possess nine-tenths of the strength in the world and all the other countries possess but one-tenth.

(10) The tribe of Judah possesses nine-tenths of the valor in the world and all the other countries possess the remaining tenth.

(11) The Land of Israel possesses nine-tenths of the wisdom in the world and all other countries possess but one-tenth.

(12) The Jews possess nine-tenths of the Torah (learning) in the world and all the other peoples possess but one-tenth.[16]

Speaking in the same vein on another occasion he said: "There is no greater love than the love of the Torah; there is no greater wisdom than the wisdom of the Land of Israel; there is no greater beauty than the beauty of Jerusalem; there is no greater wealth than the wealth of Rome; there is no greater valor than the valor of the Persians; there is no greater immorality than the immorality of the Arabs; there is no greater rudeness than the rudeness of the land of Elam; there is no greater flattery than the flattery of Babylonia; there is no greater witchcraft than the witchcraft of Egypt."[17]

The following statements of Rabbi Nathan concerning the creation of the world are also very interesting:

"The whole world is beneath one star. One can see this by looking at a star. If a man walk to the East, the star is above him; if he walk in another direction the star is still over him. During the summer the sun is high in the sky and the whole world is hot but the water from the springs is cold; but during the winter the sun is low in the sky and the whole world is cold but the water from the springs is warm.[18]

38

RABBI MEIR

T HE REMNANT OF RABBI AKIBA'S disciples together
with those scholars who were ordained by Rabbi Jehudah ben
Baba were the main pillars of the Sanhedrin at Usha. Rabbi
Meir was one of the most important of these.

Nothing is known of Rabbi Meir's family; even his name is
not known for certain. Some authorities maintain that his real
name was not Meir but Nehorai and that he was called Meir
because "he illuminated the vision of the scholars with his
learning." Others say that his name was Miasha or that he was
really Rabbi Eleazar ben Arach.[1] It is interesting to note
that the names Meir and Nehorai have the same meaning. Meir
is the Hebrew for "one who gives light" and Nehorai is its
Aramaic equivalent. However, it is also noteworthy that
the Talmud cites a dispute between Rabbi Meir and Rabbi
Nehorai.[2]

A legend relates that Rabbi Meir was descended from a
Roman general who was sent to subdue Palestine and who was
converted to Judaism. It is therefore remarkable that despite his
uncertain origin, Rabbi Meir became the son-in-law of Rabbi
Chanina ben Teradion who gave him his brilliant daughter,
Beruriah, in marriage.

The first years of Rabbi Meir's activity must have occurred

328

after the destruction of Betar and before Emperor Antoninus Pius alleviated the condition of the Jews. Since Rabbi Meir was a pupil of Elisha ben Avuyah during the time of Hadrian's decrees against the study of the Torah, it may be assumed that together with other scholars he fled to Babylonia for a time and returned with the accession of Antoninus Pius to the throne of Rome.

At first Rabbi Meir was a pupil of Rabbi Ishmael and later he studied with Rabbi Akiba. He was also a pupil of Elisha ben Avuyah and he maintained a close friendship with a Gentile philosopher Abnimos Hagardi, who was a great friend of the Jewish people and who revered the Torah.[3]

Rabbi Meir's devotion to Elisha ben Avuyah has been described before. His friendship for Abnimos Hagardi was equally great and when the parents of his friend died he visited him and condoled with him.[4]

It thus becomes evident that Rabbi Meir was interested in the Gentile sciences as well as Jewish learning and he was probably acquainted with the Greek writings of his time. The three daily benedictions which Rabbi Meir instituted (for not being born a Gentile, for not being born a woman, and for not being created a boor) he did not receive by tradition from previous scholars, but he probably imitated the Greek philosopher Socrates who recited three similar benedictions to his idols. This supposition is further substantiated by his devotion and friendship for Elisha ben Avuyah and Abnimos Hagardi. It is impossible to think that these two did not acquaint him with Greek literature or that Greek letters should have made no impression upon him, even where they did not conflict with the tenets of Jewish religion. This influence is also evident from his statement that "just as a judge covers his face with a veil even so did the generation of the deluge believe that God covered his face with clouds."[5] Saying this Rabbi Meir must have had in mind the Greek goddess of Justice (Themida) who is pictured with eyes covered.

All of Rabbi Meir's statements were concise and were interwoven with fables from which he deduced legal opinions as well as using them to illustrate legends.[6] When Rabbi Meir died it was said that the mastery of fable had departed.[7]

Rabbi Meir's first public statement resulted in a conflict of opinions. A meeting was held at that time in the valley of Rimon to determine the question of the leap year because the calculations of the calendar were confused. Rabbi Jochanan the Sandalmaker opposed the calculations of Rabbi Meir, and when the latter insisted on his opinion and quoted Rabbi Akiba, Rabbi Jochanan said to him, "I have always served Rabbi Akiba as a disciple while you were only one of the audience." Rabbi Jochanan implied that he was better informed as to the opinions of Rabbi Akiba, but Rabbi Meir scoffed, "You are only an Alexandrian." (The term Alexandrian suggested a person who was limited in his understanding of the words of his master.)

This clash, however, did not engender any hatred between the scholars for they all realized that peace was essential at that time for the observance of the commandments of the Torah. Therefore, none of those gathered departed until peace was restored between the disputants.[8] Only much later did a sharp conflict take place between Rabbi Meir and the Nasi, Rabban Simeon ben Gamaliel, which ended with Rabbi Meir's departure from Palestine to settle in a city of Asia Minor.

Some of Rabbi Meir's statements definitely show the influence of his contact with Elisha ben Avuyah and Abnimos Hagardi. Thus when he said that "even a Gentile who devotes himself to the Torah is like a High Priest"[9] he probably had in mind his friend Abnimos; and when he said that "all Jews are God's children when they behave like children as well as when they misbehave"[10] he no doubt thought of Elisha ben Avuyah.

Rabbi Meir considered learning to be the most important thing in life. A man must always devote more time to learning than to worldly affairs, he said, and whoever devotes himself to learning for its own sake attains various stages of perfection, and he is justified in believing that the world was created for his sake. Such a person is beloved of God and men, people are as pleased with him as is God; he is modest and pious, just and devoted, he refrains from sin and his advice is sought, for the Torah confers on him the understanding of its mysteries.[11]

When the inhabitants of the city of Sepphoris disapproved of his custom of greeting mourners on the Sabbath, because he believed that the Sabbath was not a day of mourning, Rabbi Jose ben Chalafta, Rabbi Meir's friend, defended him and said that he was "a great man, a holy, and a modest man."[12] Still greater praise of Rabbi Meir was expressed by Ravina who said that whoever saw Rabbi Meir in the academy could imagine seeing him pull up the largest mountains and crushing them one against the other, for then a person could gain knowledge even from Rabbi Meir's cane.[13]

Rabbi Meir was attached to Palestine by the bonds of deep love and he spoke with great enthusiasm of the Hebrew language. He greatly treasured these two national assets and declared that whoever settles in the Land of Israel and speaks the Hebrew language is certain to deserve a share in the world to come.[14] He was also a master of legal argumentation and later generations admitted that in his day there was none to equal him. But his legal opinions were frequently rejected because his intent could not be fathomed. Applying pilpulistic reasoning he could prove that which everybody held to be clean as unclean and vice versa.[15]

An anecdote was therefore current at that time that Rabbah ben Shilah once met the prophet Elijah and asked him what God was doing. Elijah replied that God was pondering the words of all the scholars except those of Rabbi Meir, because he was a pupil of Acher.[16]

It is necessary to remark, however, that Rabbi Meir never tried to lighten the burden of the law so that people might not say that he allowed liberties to be taken with the law because of his knowledge of secular sciences. He was therefore strict in his interpretation as, for instance, when he ruled that a *Ketubbah* (marriage certificate) that promises less than two hundred dinars for a virgin or less than one hundred dinars for a widow is not valid,[17] or that a bill of divorce differing even by one word from the prescribed form is invalid and any children the woman may have by a subsequent marriage are illegitimate.[18]

He frequently brought up for discussion legal situations that may occur only very rarely or never at all. In doing so

Rabbi Meir tried to provide complicated exercises for his pupils as, for example, the case of a man who had two groups of daughters from two wives, and one of the daughters was married but he did not know whether it was the oldest of the first group or the oldest of the second, or possibly the youngest of the older group who was older than the oldest of the younger group.[19] Another time he suggested the problem of an ox belonging to a deaf person, a foolish man, or a minor that gored the ox belonging to an intelligent man.[20] The following was another example of this type of questions: the law forbids the slaughter an animal and its offspring on the same day; but a man who slaughtered an animal and its third generation offspring has broken no law. If however this person proceeds to slaughter the daughter of the old animal (and the mother of the young) he breaks the law twice but he is to be punished only once.[21]

When Rabbi Meir died, his colleague, Rabbi Jehudah bar Elai, asked that his disciples no longer be admitted to the academy because of their attitude of spite; they came not to learn but to ask perplexing questions which could not be answered.[22]

It would be difficult to list here all of Rabbi Meir's legal opinions since the *Mishnah* alone contains over 300 laws that bear his name. In addition it is traditionally accepted that all laws whose authorship is not mentioned are generally those of Rabbi Meir. We are more concerned here with his ethical maxims that reflect a great love for the Jewish people, the Torah, and the Land of Israel. Of special interest are his ideas about death.

Death was not considered as an uncommon and cruel phenomenon during the time of Rabbi Meir. The constant wars and the bloody persecution of the Jews hardened the people to consider death with indifference. If a man lost his life for his observance of Judaism, his relatives were comforted by the belief that he had sacrificed himself for the sake of God. Rabbi Meir probably witnessed the death of Rabbi Akiba as well as the execution of many others. Later he witnessed the death of his father-in-law, Rabbi Chanina ben Teradion. Rabbi Meir therefore evolved a philosophic outlook on death and he frequently turned to the Book of Job. Rabbi Jochanan relates that every time Rabbi Meir finished reading that book he would say: "The end of a man is death; the end of animals is slaughter; everything in the world is doomed to die. Happy is he who is raised in the knowledge of the Torah and who strives for it thus causing satisfaction for his Creator. Such a man prospers in his good name and he leaves the world in good repute as King Solomon said: "A good name is better than fragrant oil and the day of death is better than the day of birth."[23]

The same idea lies at the root of his statement that the Biblical description of the creation of the world that ends in saying that God saw all that He created and that it was "very good" implies that death is "very good." After the creation of the world God was satisfied with its growth and development as well as with the death of its inhabitants.[24]

Rabbi Meir's attitude toward an *am ha'aretz* was unusual. It is told that he always rose at the sight of an old man even if the man was an *am ha'aretz*. When he was asked why he accords such honor to an old *am ha'aretz*, he replied, that if God chose to grant such a man so many years of life, he must have deserved it and he therefore also deserved that people should accord him honor.[25]

But despite the honor he accorded them, Rabbi Meir felt an overwhelming hatred of the *am ha'aretz* saying, "When a man marries his daughter to an *am ha'aretz* it is as if he bound her and placed her in front of a lion who steps on his victim before devouring her. An *am ha'aretz* may also beat his wife and love her at the same time without shame.[26] Another time he expressed his hatred of an *am ha'aretz* in even sharper terms when he said that "one who allows an *am ha'aretz* to sleep in his house and finds him awake when he enters the house, must consider the house to be unclean."[27]

Rabbi Meir's social orientation may be gleaned from his statement that a bill of debt that includes a clause about interest is invalid and even the principal may not be collected.[28] The charging of interest he considered to be on a par with robbery and the repentance of a man who had committed robbery could never be accepted.[29]

Rabbi Meir studied with three masters (Rabbi Ishmael, Rabbi Akiba, and Elisha-Acher) and of this he said: "A man who learns the Torah from one master may be compared with a person who owns one field, part of which is sown to wheat, part to barley, another part is planted with olives, and the remainder with other trees. Such a man will see no blessing in his field. But one who learned from two or more masters may be compared to a person who owns several fields, one of which is sown to wheat and another to barley, one is planted with olive trees and another field is planted with other kinds of trees. Such a man will find blessing in his fields.[30]

Rabbi Meir's wife was the daughter of Rabbi Chanina ben Teradion. He had two sons, both of whom suddenly died on a Saturday afternoon, and one daughter who was married to a scholar named Zivtai. He derived no income from his scholastic work and made his living as a copyist. By doing this work he earned three ducats a week, one of which he spent for food for his household; one he spent for clothing, and the third he distributed to the needy scholars. When he was asked what he was doing to assure the future of his children, Rabbi Meir replied: "If my children will be just men, God will provide them with their needs according to the verse that there was never a just man whose children were forced to beg for bread. But if they will not be just men, why should I leave money for the enemies of God?"[31]

In the matter of the observance of Judaism Rabbi Meir would tolerate no compromises; if he suspected a man of breaking even the slightest commandment, that man was already suspected in his eyes of breaking all the commandments of the Torah.[32] This attitude was parallel to the accepted rule that a false witness was capable of committing every sin mentioned in the Torah.[33]

Every man should teach his son a clean and easy trade, but at the same time he must pray to God for a livelihood for there is no trade but that some who are engaged in it are rich while others are poor. Poverty and wealth are not the result of following a certain trade but every man gets what he deserves.[34] A man may gain his livelihood by doing any kind of work, but happy is the man who sees his parents doing noble work and woe to him who sees his parents engaged in low work.[35]

Concerning prayer Rabbi Meir said that one must not speak too much when praying to God,[36] and that it is necessary to praise God for the evil as well as for the good.[37] Above all is the significance of repentance that may cause God to forgive the sins of the whole world because of the repentance of an individual.[38]

In interpreting the text of the Bible, Rabbi Meir often used fables. He thus pointed out that the prophet Obadiah was an Idumean proselyte and that his prophecy foretold the downfall of Idumea. This he compared to an ax that tries to chop down a forest but cannot do so until it first obtains a handle from the trees of the forest.[39]

The tree of knowledge of which Adam ate, Rabbi Meir declared to be a wheat plant (!), and a foolish man may be said to have never eaten bread made of wheat.[40] When one comes to a strange city, he should follow the customs of that city. When Moses ascended to heaven he neither ate nor drank, but when the angels descended to earth they consumed food.[41]

Rabbi Meir's opinions regarding relations between man and wife illustrate that it was very difficult at that time to preserve women from the Roman soldiers, who evidently considered them as their possession. Rabbi Meir said: "Just as there are different tastes regarding food, even so there exist different attitudes to women. One man will throw out the fly that falls into his beaker but will drink no more of it, while another man will cast out the fly from his beaker and will continue to drink from it.[42]

Whenever Rabbi Meir saw a man leaving on a journey he would say: "Go in peace, you who are doomed to death." Due to the insecurity of the highways at that time it could be assumed that any man going on a trip was sure not to return alive; and when he saw two people going on a journey he would say: "Go in peace, men of discord," for he was certain that when two people travel together they are bound to quarrel. But when Rabbi Meir saw three people going on a journey he would say, "Go in peace, oh children of peace," because he felt certain that if two of them were to quarrel, the third would reconcile them.[43]

With the death of Rabbi Meir, his contemporaries claimed that a definite type of person had died out. Rabbi Tarphon was said to have been the tallest man of his generation and Rabbi Meir only reached up to his shoulder. After Rabbi Tarphon died, Rabbi Meir remained the tallest man of his generation and the Nasi, Rabbi Jehudah, only reached to his shoulder.[44]

All of Rabbi Meir's days were one long series of uncommon afflictions and suffering. Together with other Jews of his time he had to bear the burden of persecutions which he probably felt more keenly than the others. This may be gathered from his story that when he was attending the academy of Rabbi Akiba, everybody recited the *Shema* in such low tones that they could not hear their own murmuring for fear that the military guard who was stationed at the door to watch all their movements might hear them pray. It would seem that the study of the Torah was not entirely forbidden at that time but reciting the *Shema* was prohibited.[45]

But in comparison with the suffering that followed, the early difficulties seemed no more than child's play. Rabbi Meir had to witness the terrible death of Rabbi Akiba as his flesh was torn with iron flails; later he saw his father-in-law, Rabbi Chanina ben Teradion, burned at the stake, his mother-in-law executed, and his sister-in-law sent to a house of ill-repute for the gratification of Roman officials.

Rabbi Meir was known for his modesty toward women and he frequently scorned those who succumbed to their passions. He said that human intelligence should be able to control all passions; nevertheless he once had an experience of which he was later very much ashamed. As he walked along the bank of a river, the Evil one appeared before him in the guise of a beautiful woman on the other shore of the stream and tempted him so luringly that he lost all control of himself and decided to cross to the other side of the river. But no boat was available and there was only a board floating in the middle of the stream. Picking up a rope he found on the shore, he tried to reach the board and when his attempt was unsuccessful he waded into the water trying to reach the board. But the woman on the other side of the stream meanwhile vanished and he returned to the shore shamefaced at having succumbed to the vision.[46]

Beruriah, the wife of Rabbi Meir and the daughter of Rabbi Chanina ben Teradion, was the only woman ever mentioned in the Talmud for her scholarship, and learned men respectfully listened to her opinions on legal as well as secular matters.[47] When Rabbi Jose of Galilee once asked her opinion in some matter, she made fun of him for speaking at such length and thus breaking the commandment of the scholars not to speak too much with a woman. She is also said to have complained against a pupil of her father who studied very quietly, that only when one studies aloud can he understand his learning.[48] She was the spiritual support of Rabbi Meir and comforted him in time of need. It is thus related that Rabbi Meir once lived in the neighborhood of a group of rude people who plagued him greatly and he cursed them. His wife chided him for cursing them and said that one should never condemn sinful people but rather condemn their sins. Rabbi Meir began to pray to God to reform these people and his prayer was granted.[49]

Like her husband, Beruriah also felt confident of her willpower and scorned those who said that women were light minded. Rabbi Meir warned her against this attitude saying that some day she might prove this rule, but she insisted that no woman who held fast to her opinions need be led astray. Rabbi Meir then persuaded one of his pupils to attempt to seduce her; he was certain that his pupil would not go further than the attempt and he could then prove to his wife the truth of the opinion of the scholars regarding women, when they said that even an educated woman could be led astray. But Rabbi Meir's disciple betrayed him, and when Beruriah found out that the affair had been planned beforehand she hanged herself out of chagrin.

We have previously mentioned that Beruriah's sister was

condemned to be sent to a house of ill-repute located in Antioch where lived the officials of the Roman administration of Palestine. Beruriah begged Rabbi Meir to save her sister and he went to Antioch, dressed as a Roman noble in order to deceive the guard of the house as well as his sister-in-law as to his identity. Legend recounts many wonders that occurred during this attempt. When he was convinced that Beruriah's sister had preserved her purity, he took a measure of gold and offered it to the guard to release her. He told the guard to keep half of the gold and to use the other half to bribe the officials if *he* were caught. The guard feared that money would be of no avail if he were caught and Rabbi Meir advised him to pronounce the words: "God of Meir, save me!" and he would certainly be saved.

The guard still refused to believe that these words would help him when in danger but Rabbi Meir proved this to be so. Around that house there were savage, man-eating dogs and Rabbi Meir began to tease them. The dogs pounced, ready to devour him and he exclaimed, "God of Meir, answer me!" and the dogs immediately left him in peace. Seeing this the guard was convinced that he could safely accept the bribe.

When the guard was finally caught and sentenced to be crucified, he pronounced these words and was saved. The executioners marvelled at this and asked him what incantation he knew that could save him from the cross and he told them everything that he knew. They then began to search for Rabbi Meir and engraved his image on the gates of Rome (more probably Antioch) and issued a commandment that whoever recognized the man who resembled the image should seize him and bring him before the imperial authorities. One day Rabbi Meir was recognized and an attempt was made to seize him.

There exist numerous versions concerning the manner in which he escaped his pursuers. One version states that he fled into a house of ill-repute and his pursuers were convinced that they were mistaken and that it could not have been Rabbi Meir for he would not enter such a house. Another version relates that in his flight he came upon a pot of unclean food; he then placed his finger in it and ate some of it. Obviously he did not put into his mouth the finger he had placed in the unclean food, but from a distance, his pursuers could not distinguish what he did and they felt certain that it was not Rabbi Meir that they were following. Another version relates that the prophet Elijah appeared in the guise of a harlot and embraced Rabbi Meir and thus deceived his pursuers as to his identity.[50]

On one of his journeys Rabbi Meir spent a night in an inn and he saw that the proprietor woke the guests at night and told them to proceed on their way. The proprietor then escorted each of the guests part of the way. Rabbi Meir understood that the proprietor was in league with a band of robbers, and when his turn came he said that he could not go because he was waiting for his brother to accompany him. The proprietor asked Rabbi Meir what the name of his brother was and where he lodged, and Rabbi Meir answered that his name was *Ki Tov* and that he lodged in the synagogue. The man then stood all night in front of the synagogue calling: "It is good, come out; your brother is waiting for you," but no one came out and he received no answer.

In the morning Rabbi Meir was ready to leave and the innkeeper said to him: "Where is your brother? Why don't you wait for him?" Rabbi Meir replied: "The light of day is my brother for the Bible says that the light of day is good, and this verse was in a book of the Bible in the synagogue all night."[51]

Beruriah, Rabbi Meir's wife, exerted a great influence over him and it is therefore interesting to relate how she informed him of the sudden death of their two sons. It happened on a Sabbath before sunset when Rabbi Meir was in the academy engaged in his studies that his sons suddenly died. Legend does not mention the cause of their death. Beruriah placed the bodies of her sons on the bed and covered them with a sheet without saying a word to anyone. When Rabbi Meir returned to his house he immediately asked where his sons were and she replied that they were probably in the academy. He was surprised and said: "I have looked everywhere in the academy but I did not see them."

Somewhat later he asked for his sons again and she replied that they had probably tarried in conversation on the way home and would soon return. Then Beruriah turned to Rabbi Meir with the following question: "I was once given a valuable treasure to guard until it would be called for. Today the man came to claim his treasure; should I return it?" Rabbi Meir at once replied: "Of course you must return that which was given to you to guard. I do not understand why you have to ask me such a question." Beruriah then took Rabbi Meir by the hand and led him to the bed where their dead sons lay and she said: "This is the treasure God gave me to guard and today he claimed it." Rabbi Meir began to weep bitterly but she said to him, "Did you not say that it was necessary to return a treasure that was given to one to guard?"[52]

Wonderful stories are told of Rabbi Meir's modesty. One of these is very similar to the one told about Baba ben Buta of how a woman threw a candlestick at him at the command of her husband.

The story concerning Rabbi Meir relates that there was a woman who loved to hear his lectures and on a certain Sabbath she tarried long in the academy listening to him. When she returned home late, her husband expelled her from the house and threatened to divorce her if she would not spit in Rabbi Meir's face. When Rabbi Meir heard of this he summoned the woman and said to her: "I have an ailing eye and the doctor said that if a woman were to spit in it seven times it would be healed." At first the woman refused to do as Rabbi Meir asked her but when he insisted, she was persuaded and did as she was asked. Rabbi Meir then said to her: "Go and tell your husband that not once but seven times did you spit in Rabbi Meir's eye."[53]

39

RABBI JEHUDAH BAR ELAI

WHEN THE SCHOLARS GATHERED in Usha, they honored the outstanding man of that city, Rabbi Jehudah bar Elai. At that gathering he spoke of the various customs and commandments that were nearly forgotten during the days of Hadrian and he gained the appelation of "first speaker on every occasion" and this name was associated with Rabbi Jehudah all the days of his life. Various sources indicate that he was the only scholar of that time whose opinions concerning *Halakhah*, *Aggadah* and the contemporary problems of life were listened to with respect. Nearly 3,000 statements of Rabbi Jehudah are quoted in the *Mishnah, Beraita, Tosefta, Safra, Sifri,* and *Mekhilta*. All statements, credited to Rabbi Jehudah without any further designation, are the statements of Rabbi Jehudah bar Elai.

These statements concerning accepted laws quoted the opinions of his teachers, or traditional interpretations they had received from their predecessors, as it was customary at that time to quote opinions of authorities dating back before the destruction of the Temple.

Rabbi Elai, the father of Rabbi Jehudah, was a *tanna* of the *Mishnah* and a contemporary of Rabban Gamaliel of Jabneh.[1] He was a disciple of Rabbi Eliezer ben Hyrcanus[2] and of Rabbi Ishmael ben Elisha.[3] Rabbi Elai was the first teacher of his son

Jehudah; later he sent him to the academy in Jabneh to receive instruction from the same men he had studied with in his youth. Rabbi Jehudah studied with Rabbi Akiba and even more with Rabbi Tarphon. He thus accumulated a large volume of information that he later quoted in the name of his masters.

Rabbi Jehudah was an opponent of Rabbi Meir. This opposition was so strong that after the death of Rabbi Meir Rabbi Jehudah asked that Rabbi Meir's disciples should not be admitted to the academy because "they are spiteful and they come not to learn but to ask questions that cannot be answered."[4]

The following was a favorite maxim of Rabbi Jehudah: "Be cautious in learning, for error may lead to sin."[5] This maxim he further elaborated and said: "The errors of a scholar are considered as intentional sin while the intentional sin of an *am ha'aretz* is considered as an unconscious transgression."[6] He also said: "He who makes the Torah the outstanding purpose of his life and relegates his worldly occupations to a secondary position will come to be considered by the world as of importance; but a man who makes his worldly occupations the central motive of his life and relegates the Torah to a secondary place will himself come to be considered as of no importance. It is like choosing between two highways, one of which is made of fire while the other is covered with snow. If one goes on the fiery road he may be burned, and if he goes on the snowy road he may be frozen. It is therefore necessary to follow a middle course and to beware of the heat of the fire and the frost of the snow."[7]

Rabbi Jehudah highly valued the worth of labor and he said that it honors those that engage in it.[8] Among the duties of a father toward his son he also included that of teaching him a trade and he added that "one who does not teach his son a trade may be compared to a person who teaches his son to be a robber."[9] But despite his attitude toward labor he still ascribed the highest importance to learning and he said: "Previous generations definitely established the time to be devoted to learning, but the time to be devoted to their occupations and their personal interests was left undetermined. They therefore found time for both. But later generations determined the time for their labors and did not definitely establish the time to be devoted to learning. They therefore found time for neither."[10]

When the question was discussed whether it was more important to study the commandments or to practice them, Rabbi Jehudah said that the fulfillment of the commandments was of greater significance than learning, and when he saw that a dead person had to be buried or a bride had to be led to the canopy, he commanded his disciples to interrupt their studies and to attend the funeral or the wedding.[11]

Rabbi Jehudah learned most from Rabbi Tarphon and he frequently related things he had learned from him. Thus he told of the occasion when, as a small boy, he read the *Megillah* in the presence of Rabbi Tarphon and other scholars[12] or the various customs Rabbi Tarphon saw him performing during the lighting of the candles or in the matter of removing objects through the window of a house on the Sabbath.[13]

It has been stated that Rabbi Jehudah bar Elai was "the first to speak" in Usha because he was a native of that city. He maintained this position even after the Sanhedrin returned to Jabneh for a short time as a result of Rabbi Jehudah's friendly attitude toward Rome.

How his attitude became known to the Romans is related in the following story. Rabbi Jehudah, Rabbi Jose ben Chalafta, and Rabbi Simeon ben Yochai once sat in the academy together with Rabbi Jehudah ben Gerim. A discussion developed regarding the achievements of the Romans in Palestine and Rabbi Jehudah bar Elai praised the Romans for paving highways and building baths and bridges. Rabbi Jose ben Chalafta heard these praises and remained silent. He did not agree with Rabbi Jehudah, but he was afraid to contradict him. Rabbi Simeon ben Yochai could control himself no longer and he said: "What is there to praise? Whatever the Romans did, they did for their own benefit. They paved streets in order to settle their harlots there; they built bath houses in order to anoint themselves; they built bridges in order to collect tolls."

Unintentionally perhaps, Rabbi Jehudah ben Gerim re-

peated these words in the presence of others, and the Roman
authorities finally heard of the discussion and were greatly
displeased with it. They commanded that Rabbi Jehudah bar
Elai, who praised the Roman achievements, should be honored. Rabbi Jose ben Chalafta, who remained silent and did not
express his agreement with Rabbi Jehudah, they interned in his
native city of Sepphoris and he was forbidden to leave it. Rabbi
Simeon ben Yochai, who denounced the Romans, was condemned to death.[14]

Rabbi Jehudah was allowed to continue as head speaker
and he later became a tutor in the house of the Nasi. It must be
borne in mind that although the decrees against the Jews were
abrogated, the Roman government still looked unfavorably on
the dynasty of the Nasi that had derived from the royal house
of David, and government circles understood that Jews did not
consider themselves subjects of Rome but looked to the Nasi as
to their God-anointed ruler. But the Romans had great confidence in Rabbi Jehudah bar Elai and they overlooked the royal
honors the Jews accorded to the Nasi. The Roman attitude now
was one of toleration and they allowed the Jews to "play" with
a Nasi as long as they paid their taxes regularly.

Despite Rabbi Jehudah's prominence among the Jews and
his favorable position among the Romans, he suffered great
poverty. His wife was always dressed in old woolen garments
and they had only one heavy coat. When Rabbi Jehudah had to
go into the street he put it on, and when his wife had to go to
market she wore it. Poverty was very common even then and
it was told that six people had to share the same blanket.[15]
Many people wanted to aid Rabbi Jehudah but he refused all
assistance. Once when the Nasi declared a fast day and Rabbi
Jehudah failed to appear at prayers following the fast because
he had no garment to wear, the Nasi sent him some garments
but even these he refused.

But Rabbi Jehudah's face never betrayed his poverty. It is
related that once he sat before Rabbi Tarphon and the latter
said to him: "You appear to be merry today." Rabbi Jehudah
replied: "Your slaves went into the field today and they
brought me some greens that I ate without salt. This is the

reason why I am merry. You may also imagine how much happier I would be if I had some salt to eat with the greens."

At another time a Roman matron said to him: "You are a scholar but you look like a drunkard." Rabbi Jehudah replied, "I swear by my faith that I drink no wine except for the *Kiddush* and *Havdalah*; when I drink the prescribed four glasses of wine on the Passover I suffer from headaches until *Shavuot*." A Sadducee who met Rabbi Jehudah said to him, "You look like a usurer or a swineherd." But Rabbi Jehudah answered, "I am a Jew and therefore I can be neither."[16]

From what has been related so far we may conclude that Rabbi Jehudah was a man of modesty and of extreme piety.[17] He said, "Better eat an onion and sit in the shade, and refrain from eating geese and hens and your heart will not palpitate. It is better still to eat less and drink less in order to live better."[18]

Rabbi Jehudah's attitude toward the political situation of the Jews is expressed in his statement regarding the Biblical verse that sometimes compares the Jews to the dust and at other times to the stars. When the Jews fall, he said, they fall as low as the dust, but when they are elevated, they are raised to the stars.[19]

Like some other *tannaim*, Rabbi Jehudah was ready to overlook his own dignity when peace between husband and wife was at stake. Thus it happened that a man once vowed not to taste his wife's cooking until Rabbi Jehudah would first partake of it.[20]

The following expressions of Rabbi Jehudah are also characteristic of his trend of thoughts:

"Do you want to know what man is worthy to speak to God for his congregation, when a fast has been declared to avert a calamity? Such a man must have many children and not enough food for them; he must be a hard worker and his house empty of furniture; in addition he must have a fine voice and good diction. He must be modest and beloved of the people. He must know the Scriptures, the *Mishnah*, *Halakhah*, and *Aggadah* as well as all the benedictions."[21]

"When a man is sick with croup it generally begins with the intestines and it ends with his mouth. Even so is the

development of sin: the kidneys mislead, the heart understands, the tongue speaks, and the mouth ends it all."[22]

"Charity is a great virtue and it brings redemption nearer.
God created ten kinds of strength each of which is stronger
than the preceding one and acts as a cure for it. A mountain is
strong but iron cuts it; iron is strong but fire melts it; fire is
strong but water puts it out; water is strong but the clouds carry
it away; clouds are strong but the wind disperses them; wind
is strong but the human body withstands it; the human body is
strong but fear breaks it; fear is strong but wine dispels it; wine
is strong but sleep does away with its effects. The strongest of
all is death but charity saves one from death."[23]

40

RABBI JOSE
BEN CHALAFTA

RABBI JOSE BEN CHALAFTA was one of the outstanding disciples who survived Rabbi Akiba. With a group of other disciples he was ordained by Rabbi Jehudah ben Baba in the mountains between Usha and Shefarom, when the Roman government forbade ordination. Rabbi Jehudah ben Baba paid with his life for this act.

Rabbi Jose was said to have descended from an aristocratic line. When a list of genealogies was found in Jerusalem, Rabbi Jose traced his descent from Jehonadab ben Recheb[1] who aided Jehu, the king of Israel, to destroy the house of Ahab and to eradicate idolatry from among the ten tribes. It may be assumed that Rabbi Jose's grandfather came to Palestine from Babylonia and his racial purity was therefore unquestioned. Rabbi Jose was very proud of this and said: "All lands are as sour dough when compared to the Land of Israel, but the Land of Israel is as sour dough when compared to Babylonia."[2] In saying this Rabbi Jose implied that the purity of the race was better preserved in Babylonia than in Palestine, where the immorality of the Romans influenced the general behavior.

Rabbi Chalafta, Jose's father, was one of the most prominent people in the period preceding the decrees of Hadrian. It seems probable that he was head of the court in Sepphoris located eighteen miles from Tiberias.[3] Rabbi Jose told that his father saw Rabban Gamaliel the Elder before the destruction of the Temple. His father was also Rabbi Jose's first teacher and he frequently quoted laws in his name.[4]

Once the question arose whether it was permissible to use a Greek translation of the Scriptures. Rabbi Jose related that his father once came to the house of Rabban Gamaliel II and found him perusing a Greek translation of the Book of Job; he then said, "I remember seeing your grandfather, Rabban Gamaliel the Old, standing on the Temple steps and he was given a Greek version of the Book of Job. He then commanded the master builder to put the book into the walls of the Temple.[5]

Rabbi Jose followed the method of Rabbi Akiba in his legal opinions,[6] because he was a disciple of Rabbi Akiba, but at various times he was also a pupil of Rabban Gamaliel II, Rabbi Joshua ben Chananiah, Rabbi Ishmael ben Elisha, Rabbi Tarphon, and Rabbi Jochanan ben Nuri. For a time he also studied with Abtolemos who was a *tanna* at the time when the *Mishnah* was created but whose name is mentioned only three times.[7]

Together with other scholars who survived the persecutions of Hadrian, Rabbi Jose witnessed the afflictions visited upon the Jews of Palestine after the execution of many of its outstanding leaders. He witnessed as well the destruction of his native city Sepphoris. After the city was restored he told that the destroyed city contained 180,000 markets (!) where cooking utensils were sold exclusively.[8]

After the death of Rabbi Akiba, all the academies were closed until Hadrian's death brought a respite from the decrees. It was at this time that the famous discussion concerning the achievements of the Romans took place, and Rabbi Jose, who was present at the discussion, remained silent or expressed his disapproval with a gesture and was thus interned in his native city of Sepphoris. During his internment the city was rebuilt and he became its representative. It also appears that at a later date, the decree against Rabbi Jose was annulled and he was again free to participate in the deliberations of the Sanhedrin.

Both the Nasi Rabban Simeon ben Gamaliel II, as well as

his son Jehudah, established all laws according to the decisions of Rabbi Jose ben Chalafta. This was especially true when other scholars disputed Rabbi Jose's contentions. When the Nasi Rabbi Jehudah was asked why the law is always enacted according to the opinion of Rabbi Jose, he replied: "Just as the distance between the most holy and the ordinary is great, even so is there a great difference between our generation and the generation of Rabbi Jose." Rabbi Ishmael, the son of Rabbi Jose, expressed himself in a similar vein when he declared: "The difference between our generation and the generation of my father is as great as the difference between dust and gold."[9]

The arguments of Rabbi Jose are referred to as *nimukim*, deeply considered convictions.[10] His method was to eliminate all disputes and to explain all contradictions.[11] The opinion prevailed that Rabbi Jose was an unusually pious and guarded man. The rumor that he once secretly performed ablutions on the Day of Atonement is therefore unbelievable.[12]

The Talmud relates that the prophet Elijah frequently appeared to Rabbi Jose and spoke to him man to man.[13] Rabbi Jose nevertheless allowed himself to make a statement contradicting the basic tenets of the faith. He said that "the *Shekhinah* (the majesty of God) never descended to earth, and Moses and the prophet Elijah never ascended heaven."[14] The Talmud attempted to explain the words of Rabbi Jose that were in direct contradiction to the text, concerning the granting of the Torah and the ascension of Elijah. It was then said that the *Shekhinah* never descended lower than ten handsbreadth above ground and that Moses and Elijah never ascended higher than ten handsbreadth above the ground. In contradiction to the accepted belief that God judges the world four times a year, Rabbi Jose maintained that He judges humanity every day.[15]

Rabbi Jose's modesty was a subject of admiration long after he died, and everyone was convinced, (considering his reverence for the authorities that preceded him) it could be assumed that despite his age and his superior scholarship, he would have respected the Nasi Rabbi Jehudah as his master had he lived.[16] This conviction was reenforced by the fact that Rabbi Jose always spoke with the greatest respect of his colleagues.[17] Rabbi Jose said of himself that he never rescinded his word nor did he ever do otherwise than the scholars commanded.[18]

Rabbi Jose gained his livelihood by tanning animal skins. According to the concepts of that time, this occupation was considered as a low type of work.[19]

From numerous statements in the Talmud, we may conclude that Rabbi Jose was versed in the natural sciences. He described numerous strange animals mentioned in the laws which the scholars were at a loss to identify. He was also an accomplished historian and he composed a chronology of Jewish history from the time of the creation to his own day and called it *Seder Haolam*.

Rabbi Jose frequently related the customs of previous generations and he based his own opinions on those customs. He thus elucidated customs concerning the scapegoat,[20] the sanctification of the new month,[21] regulations pertaining to women who bring offerings to the Temple,[22] and numerous others.

The miracles accompanying the creation of the world Rabbi Jose described in an unusually poetic manner. People, he said, look but they know not what they see; they stand and know not what they stand on. Consider the earth for instance. What is the earth supported by? The earth is supported by pillars; the pillars of the earth are based in water; the water rests on mountains; the mountains hang in the air; the air rests on storm, and the storm is held in the arms of God.[23]

His concepts of justice are exemplified by the statement that a witness who has proved false in money matters may testify in cases affecting life.[24] He maintained that a court may admit the testimony of such a witness on the ground that if a man states a falsehood once it is not proof that he will testify falsely every time.

At some other time he said: "See how blind usurers are. If a man should call another person wicked he would be ready to kill him, but usurers bring witnesses and a scribe, and they sign their own names to a statement, and they deny the Jewish God who commanded not to loan money for interest.[25]

Rabbi Jose often disputed with infidels, and among them was one matron who asked innumerable questions. Once she asked him what God was doing all the time, and he replied that God was busy making ladders on which he raised some people and lowered others; to some He gives money and from others He takes it away to give it to others. The matron was dissatisfied with this answer and Rabbi Jose then told her that God was also busy arranging marriages.

Hearing this the matron exclaimed: "Is this all that your God does? I can do the same. I have a host of men and women slaves and in one hour I can marry them all to one another." Rabbi Jose replied, "That which seems easy in your eyes is as difficult for God as the rending of the sea." The matron then chose 1,000 men slaves and 1,000 women slaves and arranged them in two lines and declared, "This slave will marry this woman servant and this woman servant will marry that slave." In this manner she married them all in a short time.

The following day they all came to her with various complaints. One had a broken head and another had a black eye or a broken leg. When the matron asked what had happened, they protested that she had chosen the wrong mates for them. The matron then realized that marriage between two human beings was not as simple as she thought it to be.[26]

Rabbi Jose had five sons: R. Ishmael, R. Eleazar, R. Chalafta, R. Abtilas, and R. Menachem. All of them figured among the scholars of their time and Rabbi Jose proudly said that he had planted five cedar trees among the Jews.[27]

It is also noteworthy that Rabbi Jose was opposed to afflicting the human body, and he declared that an individual may not establish fast days for himself, for if such a person needs the aid of others they will refuse it saying that he is used to fasting.[28]

When Rabbi Jose ben Chalafta died it was said that "the pipes of Lodakia flowed with blood." The reason given for this phenomenon was Rabbi Jose's readiness to die for the fulfillment of the commandment of circumcision.[29] Another text declares that "the pipes of Sepphoris flowed with blood."[30]

When Rabbi Jose died it was said that understanding ceased among the Jews.[31]

41

RABBI SIMEON BEN YOCHAI

R̲ABBI SIMEON BEN YOCHAI was gifted with numerous
virtues which made him a favorite among the people of his
district. He also possessed much knowledge and followed a
strictly logical method of reasoning. His activity as a leader
dated from his return from exile when, together with a group
who escaped the wrath of Hadrian's decrees after the death of
Rabbi Akiba until he was ordained by Rabbi Jehudah ben Baba.
The position of his father Yochai was not very clear, and from
some statements it would seem that he was an official of the
Roman administration whose duty was to report all those who
did not act in accordance with the Roman law. This seems to be
implied in the story that Simeon came to Rabbi Akiba in prison
and asked to be taught by him. When Rabbi Akiba refused,
Rabbi Simeon said to him: "If you will not teach me I will tell
my father, and he will report you to the government."[1]

It is therefore remarkable that although Yochai was an
adherent or an official of the Roman government, his son Rabbi
Simeon was an enemy of Rome. The authorities were probably
aware of his attitude and sought an opportunity to capture
him. When the scholars returned during the reign of
Antoninus Pius and resumed their scholarly labors, Rabbi
Simeon ben Yochai gained the disfavor of the authorities

because of his criticism of the Roman government and he was condemned to death.

Numerous miracles are related concerning the escape of Rabbi Simeon ben Yochai. One of these stories states that he escaped with his son Eleazar and that together they hid in the academy for a long time, and food was secretly brought to them from their home. But when the authorities intensified their search for Rabbi Simeon, he feared his wife might not be able to withstand the stringent questioning and might reveal their hiding place. Father and son decided to hide in a cave and there they were fed in a miraculous manner for a number of carob trees began to grow about the cave and a spring of water appeared.

In that cave—it is further related—they sat naked and buried to the neck in sand and continued their studies. Only when prayer time arrived did they emerge from the sand and don their garments for the prayer. With praying finished they again disrobed, in order not to wear out their garments, and continued sitting buried in sand.

Thus they sat for thirteen years until one day Elijah appeared and said, "Who will announce to Rabbi Simeon ben Yochai that the emperor has died?" Rabbi Simeon and his son then left the cave and when Pinchas ben Yair, Rabbi Simeon's son-in-law, heard that they had emerged from the cave, he went to meet them and took them to his house.

As he was leaving the cave, Rabbi Simeon met Rabbi Jehudah ben Gerim, who thirteen years earlier had repeated Rabbi Simeon's remarks which led to his being sentenced to death, and he exclaimed: "Is this person still alive?" As he said this he stared at Rabbi Jehudah with his burning eyes and the latter fell down dead.

Rabbi Simeon then began to cure the body of his son, and Rabbi Pinchas ben Yair attended to Rabbi Simeon. The body of Rabbi Simeon was creased and swollen from the many years of sitting in the sand and from the diet of St. John's bread and water. When Rabbi Pinchas saw this, he began to weep and the tears falling on Rabbi Simeon's body caused him great suffering because of their salty tang.

This happened in the city of Tiberias where Rabbi Pinchas then lived. Rabbi Simeon bathed in the warm springs of that city and his body healed rapidly. Out of gratitude he wanted to confer some favor on the city saying: "Since a miracle occurred to me here I would gladly do something for this city." His son then said: "For the many favors this city has extended to us we should declare it to be permissible for Jewish residence."

It was believed that Tiberias was situated on the site of an old cemetery, and many priests as well as other pious Jews had refused to reside there so as not to be contaminated by the impurity of the dead. Rabbi Simeon ben Yochai, however, declared the city to be clean and fit for residence.[2]

One must bear in mind that Tiberias was founded by Herod Antipas, a grandson of Herod the Great, on the site of the ancient city Hamath. When the ancient city was deserted the ground was used as a cemetery. Priests and pious Pharisees therefore refused to settle in the city despite the fact that Herod Antipas had freed its inhabitants of all taxes. Only such people who were forced to reside in the city because of their occupations settled there, and even these considered their residence in Tiberias as a sin because of the contamination of its soil. Rabbi Simeon ben Yochai therefore favored the city when he decreed it to be clean and fit for the residence of even the most pious.

Meanwhile Palestine was again agitated by political unrest. Despite the relatively favorable attitude of Antoninus Pius, the Jews were influenced by the Parthians who ruled in Babylonia and were independent of Rome, and again revolted against Roman rule. The Parthians were anxious to free themselves from the threat of Roman invasion and attempted a struggle with Rome in which the Jews aided them (or, as others maintain, the Jews began the struggle and were aided by the Parthians).

The Jews felt confident they would be liberated with the aid of the Parthians. The Roman empire was then occupied with the simultaneous revolts of the Germans and the Dacians. It was therefore said that "Whenever one sees the horse of a Parthian tied to a tombstone in Palestine, he may expect the early coming of the Messiah." Another statement of the scholars declared that "They who have destroyed the Temple will in the end fall into the hands of the Parthians."[3]

This rebellion lasted for four years until the Romans again triumphed under the leadership of Atidius Cornelianus. It may be surmised that the Jews again had to withstand persecution and oppression. The first decree abrogated the right of the Jews to be tried before a Jewish court in civil disputes. This decree was not considered as a great calamity, and Rabbi Simeon ben Yochai even declared his satisfaction with it because "Jews no longer have the wise men required to decide in such matters."[4]

The Roman imperial throne was also in an uncertain state at that time. At first Hadrian appointed Antoninus Pius as his successor. Later he met Marcus Aurelius, who was a military leader, and he liked him as well. Hadrian then commanded Antoninus Pius to appoint Marcus Aurelius as his successor. Marcus Aurelius then assumed the name Antoninus, and after the death of Antoninus Pius, the Roman senate decided that his son, Lucius Varus, should share the throne with Marcus Aurelius. And thus it was that two emperors reigned simultaneously.

During this war against Rome, the Parthians advanced into the Roman provinces northwest of their possessions as far as Syria. Under the leadership of their King Valagesias, they captured the Roman governor Atidius Cornelianus and put him to death. They then occupied one Syrian city after another and for a time it seemed that the Romans would be expelled from Palestine forever. But these victories were not lasting, and when Emperor Lucius Varus arrived with reenforcements of Roman legions, the Parthians were driven out of all the positions they had formerly occupied.

It would seem that the scholars remained neutral in this war. No mention is made either of their participation or of their opposition to it. But since Emperor Varus reenacted some of Hadrian's decrees forbidding the observance of the Sabbath and the practice of circumcision, it may be assumed that the masses actively participated in the struggle, with the consent of the scholars or against their wishes. It is also apparent that the Nasi, Rabban Simeon ben Gamaliel, no longer lived at that time and that no other Nasi had yet been elected.

When Varus died, Rabbi Simeon ben Yochai was sent to Rome to intercede with Emperor Antoninus Marcus Aurelius to nullify the decrees of Varus. Although they knew that Marcus Aurelius was not favorably inclined toward the Jews they trusted his sense of justice, for he was known as a kindly and philosophical man.

To accompany Rabbi Simeon, the scholars sent Rabbi Eleazar, the son of Rabbi Jose ben Chalafta, who could speak Latin. Both arrived in Rome and with the aid of Roman Jews who wielded a considerable influence in government circles, they successfully completed their mission.

Legend relates the following miracle to have occurred during this journey. The emperor's daughter Lucilla was then possessed by a "devil" or *dybbuk* named Bar Tamalion. Rabbi Simeon ben Yochai expelled the spirit, and as a reward the emperor told him to enter the treasury and choose the most valuable gift. Rabbi Simeon entered the royal treasury, found the document of Varus's decrees against the Jews, and forthwith tore it up before the emperor.[5]

Rabbi Simeon ben Yochai was a pupil of Rabbi Akiba for thirteen years and he did not leave him until the day of Rabbi Akiba's martyr death. But once Rabbi Akiba expressed his preference for Rabbi Meir and Rabbi Simeon was displeased. Even Rabbi Akiba's later statement that Rabbi Simeon should "be satisfied that God and I know how to appreciate your power" failed to reconcile him.[6] Rabbi Simeon remembered this incident long after Rabbi Akiba died and he allowed himself to say that which no other disciple allowed himself; he declared that Rabbi Akiba's interpretation of four biblical verses were not correct and that his own explanations were more acceptable than Rabbi Akiba's.[7] Another time he addressed his pupils in the following words: "My children, copy my manners for mine are copied from Rabbi Akiba's best manners."[8]

Rabbi Simeon's system of study was highly original and he always sought the reason behind the interpretations of the

Torah text. He always asked: "Why does the Torah command us to do this?" In this respect he was an exception in his generation. He based his opinions on reason, irrespective of whether they were in agreement with the opinions of scholars of previous generations. In such cases he showed no reverence for his contemporaries nor for authorities of an earlier day. Intentionally he sought to do away with ideas that others had planted when he was convinced of their error.

The Torah commanded that the garment of a widow may not be taken in pawn and the *Mishnah*[9] declared that this law applied equally to rich as well as to poor widows. But Rabbi Simeon declared that this regulation applied only to poor widows because rich widows undoubtedly owned other garments. Unable to base his opinion on purely humanitarian grounds, he explained that in the case of a poor widow who may not have any other garments, such a pawn would have to be returned every evening, and the repeated visits of the pawnbroker may cause suspicion to be cast on the character of the widow.

Rabbi Simeon also sought to lighten the burden of the observance of the Sabbath in contradistinction to other scholars who heaped prohibition upon prohibition. He thus allowed the moving of household furniture if care were taken not to dig up the ground in doing so.[10] He ruled similarly concerning other types of work prohibited at that time.[11]

Fully cognizant of his worth Rabbi Simeon never pretended modesty. On the contrary, he sometimes expressed himself in a manner that might indicate pride. Thus he said: "There are few good people in the world. If there are a thousand such then I and my son are among them. If there are one hundred such then I and my son are among them. If there are only two such then I and my son are they."[12] On the same occasion he further stated: "Because of my merit I can redeem the world from judgment for all sins committed since the time of my birth until this day. Were the merit of my son Eleazar to be joined to mine, I could free the world from judgment for all sins committed since the creation of the world until this day."

As did other scholars of his day Rabbi Simeon also sought

to preserve peace between husband and wife, but he never sought to attain this end at the expense of his own dignity. Recall the previous story of how Rabbi Meir allowed a woman to spit in his face when her husband commanded her to do so. Another man refused to eat his wife's cooking until Rabbi Jehudah and Rabbi Simeon tasted it. Rabbi Jehudah then agreed to do so, but Rabbi Simeon said: "Were the man to starve, and were the woman to remain a widow, and her children die I would not do this."[13]

In this connection it is interesting to relate an incident that occurred while Rabbi Simeon ben Yochai was in Sidon. A married couple who had lived together for ten years and had no children came to him to obtain a divorce. Rabbi Simeon said to them: "Since you do not want to part in anger, you must do now as you did at the time of your wedding. At your wedding you made a feast; you must also make a feast at your parting."

The husband and wife did as Rabbi Simeon advised them. During the feast the husband became merry with drink and he said to his wife: "Choose that which is most beautiful and dearest to you in the house and take it with you when you return to your father's house." When the husband fell asleep she ordered the slaves to carry him on his bed to her father's house. When he awoke and found himself in strange surroundings he asked his wife, "Where am I?" and she replied, "You are in my father's house."

The man further asked, "What have I to do in your father's house?" and his wife replied, "You asked me to take that which I held dearest in your house, and I could find nothing dearer to me than yourself." They then went to Rabbi Simeon ben Yochai a second time to ask him what to do. He advised them not to part for he was certain that God would reward such a wife with children. He also promised to pray for them.[14]

Rabbi Simeon's attitude toward the Romans was always one of condemnation. He could never forget the suffering the Romans inflicted upon the Jews, nor the fact that all scholars had to flee Palestine to save their lives. Even when they were allowed to return during the rule of Antoninus Pius, they were forced to wander from city to city. At first they settled in Sidon, later in Usha, and finally in Jabneh. When Rabbi Simeon expressed criticism of the Romans he was forced to hide in a cave. All of these events aroused within him a hatred for all Romans, and he declared that the best among the Romans was like a snake whose head should be crushed.[15] Another time he said that only Jews could be considered as human beings.[16]

As a result of these events and also because of his personal misfortunes, Rabbi Simeon ben Yochai became embittered and he ruled that as long as Jews are in exile no one must laugh wholeheartedly.[17] When in later life he suffered because of his self-incarceration he ruled that even wicked people who curse their fathers and deserve to forfeit their lives according to law, should not be reported to the authorities.[18]

Rabbi Simeon valued the Torah above all else and declared that "Three who have eaten at one table and have not said over it words of the Torah are as if they had eaten of the sacrifice of the dead."[19] He further said that no scholar may partake of a feast the purpose of which is not to fulfill some commandment,[20] and that people who do not engage in learning are to be punished.[21]

"Three valuable gifts God granted to the Jews," he said, "and all three are bound up with suffering. These three gifts are: the Torah, the Land of Israel, and the world to come."[22]

"If I had been present on Mount Sinai when the Torah was given to the Jews," he said, "I would have asked God to grant us two mouths, one for the study of the Torah and the other for all other purposes." But he added immediately that two mouths might be even worse than one, for if one mouth can cause so much trouble by carrying reports, how much worse would the world be if people possessed two mouths.[23]

Being imbued with such a great love for the Torah, Rabbi Simeon abhored all those who rebelled against its commandments and he said: "Whoever wishes to taunt a wicked man may do so without compunction,"[24] for the gain of a wicked man is the loss of a just man.[25]

Speaking of relations between people, Rabbi Simeon

declared that deceiving one's neighbor with words is even more wicked than obtaining his money under false pretenses.[26]

The saintliness of Rabbi Simeon ben Yochai was revered among Jews long after his death, and it was said that during his lifetime no rainbow ever appeared, because no flood could have descended upon the world due to his merit.[27] It is also related that when Rabbi Joshua ben Levi died, he entered paradise and there he found Rabbi Simeon ben Yochai reclining on thirteen golden thrones. Rabbi Simeon asked him: "Did a rainbow ever appear during your lifetime?" and Rabbi Joshua said that it had. Rabbi Simeon remarked: "If so, then you were not a very just man."[28]

Upon returning from his hiding place in the cave Rabbi Simeon ben Yochai settled in Meron where he lived until his death. The anniversary of his death is observed in Meron to this day.

During all the years that Rabbi Simeon ben Yochai and his son Rabbi Eleazar remained secluded in their cave, they pondered the mysteries of the Torah. It must be borne in mind that no books except the Bible were then available. The *Mishnah* was then still being repeated orally, and if someone wrote down interpretations of the Torah, these were not circulated in order to prevent such writings from assuming the sanctity of the written scriptures. It is therefore quite certain that Rabbi Simeon possessed no written books in his cave.

Leading an isolated existence and deriving nourishment from a carob tree and a spring of water for thirteen long years the thoughts of Rabbi Simeon and his son naturally turned to the mysteries of the creation of the world and to original interpretations of the Biblical texts. The proximity of the desert, the encounters with wild animals and poisonous snakes, and their miraculous escapes, all these no doubt still further accentuated their interest in the imponderable aspects of life.

When they emerged from the cave later and resumed their teaching in the academy, they expressed many of the mystical conclusions and observations they had gathered during the years they lived as hermits. These ideas they wrote down, or repeated orally to their pupils who gathered them into book form. But since these ideas had no direct bearing on current legal regulations they remained unknown for centuries, until a Jewish scholar discovered them and compiled the famous *Zohar*.

42

RABBI ELEAZAR BEN SHAMUA AND RABBI JOCHANAN THE SANDALMAKER

AFTER RABBI AKIBA'S 12,000 (or 24,000) pupils died and he was imprisoned for treason against the Romans, only a few disciples remained at his side until the time of his execution. Two of these, Rabbi Eleazar ben Shamua and Rabbi Jochanan the Sandalmaker, exemplified the spirit of Rabbi Akiba's last disciples. After the death of Rabbi Akiba, they decided to go to Netsivin where Rabbi Jehudah ben Bathyra conducted an academy, but when they reached Sidon and looked back upon the Land of Israel they were leaving behind, they both wept in grief and returned.

These two were the last of Rabbi Akiba's disciples and Rabbi Eleazar ben Shamua was the more prominent of the two.[1] All statements in the *Mishnah* and *Beraita* quoted in the name of Rabbi Eleazar (without further identification) are the opinions of Rabbi Eleazar ben Shamua.[2] It was said that Rabbi Eleazar was a pupil of Rabbi Joshua ben Chananiah, Rabbi Jose of Galilee, and Rabbi Tarphon before he became a disciple of Rabbi Akiba.

Despite his love for Palestine, Rabbi Eleazar ben Shamua was later forced to seek refuge in a strange country where the persecutions of the Romans were not so severe. When the political situation improved and the Jews were allowed to engage in the Torah again, Rabbi Eleazar did not return to Usha with the other scholars. Rabbi Jochanan the Sandalmaker also remained in a foreign land. Rabbi Eleazar then founded an academy in one of the cities of Galilee and this institution gained such fame that the Nasi, Rabban Simeon ben Gamaliel, sent his son Jehudah to study at this academy. It was said that Jehudah remained there for many years and did not even return to his home for the holidays.

Years later the Nasi Rabbi Jehudah related that when he came to the academy the other pupils surrounded him angrily and would not allow him to study.[3] The academy was very crowded and six people were forced to sit in the space of one ell.[4] In his later life Rabbi Jehudah visited Rabbi Eleazar ben Shamua to inquire concerning the essence of some of his teachings.[5] From this we may conclude that even after he was Nasi, Rabbi Jehudah still consulted Rabbi Eleazar in all difficult questions.

The name of Rabbi Eleazar ben Shamua is also listed among the ten martyrs and he was said to have been 105 years old at the time of his death. It was remarked that he never prayed aloud nor quarrelled with other people and that he fasted for 85 (!) years. When he was asked what he had done to merit such a long life, he declared that he never used the synagogue as a place for idleness, he never humiliated others, and he did not pronounce the priestly blessing without reciting the benediction first.

The following maxim characterizes Rabbi Eleazar's conception of the proper type of human behavior. He said: "Let the honor of your disciple be dear to you as your own honor, and the honor of your friend should be like your reverence for your master, and your reverence for your master should be like your fear of God.[6] Like other scholars he also spoke frequently of the value of peace and he said: "All the teachings the prophets sought to implant in the hearts of the people had but one aim—peace."[7]

Rabbi Eleazar frequently repeated the following parable: "There exist three types of scholars and they may be compared to three kinds of stones. One type of scholar is like a stone pointed at one end; another type may be compared to a two-pointed stone, the third type is like a stone hewn on all sides. Who may be likened to a stone pointed at one end? One who has studied *Midrash* and if he is questioned about the *Midrash* he is able to reply. Who may be likened to a two-pointed stone? One who has studied *Midrash* and *Halakhah* and when he is questioned he is able to answer from both. Who may be compared to a hewn stone? One who studied *Midrash*, *Halakhah*, *Aggadah*, and *Tosefta*. Whatever such a scholar is asked he is able to answer."[8]

There is a legend connected with the life of Rabbi Eleazar for which it is impossible to find any historical substantiation. This legend[9] relates that Rabbi Eleazar ben Shamua once strolled on the seashore and saw a ship tossed about by the waves. Before it could be clearly discerned, the ship sank with all on board except one man who clung to a board and reached dry land without any clothes. Just then a group of Jews passed by on a pilgrimage to Jerusalem. (Although the Temple was destroyed, Jews continued to make pilgrimages to Jerusalem as often as the Romans allowed them.) The survivor appealed to them and said: "I am one of your brother Esau's children, and I beg that you give me a garment to cover my nakedness. The sea has destroyed my ship and I could save none of my possessions." To this the Jews replied, "If you are one of Esau's children, then it were better that your whole people had been destroyed."

The survivor looked around and seeing Rabbi Eleazar ben Shamua said to him, "It is discernible that you are a prominent man among your people, and you will no doubt understand that it is not proper to allow a man to go about naked. I beg you therefore to do a good deed and to give me a garment because the sea had taken all my possessions." Rabbi Eleazar was wearing seven garments and he immediately removed one of them and gave it to the man. He then took him to his house and gave him food and drink and two hundred ducats, and he mounted him on one of his asses and escorted him a distance of 14 miles to his house.

Some time later the king (?) died and another king was chosen in his place. The new ruler issued a decree against that country (?) to have all the males killed and to do with the women as they chose. The inhabitants of that country asked Rabbi Eleazar ben Shamua to intercede with the king on their behalf, and they gave him 4,000 ducats to offer as a gift to the king. Rabbi Eleazar proceeded to the palace of the king and when he entered the throne room, the king descended from his throne and bowed before him asking, "What is your request?"

Rabbi Eleazar said: "I want you to have mercy on the kingdom and to rescind your decree." The king then replied: "It is written in your Torah that an Edomite or a Moabite may not be included in the congregation of God because they did not meet the Jews with bread and water when they came out of the land of Egypt. The Torah also states that you may not humiliate an Edomite because he is your brother. But your people dealt otherwise with me and because they did not observe this commandment of the Torah they have forfeited their lives."

"Nevertheless you must forgive them," Rabbi Eleazar said. "You must have mercy on them, for if they did not act according to the commandment of the Torah they did so out of foolishness and God will forgive them." Saying this Rabbi Eleazar handed the king the 4,000 ducats the people had given him. Then the king said, "The 4,000 ducats you may keep, instead of the 200 ducats you gave me. Because you gave me food and drink I will also forgive the sins of that country. You may also enter my treasury and choose the most beautiful garments to replace the one garment you gave me to wear."

The name of Rabbi Jochanan the Sandalmaker is mentioned only three times in connection with legal matters. When the question arose concerning the case of a woman who received *Halitzah* in the presence of witnesses, one of whom later proved to be a relative of the woman, or disqualified as a witness for some other reason, and it was decided that such *Halitzah* was invalid, Rabbi Simeon ben Yochai and Rabbi Jochanan the

Sandalmaker declared that such *Halitzah* was valid. During this debate Rabbi Jochanan related his ruse in visiting Rabbi Akiba in prison to ask his opinion in this question.[10]

A maxim of Rabbi Jochanan stated: "Every assembly conducted for the sake of God will remain permanent, but assemblies not for the sake of God will not last."[11]

Opinions differ concerning his appellation of "Sandlar" (sandalmaker). The book of genealogies (*Yuhasin*) declares that Rabbi Jochanan was either a sandalmaker or that he drilled pearls to be strung, but some modern philologists dispute this point of view and interpret the name "Sandlar" to indicate that he was a native of Alexandria.

43

RABBI NEHEMIAH
AND OTHER DISCIPLES
OF RABBI AKIBA

THE LAST DISCIPLES OF RABBI AKIBA began the work of compiling the *Mishnah* as they received it from their master. One of these was Rabbi Nehemiah who participated in the first gathering of scholars after the death of Emperor Hadrian.[1] He was also present at the convocation at Usha although he did not actively participate in it.[2]

Little is known of the life and activities of Rabbi Nehemiah except the fact that he was very poor and a potter by trade.[3] The name of his father is also unknown although it is certain that he was a prominent scholar, because Rabbi Nehemiah once quoted his opinion in a legal matter.[4] Rabbi Nehemiah opposed the methodology of Rabbi Jehudah bar Elai and contradictory reports concerning his personality circulated in later generations. One opinion claimed that all anonymous statements in the *Tosefta* were those of Rabbi Nehemiah.[5] When the book of genealogy of the noble families of Jerusalem was discovered, it was found that Rabbi Nehemiah was a descendant of Nehemiah the Thirshata.[6]

Another belief current in later generations maintained that Rabbi Nehemiah was really the *tanna* Rabbi Nehorai. In explanation it was said that he was called Nehorai because he shed light on doubtful legal questions.[7] But Rabbi Nehorai had also been previously identified with Rabbi Eleazar ben Arach.[8] These beliefs therefore lack all substantiation because we also find a text quoting a dispute between Rabbi Nehorai and Rabbi Nehemiah, and on another occasion the opinions of both are listed side by side.[9]

The following statements reflect Rabbi Nehemiah's ethical precepts: "Suffering is good for people. Just as sacrifice placates God and stills his anger, even so does human suffering placate the Almighty. Moreover, human suffering is even more effective than the offering of sacrifices."[10] "The sin of unfounded hatred is punished by domestic discord, frequent miscarriage, and the early death of children."[11] "He who undertakes to fulfill even one commandment honestly deserves that the Holy Spirit should rest upon him. Thus we see that our forefathers left Egypt and believed in God, and the Holy Spirit rested upon them and they merited the privilege of praising God."[12]

Speaking of the coming of the Messiah, Rabbi Nehemiah declared that "brazenness will then increase and honored men will follow devious ways. The vineyards will bear fruit, but wine will be scarce. Government will be transformed into the rule of cliques and there will be no man capable of pointing out the right path."[13]

In his exposition of the Scriptures, Rabbi Nehemiah based his opinions on logic as well as on grammatical structure. He said: "The words of the Torah are sometimes insufficient in one place and superfluous in another."[14] When scholars expressed differing opinions regarding the duration of the time known as *bein hashemashot* (twilight), Rabbi Nehemiah declared that it lasts as long as it would take a man to walk 1,000 ells.[15]

Another important *tanna* of that time was Rabbi Joshua ben Korcha. Talmudic commentators such as Rashi, Rabbenu Gershom Meor Hagolah, and Rashbam claim that he was the son of Rabbi Akiba, who was nicknamed "Kereach" (the bald) because of the statement of Ben Azai who said that all Jewish scholars are worth no more than the skin of garlic except the bald one (referring to Rabbi Akiba). As a result of this Rabbi

Joshua came to be called Ben Korcha, the son of the bald one.[16] But *Tosefot* argue that this could not be the case and that Ben Azai's reference to Rabbi Akiba as "the bald one" did not suffice to justify Rabbi Joshua's appellation of Ben Korcha instead of ben Rabbi Akiba. The chronological order of the generations is also against such an assumption. When Rabbi Joshua was dying, the Nasi, Rabbi Jehudah, asked him for a blessing and Rabbi Joshua said: "I wish that you may live at least half as many years as I did."[17] Had Rabbi Joshua been the son of Rabbi Akiba this blessing would have been meaningless.

Rabbi Joshua's name is mentioned only four times in the *Mishnah,* but the Talmud frequently quotes his legal opinions. Rabbi Joshua was in favor of allowing witnesses to appear one after the other[18] and he declared that a messenger had the same legal powers as his sender.[19] He believed in the strict enforcement of all scriptural commandments, but he was lenient concerning the fulfillment of the rabbinical regulations.[20]

Some of his moral maxims are noteworthy: "He who studies the Torah but does not review his studies may be compared to a man who sows a field but does not harvest the crop."[21] "He who hides his eyes from charity is like one who worships idols."[22]

Brigandage was very prevalent at that time, and the government found itself powerless to suppress it. Whether these were ordinary robbers or rebels whom the government declared to be bandits is hard to determine today. It is interesting to note, however, that the government appointed Rabbi Eleazar, the son of Rabbi Simeon ben Yochai, who hid with his father in a cave for many years, to exterminate the brigands. This office was similar to that of his grandfather Yochai and was commented on previously.

Rabbi Eleazar had been a pupil of Rabbi Joshua ben Korcha for some time and when Rabbi Joshua heard of his pupil's new position he sent him the following message: "Who gave you the right to exterminate God's people?" Rabbi Eleazar replied: "I only pull out the weeds from the vineyard." To this Rabbi Joshua retorted: "The owner of the vineyard can destroy the weeds himself."[23]

Rabbi Joshua ben Korcha lived to a ripe old age; according to some he was 160 years old at the time of his death. The Nasi, Rabbi Jehudah, once asked him to explain the cause of his long life but Rabbi Joshua was offended and asked: "Are you tired of seeing me alive?" Rabbi Jehudah assured him to the contrary and explained that he was interested from a scientific point of view. Placated, Rabbi Joshua answered: "All my life I never looked at a wicked man."[24]

Among the scholars who met in Jabneh and later in Usha after the destruction of Betar, was also Rabbi Eliezer, the son of Rabbi Jose of Galilee.[25] It was said that whenever Rabbi Eliezer spoke of the *Aggadah* it was advisable to pay close attention.[26] He rarely participated in legal discussions but gained his fame by compiling a list of thirty-two rules of logic according to which the *Aggadah* was being interpreted. Aside from two or three laws ascribed to him, there is also a statement of Rabbi Eliezer which says: "If one begins to fulfill a commandment but does not complete it, and another man finishes the work, credit is given to the one who finished the work."[27]

44

RABBI JEHUDAH HANASI

As a result of the persecution of the Jewish faith that was renewed after the death of emperor Antoninus Pius, Rabban Simeon ben Gamaliel II had to move his academy from Usha to Shefarom. The new decrees promulgated during the joint reign of Lucius Varus and Marcus Aurelius did not strike at the study of the Torah but only at the observance of its commandments, particularly as they concerned the observance of the Sabbath and the practice of circumcision. When Rabban Simeon ben Gamaliel II died, his son Rabbi Jehudah was appointed Nasi. Although documentary evidence is lacking, it is apparent that the assumption of office by the new Nasi took place with the consent of the authorities. Roman suspicion of the Nasi's descent from the royal House of David had subsided by that time and no attempt was being made to offer the office to a man of less aristocratic lineage.

The Talmud always refers to Rabbi Jehudah the Nasi only by his title of Rabbi. Because his contemporaries were convinced that he was the most pious man since the days of Moses, he was also called *Rabbenu Hakadosh*, our holy teacher. His whole life was encompassed by legends of miracles said to have occurred from the day of his birth until many weeks after his death. It was said that he was born on the same day that

Rabbi Akiba was executed.[1] Hadrian's decrees against the practice of circumcision were then in full force and both the child and its parents had to forfeit their lives. One *midrash* relates that Rabbi Jehudah's parents were reported to the government for having circumcised their son. Parents and child were then brought before the emperor (actually the imperial representative then residing in Palestine), but a gentile neighbor who was a member of a prominent Roman aristocratic family pitied the child, and she gave her own son to Rabban Simeon ben Gamaliel to show to the judges.

Because of the turbulence of the times, it is impossible to know definitely where Rabban Simeon ben Gamaliel and his wife resided when Rabbi Jehudah was born. The son of the Nasi and destined to follow his father in that post, Rabbi Jehudah was provided with the best tutors who acquainted him with all the sciences. Gifted with great talents and a natural curiosity, he absorbed much learning and assimilated it within his personality. In his youth Rabbi Jehudah studied with his father[2] and later he was a pupil of the academies of Rabbi Jehudah bar Elai, Rabbi Eleazar ben Shamua, and others.

Rabbi Jehudah evinced a great love of the Bible and all his life he sought to establish Hebrew or Greek as the spoken language among the Jews. He was grieved to hear the Jews speak a mixture of languages,[3] but in his own household everyone spoke Hebrew. Rabbi Jehudah owned a woman slave (frequently mentioned in the Talmud as "the servant in the house of Rabbi") who was an authority on the Hebrew language and who was often consulted by some of the scholars in the matter of the Hebrew names of various subjects.[4]

Like his predecessors Rabbi Jehudah also devoted much time to the study of the natural sciences. His position as Nasi obligated him to determine the dates of the new months and the holidays, and he had to know astronomy. Likewise he had to know the nature of various plants and animals in connection with the dietary laws and the regulations pertaining to cleanliness. These sciences attained a higher stage of development among the Gentiles who were not bound by the regulations of the Torah, so that Rabbi Jehudah declared that whenever a law was not involved, the opinions of gentile naturalists were to be considered as more valid than the opinions of Jewish scholars.[5]

Rabbi Jehudah the Nasi was very rich and his wealth was often described with fantastic exaggeration. For instance, it was said that his cattle fed from golden troughs and that his stables contained more gold than the treasure rooms of the Persian king.[6] Because of his prominent position he had to conduct a lavish court in the manner of a royal prince, but it is known nevertheless that he used little of his wealth for his personal use.[7] Whenever necessary he gave generously for charitable purposes, for the maintenance of needy students, and to feed the poor.[8]

A great famine occurred throughout all the provinces of the Roman empire at that time. Rabbi Jehudah opened his storehouses to distribute grain to the poor, but at first he commanded that only those who had studied the Torah should be given bread. One of his disciples, Rabbi Jonathan ben Amram, appeared dressed as an *am ha'aretz* and when Rabbi Jehudah refused to give him bread he said: "Does not even a crow or a dog have the right to be fed?" Rabbi Jehudah then agreed that no distinction should be made in the matter of the distribution of bread, and he commanded that it be given to all who asked for it.

Despite his great personal success Rabbi Jehudah never showed the least sign of pride. None of the scholars so readily acknowledged the value and superiority of others as he did.[9] One of his most favorite maxims was: "I have learned much from my teachers; I have learned even more from my friends, but I have learned most from my pupils."[10] When certain activities of other people were being judged and criticism leveled against them, Rabbi Jehudah carefully weighed his opinions before passing judgment. When a man was brought before Rabbi Jehudah for trial on the grounds that he did not observe the regulations of the sabbatical year, Rabbi Jehudah carefully listened to the accusation as well as to the arguments of the defendant and said: "What else could you expect the poor man to do when he was hungry?"[11]

Like his grandfather, Rabban Gamaliel of Jabneh, Rabbi

Jehudah realized that the regulations of the sabbatical year were a heavy burden upon the poorer people and felt they should be modified. The poorer elements of the community usually remained without bread on the sabbatical year, and it was obvious that they had to resort to eating the fruit that had ripened in that year. Rabbi Jehudah was ready to open the subject for discussion with Rabbi Pinchas ben Yair but realizing that he would be overruled said nothing.[12] Nevertheless he succeeded in repealing several prohibitions of the sabbatical year still in effect at that time. Rabbi Jehudah acted similarly to reduce the burden of the tithes,[13] and he also declared that the population should not be burdened with too many fasts.[14]

Rabbi Jehudah Hanasi never insisted on his personal prerogatives, but he severely punished all infringements on the dignity of the office of Nasi. Rabbi Jehudah devoted much effort to the attainment of this goal and he was successful. The office of Nasi therefore attained a great measure of authority. Wherever Jews lived, the word of the Nasi was listened to attentively. His pronouncements were considered as law and no one dared to criticize his actions. In Babylonia as well as in Palestine, and in all the other countries, his decisions were unquestioned. As a result the organization of Jewish life proceeded in better order than ever before, and it was said that "from Moses until Rabbi Jehudah Hanasi there was not another man who combined learning and greatness of spirit to such a degree.[15]

Because of his descent from Hillel of Babylonia and from King David, Jews accorded him all the greatest honors. He was the recognized leader of the people and his word carried more weight than that of all the other members of the Court together. His opinion determined whether a disciple should be ordained, irrespective of the opinions of the other scholars. At that time it was also ruled that "When a court appoints one to an office without the sanction of the Nasi, such appointment is invalid; but when the Nasi appoints a person to an office without the sanction of the court, the appointment is valid."[16]

The court of Rabbi Jehudah Hanasi had no superior judge (*Av Beit Din*) and the post of *hakham* was also done away with.

These changes eliminated conflicts and disputes among the Nasi and the other scholars. Rabbi Jehudah also knew how to keep his decisions within certain bounds. He always sensed possible opposition to new and radical legislation and avoided enacting it. Due to the changing developments in the political situation in Palestine, he felt compelled to introduce some reforms in Jewish religious life. He thus abolished the time-honored custom of lighting fires on the mountain tops to announce the beginning of a new month, which determined the dates of the holidays, substituting instead the dispatch of messengers to the communities.[17]

The cause of this innovation was the renewed animosity between the Samaritans and the Jews which again flared up after a period of friendship when they were both equally oppressed by the Romans. In order to confuse the Jews in the celebration of their holidays, the Samaritans often lit fires on the mountain tops at the wrong time. As Rabbi Ishmael ben Jose was making a pilgrimage to Jerusalem he passed through Shechem. The Samaritans ridiculed him for making a pilgrimage to a ruin that God had rejected and declared that it would be more reasonable to offer prayers on Mount Gerizim that had been blessed by God. Rabbi Ishmael replied that the Samaritans probably venerate Mount Gerizim because it was there that Jacob buried the idols he had taken from Laban's house. This reply incensed the Samaritans and they were ready to kill Rabbi Ishmael who escaped with great difficulty.[18]

The observance of the sabbatical year and the payment of tithes at that time had become a severe problem due to the prevalent poverty. Rabbi Jehudah modified the regulations governing the sabbatical year and the tithes. Moreover, he could see no justification for the continued payment of tithes to the Priests and Levites after the Temple was destroyed. He therefore declared the environs of many cities (not included in the first conquest of Canaan by Joshua) as foreign territory and not subject to those commandments operative in Palestine only. The inhabitants of those districts were thus freed from the burden of both the sabbatical year and the tithes.[19]

The conditions of Jewish life had also changed to such an

extent that it became necessary to think of modifying the restrictions of the Sabbath, in order to allow people to go from one city to another; for example, from Geder to Hamthan.[20] Rabbi Jehudah also simplified the procedure for accepting proselytes[21] and he attempted to modify the observance of the ninth day of *Av*. His reforms in this case are not entirely clear. The Talmud relates that he wanted to do away altogether with the observance of the ninth day of *Av*. Later scholars doubted such an intention and declared that he merely wanted to abolish the fasting when that day coincided with the Sabbath. Since fasting was prohibited on the Sabbath he wanted to do away with the fast on such a year.[22]

Rabbi Jehudah ruled that students considered capable of heading an academy should not be allowed to open one without the permission of the Nasi.[23] He also instructed his son Rabban Gamaliel, who was to be his successor, to conduct himself with dignity and to inspire fear among his disciples.[24]

Speaking to one of his disciples (Rabbi Chiya) Rabbi Jehudah declared that he would honor the wish of any person except those of the Men of Bathyra because they had renounced the office of Nasi in favor of Hillel. "But," he added, "were the Exilarch Rav Huna to come from Babylonia, I would not renounce my office, but I would give him the seat of honor for he is descended from a son of King David while I am descended from a daughter of the king."

Sometime later, when this conversation had been forgotten by all, Rabbi Chiya entered the academy of Rabbi Jehudah and announced: "The Exilarch Rav Huna of Babylonia has arrived." He noticed that Rabbi Jehudah's face changed color from great agitation and he immediately added: "The dead Rav Huna and not the living one has arrived." (Rav Huna commanded in his will that his body be interred in Palestine, and it was the arrival of the body that Rabbi Chiya announced.)

Rabbi Jehudah Hanasi was greatly angered at this attempt to confuse him for even a moment, and he punished Rabbi Chiya by denying him entrance to the academy for thirty days.[25]

Another angry outburst of Rabbi Jehudah (against Bar

Kapara) is related in the following story. Rabbi Jehudah had a son-in-law, Ben Elasha who was a wealthy man but not a learned one. On the occasion of a feast that Rabbi Jehudah tendered in his house, the guests proposed riddles for the others to solve, but Ben Elasha remained silent. Bar Kapara then said to him: "Why are you silent, brother?" And Ben Elasha replied: "You know that I know not what to say." Bar Kapara suggested that he should ask the following riddle: "The grebe looks down from heaven, it hovers in all the corners of the house, it frightens all the birds. Young ones see it and hide, old ones remain standing in fright. Whoever escapes cries out in pain, and he who is caught, is caught in his own sin."

This riddle was aimed at the leadership of Rabbi Jehudah and he understood that it could not have been thought up by his son-in-law. Rabbi Jehudah also noticed Bar Kapara smiling and he felt certain that he was the author of the riddle. In great anger he exclaimed: "I do not want to know you any longer, old man." This was a great blow for Bar Kapara who could never obtain ordination after that, although he deserved it more than many others.[26]

It was the same with Shmuel Yarchina'ah who was one of the greatest scholars of the time, but who never received ordination. He had served Rabbi Jehudah Hanasi for many years as physician and cured him of a dangerous disease. It is unknown what Shmuel Yarchina'ah's offense was, and it is also possible that he did not receive ordination because of an insufficient knowledge of the law. He devoted himself mainly to the sciences such as astronomy and astrology. Shmuel consoled himself with the belief that since the time of Adam it had already been foretold that he would be a learned man but not ordained, and that he would bring about the cure of Rabbi Jehudah Hanasi.[27]

Rabbi Jehudah was prone to anger as a result of his sickness which caused him great suffering. These outbursts of temper brought about a subdued discontent among his disciples as well as among the members of his household. This discontent was never voiced except on one occasion during a feast in the Nasi's house. When everyone was merry with wine, Rabbi Jehudah asked the two children of Rabbi Chiya, Jehudah and Hezekiah, to speak. The two boys began describing the time of the coming of the Messiah saying that the Messiah would not arrive until the two ruling houses, of the Nasi and of the Exilarch of Babylonia, would be done away with for these hinder the redemption. Rabbi Jehudah was greatly grieved to hear this, but being in a good mood he did not remove the boys from the house, and merely remarked: "Children, you cast thorns in my eyes."[28]

The whole generation of Rabbi Jehudah was unanimous in its veneration of the saintliness of the man and he was therefore called *Rabbenu Hakadosh* (our holy teacher). His personal qualities and his nobility in his relations with people caused him to be the beloved friend of a Roman emperor (according to some historians it was a Roman governor) who secretly visited him to learn about Judaism until he was convinced of the truth of the Jewish faith and became converted. One must bear in mind that the Romans looked with contempt upon the Jews at that time. A Jew who could win the friendship of a Roman emperor or governor had to be a shining example among millions. Under these circumstances it is understandable why the Jewish people idolized Rabbi Jehudah, and when Rabbi Simeon ben Menasia listed seven virtues that every just man must possess he immediately added that all of these were united in Rabbi Jehudah and his family. These are: beauty, strength, honor, wisdom, a manly beard, old age, and successful children.[29]

People therefore believed that one who sees Rabbi Jehudah in his dream could expect wisdom,[30] and later scholars declared that he drew his wisdom from deep wells,[31] and that the prophet Elijah sat among the disciples of Rabbi Jehudah to hear him teach the Torah.[32]

When he was asked "Which is the right way for a man to choose?" Rabbi Jehudah replied that every way is good when it is fit for the people who follow it and if they can take pride in it. To elucidate his meaning he immediately added: "Be careful in the case of a light commandment as in that of a weighty one for you know not the value of the commandments. Everyone

must therefore weigh the loss incurred in fulfilling a commandment against its reward, and the reward of a sin against its
punishment."[33] "When a man commits a good deed he should
be joyful, because it is certain to lead him to other good deeds;
but one who commits a sin must feel sorrowful because he will
be lead to commit other sins."[34]

Evil nature and its relation to the sinner, Rabbi Jehudah
said, may be compared to two persons who enter a house and
one of them is caught in the act of stealing. When the guilty
person is asked, "Who was with you?" he could say that he
alone was responsible, but seeing that he was to be condemned
to death he also involves his friend. Evil nature acts similarly
and when one of man's limbs sins and loses its share in the
world to come, all the other limbs are also lost.[35]

"One who enjoys the pleasures of this world," Rabbi
Jehudah continued, "is denied the pleasures of the world to
come; one who is denied the joys of this world is certain to
share in the pleasures of the world to come. A just man who
meets with difficulties in this life may be compared with a cook
who prepares a feast for himself; although he has to work hard
to prepare the feast he realizes that he will enjoy it later.
Wicked men who meet with difficulties may be compared with
a cook who prepares a feast for others; he has to work hard but
he does not enjoy the fruit of his labor."[36]

But it is remarkable that despite Rabbi Jehudah's conviction that all man's activities must be directed toward attaining
a share in the world to come, nevertheless he once expressed
himself in the following terms: "One hour of repentance and
good deeds in this world outweighs all the life in the world to
come."[37] This statement was interpreted to refer to the satisfaction one derives from repentance or good deeds that is more
important than the joy of anticipating a world to come.

Speaking of the Torah, Rabbi Jehudah compared it to
water. Just as an adult is not ashamed to ask a child for a drink
of water, even so a man should not be ashamed to ask one
lesser than himself to clarify some doubtful passage of the law.
The Torah may also be compared to water in another manner.
One who is thirsty diligently searches for water to quench his

thirst, and a student must be diligent in his attendance at the academy.[38] No man can hide his learning, and even if he engages in secret study, the Torah will announce itself to all.[39]

Because of his great veneration of the Torah and its followers Rabbi Jehudah despised the uneducated and declared that only students may eat the flesh of animals or fowls, but the uneducated must not eat such flesh for they themselves are not different from animals.[40] He believed that all the evil visited upon the world was in punishment of the sins of the *amei aratzim.*[41]

As did many of his predecessors Rabbi Jehudah believed in peace, and he said that "Even if the Jews were to worship idols but live in peace, God himself would be powerless to harm them."[42] He attached great significance to labor and declared: "Great is the value of labor. When people see a man not engaged in some occupation, they wonder where he gets his income. Such a man may be compared to an unmarried woman who adorns herself before going out and thus attracts the unfavorable comment of the people. Similar attention is attracted by a man who does not work."[43]

After the daily prayers Rabbi Jehudah recited a prayer of his own in which he asked to be preserved from meeting with arrogant people, from showing arrogance, and to be spared from untoward events, evil thoughts, wicked friends, bad neighbors, severe laws as well as from severe judges.[44] Rabbi Jehudah was always ready to acknowledge the truth of others' views, but if one of his pupils corrected him in public, he never forgave him even though he may have agreed with the correction.[45]

The following story is related in the Talmud concerning the kindness of Rabbi Jehudah. As he once sat in front of the Babylonian synagogue in Sepphoris, a calf was led by to slaughter. The animal fawned upon Rabbi Jehudah and bleated pitifully as if asking him to save it from slaughter, but he said to it: "I cannot save you. You must follow where you are led, for you were created for the purpose of slaughter." It was then announced in heaven that since Rabbi Jehudah did not pity God's creature, he was to be punished and consequently suffered from toothache for thirteen years. Sometime later his daughter saw an insect in the house and wanted to kill it, but Rabbi Jehudah said to her: "Leave it be. God created it and He pities all his creatures." It was then decided in heaven to show mercy on Rabbi Jehudah because he had shown mercy to a living creature.[46]

When Rabbi Jehudah was about to die, he commanded his children that the conduct of the house should not be altered in any manner. He then raised his hands heavenward and said: "Creator of the world, you know the truth. All my days I have devoted to the Torah and I have not enjoyed the pleasures of this life in the slightest measure." As his death drew near, the scholars declared a fast and fervently prayed to God. They also said that whoever announced the death of Rabbi Jehudah was to be pierced with a sword. Later they sent Bar Kapara to see Rabbi Jehudah, but when he arrived Rabbi Jehudah was dead. Bar Kapara rent his garments and returning to the academy, he said: "Angels and men have contended for the Holy Ark but the angels triumphed and the Ark has been taken away." He was then asked, "Is Rabbi Jehudah dead?" and Bar Kapara answered, "You have said it. I could not bring myself to utter the word."[47]

Many of the stories of Rabbi Jehudah's activities related in the Talmud and the *Mishnah* reveal an intimate friendship between him and the Roman Emperor Antoninus, and it was said that the emperor often visited Rabbi Jehudah's house through a secret tunnel.(!) During these visits they engaged in friendly arguments concerning religious questions. The confidence of the emperor in the Nasi was said to be so great that he often asked Rabbi Jehudah's advice in such matters as the succession to the Roman throne, and his conduct toward his daughter who had deviated from the ways of morality.

Most of these stories are related in Tractate *Avodah Zarah* and as proof of their factual basis we may cite the writings of the Christian church father Hieronymus, who lived at a time when these events were still fresh in the memory of the people. Other historians, however, find it difficult to establish defi-

nitely which emperor this was. During the lifetime of Rabbi
Jehudah two or three emperors ruled who added the name
Antoninus to their given names. But the personalities of none
of these emperors fit the legendary description of a great
friendship with the Jewish leader. Antoninus Pius, who was
the first to ameliorate the condition of the Jews in Palestine by
modifying Hadrian's decrees could not have been the hero of
these legends because he was not really a friend of the Jews.
Furthermore, the period of his reign does not coincide with the
period given in these legends.

Still other historians deny the truth of the legend and
maintain that the growth of Christianity which by then had
gained adherents among some Roman emperors caused the
Jews to ally themselves with the Roman opponents of Christianity and to fabricate the story of the emperor's friendship.
Some who recognize the factual basis of the legend claim that
it involved a Roman governor named Antoninus and not the
emperor.

Another version of the legend relates that there was a
secret passage from the governor's palace in Caesarea to the
house of Rabbi Jehudah and that the governor was always
accompanied on his visits by two slaves. Fearing that the slaves
might disclose his friendship with the Nasi and lower his status
in Rome, the governor killed one of the slaves on his arrival at
the house of the Nasi and the other on his return to the palace.

Antoninus objected to the presence of outsiders during his
visits, and once when he found Rabbi Chanina bar Chama
there he asked in anger, "Who is this person?" Rabbi Jehudah
answered, "This is not a human being but an angel." "If so,"
Antoninus said, "let him go out and awaken my slave who is
sleeping at the door." Rabbi Chanina went out and with his
prayers caused the dead slave to come to life again.

Antoninus consulted Rabbi Jehudah concerning his family
problems and in order that no one else might understand the
subject under discussion they frequently conducted a "correspondence of flowers." When Gira, the daughter of Antoninus,
began to conduct herself immorally, Antoninus sent Rabbi
Jehudah the herb Gagira, thus informing him of the situation

and requesting his advice. Rabbi Jehudah responded by sending the herb Chusbarta to express his opinion that he was
justified in killing her. In reply Antoninus sent a flower named
Karthi indicating his inability to execute a member of his
family, and Rabbi Jehudah sent him an herb, Chasa, to advise
him that he should keep the whole matter secret.

Another time Antoninus sent this message to Rabbi
Jehudah: "The treasury is empty. Tell me what to do." Rabbi
Jehudah led the messenger into his garden and in his presence
he pulled out some large radishes and planted new seed in
their place. When the messenger asked for his reply, Rabbi
Jehudah said that none was needed. The messenger returned
to Antoninus and reported that Rabbi Jehudah gave no answer
to the question. "Did he do anything in your presence?"
Antoninus asked, and the messenger related what he had seen.
Antoninus understood the message and he discharged some
officials and appointed others in their place. In a short time the
royal treasury was again filled with gold.[48]

Antoninus once said to Rabbi Jehudah: "I would like to see
my son Severus succeed me to the throne, and I also want to
make Tiberias a free city, but I can only do one of those things
and I don't know which to choose." Rabbi Jehudah advised him
to appoint Severus as his successor and *he* would later declare
Tiberias a free city.

Several episodes related in the Talmud indicate that after
a while relations between Antoninus and Rabbi were no longer
kept secret. It is told that Antoninus sought to serve Rabbi
Jehudah every time he visited and when he was taking his
place in the litter to be carried to the academy, Antoninus
would bend down so that his back might serve as a step for
Rabbi Jehudah. When Rabbi Jehudah objected to this servility
because it lowered the dignity of the royal office, Antoninus
remarked: "I wish that I could be a rug under your feet in the
world to come." Antoninus also sent sacks full of gold to Rabbi
Jehudah and covered them with wheat to hide the fact from the
populace that he was giving government money to the Nasi.
Rabbi Jehudah asked: "Why do you do this? I do not need it."
Antoninus replied: "Let it remain for those who will come after

you and they can pass it on to future generations." It is also told that Antoninus leased two thousand acres of land in Palestine to Rabbi Jehudah.[49]

Some versions of this legend declare that Antoninus was converted to Judaism, but this is contradicted in other places. Antoninus is reported to have remarked to Rabbi Jehudah: "You promise that in the world to come I will partake of the Leviathan, but now you do not even allow me to eat the Paschal lamb." Rabbi Jehudah pointed out that the uncircumcised were forbidden to eat of the Paschal lamb. Antoninus then underwent circumcision and it was said that when Messiah comes, he would be in the front rank of the proselytes. Incidentally, it was also told that Antoninus presented a menorah to the synagogue in Tiberias. When Rabbi Jehudah heard of the gift he exclaimed: "Praised be God who inspired him with this idea!" The fact that he did not say, "Praised be *our* God!" was interpreted by some to prove that Antoninus had not embraced Judaism.[50]

Antoninus frequently invited Rabbi Jehudah to his house and Rabbi Jehudah often arranged feasts in honor of Antoninus. At one such feast that took place on a Sabbath, only cold food was offered. Antoninus ate the food and praised it highly. At another feast given on a weekday hot dishes were served, but Antoninus declared that the cold foods offered on the Sabbath were tastier. Rabbi Jehudah explained that the hot food did not contain a certain herb only mixed with the cold food. When Antoninus asked in surprise what that herb was, Rabbi said that it was called *Sabbath*.[51]

Antoninus often engaged Rabbi Jehudah in philosophic and religious discussions asking questions such as: "Whence does man derive his soul?" or "Since when does evil nature rule humanity?" Often he was not satisfied with Rabbi Jehudah's replies and offered his own explanations which Rabbi Jehudah admitted to be correct.[52]

During one of these discussions, Antoninus argued that both body and soul may escape punishment on the day of judgment. The body may claim that it could not sin had it not been imbued with a soul, and the soul could reason likewise.

Rabbi Jehudah explained what could be done in such a case with the following example from human behavior: The owner of a garden hired two watchmen, one of whom was blind and the other lame, to guard the fruit. The lame one saw the fruit on the trees and wanted to eat some. He then said to the blind watchman, "Lead me to the tree and we will both eat the most beautiful fruit." The blind man then carried the lame one on his shoulders and they ate all the fruit. Later the owner of the garden arrived and asked: "Who ate all the fruit of the tree?" The blind man said: "You cannot blame me for you know that I cannot see." The lame watchman similarly declared: "You cannot blame me for I could not walk to the tree." The owner then placed the lame one on the back of the blind one to show them that he understood how they had reached the fruit and he punished them. God does likewise when body and soul attempt to escape punishment by placing the blame on the other.

When Antoninus died Rabbi Jehudah sighed and exclaimed sorrowfully: "Society has now broken down."

The greatest achievement of Rabbi Jehudah that immortalized his influence and gave him a place in our history almost rivaling that of Moses was his editing of the *Mishnah* in which he compiled all the laws and customs of Jewish life as they were then accepted orally by the people as interpretations and supplements to the commandments of the Torah. The traditional oral explanations were handed down from one generation to another by the priests, the Levites, and the scholars. These laws and opinions were never systematically written down in order to prevent their rivaling the sanctity of the Scriptures, but individual scholars kept short notes of what they heard from their teachers and these notes circulated extensively until they were gathered and edited by Rabbi Jehudah. Many of these traditional interpretations were accepted as legally binding as early as the time of Simon the Just, but during the years they were amplified and developed until there arose differences of opinion which seemed contradictory.

The first *Mishnah* of tractate *Berakhot* thus begins with a question: "When does one have to recite the Shema?" The

Mishnah expresses no doubt regarding the necessity of reciting the *Shema,* but is merely concerned with the length of time allowed for this prayer. The majority of the laws and customs cited in the *Mishnah* are not referred to any one person's authorship. Who the original author of a basically accepted law had been was considered irrelevant. As the years went by, the authors were often forgotten and the *Mishnah* merely endeavored to establish the origin of the laws in the scriptural texts, deriving them literally or through exposition.

Throughout the centuries that elapsed from the time of Simeon the Just until the days of Rabbi Jehudah, many scholars were killed and with them the distinct knowledge of many laws was lost. Numerous customs also fell into disuse in the course of time. The remaining scholars would then assemble witnesses to testify concerning doubtful interpretations of laws and the manner of their observance. In compiling the *Mishnah* Rabbi Jehudah sought to achieve a similar goal.

The persecutions that grew through the ages severed Jews from contact with the surrounding environment forcing them into the narrow bounds of their own intimate group life and blinding them to what was going on outside. They then devoted all their spiritual energies to the Torah; they reckoned every word and letter in the Torah and surrounded even minor words and seemingly unnecessary letters with numerous interpretations.

These interpretations and elucidations were called *Mishnah* because it was a more complete and improved code of laws for the conduct of mankind. Many of the Biblical commandments were rather vague in their context and required further elucidation. Nevertheless when Rabbi Jehudah compiled the *Mishnah* in six "orders" divided into sixty tractates, some laws remained that were not included for reasons unknown to us and these were later included in the Talmud as *Beraita* or in *Tosefta.* The Mishnaic method of interpretation thus became the nerve center of Jewish jurisprudence, and the Jerusalem Talmud explains[53] even where tradition and biblical text were contradictory it was sought to find some way to derive the tradition from the text in order not to impair the sanctity of the scriptural text. Actions forbidden at one time were permitted at a later date, but both the prohibition and the permission were derived by expounding the same text. A case in point involved the timing when cultivation of the fields on the year preceding the sabbatical year had to cease.[54]

This approach was maintained toward all laws irrespective of whether they were based on traditional interpretation or on the regulations of the Elders enacted from time to time since the days of the Great Synagogue. A similar attitude was observed toward customs that were originated by teachers of the law or were commanded by the Torah and had become hallowed by time. The *Mishnah* did not differentiate between these two types of laws.

Much has been said concerning the difference between the schools of Hillel and of Shammai and that for a time it seemed as if two separate sets of laws would be established. Such fears, however, could be entertained only by the superficial observer for despite all differences both schools had only one aim, to attain the truth.

As Rabbi Jehudah grew old he felt concern for the fate of the traditions, and he feared that they would be forgotten by later generations. He decided therefore to have them written down and edited. He had no such fears concerning the Torah and felt sure that its spirit would remain alive even if the books of the Torah were to be destroyed. The constant oppression and the weakening human spirit did fill him with foreboding concerning the observance of the numerous traditions.

As Rabbi Jehudah gathered the various laws to include in the *Mishnah* he omitted the explanatory arguments and conflicting opinions which had been added. He also sought to retain the original style and form of the laws and he included laws and customs no longer observed in his day. All these he tried to present in the clearest possible manner.[55] The *Mishnah* thus bears the marks of organic unity (despite the many disputes which took place during the formulation of the laws) and it appears to be written by one man. Any contradiction that may be found in it was considered superficial because "every-thing which a scholar may learn someday had previously been said to Moses on Mount Sinai."[56]

The *Mishnayot* (pl. of *Mishnah*) of Rabbi Jehudah could be classified under two headings: *Halakhah* (law) and *Drashah* (exposition). The word *Halakhah* signifies "conduct" and it refers to traditionally accepted customs irrespective of whether they are based on Biblical commandments in their essence or in detail. It was an accepted axiom of the Jewish faith that all of these *halakhot* were orally given to Moses on Mount Sinai. Differences of opinion that existed regarding some of these, were settled by a *bat kol* (public opinion) which declared that the contentions of both sides were the words of the living God.[57]

The Graeco-Jewish philosopher Philo described the cus-toms of the Jews in his books and he defined those customs (*minhagim*) as unwritten traditional interpretations of the laws. From this we may conclude that the origin of a *Halakhah* was a popular custom. In time, however, laws and customs became differentiated into separate types of observances. When we assume that custom was the foundation of law, we must bear in mind that customs become antiquated and lose their original purpose. We therefore find in the *Mishnah* numerous laws whose intent is no longer clear. In such cases it was the established rule of the court to observe the accepted procedure of the populace. A rule was established that customs that are contradictory to old laws should not be abolished and it was said that "custom outweighs the law."[58] Another rule declared that "a person may be punished for the infraction of a custom as well as for breaking a law."[59]

The laws of the *Mishnah* developed to a large extent out of analysis of the words of the Torah. This method was then considered to be the most valid and the only one capable of bringing out the simple meaning of the text. The biblical verse "on the morrow after the Sabbath" (Lev. 23:15) was thus explained to mean the morrow of the first day of Passover and not the morrow of the Sabbath as the Sadducees claimed. The interpretation of the Sadducees would cause *Shavuot* to occur always on a Sunday. Similarly they explained the biblical injunction that a man must marry the childless widow of his brother to be operative only if the woman had no children at all despite the text of the Bible which reads "if he has no son." These two interpretations must have been accepted long before the compilation of the *Mishnah* because the Septuaginta, the Greek translation of the Torah, rendered these verses in accordance with the mishnaic explanation.

After the destruction of the Temple, this method of exposition gained in popularity and every word was minutely analyzed. The seven rules of interpretation that Hillel the Older set up increased in time to thirteen (formulated by Rabbi Ishmael) and they were expanded later by Rabbi Jose of Galilee to thirty-two. Rabbi Akiba attached significance to every word and letter in the Bible. A contributing factor that influenced this form of reasoning was the fact that the text of the Bible was then written without vowel signs. Although everyone knew the traditionally correct reading of the text, tradition was frequently overlooked and the ambiguity caused by the lack of vowel signs allowed for interpretations contrary to the spirit of the text.

When Rabbi Jehudah began to compile the *Mishnah,* two generations had passed since the first tractate *Eduyot* was composed. In the intervening years many laws developed along new lines due to historical developments that could not have been foreseen. Rabbi Jehudah carefully weighed all the pros and cons concerning all laws before he determined their final form. Although he used the *Mishnah* of Rabbi Akiba extensively he did not include all the laws listed in it, because his decisions were based on the opinions of the majority of his contemporary scholars. He also changed the order of Rabbi Akiba's *mishnayot* which arranged the laws according to their authors and not according to subject matter.

Rabbi Jehudah rearranged the *Mishnah* according to subject groups. The first group dealt with prayers and benedictions; the second dealt with the laws of cultivation of the soil and the attendant regulations; the third dealt with the regulations governing the observance of the Sabbath and the holidays, fast days, and other historical memorial days; the fourth group included laws pertaining to family life, vows, and Nazarites; the fifth dealt with money matters, the Sanhedrin, and relations between man and the community; the sixth included the laws of the sacrifices and the regulations of cleanliness. But Rabbi Jehudah was not altogether successful in classifying the material as he wished. The great volume of subject matter at hand could not easily be made to conform with rigid classifications, and thus we find problems of money matters among the laws of marriage or the regulations of the holidays; dietary laws are frequently found among regulations pertaining to the offering of sacrifices.

Historians differ as to the motives that prompted Rabbi Jehudah to compile the *Mishnah*. Some maintain that he undertook the work in order to preserve the traditions from being lost. Others claim that his primary motive was to define the laws once and for all and to remove any possible ambiguities. Such conflicting opinions as are found in the *Mishnah* or cases where the final decision concerning a law was not laid down, these historians explain as being later-day additions.

The *Halakhah*, constituting the greater part of the *Mishnah*, is accompanied by all the arguments advanced concerning the law as well as by the fundamental cause that brought about enactment of law, often derived from scriptural text that had no direct bearing on that law. In explanation of this view, the Talmud states that Rabbi Jochanan ben Zakkai studied the disputes of Abayei and Rava[60] implying that he foresaw the possible future argumentation of these two scholars. Since Rabbi Jochanan lived nearly two hundred years before Abayei and Rava no other view can be taken of this statement.

The second important component of the *Mishnah* is the *Derashah* (exposition) consisting of interpretations of words to substantiate the opinions of the *tanna*. These *Derashot* (pl. of *Derashah*) are generally preceded by the words "I am instructed to say" (*talmud lomar*) or "it is intended to teach you" (*lelamedkha*). It is noteworthy, however, that in some cases the law is stated fully in its final form, while at other times all the interpretations of the words and even of the letters are quoted.

The *Mishnah* was written in a Hebrew slightly modified from the language of the Bible. Because of the practical problems with which it concerned itself, it had to depart from the poetic idiom of the Scriptures, and in order to express the numerous new concepts words had to be borrowed from the languages then currently spoken in Palestine such as Chaldean, Aramaic, Greek, and Latin. The foreign words introduced into the *Mishnah* were modified to conform to the spirit and grammar of the Hebrew language. The same words were not always used to define one concept because the editor of the *Mishnah* sought to retain the original idiom of the *tanna* who expounded the law, and they employed the idioms current in their own time. The style of the *Mishnah* illustrates Rabbi Jehudah's keen sense of the Hebrew language. In his own household Hebrew was spoken exclusively and to determine the correct spoken form of some Hebrew word, many went to hear Rabbi Jehudah's servant speak. Hebrew was still the spoken tongue of the majority of the Jews and it was flexible enough to express the finest abstract concepts.

It is impossible to point out those *halakhot* in the *Mishnah* quoted from the original statements and those that Rabbi Jehudah phrased in his own words. Only a skilled philologist could recognize the stylistic nuances between the original statements and those that were rephrased. The beginning of every book of the *Mishnah* quotes the most important laws of that group. It is therefore assumed that these are quotations from earlier *tannaim* given in their original wording with the name of the *tanna* omitted. This is also the case when the authorship of the *tanna* was acknowledged. However there are statements in the *Mishnah* ascribed to certain *tannaim* that are recognizable as not being direct quotations. In such cases Rabbi Jehudah was probably more interested in the essence of the opinion rather than in its exact wording.

There are indications that the text of the *Mishnah* underwent modification during the lifetime of Rabbi Jehudah. Some of these were probably made by Rabbi Jehudah himself. This may account for the different version of the *Mishnah* that sometimes occurs in the Jerusalem Talmud. Others claim that the text of the *Mishnah* as it is quoted in the Babylonian Talmud is its final form, and that it was brought to Babylonia by Rav (Abba Arecha) after Rabbi Jehudah introduced improvements. It can be justifiably assumed that certain changes were introduced into the *Mishnah* after the death of Rabbi Jehudah. As a result of these changes a number of corrections were made by various scholars who understood that it was impossible to preserve the original text of the *Mishnah* without variations. The tendency to change the text is evidenced by the warning of Rabbi Jochanan (the editor of the Jerusalem Talmud) who said: "No one may add to the language which the early ones used."[61] Other scholars warned against confusing the names of the *tannaim* and ascribing a saying of one *tanna* to another. Such errors, they said, amounted to committing the sin of "changing eternal boundaries."[62]

The following story is characteristic of the attitude toward changing the text of the *Mishnah*. Levi ben Sisi once asked Rabbi Jehudah to improve a certain sentence in the *Mishnah* and Rabbi Jehudah was angry with him for making such a request. Levi nevertheless changed the text as he saw fit.[63] Others no doubt followed Levi ben Sisi's example for we frequently find in the Jerusalem Talmud the statement, "we studied the *Mishnah* in this form" or "there are those who study it otherwise." It is evident that changes had been introduced in all these cases.

This practice was later adopted by the *amoraim* when they found that the *Mishnah* conflicted with views they were trying to prove, and the corrections remained permanent despite the accepted rule against introducing changes. This practice was more prevalent in Babylonia because *pilpul* was more popular in that country. Sometimes these changes were not incorporated into the body of the *Mishnah* and thus we find the Jerusalem Talmud using the phrase: "The *Mishnah* should have read otherwise."

Taking all these into consideration, we may conclude that the text of the *Mishnah* often caused misunderstandings among the scholars who failed to comprehend the original meaning.

The introduction of changes continued for a long time until the Talmud was ready to be compiled. Conflicting versions became popular and Rabbi Zeira (a pupil of Rabbi Jochanan) complained that indifference was shown to the original text of Rabbi Jehudah.[64] In addition the Talmud declares that some sentences in the *Mishnah* were not put there by Rabbi Jehudah.[65]

45

CONTEMPORARIES OF RABBI JEHUDAH HANASI

THERE WAS AN ENTIRE GROUP of scholars who lived and exerted an influence during Rabbi Jehudah's lifetime but who conducted independent academies and frequently even opposed Rabbi Jehudah. This group marked the transition from the *tannaim* who lived after the completion of the *Mishnah* to the *amoraim*, who were the authors of the *Gemara*.

Rabbi Simeon ben Menasia

Rabbi Simeon ben Menasia belonged to this group of transition scholars. He was a member of a society of pious men called "The Holy Congregation" because of their habit of dividing the day into three parts, one of which they devoted to learning, the second to prayer, and the third to work. Other members of this society divided the year into two parts; they devoted winter to study and the summer to labor in their trades. It was this group that Rabbi Jehudah had in mind when he declared that "man should gain knowledge of an occupation as well as knowledge of the Torah."[1]

Rabbi Simeon was a disciple of Rabbi Meir and he always quoted his master in legal matters.[2] Some of his references to Rabbi Simeon ben Yochai indicate that he had also studied with him.[3] Rabbi Simeon ben Menasia was diligent in spreading the praise of Rabbi Jehudah despite the fact that at times he disagreed with his opinions.[4] He listed seven virtues every pious man must possess and he immediately noted that Rabbi Jehudah and his family combined all of these in their personalities.[5]

Rabbi Simon ben Menasia's sense of justice is expressed in his dictum concerning the proper conduct of a judge during a trial. He declared that a judge must endeavor to conciliate the contending parties before he has heard their grievances, or before he has made up his mind where justice lies. But after he has heard their arguments and decided which of them was right and which was wrong, he no longer has the right to attempt conciliation but must pass sentence.[6]

Concerning the Sabbath, Rabbi Simeon ben Menasia said that the Biblical verse "Behold I have given you the Sabbath" indicates that people have the right to regulate the Sabbath more than the Sabbath should regulate their lives. He therefore concluded that it was permissible to desecrate the Sabbath to save a human life in order that the person might live to observe many Sabbaths in the future.[7]

A fantastic remark of Rabbi Simeon ben Menasia concerning the punishment of the original sin was interpreted by some as ridiculing those scholars who believed that God sent angels to cut the feet off the snake after Adam had eaten the fruit of the tree of knowledge. Rabbi Simeon ben Menasia said: "It is regrettable that we have lost an excellent servant in the snake. Had Eve not been led to sin, the snake would not have been cursed and every Jew could keep two snakes in his house—one of which he could send to the East and the other to the West. The snakes could then have brought him diamonds and other wealth from the ends of the earth and none could have harmed him. Snakes could also have been used for all kinds of labor instead of camels and asses; snakes could even have carried fertilizer into the gardens."[8]

Rabbi Pinchas ben Yair

Rabbi Pinchas ben Yair was another contemporary of Rabbi Jehudah. According to the Talmud he was the son-in-law of

Rabbi Simeon ben Yochai; but according to the Zohar, he was his father-in-law. In mental brilliance Rabbi Pinchas was the equal of Rabbi Simeon ben Yochai and it was said that whenever Rabbi Simeon asked a question during their studies, Rabbi Pinchas immediately had twelve answers; when Rabbi Pinchas asked a question, Rabbi Simeon answered at once in twenty-four different ways.[9]

But Rabbi Pinchas gained his reputation not because of his scholastic attainments but because of his piety, concerning which many wonderful stories are related. The Talmud therefore contains none of Rabbi Pinchas's legal opinions but much is told of his observing the commandment of offering tithes with such painstaking care that even his ass would not eat grain that had not been tithed. Although he declared that the city of Ashkelon was not included within the boundaries of Palestine and should therefore have been considered free from the commandment of offering tithes, he nevertheless insisted that Jews who lived in that city must abide by this commandment.[10] His belief in the significance of this commandment was so great that he ascribed all punishment visited on the people as having been caused by the avoidance of offering tithes.

It is thus related that he once came to a city where the people complained of a plague of mice that were devouring the harvest. Rabbi Pinchas warned them against shirking the offering of tithes and when the inhabitants of that city began to pay closer attention to the fulfillment of this commandment they were rid of the mice. At another time some people came to him and complained that the city well did not yield enough water. Rabbi Pinchas said: "This is certainly a punishment for your disregarding the tithes." The people vowed to change their ways and the well began to yield sufficient water for all their needs.[11]

Rabbi Pinchas's ass was said to be able to discern which grain had been tithed and which had not. When it was stolen, it refused to eat for three days. The thieves realized that it would starve to death and they released it, whereupon it returned to its master. Rabbi Pinchas was glad to get his animal back and he commanded that it be fed at once, but when some barley was offered to it the ass recognized that the barley had not been tithed and refused to eat. Rabbi Pinchas's pupils then said to him: "Did you not teach us that in doubtful cases it is unnecessary to offer tithes from grain that is to be fed to animals?" and Rabbi Pinchas answered: "What can you do to this animal who insists on the strict observance of the law?"[12]

Rabbi Pinchas listed a number of human virtues, each of which grows out of the preceding one and leads ever higher to the final stage of perfection. Observance leads to modesty, modesty leads to fear of God, fear of God leads to piety, piety leads to the holy spirit, and the holy spirit leads to resurrection.[13]

Rabbi Pinchas complained as well about the low moral state of the Jewish people, and he declared that since the destruction of the Temple scholars are shamed and decent people go about with bowed heads; the desire to do good deeds is weakened, and men of strong arms and arrogant tongues have gained the upper hand. Nevertheless, no one wishes for anything, for all things have lost their worth, and any man who is dissatisfied may look only to God.[14]

The Talmud relates that on one of his journeys to redeem captives, Rabbi Pinchas came to the river Ginai and could not cross it because there was neither bridge nor boat at hand. He then addressed the river: "Make way that I may cross!" The river answered: "You are about to do the will of the Creator and I always do His will, but you are not certain whether your journey will be successful, while my path has been laid out by God. I, therefore, need not change my course." Rabbi Pinchas ben Yair then commanded: "If you will not make way for me, I will decree that your sources dry up." On hearing this threat the river grew frightened and at once parted for Rabbi Pinchas.

There then came a man who carried a sack of Passover wheat on his back. Rabbi Pinchas commanded the river to let him also pass because he was on his way to fulfill a commandment. This time the river parted its waters at once. Meanwhile, a wanderer came and joined the other two, and Rabbi Pinchas again asked the river to let the wanderer pass so that it might not be said that a companion of his was discriminated against, and the river parted its waters for the third time.[15]

When the disciples of Rabbi Pinchas heard of this occurrence, they asked their master whether they would ever be able to perform the same miracle and he replied: "If you will feel certain that you never harmed a Jew nor shamed any person, you will be able to perform the same."[16]

It is further related that Rabbi Pinchas never ate at a stranger's table and that after he became of age he did not eat even at his father's table. When Rabbi Jehudah heard that he had arrived in the city he invited him to dine with him, and Rabbi Pinchas accepted the invitation. Rabbi Jehudah was overjoyed at this and openly showed his pleasure. Seeing Rabbi Jehudah's joyful expression, Rabbi Pinchas said: "You seem to think that I had vowed not to derive any benefit from Jews, but the situation is entirely different. It is true that Jews are a holy people, but there are some who would gladly give you food but have none, while others have enough but do not want to share it. Therefore I decided never to take any food that was offered to me."

When Rabbi Pinchas reached the door of Rabbi Jehudah's house he saw there two white mules and he exclaimed: "The Angel of Death is in this house, how can I eat here?" (His reference to the mules as the Angel of Death is explained by the fact that people of that time believed that a blow of a white mule could never be healed.)

As Rabbi Jehudah heard Rabbi Pinchas's exclamation, he came out of the house and said: "If you are not satisfied with my keeping white mules, I will sell them."

"You must not do so," Rabbi Pinchas replied, "for that would amount to putting a stone in the way of a blind man so that he may stumble on it."

"Then I will disclaim ownership of the animals so that anyone may take them, and then you may come into my house," Rabbi Jehudah continued.

"You must not do that either, because of the loss that you will suffer," Rabbi Pinchas responded.

"In that case I will have their hooves removed so that they may harm no one," Rabbi Jehudah countered.

"If you do so, you will commit the sin of causing suffering to an animal," Rabbi Pinchas objected.

"Then I will kill the mules in order that you may enter my house," Rabbi said.

"You must not do that either," Rabbi Pinchas said, "for it is against the law to damage objects of value."

In the end Rabbi Pinchas did not enter the Nasi's house, and since that time the two became estranged and never met again.[17]

Rabbi Eleazar Hakapar and Bar Kapara

The *tanna*, Rabbi Eleazar Hakapar, who was also a contemporary of Rabbi Jehudah was famous for his saying that "envy, desire, and ambition drive a man out of the world." He also declared that "those that are born are destined to die, the dead are destined to rebirth, the reborn are to be judged; to know, to make known, and to be aware that God is the Creator, the Discerner, the judge and the witness, the plaintiff, and the highest authority at the trial. In His presence there is neither injustice nor forgetfulness, neither respect of persons nor taking of bribes. All is according to reckoning. Let not your nature persuade you that the grave will be a refuge, for against your will were you created and against your will were you born, against your will you live, and against your will you must die and give account and reckoning before the King of Kings."[18]

In his warning against pride, Rabbi Eleazar Hakapar said: "You must not strive to be like the highest stair but rather like a doorstep upon which everyone treads, for when the house is being destroyed the doorstep remains in place to the very end."[19]

Like other contemporaries of Rabbi Jehudah whose names did not appear in the *Mishnah* despite the fact that they were considered to be authorities on legal questions, Rabbi Eleazar

Hakapar also figures only in the Beraita.[20] There are grounds to believe that Rabbi Eleazar's father was also a learned man, for we find Rabbi Eleazar referred to as Rabbi Eleazar ben Rabbi, and Rashi interprets this to indicate that his father was held to be a great man. Rabbi Eleazar Hakapar had a son, Eliezer. Historians are confused concerning the identity of this son; some say he was the well-known Bar Kapara, while others maintain that both names refer to the same person. Thus some statements in the Talmud are sometime attributed to one and on other occasions to the other. This confusion of names is ascribed by some talmudists to the editors of the Talmud.

We find a clear indication of the economic conditions of that time in Rabbi Eleazar Hakapar's statement that "a man must constantly pray to God to preserve him from poverty." Rabbi Eleazar was convinced that poverty was bound to affect every family, and that if one were spared the anguish of poverty, his sons or grandsons were sure to be affected by it.[21]

Because of the great development of Jewish religious life in Babylonia, there were many scholars who feared that in time that country would become a serious competitor to Palestine similar to the case of Alexandria generations earlier. Rabbi Eleazar therefore declared that "all the synagogues and academies of Babylonia will in the end be transported to Palestine."[22] Like his contemporaries he also valued peace because "all the benedictions of the Shemoneh Esrei end with the blessing of peace."[23]

During a discussion of these virtues of the Jews that had gained them their redemption from Egypt, Rabbi Eleazar declared that this was due to the fact that "they avoided immorality and slander and did not change their language."[24] This statement was a sharp protest against the conduct of many Jews of that time who reported one another to the authorities, and who abandoned the Hebrew language in favor of Greek.

Bar Kapara was a contemporary of Rabbi Eleazar Hakapar. Despite the contention of some Talmudic critics that both Rabbi Eleazar and Bar Kapara are the same person, we can not assume this point of view because we find a dispute in the

Talmud between these two concerning the regulations of slaughtering fowl. Rabbi Eleazar declared that the regulations governing slaughter were introduced by the rabbis, while Bar Kapara maintained that it was a commandment of the Torah.[25] The given name of Bar Kapara has not been definitely established. *Yuhasin* calls him Simeon, *Arukh* refers to him as Eleazar and the *Midrash* mentions him as Abba.[26] Others explain this ambiguity as due to the fact that he was named after his father who died before he was born.

Bar Kapara compiled a collection of laws, but these did not become as popular as the *Mishnayot* of Rabbi Jehudah, and many of them were lost in time. Of the remainder only a few were included in the Talmud as *Beraitot* and these were always introduced by the words "Bar Kapara taught." But it must be borne in mind that Bar Kapara's opinions were highly respected among the students of the academies and they were called the *Mishnah* of Bar Kapara.[27]

Aside from his prominence in *halakhah* Bar Kapara was famous for his expositions, and his clever interpretations and deductions from Biblical passages were repeated in the academies of Palestine and Babylonia. The following are some examples of his aphorisms and treatment of Biblical texts:

"In Isaiah (9:6) we find an exceptional case where a final *mem* is used in the middle of a word. What could we conclude from this? God had decided to make King Hezekiah the Messiah and to transform the wars of Sancherib into the wars of Gog and Magog. The *Midat Hadin* (emanation of justice) thereupon said to Him: 'Creator of the world! Why would you do so? King David sang your praise and You did not make him Messiah. You have already performed many miracles for Hezekiah. You saved him from Sancherib and You healed him of his sickness. Why should You give him this additional honor?' God's will was thus frustrated. The earth then said to God: 'I will sing your praise instead of Hezekiah but appoint him Your Messiah,' but this was not accepted. The angel in charge of the whole world (*sar ha'olam*) then proclaimed: 'Creator of the world! Do as you see fit,' and a *bat kol* announced: 'This is my secret! This is my secret!' "[28]

In one of his lectures he hinted that people must always be ready to give an account of their deeds: "A woman whose husband went on frequent journeys always adorned herself in her best garments. Seeing this, her neighbors asked: 'Your husband is not at home; why do you adorn yourself?' and she replied: 'My husband is a sailor and as soon as he earns something he will return home. It is therefore possible that he will arrive at any moment, and it is best that he should find me adorned to meet him.' "[29]

The following are noteworthy among Bar Kapara's maxims:

"Love peace and despise disputes. Beware of anger, for anger will lead you to sin."[30]

"He who honors his neighbor because of his wealth will in the end part from him in shame, but he who shames his friend for the sake of the fulfillment of a commandment will in the end part from him in honor."[31]

"The activities of just men are of more importance than the creation of the earth and sky."[32]

"An angry man possesses nothing except his anger."[33]

Many anecdotes were current in the academies of Palestine and Babylonia concerning the relations between Bar Kapara and the family of the Nasi Rabbi Jehudah. It was previously related how Bar Kapara persuaded Ben Elasha, the wealthy but dull son-in-law of Rabbi Jehudah, to propose a riddle to the guests assembled at a feast that criticized the conduct of the Nasi. It was also related that every time Rabbi Jehudah laughed, some punishment was visited upon the world. But since the Rabbi frequently laughed at the witticisms of Bar Kapara, he offered Bar Kapara forty measures of wheat one day if he would remain serious on that day. Bar Kapara then brought a great basket smeared with tar and turning it upside down, he asked Rabbi Jehudah to fill it with grain. At another time Bar Kapara made a bet with Rabbi Jehudah's daughter that he could make her father sing and her mother to dance for him. The following day he attained his aim by a clever stratagem. Ben Elasha, who was present, resented the fact that his father-in-law did everything that Bar Kapara wanted him to do and together with his wife he left the house in displeasure.[34]

Despite the fact that he was not ordained, Bar Kapara was the teacher of nearly all of the first generation of *amoraim*. Of Bar Kapara's private life we know only that he was poor and that he gained his livelihood from manual labor. There are vague hints that worked on a small rocky island in the sea.

It is told that Bar Kapara once had a dream that he asked Rabbi Jehudah to interpret. In his dream he saw his nose fall off his face. Rabbi Jehudah declared that it was a sign that God had been angry with him but the anger had now passed. Another time he dreamed that his hands were cut off, and Rabbi Jehudah interpreted it as a sign that he would no longer have to work with hands for his sustenance.[35]

A legend relates that Bar Kapara once saw a ship sink and only one of its passengers was saved from drowning. He pitied the man and took him to his house where he gave him food and some money. Years later some Jews were taken captive and Bar Kapara was sent to ransom them with the sum of 500 ducats. When Bar Kapara arrived at the palace, he found that the man whom he had saved was a high official of the government.

When the man saw Bar Kapara he ran to greet him and asked him what his mission was. Bar Kapara told him that he had come to ransom the captive Jews and he showed him the money that he had brought, but the man said to him: "You may keep this money as payment for the five *shekalim* which you gave me, and because you gave me food and drink I will free your brothers without ransom."[36]

Since that time Bar Kapara's situation improved and he could easily provide for his household as well as feed a number of students at his table.[37]

46

RABBI CHIYA RABBAH BAR ABBA

RABBI CHIYA BAR ABBA I, usually referred to in the Talmud as Rabbi Chiya (without his patronymic) or Rabbi Chiya Rabbah (the great),[1] to distinguish him from Rabbi Chiya bar Abba II (who was an *amora*,) was a colleague and pupil of Rabbi Jehudah. His influence was exerted after the *Mishnah* had been completed, preceding the beginning of the epoch of the *amoraim*. Rabbi Chiya was born in a town near Sura in Babylonia about 190 years after the destruction of the Temple. Some said that his family was descended from Shefatiah, the son of King David,[2] while others traced its origin to Shimei, the brother of King David. A passage in the Talmud relates that Rabbi Jehudah wanted to marry his son to the daughter of Rabbi Chiya and just before the wedding, the bride suddenly died. Rabbi Jehudah considered this to be a sign from heaven and he suspected some fault in Rabbi Chiya's family. The origins of the two families were investigated and it was discovered that Rabbi Jehudah was descended from Shefatiah ben Avital, while Rabbi Chiya was descended from Shimei, King David's brother.[3]

Little is known of the youth of Rabbi Chiya, or of the other Babylonian scholars who lived in his time. It appears that the Jews of Babylonia maintained great academies, for when Rabbi

Chiya arrived in Palestine together with his sons, they were already well versed in the Torah. Since they had never visited Palestine previously, they must have gained their knowledge in academies in Babylonia.

The statement in the Talmud that "when the Torah was once forgotten Ezra came from Babylonia to renew it and then came Hillel the Babylonian who renewed it again." This is followed by "when the Torah was again forgotten, Rabbi Chiya came with his sons and they renewed and expanded it," therefore appears incomprehensible.[4] When Rabbi Chiya arrived in Palestine, learning was at a high level of development. Rabbi Jehudah was Nasi and he had many disciples so there could hardly be any talk of the Torah being forgotten. The family of the Nasi occupied the undisputed leadership of the people and had learning been at a low ebb, the Nasi would not have allowed a recent arrival from Babylonia to become the "savior" of the situation.

However, there is no doubt that Rabbi Chiya was an important figure in Jewish life. He often lectured at the door of the Nasi[5] and his colleagues often referred to him as "the lion of the company."[6]

Characteristic of the determination not to allow learning to disappear is Rabbi Chiya's statement: "If the Torah were to be forgotten, I would take flax and weave nets with which I would capture deer. The flesh of the deer I would give to the orphans and from the skins I would make parchment on which to write the Torah. Then I would go to cities where there are no teachers; I would have the five books of the Torah written down and I would teach them to the children; later I would teach them the six orders of the *Mishnah*. All that I would do to prevent the Torah from being forgotten." When Rabbi Jehudah heard of this he said: "See what great deeds Rabbi Chiya promises to perform."[7]

Upon his arrival in Palestine, Rabbi Chiya was received with love and honor by Rabbi Jehudah and ate at his table.[8] When he helped the Nasi with the formulation of a law, Rabbi Jehudah applied the verse of Isaiah (46:11) to him "from a far land my counsellor has come."[9] The great respect in which

Rabbi Jehudah held Rabbi Chiya was shown on numerous occasions; when they arrived at the academy, Rabbi Jehudah asked Rabbi Chiya to enter first[10] and during a discussion on the question of cleanliness, Rabbi Jehudah declared: "Leave my words and listen to the words of Rabbi Chiya."[11]

Rabbi Jehudah always confided all his scholastic innovations to Rabbi Chiya and when he once forgot some of these during his sickness, Rabbi Chiya repeated them to him. Rabbi Jehudah then declared: "You have made me again what I had been!"[12]

Outstanding among Rabbi Chiya's legal achievements are his formulations of the laws governing interests.[13] He also made many innovations and wrote them down in a book, but these were not accepted by the people and they were named *megillat setarim* (the scroll of secrecy).[14] Rabbi Chiya participated in the compilation of the *Tosefta* and together with his pupil Rabbi Oshaiah, he shared in gathering the *Beraita*. It was an accepted rule at that time that any *Beraita* that was not expounded by either Rabbi Chiya or Rabbi Oshaiah was of doubtful authenticity.[15]

Rabbi Chiya frequently accompanied Rabbi Jehudah on the latter's travels in the fulfillment of his duties as Nasi or to the imperial court in the interests of the people.[16] Whenever Rabbi Jehudah was displeased with him he merely remarked: "I think that someone is calling you outside." Rabbi Chiya would then understand the hint and would remain away from the academy for thirty days.[17]

Rabbi Chiya resided in Tiberias most of the time and there he conducted an academy. Frequently he would be empowered by Rabbi Jehudah to determine the day of the new month and to establish leap years, and he would then be sent to other communities to inform the inhabitants of these decisions. Rabbi Jehudah lived in Sepphoris in the Galilee, but the law prescribed that the determination of a new month or a leap year had to be made in a city of Judea.[18] A special court was therefore established in Ein Tuv and Rabbi Chiya went there to represent the Nasi at these functions.[19]

To earn his livelihood Rabbi Chiya engaged in commerce,

and in partnership with Rabbi Simeon, the son of Rabbi Jehudah, he traded in silk which was then marketed in Tyre.[20] Later he also traded in flax.[21] He was successful in his commercial ventures and he had to entrust the conduct of some of his business to his nephew Rav (Abba Arecha). Rabbi Chiya was also considered to be an authority on coins. It is told that a woman once came to him concerning the authenticity of a coin and he declared it to be genuine. The following day the woman brought the same coin and he said that it was false, but since he had declared it to be genuine on the previous day he commanded Rav to exchange it for a good coin and to write down the loss as an unsuccessful transaction.[22]

Despite his success Rabbi Chiya never boasted of his wealth and when the poor came to his house, he would say to his wife: "Give them bread and in the future they may return it to your children." His wife objected by saying: "You curse your own children," but Rabbi Chiya replied: "I do not curse them but such is the changing fate of the world."[23]

Of Rabbi Chiya's family life it was related that his wife twice gave birth to twins, and because her labor pains were so great, she vowed never to bear children again. Dressed in different clothes and with her face covered by a veil to prevent her husband from recognizing her, she came to his academy and asked him whether a woman was legally compelled to bear children. Rabbi Chiya declared that she was not compelled to do so. The woman then drank a medicine that women of that time used to avoid bearing children.[24]

Rabbi Chiya was devoted to the Torah and he would repeat a special prayer of his own asking God to make the Torah his life work and to preserve him from an ailing heart and from failing vision.[25] When he was asked what a woman's aim in life was if she was not obliged to engage in study, he replied that "women should bring their children to the academy, and they must also accompany their husbands to the synagogue and wait there until they have come out after prayer."[26]

To avoid seeing others put to shame, Rabbi Chiya sometimes sacrificed his own dignity. It once occurred that while lecturing at the academy, Rabbi Jehudah noticed the odor of garlic. Being in an angry mood that day Rabbi Jehudah exclaimed: "Whoever had eaten garlic should leave the academy." Rabbi Chiya was the first to rise and leave the building. The others saw him leave and knowing that he could not have been guilty of the offense, they all followed his example and left in order not to put the offender to shame.[27]

Much was spoken of Rabbi Chiya's saintliness and it was said that since his arrival in Palestine, storms no longer occurred and the wine never turned sour.[28]

Another legend related that the prophet Elijah appeared to Rabbi Jehudah and informed him that in the eyes of God Rabbi Chiya and his sons had the same merit as the Patriarchs and that all their prayers would be answered. It then occurred that no rain had fallen for a long time. Rabbi Jehudah declared a fast and he ordered Rabbi Chiya to pray before the pulpit. As soon as Rabbi Chiya reached the words "He causes the winds to blow," a strong wind arose and when he pronounced the words "He causes the rain to fall," rain began to descend. When Rabbi Chiya reached the words "He causes the dead to come to life," everyone in heaven was disturbed, for it seemed that the hour of resurrection was at hand, and it was asked in heaven who had revealed the secret to the people. When it became known that Elijah had revealed the secret, he was punished with sixty fiery lashes. Elijah then descended to earth in the guise of a fiery bear and scattered the congregation from the synagogue.[29]

Legend further relates that when Rabbi Chiya was about to die, the Angel of Death was afraid to touch him. He therefore assumed the guise of a poor man and knocked on the door. Rabbi Chiya heard this and said to the members of his household: "There is a poor man at the door. Give him some bread." The Angel of Death appealed to Rabbi Chiya and said: "I have heard you pity a poor man and order that he be given bread. Why then do you also not have pity on me? You know that I was sent to take your soul. Give it to me that I should not have to come here again."[30]

When Rabbi Chiya died—the Talmud continues—fiery stones fell from heaven.[31]

47

RABBI SIMEON BEN CHALAFTA

Rabbi SIMEON BEN CHALAFTA was one of the outstanding colleagues of Rabbi Jehudah Hanasi during the latter's old age. He was a member of a family of scholars and the Talmud referred to his father as Ben Rabbi (the son of a rabbi) to indicate that at least three generations had been ordained. The family of Rabbi Simeon were loyal adherents of the dynasty of the Nasi for many generations. Rabbi Chalafta (sometimes called Chalfuta, Chulafta and Tachlifa) was a son of Rabbi Jose ben Chalafta who prided himself on having planted five cedar trees in Israel, referring to his five sons of whom Chalafta was one.[1]

Rabbi Simeon ben Chalafta was one of the last disciples of Rabbi Meir. Later he attended the academy of Rabbi Jehudah and was befriended by the Nasi because of the loyalty of his family to the office of Nasi. Rabbi Simeon lived in the town of Ein T'enah located between Sepphoris and Tiberias. He regularly visited Rabbi Jehudah once a month when the latter lived in Sepphoris and also after he moved to Tiberias. As Rabbi Simeon left the house of the Nasi, Rabbi Jehudah once sent his son to follow and obtain his blessing. Rabbi Simeon blessed him with the following words: "May God grant that you should never put others to shame nor be put to shame yourself."[2]

As Rabbi Simeon grew older it became more difficult for him to make the trip, and he finally gave up his visits to the house of the Nasi. When Rabbi Jehudah asked him: "What is the cause of your absence that I cannot greet you any more as my fathers used to greet your fathers?" Rabbi Simeon replied: "The stones on my way have become larger and I can no longer step over them. Things nearby appear to be far and I cannot see them; that which is distant must now appear to be near so that I may hear it, and in addition to my two feet I need a third one to lean on."[3]

Rabbi Simeon maintained a close friendship with Rabbi Chiya bar Abba and with Rabbi Simeon, the son of the Nasi. It is related that all three of them were once in doubt concerning the meaning of some Hebrew words, but passing an Arab merchant they discovered the meaning of the words from his conversation.[4]

The *Mishnah* quotes Rabbi Simeon only once to the effect that "God has no better medium for blessing than peace."[5]

The friendly relations between Rabbi Simeon and Rabbi Chiya were quite understandable. They were both students in the academy of the Nasi and when Rabbi Chiya was informed of Rabbi Simeon's poverty he leased him one of his fields from which Rabbi Simeon later derived a comfortable income. Before he leased the field, Rabbi Simeon was in great need and his situation was aggravated by the fact that he refused all aid. It was said that out of great pity, Rabbi Jehudah would place small heaps of grain on the street; since these no longer belonged to anyone, Rabbi Simeon would gather them.[6] When on a certain Friday Rabbi Simeon found himself without a morsel of food in the house, he left the city to pray that God might send him aid. He was then handed a diamond from heaven, and this he pawned and obtained enough money to provide for the Sabbath, but his wife refused to partake of the food until he promised to return the diamond immediately after the Sabbath.[7]

Another *Midrash* relates this story in a somewhat different version. Rabbi Simeon ben Chalafta and Rabbi Chiya are said to have been in the academy at Tiberias on the eve of a holiday. While engaged in study they suddenly became aware of a great commotion in the street and Rabbi Simeon asked what was causing it. Rabbi Chiya replied: "Those who have money now go to buy the things they need for the holiday; those who have none go to their employers to obtain the necessary money," Rabbi Simeon then said: "I will also go to my employer to ask for money for the holiday." By this he meant that he would pray to God whom he always served.

He left the academy and proceeded to the caves outside the city where he prayed to God. Suddenly a hand appeared and handed him a pearl. Rabbi Simeon took the pearl to Rabbi Jehudah who advised him not sell it until he had ascertained its worth. Meanwhile Rabbi Jehudah gave him three ducats with which to purchase his holiday needs.

When Rabbi Simeon came home with his purchases his wife asked him: "Where did you get the money? Did you not steal it?" and he related to her what had happened. Rabbi Simeon's wife was displeased and said: "Would you have a pearl missing from your crown in the world to come?" Rabbi Simeon asked her what he should do and she advised him to return the purchased articles and with the money to redeem the pearl and to return it to heaven.[8]

Another story is told of Rabbi Simeon ben Chalafta that on one of his journeys he met two hungry lions. Rabbi Simeon was greatly frightened but before the lions could attack him he was handed two pieces of meat from heaven, one of which he gave to the lions and the other he brought to the academy to ask the scholars whether it was clean and fit to eat. He was then informed that "no unclean thing can come from heaven."[9]

Rabbi Simeon's opinions are quoted in the Talmud, and it was characteristic of his religious conception that he declared that children 9 or 10 years old should be required to fast on the Day of Atonement."[10]

Once Rabbi Simeon went with Rabbi Chiya to the valley of Arbel to watch the sunrise and determine how long it takes from the first break of dawn until full daylight. On that occasion Rabbi Simeon said: "See how slowly dawn turns into day. Equally slow is the coming of aid to Jews."[11]

Rabbi Simeon declared that since flattery had become so prevalent, men now follow devious ways, and their activities have sunk to such a low level that one may no longer boast to his friend that his actions are more important.[12] Another time he said: "The courageous usually triumphs over the modest." He came to this conclusion from the fact that God seemingly changed his mind and did not destroy the city of Nineveh as he had announced through the prophet Jonah because "he who is daring in his prayers can obtain his wishes even from God."[13]

He also said: "One who has studied Torah but does not fulfill its commandments commits a greater sin than one who has never studied. It is as if one hires two watchmen for his garden one of whom plants beautiful trees and later breaks them; the owner of the garden is more angry with him than with the watchman who planted nothing."[14]

In addition to the stories told of Rabbi Simeon's poverty there were other legends about wonderful events that happened to him. Once while going to attend a circumcision dressed in his best garments, he attracted the attention of children in the street who surrounded him and would not let him pass until he danced before them. Rabbi Simeon pleaded with them that he could not dance because of his great age and when they refused to leave him, he scolded them and said that the gatepost of the house would collapse. He then sent them to call the owner to come out of the house at once. When the owner appeared, Rabbi Simeon warned him to remove all his possessions from the house and as soon as that was done the gatepost collapsed.

At the feast which followed the circumcision, the father served valuable old wine and said: "If I live I will serve the same kind of wine at the wedding of my son," and Rabbi Simeon replied: "Even as the child was today inducted into the covenant of Abraham, he will grow to go to the canopy and we will both drink again."

On his way home Rabbi Simeon met the Angel of Death who addressed him with the following words: "Is it because you are a just man that you are not afraid to go alone at night?"

When Rabbi Simeon asked the Angel whither he was bound, the Angel replied that he was going to take the soul of the child who had been circumcised that day. Rabbi Simeon scolded the Angel of Death for wishing to prove him a liar since he had already promised to drink at the boy's wedding, and with these words he annulled the decree of death against the child.[15]

Rabbi Simeon ben Chalafta also devoted himself to the natural sciences and he cured a bird whose back was paralyzed. When one of his hens lost all her feathers, he warmed the bird in an oven and covered it with a cloth and thus caused its feathers to grow again.[16]

It is also related that Rabbi Simeon had a garden in which there was a hollow stump of a tree where a bird made its nest. Rabbi Simeon destroyed the nest but the bird repaired it again, and when he boarded up the hollow, the bird brought some herbs and placed them on the nails in the board and the nails were corroded. Rabbi Simeon then cursed the herb that it might grow no more for fear that thieves may discover it and use it to break locks.[17]

48

LEVI BEN SISI

LEVI BEN SISI WAS THE MOST prominent of Rabbi Jehudah's last disciples. He is usually referred to without his patronymic and although he was often called a Great Man,[1] it appears that he was not ordained, for we find no instance in the Babylonian Talmud where he is referred to as Rabbi. This title was attached to his name in the Jerusalem Talmud and in the *Midrashim*.[2] It is difficult to understand why Levi had not been ordained because he conducted his own academy and his legal opinions were quoted by many scholars of that time such as Rav (Abba Arecha), Shmuel Yarchina'ah, Rabbi Jochanan, and Resh Lakish. This question becomes even more perplexing when one considers that his father was ordained and that no cause is mentioned for his lack of ordination.

Levi ben Sisi was born in Palestine about 160 years after the destruction of the Temple. Some historians give the city of Lud as his birthplace. He was one of Rabbi Jehudah's brilliant pupils and he tutored Rabbi Jehudah's son, Simeon. The relations between Levi and his pupil were not friendly probably because Simeon insisted on choosing his own subjects of study.[3] These unfriendly relations probably continued until Rabbi Jehudah's death. There are some indications that Levi was a candidate for the post of *hakham* in the academy, but this office was bequeathed to Simeon in his father's will.[4] For this reason, or because it took so much time to administer his great wealth, Levi did not frequently attend the academy.

The attitude of Rabbi Jehudah toward Levi ben Sisi was inconsistent. When Rabbi Simeon ridiculed some question of Levi's, Rabbi Jehudah declared that it was a wise question,[5] and he once appointed Levi to an office in the academy.[6] At some other time Rabbi Jehudah was annoyed with Levi's questions and he exclaimed: "It seems to me that this man has no brains in his head."[7]

At Rabbi Simeon's wedding, Levi was honored with reciting the benediction,[8] and when representatives of Simunia, on the lower Galilee, came to Rabbi Jehudah and asked him to recommend someone to fill the post of lecturer, judge, teacher, and scribe, Rabbi Jehudah recommended Levi ben Sisi. The men of Simunia then seated Levi on a great platform and questioned him concerning the laws of *halitzah* but Levi could not answer their questions. Thinking that he was unacquainted with legal matters, they asked him the meaning of a verse of Daniel and he could not give that either. They then came to Rabbi Jehudah and said: "Was it for such a man that we asked you?" but Rabbi Jehudah replied: "I swear by my life that he is my equal in learning."

Later Rabbi Jehudah sent for Levi and asked him the same questions that he answered correctly. "Why did you not answer them before?" Rabbi Jehudah queried, and Levi replied: "When they placed me on the platform, I became confused and did not know what to say."[9]

Levi ben Sisi also devoted himself to athletics and he could perform acrobatic tricks such as throwing eight knives simultaneously and catching them in his hand. He also performed other athletic feats despite the fact that he was lame.[10] There is also evidence that he paid close attention to his appearance and even painted his eyelids, although he believed that the practice was dangerous and might cause death.[11]

Like Rabbi Jehudah, Levi ben Sisi also compiled six "orders" of *Mishnayot* that are mentioned in the Talmud under various names such as "the books of Levi,"[12] "the holiness of the house of Levi,"[13] and "the writings of Rabbi Levi."[14] On other occasions opinions are introduced by the words "Levi taught" or "Levi taught in the *Mishnah*." Rashi likewise states that "Levi compiled the *Beraita* in six orders like Rabbi Chiya and Rabbi Oshaiah."[15]

As long as Rabbi Jehudah lived, Levi returned to Palestine after each trip abroad.[16] Although he was not on friendly terms with the son of the Nasi, he frequently sent gifts to the house of the Nasi, and once he sent wine made out of dates that was purified thirteen times.[17] Only after the death of Rabbi Jehudah, when Levi remained without friends in Palestine, did he remember his comrades in Babylonia and he thought of finding a new field of work in that country. When Levi arrived in Nehardea, he was received with open arms and assisted in founding an academy.[18]

The rumor rapidly spread that a "great man" had arrived and many people came from far and near to hear his lectures and to ask his opinion. Wonderful stories began to circulate about him. One of these related that when foreign soldiers wanted to rob the city, Levi took a book of the Torah and ascending the roof of the house addressed God: "Creator of the world! If I have ever transgressed against one of your commandments let the enemy enter the city, but if I have not, then cause them to depart." The foreign soldiers immediately vanished from the city.[19]

Levi's lameness was explained to be the result of an acrobatic trick that he had attempted to perform before Rabbi Jehudah. A more interesting explanation tells that it was a punishment for his arrogance toward God. Once a severe drought affected the land. A fast day was declared but still no rain fell. Levi is said to have made the following remark to God at that time: "You sit on high and You have no mercy on Your children!" As soon as he finished this statement he became lame.[20]

In his will Rabbi Jehudah commanded that his son Gamaliel succeed him in the office of Nasi, that Simeon should be *hakham* in the academy, and Rabbi Chanina bar Chama should be head of the court in Sepphoris. Rabbi Chanina refused to accept this post since Rabbi Ephes, secretary to Rabbi

Jehudah, was his senior by two years. Rabbi Ephes then became head of the court and Rabbi Chanina together with Levi sat outside the academy. After the death of Rabbi Ephes, Rabbi Chanina became head of the court and Levi remained alone. Levi also refused to recognize the authority of Rabbi Chanina because they were both of the same age, and because he considered himself the equal of Rabbi Chanina in learning. It was at that time that Levi left Palestine and went to Nehardea.

In Nehardea he won the friendship of Abba bar Abba, the father of Shmuel Yarchina'ah. Together they prayed and studied and, at the request of Abba, Levi examined his son Shmuel.[21] After that, whenever Shmuel had any doubts he turned to Levi.[22]

In Nehardea Levi introduced new regulations. He ruled that women may appear in public on the Sabbath adorned in their jewelry. This regulation was accepted and the Talmud relates that twenty-four women wore jewelry on the first Sabbath.[23]

Levi ben Sisi had ten scholarly sons whose names are listed in the Talmud. According to some authorities Rabbi Joshua ben Levi also was his son. When Levi died he was mourned by Abba bar Abba who pointed out the greatness of the generation of Rabbi Jehudah's contemporaries of whom Levi had been the last. In his eulogy Abba bar Abba said: "The life of Levi ben Sisi may be compared with the story of a king who had a vineyard where there were 100 vines, each of which yielded 100 barrels of wine yearly. In time the vines dried up and with every passing year fewer remained, until in the end there was no more than one vine left. The king loved this last vine as had he once loved his whole vineyard. Even so was Levi ben Sisi beloved of God like an only remaining vine."[24]

With the death of Levi ben Sisi the epoch of the *tannaim* came to a close and the period of the *amoraim* began.

PART II

JERUSALEM
TALMUD

49

INTRODUCTION

ANY TREATISE ON THE *AMORAIM* must begin with the *amoraim* of Palestine, who were the direct heirs of the *tannaim* and the last link in the long chain of development of oral law that stretched from the days of the Men of the Great Synagogue down to their time.[1] The *amoraim* of Babylonia, on the other hand, marked the beginning of a new historical epoch for the Jews of that country that continued for centuries after the spark of spiritual life had expired in Palestine.

With the completion of the *Mishnah*, whose authority was recognized both in Palestine and in Babylonia, the Jewish law assumed its final form. In both countries the *Mishnah* was recognized as the final decision in all problems of life, but the subsequent development of the laws followed different lines in each country. None, however, dared to question the interpretations of the *tannaim* even when these concerned Biblical verses with no direct relationship to religious problems.

When one considers the teachings of the *tannaim* and *amoraim*, it becomes obvious that they sought to establish a worthy continuation to the teachings of the prophets, who aimed to elevate Jewish ethics to the highest possible level. They therefore interpreted the commandments of the Torah in such a manner as to inculcate the people with feelings of justice, love of peace, and love of one's neighbor. This aim led some of the scholars to believe that study of the Torah and the fulfillment of its commandments was most important in life, even though one did not agree with the commandments. Others said that after the coming of Messiah, all command-ments would be done away with, and there would no longer be any need for written laws.[2]

There is a *midrash* extant that states that those Jews who had left Egypt and wandered in the desert belonged to a "generation of knowledge," because they possessed a measure of civilization and were not, as might be assumed, simply untutored slaves who had just acquired freedom. Many critics ironically nod their heads at this *midrash,* but on closer obser-vation of the commandments of the Torah it becomes obvious that those Jews did possess a high measure of culture.

Like other civilized peoples of that time, the Jews while still in Egypt understood the art of weaving. Even if we assume that their garments were not made of the finest material, skill was nevertheless required to weave the linen of which their garments were made. They understood the art of agriculture and the various occupations involved in it, such as plowing, sowing, harvesting, threshing, grinding, and baking. They were also acquainted with animal husbandry and its attendant occupations. While still in bondage, they learned to make bricks out of clay, and they built houses and cities. Woodwork, masonry, metalwork, winemaking, and hunting were also not strange to them. They knew how to find water in the depths of the earth and how to maintain fires. They made decorations of precious metals and pressed oil out of olives.

In their social relationships they maintained a civilized system of order that included representatives and judges, policemen and arrests. They understood how to divide time into weeks, months, and years. In commerce they used money, as is obvious from the stories of Abraham's purchase of the cave of Machpelah, and of Jacob's purchase of a tract of land from the sons of Chamor for which he paid 100 *kesitah.* In general we may say that people of that time possessed a high level of intelligence and that the Jews were not behind the others. When other nations were governed by law, we may assume that the Jews did not live in lawlessness.

In the case of some commandments, the Torah merely added legal sanction to customs already in practice. Thus, Rashbam (Samuel ben Meir, the grandson of Rashi) states in his interpretation of the Torah that rules governing robbery, sexual relations, covetousness, courts, and hospitality were accepted among the Jews even before the Torah was granted. In this case the Torah merely strengthened the accepted conduct and insured the future observance of these laws.

All the civilized peoples of that time, including the Jews of the period preceding the granting of the Torah, were called the "sons of Noah." As such they had to observe only seven commandments, namely: to deal justly, not to desecrate the name of God, not to worship idols, not to commit adultery, not to commit murder, not to rob, and not to eat flesh cut from a living animal. Some maintain that the prohibitions against consuming the blood of a living animal, castration, witchcraft, mating different breeds of animals, and planting mixed seeds were included in the aforementioned seven commandments.[3]

The Talmud declares that even Adam was commanded to obey these commandments, with the exception of the one forbidding the eating of the flesh of a living animal, since the consumption of meat was altogether prohibited until the deluge. Others said that the "sons of Noah" had thirty commandments to observe.[4] But these probably included many observances that were derived from the original seven commandments. It is quite understandable, that in order to conduct trials it was necessary to know which people to select as judges. Likewise, in the matter of adultery, regulations had to be established defining which women were forbidden. The concept of robbery also required definition, since borrowing money and not repaying it, and not paying the wage of a laborer were then considered to be robbery.

The offering of sacrifices from animals, fowl, and fruit was customary since time immemorial. Cain had offered a sacrifice from the fruit of his fields, and Abel offered his best sheep. After the deluge Noah erected an altar and offered sacrifices.

Abraham and Jacob likewise erected altars for the offering of sacrifices. When Moses asked Pharaoh to release the Jews, he said that they had to go to the desert to offer sacrifices to God. Rabbi Saadiah Gaon declared that since sacrifices and circumcision preceded the establishment of the Sabbath, both of them superseded the Sabbath. During the later development of divine service, which at that time consisted of sacrificial offerings, the belief grew among many peoples that ordinary men could not fulfill this task since they were not acquainted with all the regulations governing the offerings. This led to the establishment of a separate group of people who devoted themselves solely to sacrifices and who abstained from ordinary labor. For the support of these people, tithes were offered by all. Thus we find Abraham giving tithes to Malchi-Zedek, who was a priest of "the highest God"; Jacob vowed to tithe all his possessions, if God would bless his journey and provide him with bread and garments.

The firstborn son initially performed the divine service. This procedure was also accepted among the Jews until the tabernacle was built. Later, the performance of this office was taken out of the hands of the first born and entrusted to the descendants of Aaron. Further development necessitated the establishment of a class of assistants to the descendants of Aaron, and the Levites were added to the service. The priests performed the offering of sacrifices and they received the first fruit, the firstborn animals, and similar gifts. The Levites who worked in the tabernacle were granted tithes, one-tenth of everyone's income. Of this, the Levites had to give one-tenth to the priests. But the rights of the firstborn were preserved in the government of the family as a representative of the father. The firstborn also received a double share in the inheritance. If a man had children by two wives, one of whom he loved and the other he hated, and the firstborn was a son of the despised wife, the father nevertheless had to recognize the rights of this son to a double share in the inheritance. The custom of the priests blessing the people is very ancient. The first priest to do so was Malchi-Zedek who blessed Abraham. Thus it is also related that Aaron blessed the children of Israel even before the Torah explicitly commanded him to do so.

Even before the deluge, Noah could differentiate between animals that were considered as clean and those that were considered to be unclean. The Talmud questions this, and the answer was given that when all the animals sought safety in the ark, it admitted only one pair of some kinds of animals and seven pairs of other kinds. By this method it was known which were the clean and which the unclean animals.[5]

Soon after man began to develop family life, he recognized his near relatives as part of himself. When rights of property were established he enacted laws to secure his possessions for his relations, and he likewise made certain that after his death his possessions would remain within the family. In this manner laws of inheritance were established. Abraham complained to God saying: "Since you gave me no offspring, the manager of my house will inherit me." Jews also practiced the same custom accepted among other peoples in denying a daughter a share in the inheritance. Every father gave his daughter her share as a dowry when she married. Since daughters could marry men of other tribes, they could not share in the inheritance of their fathers so that the possessions of one tribe should not pass to another tribe.

Long before the Torah was granted, the descendants of Abraham observed the commandment of circumcision. It may even be assumed that the descendants of Ishmael and the sons of Keturah observed this commandment with greater strictness than did the Jews who did not practice circumcision while in the desert for forty years.

Among other civilized concepts man also learned to observe vows and oaths. He understood his duty of abiding by his word whether that concerned himself or others. All of these concepts civilized peoples observed long before the Torah was given. The Patriarch Abraham swore to Abimelech not to harm him or his descendants. Jacob vowed and later swore to Laban not to trespass his boundaries with evil intent.

The slaughter of animals for food was always considered

to be a natural procedure and was practiced from time immemorial. It may also be assumed that such slaughter was always
done by cutting the throat of the animal. This method was
probably adopted as a reaction against the savage method of
beasts of prey that break the necks of their victims. Since the
commandments of the Torah aimed to refine the people and are
based on mercy, it was strictly forbidden to cause unnecessary
suffering to any living creature.[6]

Since ancient times man recognized the concepts of purity
and impurity. As soon as man could aesthetically comprehend
the concept of cleanliness, he avoided coming in contact with
things that were unclean. It was then believed that evil spirits
inhabited the unclean objects, and that they would gain control
of the clean body that touched the impure one. Thus Jacob
commanded his household when he left Shechem: "Cast out
the strange idols from your midst, clean yourself, and don
other garments." People likewise avoided coming in contact
with a woman during her menstrual period or with unclean
animals or insects.

Bathing in water was the accepted mode of purification. In
this manner all impurity was washed away. Before giving the
Torah, God commanded the people to consecrate themselves
and to wash their garments. This was also the reason why a
proselyte had to immerse himself in water and even though he
was circumcised, he was not accepted as a proselyte until after
immersion. Menstruating women were also required to bathe
before being considered pure. This appears to have been an
ancient custom observed by all civilized peoples.

There is no doubt that all of these commandments later
evolved into numerous supplementary observances. With the
development of society, punishments were determined for
infractions of these commandments. But no matter how earnestly the scholars wanted the commandments of the Torah to
be observed, they nevertheless warned against observing a
commandment at the expense of committing a sin, as in the
case of stealing an object in order to do some good deed with
it.[7] But in some exceptional instances, the ignoring of one
commandment could aid in the fulfillment of another, as when

study of the Torah was interrupted in order to perform some philanthropic deed.[8]

Ordinarily there was no prohibition which could not be broken in order to save a life, with the exception of committing murder, worshipping idols, or committing a sexual offense in order to save one's life.[9] These three sins were considered to be so great that even if one's life depended on one of them, it was forbidden to employ them.[10]

Observance of the Sabbath was treated differently. Even though it was also considered to be very important and one who desecrated the Sabbath was to be punished by death, it was nevertheless accepted that the Sabbath could be desecrated in order to aid one whose life was in danger.[11] The *tanna* Rabbi Simeon ben Menasiah thus said that "the Sabbath was given to the people and not the people to the Sabbath."[12] In order to save the life of a person, Rabbi Nathan said that "it is permissible to desecrate one Sabbath in order that he may observe many Sabbaths to come."[13]

The Talmud declares that the basic purpose of religious regulations was to enable people to live and not to kill them.[14] It likewise states that he who destroys one Jewish soul is like one who destroyed a whole world, and he who maintains one Jewish person alive is like one who saved a whole world.[15]

People were forbidden by the scholars to harm themselves even as they were forbidden to harm others.[16] When the Torah said that fruit trees should not be cut down during the siege of a city, the scholars added that one may not cut down a fruit tree even in his own garden, and he who did so was to be punished.[17] On other occasions the scholars said that endangering one's life was worse than committing a sin.[18]

The Talmud further declares that the Torah was concerned with the honor of the people. In its eyes the worth of man was so great that one could sometimes overlook a commandment because of it.[19]

Thieves were usually enslaved after they were forced to repay twice the price of the stolen goods. If a living animal was stolen, the thief had to pay four or five times its value. At times thieves were also sentenced to death or flogging. The death sentence was imposed by the Torah for abducting a person and selling him into slavery. Nevertheless the Torah showed consideration even for the thief, and the scholars declared that the reason why a thief had to pay five times the value of a stolen ox and only four times the value of a stolen sheep was that an ox can be led easily, but a sheep has to be carried and this accounted for the lighter punishment for one stealing a sheep.[20]

Other punishment, aside from death and flogging, were meted out to offenders against God or man. Prisons already existed and when one was flogged for an offense and later committed a similar offense, he was imprisoned.[21]

Self-inflicted torture as a religious ritual had been known for a long time. The forms of this torture were numerous. Some renounced food and drink while others avoided pride. The drinking of wine was considered a luxury and he who wanted to deny himself pleasure for the greater glory of God renounced the drinking of wine. Shaving one's head or letting one's hair grow wild were at various times considered ways of breaking pride. The scholars differed in their evaluation of these forms of self-torment. Some praised them while others condemned them as sinful.[22] The majority of the scholars agreed with the opinion of Rabbi Jose that one should not torment himself with too many fasts.[23]

The custom of mourning for dead relatives, as it is accepted in the form of a Biblical commandment, was a subject often questioned by the scholars. From the story of Joseph they deducted that mourning should last seven days. Others reached the same conclusion from the verse "I shall turn your feast days into mourning," and they said that even as each holiday lasts seven days so also must mourning last for seven days. There were also differing opinions among the scholars on whether mourning was a biblical commandment or whether it was instituted by the Rabbis. The Jerusalem Talmud declares that "Moses instituted for the Jews seven days of mourning and seven days of merrymaking."[24]

For seven centuries, from the time of Simon the Just, until the last *amora*, Greek, Roman, and Persian culture had a great influence on Jewish life. For that reason one comes across ideas that arose at different times under different circumstances and were differentiated in their spirit and character. At times it is difficult to discover which event preceded and which followed and to separate fact from legend.

Our spiritual heroes often rise to great spiritual heights. Their ideas are rooted in the past but are able to look to the future as well. Their roots cleave a path through stern reality to the high ideals of mankind as a whole, and emphasize those means that help realize those ideals.

It is this talmudic forest whose trees contain the seed for the plants of future generations. It is also the source from which later lawgivers derived their notions as well as the form for the pursuit of learning in all its branches.

50

LIFE IN PALESTINE DURING THE CREATION OF THE JERUSALEM TALMUD

SOME ENLIGHTENED PEOPLE ARE of the opinion that while death and destruction raged in Palestine, the scholars of that country secluded themselves within the walls of the synagogues and debated irrelevant religious problems. Such a view is highly superficial. Between wars and in addition to talmudic discussions, people pursued their normal occupations. They sowed their fields, they engaged in various trades, and they developed a highly complex Jewish cultural life.

There are only a few sources of information concerning the mode of life of that time. The Talmud is the most trustworthy of these, although it was written much later, when many of the previous customs were nearly forgotten. In addition to the Talmud there are less faithful descriptions in the writings of Josephus Flavius, the geographer Strabo, and the naturalist Pliny.

During all these centuries, the overwhelming majority of Jews were farmers. These tillers of the soil were little affected by the numerous incursions of the Romans. In the worst cases their cattle and produce were stolen, but the farmers and their families were not molested. Even when the Romans were determined to destroy Judaism they understood that the farming population was the foundation of the productive forces in the country and should be spared. It is therefore certain that even when many Jews were exiled from the country, the farmers were left to till their fields.

It must also be borne in mind that the Jewish farmer of that time was more religious than patriotic. As long as the Romans did not interfere with his offering of sacrifices, he was satisfied and probably indifferent as to whether he paid his taxes to the Jerusalem aristocrats who looked down upon him, or to the Romans.

When the Hasmoneans ruled Palestine they acquired a number of seaports, but the merchants and sailors of these cities were largely Phoenicians. Jews were then in the initial stages of learning the arts of commerce and navigation and their share in these occupations was negligible. Even the Jews of Galilee who were close neighbors of the Phoenicians excelled in agriculture and fruit-growing rather than in commerce, and Josephus described their land as "covered with fields of grain and resembling a large garden."

The Bible described Palestine as a land of milk and honey but this blessing was not always realized. The biblical curse that the heavens "shall be like copper over their heads and the earth shall be like iron under their feet" often approached nearer the truth when periods of drought affected the land. Nevertheless, the tillers of the soil always managed to secure their bread despite the fact that the country was rocky and sandy to a large degree. The Jews loved their land and all were convinced that it was the most beautiful in the world. They learned to improve the soil and to fertilize it artificially, to clear it of stones, and to destroy obnoxious weeds. The fields were surrounded with cactus fences to prevent the cattle from straying and those fields that were located on steep hills were terraced. Every handbreadth of land was utilized and there were no more diligent workers than the farmers of Palestine. Agriculture was highly regarded by all and was especially revered by the Romans. Whereas in other lands the Romans encountered difficulties in persuading people to till the soil, Palestine farmers were happy if they were allowed to pursue that labor.

The fertility of the soil of Palestine varied in different

regions of the country. Jericho and its environs was praised by the writers of all times as "the city of dates." Other districts excelled in wheat growing. It was said that the grain growing about the city of Hapharaim attained such height that it provided sufficient straw for the needs of the whole country. The wheat of Galilee was also famous for its quality and some said that it even excelled the wheat of Judea. Rye, oats, barley, sorghum, and other grains grew in abundance. Bread made of barley meal was considered to be the staple food of the poorer elements. There was a great abundance of this meal and considerable quantities of it were exported to other countries in exchange for rice that was later grown in Palestine.

In ordinary years the grain crop was between five- and ten-fold that which was sown, but in years when the rains came in good time, and the sun did not scorch the germinating seed, the crop was sometimes as much as a hundredfold. In years of bumper crops Palestine exported grain, but during lean years grain had to be imported from Egypt. Palestine abounded in all kinds of greens and vegetables such as cabbage, cucumbers, onions, garlic, radishes, and various beans. In time new vegetables previously not grown there were introduced and were avidly consumed. Due to the stringent regulations governing the offering of sacrifices, people often abstained from eating meat except on Sabbaths and holidays or other festive occasions. After the destruction of the Temple, when the offering of sacrifices was done away with, many people gave up meat altogether as an item in their diet.

Many varieties of fruit trees thrived in Palestine including figs, grapes, olives, carobs, oranges, *etrogim*, plums, cherries, walnuts, almonds, dates, mulberries, pomegranates, apples, and pears. In addition to these, new improved varieties were introduced and cultivated. Palestine was especially renowned for its wine, dates, and wheat. The coins that were minted by the Hasmoneans bear images of wheat, bunches of grapes, and date palms as symbols of the fertility of the land. The vineyards of Judea were considered the most beautiful in that part of the world. Between the rows of trees and vines flowers were planted and filled the air with their fragrance. Raisins and date honey were commonly used as food. Olive oil, which was plentiful, was exported in great quantities, and just as Judea was renowned for its wine, Galilee was famous for the quality of its oil. The oil was used as food and also for medicinal purposes and was widely sold in Sidon, Syria, and Egypt.

Pliny, the Roman natural philosopher, declared that Judea was famous for its dates just as Egypt was known for its incense. In the Talmud Rabbi Jacob ben Dostai tells us that on his way from Lud to Ono, a distance of three miles, he waded ankle deep in fig honey.[1]

The shores of the Dead Sea were covered with balsam and the districts of Gilead and Jericho were especially noted for it. Balsam was used as a medicine and also as incense. It was a very expensive commodity, and the Romans declared that the Jews did not plant it elsewhere in order to maintain its rarity and to be able to sell it for a high price. After the destruction of the Temple the Romans said that the Jews uprooted all the balsam trees in revenge on the Romans.

Sheep and cattle abounded in the land as a result of the need for sacrifices. There were many Jewish shepherds at that time and some of these also traded in cattle or in wool. This was especially true in the regions east of the Jordan. The women of Judea spun the wool and the women of Galilee spun flax and the garments were sold in the nearby cities. Many of the known varieties of fowl were introduced into the country at a later date. This is obvious from their Hebrew names that were never mentioned in the Bible. Geese, ducks, and chickens were among the imported species, and since they were not used for sacrificial purposes they were used as food. Many people also raised cattle and goats; considerable quantities of dairy products were consumed and exported.

Although some Jews engaged in hunting animals and birds, the number of these was not great due to the numerous laws regarding unclean animals and the restrictions affecting slaughter. But many people engaged in fishing especially in Galilee. The sea of Gennesaret (Sea of Galilee) abounded in many varieties of the best edible fish and scores of fishing villages dotted its shores. A great part of the catch was also exported.

The Dead Sea occupied a prominent place among the natural resources of the country. Various minerals were extracted from its waters (salt of Sodom) as well as asphalt. These were sold far and wide and were used for medical purposes and also in the manufacture of cosmetics. Historical descriptions of Palestine also mention metal mines. Iron was mined in the Lebanon mountains and in the region north of Idumea. Josephus Flavius mentions an iron mountain extending to the boundary of Moab and in later years this metal was also mined in Trans-Jordan.

The trades and occupations of the Jews of that time are a subject of endless interest. The Talmud is the best historical source on this subject and it lists the following occupations as being most widely engaged in: tailoring, shoemaking, building, quarrying, carpentry, hairdressing, metal working, weaving, dyeing, tapestry-weaving, bee raising, pottery, glass blowing, engraving, tanning, ink and arms manufacturing.

But although all these trades were commonly practiced and Jewish artisans were accorded social recognition, they did not constitute a majority of the population. Farming engaged the efforts of the majority of the nation. This is evident from the fact that the Talmud devoted itself more to the interests of the farmers than it did to the interests of the artisans.

From the available historical data, we may conclude that the Jewish artisans could not compete with the artisans of foreign countries, and when vessels or garments of higher quality were desired they had to be imported. This is also substantiated by the fact that the Talmud refers to all superior vessels or garments by their Greek names. This was also true of vegetables for some time, but as the years went by the superior varieties were also cultivated in Palestine. However, there was a common conviction that articles of foreign manufacture were superior in quality, and people of means bought their garments and decorated their houses with foreign imports.

Among the farming population the poorer peasants were

in a majority. These were referred to in the Talmud as *baal habayit* and they usually possessed only a small tract of land from which they barely eked out a living. Together with the members of his family such a peasant would work in his field from dawn till sunset. Most of his produce he used for his own household and the remainder, after he paid his taxes and tithes, was bartered in nearby cities or sold for money. Under such circumstances, the poorer peasants suffered every time a drought occurred or some other calamity overtook the country. He was then forced to hire himself out as a farmhand or to pawn his land to a richer farmer. But even when no unforseen calamities occurred, the poor peasant often had to become a wage-earner by working for another farmer. The parceling out of the land when it was divided among the heirs left each of them with such a small holding that many were forced to hire out even during normal years. Those who could find no employment were forced to turn to begging or to brigandage.

In Galilee and Judea a small class of rich farmers owned considerable parcels of land and had a comfortable income. It was these people who lent money to the poorer peasants and in time increased their holdings by seizing the land in payment of outstanding debts. They were also the grain merchants, and the Talmud refers to them as *atirei nekhesin* (men of much property). Although their number was small, they were socially prominent and exerted an influence on the administration of the land. They were generally the officials, the elders, and members of priestly families who accumulated the land of the poor. It is told that they engaged *ikonomusin* (managers) and *apitropsim* (overseers) to supervise the cultivation of their fields and vineyards while the owners remained in the city or traveled about in connection with their business ventures.

Thus the Talmud relates that Rabban Gamaliel II, also known as Rabban Gamaliel of Jabneh, employed a great number of laborers[2] and he also leased a part of his lands.[3] Such a procedure was engaged in by people who did not live on their land. Rabban Gamaliel was presiding officer of the Sanhedrin and had to reside in the city. He administered his lands through the agency of an *ikonomos* or an *apitropos*.

Hired laborers were engaged for a definite period of as much as a year or as little as a day or half-a-day but never for more than six years. Among the laborers were men who owned small plots of land as well as those who owned no land at all. Those unskilled in agricultural work hired out as common laborers and engaged in the most difficult work.

The scholars always sided with the laborers when they had complaints against their employers. They also established definite regulations concerning the food and drink to which the laborers were entitled, and although it is possible that most of these rules defining the rights of the workers remained theoretical, it is nevertheless certain that the social differentiation between poor and rich was not as sharp among the Jews as it was among the other nations of that time. The persecution at the hands of the Gentiles to which Jews poor and rich were subject partly accounted for this state of affairs.

Contract farming was also a known phenomenon. A contractor would undertake to cultivate a field and he was responsible for all the operations. He would buy the seed, hire the laborers and work together with them. He was responsible for the payment of the taxes to the government and the tithes to the priests as well as for all other expenditures. In compensation he received half the crop. In addition there were *arisim* (tenants) who received the seed, the tools, and the animals required for cultivation from the owner. Tenants supplied only their labor.

Artisans and peasants in Palestine were free men. They could choose their own occupation and when they hired out they were free to leave at any time, and the employer was legally bound to pay whatever wage was coming to them for the work they had accomplished. The condition of the slaves was entirely different. In some respects the slaves were in a better position than the hired laborers, but socially they occupied the lowest level. The slave was assured of his food and shelter, but he was not free to choose his occupation and he was dependent on the whims of his owner who could force him to work day and night.

The condition of the Jewish slave was peculiar. It was only

on rare occasions that a Jew bought a Jewish slave. When the Gentiles from the surrounding countries brought Jewish slaves to sell, they were ransomed, and immediately freed. But there were occasions when a Jew was in debt and he voluntarily sold himself into slavery to be able to repay his debt. Similarly, when a man was caught stealing he had to pay twice the value of the article stolen, and the court could sell him into slavery if he could not pay the required sum. Like the artisan and farm laborer, the Jewish slave sold only his labor, but he did not have definite working hours and he could be called upon to perform some task at any hour of the day or night. However, he enjoyed the privilege of resting on the Sabbath and the holidays together with his owner.

Because of the preferred treatment an owner had to accord a Jewish slave there were not many who were anxious to own one, and a saying current at the time declared that "He who buys a Jewish slave buys an overlord." But there undoubtedly existed slave owners who did not grant their Jewish slaves any privileges, and on the year of the Jubilee the courts had to force them to liberate their Jewish slaves. Human nature had not changed much during the centuries and it is apparent that the generations during talmudic times had to contend with the same problem recorded by Jeremiah (Chapter 34) where King Zedekiah commanded all Jewish slaves to be liberated and their owners soon enslaved them again.

Jewish slave owners were enjoined to treat their non-Jewish slaves with humanity. Although the owner could beat his slave at will, he was strictly warned not to starve him, and in case the slave was crippled through the loss of an eye or a limb, he was immediately liberated. If a slave died as a result of a beating, the Torah commanded that the owner be put to death; but when the slave survived his punishment by a day or more, the owner was not to be put to death.

Judging from numerous circumstances, we may conclude that Jewish slaves felt a greater kinship to their owners than the non-Jewish slaves. They participated actively in the various rebellions against Rome, and Josephus relates that during the war that ended with the destruction of the Temple, Bar Giora proclaimed the liberation of all Jewish slaves as the first step in his mobilization of an army. At the same time the Romans announced that all non-Jewish slaves who betrayed their owners would be granted their freedom.

Non-Jewish slaves were brought from the markets at Tyre and Sidon. Their treatment in Palestine would compare favorably with their treatment in other countries. Every slave was branded on the forehead or he was given a cap with a bell on it to wear so that he might be recognized. Compared with the treatment of slaves in other lands, these measures were relatively humane.

Slaves were the unrestricted property of their owners. If the owner so desired he could marry a slave to his mother or sister. But the marriage of a slave was of no significance and the owner retained his rights of possession. Children of slaves also belonged to the owner and could be sold at will. All possessions of a slave automatically belonged to his master who also could claim any object found by the slave. In addition the owner could rent his slaves' labor power to others without consulting the slaves.

The *Midrash* relates the case of a man who persuaded his neighbor to divorce his wife because of her immoral conduct. When the husband complained that he could not divorce her because he did not have enough money to repay her dowry, the man offered to loan him the necessary sum. After the woman was divorced, the creditor married her and enslaved her previous husband for inability to repay his debt. The man thus became the slave of his ex-wife and was forced to witness her relations with his creditor.

But if the position of the male slave was unenviable, the condition of women slaves was even worse. In addition to their labor they were held at the disposal of the owner and his sons. It is therefore remarkable that some women were sold by their own parents into such life.

There undoubtedly were many Jews who treated their slaves in a more humane manner. In many homes the slaves were employed in skilled work and were trusted with all confidence. Some of them were tailors or barbers; others were bakers and cooks. In some cases the owners even entrusted the education of their children to the slaves. Among the women slaves were singers and dancers who entertained their owners and their guests.

The *Mishnah* tells that Rabban Gamaliel of Jabneh owned a slave named Tabbai whom he respected greatly and for whom he mourned a long time after his death. Another slave of Rabban Gamaliel was called "father" and his wife was referred to as "mother." It is quite probable that these were not isolated instances and that the lot of the slave of a Jew was better than that of a slave belonging to a non-Jewish owner.

It must be borne in mind that the whole Jewish people was not in constant mourning for the destruction of the Temple and the cessation of the sacrifices. It is even related that when Jerusalem was destroyed, the people of Betar celebrated the occasion. It is also quite certain that the institution of sacrifices had lost much of its significance in the minds of many leaders, and some of them were satisfied that Jabneh had been saved as a cultural center. Others, however, were convinced that the destruction of the Temple was temporary and that it would soon be restored even as the First Temple was rebuilt a short time after its destruction. This belief found a deep echo in the hearts of large sections of the population who looked upon themselves as people whose house had been burned and who were waiting for the construction of a new house. There is also no definite proof that the institution of sacrifices ceased with the Temple and that small groups did not gather secretly to offer sacrifices. It is even possible that they brought their offerings to the site of the demolished altar. The fact that the regulations pertaining to the priests and the tithes were observed for a long time after the destruction is ample proof of the expectations of the people of a rapid restoration.

This was not an impossibility under the political conditions then prevailing. It was quite likely that some emperor might eventually grant permission to rebuild the Temple out of respect for the Jews or through the intercession of some influential person who could also pay for the right. But these hopes vanished with the rebellion of Bar Kochba against Hadrian. Over half a million Jews were killed in the uprising and hundreds of thousands were sold into slavery. The country was devastated and a temple to Zeus was erected in Jerusalem. Jews were not even allowed to approach the gates of the city.

But this was not the final expulsion from Palestine. Jews continued to reside in other cities and subsequent Roman emperors allowed them to visit Jerusalem on the ninth day of *Av* to mourn for the destroyed Temple.

Various historical events of that time are described in the Jerusalem as well as in the Babylonian Talmud and also in the *Midrash*. Most of these descriptions were not clearly understood until recently when certain Jewish historians made a careful study of these sources. Whenever the talmudic descriptions are not in agreement with the facts as they are related by Roman historians, it is safer to rely on the talmudic sources.

That the destruction following the conquest of Jerusalem by Titus was not complete was also a result of other factors. Many people did not actively participate in the rebellion and after the war they rearranged their lives to conform with the situation that had been created and they kept peace with the Romans. But the zealots who participated in the war were branded as bandits after the conflict. Their desperation in the struggle also hurt the interests of the others and hastened the ultimate destruction.

Titus and the rulers who immediately followed him did not intend to interfere with the religious practices of the Jews. According to Josephus, Titus even commanded the Temple be spared, and that it was Princess Berenice who set fire to it out of conviction that the Jews would never surrender as long as it remained in existence. After the revolt was quelled Titus did not wish to do any further harm. In all religious matters the Jews remained free, and they retained the right of judgment in religious and also in secular cases. Even non-Jews often appeared before a Jewish court when in dispute with a Jew, and the Roman authorities allowed Jewish courts to handle all cases when both parties consented to be tried by it. The Church-father Origines even declared that Jewish courts tried cases involving life although they were not authorized to do so.

The teachings of the Pharisees then developed to an extent that would have been impossible had the Temple been in existence. The Sadducees disappeared altogether and the oral law became the dominant influence in Jewish life. All national life concentrated around religious regulations that were strictly observed. In their devotion to the Torah and in the observance of its commandments, the people found consolation for the destruction of the Temple; Jabneh took the place of Jerusalem and the offering of gifts to the scholars in Jabneh took the place of the offering of sacrifices on the altar.

Sixty years after the destruction of Jerusalem during the reign of Hadrian, another uprising took place that affected the whole people. The cause of this uprising can be found in the events that occurred during the reign of the preceding Emperor Trajan. During his reign, Babylonia rebelled against Rome and the Jews extended aid to the insurgents. (The Talmud refers to this revolt as "Polemos Quietus.") A number of Jews from Palestine also joined this uprising in the hope that the defeat of the Romans would lead to the liberation of Palestine.

Trajan entrusted the conduct of the war to General Lusius Quietus and he commanded him to execute all the Jews who fell into his hands. After he quelled the revolt, Quietus was appointed governor of Palestine. Jewish uprisings occurred simultaneously in Egypt, Cyrenaica, and Cyprus and the rebels vented their pent-up anger on the neighboring Greek population and slaughtered many of them. Greek authors of that time speak of hundreds of thousands of slain Greeks, but these numbers were undoubtedly highly exaggerated. Marcius Turba was dispatched to quell the revolt and he triumphed over the Jews in *Bikat Yadaim* (Alexandria). A Talmudic legend describes the slaughter that followed by saying that twice as many people were killed at that time as had originally left Egypt.

Hadrian was by nature a peace-loving and kindly man and he is said to have permitted the restoration of the Temple, but the Samaritans objected and he withdrew his permission. One legend states that when the foundations for the new Temple were being laid, flames burst from the diggings and consumed the laborers. The Jews then asked that the work be stopped because they believed that this was an omen of God's will that the Temple not be rebuilt. However, it has been historically established that the relations between Samaritans and Jews during the reign of Hadrian were friendly, and they also participated on the side of the Jews during the uprising.

Recent historical investigations ascribe the rebellion to Hadrian's prohibition against circumcision. Both the Jews and the Samaritans observed the law of circumcision and they therefore united against Rome. It seems inexplicable that the Romans, who did not interfere with the religious customs of their subject peoples, should have prohibited circumcision. But the Christian historian Schuerer explains it in the following manner: Emperor Domitian issued a law against castration as a barbaric custom. This law Hadrian extended to include circumcision, and the death penalty was established for those who broke the law. This explanation is obviated by the fact that Antoninus Pius again allowed the Jews to practice circumcision, and his edict declared the practice to be an old Jewish custom not to be confused with castration. In issuing this edict he was also influenced by the stubbornness with which the Jews clung to this practice.

When Moses sent spies to Palestine they reported that the cities of Palestine were well fortified (Num. 13:28). Moses informed the Jews that they would find "cities great and fenced up to heaven" (Deut. 9:1). It is therefore remarkable that after so many invasions and wars, people believed that many of the gates and fortresses dated back to the days of Joshua ben Nun. The Bible mentions that the Jews lived in *ir* (city), *chatzer* (court) and *kefar* (village). The Talmud makes no mention of *chatzer* but contains the additional concept of *kerach* (large city) and in addition to *ir* (city) it makes mention of *ayarah* (town). There are differing opinions concerning the exact meaning of *chatzer*. Some declared it to be a suburb; others maintained that it referred to an enclosure or a group of houses where a large number of people lived. There are also references to cities named Hatzar (Num. 34:4; Joshua 19:3), and these probably developed from small groups of houses. The name Kefar appears both in the Bible and in the Talmud. The size of a Kefar was not definitely determined but Josephus declares that the smallest Kefar in Palestine contained 15,000 inhabitants. However, this statement may be discounted as exaggerated. There were also cities in Palestine that developed from villages as is indicated by their names: Kefar Haamoni, Kefar Chananiah and Kefar Aziz.

When the scholars tried to define the difference between a city and a village they said that a city is a place where there are always ten *batlanim* (idlers) available for various religious functions which require that number.[4]

The name *kerach* was derived from the Aramaic. The name signifies a fortified city. The Talmud sometimes refers to the same city by all three names (*kerach, ir, kefar*), but it is obvious that *ir* usually referred to an unfortified city.

The fortified *kerach* was surrounded by a wall as protection against sudden attacks and was generally situated on the top of a mountain or on a rocky hill difficult of access and easy to defend. Whenever an *ir* was fortified it was expressly referred to as a walled city.

A *kerach* was limited in area by its walls and could not grow indefinitely; the name therefore described the strength of the city and not its size. Whenever we find statements such as "the great *kerach* of Rome," these refer to the defenses of the city rather than to its size.

The Talmud relates that when God wanted to determine the size of Jerusalem the angels said: "You have created so many *kerachim* of the gentile nations without determining their size. Why should you do so for your own city?"[5] This legend is interpreted by some to indicate that *kerach* referred to gentile cities or to those whose garrisons were largely non-Jewish. The Talmudic reference to Betar, which was a Jewish city, as *kerach* they hold to be an exception.

The walled cities of Palestine were thus named *kerachim* and were considered as gentile places of residence. There were ten such cities that bore the collective name of Decapolis. In the course of time they developed into separate centers of activity apart from the rest of Palestine,[6] although some of them were surrounded by Jewish settlements.[7] The administrators of these cities discriminated against the Jews who were denied privileges enjoyed by the other inhabitants. This was also a distinction between a *kerach* and an *ir* which was not autonomous. The *kerach* was a garrison town; this is evident from the reference in the Talmud to *Burganin*, the barracks for soldiers or the government tax collector.[8]

This fact explains the Talmudic saying that a man who is about to enter a *kerach* should pronounce the following prayer: "May it be Thy will to lead me into this *kerach* in peace." Once within the city, one was supposed to pray: "I am thankful to You that You brought me into the city in peace." Upon leaving, one said: "May it be Thy will to lead me out of this city in peace," and after one was outside the city limits he was to say: "I thank You for leading me out of the city in peace and I pray that You shall further lead me and protect me in peace, and that You shall save me from an enemy who may lurk by the roadside."[9]

This prayer evolved because of the danger of entering and leaving a *kerach*. It was composed during the rule of the Romans who afforded no protection to Jewish travellers when they did not molest them themselves. But despite the danger, Jews constantly were forced to visit these cities because of their business enterprises. Sometimes they only had to pass through these cities, as in the case of sea journeys when the ships touched at these ports. The scholars therefore at times forbade entrance into these cities or even into towns located in their neighborhood, but these prohibitions were usually ignored out of necessity.[10]

Even wicked kings who ruled the land with brutal force and persecuted the Jewish religion could gain the admiration of the people by building a new city. This act was enough to justify many of his cruel deeds. Such was the case of Omri, the king of Israel, who encouraged idolatry; nevertheless the Talmud declared that he gained the kingdom for four generations of his successors because he built the city of Samaria.[11]

The number of cities in Palestine was usually highly exaggerated. Speaking of the conquests of Alexander Jannai, Rabbi Jochanan declared that the occupied area held 600,000 cities each of which was inhabited by 600,000 people. The total number would thus be larger than the population of the whole world today. Similar exaggerations are found in the writing of Josephus who said that there were 1200 cities in Galilee alone and in the writings of the Greek historian, Dio Cassius, who related that during the Bar Kochba uprising the Romans conquered 950 fortified cities.

We may conclude, however, that the large cities were subdivided into quarters each of which was significant in itself. From the descriptions of ancient Jerusalem we know that the city was divided into an upper and a lower part. During this period, Jerusalem was in ruins and uninhabited, and when the scholars attempted to describe the beauty of the city they were forced to rely upon their imaginings of a future Jerusalem after Messiah would come.

But the descriptions of ancient Jerusalem were not exaggerated. The image of the city lived in the memory of all the people, and they sought to make other cities resemble Jerusalem in appearance. Most of the Palestinian cities were built on mountain tops and the synagogues were erected at the highest point so as to be seen from all sides. The court that dispensed justice and controlled the observance of Torah commandments also held its sessions there. The academies were located nearby and the sexton of the synagogue blew the *shofar* there to announce the beginning of the Sabbath. The watchtower was also located in that vicinity to observe the countryside over a great distance and to warn of an enemy's approach.

Nearly all Palestine cities had suburbs known in Hebrew as *migrash* or *parvar* (II Kings 23:11). Houses in these suburbs were considered part of the city for purposes of taxation and maintenance of order, but in time of war they were abandoned except those houses bordering on the city walls.

The scholars established a rule by which all inhabitants of a city were compelled to aid in building a wall with gates about the city. This rule was enforced in those towns near the border of the country that were subject to attacks. Every city also had one or more marketplaces and was traversed by streets.

Of the greatness of Jerusalem, a *midrash* relates that the city contained twenty-four palaces, each of which had twenty-four entrances. Near every entrance there were twenty-four large marketplaces, each of which was divided into twenty-four smaller ones. Each small marketplace had twenty-four courts in each of which there were twenty-four houses.[12]

Every marketplace was usually designated by a name describing the type of merchandise sold there. Thus there were poultry markets and fish markets. Others were named after the people who lived in the neighborhood such as "the market of the Arameans," "the market of Rabbi Yitzchak" and "the market of Rabbi Chanin." In addition every city had corners (*keranot*) where different stores were located and where idlers (*yoshvei keranot*) congregated waiting for the odd job.

The *mavo* (entrance) to the city also served as a market place and frequently resembled a court extending for some distance and leading up to various houses and courts within the city. The *mavo* was significant and played an important role in the development of rules pertaining to *eruvin*.[13] The inhabitants living in the neighborhood of the *mavo* were also responsible for its upkeep.

The Romans were great city builders and they generally laid out new cities in squares. Jewish scholars therefore developed the theory that cities should be built in that form in order to facilitate defining the 2000 ell limit outside the city which was the allowed distance walkable on the Sabbath.[14] Jews also built the walls surrounding their cities with uneven surfaces. The unevenness of the walls increased their defense capacity and when the enemy attempted to demolish them with iron rams, the upper stones would fall on the attackers. The numerous corners and turns in the walls were also strategically important and hard to conquer.

As a result of the limited space within the walled area, houses were built close together and some of them were built into the protecting walls. Such houses generally served as gates to the city. Thus we find that during the conquest of Jericho,

Rahab's house was built into the city wall, and it was also said of one of the *amoraim* of Palestine that the gate of the city led into his house.[15] Some cities had double walls for greater protection. The Romans frequently erected imposing gates on each side of a city, but such gates were built only in the gentile-inhabited cities. Jewish cities, on the other hand, presented a poor appearance architecturally, both in the construction of their houses and protecting walls.

Life in the cities differed greatly from that in the villages so far as food, clothing, and general behavior was concerned. Life in the cities was more refined in all its aspects when compared with the primitive mode of life in the villages. For the convenience of the city dwellers there were markets and inns where food supplies were sold and travellers were accommodated. These two institutions also served as the foundation for commerce in the country. On certain days of the week the villagers would bring their produce to the cities and would buy those necessities which they could not raise themselves. These market days were called *yemei hakenisah* (days of entrance) and occurred on Mondays and Thursdays. In honor of the visitors a chapter from the Torah would be read in the synagogue on those days and other religious needs of the villagers would be fulfilled. The court held its sessions and the scholars lectured on religious questions. Friday was another market day when the villagers brought food supplies such as fowl, cattle, fish, and wine for the Sabbath. The artisans also had their shops in the city and villagers paid for those articles with their farm produce. Among these were also the scribes, the doctors, and the teachers.

This trade was defined in the Talmud as "give and take" (*masa u'matan*) because it largely consisted of barter. It was only rarely that the villagers possessed any money. Cities were generally built near a supply of water, but when there were no springs or wells in the vicinity, water would be brought in pipes or aqueducts from some distance. Many cities also had reservoirs to store water in anticipation of drought or the drying up of wells, and the people knew how to utilize water pressure to raise it to higher levels. Some cities had canals for drainage purposes and these canals were also used to bring water to the fields for irrigation purposes. Wells were also well known at that time.

The plentiful supply of water in Palestine enabled people to maintain cleanliness and its effect on the health of the population was noticeable. The need and the justification for bathing was recognized by the Talmud in the following words: "If a city dweller does not allow his wife to bathe at least once a week, or a villager does not allow his wife to bathe at least once in a fortnight the woman may demand a divorce and the full payment of her dowry; likewise if a villager forces his wife to go barefoot three months in succession, or if a city dweller commands his wife to go barefoot one day."[16]

Every city was surrounded by fields and in some cases part of the fields were within the city walls. This was also true of wine cellars and threshing floors that were sometimes found within the confines of the city walls. Although numerous trees grew within the cities, orchards and produce gardens were outside the walls. The roads leading through the gardens were often lined with avenues of trees. Torches and oil lamps were used to illuminate the entrances to the courts and were provided by the owners of the houses at their own expense.[17]

In addition to the weekly marketdays, every city had special fairs once a month or every half year. At these fairs various kinds of merchandise from distant places and foreign lands were sold and money changers (*shulhanim*) were present to exchange the coins of the foreign merchant who came to buy Palestinian products.

Aside from their economic significance, marketplaces were also social centers where people congregated to look at the displays of merchandise and at the artistic arrangement of fruit. The grains most commonly sold for breadmaking were rye or wheat. In addition there were articles of apparel, flax, wine, wool, leather, and slaves. Stores, in addition to the markets, provided the city dwellers with all their needs. These stores contained all possible articles including arms. In the smaller towns and villages there were also peddlers who carried their wares from house to house and many villagers preferred to sell their goods in this manner out for fear of being cheated in the cities.

The more refined tastes of the city people was apparent also in the food they consumed, and the Talmud mentions the difference in the flour they used compared with the flour used by the villagers.[18] A delicacy frequently used at that time consisted of dough baked in honey, but in the cities this was made with much honey while in the villages only a trace of it was used.[19] The villagers also ate a coarse bread that was not liked in the cities.[20] Similar differences were apparent in their garments. The garments of the villagers were primitive and are referred to in the Talmud as *bigdei b enei chakla'i* (garments of the farmers); in the cities various styles were used and it was often impossible to distinguish between the garments of men and women.[21]

Difficult as conditions were in the cities, the farming population met with still greater hardships. Their struggle for existence was more arduous and they were also exposed to ridicule. Villagers were known as *am ha'aretz* and even those scholars who showed respect for the city artisans often expressed disdain for the *am ha'aretz*. In later years the name *am ha'aretz* was no longer used and *ben kefar* (villager) was substituted instead, but even then it was pointed out that a great difference existed between the city dweller and the villager. The contempt in which the villager was held is apparent from many descriptions and popular sayings of that time. From these it is obvious that only city dwellers were considered civilized and the rural population was believed to be ignorant.

Cities were held to be the home of wisdom and only their inhabitants knew how to show proper respect to scholars and to prominent men. Whenever a villager did not accord the proper respect to one greater than himself, he was not punished and it was ascribed to his ignorance.

The most striking analysis of the difference between city and village inhabitants is contained in the statement of the scholars concerning the prophets Isaiah and Ezekiel both of whom described their visions of God and his heavenly retinue. Isaiah described what he saw as a city dweller who had frequent opportunities to see the king, but Ezekiel described his vision like a villager who may have seen the king only once in his life.[22]

All political upheavals of that time originated in the cities, for only there did the people show any understanding of political events. Villagers were not much concerned with political matters and they suspected everyone of trying to rob them. This state of mind resulted partly from the fact that the country was overrun by Jewish as well as non-Jewish bands of robbers in addition to soldiers, tax collectors, and others who in fact *did* frequently rob them.

The entire mode of life of the villagers was thus on a low level. Their food was poorer, their garments coarse, their furniture made of unplaned boards. The regulations of the Talmud concerning cleanliness of vessels specifically mentions the "bowl of the villagers" which was different from those used in the cities.[23]

Villagers were allowed to celebrate Purim earlier than the city dwellers. Although the Book of Esther expressly states that Purim should be observed on the 14th and 15th days of *Adar*, the *Mishnah* declared that villagers may read the Book of Esther on marketday when they come to the city on a Monday or Thursday even when those days are only the 11th, 12th, or 13th of the month.

As soon as darkness fell, all villagers were afraid to leave their homes because of wild animals that roamed the land,[24] and also for fear of soldiers and robber bands. But whereas the soldiers would only rob the farmer and force him to provide all their needs, the robber bands who roamed the land in peacetime as well as during years of war, frequently killed their victims if any resistance was offered. Rabbi Jose ben Chalafta therefore said that the life of a villager might be compared with those of desert wanderers who were never sure of their lives, and whose wives and children could always be seized.[25]

The doors of city houses were usually locked and there was always a bell to announce visitors. But the houses in the villages were always open and visitors with honest intentions could always be sure of generous hospitality.

But despite the hardships of village life, their mode of life had certain advantages. Due to the crowded conditions in the cities contagious diseases were common and frequent bathing did not counteract them. The disease germs bred in the walls of the houses, as may be seen from the biblical laws concerning leprosy.

The scholars ruled that every city must possess the following ten conveniences for its inhabitants: a court, a charity fund, a synagogue, a bathhouse, a comfort station, a doctor, a barber, a scribe, a butcher, and a teacher.[26] But all of this did not suffice in time of epidemics and the inhabitants sought refuge in the villages.

By far the greatest difference between city and village was to be found in matters of administration. The cities maintained courts and a police force to keep order; everyone was also taxed a definite sum for the city government and also for charitable purposes. In the villages, on the other hand, anarchy reigned and he who was more powerful could do as he pleased.

Jews showed a dislike for dogs and only in rare cases were dogs allowed in the cities and then they had to be chained. The opinion was common that one who keeps a dog is like one who raises pigs, and stories were related of pregnant women miscarrying when frightened by dogs barking.[27] But in the villages dogs were common, especially for herding purposes.

Many people traveled through the villages in connection with their business enterprises or to announce the regulations of the Sanhedrin. There were also those who traveled about to acquaint themselves with different peoples and lands. All of these found shelter and hospitality in the villages where they stopped overnight for fear of robbers who roamed highways. Tax collectors were especially subject to such robberies, when it was known that they carried considerable sums.

51

RABBI JEHUDAH N'SIAH I
AND HIS SUCCESSORS

RABBI JEHUDAH HANASI (*Rabbenu Hakadosh*) was succeeded by his son Rabban Gamaliel to the post of Nasi and he
maintained that post only for a short time, certainly not more
than ten years, and was followed by his son Jehudah, whom
the Talmud calls Rabbi Jehudah N'siah (or Rabbi Judan) to
distinguish him from his grandfather. Historically he is known
as Rabbi Jehudah N'siah I, because he was followed by others
of the same name.

Rabbi Jehudah N'siah I was the last of the descendants of
Hillel who was both head of the Sanhedrin and in charge of the
secular administration of the Jewish population. After his death
these two offices were separated and were held by different
persons. It is impossible to establish the definite dates of these
events due to the confusion of the records resulting from the
repetition of names. Frequently it is impossible to determine
whether it is the grandfather or the grandson of whom the
records speak. But despite these discrepancies, it is safer to
trust Talmudic sources even when they disagree with Roman
historical dates.

There are numerous indications that Rabbi Jehudah N'siah
was a pupil in his grandfather's academy. At that time it was
still permissible for a grandson to bear his grandfather's name

during the latter's life. As additional substantiation of this fact, we find a statement in the Talmud that Hillel, the younger brother of Rabbi Jehudah N'siah, questioned his grandfather in some religious matters.[1] This leads to the belief that the older brother must certainly have been a pupil of Rabbi Jehudah Hanasi. The Talmud also cites differing opinions between grandfather and grandson regarding the necessity of offering tithes from fruit bought from a stranger or from a pagan, and this is held to be further proof of the scholastic relationship between the two.[2] But despite these deductions we can only say with certainty that Rabbi Jehudah was a pupil of his father, Rabban Gamaliel, and of Rabbi Chiya.[3]

Rabbi Jehudah N'siah permitted the use of oil bought from pagans,[4] and also attempted to introduce other reforms pertaining to the laws of marriage and divorce. In these reforms, however, he was thwarted by the opposition of the Sanhedrin. When his disciple, Rabbi Simlai, wished to repeal the prohibition against the use of bread bought from strangers and consequently possibly untithed, Rabbi Jehudah objected on the ground that people would say that the court was repealing all prohibitions.[5]

In previous years enough olives were raised in Palestine so that it was unnecessary to buy oil from pagans since such oil was considered undesirable in the same way that wine made by pagans was not used for fear that it had been also used for idolatrous purposes. But during the numerous wars fought in the country, the Romans destroyed most of the olive groves, and the inhabitants had to resort to buying oil. For this reason Rabbi Jehudah N'siah allowed the use of such oil.

The origin of the prohibition against the use of oil bought from pagans, dates back to the time of Daniel, according to Rav (Abba Arecha). Others maintain that this prohibition was one of the famous eighteen decrees promulgated by the scholars prior to the destruction of the Temple. It is related that Rav refused to use such oil even after the prohibition against it was repealed. His friend Shmuel reproved him: "You should eat this oil, otherwise I will declare you to be a 'dissenting elder' who refuses to obey the decisions of the court."[6]

It appears that the people clung to the stricter interpretations of the law, and the laxity of the religious conduct of the household of the Nasi was the subject of comment throughout the country. When Rabbi Jehudah realized that his household was the talk of the country, he commanded that a stricter religious discipline be applied in order to avoid criticism.

The following instances are related in the Talmud. Rabbi Jehudah N'siah and his brother Hillel were once bathing in the bathhouse at Kabul. The custom of that city did not allow two men to bathe together, and when Rabbi Jehudah heard the people murmuring against him, Hillel immediately left the bathhouse to avoid all cause of criticism. At another time the two brothers spent the Sabbath in Biri, a city to the north of Safed, and on that day they walked about the streets in their overshoes. They then heard the people exclaiming that such a thing had never been seen before and they immediately removed their overshoes and gave them to their servants to carry.[7]

The people criticized the household of the Nasi for many of its customs which differed from those commonly accepted, but the scholars informed them that some things that were prohibited for the rest of the population were permissible for the Nasi and those about him because they were "close to the government." They were thus allowed to decorate their wall with various paintings, to use mirrors, to grow their hair long, and to study Greek.[8]

Among other attempted reforms, Rabbi Jehudah N'siah also sought to do away with the fast on the ninth day of *Av*. Others maintain that he merely wished to do away with the fast on those years when the ninth day of *Av* fell on a Saturday and that it would have been unthinkable for him to try to abolish the fast altogether, since it was enjoined by the Bible. Rabbi Jehudah also declared that there was no need for fasting in times when there were no religious persecutions and Jews lived peacefully.[9]

It was noted already that the events of this period are highly confused. Much information is lacking and we do not know with any degree of certainty where the last of the N'siim maintained their academies. It was said that Rabbi Jehudah N'siah's academy was located in Sepphoris; others maintain that it was in Tiberias. The city of Tiberias was held to be unclean because of the belief that it was built on the site of a cemetery. Rabbi Jehudah thus removed the taboo from this city by holding his academy there. Even the ceremony of the "consecration of the month," always held in a city of Judea, Rabbi Jehudah performed in Tiberias.[10]

Like his grandfather, Rabbi Jehudah N'siah was also called Rabbi or Rabbenu. This appellation applied to both grandfather and grandson still further confuses the records. The historian Graetz thus maintains that the Talmudic story of the friendship of Rabbi and Emperor Antoninus actually refers to Rabbi Jehudah N'siah and Alexander Severus.

History records that Alexander Severus was a Roman of Syrian birth. He ruled from 222 until 235 C.E. and was friendly to the Jews. His bedroom was said to contain the statues of Orpheus, Jesus, and Abraham. On all occasions he repeated the maxim of Hillel: "That which you would not have done to yourself, do not unto others." He also commanded that this maxim be engraved on the gates of all courts, and whenever his legions were about to march, a herald pronounced these words to the soldiers that they might remember them.

Being a friend of Jews and Christians (who were then still considered to be a Jewish sect) he always held them up as examples of honesty and moral conduct. The Greeks of Antioch and Alexandria therefore ridiculed him and called him "Imperator Archisynagogos," but although the emperor knew of this attitude of the Greeks he did not deviate from his path. He presented the synagogue at Tiberias with a golden menorah and he gave the Nasi a large field to help maintain his pupils. The friendly attitude of the emperor brought about more cordial relations between the Romans and the Jews and Christians. The Christian church father Origines complained in his writings that the emperor thought more like a Jew than a Roman.

It was characteristic of Rabbi Jehudah N'siah that he did not distinguish between scholars and ordinary people in administrative matters but taxed everyone equally for the government of Tiberias. This was against the accepted axiom that one who undertakes the burden of the Torah should be freed from the burden of the government. Many scholars therefore spoke against the Nasi and on one occasion, as they studied the laws pertaining to a Nasi who commits a transgression, Rabbi Simeon ben Lakish asked: "If a Nasi has committed a transgression, should he be flogged or not?" He was answered that a court of three judges could condemn such a Nasi to be flogged, and that it was not even necessary to convoke the small Sanhedrin of twenty-three members to try him.

Later Rabbi Simeon ben Lakish asked further whether a Nasi who had been flogged could be reinstated to his office. One of the pupils, Rabbi Haggai, replied that such a Nasi could not be reinstated for fear that he would execute his judges.

When Rabbi Jehudah N'siah heard of this discussion he understood that it was directed against himself, and he sent one of his non-Jewish soldiers to seize Rabbi Simeon ben Lakish, but Rabbi Simeon escaped.

The following day Rabbi Jochanan came to the academy and before the studies were begun he pretended to look in all the corners of the buildings. When he was asked by the Nasi what he was searching for, Rabbi Jochanan answered: "I search for Ben Lakish; we cannot begin our studies without the key."

"Where is Ben Lakish without whom we cannot pursue our studies," the Nasi asked, and Rabbi Jochanan replied that he was hiding in Magdala. They then decided to go to Magdala the following day to bring Ben Lakish back.

Rabbi Jochanan at once sent a messenger with the good news to Ben Lakish and when they met on the following day, Ben Lakish said to the Nasi: "You have this day done an act similar to that of the Creator. When God wanted to free his people from bondage he did so Himself and not through a messenger or an agent." The Nasi asked him why he proposed his questions in the academy in a manner to insult the Nasi, and Rabbi Simeon ben Lakish replied: "You must not think that I will refrain from studying God's Torah out of fear of you."[11]

Another time Jose the Maonite expounded the fifth chapter of Hosea and remarked that there would come a time when God would bring the priests to trial and ask them why they did not observe his Torah after He had granted them twenty-four priestly gifts. The priests would then reply: "Creator of the world! You have given us nothing." God would then go to the Jews and ask them: "Why do you not give the priests the twenty-four gifts which I have commanded in my Torah?" and the Jews would reply: "Because the servants of the Nasi take everything away from us."

The Nasi wanted to punish Jose the Maonite for these words, but Rabbi Jochanan and Rabbi Simeon ben Lakish pleaded with him and said: "Jose the Maonite wished to explain a difficult passage in the Bible; would you punish him for it?" The Nasi summoned Jose the Maonite and during their conversation he asked him the meaning of the verse "As is the mother so is her daughter" (Ezekiel 17:44). Jose replied: "As is the generation, so is its Nasi and as is the altar such are its priests.[12]

Rabbi Jehudah N'siah I was succeeded by his son Rabban Gamaliel IV; Rabban Gamaliel IV was followed by his son Rabbi Jehudah N'siah the Second.[13]

Nearly eighty years passed between the rule of Rabbi Jehudah N'siah I until the administration of Rabbi Jehudah N'siah II. Lack of documentary information makes it impossible to fit the events of these years into the historical frame work of the Roman empire. It is also entirely possible that due to political changes, there was an interregnum in the rule of the N'siim. It is also noteworthy that Rabbi Jehudah N'siah II was only nominally Nasi, for although he was recognized by the government as head of the Sanhedrin, the people recognized Rabbi Ami and Rabbi Jochanan as religious authorities. We may assume that even Rabban Gamaliel IV did not make any religious decisions without consulting the opinion of other scholars. Rabban Gamaliel was looked upon as a mediocre man and a similar attitude was shown toward Rabbi Jehudah N'siah II who always sought the advice of Rabbi Ami. When Rabban Gamaliel asked Rabbi Avahu whether it was permissible to go to a gentile fair to buy slaves, the latter sharply responded in the negative.[14]

On another occasion, when the land was affected by a drought, Rabbi Jehudah N'siah declared thirteen fast days but still no rain fell. He was ready to declare still more fast days, but Rabbi Ami sent a message saying that since the first thirteen fast days did not produce the desired effect, additional ones would probably be of no avail.[15]

Rabbi Jehudah N'siah was a pupil of Rabbi Jochanan. He admitted this himself, and the Talmud also relates that on a certain evening Rabbi Jochanan came to the gardens of Rabbi Jehudah to teach his men how to clean the plowshares.[16] It is further told that when the pupils of Rabbi Chanina explained a law contrary to the opinions of Rabbi Jochanan, Rabbi Jehudah sent soldiers to enforce the decisions of Rabbi Jochanan.[17]

Meanwhile scholarship declined in Palestine. The political unrest in the country and the growing weakness of the Roman Empire resulted in a chaotic state of affairs. Emperors changed frequently and the central government lost much of its ability to govern lands as distant as Palestine. Babylonia then developed into a center of Jewish learning, and in Palestine academies existed only in Galilee. But the Jews of Babylonia continued to cherish a great love for the Land of Israel, and they still believed that one who would be a scholar must go to Palestine. Various anecdotes about the inhabitants of the other country then became current.

Determining the day of the new month was then a most important religious question. This day could then be determined only on the testimony of witnesses who declared that they had seen the new moon. It had become a very difficult procedure due to the interference of the Romans and also because of internal enemies. The beginning of the months of *Tishri* and *Nissan* were especially significant because the date of the Passover and leap years were then established. Rabbi Ami insisted on maintaining the old procedure, but Rabbi Jehudah N'siah reminded him of the ruling of Rabbi Jochanan that one must be so strict with the witnesses who testify about the new moon, because even if they had not seen the new moon in time, they might declare that they had.[18]

It is told that Rabbi Jehudah N'siah devoted much time and energy to the establishment of schools for children and academies for adults in all corners of the land. To achieve this aim he sent out three scholars (Rabbi Ami, Rabbi Asi, and Rabbi Chiya bar Abba) to investigate the situation and he instructed them that wherever they found a city without a school or an academy, they should call the elders and inform them that any city where children do not study should be destroyed.[19]

The administration of Rabbi Jehudah N'siah occurred during the reign of Diocletian who was born in Dacia and rose from common people. Diocletian decided that it was too great a task for one man to conduct the numerous Roman wars and to rule the empire at the same time. He therefore selected men to assist him; these were called "Anti-Caesar."

Some historians claim that Diocletian was friendly to the Jews and it is true that there is no record of any unusual persecution during his reign. But the Christian church father Eusebius relates that Diocletian persecuted the Christians. This is hard to explain in view of the fact that the Christians were then still considered to be a Jewish sect. This hatred of Christianity is ascribed to Diocletian by some historians as due not to religious fanaticism but to the realization that the Christians aimed to destroy the ruling religion. He therefore forced them to worship idols and commanded that all Christian churches be closed. From Jewish sources we learn that Diocletian also persecuted the Samaritans in Palestine and forced them to offer sacrifices to Roman idols. It is even said that he forced all the peoples of the empire, with the exception of the Jews, to worship idols and to pour wine before their images. The Samaritans obeyed and since that time the wine of Samaritans was prohibited to Jews as unclean.[20]

The favorable position of the Jews aroused the envy of their neighbors and in order to undermine the friendship of the emperor it was reported to him that the Jews ridiculed his low origin and referred to him as the "swineherd."

A Talmudic legend relates that when Diocletian was a swineherd, the pupils of Rabbi Jehudah N'siah mocked him and even beat him. After he was elected emperor, he remembered the insults that he had borne and when he visited a Palestinian city a few miles from Tiberias, he sent a letter to the Nasi commanding that he appear before him on a Saturday night together with a group of his scholars. The messenger was instructed to deliver the letter on the eve of the Sabbath so that the Nasi would have no opportunity to flee. Heavy punishment was threatened for the Nasi and the scholars should they delay their appearance.

The legend continues that a miracle occurred and the Nasi together with his companions appeared before the emperor on time. A spirit named Antigris carried them to the emperor immediately after the *Havdalah*. When their coming was announced, the emperor declared he would not see them until after they had bathed, and he commanded that a bath be heated for them for seven days and seven nights so that they might die of the heat. But the same spirit cooled the bath before they entered it, and when they finally appeared before the emperor he asked them whether they had allowed themselves to ridicule the emperor because of their assurance that miracles would occur. The scholars replied that the Jews had only ridiculed the swineherd Diocletian and not the emperor Diocletian.[21]

We have noted before that the family of the Nasi was no longer outstanding in scholarship and its religious authority had almost entirely vanished. But the adherence of the people to the dynasty of the Nasi remained steadfast. As long as the Nasi was descended from Hillel, who traced his descent from King David, the people felt their ruler was of the royal house of David whose power was temporarily limited by the Romans. The people considered it to be their duty to provide the needs of the Nasi and to maintain him in the greatest honor. As long as one of the seed of David still lived, their independence was not entirely lost.

The Roman government sought to squeeze as much money as they could out of the Jews and although the Jews avoided the tax collectors as much as possible, for the needs of the Nasi everyone gave as much and even more than was asked. When the Nasi sent his messengers to announce the religious decisions of the Sanhedrin, they were received with great honor and given valuable gifts for the Nasi that he might be able to conduct his office without concern.

When Rabbi Jehudah N'siah I died, Rabbi Jannai Rabbah announced to the academy that all regulations affecting the priests were abrogated for that day and that the priests could participate in the rites for the dead. But when Rabbi Jehudah N'siah II died no such reverence was shown and some of the scholars even allowed themselves to joke at the funeral.[22]

Rabbi Jehudah N'siah II was followed by three N'siim of the house of Hillel concerning whom we would have known nothing were it not for the Christian church father Epiphanos who wrote about them. Epiphanos thus saved the history of these N'siim from oblivion even as Josephus had saved for future generations the chronicle of many of the events that transpired during the time of the Second Temple. Ephiphanos appears to have been born a Jew and he describes the history of the N'siim in the belief that those were the last days of the Jewish faith. In this respect he also resembled Josephus who believed that he was writing the history of a people doomed to extinction.

Rabbi Jehudah N'siah II was followed by his son Rabban Gamaliel V. Rabban Gamaliel was succeeded by Rabbi Jehudah N'siah III who was thirteen generations removed from Hillel. The talmudic records on this Rabbi Jehudah are very meager and his being mentioned together with Rabbi Jeremiah[23] and Rabbi Ami[24] is our only basis for concluding that the reference is to Rabbi Jehudah III. The events mentioned in connection with his name also do not coincide with the period of his predecessors.

Due to the political alignment in Palestine, Rabbi Jehudah III lived in Caesarea where Rabbi Avahu headed the academy. Previous N'siim lived either in Sepphoris or in Tiberias.

But despite the unfavorable political and economic situation of the Jews, the Nasi still occupied an exceptional position and was politically immune. His decisions in religious matters were binding. The Nasi had to assist in the collection of taxes from the Jews and had the right to collect money for the needs of his own household. He also had the right to ordain his disciples and to excommunicate those who joined the Christians.

Until the year 325 C.E. the Christians were considered to be a Jewish sect and they had a large following in the country. Debates between the orthodox and Christian Jews were a common occurrence and both groups sought substantiation for their beliefs in the Bible.

Oppressed by heavy taxes and other political and economic persecutions, the condition of the people grew worse from day to day but their spirit remained unbroken as long as their religious life could continue in its traditional channels. In this respect the situation took a radical turn for the worse with the accession of Constantine to the throne of Rome 306–337 C.E. Constantine embraced Christianity and established it as the state religion. Persecution of the Jews on religious grounds was intensified. The council of the Christian Patriarchs was held at Nicea in 325 C.E. and this gathering severed all bonds with the Jews. The emperor lent his aid to the Christian church in its persecution of all other religions. Constantine II, who ruled together with Emperor Gallus (337–349), revived the policies of Hadrian by not allowing the Jews to practice their religious commandments. Gallus was especially known for his brutality to the Jews. Upon his return from a war in the east he laid waste the southern half of the country, and it seemed that this region with its many educational institutions headed by the disciples of Rabbi Jehudah would never be rebuilt.

Under these circumstances the secular power of the N'siim was reduced to a minimum. The population lost much of its interest in legal matters and devoted itself primarily to *Aggadah* with its fantastic interpretations. The scholars of Palestine lost the creative powers of the previous generations. There was also not much time to devote to such matters, for everyone was attempting to escape from the country. The population became impoverished and Rabbi Levi said: "Years ago when people had money they were interested in the *Mishnah*, *Halakhah*, and Talmud; but now that they are poor they do not want to hear of legal matters and are only interested in blessings and consolation."[25]

The study of the Bible, however, continued. Those who leaned toward Christianity studied it to prove their contentions, and the others studied it to be able to refute the Christians. Thus Rabbi Avahu who was a disciple of Rabbi Jochanan declared: "The people of Palestine study the Bible and are acquainted with all its books, and they can explain every one of its verses because of their constant debate with the *Minim* (Jewish Christians) on the basis of the Bible."[26]

The study of *Halakhah* thus declined and only those who remembered the days of Rabbi Jehudah N'siah I understood it fundamentally. The other scholars were mediocre people and exhibited no penetrating logic. They merely gathered the statements and opinions of the previous generation without analyzing their content and without questioning their validity. They did not seek to solve the problems that arose in their day, nor did they ponder the words of their predecessors. They were satisfied to know the simple meaning of the laws they had received.

The situation was entirely different in Babylonia. There, sophistry was engaged in extensively and for this reason the Palestinians often mocked the Babylonians saying that "there is no study of the Torah that can compare with the study of the Torah in Palestine, and there is no wisdom like the wisdom of Palestine."[27]

Although the Jews of Palestine realized that scholarship was on the decline, they were still proud of their heritage and convinced that the handful of scholars in Palestine outweighed those of Babylonia, they said: "The small group of scholars in Palestine is of greater significance than a large Sanhedrin in a foreign country."[28] Palestine scholars did not allow their pupils to emigrate, and when Rabbi Simeon bar Abba asked Rabbi Chanina bar Chama whether he should go to Babylonia and requested a letter of recommendation, Rabbi Chanina refused to give him such a letter, not wishing to see a promising pupil leave the country.[29]

The increasing lack of interest in *Halakhah* and the difficult situation of the country led to the emigration of many scholars despite the opposition of others. This attitude toward *Halakhah* is illustrated in the following story: "Rabbi Avahu and Rabbi Chiya bar Abba once came to a city where Rabbi Avahu lectured in *Aggadah* and Rabbi Chiya expounded *Halakhah*. All the inhabitants of the city came to hear Rabbi Avahu but Rabbi Chiya had no audience. Rabbi Chiya was greatly hurt and Rabbi Avahu consoled him by saying that few people buy valuable diamonds and pearls but everybody buys cheap toys."[30]

But Palestine still maintained a position of authority. Legal decisions were sent from Palestine to Babylonia[31] touching upon various prohibitions and permissions and also on money matters.[32] No one in Babylonia dared to question the validity of these decisions.[33] The decisions of the Palestine scholars in the matter of determining the date of the new month and of leap years were especially adhered to even after Babylonian scholars had learned to calculate the calendar and could determine these dates without having to wait for word from Palestine that the new moon had been seen.[34]

Thirteen generations after Hillel the Old, another Hillel, the son of Rabbi Jehudah N'siah III, was elected Nasi. Of his activities we only know that in 359 c.e. he finally solved the problem of a calendar by basing it on exact calculations. The new calendar was to be permanent and all holidays were to be determined by it. The book of genealogy lists the following as the last N'siim: Rabbi Hillel II, Rabbi Gamaliel V, Rabbi Jehudah N'siah IV, and Rabbi Gamaliel VI (or Bathra'ah—the last). About sixty years elapsed from the time of Hillel II until Rabbi Gamaliel VI, and this period was a very difficult one since it coincided with the rise of Christianity to power.

The political decline of the Jews began during the reign of Constantine the Great and continued at an accelerating pace. During the first years of his rule Constantine was quite tolerant to the Jews and repealed the limitations imposed by Diocletian. He was then convinced that every man should have the right to choose his own faith and freed the Jewish scholars and all "the servants of the synagogue" from payment of taxes to the government. He recognized the Nasi as the head of the Jewish religious community and teachers of Jewish law were commanded to obey his edicts. But the emperor's liberalism was not of long duration. Soon after he embraced Christianity, he fell under the influence of religious fanatics and was guided by them in his policies toward the Jews. The emperor's religious advisers followed the leadership of Bishop Sylvester of Rome, Bishop Paul of Byzantium, and Bishop Eusebius of Caesarea. It was they who influenced the emperor to believe that the Jews were a cursed and forsaken people condemned to suffering. They insisted that since the emperor had seen the light and had embraced the only true faith, he must abstain from the sin of protecting the Jews.

Constantine then ruled that Jews could not convert others to their faith, and if they did, both parties were to be punished. A free man who embraced Judaism was to lose all his property, and a non-Jewish slave who was circumcised against his will was to be liberated. If a Jew who embraced Christianity was persecuted by other Jews, his tormentors were to be burned at the stake.

All those years of persecution were broken for a brief moment by the short-lived reign of Julian the Apostate who ruled for eighteen months (November 361–June 363). In his struggle against Christianity Julian befriended the Jews. He reduced the burden of taxation, did not allow them to be insulted, and he called the Nasi "Honored friend and brother." In a letter to the Nasi Rabbi Hillel, he promised to improve the condition of the Jews and to permit the rebuilding of the Temple after his return from the war with the Persians.

After Hillel II the post of Nasi was occupied by his son Gamaliel V. The Christian church father Hieronymus relates that Emperor Theodosius the Great who ruled from 378 until 395 took the part of the Nasi against the Roman consul in Palestine, who infringed upon the Nasi's rights, and had him executed.

Rabbi Gamaliel V was succeeded by Rabbi Jehudah N'siah IV. The son of Rabbi Jehudah, Rabbi Gamaliel VI, was the last Nasi. In his time the Roman Empire was divided into two

parts—Eastern Rome with the capital at Constantinople
(395–1453) and Western Rome with its old capital (395–476).
Rabbi Gamaliel (the last) is mentioned in the decrees of
Emperor Honorius (395–424) and of Theodosius II (408–450).

A decree of the year 426 still exists commanding that all
the payments made by the Jews of Palestine to the Nasi should
henceforth be paid to the imperial treasury. This decree was
probably issued at the death of Rabbi Gamaliel VI who died
childless and with him the dynasty of Hillel came to an end.

Thus we find that although the Nasi was recognized by
the government at all times, his significance in the eyes of the
Jews diminished toward the end. In religious matters he was
no longer the highest authority and his political influence with
the Roman officials was negligible. His only important religious
functions were the consecration of the new month, the sending
of messengers to report the appearance of the new moon,
questioning witnesses, and the determination of the holidays
and the leap years. Traditionally all of these had to be determined in the presence of the Great Court in Palestine in order
to be valid.

The Romans frequently seized the messengers who were
sent to announce these matters to the scholars in Babylonia that
was outside the boundaries of the Roman Empire. Whenever
caught, the messengers were hanged and few people volunteered for such dangerous work. Although the Babylonian
scholars could calculate the time of the holidays and the leap
years, they were not allowed by tradition to determine these
occasions on the basis of their calculations. Thus it once
occurred that throughout the month of *Adar*, it was impossible
to send messengers to Babylonia to announce that a leap year
had been declared. Only late in the summer were people found
who were willing to risk their lives on this mission, and the
Babylonian Jews observed the month of *Av* twice in order that
the New Year might coincide with the one celebrated in
Palestine. The messengers were given a coded letter so that in
case they were caught, the Romans should not be able to
understand its contents. The letter read and was interpreted as
follows: "A pair (two witnesses) came from Reketh (Tiberias)

and were caught by the eagle (the Romans) who found in their possession things that are made in Luz (*tzitzit*). Through God's mercy and because of their own merit they escaped in peace (from the hands of the Romans). The descendants of Nachshon (the Nasi who was descended from the tribe of Judah) wanted to decide upon a crescent (declare a leap year), but the Idumean (the Roman) did not permit them. But the men of the assemblies gathered and declared a crescent for the month that Aaron died (the month of *Av*)."[35]

The function of determining new months and leap years lent some prestige to the Nasi and he had to be looked up to as the religious leader. But when Rabbi Hillel II established a permanent calendar, he did away with the last important role of the Nasi. The office of Nasi thus became an empty title. The government looked on the Nasi as a Jewish official, but the Jews could see no use in maintaining the office. Emperor Theodosius issued a decree that "whoever insults the Nasi should be heavily punished." From other sources we may conclude that this decree was aimed primarily at the Jews.

We have previously recounted some of the laws promulgated by Constantine against the Jews, especially in relation to their attitude toward converts to Christianity. When he was informed that the Jews were planning a revolt against Rome, he issued a decree prohibiting them from approaching the gates of Jerusalem. He also exhibited a certain sense of justice in not repealing a previous order that freed scholars and servants of the synagogue from taxes. In 336 he also ruled that Jews who embraced Christianity must not insult nor do harm to their previous coreligionists.

This law was very timely because new converts to Christianity persecuted the Jews, and before the governor or the emperor could redress the problem, much harm had been done. Such was the case of Joseph of Tiberias who was considered one of the scholars of the court of the Nasi. The Nasi trusted him and sent him to gather the offerings of the people. When Joseph came to Cilicia in Asia Minor, it became obvious from his lectures that he was no longer an adherent of Judaism, and the people would pay no attention to him. Joseph then said that he had been thrown into a river and was saved only through a miracle. After he openly embraced Christianity, the priests interceded for him with the emperor and he was placed in charge of the new converts. Making use of the emperor's confidence, Joseph fabricated numerous false stories about the Nasi and he particularly tried to convince the emperor that the Jews were planning a revolt.

The rumor of a planned revolt must have been based on some truth for in 351 another attempt was made to overthrow the Romans. The records of that rebellion, both Jewish and non-Jewish, are very inadequate, but even from these meager sources the following events emerge.

The uprising began in the city of Sepphoris, a natural fortress. The Jews overwhelmed the Roman garrison on a dark night and with the weapons they had seized they attacked other cities and succeeded in capturing Tiberias and Lud. Constantine II (350–361) dispatched several legions to subdue the uprising, and mercilessly persecuted the rebels. Sepphoris was entirely destroyed. Tiberias, Lud, and southern Palestine were laid waste. The pursuit of the rebels continued until they were all wiped out.

The Roman commander Arsikanus was especially severe with the inhabitants of Sepphoris who were forced to hide in the caves about Tiberias. Some of them tried to mask their faces in order not to be recognized, but numerous informers reported them to the authorities.[36]

Because of the great perils that attended the announcement of the new months and leap years, Rabbi Hillel II decided to do away with the traditional procedure and he established a permanent calendar. It was thus no longer necessary to question witnesses concerning the appearance of the new moon nor to send messengers to announce the findings to the Jews of foreign countries. In the matter of holidays, Jews in foreign countries were freed from the decisions of the Great Court in Palestine.

52

THE AGGADAH
AND ITS AUTHORS

THE AGGADIC PART OF THE TALMUD consists of interpretations of Biblical texts as well as legendary and poetic descriptions of historical events insofar as these were not concerned with the law. It was the aim of the *Aggadah* to inspire people to higher moral concepts and to revive their courage during times of oppression.

Throughout the numerous generations of *amoraim* there were many scholars who underestimated the worth of the *Aggadah* and even opposed it. Such opposition, however, remained ineffective. The demands of the people were stronger than scholastic theories. The masses yearned for words of consolation and they eagerly listened to the teachings of the *Aggadah*.

The economic and social pressure resulting from political developments, the constant impoverishment of the people, and the burden of submission to foreign rulers weakened the interest in *Halakhah*. A much more receptive attitude was maintained toward *Aggadah* which nurtured fantasy, and in times of sorrow inspired hope for a brighter future. Even during the brief period when the situation of the Jews of Palestine improved during the reign of Alexander Severus, Rabbi Jehudah, then Nasi, complained of the suffering inflicted by the government that forced him to take the people's last earnings for the payment of taxes. In an attempt to increase its taxes, the Roman government once decreed that Jews should cultivate their fields on the sabbatical year and the scholars had to give their consent, otherwise the people would have been unable to pay their taxes.

But such respites in the long chain of oppression were short-lived and intended to allow the people only a short hiatus to prepare them to bear patiently other decrees that inevitably followed. It is also remarkable that the rich as well as the poor suffered whenever the Romans intensified their oppression. The rich were sentenced to death for not giving all that was asked of them, and the poor met a similar fate for not having anything to give.

All of these facts we learn from casual remarks in the Talmud and the *midrashim* that are attached to various legal opinions. The scholars of that time did not appreciate the importance of recording the events, and when it was remarked that future generations would not know what had occurred, the answer was given that "even if we should want to record everything we could not do so."

Considering the unbearable position of the Jews at that time, it is quite understandable why they thirsted for consoling words and why they so eagerly turned to the *Aggadah*. But the masses were not alone in this respect; their leaders also sought momentary respite from the bitterness of their fate. The *Aggadah* offered them all that. It promised a glorious future for the Jews, it taught them to value their faith, and it assured divine justice and retribution for all the wrongs they were suffering. The *Aggadah* extolled the virtues of the Jewish nation; it listed the virtues of the Torah and of those who adhered to it; it related the events of the past and inspired courage to face the future.

Not all the legends repeated by the scholars were written down and many of them were lost. Others were not concerned with problems of conduct and were considered unimportant. But all those legends that have come down to us are a rich source of ethical maxims and words of wisdom with a definite lesson for every eventuality. In addition they also explain many passages of the Bible that otherwise would remain inexplicable. Some of the legends may appear to be of minor worth today, but this is usually because we do not understand them. Others are based on events of which we have no record or on events we cannot even conceptualize today.

The authors of the *Aggadah* are usually also known as *ra'atan* (teachers of the *Aggadah*). Some of these also engaged in legal discussions and looked to the *Aggadah* as a means of refreshing the minds of their pupils when they showed signs of weariness of its sophistry. There were some scholars who looked at the teachers of *Aggadah* with a lack of respect; they refused to call them "Rabbi" and merely referred to them as "the men of *Aggadah*."

Aside from these purposes, the *Aggadah* also served to protect the Jews from the Christian teachings becoming common at that time. It taught them how to answer and to refute arguments that the Christians had based on the Bible. As long as the Christians were considered a Jewish sect and they preached moral principles that did not threaten the fundamental tenets of the faith, they were tolerated. But when they began to claim that God had repudiated the Torah and for this reason had destroyed the Temple, they became a threat to the Jewish religion. When the Christians sent apostles to win the nations to their faith and these apostles were successful because they repudiated the Sabbath, the laws of cleanliness, and circumcision, the scholars feared that Jews also might be misled.

One must also bear in mind that the Jewish method of interpreting the Bible was also used by many early Christians. The difference consisted in that the *Aggadah* never assumed the authority of law among Jews, while many of the principles of Christianity were founded on such interpretations. Not only Jewish-born Christians but also non-Jews who embraced Christianity used this method of expounding the Old and the New Testaments, and even in their attacks on Jews they based themselves on the texts of the Bible.

The Church father Theophil of Antioch, who was born a non-Jew, thus explained that God was called "Makom" because He contained the whole world within himself, but that the world was too small to be the "Makom" (place) of God. Likewise he said that when the animals were created they were powerless to do any harm, and only the sin of Adam gave them this power. Another time he declared that when God said to Adam "Where art thou?" it might seem that He did not know where Adam was, but in reality His question was to open a dialogue with Adam and to give him an opportunity to repent.

The Church father Origines declared that the *seraphim* the prophet Isaiah saw in heaven were the Messiah and the personification of the Holy Spirit. He also explained the functions of the angels mentioned in Scriptures: Raphael was appointed to heal the sick, Gabriel was in charge of wars, and Michael was in charge of the prayers of man.

Hieronymus, the greatest of the Church fathers, to whom Jews owed a debt of gratitude for preserving the Bible, held forth on the piety of Noah who lived in a generation of wicked men. The passage stating that God created a garden eastward (*mikedem*) of Eden, he explained to indicate that the garden of Eden was created before the rest of the world.

It is pointless to cite any more interpretations of the Christian patriarchs (who were born non-Jews) of the texts of the Bible insofar as they resemble those of the Jewish scholars. It is obvious, however, that most of these interpretations were taken from Jewish sources.

Nearly all Christian teachers attempted to prove their contention from the verse "Let us make man." The use of the plural in this verse, they said, indicated that God consulted with His son when He decided to create man.

Rabbi Shmuel bar Nachmani quoted his teacher Rabbi Jonathan in this matter and said that when Moses had to write this passage in the Torah he said to God: "Lord of the world! Why do you give an opportunity (for others) to claim that You had a partner in the creation of man?" and God answered: "You write as I tell you and those who err shall err."[1]

The Church father Justinus the Martyr once asked a Jew with whom he was debating religious matters: "If the commandment of circumcision is so important in the eyes of God, why did He not impose it on Adam?" The same question was once asked by a *min* (a Jew who embraced Christianity) of Rabbi Oshaiah, and the latter replied: "Why does a man shave the hair on his head but not his beard?" The *min* answered: "Because the hair on a man's head was already growing when he was still a foolish child."

"Why then does one not gouge out his eyes or cut off his hands because they were also with him when he was still foolish?" Rabbi Oshaiah continued, "The truth of the matter is that whatever was created by God during the six days has to be improved. Thus wheat has to be ground before it can be used. Likewise the human body has to be improved."

Outstanding among the teachers of the *Aggadah* was Rabbi Simlai, a disciple of Rabbi Jehudah N'siah I and a friend of Rabbi Jehudah II whom he accompanied on all his travels. He was a constant companion of the Nasi who always relied upon him. Rabbi Simlai loved the *Aggadah* and although most of his statements were lost, we may conclude from the few that remained that his expositions consisted of wise and witty sayings.

Rabbi Simlai said: "God gave Moses 613 commandments; King David reduced them to eleven; the prophet Isaiah reduced the commandments to six; Micah limited them to three, and Amos condensed all 613 into one commandment. Rashi comments that in earlier generations people were very pious and could observe all 613 commandments, but later generations were not so pious, and when it is impossible to observe all the commandments it is necessary to be satisfied with fewer."[2]

Characteristic of the condition of his times is his explanation of the passage in Hosea (2:7), that refers to scholars who shame the Torah with their deeds, such as people who preach that one must not loan money for interest, and yet they do so themselves, that one must not rob, yet they rob others, or that one must not steal, and yet they steal from others.[3]

Rabbi Shmuel bar Nachmani, several of whose *halakhic* opinions are cited in the Talmud, was even greater than Rabbi Simlai in this form of exposition. He loved to compare the virtues of the Jews with those of other peoples, and at the same

time he praised the Torah and its followers. But the moral life
he held to be "even more important than the study of the
Torah." He sought to explain and justify the sins of the leaders
of the nation. He always maintained that the story of these sins
must not be taken literally and those who believed that such
people as Reuben, the son of Jacob, the sons of Eli, or King
David could have sinned, were in error.[4]

Even in legal matters he based his arguments on the
aggadic method of interpretation. Thus he said: "How do we
know that a court need not listen to the defense of one who
incites to idol worshipping? We may learn this from the case of
the snake God cursed for persuading Eve to sin, without even
giving it an opportunity to defend its act."[5] When the *Mishnah*
ruled that during a public fast ashes had to be placed on the
Ark, Rabbi Shmuel bar Nachmani said that it was necessary to
do so in memory of Isaac who allowed himself to be sacrificed
and that God might consider the ashes on the Ark as if they
were those of the ram that Abraham sacrificed instead of his
son.[6]

Another bright star in the firmament of the *Aggadah* was
Rabbi Levi. He lived during the second and third generations of
amoraim in Palestine. The name of his father is unknown to us,
for he is always referred to only by his own name. Like Rabbi
Shmuel bar Nachmani he also found substantiation for legal
decisions in the interpretations of Biblical texts. For a long time
Rabbi Levi was not appreciated among the scholars. His work
then consisted in calling the people to attend the lectures of
Rabbi Jochanan. But once Rabbi Jochanan was late and Rabbi
Levi addressed the audience to fill the time until the arrival of
Rabbi Jochanan. His words were greatly liked and since then he
was allowed to lecture every Saturday in the academy of Rabbi
Jochanan.[7]

Even Rabbi Zeira, who often mocked the "men of
Aggadah," asked his friends and colleagues to attend the
lectures of Rabbi Levi.[8] Rabbi Levi's interpretations followed an
original method and he explained the significance of Biblical
words according to their meaning in other languages, particularly Arabic and Greek. He also employed fables based on the

behavior of men and animals. Thus he related that the lion, the king of the animals, was once angered by his subjects. The animals gathered to decide who should conciliate him and the fox undertook the task. At other times he delivered maxims to guide men in their conduct saying that man should eat according to his income, dress poorer than his income allows, and furnish his home better than his income permits.[9]

Of the verse "If the anointed priest shall sin" he said: "Woe to the city whose doctor is sick and he who has to cure others is himself blind in one eye." He also said: "The heart and the eye are agents of sin. The eye sees and the heart desires."[10]

"Six limbs serve man," he said, "three of these he can control but the other three are outside of his control. Man cannot control his eye, for it sees even against his will. The same is true of the ear that hears even when one does not want to. Likewise the nose smells odors that one does not like. The mouth, on the other hand, can be controlled. It may be used for the study of the Torah or it may be employed in gossip. Man also controls his hand to fulfill commandments with it or to steal. The same is true of the foot that leads man wherever he chooses, either into the synagogue and the academy, or to see forbidden games."[11]

In many of his speeches Rabbi Levi sought to inspire the people with courage to bear all vicissitudes, in the belief that God would avenge them. At times he also hinted that the Jews were themselves to blame for much of their suffering. Thus he said that when Messiah came God would throw the pagans into Gehenna and He would say to them: "Why have you inflicted pain upon my children?" They would then answer: "We would not have inflicted pain upon them if they had not slandered each other."[12]

The passage "A good name is better than precious ointment and the day of death than the day of one's birth" (Ecclesiastes 7:1), Rabbi Levi explained with a parable. Two ships were once on the great sea. One of them was leaving the shore while the other approached it. It was seen that the people on the ship leaving the shore were happy while some of those on the ship nearing the shore were sad. A wise man remarked:

"We see here a strange sight. People who leave the shore should not be happy, for they know not how long they will be at sea and what winds they will encounter, but people who near the shore should be happy in the realization that they have safely reached dry land. It is likewise with the life of man. One should not reckon the years he has lived but rather should he reckon the time that still separates him from death."[13]

Rabbi Levi said: "When God commanded Noah to include two of each kind in the ark, falsehood came and wanted to enter, but Noah said to it: 'You cannot enter, for you have no mate.' Falsehood then went to search for a mate; it met sin and asked whether it would enter the ark. Sin asked what it would receive for doing so, and falsehood promised that everything it would earn it would give to sin. When they left the ark, sin seized everything falsehood had gained, and when falsehood objected, sin reminded it of their compact. Falsehood thereupon said: 'How could you believe that I meant to do as I promised?' "[14]

Another prominent teacher of *Aggadah* was Rabbi Jehudah bar Simeon or Rabbi Jehudah ben Pazi, as he is called in the Jerusalem Talmud. (Sometimes also called Rabbi Jehudah ben Simeon ben Pazi.) Like some other teachers of *Aggadah*, his legal statements in the Talmud are of minor importance. Many of his expositions were not original but repetitions of those of former scholars improved and amplified for the better understanding of his audiences.

Speaking of Adam, Rabbi Jehudah said: "God almost decided to give the Torah through Adam and He thought: 'This man whom I created and who is not of woman born, should I give the Torah through him?' He immediately decided not to and said: 'I gave one commandment to this man not to eat of the fruit of the tree of knowledge and he failed to obey me. How then can I give him the Torah with its 613 commandments?' "[15]

Another time Rabbi Jehudah said: "Adam was destined to live forever. Why then was he condemned to die? To inspire people with the fear of God."[16]

Rabbi Jehudah bar Simeon sought to introduce such novel interpretations into the texts of the Bible as would surprise the hearer by their originality and their wondrous nature. Of the passage in Genesis, "And the earth was without form and void," he said that "without form" referred to Adam who was as nothing after he sinned and "void" referred to Cain who voided the act of creation by killing Abel. "Darkness" referred to the generation of Enosh. "The face of the deep" referred to the generation of the deluge. God's words "Let there be light" referred to Abraham; "and God called the light day" referred to Jacob; the evening referred to Esau and the morning to Jacob. "One day" referred to the Day of Atonement that God gave to Israel.[17]

Telling of Sarah and the miracles that occurred to her, Rabbi Jehudah declared that many other childless women bore children at the time that Sarah gave birth to Isaac; the blind regained their sight and the deaf their hearing and many foolish men gained wisdom."[18]

Rabbi Jehudah referred to the political situation of the Jews on numerous occasions but he could not speak openly on this subject and limited himself to vague references to the oppressors. "The devouring fire" spoken of by Isaiah (33:4) he explained to mean the enemies of the Jews who would burn the world and all of humanity if they could.[19] On the same subject he also said: "The Jews say to God: 'How many decrees have been enacted against us to make us turn away from your holy name but they were to no avail, for we still come to Your synagogues and academies to announce to the whole world twice each day that You are our only God.'"[20]

Once Rabbi Jehudah was asked concerning the Trinity and the verse of Zachariah (13:8) that "it shall come to pass that in all the land two parts therein shall be cut off and die but the third shall be left therein." Some Christians explained this verse to indicate that those people who believed in two kinds of gods, such as the Persians who believed in a god of light and a god of darkness, shall perish and only those who believed in the Trinity would be saved. Rabbi Jehudah agreed with them concerning the Persians but the "third" he explained as referring to the Jews who are made up of three groups (Priests, Levites, and Israelites) and who praise God by thrice saying *kadosh*.[21]

With exaggerated love Rabbi Jehudah bar Simeon spoke of the Jews and said: "A king once had an orchard in which there grew figs, vines, pomegranates, and apples. The king leased the orchard and went away. Sometime later the king returned to see how his orchard was thriving, and he found it full of thorns and weeds. In great anger he called men and commanded them to cut down the trees, but when he looked closely between the thorns, he noticed a beautiful rose. He bent over it, inhaled its fragrance and said: 'Because of this rose I will save the whole orchard.' "

Such was also the case with the world. Twenty-six generations after the creation of the world God saw that its conduct was bad and He decided to annihilate it. But among the thorns He saw a rose, the Jews, who accepted the ten commandments and for their sake He spared the whole world.[22]

The passage "after God you shall follow" Rabbi Jehudah questioned and said: "How can one imagine people following God who makes a way in the sea and a path in mighty waters? How can one cling to the *Shekhinah* which is made of fire and surrounded by a river of fire? This can only mean that one should imitate the deeds of God. When He created man He immediately planted a garden in Eden, where Adam was. For this reason the Jews were also commanded to plant trees when they came to Palestine."[23]

Rabbi Jehudah further said: "Of three places in Palestine the pagans cannot say that the Jews have taken without paying: the cave of Machpelah, the Temple, and the grave of Joseph. The Bible expressly states that Abraham bought the cave of Machpelah for four hundred silver shekels. The site of the Temple was bought by David from the Jebusite for six hundred golden shekels, and of the grave of Joseph it is said that Jacob bought a plot of land from the sons of Chamor for one hundred *kesitah*."[24]

Another prominent aggadist was Rabbi Jose ben Chalafta who was also an authority in *Halakhah* and who strove to eliminate the differences between the school of Shammai and the school of Hillel. He expressed a wish that his share in the life to come should be among those who eat three meals on the Sabbath, who praise God daily, who pray at sunrise, who die of intestinal trouble or on their way to fulfill a commandment, who greet the Sabbath in Tiberias and end it in Sepphoris, who seat their pupils in the academy and do not let them stand, who are in charge of charities but not participate in their distribution so that no suspicion is directed against them.[25]

In their persecution of the Jews, the Romans sought to prevent them from resting on the Sabbath. Rabbi Jose therefore said that "he who observes the Sabbath joyfully, him will God give boundless rewards." Fasting was prohibited on the Sabbath but the persecutions were such that people often had no opportunity to eat on that day and Rabbi Jose said: "He who fasts on the Sabbath will be forgiven all the sins of his seventy years. Nevertheless, he will also be punished for disobeying the commandment that one must enjoy himself on that day."[26]

Rabbi Jose's opinions of prophecy was unusual. "All the prophets," he said, "spoke they knew not what, for the spirit of prophecy spoke out of them, and the prophets did not say what they themselves wanted to say. The only ones who did know what they said were Moses and Isaiah."[27] His appreciation of the greatness of God was also expressed in his statement that were all the scholars of the world to attempt to create the smallest creature, they would not be able to inspire it with the breath of life.[28]

It appears that some gentile scholars asked why God did not choose as sacrificial animals those that symbolized His greatness. Rabbi Jose replied that God purposely chose the hunted, and not the preying animals, as sacrifices. The ox runs away from the lion; the goat flees the tiger; the sheep flees the wolf. God chose to honor the hunted animals in order to show his love for the weak.[29]

Prayers had already supplanted sacrifices at that time and many people apparently did not pray in the belief that if God had desired prayers He would not have allowed the Temple to be destroyed. Rabbi Jose then declared that God also prayed. He arrived at this conclusion from the verse of Isaiah "I will make them joyful in my house of prayer" (56:7). The use of the words "my house of prayer" instead of "their house of prayer," Rabbi Jose held to be proof that God also prayed.[30]

"It sometimes occurs," Rabbi Jose said, "that a man prays

to God to help him because of his merit, and God heeds his prayer because of the merit of others; or a man prays to be aided because of the merit of others, and God aids him because of his own merit. Thus we find that Moses prayed to God to remember the merit of the fathers, but his wish was fulfilled because of his own merit. King Hezekiah prayed to God to aid him on his own merit, but God aided him because of the merit of King David."[31]

Another prominent aggadist was Rabbi Simeon ben Jozadak. Some are of the opinion that there were two people with this name because references in the Talmud to this man concern events occurring over a period of several generations. We may be justified in assuming, however, that there was only one man because the name Jozadak is rare and appears only once in the Bible and in the Talmud. Any discrepancies that have arisen may be ascribed to errors of the copyists.

Two of his statements deal with the honor due to scholars, and with the Torah that confers eternal life upon its followers. One of these states that "any scholar who is not vengeful as a snake is not a scholar."[32] The other statement says: "Every word that is quoted in the name of a scholar causes the lips of its author to move in the grave."[33] He also said: "A letter may be omitted from the Torah if in this manner the name of God will be publicly honored."[34]

Aside from the teachers of *Aggadah* who were already named there were other *amoraim* who devoted themselves to it. Rabbi Berachiah, a disciple of Rabbi Simeon ben Gamaliel, said of the creation of the world: "When God wanted to create man he foresaw that both good and wicked men would be descended from him. He then thought: 'If I will create man, he will have wicked descendants, but if I am not to create him how will there be just men?' God then removed the ways of the wicked from his view and donning the 'measure of pity' He created man."[35]

More interesting is Rabbi Berachiah's interpretation of the verse "Blessed is he whose transgression is forgiven" (Psalms, 32:1). He said: "Happy is he who can rise above sin and not that sin should rise above him."[36]

53

RABBI JOCHANAN, COMPILER OF THE JERUSALEM TALMUD

THE LIFE OF THIS PROMINENT *amora* consisted of an unbroken chain of misfortunes. His parents he did not know, for his father had died before Jochanan was born and his mother died during his birth.[1] When he came of age and married, Rabbi Jochanan became the father of ten sons all of whom died before him. Rabbi Jochanan then carried about the tooth of his tenth son who had died and pointed out on all occasions that "this is a bone of my dead tenth son."[2]

The occupation of Rabbi Jochanan's father was hinted at when Rabbi Jochanan was called "the son of the blacksmith."[3] Since his father died before his birth, Rabbi Jochanan lived with his grandfather, who made him the pupil of Rabbi Simeon bar Eleazar.[4]

Rabbi Jochanan was gifted by nature with the highest physical and spiritual qualities. He possessed deep understanding exceeding that of others and he was renowned for his beauty.[5] His diligence was also uncommon and love of the Torah filled his whole being. Only once did he forsake study of the Torah when his friend Ilfa, who was older and probably better educated than Rabbi Jochanan, suggested that they engage in a partnership business. However, this venture did not last long, and Rabbi Jochanan soon realized that it was undesirable to leave the permanent values of the Torah for the transitory gains of commerce. He then parted with his friend Ilfa and returned to the academy.[6]

The years of Rabbi Jochanan's youth coincided with the period of the last *tannaim* and he often told of how in his early youth he attended the academy of the Nasi Rabbi Jehudah where he sat seventeen rows behind Rav (Abba Arecha) and listened to the debates between the two when their words flew like coals of fire, but which he could not understand because of his unripe age.[7]

Later Rabbi Jochanan became a pupil of Rabbi Jannai Rabbah,[8] but also attended the lectures of Rabbi Chanina bar Chama.[9] When he began to lecture in the academy of Rabbi Bana'ah, Rabbi Chanina pronounced a benediction and praised God that he had been allowed to see the fruit of his labor.[10] But even after he already ranked among the scholars, Rabbi Jochanan still heeded the words of older scholars and for a period of thirteen years often attended the lectures of Rabbi Oshaiah in Caesarea.[11]

It can be seen then that Rabbi Jochanan was ready to learn from everyone, but the foundation of his learning was the *Mishnah* of the Nasi Rabbi Jehudah. The *Mishnah* he considered as his highest authority and he often repeated that "I have nothing but the *Mishnah*."[12] He considered every word of the *Mishnah* to be holy and he believed that nothing could be added or subtracted from it.[13]

Rabbi Jochanan weighed and analyzed every word in the *Mishnah* just as other scholars had done with the text of the Torah. Statements of earlier scholars were sacred in his eyes and he said, "The hearts of earlier scholars were as wide as the gate of a palace"[14] and "The least fingernail of an earlier scholar was of greater worth than the whole body of the later ones."[15]

He delved as well in antiquities and no other *amora* ever strove as hard as he did to retain for later generations all the old traditions and what they signified. He therefore said: "Whatever is written in the *Mishnah* has been commanded to Moses from Mount Sinai."[16]

Many customs of that time were considered by the other

scholars to have been originated by the *sofrim* for various purposes, and any man who broke one of these customs was said merely to have transgressed a rabbinic commandment. But Rabbi Jochanan declared that even such customs as those regulating the quantity of matter in the use of certain articles[17] or the customs of beating willow branches and pouring water during the feast of *Sukkot* were laws given to Moses on Mount Sinai.[18] Likewise he declared that the biblical prohibition against eating the first fruit of trees was also mandatory outside of Palestine as a Mosaic law.[19] It is also characteristic that he always spoke highly of the rabbinical commandments because he considered all of these to be part of the same sacredness as the biblical commandments,[20] and in this connection he said: "The words of the scholars are very near to the words of the Torah, and often they are even more loved by the people than the words of the Torah."[21]

Aside from his great learning Rabbi Jochanan was also renowned for his moral qualities equalled by few others. Because of his love for learning he despised wordly advantage, and he preferred a life of suffering if only he would not be disturbed in the sacred work. From his father, or from his grandfather, he inherited a small field between Sepphoris and Tiberias, and even this he sold in order to be free from mundane cares.

The death of his sons he suffered patiently and he found consolation in his studies. He was kind to all, even to his slave whom he gave meat to eat and wine to drink. When he was asked why he treated his slave so well he replied: "The slave was born in the same manner that I was born."[22]

But although he led a pious life he believed that for the welfare of the community, or even for that of an individual, it was permissible to depart from the strict letter of the law. It was thus related that, weak from hunger, he once ate food without ascertaining whether it was clean. Another time he ruled that it was permissible to desecrate the Sabbath to save the life of a sick man who would later live to observe many Sabbaths.[23] He also appeared indifferent to the people's painting various images on the walls of their houses under the influence of their

Greek neighbors, although this was against the injunction of the Bible not to make any graven images.[24]

He was likewise tolerant in his interpretation of biblical passages. Thus he explained that the injunction not to let "thy brother's ox or his sheep go astray" (Deut. 22) applied even to the possessions of one who had renounced Judaism.[25] He also sought to modify the rule that forbade Jews to eat the flesh of an animal slaughtered by a Samaritan, if the slaughter was carried out in the presence of a Jew who could testify that it had been performed according to law. It was said that even Rabbi Jochanan once ate such flesh.[26]

Due to the difficult political and economic circumstances of the country, many sought to emigrate and settle in neighboring lands. In an attempt to stem the tide of emigration, the Talmudic teachers declared that any scholar who left the country to settle in a foreign land was to be excluded from their society. Rabbi Jochanan, on the other hand, was opposed to this measure.[27]

As an example of his tolerance, Rabbi Jochanan also preached patience toward sinners. This was especially true in the case of relations with the Romans. The Romans showed contempt for the Jews and the latter repaid them with the same measure. Since the Romans ridiculed Jewish wisdom and learning, the Jews underestimated the value of the gentile sciences. It was then that Rabbi Jochanan declared that God had granted a share of wisdom to the gentile nations, and it was therefore possible for them to say wise things.[28]

He shared the reverence of other *amoraim* for the scholars and he often said that they were the "master builders" of the world.[29] He expressed a similar sentiment when he said that "the Torah was like a fortress about the Jewish people and the scholars were its bastions."[30] This was only true, he added, when a scholar served the Torah with all his might and renounced all worldly interests for the sake of spiritual interests,[31] when he ignored all earthly gain,[32] and when he did not desecrate the honor of the Torah by vain pride.[33] Only one who possessed these qualities could, in Rabbi Jochanan's opinion, be considered a "master builder" of the world and a worthy guardian of the Torah. Such a man could be compared to a myrtle growing in the desert.[34]

And when Rabbi Jochanan thought that he had not sufficiently stressed the worth of the Torah, he added that even a bastard, who according to law could not be admitted into a Jewish family until the tenth generation—even he, if he is a scholar—is more important than an ignorant High Priest.[35]

The contemporaries of Rabbi Jochanan also gave preference to the rich, and of this attitude he said: "Not wealth nor noble descent are the measure of a man's worth, but only his knowledge of the Torah."[36]

Patiently he suffered misfortune and without complaint he bore his poverty, but he could not brook opposition to his opinions, and he could easily become an enemy of one who opposed him in these. While he was still in Sepphoris, he could not tolerate the *amora* Rabbi Chanina bar Chama who disagreed with him. When he realized that he would never convince Rabbi Chanina of his own correctness, he left Sepphoris and settled in Tiberias.[37] Rabbi Jochanan also clashed with his pupil Rabbi Eleazar ben Pedat who refrained from quoting his name when he repeated his opinions.[38] Rabbi Jochanan then said: "Whatever Rabbi Eleazar says he probably heard from me."[39]

Once Rabbi Eleazar repeated a law he had heard from Rabbi Chanina concerning the share of a firstborn son in the inheritance of his father. Rabbi Jochanan then remarked: "It is strange that during all the years I sat at the feet of Rabbi Oshaiah, I have not heard this law." In saying this he meant to hint that Rabbi Eleazar quoted Rabbi Oshaiah in order to lend weight to his own opinion. To this Rabbi Eleazar replied: "Why is it strange? It is a common matter that one should hear something from his master that another has not heard."[40]

But most characteristic of Rabbi Jochanan were his relations with his brother-in-law, Rabbi Simeon ben Lakish. Rabbi Simeon was a devoted friend of Rabbi Jochanan who often boasted that he introduced him into the mysteries of the Torah. Nevertheless he would tolerate no disagreement on his part and whenever Rabbi Simeon opposed him, Rabbi Jochanan complained that "even the members of my own family are against me."[41]

However, these shortcomings of Rabbi Jochanan were overlooked by the people who saw only his great achievements toward increasing the worth and the influence of the Torah, and his own importance grew in their eyes as a result of his efforts. Rabbi Oshaiah, who was probably the head of the academy in Tiberias, died meanwhile and Rabbi Jochanan succeeded to this office. Hosts of disciples then flocked to him and his name became known throughout the land, even as far as Babylonia.

Rabbi Jochanan showed great reverence for the scholars of Babylonia and he was angered when he heard them slighted. His words were also held in great respect in that country and it was sufficient for him only to inform them what the law was and his opinion was accepted.[42] Rabbi Chisda was the only one in Babylonia who dared to disagree with Rabbi Jochanan, and he declared that even if he were to receive instructions from Rabbi Jochanan he would disobey them.[43] On another occasion, while disputing with a disciple of Rabbi Jochanan, he similarly questioned: "Who heeds you or your master Rabbi Jochanan?"[44]

Rav (Abba Arecha) and Shmuel (Yarchina'ah) were at that time the heads of the academies in Babylonia. When Rabbi Jochanan addressed messages to that country, he always wrote to Rav as "our teacher in Babylonia." But after the death of Rav he refused to recognize Shmuel as an authority in legal matters and in his letters addressed him as "our friend in Babylonia." Shmuel was offended by this attitude and as proof of his authority in *Halakhah* he sent to Rabbi Jochanan a calculation of the seasons and a calendar of leap years for sixty years. But Rabbi Jochanan said that one may be an expert in reckoning the seasons and yet not be an authority in *Halakhah*. Shmuel then sent him "thirteen camels" (?) laden with questions pertaining to the laws of cleanliness and only then did Rabbi Jochanan exclaim: "There is a teacher in Babylonia."[45]

Rabbi Jochanan found a staunch adherent in Rabbi

Jehudah N'siah I, the grandson of Rabbi Jehudah. Rabbi Jehudah realized that the needs of his office as well as his personal benefit required such an attitude, and knowing Rabbi Jochanan's sensitive nature in everything that touched his personal honor, the Nasi refrained from offending him in any manner. The Nasi also supported Rabbi Jochanan with the authority of his office and provided for all his needs.[46] The power of the Nasi was then still great enough to enable him to enforce his regulations with the aid of the government. This power greatly aided Rabbi Jochanan in putting his religious regulations into effect.

Rabbi Jochanan particularly strove to impress upon the people the significance of prayers that had been introduced some time before, but apparently were now neglected. Everybody realized that since the destruction of the Temple prayers had come to take the place of sacrifices. It therefore became necessary that a man of Rabbi Jochanan's authority should establish the proper significance of prayers.

Rabbi Jochanan then declared that "he who wears phylacteries, pronounces the *Shema*, and recites his prayers, is like one who has built an altar and has offered a sacrifice."[47] He also ruled that every man should pray in a place specially appointed for this purpose,[48] for "whoever establishes a special place where he recites his prayers, his enemies shall fall before his feet, and when a congregation prays together it is a time when God is ready to fulfill the wishes of the supplicants."[49] When a man is told to be the messenger of the congregation, he is not told: "Go and pray for us!" but rather he should be told: "Go and offer a sacrifice for us, pray for our needs, and fight our battles!"[50]

Rabbi Jochanan was a pupil of Rabbi Jehudah in his early youth. In his later years he paid tribute to his master by saying that he would never have reached his position as a scholar if he "had not seen Rabbi Jehudah's finger portruding from under his mantle."[51]

Regarding Rabbi Jochanan's birth there exists a legend that on the Day of Atonement a pregnant woman was seized with a great craving for food. Rabbi Jehudah was consulted and he suggested that the woman be reminded that it was the Day of Atonement. When this was done, her craving for food vanished and she completed her fast. This woman was said to be the mother of Rabbi Jochanan.[52]

Rabbi Jochanan was raised in the house of his grandfather and partly in the home of the Nasi who prophesied that he would someday be a teacher among Jews.[53] He survived all his comrades and even the grandson of Rabbi Jehudah. Since he lived until the fourth generation of *amoraim*, he witnessed the decline of the Nasi and the loss of his prestige.

It is told that whenever Rabbi Jochanan was immersed in his studies, he was not aware of what transpired about him. Thus he once sat before the synagogue in Sepphoris engaged in his studies. A high Roman official happened to pass by, but Rabbi Jochanan did not notice him and did not accord him his honors. The servants of the official were ready to attack Rabbi Jochanan, but the Roman prevented them from doing so, for he understood that it was not out of lack of respect that the honor was denied to him.[54]

Rabbi Jochanan was a strong and stout man.[55] As he was once ascending some stairs, supported by Rabbi Ami and Rabbi Asi, the stairs caved in under his weight and his two disciples carried him up in their arms. The scholars then asked him: "If you are so strong, why do you lean on others?" Rabbi Jochanan replied: "I must spare my strength for my old age."[56]

But above all Rabbi Jochanan was gifted with great beauty.[57] It was also remarkable that he was beardless and once as he was once bathing in the river a passerby mistook him for a woman and waded after him into the water.[59] The Talmud further relates that Rabbi Jochanan himself declared: "I am the only one of the beautiful men remaining in Jerusalem." When people spoke of his beauty, they said: "If one would have some conception of the beauty of Rabbi Jochanan, he must take a silver beaker just out of the hands of the silversmith and fill it with red flowers; he should then surround it with a wreath of red roses and place it between the sun and the shade; the reflection of the beaker on the ground will then resemble the beauty of Rabbi Jochanan."

His diligence in his studies so weakened Rabbi Jochanan that he could not wear the phylacteries all day. During the winter he wore phylacteries on arm and head, but during the summer when his head felt weak he merely wore the phylacteries on his arm. But in order that others should not copy his example, he explained to his disciples that it was only due to his weakness that he took these liberties.[59]

Of all the books of the Bible, Rabbi Jochanan preferred the Book of Job and after each reading he exclaimed: "Death is the end of man; slaughter is the end of animals; all that exists is doomed to die. Happy is he who was raised in the Torah and who devoted his efforts to it. Such a person brings joy to his Creator when his good name grows and when he leaves the world with a fair name."[60]

Rabbi Jochanan's attitude toward prayer has already been noted and his insistence that people should pray in congregations. To this he added that when God comes into a synagogue and does not find a *minyan* of ten Jews He is angered thereby."[61]

Whenever Rabbi Jochanan finished his prayers, he concluded with the following words: "May it be Thy will, oh Lord our God, that You should see our shame and observe our plight and that You should don Your great mercy and cover Yourself with Your strength and wrap Yourself with Your righteousness and gird Yourself with Your forgiveness and may the measure of Your goodness and Your modesty come before You."[62]

Rabbi Jochanan is also said to have shown respect to every person and whenever he saw an old man, he rose before him even if the man was of another faith. He would then say: "So much suffering the man withstood and if in spite of all he lived to old age, he deserves that honor be accorded to him."[63]

But his attitude toward the scholars of Babylonia was contradictory. The political and economic situation of Palestine had resulted in the establishment of a Jewish center in Babylonia. The might of the Romans broke at the gates of Babylonia, and the Jews enjoyed numerous liberties in that country. When young men came from Babylonia to study in the

academy of Rabbi Jochanan, he befriended them, but nevertheless sometimes allowed himself to make fun of them. When
asked why he did so, Rabbi Jochanan replied: "The prophet
Hosea allowed himself to mock the Jews of the foreign lands
when he said that they are despised in the eyes of God who
exiled them to foreign lands for their disobedience. Then why
should I not allow myself the same?"[64]

But Rabbi Jochanan's mockery was good-natured in character. This, for instance, was the case while he was explaining
some passages to one of his pupils but realized that the latter
did not understand what he was told. He then asked him:
"Why can't you understand what I am teaching you?" The
pupil replied: "It is because I am exiled from my home."

"And where is your home?" Rabbi Jochanan further
asked.

"In Bursif," the pupil replied.

"Oh, in Bulsif!" Rabbi Jochanan mocked, for the Babylonians pronounced the letter r with difficulty.

Another time he remarked to his pupil Rabbi Chiya bar
Abba: "How could you become interested in learning in
Babylonia, where you were always busy eating dates?"[65]

On the same subject he also said: "Even if all the Jews had
returned from Babylonia together with Ezra, the *Shekhinah*
would still not have rested on the Second Temple, for the
Babylonian Jews suffered from the biblical curse that God had
given them a heart full of unrest which would not calm even
with their returning to Palestine."[66]

But Rabbi Jochanan also had kind words to say about
Babylonia. Thus he explained the name Babylonia to mean
"varied" or "confused" and he pointed out that the Jews of
Babylonia engaged in the study of all branches of the Torah
such as Scriptures, *Mishnah* and *Gemara*.[67]

Frequently he would say: "Why did God choose to exile
the Jews to Babylonia? This may be compared to a man who is
angered with his wife and sends her away from his house; he
then sends her to her mother's house. God did likewise with
the Jews; He exiled them to the land whence their mothers
came."[68]

The political situation of that time is mirrored in the sayings of Rabbi Jochanan. Whenever the scholars wanted to discuss this problem, they generally did so by speaking of the time of the coming of Messiah. In analyzing their discourse a clear picture of the events of that time begins to emerge. These discussions also served to revive the courage of the people in the face of their misfortunes which were explained to be the "pains of Messiah" preceding the redemption. Hundreds of statements by Rabbi Jochanan reveal to us the conditions of his time and his philosophy of life which is of worth for all times.

"In the generation that will mark the coming of Messiah," Rabbi Jochanan said, "scholars will diminish and all men will sigh with sorrow. There will be many misfortunes and numerous evil decrees will be promulgated daily; before one decree can be enforced, another one will be enacted."[69]

When Rabbi Jochanan told the story of Jacob waiting for Esau and who meanwhile prayed to God: "Spare me from the hand of my brother, from the hand of Esau," he remarked: "Such is the way of an evil kingdom when it desires to seize the property of men; it appoints one to be an overseer and another to be tax collector. All this is done in order to take away from the people that which they possess."[70]

It is also related that Rabbi Jochanan never smiled and that he was always sorrowing. He declared: "One must never laugh as long as the Jews are in exile, and the promise that the gentile nations will see the miracles that have been performed for the Jews has not yet been fulfilled."[71]

His reverence for the Torah has been stated many times. In this category belong his statements that "The Torah clings to that person who in his modesty acts as if he did not exist at all,"[72] and "If one has learned much but does not observe the commandments, it would have been better had he not been born."[73]

"Out of reverence for the Torah," he said, "it is a shame for a scholar to go about in patched shoes, and it is a sin punishable by death for a scholar to go about in a soiled garment."[74]

The praise which he expressed for prayer in congregations, he somewhat modified in his old age when due to weakness, he often wore only the phylacteries of the arm and he said: "Whoever prays at home is like one who has surrounded his prayer with an iron wall."[75]

Rabbi Jochanan had ten sons, all of whom died during his lifetime. In order to console him, one of the scholars said that God will forgive the sins of one who buries his sons during his lifetime. But Rabbi Jochanan denied this and said that "sickness and the death of children are not a punishment that God visits upon a person out of love,"[76] but rather it is true that "he who leaves no sons to inherit from him, has incurred God's anger."[77] He believed instead that exile, iniquity, the hardships of wandering, and discontent are conditions that pardon man's sins.[78]

Various authorities of his time forbade the writing down of Talmudic legends, but Rabbi Jochanan declared that one who studies the legends from a book will not forget them so readily.[79] In another instance he inveighed against writing down the *Halakhah* and said that "whoever writes down the laws is like one who has burned the Torah, and he who studies law from a book will receive no reward."[80]

During the numerous clashes between the Romans and the Parthians who ruled in Babylonia, Rabbi Jochanan always hoped for a Parthian victory, and he often repeated the statement (credited to Rabbi Jehudah) that the Romans would in the end be vanquished by the Parthians.[81]

This statement he further amplified by reasoning: "If the First Temple that was built by Jews and destroyed by the Chaldeans, caused the Chaldeans to be conquered by the Persians; the Second Temple that was built by Persians and destroyed by Romans, would certainly cause the Romans to be conquered by the Persians."

Rav (Abba Arecha), on the other hand, looked forward to a Roman victory. But neither the Romans nor the Parthians were victorious for the Persian *Chabarim* (Zoroastrians) took over the government of Babylonia. When Rabbi Jochanan heard of this all his hopes were crushed.[82]

A period of turbulence and upheaval at that time affected

all the countries where Jews lived. After the death of Alexander Severus, Rome underwent a period of unrest and changed emperors rapidly. In Babylonia a prince of the house of Sassan, named Ardeshir (or Artachshaster) revolted against Artaban, the last of the Parthian dynasty. The struggle in Babylonia was more of a religious nature. Artaban had been favorably inclined toward the Greek form of worship that had come into the country and the population revolted against the innovation. The rebel Artachshaster therefore established a new dynasty in place of the old one that had ruled the country for 466 years.

The new rulers of Babylonia, historically known as the Sassanides, are referred to in Jewish writings as *Chabarim.* These were worshippers of fire and believed in a dual deity of light and darkness. Zealously they persecuted all who refused their teachings and were especially vengeful toward the Greeks and Christians. The Jews also met with suffering, but they were not persecuted with such fury as were the Greeks and Christians. The latter were offered a choice between acceptance of the law of Zoroaster or emigration. Those who stubbornly clung to their beliefs were executed.

Jews were deprived of the right to judge in cases affecting life but as long as they remained neutral to the dominant religion they were somewhat tolerated. This attitude was not a result of openmindedness but rather due to the fact that the Jews offered a great resistance to the *Chabarim.* Since they lived in Babylonia in compact masses, it was difficult to subdue them.

The affliction of the Jews under this new rule could nevertheless easily compare with their plight under the Romans. They remained undisturbed in their religious life only as long as they did not use fire for any purpose. When they lit candles on the Sabbath eve or on *Hanukah*, these had to be hidden and anyone caught keeping fire in his house was condemned to death.

The Jews of Palestine at that time felt that *their* plight was unbearable, but the Jews of Babylonia were convinced that conditions in Palestine were more favorable. When the news of these developments reached Palestine, Jews there began to say that the Romans were honorable men even in their oppression while the *Chabarim* were no more than barbarians.

When Rabbi Jochanan became convinced that no help would come from Babylonia, he began to look for aid from Tiberias, the last home of the Sanhedrin.[83] In order to encourage the people and persuade them to remain in the country, he declared that God said: "I cannot enter the heavenly Jerusalem until I have come to Jerusalem on earth,"[84] or "he who walks four ells in Palestine is certain of his share in life to come."[85]

Another time he said: "What good deeds had Omri, king of Israel, done that he merited the crown? It was because he added the city of Samaria to the kingdom of Israel."[86]

Regarding the old age of Rabbi Jochanan, it is told that for a period of three-and-a-half years he did not come to the academy out of grief for his brother-in-law who had died.[87] When he realized that his own death was approaching, he instructed those who were to bury him that he be interred in a shroud that was neither black nor white. For if he were buried in a black shroud he might, at the resurrection, come to life among just men and he would be put to shame. Likewise if he were buried in a white shroud, he might come to life among wicked men and he would be shamed by the garment of a just man.[88]

He apparently lived to a ripe old age. The *Epistle* of Rav Sherira Gaon declares that he survived Rabbi Jehudah Hanasi by 68 years and that he died in the year 279 C.E.

Aside from the statements of Rabbi Jochanan quoted so far in connection with various times of his life, many expressions also exist that are concerned with the interpretation of biblical passages. Although most of these are of value only in exposition, some of them contain important philosophic observations concerning the conduct of men and the ways of the world.

At a certain period of Rabbi Jochanan's life, it was forbidden for Jews to determine the month through lunar observation, and the Romans were especially strict in preventing them from celebrating their holidays, but at the same time they did not interfere with their observance of the Sabbath. Under the influence of Rabbi Jochanan, the court in Tiberias therefore decided to observe the Day of Atonement on a Sabbath, although it really was to occur on a weekday, in order to deceive the Romans. The exact date of this occurrence is unknown, as is the duration of this decree. One can only guess under whose administration this took place, for only hints are given.[89] Historians are equally confused as to the exact date and the motive that prompted Rabbi Jochanan to instruct the Jews of Babylonia also to observe the Day of Atonement on a Sabbath, although the latter were not under Roman rule and could have celebrated the Day of Atonement in its proper time. A possible explanation of this is hinted at in the statement of Rabbi Jochanan who said that the angels gather about God and ask: "When is the New Year and when is the Day of Atonement?" and God answers them: "Why do you ask me? Let us go to the court on earth and find out."[90] By this statement Rabbi Jochanan meant to imply that the court in Tiberias had the complete right to determine holidays as it saw fit under the circumstances.

The following is a similar statement concerning the determination of holidays. If the court had said that today is the New Year, then God says to the angels: "Erect a platform and let the prosecutor and the defense appear before me, for my children have said that today is the New Year and so it shall be." If the court decided to postpone the New Year until the following day, then God says to the angels: "Take this platform away and remove the prosecutor and the defense for my children have postponed the New Year until the following day, and so it shall be."

Rabbi Jochanan was always poor even when he headed the academy and he received assistance from the Nasi. He then said: "When one depends on the charity of men, the color of his face changes to pale blue." In general we may assume that it was very difficult to earn a livelihood at that time from his statement that "It is difficult to earn a livelihood, twice as difficult as the pains of a woman in childbirth, more difficult than the arrival of the redemption."[91]

It appears that it was customary at the time for city people to do the work of the scholars that resided there. When Rabbi

Jochanan was asked how great a scholar one must be to deserve such a service from his townsmen, he replied: "Only a scholar who renounces all worldly occupations and devotes himself solely to heavenly matters deserves this service; the obligation rests on the people to provide him only with his daily bread but not with luxuries."[92]

He added: "One should eat an onion and sit in the shade, and not eat geese and hens so that his heart should not lust after such food."[93]

There are grounds to assume that he also believed in hypnotism and in the ability of a person to convince himself that he was in a healthy or a sickly state. Thus it is told that when Rabbi Chama bar Abba fell sick, Rabbi Jochanan came to visit and asked him: "Do you accept your suffering with love?" by which he meant that suffering atones for the sins of man who enters the world to be absolved of wrong doing. But the sick man replied: "I do not want the suffering nor its reward." "Then give me your hand," Rabbi Jochanan said. Rabbi Chama gave him his hand and he was healed.

Another version of this story relates that Rabbi Jochanan came to visit Rabbi Eleazar ben Pedat who had fallen sick, and he found him lying in a dark room. Rabbi Jochanan then bared his arm which illuminated the room and he saw that Rabbi Eleazar was weeping. "What is the cause of your weeping?" he asked. "Is it because you have not studied as much as you had wanted to? We have a rule that it is all the same whether one studies much or little and that only the good intention counts. Do you weep because you cannot earn your livelihood? One cannot deserve two tables, the table of the Torah and the table of worldly goods. Do you weep that you leave no son? Then look at me and know that I carry a bone (tooth) of my tenth son."

To this Rabbi Eleazar replied: "I weep because I am reminded that beauty such as yours will rot in the ground." "For this one should weep," Rabbi Jochanan responded, and they both wept.[94]

Still another form of this story is told concerning Rabbi Jochanan and Rabbi Chanina.[95] Rabbi Jochanan was punished by becoming afflicted with a disease for three-and-a-half years. Rabbi Chanina came to visit him and asked: "What ails you?" to which the other replied: "It is more than I can bear." "You must not say so," Rabbi Chanina answered, "you should rather say that God is just." It is further related that when Rabbi Jochanan's pains increased, Rabbi Chanina prounounced an incantation and the pain ceased. We may conclude from this *midrash* that Rabbi Jochanan believed in incantations.

It must be remarked, however, that this matter is not entirely clear, for Rabbi Akiba had already declared that "one who attempts to heal a wound with incantations loses his share in the life to come."[96]

When people wondered how a man like Rabbi Jochanan, who lived in poverty and who devoted all his energies to study, nevertheless retained good health, he said: "My father comes from a healthy family and I can do without meat, but under present conditions it is best that any man who has money should immediately buy meat."[97]

The following statements of Rabbi Jochanan illustrate his great love for the Torah:

"One who has many pupils but does not allow them to serve him is as if he had denied them his kindness,[98] for serving the Torah is often more important than study itself.[99]

"When Jews devote themselves to the Torah and to charity, their evil natures are under their control and not they under control of their evil natures.[100] Study is of such importance that one who engages in it in this world is conducted into the academies of Shem and Eber, of Abraham, Isaac, and Jacob, of Moses and of Aaron, in the world to come.[101]

"Three types of people are so rare that when they come along God speaks of them and wishes people to note their qualities. The first is an unmarried man who lives in a great city and does not sin; the second is a poor man who returns what he finds to its owner; the third is a rich man who offers the tithes of his fruit so that no one should know of it.[102]

"There are three types of attractions: One is the attraction of a place in the eyes of its inhabitants; another is the attraction of a woman in the eyes of her husband; the third is the attraction of something bought in the eyes of its buyer."[103]

Rabbi Jochanan attached great importance to repentance and he said that "Whoever believes that King Menasheh, the son of Hezekiah, has no share in the world to come, weakens the hands of penitents by making them believe that repentance is of no avail."[104]

Among other interesting statements of Rabbi Jochanan:

"Great is the day when God will gather the exiled Jews — as great as the day on which He created heaven and earth.[105]

"Deception with words is even worse than deception in money matters.[106]

"The prophets spoke only for those who give their daughter in marriage to a scholar, or who conduct the business of a scholar, or who share their wealth with scholars.[107]

"The observance of six types of commandments rewards men in this world, while the principal of the good deed is rewarded in the world to come. These commandments are: hospitality to strangers, visiting the sick, careful prayer, rising early to go to the academy, raising children to the knowledge of the Torah, and judging everyone according to his good deeds."[108]

When Rabbi Jochanan died, Rabbi Yitzchak ben Eleazar eulogized him in the following words: "This day is as difficult for the Jews as if the sun had suddenly set at midday."[109]

Rabbi Jochanan is called the editor of the Jerusalem Talmud. This does not imply that he gathered and edited all the statements and opinions found in it, but rather that he conceived the idea that since Jewish life had expanded to such a great extent, that the *Mishnah* was no longer sufficient and therefore it was necessary to gather everything the scholars had said in comment on the *Mishnah*. This became the foundation for the Jerusalem Talmud.

54

RABBI SIMEON BEN LAKISH

THE ACADEMY OF RABBI JOCHANAN was open to all those who sought learning. Men of two generations prided themselves on being disciples of Rabbi Jochanan. Among these were some who had seen and heard Rabbi Jehudah Hanasi but remained disciples, while he grew in stature to become one of the most outstanding *amoraim*. Among his disciples were also some who headed academies themselves, but who came to the academy of Rabbi Jochanan in Tiberias as often as they could in order to be able to call themselves his disciples although they were not compelled to do so.

Rabbi Simeon ben Lakish was one of the most prominent of these colleagues and disciples of Rabbi Jochanan. In the Talmud he is more commonly referred to as Resh Lakish.[1]

Very little is definitely known of the youth of Resh Lakish and numerous terrifying legends surround his early years. It was said that he befriended robbers and that he was a robber himself. While going about the banks of the Jordan armed from head to foot he saw a woman bathing, and he entered the water. But the figure he saw bathing was not a woman. Instead it was Rabbi Jochanan who remarked to him that such unusual strength as he seemed to possess should rightfully be devoted to the Torah. Resh Lakish replied: "Such beauty as you possess, should belong to a woman." Rabbi Jochanan is said to have told him: "If you will turn to learning, I will give you as a wife my sister who is more beautiful than I am." Resh Lakish then promised to give up his occupation and to turn to learning, and he married the sister of Rabbi Jochanan.[2]

The legend is highly questionable and does not agree with other accounts of Resh Lakish's youth. Thus it was accepted as a fact that in his youth he was a companion of Rabbi Jochanan in the academy of Rabbi Jehudah and that would make any such error as the legend ascribes to him completely unbelievable. Nor is there any mention anywhere as to who the teacher of Resh Lakish had been, for although he attended the academy of Rabbi Jehudah together with Rabbi Jochanan, they were both very young at that time and could not have been direct pupils of Rabbi Jehudah. However in later life they both declared that were it not for their contact with Rabbi Jehudah, they would not have attained their status as scholars.[3]

It appears that both Resh Lakish and Rabbi Jochanan, attained prominence rapidly, but Resh Lakish continued to be considered a disciple of the latter despite the fact that his importance was great enough for problems to be brought to him for decision in the absence of Rabbi Ephes who was a disciple and a member of the household of the Nasi.[4] In scholarship, however, the two were considered to be of the same rank by the Nasi and by Rabbi Oshaiah Rabbah.[5]

In the academy of Rabbi Chanina bar Chama, it was customary for Rabbi Chanina to begin a lecture and for Resh Lakish and Rabbi Jochanan to finish it.[6] Resh Lakish was also held in great esteem at the court of Rabbi Oshaiah Rabbah[7] and he called Rabbi Oshaiah the "father" of the *Mishnah*.[8] Resh Lakish was also a friend of Rabbi Joshua ben Levi, whom he quoted on numerous occasions. All this would indicate that Resh Lakish and Rabbi Jochanan were friends since youth. They were both considered as equals and were referred to as "the two great men of the world."[9]

Some scholars considered Resh Lakish to be superior to Rabbi Jochanan in the use of clear logic. Ula, one of his pupils, declared: "He who sees Rabbi Simeon ben Lakish expounding in the academy will imagine that he sees a man uprooting mountains and crushing them one against another."[10] Rabbi Jochanan likewise said: "Whenever Resh Lakish is absent from the academy I feel as if I lacked my right hand."[11] Resh Lakish was not an ordinary disciple who assents to all that is said. On the contrary, he frequently raised doubts concerning opinions that were expressed and Rabbi Jochanan complained that Resh Lakish would ask twenty-four (!) questions in every matter and that he had to search for replies to all those questions.[12] It is also remarkable that the questions of Resh Lakish were often of such penetrating keenness that Rabbi Jochanan was compelled to change his previous opinion,[13] and in at least one instance, when the question of *Eruvin* was being discussed, the opinion of Resh Lakish prevailed.[14]

Resh Lakish based all of his opinions on the *Mishnah* and he rarely employed arguments not substantiated by the *Mishnah*.[15]

Rabbi Simeon ben Lakish was known for his honesty in worldly matters, and any person with whom he had dealings was considered to be as honest as himself and to be trusted unquestioningly.[16] In his loyalty to his friends he was ready for self-sacrifice and it was told that when Rabbi Isi was captured by bandits, Resh Lakish hastened to save him, saying that he must do so even if his own life was endangered.[17] His diligence was incomparable and he was said to study every subject forty times.[18] He boasted himself that even Rabbi Chiya bar Abba was not more diligent than he.[19]

But despite all these qualities he never attained the leadership of an academy, and he always remained a disciple of Rabbi Jochanan. When differences of opinion occurred, the matter was always decided according to Rabbi Jochanan with the exception of three cases concerning *Halitzah* which the Babylonian scholars decided according to Resh Lakish, but this was due to the fact that there was no dissenting opinion from Rabbi Jochanan.[20]

Resh Lakish was not a reserved man, and when it seemed to him that not enough attention was paid to his words, he would shout in a loud voice.[21] He also did not restrain himself from passing judgment when he saw something wrong, and he did not spare his colleagues, nor even the Nasi, in this respect.[22]

Sometimes Rabbi Jochanan expressed an opinion in a matter of law and Rabbi Jannai Rabbah praised him for it; Resh Lakish then ironically remarked that Rabbi Jochanan's words were incorrect.[23]

Much time and energy was devoted by the scholars in gathering the *Beraitot* (the tannaitic traditions not incorporated in the *Mishnah*), and it was even attempted to lend the authority of law to these. Resh Lakish opposed this tendency and refused to recognize the authorship of those *Beraitot*. He therefore ruled that any *Mishnah* that had not been studied by a group of scholars should not be depended upon.[24] In this respect he would not even listen to Rabbi Jochanan and he refused to accept any new *beraita*, saying that it was not needed and that Rabbi Jehudah had left a complete *Mishnah*.[25]

Because of these ideas, Resh Lakish was disliked by his contemporaries who looked upon him as a troublemaker.[26] Thus he was the first to declare that the events related in the Book of Job were imaginary, that there never was a man named Job nor ever would be, and that the whole book was only intended to teach people moral principles.[27]

Another time he declared that the Jews had borrowed the names of the angels from the Babylonians, because until the time of the Prophets who lived in Babylonia, the Bible spoke of angels without mentioning names.[28]

The reason why Resh Lakish never came to head an academy either in Tiberias or in any other city despite the fact that he was considered worthy for such a post is explained by his past, when he interrupted his scholarly career and followed ways not befitting a scholar. Like Rabbi Jochanan who left the academy for a short time to engage in commerce, Resh Lakish also abandoned his studies for a time but not to engage in commerce. Instead he became a gladiator.[29]

At some other time Resh Lakish hired out as a garden watchman. Because of his unusual strength and his ability to deal with animals, he was believed able to drive away any marauders. But it is further told that thieves once came to that garden and took as much fruit as they could carry and Resh Lakish did not seize them and bring them to court; instead he argued with them and threatened them with excommunication.[30]

Once Rabbi Jochanan was robbed of all his possessions and when Resh Lakish came to the academy and asked him something, he did not reply. Resh Lakish inquired for the cause of his silence and the latter replied: "My heart is with the wealth that the robbers have taken from me." Resh Lakish then pursued the robbers and retrieved the stolen objects.

Because of these stories there were rumors that Resh Lakish associated with thieves. The truth of the matter was that because of his poverty (for he had no income from his scholastic endeavors) he sometimes hired out as a gladiator and at other times as a watchman, but he is not known to have done any harm and even the robbers against whom he was supposed to protect were merely threatened with excommunication and not with the punishment they deserved. Rabbi Jochanan brought Resh Lakish back to the Torah, as previously related, but even after he abandoned his earlier calling, the people never forgot it. When Rabbi Jochanan was called upon to answer a question pertaining to knives and how they are contaminated, Resh Lakish found the correct answer and Rabbi Jochanan remarked: "A thief understands the matters of his trade." He said this although Resh Lakish was then already his brother-in-law and was held to be his equal in learning.

Like Rabbi Jochanan, Resh Lakish also disliked the Babylonians who prided themselves on the fact that when the Jews returned from Babylonia to Palestine, only the poorer families left while the more aristocratic remained behind. To this Resh Lakish remarked: "If someone told me that there are genealogies of the families in Babylonia I would go and bring them, but even if all the scholars gathered for this purpose they could not bring them thence."[31]

On another occasion he chided the Babylonian Jews for remaining in an unclean land and not returning to Palestine with Ezra. Speaking with Rabbah bar Bar Chana he said: "God is displeased with you, people of Babylonia, that you did not come to Palestine in great masses at the time of Ezra."[32]

Nevertheless he sometimes also praised the Babylonians and said: "When the Torah was forgotten among Jews, Ezra came out of Babylonia and reestablished it anew; later Hillel the Babylonian came and revived it and when it was forgotten for the third time, there came Rabbi Chiya and his sons and they reestablished it."[33]

More than all other *amoraim*, Resh Lakish revered Rabbi Chiya. He is said to have maintained 300 fasts in order to see Rabbi Chiya in his dream but to no avail.[34]

When he complained about this and said: "Have I not studied as much Torah as he did?" a *bat kol* replied: "You have studied as much Torah as he did, but you did not help spread the Torah as much as he did."[35]

The grandson of Rabbi Jehudah, who was then Nasi, disapproved of the privileges of the scholars and he demanded that they should also bear the burden of taxation, share in the expense of strengthening the gates of the city, and paying the city watchmen. Resh Lakish protested against this demand which would have placed the scholars on the same level as the rest of the population, especially since it was an old custom to liberate scholars from the burden of taxes.

To the other differences of opinion that existed between Rabbi Jochanan and Resh Lakish, we may add the following: When Rabbi Jochanan declared that "the least fingernail of the scholars of old was worth more than all of the whole bodies of those of today," Resh Lakish replied: "On the contrary, the worth of today's scholars is greater, for they devote themselves to the Torah, and they ignore the persecution of the government."[36]

The final altercation between the two has already been mentioned. It occurred around the question of the contamination of knives, when Rabbi Jochanan exclaimed to Resh Lakish that "your business involved knives and therefore you understand their nature." It is remarkable that Resh Lakish was never offended by references to his old occupation. Frequently he even spoke of it himself, and he often introduced his remarks by comparing the situation in question to "two athletes." It is also told that on one occasion he witnessed a public performance where people ate and drank and danced, and aroused by past memories of his career, he participated in the gaiety.[37]

He was once asked whether it was permissible to drink water that had remained uncovered, for fear that a snake might have drunk of it and thus have poisoned it. He did not reply directly to this question, but instead he said: "When one sells himself to the gladiators he does so for a high price because he will have to risk his life. Will you sell your life so cheaply?"[38]

But the final remark of Rabbi Jochanan offended Resh Lakish to such an extent that he fell sick from worrying, and he died soon after. Of this last clash between the two it was related that Rabbi Jochanan said to Resh Lakish: "Are you not glad that I have brought you under the wings of the Torah?" and Resh Lakish replied: "What good has it done me? There I was called Rabbi and here I am called Rabbi."

When Resh Lakish was sick, his wife ran to Rabbi Jochanan and implored him to save his life, but Rabbi Jochanan remained stubborn until after his death. Afterward he was greatly troubled by his conscience; the "right hand" of his learning was lacking. The scholars then gathered and said: "Who will go to console Rabbi Jochanan?" Rabbi Eleazar ben Pedat volunteered and as he sat with Rabbi Jochanan, he remarked to every one of his statements: "There is a rabbinical saying that can substantiate your words." But Rabbi Jochanan was annoyed at this and said: "Do you think of taking the place of Resh Lakish? Ben Lakish asked twenty-four questions to every statement that I made, and I had to find twenty-four answers to them. The law was thereby clarified. But you merely say that there is a rabbinical saying which substantiates my words, as if I did not know that myself."[39]

Many of the expressions of Resh Lakish contain truths of permanent validity. Thus he said: "He who mocks others will be doomed to Gehenna"[40] or "If one is angry, even though he is a scholar, his learning will depart from him, and if he is a prophet, the spirit of prophecy will abandon him."[41]

The Nasi once appealed to Resh Lakish saying: "Pray to

God for me, for the government mistreats me" and Resh Lakish replied: "If you take nothing from others, you will have to give away nothing that is yours."[42]

"He who slanders his neighbors," Resh Lakish continued, "his sin reaches to heaven, and the verse 'Surely the serpent will bite without enchantment and a babbler is no better' implies that just as no magic can cure the bite of a serpent even such is the harm done by a slanderer. When Messiah will come all the animals will gather and say to the serpent: 'If a lion kills his prey, he devours it; a wolf eats that which he has killed, but what pleasure does a snake derive from its bite?' The snake will then answer: 'What pleasure has man out of a gossiping tongue?'"[43]

Resh Lakish said: "He who raises his hand against his neighbor, even though he did not strike him deserves to be called a wicked man,[44] and "He who suspects his neighbor wrongly will be punished in that he will do that which he suspected the other of doing." And so it was with Moses, when God commanded him to announce to the Jews that He would redeem them from the bondage of Egypt. Moses then said: "How can I say this; they will not believe me?" God then said to Moses: "Jews are a trusting people." And when Moses came and spoke to the Jews they believed him. Jews are also descended from believers, for when God said to Abraham, who was then childless, that his children would be like the stars in the sky, he believed Him. Only Moses doubted the word of God when He commanded him to speak to the stone and instead smote it with his cane."[45]

Repentance — Resh Lakish believed — ranked above all, for one who repents is forgiven, even such sins as were committed purposely and have come to be considered as errors. For a penitent they are sometimes even reckoned as good deeds.[46] Since everybody knew of his belief in repentance, it was related that on the day of his death, two thieves who had been his friends died and their share in the life to come was granted to Resh Lakish.[47]

Nevertheless, Resh Lakish continued, sinners are so hardened in their wrong doing that even at the gates of death they do not think of repentance.[48] And when one wants to point out the shortcomings of another, he should be told: "Adorn yourself first and then you will adorn others."[49]

Concerning judges and courts, Resh Lakish declared that "one should only heed the judges of his own generation,"[50] and "he who appoints an unworthy judge is like a man who plants a tree that Jews might worship idols under it."[51] "When a court has to pass sentence it must consider small matters of the same importance as great ones."[52]

On another occasion Resh Lakish said: "He who is merciful when he should be harsh, will in the end be harsh when he should be merciful." Thus we find that King Saul was merciful to the Amalekites but later ordered the obliteration of the city of Nob together with its priests.[53]

When a man lends his neighbor a sum of money to help him rehabilitate himself, he does a kinder deed than if he had given the money in charity. It is better still if one invests the money in partnership, for this makes the other man happy that he has neither to borrow nor to take charity.[54]

"One who wishes to sin is aided in doing so, and one who wishes to turn to better ways is assisted from heaven."[55]

The biblical verse "The eye of an adulterer guards the night," he interpreted to mean that one is an adulterer even if he lusts only with his eyes."[56]

The Torah says that "If you abandon me one day I shall abandon you two days." This he compared to two men, one of whom is coming from Sepphoris and the other from Tiberias. On the road they pass and continue on their way. But after each has walked one mile, they are already two miles apart.[57]

Of the worth of scholars Resh Lakish said:

"A scholar may not spend his time in fasting, for he thereby loses time and energy that should be devoted to study."[58]

"A scholar should be as shy and modest as a bride and like her he must also guard his conduct that no shadow of immorality should fall upon him."[59]

"When two scholars heed each other in matters of *Halakhah*, God also hears their voices and grants their desires, but when they don't, they cause the *Shekhinah* to depart from among the Jews. Two scholars who encourage each other are beloved of God."[60]

"It is customary that when two merchants exchange their products, one offers silk and the other pepper; in the end they each have but one article. It is otherwise in learning. One studies the order *Zeraim* and the other studies the order *Nezikin*. One scholar then says to the other: "Teach me *Zeraim* and I will teach you *Nezikin*. In the end they both know double that which they knew at the beginning. Can one possibly imagine a better trade in the world?"[61]

Poor as the political situation of the Jews was at that time, people nevertheless did not give up their hope that redemption was bound to come, and that the first step of the liberated Jews would be to restore the Temple. But "even if the moment of the restoration of the Temple were at hand, children should not be disturbed in their studies."[62]

Resh Lakish was very particular where the dignity of a scholar was concerned and when a certain wealthy man offended the *amora* Rabbi Jehudah bar Chanina, whom Resh Lakish often quoted in matters of law, but later wished for reconciliation, he told him to donate a pound of gold. On another occasion Resh Lakish said: "He who expectorates in the presence of his Rabbi deserves to be punished by death."[63] "But if a scholar commits an error he should not be reproved in public."[64]

Sometimes—Resh Lakish said—new interpretations lead to hindrance in the study of the Torah. Thus God commanded Moses to make new tablets to replace those that he had broken and indicated that He had approved the breaking of the first tablets.[65]

"When afflictions are visited upon the world," Resh Lakish said, "the Jews are the first ones to suffer, and when joy comes to the world the Jews are also the first to feel it."[66]

"In the eyes of God a proselyte is preferred to a Jew, even to those Jews who stood at the foot of Mount Sinai and of whom God is so proud. Why is this so? Because if it were not for the lightning and the thunder and the blowing of the heavenly *shofar* at the time of the giving of the Torah, the Jews would not have accepted it. But a proselyte who has not seen nor heard all this and embraced the Torah of his own free will— could God love anyone more than him?[67] To this Resh Lakish added that "he who denies the rights of a proselyte, is like one who denies the rights of God."[68]

"All his life," Resh Lakish believed, "man should devote to study and even nights were created by God for that purpose."[69] While strolling once during a Sabbath, Resh Lakish was so immersed in pondering some problem that he unconsciously walked beyond the limit allowed on that day.[70]

55

JEHUDAH AND HEZEKIAH, THE SONS OF RABBI CHIYA

RABBI CHIYA RABBA BAR ABBA had two sons, Jehudah and Hezekiah. These at one time incurred the displeasure of the Nasi Rabbi Jehudah. As they sat at the table of the Nasi without uttering a word, he commanded his servants to serve them wine to loosen their tongues. His command was obeyed and as the two young men became merry with wine they exclaimed: "Messiah will not come as long as the two ruling houses in Israel, the house of the Exilarch in Babylonia and the house of the Nasi in Palestine, are not destroyed." As proof of their statement they quoted a passage from the Bible. In great anger the Nasi replied: "Will you throw thorns in my eyes?"[1] As a result of this altercation the two young men never received ordination although they were both called "*amoraim* of the West."[2] The older brother, Jehudah, is sometimes referred to as Rabbi in the Talmud, but this appears to be an error.

The two brothers died in their youth. It was also said that their birth was unusual, and although they were twins, one of them was three months older than the other (!). The older brother was born at the beginning of the seventh month of pregnancy, while the younger one was born at the end of the ninth month.[3]

Together with their father Rabbi Chiya, the two young

men came to Palestine from Babylonia when they were already of age and well versed in learning. It was said then that learning in Palestine was in a decline and that Rabbi Chiya and his sons reestablished it in the minds of the people.[4] It was also related that as long as they lived, it was not necessary to thresh the flax in the country, and because of their merit the wine never turned sour.[5] When the land was afflicted by a drought, the Nasi declared a fast day and he commanded Rabbi Chiya and his sons to pray for rain out of conviction that God would not refuse their prayer.[6]

After the death of their father the two sons became tillers of the soil,[7] and being so far removed from the academy, they once expressed concern lest their father be troubled in his grave at their neglect of their studies.[8] These remarks are not entirely clear for although they were not ordained, they were both known as prominent scholars. Jehudah's name is often mentioned in the Talmud in connection with various legal matters. Hezekiah was mentioned even more frequently and it appears that he compiled a collection of *bereitot*. His opinions are quoted in the Babylonian Talmud with the introductory words "We have learned in the house of Hezekiah" and in the Jerusalem Talmud they are prefaced by the words "Hezekiah taught."

Jehudah, the older brother, was a son-in-law of Rabbi Jannai Rabbah and he died during the lifetime of his father-in-law. Jehudah habitually spent his days in the academy returning home only at nightfall. When he once failed to appear at the usual time, Rabbi Jannai ordered his bed to be covered believing him to have died.[9] The reverence with which Rabbi Jannai regarded his son-in-law may be gauged from the following story of their relations. Jehudah always visited his father-in-law each Friday, and Rabbi Jannai would seat himself on top of a high mountain to observe the approach of his son-in-law. As soon as he saw him coming in the distance, he would rise out of respect. His disciples asked him for the meaning of his action and he explained that his son-in-law equalled Mount Sinai in sanctity and that no one was allowed to sit down in front of Sinai.[10]

Jehudah's statements on various problems can best be

understood when one considers the events of that time—the persecution at the hands of the Romans, the denial of their rights, the destruction of their academies, and the unbearable taxes imposed on them. These persecutions were believed to be a punishment for the sins of man. When many people repented their sins, and the persecutions continued, Jehudah said: "Repentance avails against half of the punishment while prayer may undo all of it."[11] To this he often added that "the suffering of exile brings forgiveness for the second half of the sins, so that one should not suffer in the world to come."[12]

Because of the numerous afflictions it was at that time customary for a congregation to request one of its members to pray to God for deliverance, but when no aid was in sight many lost their faith. It was then that Jehudah declared that a "scholar who devotes himself to learning despite his needs, his prayers will surely avail."[13]

Like most of his contemporaries Jehudah highly praised the worth of the Torah and compared it to a healing balm that cures all diseases unlike ordinary cures that are effective only for one limb.[14] Hezekiah expressed a similar sentiment when he said of the Torah that "its words are a crown for one's head, an adornment for one's neck, a joy for one's heart, salve for one's eyes, and balsam for one's wounds."[15]

The following are the most characteristic statements of Hezekiah:

"Most important of all is peace. All the commandments a man must observe if they are at hand. When one meets with a situation, he must act in a certain manner, but if he does not meet with it, he is absolved. But where peace is concerned one must go out of his way to seek for it. The value of peace is so great that the Bible refers to all the wanderings of the children of Israel in the desert in the plural (*vayisu vayachanu*) because they traveled in discord and they rested in discord, but when they reached Mount Sinai the singular is used (*vayichan yisrael*) for then they were at peace and united in one wish; it was then that God said: 'Now the time has come that I should give the Torah to my children.' "[16]

"The prophets did well when they described the power of God by comparing the creation to the Creator. Thus they compared the voice of God to the roar of a lion or to the sound of mighty waters, for the human ear can conceive only that which it can hear. Man should likewise be shown only that which he can see."[17]

"He who would add to what he has heard in order to strengthen its impression only succeeds in detracting from it. Thus God commanded not to eat of the fruit of the tree of knowledge, but when Eve spoke to the serpent she added that He had also commanded not to touch the tree. The serpent then pushed Eve until she touched the tree and seeing that she had not died the serpent said: "Touching the tree has caused you no harm, neither will you suffer any harm by eating of its fruit.' "[18]

After the Jews had made the golden calf, Moses prayed to God to forgive their sin and he reminded Him of His promise to Abraham, Isaac, and Jacob to increase their offering like the stars in the sky. Hezekiah formulated the prayer of Moses in the following words: "Had You sworn by heaven and earth, You could break your oath for heaven and earth may be done away with, and You would be free of your oath. But since You swore by Your own name and You are eternal, Your oath is therefore eternal and You must forgive them."[19]

We do not know where Jehudah lived, but mention is made that Hezekiah resided in Tiberias.[20] Although Hezekiah was not ordained, he had prominent disciples among whom was Rabbi Jochanan. As long as Hezekiah lived, Rabbi Jochanan did not head an academy.[21]

Both brothers died about the same time and they were buried near their father Rabbi Chiya. Jehudah, the older brother, was buried on the right side of Rabbi Chiya and Hezekiah, the younger brother, on his left side.[22]

56

RABBI JANNAI RABBAH

RABBI JANNAI RABBAH LIVED in the city of Achbara (Achbaria) located in upper Galilee, one hour's walk to the south of Safed, and there he headed an academy.[1] He was never called by his patronymic and he was often referred to as Rabbah (the Great), to distinguish him from other *"amoraim"* of the same name.

Rabbi Jannai Rabbah was a descendant of the priest Eli.[2] He was a wealthy man and he owned many fields and gardens.[3] Some talmudic teachers claimed that he owned as many as 400 vineyards.[4] His daughters were very proud and the man who would marry one of them had to pay him a pot of gold.[5]

The disciples of Rabbi Jannai cultivated his fields and vineyards and thus they earned their livelihood. It appears that this condition continued long after Rabbi Jannai died. The laws studied in his academy are known in the Talmud as "the *halakhot* of the house of Rabbi Jannai."

Some historians claim that Rabbi Jannai had been a pupil of Rabbi Jehudah Hanasi, but there is no proof of this. It is certain however that he was a disciple of Rabbi Chiya, who foretold that he would become a leader among Jews.[6] In later life he was a colleague of Rabbi Chiya; and Rabbi Jehudah, the son of Rabbi Chiya, was his son-in-law.[7] When the Nasi died, Rabbi Jannai announced that all regulations pertaining to Priests were done away with for that day and that every Priest could participate in the burial.[8]

It was also told that in his old age Rabbi Jannai once met Rabbi Jehudah N'siah II and fingering the mantle of the Nasi, he remarked: "Your mantle looks like a sack upon you," thereby hinting that the robe of office did not befit the man. Later he asked the Nasi a question concerning the laws of inheritance and dissatisfied with the reply, he said to Rabbi Simlai upon whom he was leaning: "Lead me hence. This man has studied nothing."[9]

It appears that no decrees of unusual severity were issued at that time although the emperors of the period—Caracalla, Makrinus, and Heliogabalus—were known for their cruelty. Graetz suggests that the statement of Rabbi Jannai that "we have neither the security of the wicked nor the chastisements of the righteous"[10] refers to the political situation of that day, but according to the *Seder Hadorot* this statement was uttered by an earlier Rabbi Jannai.

Only once did Rabbi Jannai depart from the strict interpretation of the commandments—when he advised the Jews to cultivate their fields on a sabbatical year. The Emperor Caracalla then led his armies through Palestine to wage war on the Parthians, and he ordered the Jews to till their fields on the sabbatical year in order to provide food for his armies. Rabbi Jannai's advice did not imply an attempt to do away with the observance of the sabbatical year, but was conditioned by the exigencies of the moment.[11]

With nostalgic longing Rabbi Jannai spoke of the days of his youth, when young men went out in groups to teach the people. In contradiction to the opinion of Rabbi Jehudah Hanasi who advised against teaching in the streets, Rabbi Jannai declared that when scholars teach in the streets they are like fields of balsam that waft their odors far and wide.[12]

Rabbi Jannai compared the Torah to a loaf of bread suspended on a rope in a house. The foolish man says: "Who can reach this bread?" but the wise man says: "Has not someone hung up this bread? I will build a ladder to reach the bread." The foolish man similarly says: "Who can learn all the Torah that my master has in his heart?" but the wise man says: "Has not my master learned his Torah from others? Therefore I will learn two sentences today and two the next day, until I learn all the Torah of my master."[13] Nevertheless Rabbi Jannai also said that one who studies all his Torah from one master will see no blessing in it,[14] and he who has studied but has not served scholars may be compared to a pagan.[15] A priest may eat his *Terumah* on the grave of another priest who was not a scholar, for he does not contaminate.[16] When Rabbi Jannai met a man who was versed in learning but had no fear of God, he said: "Woe to the people who erect the door before they build a house."[17]

Rabbi Jannai was once at home engaged in study when he suddenly heard a voice in the street calling: "Who would buy a remedy to assure him of life?" Rabbi Jannai sent his daughter to call the merchant, but the merchant said: "Neither you nor those like you need this remedy." When Rabbi Jannai insisted that he should sell him this remedy, the merchant opened a book of Psalms and showed him the verse: "Who is the man who wants life, who loves to see good days? Guard your tongue from evil and your lips from speaking falsehood." Rabbi Jannai remarked that King Solomon said the same in Proverbs: "He who guards his mouth and tongue spares himself from trouble." Finally he gave the merchant six denars for his trouble and he said to his pupils: "All my life I read this verse, but I never understood it in the same sense that I understand it now."[18]

Rabbi Jannai was one of those in charge of distributing charity in his city, but his own charity he distributed secretly.[19] When he saw a man giving charity to another in the presence of other people he said: "It were better that you had given nothing, for you shamed the poor man."[20] In this capacity he probably had many opportunities to see people break their promises to contribute to charity. He always worried because of this and he said: "When one makes a vow it is written down in a book in heaven; when the vow is not fulfilled it is also noted down in that book."[21]

"One should never tempt providence," Rabbi Jannai said, "by standing in a place of danger and expecting a miracle to occur, for no miracle may take place. If a miracle does occur, it will certainly be deducted from the reward of the man in the world to come."[22] He avoided depending on miracles to such an extent that he always tested every bridge before he crossed it,[23] and when he had to go on a journey, he wrote his will so that his family should know what to do in case he did not return.[24]

"One must always show respect for royalty," he said. "Thus we see that when Moses came to announce to Pharaoh that all firstborn sons would die, he knew that Pharaoh would come himself to ask him to take the Jews out of Egypt. Nevertheless he did not say so to Pharaoh; instead he said that Pharaoh would send his messengers."[25]

The passage stating that all the days of a poor man are evil he explained as referring to a man who is merciful.[26]

During the days of Rabbi Jehudah N'siah II, the *Beraita* and the *Tosefta* were compiled and Rabbi Jannai considered the *Bereitot* of Rabbi Chiya to be of the same importance as the *Mishnah*.[27]

Rabbi Jannai urged each man at his morning awakening to add a special prayer, thanking God for returning him to life. In addition he composed the following prayer: "Lord of the world, I have sinned before you! May it be Thy will to grant me a good heart, a good share, good desires, a good name, a good eye, a modest soul, and a humble spirit. May Thy name not be profaned through us and preserve us from being the talk of the people. Doom us not to destruction, nor our hopes to frustration, and spare us from depending on the gifts of men whose gifts are small but whose shame is great. Grant that our share be in Your Torah and among those who do Your will and build Your house and Your palace and Your city and Your temple soon in our days."[28]

Rabbi Jannai lived during the rule of four N'siim from

Rabbi Jehudah Hanasi until the rule of his great-grandson Rabbi Jehudah N'siah II. As his death approached he instructed his children not to bury him in a white shroud lest he go to Gehenna where he would appear like a groom among mourners, nor in a black shroud lest he go to Paradise where he would appear like a mourner among grooms.[29]

57

RABBI JONATHAN BEN ELEAZAR

AMONG THE DISCIPLES of Rabbi Chiya, Rabbi Jonathan ben Eleazar, sometimes called *sar habirah* or *ish habirah* (the man of the capital), was very prominent. He excelled in *Aggadah* and after he reinterpreted some biblical text, it seemed that it had never really been understood before. His deductions were primarily religious and ethical.

The times were such that the masses of the people lost much of their interest in legal disputations and preferred the legendary explanations of the Scriptures and the wondrous stories concerning the heroes of the Bible. These stimulated their imagination and momentarily removed them from their sad realities into a beautiful world of dreams. Rabbi Jonathan is therefore mentioned hundreds of times in *Aggadah*, but only once in *Halakhah*.[1]

It appears that Rabbi Jonathan ben Eleazar was a grain merchant and lived in Sepphoris. He was a close friend of Rabbi Chanina bar Chama with whom he frequently discussed various matters. The following story is characteristic of the lifetime of Rabbi Jonathan. As he once came to a merchant to buy lentils, the merchant offered him wheat at a low price but demanded a high price for lentils. Rabbi Jonathan's relative then instructed him to inquire for the price of wheat whenever he wanted to buy lentils, so that he might obtain it at a low price.[2]

Rabbi Jonathan also conducted an academy and one of his most prominent disciples was Rabbi Shmuel bar Nachmani, who often repeated the *aggadic* sayings of Rabbi Jonathan. Rabbi Shmuel came from Babylonia to Palestine to ascertain the meaning of three biblical verses of which he was in doubt. He met Rabbi Jonathan who gave him a satisfactory explanation. Another version declares that he met Rabbi Jonathan in the street, but the latter refused to answer his questions there and instructed him to visit the academy where he would teach him the meaning of these verses. Rabbi Shmuel attempted to prove that it was permissible to teach the Torah in the street and he quoted Proverbs (1:20) to prove his contention. But Rabbi Jonathan declared that the reference was not to an ordinary street, but to a highway of learning. He added further that one does not sell precious stones in a vegetable market.[3]

Rabbi Shmuel related that whenever Rabbi Jonathan came to the passage, "For the bed is shorter than a man can stretch himself" (Isaiah 28:20), he explained it to mean that the whole world is too small for God to share its rule with any other power.[4] This statement of Rabbi Jonathan is no doubt part of his argument against people who believed in dual rule out of conviction that God could not govern the world alone and required the assistance of another.

Rabbi Jonathan was always kind to those he came in contact with and there is no mention of any outburst of anger on his part. But he was strict with Rabbi Simlai, who later became one of the outstanding exponents of *Aggadah* and said: "It is a tradition of my forefathers not to teach *Aggadah* to a Babylonian nor to an inhabitant of the south, for these possess vain pride and little Torah."[5]

The problem of fair judgment in Jewish courts was then of paramount importance and of this Rabbi Jonathan said: "One who sits in judgment should consider that a sword hangs over his head and the pit of damnation opens at his feet,[6] for every judge who passes just sentence causes the *Shekhinah* to dwell among Jews, but one who is unjust drives the *Shekhinah* away and a judge who illegally deprives one man of his possessions and gives them to another will lose his life."[7]

Rabbi Jonathan's custom when passing sentence in a dispute was illustrated by the following story: He lived near a Roman home and the branches of a tree in his garden overhung the property of the Roman, who did not complain about this for a long time. One day two men came to Rabbi Jonathan to decide a dispute between them which also involved an overhanging tree. Rabbi Jonathan heard the arguments of the contending parties and told them to return on the following day when he would pass sentence. The Roman was eager to hear whether Rabbi Jonathan would order the tree cut down and how this would affect his own tree. That evening Rabbi Jonathan had his tree trimmed of all branches overhanging the property of the Roman and when the litigants appeared on the following day, he ordered them to do likewise. To the query of the Roman, he replied: "My tree has been trimmed since the previous night."

Another story concerns a woman who brought a basket of figs as a gift for Rabbi Jonathan. He refused the gift and he asked the woman to take the basket back with her; if the basket of figs had been covered when she brought it then she should take it away covered, but if it had been uncovered then she should carry it out uncovered lest people suspect that she had brought a basket of gold but was taking back a basket of figs.[8]

"He who commits a good deed," Rabbi Jonathan said, "will be rewarded for it in the world to come and he who commits an evil deed will be followed by it until judgment day."[9]

Seven different sins bring punishment upon the whole world and the innocent suffer for them together with guilty; these sins are: slander, bloodshed, false oath, immorality, pride, robbery, and envy.[10] Punishment for these sins comes when there are wicked men but the punishment first affects the just men.[11]

He who teaches Torah to the son of another man deserves to sit among the angels and one who teaches Torah to the son of an *am ha'aretz*, God will undo all decrees against him.[12] It is a worthy deed for a man to point out to his neighbor the evil of his ways and one who does so with pious intention merits the grace of God,[13] but it is a sin to slander another person. However, one who slanders quarrelsome people has committed no sin, for against such people anything may be said.[14]

We may assume that Rabbi Jonathan disapproved of the kindness of the Romans, for he declared: "The curse of Achijah of Shiloh was preferable to the blessing of Balaam. Achijah laid a curse upon the Jews that they should shake like reeds which grow in water, but water reeds are deeply rooted and no wind can uproot them; after the wind calms down the reed remains upright in its place. But Balaam blessed the Jews to be like cedar trees growing near water, and even though all other winds will not budge a cedar tree, a south wind will uproot it."[15]

When Rabbi Jonathan heard the words of the pagans who could not understand how the Jews clung to their faith despite all suffering and persecutions he said: "Other nations wish to know what is our consolation in time of need and how we withstand the anger of our God; we must tell them that even though He punishes us, He immediately heals us of our suffering and creates us anew."[16] In line with this point of view was also Rabbi Jonathan's explanation of the origins of storms: "When God remembers that His children suffer among the Gentiles a sigh escapes Him and such sighs cause storms."[17]

Rabbi Shmuel bar Nachmani quoted Rabbi Jonathan as follows: "When Moses was writing the Torah and he reached the verse 'Let us make man,' Moses said to God, 'Why do You give unbelievers an opportunity to say that You did not create man alone?' but God replied: 'Write as you are told and he who would err may err.' Later God added: 'Moses, these people whom I created consist of great ones and small ones, and I show them an example that great ones should consult small ones before doing anything even as I consulted the angels before creating man.' "[18]

When God completed the creation of the world, He looked upon it and found it good in His eyes. Rabbi Jonathan compared this to a king who was giving his daughter in marriage and who prepared a beautiful canopy for the bride. As the king looked at the canopy and his daughter he said: "Daughter, may I always be as pleased with your wedding as I am pleased now." God likewise looked at that which He had created and said to the world: "May I always be as pleased with you as I am pleased with you now."[19]

58

RABBI OSHAIAH RABBAH

RABBI OSHAIAH WAS A DISCIPLE of Bar Kapara and Rabbi Chiya Rabbah. The title Rabbah was added to his name, to distinguish him from the later *amora* of the same name.

Collaborating with his master, Rabbi Chiya, Rabbi Oshaiah compiled over seventy *Beraitot* and it became an accepted rule to doubt the authenticity of any *Beraita* not examined and explained by these two,[1] for—as Rashi explains—they were careful to repeat every word as it was originally said, unlike other scholars who often added to the texts they received.

Some scholars even referred to Rabbi Oshaiah as "the father of the *Mishnah*."[2] But primarily he was the first commentator on the *Mishnah* because he was a disciple of Rabbi Chiya who passed on to him the opinions *he* had heard from Rabbi Jehudah. The *Beraitot* of Rabbi Oshaiah are therefore referred to as "the great *Mishnayot*."[3]

Rabbi Oshaiah was descended from a family of scholars and his father, Rabbi Chama bar Bisa, was highly respected by Rabbi Jehudah who called him "a great man."[4] Rabbi Oshaiah was at first a pupil of Bar Kapara and later of Rabbi Chiya.[5] It appears that he also studied with Rabbi Ephes for some time, and he accompanied him on a journey to Antioch in the interests of the people. In addition he maintained close relations with Rabbi Jehudah N'siah I.[6]

Throughout the lifetime of Rabbi Jehudah N'siah I, Rabbi Oshaiah attended his academy at Sepphoris and it was his duty to go to Ein Tuv every month to question the witnesses concerning the appearance of the new moon in order to determine the beginning of the new month. As long as it was possible, it was customary to hear such testimony in a city of Judea and the Nasi who lived in Galilee maintained a court in Ein Tuv.[7]

Of Rabbi Chama, the father of Rabbi Oshaiah, it was said that he studied away from home for twelve years. When he returned to enter the academy one day, he did not recognize his son. In the discussion that followed, Rabbi Chama was amazed at the young man's learning and was grieved that he had been away for so long and had neglected the education of his own son. Returning home he was followed by his son but he thought the young man had followed him to continue the discussion, and he rose out of reverence. His wife then remarked: "Who has ever seen a father rise to greet his son?"[8]

Rabbi Chama was a judge together with Bar Kapara during the lifetime of Rabbi Jehudah[9] and he is frequently mentioned in the Talmud as the father of Rabbi Oshaiah.[10]

Rabbi Bisa, the grandfather of Rabbi Oshaiah, was also a scholar and at least on one occasion he sided with his grandson against his son in some legal question.[11] Various legal opinions of Rabbi Bisa were also quoted by the scholars at Caesarea.[12]

Following the death of Rabbi Jehudah N'siah I, the Nasi was no longer the head of the Sanhedrin, and Rabbi Oshaiah established an academy in Caesarea that was attended by many scholars.[13] The Christian church father Origines appears to have had religious discussions with Rabbi Oshaiah and during one of these (the *Midrash* there calls him Philosophos instead of Origines) he was asked why God had not commanded Adam to practice circumcision if this commandment was of such great significance. Rabbi Oshaiah counter-questioned: "Why do men shave the hair on their heads but not their beards?"[14] Origines replied: "Because the hair on one's head grows since childhood when man is still foolish, but the beard begins to grow when man attains wisdom."

"According to your answer," Rabbi Oshaiah said, "I could say that man should gouge his eyes, or cut off his arms, or break his legs, since these have grown with him since childhood. But the matter is entirely different, for everything that was created requires improvement. Thus there are various bitter herbs that man eats after they are sweetened; wheat cannot be eaten as it grows, but must first be ground and only then can it be kneaded and baked. It is likewise true of man that he needs to be improved."[15]

Among the prominent followers of Rabbi Oshaiah was Rabbi Jochanan who declared that Rabbi Oshaiah was as great in his generation as Rabbi Meir had been in his, and even as Rabbi Meir was often misunderstood by his contemporaries, likewise were Rabbi Oshaiah's ways often misunderstood.[16] Another disciple was Rabbi Pinchas, who gathered all the lectures of Rabbi Oshaiah and these were later included in *Midrash Rabbah* on the Book of Genesis.

Rabbi Oshaiah was a poor man and the Nasi often helped him. On a certain Purim he sent him meat and wine, and Rabbi Oshaiah told him that he had fulfilled both commandments of sending gifts to one's friends and donations to the poor.[17]

The following are some of the statements of Rabbi Oshaiah:

"He who strives for perfection in his conduct will certainly succeed, but one who is vain and proud will go to Gehenna."[18]

"Why are the words of the Torah compared to water, wine, and milk? These three liquids may be kept in cheap vessels and the words of the Torah are retained only by those who are humble."[19]

"God was gracious to the Jews in that he scattered them among the nations and thus saved them from annihilation. When they suffer in one country, they are treated kindly in another land."[20]

Speaking of the same subject on another occasion, he explained it with a passage from the Bible. When Esau came to meet Jacob, Jacob said: "If Esau come to the company and smite it (referring to the Jews in Palestine), then the other company which is left shall escape" (referring to the Jews in the lands of the Diaspora). But although the Jews in the Diaspora do not suffer as much as we do, they nevertheless fast every Monday and Thursday to intercede with God in our behalf.[21]

"When Jews obey their leaders but the leaders do not what is necessary, then the blame is with the leaders. It is as if one blackens his hands and then wipes them on the wall; the wall is blackened but his hands have not become clean."[22]

"The prophet Zachariah said: Behold I take two canes, one of them I call *Noam* (pleasure) and the other I call *Chovlim* (pain). We may say that *Noam* refers to the scholars of Palestine and *Chovlim* refers to the scholars of Babylonia who cause each other pain with their constant doubts and questions, while the scholars of Palestine are dear and pleasant to each other; they sit together and in study each improves the words of the other until the law becomes clarified."[23]

59

RABBI CHANINA BAR CHAMA

RABBI CHANINA BAR CHAMA also called Chanina the Great[1] was one of the first *amoraim* in Palestine. He was a priest and it was said that he always returned to parents the money he received at the ceremony of "redeeming a first-born son."[2] He was said to devote himself to healing and was acquainted with the nature of snakes.[3]

Rabbi Chanina was born in Babylonia and when he came to Palestine to study with Rabbi Jehudah Hanasi, he was already the father of a son who came with him. He settled in Sepphoris where the academy of Rabbi Jehudah was but for some unknown reason he was disliked by the inhabitants of the city. It was related that an epidemic once broke out in Sepphoris but did not affect the street where Rabbi Chanina lived. The people were angry and said that he refused to pray for them, but Rabbi Chanina denied that his prayer could be of any avail as long as they conducted themselves immorally. Another time a drought occurred and although a fast day was declared no rain fell. Rabbi Chanina was again blamed and it was said that because he spoke evil of the people, God refused to heed their prayers.[4]

When Rabbi Chanina arrived in Palestine, he was already well-versed in the Scriptures, but this knowledge hindered his career, for it incurred the displeasure of Rabbi Jehudah, whom he once corrected. Rabbi Jehudah at that time remarked: "Where and from whom have you learned until now?" "From Rav Hamnuna the Scribe," Rabbi Chanina replied. "Then go to Rav Hamnuna and have him ordain you," Rabbi Jehudah exclaimed.

Only when the Nasi was nearing death, did he command his son Rabban Gamaliel to ordain Rabbi Chanina and to seat him in the first row in the academy. But Rabbi Chanina refused the last honor saying that Rabbi Ephes was older and therefore deserved the foremost seat.[5] Rabbi Chanina believed that this act accounted for his long life and health, for even after he was 80 years of age, he could balance himself on one foot while removing his shoes. He added: "The fact that my mother bathed me in warm water and anointed me with oil during my childhood contributed to my long life."[6]

But although Rabbi Chanina was not ordained during the lifetime of Rabbi Jehudah, he was nevertheless highly respected by him, and whenever Rabbi Jehudah visited the emperor's representative or was visited by him, Rabbi Chanina was always at his side.

Once as Rabbi Chanina went on some mission to the Roman governor at Caesarea, accompanied by Rabbi Joshua ben Levi, the governor arose to greet the messengers. His friends asked him: "Why do you rise to greet Jews?" and the governor replied: "These Jews resemble angels."[7]

From various expressions of Rabbi Chanina we gather that he was acquainted with the science of medicine and people often turned to him for medical advice.[8] Although he believed that all actions are determined from above and that one does not even stir a finger unless it has been so determined in heaven,[9] he nevertheless declared that fevers and chills were exceptions,[10] and that ninety-nine out of one hundred people died through their own fault in not avoiding colds.[11] He likewise said: "Why do the people of Babylonia escape the skin ailment known as *ra'atan*? It is because they eat a herb called *tradin*, that grows among the thorns. This herb they mix with a special kind of wine fermented from dates."[12]

Rabbi Chanina was modest toward his master, but he consciously maintained his dignity among his colleagues. When he met Rabbi Chiya at the death of Rabbi Jehudah, a dispute arose between them as to who did more for the advancement of the Torah. Rabbi Chanina declared that if the Torah were to be forgotten entirely, he could reconstitute it with his *pilpul*.[13] It is also related that Rav (Abba Arecha) once read a chapter of the Torah to Rabbi Jehudah. Since Rabbi Chiya entered in the middle of the reading, Rav began to read from the beginning again. Then Bar Kapara entered and again he reread the chapter. He repeated this also when Rabban Simeon, the son of the Nasi, entered in the middle of the reading, but when Rabbi Chanina entered, he refused to begin the chapter anew. This offended Rabbi Chanina and on thirteen successive eves of the Day of Atonement Rav visited Rabbi Chanina to ask his forgiveness, but the latter would not become reconciled.[14]

Rabbi Chanina maintained a close friendship with nearly all the contemporary *amoraim*. One of these was Rabbi Jochanan, later the editor of the Jerusalem Talmud, who was first his pupil and later his close friend. Due to differences of opinion with Rabbi Chanina, Rabbi Jochanan left Sepphoris and settled in Tiberias,[15] but these differences did not weaken their friendship and Rabbi Jochanan often visited his master in Sepphoris.[16] When Rabbi Chanina fell sick before his death, Rabbi Jochanan went to visit him but on the road he met a man of Sepphoris and asked him: "What new things have happened in your city?" and the man replied: "A great rabbi died and everybody is hurrying to the funeral." Rabbi Jochanan then understood that Rabbi Chanina had died and he rent his garments as a sign of mourning.[17] Others told that Rabbi Jochanan carried thirteen garments to wear and that he tore all of them exclaiming: "The man who nourished me with Torah has gone."[18]

Every word Rabbi Chanina had heard directly from Rabbi Jehudah, or heard repeated in the name of Rabbi Jehudah, he considered to be sacred and would not deviate from it. In all questions that arose, Rabbi Chanina relied on the conduct of

Rabbi Jehudah in similar cases, and whenever a question arose to which Rabbi Chanina could find no answer in the *Mishnah*, he consulted his colleagues and even his disciples. Rabbi Jochanan and Resh Lakish were thus greatly surprised when he asked their opinion in a matter that could easily be explained; but Rabbi Chanina said to them: "May evil come upon me if I ever made any statement I have not previously heard from Rabbi Jehudah as many times as I have hair on my head. In all matters of law I would observe the conduct of Rabbi on three occasions in similar cases, but this matter concerning which I asked you I only witnessed Rabbi Jehudah observe twice. I therefore asked your opinion in order that it should be as if I had seen it observed a third time."[19]

This strict adherence to tradition and the constant repetition of opinions of previous authorities was disapproved of by the other scholars of the time who did not want the interpretation of the Torah to lose its vitality. Many of them therefore left Rabbi Chanina and opened academies of their own. But these differences were only theoretical and did not diminish the personal regard they felt for each other. On the contrary, Rabbi Chanina was always glad of the honor bestowed upon his past pupils.

It is told that once as he was strolling in the street he saw everyone ceasing their work to don festive garments. He asked the occasion for the rejoicing and was told: "Your pupil Rabbi Jochanan has arrived and he will lecture at the academy; everyone therefore hastens to hear him." Rabbi Chanina then pronounced the blessing of *Sheheheyanu* for he had lived to see the honor accorded to his disciple.[20]

Rabbi Chanina gained his livelihood from trade in honey. On one occasion he sold a large quantity of fig honey and from the considerable profit he realized by this transaction he built the academy at Sepphoris.[21]

His love for Palestine was indescribable. It was said that wherever he went he removed stones and other hindrances in order to smooth the road and improve it. He was said to be able to distinguish between the soil of Palestine and soil of other lands merely by taking a lump of it in his hand. When one of his young pupils, Rabbi Simeon bar Abba, asked him whether he should go to a foreign land and requested a letter of recommendation to the scholars in Babylonia, Rabbi Chanina said to him: "I cannot give it to you, for tomorrow I may see your parents (I may die) and they may complain to me that they had owned a beautiful flower in Palestine and that I had allowed it to be transplanted to a foreign land."[22]

From Rabbi Chanina's statement it is obvious that he believed that God rewards man according to his deeds and even though judgment may be delayed it was certain that God would not overlook anyone's sins, for whatever He does is done in a spirit of justice.[23] It is therefore better that should a man sin he should do it secretly, and should not profane the name of God in public.[24]

Although Rabbi Chanina believed that all man's actions were controlled from above even to the extent of stirring a finger, he nevertheless added that "fear of God" was dependent on the individual.[25] Regarding relations between people Rabbi Chanina said: "He who raises his hand against his neighbor, even though he does not strike him, has already sinned. He who strikes a Jew, is like one who struck the *Shekhinah*."[26]

"There are people," Rabbi Chanina said, "who sin on earth, but do not sin against heaven; then there are others who sin against heaven but do not sin on earth, but he who engages in slander sins both against heaven and against earth."[27]

"There are various kinds of wicked men. Some are sly and these are worse than the ordinary sinner, for they always prove their innocence. During a trial, for instance, such a man comes before the judge before the other party has arrived and presents his arguments thereby influencing the judge in his favor. A judge must therefore be careful not to heed any words until both sides are present."[28]

Like other scholars, Rabbi Chanina praised charity saying: "Charity may be compared to a garment. The stuff of a garment is woven out of single threads. Charity likewise is gathered in single coins until it accumulates into a considerable sum"[29] "In the distribution of charity, scholars should be considered first, for he who shames a scholar should be considered a heretic who does not deserve a share in the world to come."[30] "He who shows ill will toward scholars in this world will have his ears filled with smoke in the world to come,"[31] "but one who gains the approval of his teachers is certain of a share in the world to come."[32]

At the same time scholars are obliged to teach all those who wish to learn, and a scholar who refuses to read a chapter of the Scriptures or to teach a chapter of the *Mishnah* to one who requests it by saying "Leave me! I have not the strength for it," to him God says: "The time will come when you will in truth not have the strength to teach."[33]

Rabbi Chanina believed in the influence of stars (*mazal*) on human life. "The stars make one wise and also rich," he said. In contradistinction to those who said, "Jews have no stars,"[34] Rabbi Chanina declared that "Jews have stars."[35]

The Sabbath he considered to be the most important day of the week to be honored by wearing special garments. Every man, he said, should have two sets of garments, one for weekdays and the other for the Sabbath.[36] Each Sabbath eve Rabbi Chanina donned his Sabbath garments and said to his friends and disciples: "Let us go to greet the Queen Sabbath."[37]

Like his contemporaries Rabbi Chanina met with suffering but he did not allow these to influence his attitude toward life, and he always controlled his reactions. Only once did he omit his daily prayer in anger.[38] When his daughter died, he did not weep. His wife chided him and said: "Even when a hen is lost from the house one regrets it." But Rabbi Chanina replied: "One cannot bear two griefs. I suffer enough now that I am childless, must I also weep until I become blind?"[39] Rabbi Chanina also did not mourn when his son Shivchat died. He accepted it as a just act of God and merely said that his son died because "the fig was cut down before it was time."[40]

Rabbi Chanina scolded the inhabitants of his city for their immorality and he said: "During the time of Moses there was one Zimri and 24,000 Jews lost their lives on his account. In this generation we have many Zimris. Why then should we complain if God punishes us?"[41]

When asked to what he ascribed his long life, Rabbi
Chanina sometimes explained it as due to the warm baths and
the anointment with oil he received as a child. At other times
he ascribed it to the fact that he gave up the foremost seat in the
academy to Rabbi Ephes, that had been offered to him by the
Nasi, or to the special effort he had made by going out of his
way on the road from Sepphoris to Tiberias in order to greet
Rabbi Simeon ben Chalafta.[42]

60

RABBI JOSHUA
BEN LEVI

RABBI JOSHUA BEN LEVI belonged to the first and second generations of *amoraim* who were influential after the death of Rabbi Jehudah Hanasi. Among these he occupied an important position and his life history was filled with wondrous legends. It was said that he spoke to the prophet Elijah as one speaks to an equal and that he obtained whatever he requested from him. When in doubt over the meaning of some passage, he would send Elijah to inquire its meaning from the deceased Rabbi Simeon ben Yochai.[1] Often he prayed for rain and his prayer was never denied. It was even told that he spoke to Messiah who revealed the time of his coming, and when the Angel of Death finally came to take his soul, he succeeded in outwitting him and in entering paradise alive.[2]

Some people claimed that Rabbi Joshua was a son of Levi ben Sisi who had been a disciple of Rabbi Jehudah. But this appears to be unlikely since Levi ben Sisi came from Babylonia whereas Rabbi Joshua was a Palestinian. And had he been the son of the renowned *tanna*, he would have quoted his father in legal matters.[3]

Rabbi Joshua was a pupil of many of the scholars of his time. For a time he even attended the academy of Rabbi Jehudah whose legal observances he later quoted. The high esteem in which Rabbi Joshua was held is apparent from the fact that one of his statements was included in the *Bereita* to the tractate of *Avot*. This statement declares that every day a *bat kol* is heard from Mount Horeb announcing: "Woe to those who allow the Torah to be put to shame."

Rabbi Joshua lived in Judea, in the city of Lud where he was born and where he also headed an academy. We may assume that he was already prominent during the days of Rabbi Chiya, for it was told that Rabbi Chiya once visited him in Lud and in honor of the guest 24 different courses were served. Rabbi Chiya was surprised and asked what they did on the Sabbath if so many courses were offered during a week-day. Rabbi Joshua then told him that the number of courses was doubled on Saturday. Sometime later Rabbi Joshua visited Rabbi Chiya and the latter gave his pupils several golden ducats with which to buy food for a repast such as Rabbi Joshua was accustomed.[4]

Rabbi Joshua often visited Sepphoris where the Sanhedrin convened and he was a close friend of Rabbi Chanina bar Chama, the head of the academy at Sepphoris. He also accompanied him once to the proconsul at Caesarea on a mission of the people.[5] It was related that Rabbi Joshua ordained all his pupils regardless of whether the Nasi approved.[6] Nevertheless he recognized the authority of the Nasi and considered his opinions to be law.[7] When his son, Rav Joseph, married the daughter of the Nasi he considered it to be a great honor and even accorded honor to his son, always remarking that he did so out of respect for the Nasi.[8]

Rabbi Joshua was an authority in both *Halakhah* and *Aggadah*, but from some of his declarations it can be seen that he did not approve of *Aggadah*. Thus he opposed committing *Aggadah* to writing and he said that "he who writes down an *Aggadah* will have no share in the world to come; he who studies it will suffer humiliation, and he who listens to it will receive no reward."[9]

His love for the Torah and his veneration of scholars exceeded all bounds and he said: "Beware of an old man who has forgotten his learning, for the broken tablets were kept in the Ark together with the whole ones." Likewise he declared that "One who speaks evil of a scholar is doomed to *Gehenna*, and that there were twenty-four instances when a court could excommunicate a person for showing disrespect to a scholar.[10] "He who teaches Torah to his son is like one who received the Torah from Mount Horeb."[11] He also considered it to be a means of curing bodily ailments and he said: "One who suffers from a headache should turn to study."[12]

But although he wished everyone to study he nevertheless said that slaves must not be taught,[13] and he also believed that no scholar could discover anything new, for "everything a bright pupil will reveal before his master has already been said to Moses on Mount Sinai."[14]

Prayer he held to be of equal significance and he instructed his children to "rise early and hasten in the evening to the synagogue and you will gain long life."[15] Everyone should strive to be among the first ten to arrive at the synagogue,[16] and at prayer one should stand by the wall. Likewise one should never pass by a synagogue when prayers are said without desiring to enter.[17] He who answers "Amen" during *Kaddish* is certain to have all decrees against him annulled,[18] and when prayers come smoothly from one's lips, one may feel sure that they have been accepted.[19]

Repentance was held to be of great merit and Rabbi Joshua said that "the Jews have made the golden calf only in order to have an opportunity to repent and to demonstrate the power of repentance."[20]

Like many of his contemporaries Rabbi Joshua often disputed with the *minim* (early Christians), but he based his arguments on sentiment rather than on logic. This gave rise to the opinion that his opposition to *Aggadah* was a result of the fact that the *minim* often used biblical passages to uphold their views. One of the *minim* especially caused much trouble to Rabbi Joshua and he was ready to curse him, but he remembered that God had mercy on all his creatures and he refrained.[21]

The following are characteristic statements of Rabbi Joshua:

"He who slanders his neighbor is like one who has broken all the commandments of the Torah."[22]

"For two great sins there is no forgiveness: for bloodshed and slander."[23]

"An honest man never utters an improper word."[24]

"Money is of great value and even bastards are made acceptable with it. If one sees two families quarrelling and insulting each other, one of them is no doubt affected by some irregularity."[25]

Although Rabbi Joshua was of a delicate constitution and had to wear shoes on the Day of Atonement,[26] he nevertheless fasted two days in succession during the month of *Av*—the ninth and the tenth—for although the temple burned on the tenth of *Av* it had caught fire on the ninth.[27]

We have previously mentioned the "intimacy" between Rabbi Joshua and Elijah described in legends. One of these legends relates that Rabbi Joshua once met Elijah at the mouth of the cave where Rabbi Simeon ben Yochai hid for thirteen years, and he asked him when Messiah would come. Elijah replied that he would have to ask Messiah, and Rabbi Joshua said: "If I only knew where he is I would ask him."

Then Elijah said: "He sits at the gate of the great city" (referring to Antioch or Caesarea where the Romans had their camp). He also gave him a guide to recognize him saying that Messiah sat among the sick beggars.

Rabbi Joshua then approached Messiah and said to him: "Peace be with you my lord and my teacher," and Messiah replied: "Peace to you, son of Levi."

"When will the Lord come?" Rabbi Joshua asked, and Messiah answered: "Today."

Rabbi Joshua returned to Elijah and related what Messiah had said. Elijah explained that Messiah's greeting was an indication that both Rabbi Joshua and his father were assured of a share in the world to come. When Rabbi Joshua complained that Messiah had deceived him by saying that he would arrive on that day, Elijah informed him that he would have come that day, had every one obeyed the will of God as is indicated by the biblical verse: "This day, if you will heed his voice."[28]

Another legend related that a man had been devoured by a lion three miles from where Rabbi Joshua lived. This caused Elijah not to appear to Rabbi Joshua for three days, because Elijah felt that Rabbi Joshua should have prayed to God that such an occurrence should not have happened so near his home.[29]

Legend couples the name of Rabbi Joshua with the prophet Elijah on still another occasion. A certain man, Ula ben Kushab, had incurred the anger of the Roman authorities and soldiers were sent to capture and kill him. But this man hid in the house of Rabbi Joshua and the soldiers surrounded the city and threatened to destroy it, if the man were not handed over to them. Rabbi Joshua then persuaded the man to surrender to the Romans and thus save the city. He even pointed out that a law in the *Mishnah* permitted surrendering a man to the government when a whole city was threatened as was the case at Abel when Joab besieged the city, and the inhabitants gave him the head of Sheva ben Bichri who had revolted against King David.

After Ula ben Kushab surrendered to the Romans, Elijah failed to appear to Rabbi Joshua for a long time. Rabbi Joshua then fasted a number of times and Elijah finally reappeared. When he was asked why he had not appeared for such a long time, Elijah replied: "How could I appear before an informer?"

"Have I not acted according to the *Mishnah*?" Rabbi Joshua asked. But Elijah retorted: "Is this a *Mishnah* to be observed by pious people? A man like you should not have been involved in this matter."[30]

Rabbi Joshua also maintained friendly relations with the Angel of Death whom he deceived when the latter came to take his soul. He asked the Angel of Death to show him his place in Paradise, and the Angel gave him his sword to carry on the way as a token that he would not harm him. When they reached the gate of Paradise, Rabbi Joshua ran through alive. The Angel of Death seized his garment in an attempt to hold him back, but Rabbi Joshua escaped. The Angel then begged for his sword, but Rabbi Joshua refused to return it until a *bat kol* commanded: "Return the sword for the world needs it."

Glad to have regained his sword, the Angel of Death departed and the prophet Elijah went before Rabbi Joshua announcing: "Make way for the son of Levi." As Rabbi Joshua looked about, he saw Rabbi Simeon bar Yochai seated on thirteen rugs of gold. Rabbi Simeon asked him: "Are you the son of Levi?" and Rabbi Joshua replied that he was. "Has a rainbow been seen during your lifetime?" Rabbi Simeon asked, and Rabbi Joshua answered that a rainbow was seen. "Then you are not the son of Levi," Rabbi Simeon said, "for your merit should have protected your generation so that no rainbow should be needed." As a matter of fact no rainbow *was* seen during the lifetime of Rabbi Joshua, which was the best proof of his piety, but he refused to boast of it.[31]

Another time Rabbi Joshua engaged in conversation with the Angel of Death and the latter instructed him to avoid three things in order to escape death. One of these was not to stop in front of women who return from a funeral, for the Angel of Death is then among them with his sword and he has permission to do harm.[32]

As was previously mentioned, Rabbi Joshua issued ordination without the consent of the Nasi. This was not a sign of opposition to the Nasi. He merely did not want to see Babylonia become a center of ordination, for it frequently happened that those who encountered difficulties in obtaining ordination in Palestine went to Babylonia to have themselves ordained. Rabbi Joshua therefore ruled that ordination obtained in foreign countries was not valid.[33]

Rabbi Joshua taught his own children and he was accustomed to hear his grandson repeat the portion of the week every Friday. This custom he strictly adhered to and said: "He who hears his grandson read a chapter of the Torah is like one who heard the Torah from Mount Sinai."[34]

Although Rabbi Joshua insisted that the *Aggadah* should remain oral and declared that: "Only once have I read a book of *Aggadah* and since then I am afraid of evil dreams," *Aggadah* nevertheless occupied a prominent place in his lectures and a great number of them were repeated in his name. He entrusted one of his disciples with the arrangement of the *aggadot*.[35] Tanchum ben Chanilai, another one of his disciples, was considered to be an authority in *Aggadah* and was always consulted by Rabbi Chiya.[36]

The Biblical passage stating that all the days of a poor man are evil, Rabbi Joshua interpreted to indicate that any person who lacked wisdom, who was angry, or who was covetous could be considered poor. Covetousness Rabbi Joshua considered to be the worst human trait and he said that "whoever derives any benefit from a covetous person commits a sin, for King Solomon had commanded not to eat the bread of such a person."[37]

When the body of a slain person was found and it was not known who the slayer was, the Bible enjoined that the elders of the nearest city must slaughter a heifer and declare that their hands had not shed the blood of the slain man. This passage was questioned by Rabbi Joshua who said: "Could anyone suspect the elders of shedding the blood? What then did they have to declare? They had to declare that they had not seen the man or they would not have let him depart without food and without an escort."[38]

"When the enemy came to destroy the Temple," Rabbi Joshua said, "it was surrounded by 600,000 angels who were prepared to defend it. But when they saw that the *Shekhinah* was indifferent to what the enemy was doing they also departed."[39]

After the Temple was destroyed God called his angels and said to them: "What does a mortal king do when his son dies?" and the angels replied: "He hangs a sack over his door."

"Thus will I also do," God answered, "I will cover the skies with darkness and a sack shall be its garment."

Again God said to his angels: "What does a mortal king do when he mourns for his family?" and they replied: "He puts out all the lamps in his house." "Thus will I also do," God said, "the sun and the moon shall become dark and the stars shall lose their brightness."[40]

God also says to the Jews: "You have caused me to destroy my house and to exile my children, you should therefore at least pray for the peace of Jerusalem and I will forgive your sins."[41]

"If the nations of the world knew," Rabbi Joshua said, "that whenever Jews sin *they too* are punished together with the Jews, they would assign two soldiers to every Jew to prevent him from sinning. Instead they even prevent Jews from observing the commandments. When Jews sin, the whole world is punished, and when they refrain from sin the whole world is blessed for their sake."[42]

Another time Rabbi Joshua said: "Every prophecy upon which the Jews had depended was based on the prophecy of others, with the exception of Moses. All prophecy that followed that of Moses was part of his. All the commandments given by God on Mount Sinai were spoken to the Jews through the mouth of Moses, with the exception of the first two that God pronounced himself."[43]

Rabbi Joshua, who was on such "intimate" terms with the prophet Elijah and with the Angel of Death, once decided to visit Paradise and Gehenna. He spoke of this to the Angel of Death who was not at all pleased. The Angel of Death complained to the then-Nasi, Rabban Gamaliel III, but Rabban Gamaliel declared that Rabbi Joshua's request was valid, and he commanded the Angel of Death to escort Rabbi Joshua. Rabban Gamaliel also instructed the Angel of Death to ask Rabbi Joshua to send the Nasi a complete description of what he saw. The Nasi was particularly curious to know whether there were any Jews in Gehenna or any pagans in Paradise.

In his description of what he saw, the *Massekhet Gan Eden*, Rabbi Joshua relates that he went throughout the length and breadth of Paradise which was divided into seven different parts. In one part of Paradise he found Elijah and the Messiah of the House of David, who asked him what the Jews were doing. Rabbi Joshua replied: "They are waiting for your coming," whereupon Messiah wept bitterly and all the saints wept with him.

Rabbi Joshua further relates that he was not admitted into Gehenna, but was merely allowed to stand at the gate and to observe that which went on within.

"I have measured the area of Gehenna," Rabbi Joshua wrote, "and I found it to be 100 miles long and 50 miles wide. Fiery lions are stationed everywhere and whoever falls into Gehenna is devoured by these lions and afterward recreated in his previous form. Later I measured a second part of Gehenna and I found it to be of the same dimensions as the first. I then asked: 'For whom is the first part set aside?' and I was informed that it was for ten nations, and that among them was also Absalom, the son of King David, who rebelled against his father. One nation says to another: 'We have sinned in not accepting the Torah; what have you done?' and the other nation replies: 'We have committed the same sin.' Then they all turn to Absalom and ask: "What was your sin?' and Absalom replies: 'I have sinned against my father.' "

"An angel then beats them all with fiery rods and the name of the angel is Kushiel. He throws them into the fire until they are burned, and then they come out in their previous form. Finally the angel is ready to chastise Absalom, but a *bat kol* announces: 'Do not beat him, for he is descended from a people who promised at Mount Sinai to obey God's commandments even before they knew what these commandments would be.' "

"After all the sinners are chastised and burned, they emerge from the fire as if nothing had happened. This occurs seven times during each day and three times during each night. Only Absalom is neither chastised nor burned and his punishment consists in observing the others' chastisement."

Of the second chamber of Gehenna, Rabbi Joshua related the same. It also contained ten nations that were punished in the same manner as those in the first. Together with them was Doeg the Edomite who had been a guard of King Saul. The avenging angel, Lahatiel, did not chastise Doeg because of his Jewish descent. In the third chamber there were another ten nations and the name of the angel was Shaftiel. Korach and his congregation was found among these, but he also escaped chastisement and merely had to observe the punishment of the others.

The fourth chamber contained ten nations and Jerobeam ben Nebat. The punishing angel was Machtiel. Jerobeam escaped punishment because of his knowledge of the Torah and because of his descent. The fifth chamber was similar to the preceding ones and it contained Ahab, king of Israel. The name of the angel was Chutriel. The sixth chamber contained Micah who built the famous idol. He was punished together with the others by Pusiel the angel. The seventh chamber also contained ten nations, Elisha ben Avuyah, and the angel Dalkiel.

Of his visit to Paradise Rabbi Joshua also related the following:

"There are two gates of clear crystal and on top of each there stand 600,000 angels each of whose faces shines like the sky. When a saint enters, they remove the garments in which he was buried and they dress him in eight new garments made of clouds. Two crowns are then placed upon his head, one made of precious stones and the other of pure gold; in addition they place eight strands of myrtle in his hands and they say to him: 'Go eat your bread in gladness.'

"He is then led to a place of rivers surrounded with flowers. A canopy of gold is erected and from the canopy there flow four rivers: one of oil, one of milk, one of wine, and one of honey. Every canopy has a golden vine on top from which hang thirty pearls that shine like the morning star. Under each canopy is a table laden with precious stones and pearls and sixty angels stand ready to serve every saint, and they say to him: 'Eat your honey and drink your wine, for it has been waiting for you since the six days of the creation.' Even the least of the saints equals Rabbi Jochanan in beauty and is endowed with grace like that of Joseph."

"There is no night in Paradise, and each day is divided into four parts. During the first part God comes to the children and plays with them as one would with children; during the second part God comes to the young men and plays with them as one would with young men; during the third part God comes to the middle-aged men and plays with them as one would with middle-aged people; during the fourth part of the day God comes to the aged and converses with them as one would with aged people."

"There are 80,000 trees in every corner of Paradise and the least of them is more beautiful than incense trees. There are also 600,000 angels in every corner and they all sing the praise of the Creator."

"In the very center of Paradise stands the Tree of Life whose branches cover all of Paradise. Its fruits have 500,000 tastes and each taste differs from all the others and each odor differs from all the others. Above the Tree of Life there float seven sacred clouds; breezes blow from all four sides through the leaves of the Tree of Life and its scents are wafted from one end of the world to the other."

"The saints in Paradise are subdivided into seven groups. One group consists of martyrs such as Rabbi Akiba and his colleagues and disciples; the second group consists of those who were drowned for the sanctification of the name of God, such as the 400 young men and the 400 maidens who jumped into the sea when the enemy wanted to sell them into a life of shame; the third group consists of people like Rabbi Jochanan ben Zakkai and his colleagues; the fourth group consists of people whom the enemy wanted to defame after their death and a cloud descended and covered them; the fifth group is made up of penitents; the sixth group consists of young men who never sinned, and the seventh group includes modest people who suffered humiliation without replying in kind."

61

RABBI SHMUEL BAR NACHMANI

AFTER THE PERIOD OF THE REBIRTH of learning in Palestine during the lifetime of Rabbi Jochanan and Resh Lakish, a decline set in. This decline had been apparent for some time and was becoming more noticeable daily. A descendant of Hillel still occupied the office of Nasi and was thus the legal representative of the people. But the later N'siim were not noted for scholarly achievements and the veneration of the people toward them had diminished. In time they lost all spiritual authority.

Rabbi Shmuel Bar Nachmani[1] was one of the spiritual leaders of the people during this period. He left few legal decisions, but he was one of the most prominent exponents of the *Aggadah*. He repeated hundreds of aggadic statements of previous *amoraim* and his disciples quoted hundreds of his own interpretations. All questions pertaining to *Aggadah* were always referred to him for clarification.[2]

Rabbi Shmuel Bar Nachmani was born in Palestine and his grandfather often carried the child on his shoulders through Bet Shean on his way to Kefar Chanan so he should see the scholars at study and absorb the sound of their voices. This took pace during the last days of Rabbi Jehuda Hanasi and it was then an accepted belief that a child who looked at Rabbi

546

Jehudah or was in his presence for a few minutes was certain to become a scholar.

Another legend related that Rabbi Shmuel was born in Babylonia and only came to Palestine to ask Rabbi Jonathan the meaning of three biblical verses concerning which he was in doubt. But this apparent contradiction may be explained by the fact that Rabbi Shmuel spent his youth in Babylonia, where favorable circumstances prevailed, and that he later returned to Palestine. Rabbi Shmuel visited Babylonia a number of times at the request of the High Court of Palestine in order to determine "leap years" when that could not be done in Palestine. On one of these trips he spent a night in the house of Rabbi Jacob the Miller. That night Rabbi Zeira hid among the barrels in the house in order to hear Rabbi Shmuel recite the *Shema* and he later revealed that Rabbi Shmuel had repeated the *Shema* many times until he was overcome by sleep.[3] Rabbi Shmuel is also known to have been sent, together with his mother, to intercede with Queen Zenobiah for the life of a political offender.

Rabbi Shmuel Bar Nachmani lived for more than 100 years and the time of his influence extended from the days of Rabbi Jonathan, whose pupil he had been, until the rule of Rabbi Jehudah N'siah II. It appears that the Nasi did not approve of Rabbi Shmuel and when he once asked him the interpretation of the expression "by his name Jah" (Psalms 68:4), he was dissatisfied with the reply and remarked: "It is regrettable that those scholars who could interpret this passage better are already dead."[4]

A famine and an epidemic occurred at that time and the people were at a loss for which of the calamities they were to pray for deliverance. Rabbi Shmuel advised them to pray for the cessation of the famine, for "when God will give us food, He will also grant us life during which to enjoy the food."[5] He also instructed teachers to dismiss their pupil from eleven o'clock in the morning until three in the afternoon between the seventeenth day of *Tammuz* and the ninth day of *Av,* for this was a difficult period for the pupils who might become ill from too great effort.[6]

When Rabbi Shmuel grew old and realized that the Nasi

did not regard him favorably, he rarely attended the academy. During one of his infrequent visits he found the scholars debating the request of a man to annul an excommunication imposed upon him by Rabbi Jehudah ben Ezekiel. Since Rabbi Jehudah was dead at the time, the scholars were inclined to consider the petition of the man favorably. But Rabbi Shmuel said: "The maidservant of Rabbi Jehudah Hanasi once banned a man who had beaten his adult son and the scholars honored her decision; would you revoke the excommunication of our comrade Rabbi Jehudah?" His opinion was then accepted and the ban was not lifted.[7]

The following are characteristic expressions of Rabbi Shmuel:

"Everything in the world was created by God, except falsehood which is an outgrowth of human imagination."[8]

After completing the creation of the world God saw everything that He had made and "it was very good." Rabbi Shmuel declared that "very good" referred to man's evil desires, for if it were not for these no man would build a house, nor marry a wife, nor beget children, nor engage in commerce.[9]

Rabbi Shmuel devoted himself to classifying the prayers. One must pray thrice daily, he said, to conform with the three changes that occur every day. In the morning one should say: "I thank Thee my God and God of my fathers for bringing me out of darkness into light." In the afternoon one should say: "May it be Thy will to permit me to see the sun in the West even as You allowed me to see it in the East." At night one should pray: "May it be Thy will to lead me out of darkness into the light even as You had led me out of darkness into light before."[10]

Rabbi Shmuel lived during the last years of the third century C.E., when the Christians attempted to postpone the Sabbath from Saturday to Sunday. Rabbi Shmuel opposed this effort with all his might and he warned the Jews against assuming that the Sabbath could be postponed to another day. "Why did God bless the Sabbath?" he said, "because it may never be postponed to another day. Holidays and even the Day of Atonement may be postponed, when a leap year is declared, but not the Sabbath."[11]

Some of the *amoraim* believed that Sabbaths and holidays were to be devoted solely to study of the Torah, while others allowed half of these days to be utilized for personal enjoyment.[12] But Rabbi Shmuel declared that the Sabbath should be devoted to food and drink and that only in order to avoid idle talk was it allowed also to engage in study on that day.[13]

The verse "Many waters cannot quench love" (Song of Songs 8:7) Rabbi Shmuel interpreted in the following manner: Two kinds of love are referred to, the love of God for Israel which is so great that were all the nations of the world to try to thwart it, they could not do so, and the love of Israel for the Torah. Were all the nations to say: "We will sell all our possessions in order to observe the Torah and its commandments," God would reply: "Even if you were to sell all your possessions to obtain the Torah, you would only be ridiculed."[14]

The destruction of the Temple played an important role in Rabbi Shmuel's manner of thought. Nearly two centuries had already elapsed since the destruction and none thought about sacrifices any longer. Many of the scholars of the time disapproved of sacrifices or ignored the matter. The express commandments of the Torah to offer sacrifices, they easily refuted with passages from the Prophets such as Jeremiah's statement that "I spoke not unto your fathers nor commanded them concerning burnt offerings or sacrifices in the day that I brought them out of the land of Egypt" (7:22). But the Temple remained a symbol of the liberation of the people and it was always mentioned with the hope of its speedy restoration and the renewal of the service as in days of old. It is also interesting to note that the people feared to speak of the Second Temple and they therefore always referred to the First Temple. They spoke of Babylonians, but meant the Romans, they referred to Nebusaradon or Nebuchadnezzar, but really meant Titus or the reigning emperor.

Like other scholars Rabbi Shmuel also spoke of the destruction of the Temple in his lectures. Many such lectures are
included in the introduction to *Midrash Eikha Rabbati* and these
describe how Jeremiah went to the graves of the Patriarchs and
begged them to intercede with God. The belief was commonly
held at that time that Rachel rose from her grave and wept at
the fate of her children. Her weeping aroused pity in heaven
and she was assured that they would soon be redeemed from
the land of the enemy (Jeremiah 31:14). Such descriptions
delivered by good orators profoundly impressed the people.

"After the Temple was destroyed," Rabbi Shmuel said,
"Abraham came to the throne of glory; he was weeping and
tearing his hair; his garments were torn and he was covered
with ashes. Thus he went about and called upon God: 'Am I
worse than other fathers that I should suffer such shame?' "

"When the angels saw Abraham they also wept and when
God asked them why they wept, they said: 'The highways lie
waste, the wayfaring man ceaseth, he hath broken the
covenent, he hath despised the cities, he regardeth no man' "
(Isaiah 33:8).

"God thereupon answered and said: 'Since my friend
Abraham has left the world, he has not come to see the welfare
of my house, Why then does he come now?' and Abraham
replied: 'Why have you exiled my children and handed them
over to barbaric peoples who slay them with numerous kinds of
deaths? Why have you allowed the Temple, the place where I
offered my son for the sake of Thy great name, to be destroyed?' "

" 'Your children have sinned,' God replied to Abraham,
'they have not observed the commandments of my Torah and
they transgressed against the 22 sacred letters of the Torah.' "

" 'Who will bear witness against my children that they
have not observed the commandments, or that they transgressed against its 22 sacred letters?' Abraham asked."

" 'The Torah is the best witness,' God replied."

"The Torah then came out and was ready to testify against
the Jews, but Abraham said: 'Daughter, you wish to testify that
the Jews did not observe your commandments? Are you not

ashamed of such testimony? Do you not remember the day when God carried you among all the nations, and they refused to accept you until my children came to Mount Sinai and they accepted you with honor? Will you now testify against them in the hour of their affliction?' "

"When the Torah heard this, it stepped aside and God called upon the twenty-two letters to come and testify. The first of these was 'Aleph' and Abraham said to it: "You, who are the first letter of the alphabet, come to testify against my children? When God appeared on Mount Sinai and offered the Ten Commandments which begin with an Aleph, no people would accept you until my children did; would you now testify against them?' "

"In shame the Aleph stepped aside and the Bet came up to testify. To it Abraham said: 'You would testify against my children, who accepted the Pentateuch which begins with a Bet?' In shame the Bet stepped aside and the Gimel came forward, and Abraham addressed it: 'God's commandment *gedilim* (Deut. 22:12), which begins with a Gimel, was rejected by all nations until my children accepted it; would you testify against them?' After the Gimel the Dalet appeared and again Abraham said: 'Will you testify against my children? When God told Moses, 'Speak to the children of Israel,' which begins with a Dalet—did they not heed him?' "

"In shame the Dalet also stepped aside and when the other letters saw that Abraham shamed them, they refused to testify against the Jews. Then Abraham said: 'Lord of the world! When I was 100 years old, you gave me a son and when he reached the age of 37 you commanded me to offer him to you as a sacrifice. I then hardened my heart and I showed no mercy to him in order to fulfill your wish. Now you have forgotten all that and you showed no mercy toward my children.' "

"After these words Moses came and he said to God: 'Lord of the world! Have I not been like a good shepherd to your people? Like a horse I ran before them in the desert, but when the time came to enter the Land of Israel you decreed that I should die in the desert. Now I am called to mourn over their

affliction.' Then Moses said to Jeremiah: 'Proceed, and I will go
with you, for I wish to see who dares do harm to the Jews.' But
Jeremiah replied: 'I cannot go, for the road is covered with
corpses and I am a Priest.' Moses then said to him: 'Come, for
I have commanded you.' "

"Moses and Jeremiah came to the rivers of Babylon and
when the Jews saw Moses, they exclaimed: 'The son of Amram
has risen from his grave to redeem us from our enemies.' But a
bat kol was heard to declare: 'It is a decree that cannot be
changed.' "

"Then Moses said to the people: 'My dear children, I
cannot redeem you; I can only pray to God that he returns you
to your land soon.' "

"When the Jews heard these words, they wept bitterly and
the sound of their weeping shook the seven heavens. The
angels, the sun, the moon, and the stars wept with them."

"Moses returned to the Patriarchs to tell them of what the
enemy had done to their children and he said: 'Some of them
are killed, and some had their arms broken and bound behind
their backs, some were burdened with heavy chains and were
driven naked over mountains and valleys, while others died on
the way and their bodies were left to be devoured by birds and
beasts of prey. Still others were left on the sands of the desert
with their eyes gouged out to await their death.' "

"When they heard this, the Patriarchs wept and mourned:
'Woe, what has befallen our orphans that hungry and naked
they must wander in the lands of their enemies, woe that they
must climb high mountains and must wound their feet on rocks
and boulders, woe that they must carry heavy sacks of sand on
their delicate backs, woe that their arms have been broken and
their eyes gouged, woe that their throats are parched with
thirst, woe that God could witness the slaughter of children
before the eyes of their mothers and the death of mothers
before the eyes of their children.' "

"Moses then turned to the Sun and said: 'Be cursed, Sun,
that you were not darkened when the enemies entered the
Temple!' and the Sun replied: 'I swear to you, Moses, by the
name of the Eternal One, that I wanted to hide among the

clouds in order not to light the way of the enemy, but I was beaten with fiery rods and I was commanded to do my duty.' "

"Then Rachel came weeping bitterly and when the sound of her weeping was heard a voice from heaven announced: 'Cease weeping, for your children will soon return from the land of their enemies to their own home.' "

62

RABBI SIMLAI BAR ABBA

LIKE RABBI SHMUEL BAR NACHMANI, Rabbi Simlai was also a master of aggadic interpretation. Hundreds of these are quoted in the Babylonian Talmud in his name, but the Jerusalem Talmud contains only one aggadic quotation from Rabbi Simlai.[1]

Rabbi Simlai was born in Babylonia in the city of Nehardea. The exact location of this city is unknown aside from the fact that it was situated on the river Malka, somewhere between the Tigris and the Euphrates. It is also known that Jews began to settle in that city several decades after the destruction of the Temple. Various horrifying stories were at first told about Nehardea, but later it became known as the seat of prominent academies which rivalled those in Jabneh and Tiberias.

Rabbi Simlai's father was always referred to as "Abba, the father of Rabbi Simlai." However, he was a significant man in his own right and it was related that he once asked Shmuel Yarchina'ah, the mathematician of the Talmud, a question pertaining to the determination of leap years which the latter could not answer despite the fact that he had boasted that he could calculate the beginning of each month without recourse to the testimony of witnesses who had seen the new moon. On

this occasion the father of Rabbi Simlai is said to have remarked: "If you cannot answer this question, then it is entirely
possible that there are other matters which you do not know."[2]

When Rabbi Simlai arrived in Palestine he settled in Lud,
but later he moved to Galilee where he spent most of the time
in the city where the Nasi, Rabbi Jehudah N'siah I lived. The
following conversation is said to have taken place between the
two, as the Nasi once leaned on the shoulder of Rabbi Simlai
during a stroll: "Yesterday you were absent from the academy
when we permitted the use of oil bought from Gentiles," the
Nasi said and Rabbi Simlai replied: "I will yet live to see the day
when you will permit the use of gentile bread."[3]

This new regulation was announced in Babylonia by a
pupil of Rabbi Simlai, although it is also possible that Rabbi
Simlai himself was delegated by the Nasi to announce it.[4]

In later life Rabbi Simlai served Rabbi Jannai the Old[5] and
he was also a close friend of Rabbi Jehudah N'siah II.[6]

His debates with the *minim* (Christian Jews) who annoyed
him with various questions are interesting. Since the Hebrew
word *Elohim* (God) is in the plural form, the *minim* asked him
how many gods shared in the creation of the world. Rabbi
Simlai replied that the further text amply answered their
question. Thus the Bible says: "Let us make man in our image"
(plural) and this is followed by "God created man in his own
image" (singular). When his pupils said that it was easy to give
such an answer to the *minim*, but that they were not satisfied
with it, he replied that the plural was used, because Adam was
created out of earth and Eve out of Adam's rib, but in the future
no increase could be had by man without woman or by woman
without man, and both need the assistance of God.

At another time the *minim* asked him why the phrase
Elohim Kedoshim (holy gods, plural) was used in the Bible, and
Rabbi Simlai replied that the subsequent phrase *Elohim Hu* (He
is God) was a sufficient answer. To his pupils he explained that
the plural was used to indicate that God was holy with all kinds
of holiness.

The number of commandments in the Torah is 613 and
whoever transgresses against even one commandment is con-

sidered to have broken all of them. The Prophets sought to diminish the number of commandments and Hillel tried to express the essence of the Torah in one phrase: "Do not unto others what you would not have done unto you."

Rabbi Simlai said: "The 613 commandments consist of 365 negative ones, equal to the number of days in the year, and of 248 positive commandments, equal to the number of limbs in the human body."[7] One of Rabbi Simlai's pupils amplified this statement and said: "The number of positive commandments is equal to the number of limbs in a human body, because every limb implores man to commit a good deed. The number of negative commandments is equal to the number of days in the year, according to the reckoning of the sun, because each day implores man not to commit a sin during its time.

Another general statement of Rabbi Simlai declared: "The Torah begins with an act of kindness and ends with an act of kindness. When Adam and Eve realized their nakedness and were ashamed, God made them coats of skins. When Moses died on Mount Nebo and no one was there to bury him, God buried Moses."[8] Later Rabbi Simlai changed his interpretation somewhat and said: "One who would realize the kindness of God should consult the Torah, and he will see that the first act of God was to adorn Eve as one adorns a bride, when he led her before Adam. God adorns all brides as he adorned Eve; He visits the sick as He visited Abraham; He buries the dead as He buried Moses."[9]

"The Bible says: "Remember the day of Sabbath to consecrate it" and also "Observe the day of Sabbath." Rabbi Simlai explained that one should remember the Sabbath before it comes and he should observe it after it had come. How can this be done? Whenever one sees a good object or new vessel, he should reserve it for the Sabbath.[10]

Economic conditions in Palestine were very poor at that time and the population was so impoverished that no one had good garments. As Rabbi Simlai once explained the commandment to prepare special garments for Sabbath, the people wept, for they could not afford such a luxury. Rabbi Simlai then said:

"If one does not have a good garment to wear on Saturday, he should at least wear a different garment; even though it be torn it should be different from the one worn on week days."[11]

"When Messiah will come," Rabbi Simlai said, "God will take a book of the Torah in his arms and He will say: 'Whoever devoted himself to the study of the Torah, let him come and receive his reward.' All the nations will then come together, but God will say to them, 'Let each nation come separately.' "

"The first to come before God will be Edom (Rome) and He will ask them: 'What have you done in the world?' and they will reply: 'We paved highways; we built many bath houses; we gathered much silver and gold. All this we did for the sake of Your Jews that they might devote themselves to the Torah.' God will then answer them: 'Fools that you are. All that you did, you did for yourself. You paved streets that you might settle your harlots there; you built bath houses that you might anoint your bodies; you gathered gold and silver which belongs to me. But you did not study the Torah and you will receive no reward.' The sons of Edom will then leave with bowed heads."

"After them will come the Persians and God will ask them: 'What have you done?' and they will reply: 'We have built many bridges; we have conquered many cities; we have waged many wars. All this we did for the sake of the Jews, that they might have time to devote themselves to the Torah.' To them God will say: 'All that you did, you did for yourself. You built bridges to collect tolls; you conquered cities to collect taxes; your wars I waged for you, but you did not study the Torah, then why do you seek reward?' "

"But the Persians will refuse to leave empty-handed and they will say: 'Have you offered the Torah to us and did we reject it?' and God will reply: 'Seven commandments I gave to the sons of Noah and you have not observed them.' The Persians will ask further: 'Have the Jews observed the seven commandments?' "

" 'I will call your own witnesses,' God will answer, 'and you shall see that they have observed my commandments. Let

Nimrod testify that Abraham did not worship idols; let Laban testify that he did not suspect Jacob of stealing; let Potiphar's wife testify that Joseph was not persuaded to sin; let Nebuchadnezzar testify that Chananiah, Mishael, and Azariah refused to bow before an idol; let Darius testify that Daniel refused to interrupt his prayer.' "[12]

63

RABBI ELEAZAR BEN PEDAT

RABBI ELEAZAR BEN PEDAT occupied a prominent place among those who came to Palestine from Babylonia during the second and third generations of the *"amoraim."* He is very seldom referred to by his patronymic and nothing is known of his father's position in Jewish life.

Although he was not ordained, he was well educated by the time he arrived in Palestine.[1] While still in Babylonia, he was a pupil of Rav (Abba Arecha), whose legal opinions he later quoted.[2] Later he was a disciple of Rabbi Chanina bar Chama and scores of statements in the Talmud began with the words: "Rabbi Eleazar said in the name of Rabbi Chanina."

Rabbi Eleazar always named the authors of the opinions he quoted even when these were commonly known, as in the statement that declares: "He who repeats a word in the name of its authors brings redemption to the world."[3] It is therefore incomprehensible that Rabbi Jochanan complained that Rabbi Eleazar appropriated statements of others.[4] This attitude of reverence toward authorship also caused a dispute between Rabbi Eleazar and Resh Lakish, when he heard the latter state a law he had previously heard from Rabbi Jochanan.[5] In the popular mind Rabbi Eleazar was considered to be a disciple of Rabbi Jochanan, although he denied it, and when a colleague of his referred to "your master Rabbi Jochanan" he remarked: "not my master nor our master." There is also an instance in the Talmud where Rabbi Jochanan complains that Rabbi Eleazar had not greeted him.[6]

A personal misunderstanding must have existed between Rabbi Eleazar and Rabbi Jochanan, although no specific mention of it is made anywhere in the Talmud. However, there is a reference to an attempt by Rabbi Jochanan to discuss the "mysteries of the chariot" with Rabbi Eleazar who turned down the offer on the grounds of being "too young to discuss this matter."[7] Another time Rabbi Jochanan exclaimed: "It is a pleasure to observe ben Pedat lecturing. It seems as if Moses is expounding that which he heard from the mouth of God." But to this Resh Lakish remarked: "He does not speak his own words. He merely repeats what he read in a *Beraita*."[8]

Rabbi Eleazar earned his livelihood from testing coins.[9] This occupation provided him with an insufficient income and he lived in great want. Once, after he bled himself and there was not a crust of bread in the house, he ate a piece of garlic for want of something better and fainted. While swooning he asked God how much longer he would have to suffer want, but God replied: "Would you have me upset the world in order that you might be born in a more lucky hour?"[10]

From the original statements of Rabbi Eleazar in the Talmud, we gather that he was gifted with noble qualities. Thus he declared that "humility adds to one's life."[11] In his personal life he was always humble and never prided himself on his learning to others.[12] His love for the Torah was indescribable[13] and he often said: "Just as a child must be nursed by its mother every hour during the day, even so should every man devote each hour of the day to the Torah."[14]

The great poverty of Rabbi Eleazar was well known to the Nasi who sometimes sent him gifts to relieve his needs, but Rabbi Eleazar always refused to accept these. When he was invited to attend a feast at the house of the Nasi, he also refused to attend.[15]

"Charity," Rabbi Eleazar said, "atones for all sins and is more important than sacrifices."[16] "It may be compared to armor; just as armor is made up of small pieces, in charity one adds penny to penny until it grows into a considerable sum."[17]

Rabbi Eleazar was therefore entrusted with the feeding of the poor.[18] It was observed that in distributing charity, he sought to make the recipients feel they were not receiving charity. When Rabbi Eleazar was made head of the distribution of charity, he also had to collect taxes from the Jews. He then asked Rabbi Jochanan whether taxes should be levied according to wealth or according to the number of persons in a family. Rabbi Jochanan replied that taxes should be levied according to the wealth of the family.[19]

His hatred of charity for himself was so great that he said: "When Noah sent out a dove to see whether the waters of the flood had receded, it returned with an olive leaf in its beak. By this is implied that food bitter as an olive leaf, obtained from the hand of God, is to be preferred to food sweet as honey obtained at the hand of man."[20]

Rabbi Eleazar was not the only needy scholar at that time. Due to the difficult economic circumstances, there were many such as Rabbi Simeon bar Abba. It was related that Rabbi Eleazar once lost a ducat that was found by Rabbi Simeon, but he refused to take it back declaring that he had already given up the search for it.[21]

Following the death of Rabbi Jochanan, Rabbi Eleazar was elected representative of the academy and since that time the Babylonians called him "The Lord of the Land of Israel."[22]

As previously mentioned the Babylonians were not held in high repute in Palestine, and they therefore prided themselves on their countryman Rabbi Eleazar. Since he was recognized everywhere as an authority, they appealed to him in all matters and he instructed them in all matters dealing with what is prohibited and what is permissible and also in money matters.[23]

In his teachings Rabbi Eleazar followed logical reason in an attempt to find the correct interpretations and to explain apparent contradictions. He did not fear to differ from the interpretations of others, and his opinions were at times even contrary to the obvious meaning of the *Mishnah*.[24] When he sought to establish the original intentions of various laws, he set up rules that were later accepted by other scholars. These rules included the following: "One must not add to a biblical decree or to its structure."[25] "One may not declare an unclean thing to be clean nor a clean object to be unclean."[26] "Everything that derives its importance from certain circumstances loses its importance when these circumstances cease to exist."[27]

As soon as Rabbi Eleazar came to Palestine, he established close relations with the scholars of that time. He particularly respected Rabbi Chiya whose opinions served as his guide,[28] and it was accepted that the opinions of the two would always coincide.[29]

Rabbi Eleazar expressed his love for Palestine in the following statements: "He who lives in Palestine is without sin,"[30] and "Happy are they who live in Palestine for they have no sins either in life or in death."[31]

Rabbi Eleazar ben Pedat instructed the Babylonian Jews to strictly observe all holidays for two days, as it was the law at the Diaspora.[32] The problem of the second day of a holiday was then an important matter for the Jews of Babylonia. This custom of celebrating an extra day was introduced during the time when messengers of the Palestine High Court could not be sent to inform the Babylonians of the beginning of a new month. Although the Babylonian Jews could have determined the new months themselves, because they also followed the lunar calendar, the Exilarch nevertheless added a day to all holidays for fear that his calculations might differ from those of the High Court in Palestine. But at times the Romans relaxed their vigilance, and the messengers were free to announce the findings of the High Court. At such times the Babylonian Jews would ignore the extra day. It was for this reason that Rabbi Eleazar instructed all Jews who lived outside Palestine to observe the second day of the holidays.

On another occasion he sent the following message to Babylonia: "Attend to the cleanliness of your bodies; strive to study in company, and be careful in your treatment of poor children, for only from them will the Torah issue."[33]

Little is known of the achievements of Rabbi Eleazar as

head of the academy at Tiberias. Aside from the few *halakhot* in whose formulation he had participated, he was one of the outstanding exponents of *Aggadah*. His aggadic statements were of such deep significance that their value remained permanent and it was also unimportant what biblical text he had based them on, for he used the texts merely to bring out his ideas.

Thus he declared that one who returns from a journey must rest for three days before he can keep his mind on his prayers. He proved this by the fact that when Ezra came to the river Ahava, on the way to Palestine, he rested for three days before he declared a fast and prayed to God to guide his steps. When he arrived in Jerusalem he also waited for three days before he commenced his work.[34]

The statement of Hannah to Eli (I Sam. 1:16), "Esteem not thy handmaid as a daughter of Belial," he compared with the *B'nai Belial* mentioned elsewhere in the Bible, and he concluded that "the prayer of a drunken man may be compared to idol worshipping."[35] Another example of his method of interpretation is found in his declaration that there can be no other punishment for a man who lifts his hand against his neighbor except death. This he based on the verse that the earth belongs to men of strong arms.[36]

Of charity Rabbi Eleazar said: "As long as the Temple existed, a man could give a shekel for a sacrifice and his sins were forgiven; but now that the Temple is destroyed, it is best that one should give for charity, for if he will not give charity to Jews, pagans will take his possessions by force."[37] On another occasion he similarly declared that "if a poor man requires aid, it should be given to him even on the Sabbath."[38]

Of those who sought to obtain charity when they did not need it, Rabbi Eleazar said: "We should be thankful to these, for were it not for these swindlers, any man who refused to give charity when asked, would be punished at once. As it is, such a person can claim that he suspected the charity seeker of being a swindler."[39]

"Why did God create human fingers in their present shape?" Rabbi Eleazar asked. "It was done in order that a man might plug his ears when he hears improper words," he answered.[40]

Speaking of God's consideration for human weaknesses, Rabbi Eleazar said: "If a man insults his neighbor and later wishes to conciliate him, the insulted man may demand an apology in the presence of those who witnessed the insult. But when a man sins against God in public, he may repent in private."[41]

At times Rabbi Eleazar discussed the evil nature of man and said: "He who ridicules others will be punished with suffering,"[42] and "He who is arrogant toward others, deserves to be cut down like a tree, for he causes the *Shekhinah* to sorrow and in the end he will be as low as dust."[43]

More than arrogance Rabbi Eleazar despised flattery and he said: "A flatterer brings down the anger of God upon the world. Even children in their mother's womb curse him and he is doomed to *Gehenna*. He who flatters a wicked man will be delivered into his hand; if he escapes *his* hand, he is sure to be delivered into the hands of the children or the grandchildren of the wicked man."[44] "If a whole congregation is afflicted with flattery," he added, "it may be compared to an unclean woman and in the end it will be exiled."[45]

"He who departs from his word is like an idol worshipper,"[46] and "one who deceives with words, is worse than one who deceives with money."[47]

"A man who owns no land may not be considered a man, for the Bible said, 'The earth He gave to the people.' " All artisans will in the end return to the soil, despite the fact that there is no ruder work than tilling the soil. But although tilling the soil is of great importance, the position of the merchants is much more favorable.[48]

"Working for one's livelihood," Rabbi Eleazar said, "may be compared to working for the redemption. Just as redemption will be achieved through miracles, even so does one gain his livelihood miraculously, and just as one has to earn his livelihood daily, even so may he expect redemption daily."[49]

Rabbi Eleazar had a high opinion of married life and he said: "One who is not married may not be considered a man.

Thus we find that God named man after He had created both male and female."[50]

Speaking of human intelligence he said: "A man without intelligence deserves no pity, and he who gives his bread to a fool will suffer in the end and will be driven out of his home."[51]

64

RABBI AVAHU
OF CAESAREA

AT THAT TIME CHRISTIANITY began to spread throughout Palestine as a result of the encouragement it received from Roman officials who were inclined to favor it more than they favored Jewish teachings that were under the direct protection of the government. Those who steadfastly clung to the Jewish faith found themselves persecuted by their own brothers as well as by the government.

Rabbi Avahu of Caesarea lived during this period. He was known for his great beauty which was said to have resembled the beauty of the Patriarch Jacob. (According to Jewish tradition Jacob was the handsomest man of his generation and his image was engraved on God's "throne of honor.") In addition he was reputed to possess great physical strength, equal also to the strength of Jacob, who upon his arrival in Haran alone removed the stone from the mouth of the well; a feat that ordinarily required the combined effort of all the shepherds. Thus it was related of Rabbi Avahu that when the roof of the bathhouse where he was at the moment caved in, he supported it with his hands until assistance came, thus saving the lives of 101 people who were in the building.[1]

Rabbi Avahu was born in Caesarea and lived there all his life and conducted an academy. He traded in women's adornments and was very wealthy.[2] Because of this he was respected by the Roman officials whom he often presented with gifts. He led the life of an aristocrat; his house was furnished with ivory chairs, and it was said that each Saturday night he had a fatted calf slaughtered and of this he ate only the kidneys.[3] Rabbi Avahu was versed in the secular sciences and foreign languages and this contributed to his popularity in government circles. It was thus related that whenever he visited the governor, he was met with a special greeting that praised him with the following words: "Behold the greatest among his people, the leader of his nation, the shining light. Blessed be his coming in peace."[4]

But despite Rabbi Avahu's wealth and honor he was not proud and he shared his honors with other people.[5] He was often compelled to debate with Gentiles and he invariably emerged victorious.[6] During one of these debates he nearly lost his life when one Jacob Minaa gave him a poisonous liquid to drink; he was then saved by his colleagues, Rabbi Ami and Rabbi Asi. These debates forced Rabbi Avahu to study the Scriptures minutely until he became a great authority on the Bible.[7]

Rabbi Avahu began his studies with Rabbi Jochanan and from him he learned most of the Torah. In later life he remarked: "Rabbi Jochanan opened a door for me and he allowed the light to shine upon me."[8] Rabbi Jochanan also used to mention the name of Rabbi Avahu with affection and he called him "my child."[9] Rabbi Avahu also studied with Rabbi Eleazar ben Pedat. He quoted his master in the Babylonian Talmud twenty times and in the Jerusalem Talmud there are about fifty such quotations in addition to those in the *midrashim*. It appears that he also studied with Resh Lakish, but his relations with the latter were more those of friendship than the relations of a pupil with his teacher. Both often went to spread knowledge of the Torah in cities where that was needed. As they were once approaching such a city, Rabbi Avahu remarked: "Why should we go into a city of wicked men where we shall certainly be humiliated?" Resh Lakish then dismounted from the ass upon which he was riding and taking a handful of earth, he stuffed it into the mouth of Rabbi Avahu saying: "God does not want evil to be spoken of Jews."[10] Other statements quoted by Rabbi Avahu in the Talmud indicate that he also learned from other scholars.

After the death of Rabbi Jochanan, his followers wanted to choose Rabbi Avahu as head of the academy, but he refused this honor saying that Rabbi Abba of Acco was better fitted for the post. Rabbi Avahu therefore remained in Caesarea where he continued to head his own academy, and he interceded for his people with the authorities whenever necessary. When other scholars were forbidden to visit the cities for educational purposes, Rabbi Avahu was exempt from this restriction. In these travels he even reached Alexandria.

The wife of Rabbi Abba of Acco once remarked to the wife of Rabbi Avahu that her husband was equal to Rabbi Avahu in learning and that he showed respect to him merely because the latter was rich. The woman repeated this remark to her husband, but Rabbi Avahu said: "It does not matter whether Rabbi Abba needs my learning or not, both he and I praise God."[11]

The following incident was also characteristic of the modesty of Rabbi Avahu: When the land was once affected by a drought, the people sought someone whose prayer for rain should be acceptable in the eyes of God. Rabbi Avahu then learned in a dream that a certain man named Pentakake was the right man to offer the prayer. He was thereupon summoned and when asked what his trade was, he said that he was a white-slave dealer. Rabbi Avahu was curious to know what good deeds such a man could have done in order to make his prayers acceptable to God. Pentakake told him that a woman once came to him and offered her body for a sum of money to redeem her husband from prison where he was incarcerated through no fault of his own. He pitied her and gave her all the money he possessed, and when that sum was not enough he sold his belongings to help the woman free her husband. When Rabbi Avahu heard this story he said: "If this is so then you are the worthiest man to pray for rain."[12]

Rabbi Jehudah N'siah II was Nasi at that time. The Nasi

resided at Sepphoris and even though the government at times did not allow the academy to be maintained there, he was too old to move elsewhere. His son Rabban Gamaliel IV, on the other hand, settled in Caesarea where an academy could be maintained due to Rabbi Avahu's influence with the authorities.

Rabbi Avahu was devoted to the Torah. When he came to Tiberias once, he was met by the disciples of Rabbi Jochanan who noticed that his face was suffused with joy. When Rabbi Jochanan later asked what was the cause of his joy, he replied that he had found an old *Tosefta* that shed new light on the subject that he was then studying.[13]

Another time it was related that Rabbi Avahu fasted on the day that a scholar died.[14]

The following of Rabbi Avahu's ethical teachings deserve to be mentioned:

"Repentance is the greatest thing in the world; even saints cannot attain the position of penitents."[15]

"One should strive to be among the persecuted rather than among the oppressors."[16]

"One should not rule his household by fear."[17]

During a discussion on the manner in which the world had been created, Rabbi Avahu said: "God had created previous worlds which He destroyed, because He was not pleased with them, until He created the present world which is permanent."[18]

The verse "They who sit at the gates shall speak against me" (Psalms 69:13), he interpreted to refer to those who ridicule the Jews in their theatres and circuses. Rabbi Avahu then described the manner in which the theatre of his time ridiculed the Jews. They would bring out on the stage a camel whose head was bowed, and one actor would then ask another: "Can you tell me why this camel is so sad?" and the other would reply: "This is the sabbatical year of the Jews and since they do not have enough food they eat the camel's food and that makes the camel sad."

"And why is the price of oil so high?" the first actor would ask again. The other actor would then reply: "Since the Jews strictly observe their Sabbath, on which day they eat the food they have accumulated during a whole week, they never have enough wood to cook all that food, thus they use their beds as fuel; when their beds are burned, they are forced to sleep on the floor, and since that makes them dirty and dusty, they rub oil all over their bodies, and that's why oil is so expensive."[19]

Anyone who is familiar with the Bible is acquainted with the story of Saul who sought a young man who could play an instrument well in order to assuage his melancholy. On that occasion one of Saul's servants said that the son of Jesse was "skillful as a player and a mighty valiant man, and a man of war, and intelligent in speech, and a person of a good form, and the Lord is with him " (I Sam. 17:18). Rabbi Avahu interpreted "skillful as a player" to mean that David was versed in the Scriptures; "a mighty valiant man," that he was strong in *Mishnah*; "a man of war," that he was skilled in the battles of the Torah; "intelligent in speech," that he understood the value of good deeds; "a person of good form," that he understood the Talmud. Another interpretation of Rabbi Avahu to the same verse declared that "intelligent in speech" indicated that David could deduce conclusions; "a man of good form," that his face shone in *Halakhah*; and "the Lord is with him," that the law was established according to his opinion.

The following is another example of Rabbi Avahu's method of interpretation: Of the creation of the world, the Bible says that the earth "was without form, and void." This expression was then interpreted to mean that the earth was wondering at the void which pervaded it. Rabbi Avahu compared this to a king who had bought two slaves on one contract and for the same price. The king then commanded one of the slaves to be fed from the royal kitchen and the other one to obtain his own food. The second slave therefore wondered: "We were both bought on one contract and for the same price and yet I must obtain my own food or starve." The earth likewise wondered and said: "The creatures of Heaven and those of the earth were created at the same time and yet creatures of Heaven are nourished by the divine *Shekhinah* while creatures on earth must labor for their food or else they would starve."[20]

On one occasion Rabbi Avahu lectured on *Aggadah* in the same city where Rabbi Chiya bar Abba lectured on *Halakhah*. The inhabitants of the city then flocked to hear Rabbi Avahu and Rabbi Chiya felt grieved at this. But Rabbi Avahu consoled him with the following parable: "Two merchants once came to a city; one of them brought precious stones to sell while the other brought trinkets. Did not most of the people run to the merchant who sold trinkets?"[21] The Talmud further relates that on that day Rabbi Avahu showed special honor to Rabbi Chiya. On all other occasions it was customary for Rabbi Chiya to escort Rabbi Avahu to his inn whenever they chanced to be in the same city. This honor was accorded to Rabbi Avahu because he was considered the representative of the Jewish people to the Roman government. But on that day the procedure was reversed and Rabbi Avahu escorted Rabbi Chiya to his hostelry to console him in his grief at being slighted by the inhabitants of the city.

As a result of Rabbi Avahu's residence in Caesarea, the city came to be known as a seat of learning even as it was during the days of Rabbi Oshaiah Rabbah. The academy where Rabbi Avahu taught was known as Mardutha which some explained to indicate that the academy was a nest of rebellion against Rome, because Mardutha means revolt.[22] It was further related that when Rabbi Avahu studied during the night, he did not remove his phylacteries,[23] and that when he lectured his audience could see a halo about him.[24] When Rabbi Avahu died, the mourning was so great that even the pillars in the city were believed to shed tears.[25]

"Three types of sin," Rabbi Avahu said, "are never forgiven by God. These are deception, robbery, and idol worship."[26] When he heard scholars debating the cause of the destruction of Jerusalem, he declared that it was due to the neglect of reciting the *Shema* morning and evening.[27]

One of Rabbi Avahu's sons, Rabbi Chanina, was sent to Tiberias to engage in study. But the young man devoted himself primarily to charitable deeds, especially burial of the dead. Rabbi Avahu then wrote to him: "Have I sent you to Tiberias because there were not enough graves in Caesarea?

Furthermore it is an accepted rule that learning is more important than charitable deeds."[28]

Poverty was then the share of many scholars and Rabbi Avahu, who was himself wealthy, consoled the needy scholars with the following words: "A scholar who devotes himself to learning despite his poverty is certain to partake of the nobility of the *Shekhinah* in the world to come."[29] Of those who forgot their learning he said: "One who forgets anything of his learning should be demoted from his position."[30]

Like other scholars Rabbi Avahu also believed that God recognized the holidays as they were determined by the high court and he said: "When five elders gather to determine a leap year, God leaves His heavenly retinue and descends to earth in His Majesty. The angels then wonder, since they know that were the people to err God would correct them."[31]

Rabbi Avahu was once asked whether *Hallel* should be recited on the New Year and the Day of Atonement. He then declared that on these days the angels come before God and say: "Your Jews are celebrating holidays and they do not recite *Hallel*" (praise). God then answers them: "When a mortal king sits in judgment and the books of life and death are open before him, do his subjects sing his praise at that moment?"[32]

"When Jews are aided in time of need," Rabbi Avahu said, "it is as if God were also aided, for the Scriptures declare 'I am with him in affliction.' When Jews are in need it is as if God were also in need; by aiding them He also aids Himself."[33] "It is an accepted rule that God forgets nothing," he continued, "but when the punishment of Jews for their sins is concerned, He overlooks many things."[34]

Of the passage "I hear of your evil dealings from all this people " (I Sam. 2:23), Rabbi Avahu said: "The Scriptures intend to teach people ethical behavior. When one hears good things of his neighbor, he should repeat it in the name of the person he had heard if from; but when one hears evil of his neighbor and he wishes to admonish him, he should not name the person who informed him."[35]

The Biblical statement "I am the Lord your God" Rabbi Avahu explained as an indication that God was not like mortal rulers. Therefore God said "I am first" (I have no father); "I am last" (I have no brother); "Beside me there is no God" (I have no sons).[36]

During a discussion concerning wise men Rabbi Avahu said: "God gives wisdom to the wise as the Scriptures say "In the heart of every wise man I put wisdom."[37]

When a child of Rabbi Avahu died, two scholars came to console him but they remained silent fearing to grieve him by mentioning the dead child. Rabbi Avahu then explained to them that God's judgment could not be otherwise than just and he said: "When an earthly court condemns one to death, the relatives of the condemned man come to greet the judges and the witnesses to show that they bear no ill will against them and that they are convinced of the justice of the sentence, despite the fact that earthly courts are full of deception and robbery and error and they are also transitory. How much greater is the duty to recognize the justice of the judgment of God before whom there is neither deception nor robbery nor error?"[38]

65

RABBI CHIYA
BAR ABBA HACOHEN

RABBI CHIYA BAR ABBA HACOHEN is not to be
confused with the *tanna* Rabbi Chiya Rabbah who lived four
generations earlier during the time of Rabbi Jehudah Hanasi.
He came to Palestine from Babylonia together with his brother
Simeon. Since no mention is made of his teachers in Babylonia,
it is to be assumed that he left that country while still very
young. Upon his arrival in Palestine he found the first of the
amoraim Rabbi Chanina bar Chama and Rabbi Joshua ben Levi
who were then already old men. When Rabbi Chiya came to
Sepphoris he was befriended by Rabbi Chanina bar Chama
who often leaned on him when he walked through the streets;
he was also respected by Resh Lakish who engaged him to
tutor his children. Rabbi Jochanan likewise loved his pupil
Rabbi Chiya and called him "my child."[1] When Rabbi Chiya fell
ill, Rabbi Jochanan came to visit and asked him: "Do you love
your suffering?" implying thereby that suffering atones for
one's sins, but Rabbi Chiya replied: "I want neither suffering
nor its reward." Rabbi Jochanan then asked for his hand and he
cured him.[2]

Rabbi Chiya bar Abba was also respected by the Patriarch
Rabbi Jehudah N'siah II who empowered him to visit various
cities together with Rabbi Ami and Rabbi Asi for the purpose of

clarifying matters of religious conduct and also in order to appoint tax collectors in these cities for the government and for the Nasi.[3]

Rabbi Chiya suffered greatly in Palestine. Although he did not suffer want to the same extent as his brother did, he nevertheless was subject to other limitations and hindrances. Friends then advised him to leave Palestine, but for some time he refused to leave the country. Finally he was compelled by circumstances to leave because he no longer wanted to gain his sustenance from tithes, which in his eyes amounted to charity and made him feel dependent. He was at that time the *cohen* of the family Silone who gave him its tithes. When a dispute arose concerning the interpretation of a law that Rabbi Chiya wanted to interpret more leniently than the other scholars, he feared that his action would be explained as an attempt to favor the family from whom he derived his livelihood.[4] He then went to Babylonia and he was retained by no one. Rabbi Chiya asked Rabbi Eleazar ben Pedat to get a letter of recommendation from the Nasi for him and the latter immediately granted his request. In his letter to the Jews of Babylonia, the Nasi wrote: "We are sending you a great man who is our messenger and who is like ourselves."[5]

Rabbi Chiya later returned to Palestine where he remained permanently. He lived in several cities, namely in Gabala, between Bet Shean and Tiberias,[6] in Roma located in Galilee,[7] in Sepphoris,[8] and in Lodacea.[9] His permanent residence was later in Tyre which had once been a Phoenician city, but at that time it contained a Jewish community and was considered to be a part of Palestine.

It was told that at the death of Rabbi Jehudah N'siah II, priests were permitted to participate in the burial of the Nasi. Rabbi Zeira, who was also a priest, disapproved of this ruling but Rabbi Chiya forced him to touch the body of the Nasi. It appears that Rabbi Chiya was not very strict in the observance of the priestly restrictions on other occasion as well. Thus it was told that when Emperor Diocletian visited Tyre, Rabbi Chiya passed through a cemetery to see him.[10]

Rabbi Chiya bar Abba was very pious and many wondrous tales were related of the results of his prayers. Some he cured through prayer and for others he obtained long life. Once a wild animal appeared and destroyed all the trees it chanced upon. The people came to Rabbi Chiya to ask him to pray for the animal's immediate departure. He prayed and the animal suddenly heard the voice of its mother[11] and fled to the desert whence it came.[12]

This *midrash* does not name the animal and merely refers to it as *re'eim*, a young beast, concerning the nature of which commentators differed. According to another *midrash*, the *re'eim* was a gigantic animal that Noah could not take into the Ark because of its size, and he therefore tied it to the Ark so it might swim alongside. The *Septuagint* (Greek translation of the Bible) identified the *re'eim* as a unicorn. Others gave differing descriptions. It nevertheless appears now that the animal referred to in the *midrash* was really a young elephant that uprooted and trampled trees and fled when it heard the call of his mother.

Rabbi Chiya bar Abba was not an adherent of *Aggadah* and when he lectured on *Halakhah* in the same city with Rabbi Avahu of Caesarea, the people flocked to hear Rabbi Avahu whose discourse dealt with *Aggadah*. The opinion of Rabbi Chiya concerning *Aggadah* is illustrated by the incident that when he saw a book of *aggadot* and remarked: "Even though it may contain some good things, the hands of him who wrote the book should be cut off."[13] We may also assume that his knowledge of the Bible was limited.[14] One of his pupils once asked him the reason why the word *tov* (good) was mentioned in the version of the ten commandments given in Deuteronomy but not in the first version. To this Rabbi Chiya replied: "Rather than to ask me why the word *tov* is or is not used, you should ask me whether it is used at all for I do not know of it."[15]

Like his contemporaries Rabbi Chiya also revered the Sabbath above all and he maintained that because of its merit the Jews will be redeemed.[16]

"When Jews pray," Rabbi Chiya said, "they do not all end their prayers at the same time for each group prays separately.

But when all the prayers are finished, the angel who is in charge of prayer gathers them and weaves crowns for the head of God who thus adorns Himself with the prayers of Israel."[17]

"One who observes the *Shema* is like one who observes all the Ten Commandments for the latter were given at the time of the morning *Shema* and all of them are also included in the *Shema*."[18]

Other statements of Rabbi Chiya give a clear picture of the time in which he lived. Thus he said:

"Even a father and a son or a teacher and his pupil may wage hot discussions on their differences of opinion while interpreting their studies, but they do not part until they grow to love each other."[19]

"If one were to tell you that you should give your life for the sanctification of the name of God, you may say to him: 'I will do so if I am to be killed at once, but not if I have to undergo the ordeal of previous generations when heated balls of iron were placed under the arms of Jews or when their nails were pierced with wire.' "[20]

"The hatred of the Gentile nations toward the Jews may be compared to a man who is an enemy of the king and wishes to harm him, but cannot do so. Such a man at least wants to destroy the statue of the king, but fearing that he would be executed for such a deed, he undermines the wall of the monument thus causing it to fall. Gentile nations likewise fear to come out against God and therefore they persecute the Jews."[21]

Rabbi Chiya lived to a ripe old age and all of his sons grew up to be scholars. A special prayer of Rabbi Chiya is of great interest. It said: "May it be Thy will, oh Lord our God and God of our fathers, that You should turn our hearts to complete repentance, that we should not be shamed before our fathers in the world to come, that You should inspire our hearts with fear of Thy name, and that You should remove us from that which You hate, and that You should bring us near to that which You love and that You should be merciful to us for the sake of Your name."[22]

66

RABBI AMI
AND RABBI ASI

T HE TWO *AMORAIM*, Rabbi Ami and Rabbi Asi, were always mentioned together due to the great bond of friendship which united them. But before describing the lives of these two *amoraim* one must mention an event that transpired in Palmyra (Tadmor in the Bible, Tarmud in the Talmud), a city in an oasis in the Syrian desert between the Euphrates and Damascus.

In Palmyra there lived a robber chieftain who became a legitimate ruler when he aided the Romans in their war against the Persians of Babylonia. The name of this chieftain was Barnezer Odenate or Odenatus. When the Romans were defeated by the Persians and their leaders taken captive, Odenatus liberated them, preserved Roman rule in Syria, and Emperor Galianus (264 C.E.) then recognized him as co-ruler. However, this situation did not last long for Odenatus's wife (later Queen Zenobiah) hired assassins to murder him in order that she might rule in his stead. With her wisdom and her organizational talents she succeeded in transforming Palmyra into a metropolis. She was aided by the fact that it was situated at the crossroads of important caravan routes. The city was then enlarged by the construction of beautiful palaces in the Roman style.

Some historians maintain that Zenobiah embraced Judaism or that she was sympathetic to the Jewish faith. Jewish historians, however, deny this and make no mention of any kind acts toward the Jews on her part. But all Roman historians concur in their praise of her beauty, education, and good taste. She was a gifted diplomat and she succeeded in persuading all the rulers of western Asia to unite against Emperor Aurelius. Aurelius advanced against Zenobiah with a large army when he realized that she planned to liberate her country from Roman domination. In this venture he was successful and devastated her land.

It appears that the Jews of Palestine were not satisfied with the proximity of Zenobiah's kingdom and they aided the Romans. An expression current among the Jews of that time stated: "Happy is he who will live to see the destruction of Tadmor." The problem also arose as to whether converts from Palmyra were to be accepted since the population of this city was of mixed origin.

According to the Scriptures (I Kings 9:18) Palmyra was founded by King Solomon who colonized it with people from various nations. It is also known that Zenobiah was an offspring of a mixed marriage. For this reason it was accepted that "Jews would celebrate the day of the destruction of Tadmor."[1]

That the Jews participated in this war on the side of Rome is evident from numerous statements in the Talmud. Thus it is told that Rabbi Ami interceded for a man named Zeira bar Chanina who was captured in the city of Saphsipha as a warrior against Palmyra. Rabbi Ami then implored Zenobiah to spare the man's life, but she said to him: "Do you permit yourself to do anything you choose because God always performs miracles for you?" At about the same time Rabbi Asi was also captured by the soldiers of Palmyra and was condemned to death. Resh Lakish then hastened to save him saying that he would sacrifice his own life, if necessary, to save Rabbi Asi.[2]

The Palestinian Patriarch of that time was Rabbi Jehudah N'siah III. He was nearly always ignored by the scholars, and when the latter consulted him in some matter out of deference to his office, he always sought the advice of Rabbi Ami. The

Nasi once sent Rabbi Ami and Rabbi Asi to the various cities of Palestine to appoint teachers of the Bible and the *Mishnah*. They arrived in a certain city where there were no teachers and they asked the leaders of the community whether they had engaged watchmen. The city watchmen were pointed out to them, but they remarked: "These are not watchmen! The real watchmen of a city are the teachers who instruct the children."[3]

The animosity between Jews and Samaritans grew acute at that time due to the friendship of the latter toward the Romans and the Christians. Rabbi Ami and Rabbi Asi then instructed the Jews to avoid the Samaritans and to consider them as pagans in all matters, particularly in the use of their wine.[4]

Rabbi Ami and Rabbi Asi came from Babylonia where they had previously studied together.[5] Both immediately became pupils of Rabbi Jochanan,[6] and were later ordained at the same time. The day of their ordination was a feast day for the other pupils who sang their praise with the following words: "Only pupils like you should be ordained."[7]

Travel between Palestine and Babylonia was free and undisturbed at that time and scholars constantly went from one country to the other. In Babylonia the academies of Sura and Pumbedita were renowned. When Rabbi Ami quoted a law he heard in Babylonia, he would say: "Our teachers in Babylonia said . . ."[8] Rabbi Asi's coming to Palestine was said to have been caused by his desire to escape his capricious, aged mother.[9]

It has been told that Rabbi Ami and Rabbi Asi lived in great friendship. They attended the same academy, and after their ordination they enjoyed the same measure of honor. They were referred to as the Judges of Palestine[10] or the honorable Priests of Palestine.[11] Rabbi Ami was also called a great man,[12] and Rabbi Eleazar ben Pedat referred to Rabbi Asi as the example of the generation.[13]

After the death of Rabbi Eleazar ben Pedat, both headed the academy in Tiberias. It was related that when prayer time came, each one would pray alone between the columns of the academy.[14] Often they interrupted their studies and called out: "He who wants to know the law or seeks judgment, let him enter."[15]

Together with Rabbi Chiya bar Abba they once judged a licentious woman named Tamar, and they sentenced her to be beaten with rods. The woman complained to the Roman authorities that they had exceeded their rights in passing judgment affecting the life of a person. Rabbi Avahu successfully interceded for them since he was influential with the Romans, but the woman could not be persuaded to withdraw her complaint. Rabbi Avahu then sent an allegoric message to the defendants. Here is a literal translation of it: "We have conciliated the three accusers, the Good Child, the Educated one, and the Man of the Sea; the Date (Tamar) persists in its bitterness and we sought to sweeten it, but vain were the efforts of the Goldsmith." The explanation of this message is as follows: Rabbi Avahu conciliated the three judges, one of whom was named Eudokos (good child), the other Eumathes (educated), and the third Thelaseus (sea man). But the woman Tamar persists in her bitterness and would not be placated with money."[16]

Upon their arrival in Palestine, Rabbi Ami and Rabbi Asi were pupils of Rabbi Jochanan to whom they were so attached, that after his death they mourned him as one mourns a relative. They were also close friends of Rabbi Yitzchak the Blacksmith, although there exist *halakhot* in the name of Rabbi Yitzchak and Rabbi Ami alone.[17] Once when they visited Rabbi Yitzchak in his home one of them asked him to expound some matter in *Halakhah*, while the other asked him to discuss some aggadic subject. Rabbi Yitzchak replied: "What you demand of me may be compared to a man who has two wives, one young and the other old. The young wife plucks the grey hair out of his head and the old wife plucks the black hair, until he becomes bald. You likewise may cause me to say nothing by your requests; but I will tell you something that will please both of you and that will contain both *Halakhah* and *Aggadah*."[18]

During a feast in the house of Rabbi Ami, one of the guests wished to drink boiled wine that had remained uncovered overnight. Rabbi Ami said to him: "One who wishes to die should go to his own house to die."[19]

When Rabbi Ami became head of the academy in Tiberias he came into close contact with the Nasi. The latter once asked him the meaning of the verse, "Have faith in the Lord forever, for the Lord is the rock of the ages." Rabbi Ami replied that one who had faith in God would be protected by Him in both worlds.[20] It was said that the Nasi bestowed honors and ordination upon people for a price and without consideration for their merit. Rabbi Ami then said that the Nasi broke the commandment not to make gold and silver gods. During a calamity that afflicted the whole people, the Nasi decreed thirteen fast days. When these were of no avail, he wanted to decree another fast day, but Rabbi Ami objected on the ground that the people should not be taxed beyond their endurance and the Nasi had to comply with his decision.[21]

On the day of the coronation of Diocletian, Rabbi Ami dreamed that it was announced in heaven that "Magdiel was crowned today." This dream he interpreted as an omen that the emperor following Diocletian would be the last ruler of Rome. (Magdiel in the Bible preceded the last of the rulers of Edom.) This prophecy partly came true, for the successor of Diocletian was followed by Constantine the Great under whose rule Rome became a Christian kingdom.

It is told that when Rabbi Ami headed the academy, a bag of gold was once brought to him and he distributed it among the students.[22] Another version relates that he found a jar full of gold and the Romans informed him that he could use it as he saw fit, for according to Roman law a man could claim lawful ownership of any article that he found.[23]

Statements of Rabbi Ami occur in nearly every part of both the Babylonian and the Jerusalem Talmud. Although he was probably the first in his generation who ascribed sanctity to the opinions of previous *amoraim*, he nevertheless was not modest insofar as his own achievements were concerned, and he once said: "From Ami, the son of Nathan, learning will issue for all Israel."[24]

On numerous occasions he sought to lighten the burden of the laws. Thus he opposed the strictures of the scholars of Tiberias who would prohibit the spreading of fishing nets during the intermediate days of the holidays (*chol hamo'ed*) for fear that it would interfere with the festive mood of the occasion.[25] When he was asked whether Jews were permitted to participate in festivities of pagans, he wished to permit it for the sake of maintaining peace with the neighboring people, but Rabbi Abba reminded him that Rabbi Chiya had forbidden it. Rabbi Ami then remarked: "Let us praise God that Rabbi Abba called our attention to the opinion of Rabbi Chiya, else we would have fallen into idolatry."[26]

At another time a slave brought a bill of divorce for a Jewish woman and Rabbi Ami wished to declare the divorce to be valid, although it was an accepted rule that a slave may not testify. Again Rabbi Abba called his attention to a decision of Rabbi Chiya prohibiting such a procedure and Rabbi Ami said: "Let us praise God that Rabbi Abba reminded us of the opinion of Rabbi Chiya, else we would have allowed a married woman to remarry."[27]

Both Rabbi Ami and Rabbi Asi were equally respected. Rabbi Ami is always mentioned first in the Babylonian Talmud, but in the Jerusalem Talmud, Rabbi Asi is sometimes mentioned first. On one occasion Rabbi Asi addresses Ami as Rabbi. This, however, is explained by the fact that Rabbi Ami was the older of the two.[28] Both of them were known as saintly men and even when they were in dangerous places where others had suffered harm, they emerged unharmed.[29] Rabbi Asi died first in Tiberias, while Rabbi Ami spent the last days of his life in Caesarea.[30] After his death, the political situation of the Jews deteriorated to such an extent that no one could be elected to head the academy.

Rabbi Ami was also the author of the well-known statement that inspired the fantasy of many poets to the elaboration of a dramatic story. When the power of faith was being discussed, Rabbi Ami said: "We can see the greatness of people who possess faith from the story of the weasel and the well." He concluded with the following words: "If a person who believes this story is certain to be rewarded, how much greater will be the reward of one who believes in God."[31] It appears that the story of the weasel and the well was then very popular. It is also possible that it appeared in some *midrash* and that Rashi, *Tosefot* and the author of *Arukh* obtained it from that *midrash*.

"A maiden," thus the story runs, "once lost her way and

being very thirsty she bent over a well to draw some water and fell into it. A young man who chanced to pass by heard her cries. At first he was fearful lest it was some evil spirit who wished to draw him into the well, and he asked the maiden to swear by the name of God that she was human and not an evil spirit. When he drew her out of the well, his passions were aroused by her beauty, but she implored him not to sin, promising to marry him according to the laws of Israel. They then swore fidelity to each other and, as a weasel ran by, they called upon it and upon the well to witness their troth.

"The two young people then parted and the young man forgot his oath. He did not come to the maiden's father to claim her and he married another woman. His wife bore him two children one of whom was killed by a weasel and the other was drowned in a well. His wife came to believe that the children must have lost their lives as a result of the sins of their father, and then he remembered the oath he had sworn to the maiden at the well. He thereupon divorced his wife and found the maiden to whom he had sworn fidelity, nearly insane with grief. He then fulfilled his vow and married her."[32]

Regarding everyday conduct Rabbi Ami decreed that one should not take money into his mouth, nor place food beneath one's bed, nor hold bread under one's arm, nor allow a knife to stick in radishes or lemons.[33] He also gave omens through which one was to know on the new year whether he would survive the coming year, and whether a trip or some occupation to be undertaken would be accomplished successfully.[34]

One of the scholars once declared that there were three types of arrogant creatures in the world: the dog among the animals, the cock among the fowl, and the Jews among the nations. Rabbi Ami then declared that the arrogance of these creatures was a virtue rather than a fault. This he held to be particularly true of the Jews who readily offer their lives for their faith.[35]

Other expressions of Rabbi Ami indicate that he did not maintain friendly relations with pagans—thus he said that one should not teach Torah to a pagan.[36]

The Biblical verse "Let us make man," that other scholars found difficult to explain because of the implication that God was assisted in the creation of man, Rabbi Ami ingeniously explained by saying God had consulted his own heart.[37]

Rabbi Asi was once sent by the Nasi to appoint tax collectors in various cities. Many people at that time refused to accept this office because of the heavy responsibility it involved. Rabbi Asi persuaded some of them to accept the office of tax collector by the promise of fame. He also established the rule that "two brothers may not represent the same community."[38]

The opinions of Rabbi Ami and Rabbi Asi are often introduced in the Talmud by the words "both said." On other occasions, however, their opinions are quoted separately and at times they even differed.[39]

"Why are children taught the chapters on priesthood before Genesis," Rabbi Asi asked, and he gave the following answer: "God says that sacrifices are pure and children are pure; it is therefore fitting that children should begin their studies with a sacred subject."[40]

It is also related that a weaver once came to Rabbi Jochanan and told him that in his dream he had seen the sky falling but that a disciple of Rabbi Jochanan had supported it with his hand. Rabbi Jochanan asked whether he would recognize that disciple, and the weaver asked that the students pass before him. This was done and the weaver pointed to Rabbi Asi as the man who had supported the sky.[41]

When Rabbi Asi died, it was said that the gate of Tiberias collapsed.[42] Another version told of cedar trees being uprooted on the day of his death.[43]

67

RABBI YITZCHAK
THE BLACKSMITH

RABBI YITZCHAK NAPCHA (the Blacksmith) was one of the most prominent disciples of Rabbi Jochanan and a master of *Aggadah* who lived during the second, third, and fourth generations of *amoraim*. His surname, Napcha, is variously interpreted. Some claim it refers to his occupation as a blacksmith, although the Talmud is not explicit on that point, while others maintain that he was a native of a city by that name. Such a city is mentioned in the travels of Benjamin of Tudela. Rabbi Yitzchak Napcha should not be confused with another man of the same name who lived during the days of Rabbi Jehudah bar Elai.[1]

Rabbi Yitzchak Napcha is never mentioned in the Jerusalem Talmud by this name. Some Talmud critics therefore believe that Rabbi Yitzchak bar Tavlai, who is mentioned there, is really Rabbi Yitzchak Napcha. References in the Jerusalem Talmud to Rabbi Yitzchak, without any further designation, are also believed to refer to Rabbi Yitzchak Napcha.

The poverty that existed during the time of Rabbi Yitzchak is best illustrated by his remark that "the curse of God that people shall be forced to eat the grass of the fields applies only to the present generations. People suffer such hunger these days that they cannot wait for the grain to ripen in the field and they pluck and eat it while it is still green."[2] "In such times," Rabbi Yitzchak added, "people are not interested in learning and they merely wish to hear words of consolation."[3]

Rabbi Yitzchak Napcha lived in Tiberias together with his master Rabbi Jochanan and his friends Rabbi Eleazar ben Pedat and Rabbi Ami. He also maintained close bonds of friendship with other scholars who frequently visited him at home to discuss various laws and he also visited their homes for the same purpose.[4] Differences of opinion at times marked his relations with Rabbi Ami. Thus one declared that if a needle was found in the lung of an animal its flesh was kosher, while the other held it to be unfit to eat.[5] Similarly Rabbi Yitzchak decided on whether it was permissible to eat onions harvested during the Sabbatical year, while Rabbi Ami didn't know how to decide this law.[6]

That the opinions of Rabbi Yitzchak were held above those of other scholars is also evident from the fact that when the Nasi, Rabbi Jehudah II, entertained priests at his table and did not know whether it was permissible to serve them with the flesh of a firstborn animal, he first inquired Rabbi Ami's opinion and then asked the same question of Rabbi Yitzchak for a final decision.[7] It may be assumed that Rabbi Yitzchak was then a judge in Tiberias and since his teachings were popular, his decisions were accepted in all matters of *Halakhah*.[8]

At a later date Rabbi Yitzchak Napcha went to Babylonia. This journey apparently took place after the destruction of Tiberias during the Roman wars when Rabbi Ami transferred his academy to Caesarea in order to continue his teaching under the protection of Rabbi Avahu. Rabbi Yitzchak's stay in Babylonia coincided with the period that saw the influence of Rabbi Sheshet.[9]

When Rabbi Yitzchak returned to Palestine, he settled in Caesarea where he appears to have been a member of Rabbi Avahu's court. There he was once confronted with the problem of whether it was permissible to read the weekly portion of the Bible in the synagogue from a Torah containing only one of the books of the Pentateuch. Rabbi Yitzchak could not answer this question, but Rabbi Shmuel bar Nachmani reminded him of the rule that a scroll of the Torah from which even one parchment was missing, could not be used for reading in the synagogue; it thus became apparent that a scroll which contained only one of the books of the Pentateuch could not be used.[10]

Rabbi Yitzchak yearned for the restoration of Jerusalem. His heart was filled with anguish when he saw Caesarea in all its glory while Jerusalem lay desolate. He then came to the conclusion that these two cities—Caesarea and Jerusalem—could not both thrive at the same time and that the prosperity of one was inevitably bound up with the destruction of the other.[11] While speaking of these cities Rabbi Yitzchak mentioned a people, Germania of Edom—who could destroy the whole world, if God would only allow it. These people, he said, restrain the Romans. Rabbi Yitzchak was no doubt referring to the German tribes who were then conducting a struggle against Rome and of whom vague rumors reached the Jews of Palestine.

On another occasion Rabbi Yitzchak interpreted the verse "A generation comes and a generation goes, but the earth endures for ever," as referring to the various kingdoms of the world that rise and fall while the Jewish people remains eternal.[12]

Most of the expositions of Rabbi Yitzchak remained in the form of introductions to the books of the Scriptures. The following are some of the more interesting excerpts from his lectures:

"It is impossible to measure the strength of one's evil desires that are renewed daily.[13] Even when one mourns for the dead, his evil desires are with him.[14] Man is so controlled by his desires that even though these enter as visitors, they immediately possess his entire being.[15]

"He who angers his neighbor, even though he does so only with words, must conciliate him. If he has money, he must seek conciliation through money; he should also ask his friends to intercede for him and to gain forgiveness for him.[16]

Rabbi Yitzchak highly valued charity, but he considered kind words spoken to the poor to be of even greater merit than money. He therefore said: "One who gives a penny to a poor man will be blessed with six blessings, but one who speaks kind words to the poor will be blessed with all seven blessings."[17]

Like his contemporaries he also valued prayer saying: "Prayer is more important than sacrifices. Thus we see that when Samuel's father came to Shiloh, he bowed first and then he offered sacrifices."[18]

"Why were Abraham and Isaac childless?" Rabbi Yitzchak asked. He provided the answer himself by saying that "God yearns for the prayers of the holy and He caused Abraham and Isaac to be childless in order that they might pray to him."[19]

Of those who indulged in many vows in the hope of finding favor in the eyes of God, Rabbi Yitzchak said: "He who makes a vow is like a person who pierces his heart with a sword. Are not the prohibitions of the Torah sufficient that people need assume additional limitations?"[20]

Rabbi Yitzchak highly valued the study of the Torah and he said: "The fact that people forget what they have learned is for their own benefit, for if they had not forgotten what they learned, then a person could devote himself to the Torah for two or three years, and would then turn to other occupations. But since it is in the nature of man to forget, he must always continue to study."[21]

The two olives the prophet Zachariah saw in one of his visions Rabbi Yitzchak explained as referring to the scholars of Palestine, who are as gentle and as dear to each other as oil, while the scholars of Babylonia embitter each other's lives like an olive tree.[22]

Remarkably interesting is Rabbi Yitzchak's description of Moses' emotions as his death approached. When his soul refused to leave him Moses said to it: "It seems that the Angel of Death desires to take you," but the soul replied: "God will save me from death." Moses then said: "When you see the Jews weep for me, will you weep with them?" and his soul replied: "My eyes will avoid tears." "Possibly you will be forced into Gehenna," Moses said, but his soul answered, "God will

save my foot from misstep." "And where do you expect to go?"
Moses further asked, and his soul answered, "I will go before
God in the land of the living."

When Moses heard this, Rabbi Yitzchak concluded, he
liberated his soul and said to it: "Go, my soul, to your rest."[23]

Even more interesting is Rabbi Yitzchak's explanation of
Haman's accusations against the Jews:

"When Ahasuerus decided to give a feast in celebration of
the completion of the third year of his reign, Haman appeared
before him and said: 'The Jewish God abhors adultery. You
must therefore hire harlots and command all Jews to come to
the feast to gratify their desires.' When Mordechai heard this,
he warned the Jews not to come to the feast since they were
invited to encourage them to sin.

"But the Jews disobeyed Mordechai and came to the feast,
and Satan immediately appeared before God saying: 'It is time
that You destroy this people who always sins against you but
never repents.'

" 'I would do so,' God replied, 'But what will become of
the Torah?' and Satan said, 'You can give it to the creatures of
Heaven.'

"God was almost persuaded by this argument and He
ordered a parchment be brought that the decree of annihilation
might be recorded. The Torah then appeared dressed in black
and weeping bitterly. When the angels saw the Torah mourning, they also wept and said: 'If the Jews will be destroyed, of
what use will we be in the world?' The sun and moon, the sky
and the earth likewise wrapped themselves in black and
mourned. Thereupon Elijah ran and aroused the saints from
their graves and said: 'The sun and the moon are darkened; the
sky and the earth are wrapped in mourning; the Torah and the
Angels weep and you lie peacefully?'

" 'Why do you rouse us?' the saints asked and Elijah said:
'It is decreed to annihilate the Jews.'

" 'Is there not even one pious man in this generation?'
Moses asked and Elijah replied: 'There is one saintly Jew
named Mordechai.'

" 'Then go to him,' Moses said, 'and tell him to pray to God. We will also pray until God shows mercy and annuls His decree.' "[24]

68

RABBI ABBA
BAR KAHANA AND
RABBI CHANINA
BAR PAPA

As HAS BEEN PREVIOUSLY pointed out, the political
and economic situation of the Jews of Palestine was indescrib-
ably tragic at that time. But there seems to have been a constant
migration from and into Babylonia. The Roman authorities did
not object to the many Palestinian Jews going to Babylonia to
seek their livelihood, while Babylonian Jews came to Palestine
to study. This was the case despite the fact that Babylonian
Jews had by that time attained a higher degree of learning.
They enjoyed full liberty in the observance of religious regulations; they had their own courts, and they passed sentences as
they saw fit. Only rarely did they consult the High Court in
Palestine. The determination of the beginning of the months
and of the holidays was the only thing that the Jews of
Babylonia could not do. Nevertheless, they considered the
teachings emanating from Palestine as the only correct teachings and they believed that despite the destruction of the
Temple, the saying that "out of Zion" would come learning was
still sound.

Rabbi Abba bar Kahana was one of the *"amoraim"* who
came to Palestine from Babylonia at this time. He brought with
himself numerous aggadic interpretations which he repeated in
the name of Rav (Abba Arecha).[1] Some people therefore claim

that he was a disciple of Rav but the dates of the lives of the two men do not coincide, and at the time that Rabbi Abba began to study, Rav had undoubtedly already died. It is more probable that Rabbi Abba had been a pupil of one of Rav's disciples. This view is also substantiated by the fact that he sometimes quoted Rabbi Chiya bar Ashi who had been a pupil of Rav.[2]

When Rabbi Abba bar Kahana arrived in Palestine, Rabbi Chanina bar Chama was probably still alive, for we find him quoting statements in the name of Rabbi Chanina.[3]

Another reference concerns a question he asked of Rabbi Ami.[4] But little is known of Rabbi Abba bar Kahana's life and personality. On one occasion he mentioned Kefar Chitaya and we may assume that he lived there, but it is unknown whether he conducted a seminary there.[5]

Like his contemporaries Rabbi Abba was also a master of exposition. The people had tired of legal disputations, but they responded eagerly to *Aggadah*. Hundreds of Rabbi Abba's expositions exist. Many of these are not clear, for his interpretations of Biblical verses often seem incomprehensible. Only a few are cited here to illustrate his method of interpretation.

Speaking of the verse "The sun rises and the sun sets," Rabbi Abba said: "What is the intention of this verse? Does not everyone know that the sun rises and sets every day? But this verse intends to show how God conducts the world. Before the sun of Moses set, the sun of Joshua ben Nun rose; the sun of Samuel rose before the sun of Eli set, and on the day that Rabbi Akiba died, Rabbi Jehuda Hanasi was born."[6]

The verse "If a snake bite without venom," Rabbi Abba explained in a different manner than did the other scholars. The word *lahash* means both, "venom" and "whisper." Rabbi Abba interpreted this verse to mean that a snake would not bite unless it had been decreed from above, nor would a lion stalk its prey without heavenly sanction, nor would a government oppress its people unless it was so commanded from above.[7]

Of the effect of a false oath Rabbi Abba said: "Some things not consumed by fire are consumed by a false oath. Wood is burned by fire but stones are not, but a false oath will consume both."[8]

"The slightest command of the Torah," Rabbi Abba said, "is rewarded as well as the greatest. God thus determined the reward of commandments in order to encourage the people to lead honest lives. The easiest commandment is to send the mother bird away from the nest when the fledglings are taken, in order that she may not suffer the anguish of seeing them killed. The hardest commandment to observe is honoring one's father and mother. These two commandments are nevertheless rewarded by long life."[9]

The following interpretation of a Bible verse by Rabbi Abba gives a picture of the mood of that time: "The anguish of death has surrounded me" (in Babylonia); "rivers of wickedness have horrified me" (in Media); "the suffering of the grave surrounded me" (among the Greeks); "the traps of death were set for me" (in Rome). The fact that the term "death" was employed in the first and the fourth of these, Rabbi Abba explained by saying that both Babylonia and Rome undertook to annihilate the Jews; the Babylonians destroyed the First Temple and the Romans destroyed the Second Temple.[10]

As did many other scholars of that time, Rabbi Abba believed that a war between Babylonia and Rome would result in the liberation of the Jews. He therefore said: "Whenever one will see many Babylonians in Palestine, it will be a sign of the approaching redemption."[11]

In a discourse concerning the peoples who lived in the neighborhood of Palestine, Rabbi Abba bar Kahana explained the Biblical verse to indicate that the *Pathrothim* and the *Kasluchim* intermarried freely and from these mixed marriages were descended giants like the Philistines and dwarfs like the *Kaphtorim*.[12]

Rabbi Chanina bar Papa was also very prominent at that time and his name is constantly linked with Rabbi Avahu, Rabbi Yitzchak Napcha, and Rabbi Ami. In the Jerusalem Talmud as well as in the *midrashim* his first name at times appears as Hinna or Chananiah. The name Papa is an Aramaic form of the Greek name Papos.

Rabbi Chanina bar Papa was a pupil of Rabbi Shmuel bar Nachmani who praised him for his knowledge of the

Scriptures.[13] Rabbi Chanina was also a close friend of the outstanding disciples of Rabbi Jochanan and he frequently debated with Rabbi Chama bar Chanina and with Rabbi Acha bar Chanina. The Talmud contains some statements of this time whose authorship is in doubt and these are generally introduced by "Rabbi Zeira said . . . , but others claim that Rabbi Chanina bar Papa said . . . "[14]

Rabbi Chanina par Papa also differed with Rabbi Zeira in the mattered of explaining the good deeds of the Israelite King Abiyah, the son of Jeroboam.[15] The Talmud also cites some of his public lectures, but one of these is sometimes ascribed to Rabbi Simlai.

The personality of Rabbi Chanina is surrounded with numerous legendary adventures. One of these tells of an attempt by a Roman matron to seduce him. When the attempt failed she ordered that Rabbi Chanina be found and he was forced to hide all night in a bathhouse that was reported to be haunted by evil spirits, but since he had not succumbed to sin, he escaped unharmed.[16] Another time Rabbi Chanina encountered an evil spirit while he was on a mission of charity. The spirit said to him: "Have you not learned that one must not tresspass another's boundary?" meaning that evil spirits are in control at night and that no man should appear outside at that time. But Rabbi Chanina replied: "The Bible says that he who gives charity secretly appeases wrath." And he turned and fled.[17]

When the hour of his death approached, Rabbi Chanina implored the Angel of Death to grant him thirty days so that he might review his learning. The Angel of Death granted him this request and Rabbi Chanina then asked if he might see his place in Paradise and if he could hold his sword on the way. But the Angel of Death refused this last request, remembering what happened when had he granted such a request to Rabbi Joshua ben Levi. When Rabbi Chanina died, his body was surrounded by a pillar of fire and none could approach it. Rabbi Alexandri then asked the body to cause the pillar of fire to depart. "Do it for the sake of the scholars who have come to your funeral," Rabbi Alexandri said, but the pillar of fire did not depart; "Do it for the honor of your father," he continued to implore and still the pillar of fire remained; "Do it for your own honor, so that we may be able to approach to mourn you and to attend to your burial." The pillar of fire thereupon vanished.[18]

The following of Rabbi Chanina's maxims are among the most interesting:

"One who is favored with grace is also a God-fearing man."[19]

"One who enjoys something in this world without pronouncing a benediction is like one who robs God and all of Israel.[20]

"He who criticizes his master is like one who criticizes the *Shekhinah*."[21]

The verse "the lions roar for prey," Rabbi Chanina interpreted that lions refer to the unbelieving peoples (*kefirim—kofrim*) who deny God and who seek to devour the Jews who depend upon God. God also feeds the poor and the rich alike.[22]

Balaam ben Beor was considered by Jews to have been the greatest prophet among the heathens. Rabbi Chanina asked: "What is the distinction between Jewish and heathen prophets?" He replied that God spoke to Jewish prophets directly, as a king who parts the curtains of his palace to speak to his friends. To the heathen prophets he spoke indirectly, as a king who speaks to strangers through a partition.[23]

69

RABBI ZEIRA

NEXT TO RABBI JOCHANAN there was none among the *amoraim* concerning whom so many legends were related as Rabbi Zeira. These referred less to his greatness in learning than they did to his unusual personality and to the great friendship uniting him with other scholars who lived in Palestine during the fourth century of the Christian era. Rabbi Zeira came to Palestine from Babylonia when he was already well versed in learning. When he arrived, his opinions were already being quoted in the Babylonian academies and various occurrences of his life were being recounted. Rabbi Zeira was orphaned when he was very young and later mourned, saying: "I wish that I had a father and a mother; I would then honor them as much as possible in order to earn a share in the world to come."

Once he heard it told that when a shoe fell off the foot of Rabbi Tarphon's mother as she was walking outside, Rabbi Tarphon could not pick up the shoe because it was the Sabbath, and he therefore placed his hand under his mother's foot to prevent her from treading the bare ground, and thus she walked until she reached home. The scholars then added that had Rabbi Tarphon done a thousandfold for his mother, he still would not have done even half of what one is supposed to do in order to honor his parents. Later Rabbi Zeira heard it said that the mother of Rabbi Ishmael once came before the scholars to complain that her son was not according her due honor. Greatly shocked, they asked her what Rabbi Ishmael had done that she had found it necessary to complain and the woman answered: "Everytime my son comes home from the academy I want to wash his feet and drink the water, but he would not allow me to do so." The scholars then said to Rabbi Ishmael: "If this is her desire, you must honor it."

When Rabbi Zeira heard these stories he exclaimed: "Blessed be the Lord that I have no father and mother for I could not do what Rabbi Tarphon did and I would not do what Rabbi Ishmael was advised to do."[1]

In Babylonia Rabbi Zeira acquired most of his learning from Rabbi Jehudah bar Ezekiel, head of the academy in Pumbedita.[2] He was also a pupil of Rav Huna[3] and it is possible that he also attended the academy of Rav and Shmuel, although it is likely that the opinions he quoted in their names he heard from their pupils. It is also known that he studied for a time with Rav Chisda.[4]

It is told that when Rabbi Zeira served his master Rav Huna, he once brought two glasses, one filled with wine and the other with oil, carrying them both in the same hand. Rav Huna's son then remarked: "Is your other hand cut off that you carry both glasses in one hand?" Rav Huna rebuked his son and said: "Is it not enough that a man like Rabbi Zeira is serving you that you must also insult him?'"[5]

Rabbi Zeira's yearning for Palestine led him to leave his native land where he enjoyed great honor as a scholar. Before he left Babylonia he fasted frequently in order to eradicate from his mind what he had learned there in order that it might not confuse his learning in Palestine.[6] Before leaving, Rabbi Zeira also minutely examined his own conduct to determine whether he was worthy to tread the Holy Land. He then had a dream in which he saw barley and this he considered to be an omen that his sins had been forgiven.[7] Until the day of his departure Rabbi Zeira avoided his teacher Rabbi Jehudah for fear that the latter might forbid his settling in Palestine. Rabbi Jehuda believed that one who leaves Babylonia of his own will transgresses against Biblical verse that declares that the Jews would be brought to Babylonia and would remain there.[8]

As he approached Palestine, Rabbi Zeira reached a river and in his impatience could not wait until he found a boat, so he discarded his garments and swam across. A Gentile who heard of this then said to him: "The Jews were always hasty and they remain so to this day. In your haste you could easily have drowned." But Rabbi Zeira answered him: "As I stood at the border of Palestine, I wondered whether I was worthy to enter the land Moses and Aaron could not enter."[9]

Rabbi Zeira's arrival made a great impression in the country and he immediately went to greet Rabbi Jochanan.[10] But his short stature and ungainly appearance earned for him nicknames such as "the black pot"[11] and "the small dark hunchback."[12] It was later related that once every month Rabbi Zeira would light an oven and enter the fire, and that the flames were powerless to harm him. But once he was affected by an "evil eye" and was scorched by the flames which disfigured him.[13]

Upon his arrival in Palestine, Rabbi Zeira became a close friend of Rabbi Eleazar ben Pedat[14] from whom he learned much concerning the regulations pertaining to tithes.[15] He thus achieved an old ambition for it was said that while still in Babylonia, Rabbi Zeira fasted 100 times that he might find Rabbi Eleazar ben Pedat alive when he arrived in Palestine.[16] His closest friends, however, were Rabbi Ami, Rabbi Asi, and Rabbi Chiya bar Abba.[17] It appears that he knew these men in Babylonia and he merely renewed old friendships when he met them in Palestine. He was especially anxious to learn as much as possible from Rabbi Asi, who was by nature an angry man and resented too much questioning.[18] Nevertheless, it is recorded that Rabbi Zeira questioned him whenever he found his explanations unsatisfactory.[19]

Of Rabbi Chiya bar Abba, Rabbi Zeira said: "You may consider it a rule that Rabbi Chiya always repeated the exact opinions of Rabbi Jochanan."[20] Rabbi Zeira himself also scrupulously gave the names of those scholars whose opinions he quoted.[21]

Rabbi Zeira was also highly regarded by Rabbi Avahu who considered him as his disciple,[22] and when he fell sick, Rabbi Avahu promised to give a feast upon his recovery.[23]

When Rabbi Zeira settled in Palestine he hoped to obtain ordination there for no ordinations were then being conferred in Babylonia. But in many of his statements he expressed his abhorrence of people who bought their ordination, as frequently happened in Tiberias at that time. He would then purposely sit in places where scholars went by and whenever he saw one who he thought did not deserve the title of Rabbi, he would ostentatiously remain seated. To all other scholars he accorded due honor.[24]

Finally Rabbi Zeira was ordained and in Babylonia it was said that he had hidden for a long time in order to avoid ordination.[25] On the day that he was ordained, his colleagues sang his praise and the Nasi sent him gifts that he refused to accept. But when he was invited to the Nasi's table, he accepted the invitation out of respect for the Nasi.[26]

By trade Rabbi Zeira was a weaver, and he once asked Rabbi Avahu how much effort he might devote to beautifying his cloth without deceiving the buyers with its beauty at the expense of its quality.[27]

In his time, the Roman government prohibited Jews from fasting. Rabbi Zeira was greatly worried when he heard of this regulation, for he was devoted to fasting as may be seen from the earlier descriptions of his prolonged fasts.[28]

Because of his conduct Rabbi Zeira was called the Pious from Babylonia.[29] He loved peace and sought every opportunity to effect a reconciliation whenever someone offended him.[30]

The name Zeira was popular in Babylonia at that time. It appears to have been a diminutive endearing form used for children who were born late in the lives of their parents.

Rabbi Zeira's parents died when he was still young. His father was known to have been a tax collector for the

Babylonian government for a period of thirteen years. It was told that he always protected the scholars from too heavy tax burdens.[31] He is also mentioned in connection with scholarly matters when he questioned a regulation of Rabbi Joshua ben Levi.[32]

On the day that Rabbi Zeira arrived in Palestine, he met a butcher who ridiculed him, partly because of his appearance and partly because *all* Babylonian Jews were exposed to ridicule. Rabbi Zeira seemed to have been a subject for mirth in the eyes of the butcher into whose shop he came to buy meat. When he asked the price of the meat, the butcher named a sum and said that in addition to this sum, the customer must be struck a blow with the hammer. Rabbi Zeira offered a higher price for the meat if he could be spared the blow, but the butcher insisted on his original statement and Rabbi Zeira finally consented.

When Rabbi Zeira came to the academy that evening, he asked the meaning of the custom that every buyer of meat must receive a blow. All those present were surprised at his question and asked Rabbi Zeira where he had seen such a custom practiced. He then named the butcher and the scholars sent for him in order to have him punished for shaming a scholar, but they were informed that the butcher had died on that same day. When they heard this, they believed that Rabbi Zeira must have cursed the butcher, but he assured them that he had not cursed him, because he believed this to be the custom of the city. The scholars then concluded that Rabbi Zeira must be a very important man if God had administered summary punishment to one who had insulted him.[33]

The modesty of Rabbi Zeira is further illustrated by the following statement: "If the generations which preceded us were like angels then we are like men; if they were like men then we are like asses."[34] He further said that when the Torah spoke of the cure of leprosy it referred to the cure of the flesh. From this he concluded that when one is humble and lowly as the flesh, he would be cured; but one who is proud, would never be healed.[35]

Despite Rabbi Zeira's physical handicaps he always hastened to fulfill all commandments, for he had heard it said that in order to fulfill a commandment one may run even during the Sabbath when running is ordinarily forbidden. He thus declared that "the reward for learning is the haste with which one goes to the place of learning."[36] Another characteristic attribute of Rabbi Zeira was his insistence that the name of the author should always be mentioned when he was quoted. On one occasion he even forced Rabbi Asi to admit that a statement he had repeated in the name of a certain *amora*, he had really heard from a pupil of that *amora*.[37]

Rabbi Zeira considered the spoken word to be sacred and he insisted that everyone should honor his promises. He held it to be especially important to honor promises made to children so that they did not learn to tell falsehoods.[38]

But it is noteworthy that despite Rabbi Zeira's modesty he demanded that due honor be accorded to scholars and he objected to their self-debasement even when that was done during the fulfillment of a commandment. When he saw Rav Shmuel bar Yitzchak at a wedding dancing before the bride with three torches in his hands that he threw into the air and caught again, Rabbi Zeira remarked: "The old man makes a fool of himself and he also shames us."[39]

Rabbi Zeira did not tolerate the *Aggadah*. At that time there were already numerous books of *Aggadah* extant and he referred to them as "books of witchcraft." He also ordered one of his pupils not to study the *Aggadah* because he would learn nothing from it.[40]

The observance of a commandment was of lesser importance in the eyes of Rabbi Zeira than the beautification of the act and he therefore said that one may spend one-third of the cost of fulfilling a commandment in order to make its fulfillment more attractive.[41]

Rabbi Zeira stayed in the academy day and night and engaged in study. When he felt weak from overwork, he would go to the door of the academy. There he would see scholars coming and going, listen to their discourses, and he would feel refreshed.[42]

A remarkable story is related about Rabbi Zeira and Rabbah who once became drunk during Purim festivities.

While he was intoxicated, Rabbah killed Rabbi Zeira. On the following day he saw what he had done and prayed to God, and Rabbi Zeira was resurrected. The following year they made no feast for fear that the miracle might not occur a second time if needed.[43]

Rabbi Zeira lived to a ripe old age, however, and when his disciples asked him to what he attributed his long life, he said: "I was never angry at anyone in my house and I never ran ahead of one who was greater than myself; likewise I never went a distance of four ells without Torah and phylacteries. I never pondered divine matters in unclean places and I never slept in the academy, not even an accidental nap. I was never glad at the misfortune of others, nor did I ever ridicule other people."[44]

When Rabbi Zeira died he was eulogized in the following words: "Babylonia gave him birth; the Land of Israel reared him as its darling; woe to the city of Tiberias that it has lost its most attractive vessel."[45]

The following story is related of Rabbi Zeira's influence even after his death: "In the neighborhood of Rabbi Zeira's house there lived some wicked men whom he had rebuked for their evil and he prayed to God that they might improve their ways. The other scholars disapproved of this because even as they believed that it was a good deed to rebuke a person who might change his ways, so also they considered it a sin to rebuke people who were hardened in sin. After the death of Rabbi Zeira, his wicked neighbors said: 'Until now the short dark man prayed for us and protected us. Now that he is dead who will pray for us?' They thereupon repented their sins."

PART III

BABYLONIAN

TALMUD

70

INTRODUCTION

SEVEN CENTURIES PASSED FROM the days of the first *tanna* until the time of the last *amora*. This is a long time in the history of any people. No matter how conservative one may be, it would still be impossible to assume that all those years passed without profound changes occurring in Jewish life. As was the case with other peoples, these centuries also marked the birth and development of new ideas and concepts among the Jews. Some of these vanished and gave rise to others. These centuries marked far-reaching changes in the political position of the people. Now they were free in their own land, where previously they had been involved in wars; exile was succeeded by periods of peace and plenty in foreign lands.

After the return from Babylonia, where they had lived in an entirely strange environment, the Jews developed new ideas and concepts. The situation in Babylonia also changed when that country came under the sway of the Persians whose culture was equally unique. Later, the Jews fell under the domination of the Syrian Greeks as well as other cultures. It was quite natural for the Jews to be influenced by these peoples even when they did not imitate them and sought to avoid the ways of the pagans. When the conquering nations tried to undermine their belief in one God they did not succeed. The

Jews remained steadfast in their faith and were ready to sacrifice their lives for the observance of the Sabbath and of circumcision. The outside influence could be seen in some modifications in the ceremonial rituals, but the fundamentals of religion were not affected.

As soon as the repatriates from Babylonia were entrenched in the country—after the days of Ezra and Nehemiah—a new attitude developed toward the Torah. They were convinced that the destruction of the Temple and the exile was a direct result of their negligence in observing the commandments of the Torah. They therefore resolved to scrupulously observe all the regulations of the Torah. The first measure in this direction was the establishment of a rule that "many students should be maintained." To achieve this end, many schools were established in all the corners of the land. Whereas the majority of the people had heretofore been farmers and shepherds, it was now sought to transform them into a nation of scholars. The leaders of the schools were called *sofrim*, scribes, whose duty it was to explain the Scriptures and to interpret its teachings. Later the *sofrim* were known as *Hakhamim* or wise men. They thus performed a dual function of interpreting and also adapting the Torah to the needs of the time.

The religious and secular life of the people was then governed by two institutions: the Great Court and the Academy, which worked hand in hand and supplemented each other. The entire content of Jewish life centered about these institutions which laid the foundation for the spiritual life of the people. The Great Court, later known as the Sanhedrin, issued all decrees and together with the academies it became the law-giving body that regulated the moral and religious conduct of the people and strengthened its ethical concepts. One of the first activities of the Sanhedrin was the establishment of a "protective fence" (*siyag*) about the Torah. It was the function of this "fence" to prevent the people from doing anything to lead them astray from the commandments of the Torah, even when the particular deed had not been prohibited in itself.

Concerned with the moral conduct of the people, the scholars sought to prevent any possible lapses by prohibiting men to remain alone with married women in secluded places. In addition to the forms of adultery prohibited by the Bible, they also listed twenty-six degrees of relatives whom one could not marry.[1]

In the days preceding Ezra and Nehemiah, the Sabbath was not strictly observed. The *sofrim* therefore warned the people concerning its observance and surrounded it with protective barriers. The concept of work was defined in order for people to know what may and what may not be done on the Sabbath. Thirty-nine primary occupations were listed, the performance of which on the Sabbath was punishable by death. Among these were plowing, sowing, harvesting, threshing, baking, cooking, lighting and putting out fire, hunting, slaughtering animals, writing and erasing, building and destroying, sewing and tearing, carrying objects out of a house and into it.[2]

In addition to these occupations, the *sofrim* prohibited many other activities which did not constitute work in themselves but which lent a weekday atmosphere, such as climbing trees, riding on animals, swimming, judging, buying and selling, or marrying. All were forbidden in the interests of complete rest and were also forbidden on the holidays.[3]

Tools and vessels used for the performance of occupations forbidden on the Sabbath, could not be carried out on that day. As a further safeguard the *sofrim* ruled that the Sabbath was to be observed from sunset on Friday until sunset on Saturday. Blessings to be pronounced over a glass of wine at the incoming and at the departure of the Sabbath were instituted.[4] A man was likewise appointed to blow the ram's horn as a signal to the people to cease working. The first blast signaled the field workers to cease their labors; the second one called for city workers to close their shops, and the third was a signal to stop all work at home. One more blast was then blown to indicate that the Sabbath had begun.[5]

The first evening of the Passover was consecrated in the

same manner as the Sabbath. It took on the nature of a family celebration, and all members of the family gathered to eat the Paschal lamb, to relate the miracles of the redemption from Egypt, and to sing praises. Every Jew, even the poorest, was obliged to drink four glasses of wine on that evening.

In addition to the sacrifices in the Temple, prayers were introduced at that time. It appears that prayer among Jews originated during the Babylonian captivity, when the people had no opportunity to offer sacrifices. Although the forms of the prayers were not yet defined, the idea of praying took root, but it did not yet supplant the offering of sacrifices expressly commanded in the Torah.

The number of Jews who returned to Palestine from the exile in Babylonia was much smaller than the number exiled. But those who remained in Babylonia were no less religious than the ones who returned. The great national struggle characterizing the return to Palestine has never been sufficiently described. There is inadequate information concerning the time that elapsed from the coming of Ezra and Nehemiah until the rebellion of the Hasmoneans, a period of nearly two centuries. The fate of Zerubabel, who was appointed to govern the Jews of Jerusalem, is also unknown.

There exists the belief, not substantiated by any historical evidence, that Zerubabel returned to Babylonia after becoming convinced that he could achieve nothing in Palestine. Others claim that he was killed during one of the turbulent periods.

It is certain, however, that a large number of Jews refused to return to Palestine even after the Second Temple was built and a Hasmonean ruler governed the land. They did not consider their liberation as the expected redemption and hoped for miracles like those that accompanied the deliverance from Egypt. They awaited a wondrous Messiah from the House of David. They also disapproved of the new Temple which lacked the *urim* and *tummim*, the Holy Ark, and the Cherubim and the sacred fire. But the lack of authentic historical information makes it impossible to give a clear description of that time. The writings of Josephus are not entirely clear and the Talmud concerned itself more with describing the customs of the time and interpreting the verses of the Bible rather than with chronicling historical events.

It is therefore impossible to determine how learning began to develop in Babylonia. But we do know that Jewish life developed in that country at the same time that it was making rapid forward strides in Palestine. When the Second Temple was destroyed, large numbers of Jews sought refuge in Babylonia where the Romans had no control. As often as the political circumstances allowed, there was an interchange of scholars between the two countries. Thus we find Rabbi Chiya Rabbah sending his son, Nathan, to continue his studies in Palestine, while Palestinian scholars sent their children to Babylonia. But despite this interchange, the Jews of Palestine nevertheless did not respect the Babylonian Jews. Even Babylonian scholars were ridiculed until their worth became firmly established.

Most of the Jews of Babylonia lived in Nehardea and its environs because it was closest to Palestine. Some even believed that the city was once a part of Palestine and they sought to prove that the surrounding towns were included in the conquests of Joshua. Because of this doubt, the inhabitants of Nehardea celebrated Purim for two days.

The exact location of Nehardea has not been ascertained to this day. All we know is that it was located between the Tigris and Euphrates rivers and that the lands to the east were settled by non-Jews. Later, the Babylonian Jews were compelled to wander farther inland. The persecutions in Palestine forced many scholars to settle in Babylonia and the social and economic conditions in Babylonia also contributed to the establishment of academies in different cities.

Enjoying complete autonomy, the Babylonian Jews were governed by an Exilarch who represented them to the government. Like the Nasi in Palestine, the Exilarch also traced his descent from the House of David. At times the Exilarchs were held in even greater respect than the Nasiim because they were descended from King David through the male line. At the time that Rabbi Jehudah was Nasi in Palestine, Rav Huna was

Exilarch in Babylonia. Rabbi Jehudah once remarked that were Rav Huna to come to Palestine, he would accord him greater honor than he received himself.

When the conditions in Palestine took a turn for the worse, Rabbi Nathan of Babylonia declared that the verse "to those who love me and observe my commandments" (Exodus 2:6), referred to the Jews of Palestine, who were ready to sacrifice their lives for the sake of the observance of the commandments and who were indifferent to death when they were caught.

These conditions are best illustrated in a Talmudic story that relates when a Jew who was condemned to death, was asked, "Why are you being led to execution?" he would reply, "Because I have circumcised my son." Another would say, "Because I have studied the Torah." One being led to crucifixion explained that he was being punished for eating *matzah*, another who was to be flogged would explain that he had incurred his punishment for holding a *lulav*.[6] Under such circumstances, the academies in Palestine were deserted. Those who wanted their sons to gain learning sent them to Babylonia. During such times, the scholars of Babylonia would also determine the beginning of the months and the leap years, although this was traditionally the prerogative of the scholars of Palestine.

Judging by the structure of the Babylonian Talmud one might conclude that it is obscure and that its editors compiled its contents without considering sequence. But such a conclusion would be erroneous since every word was carefully weighed and measured before it was included in the Talmud. The Talmud, as we have it, is a wonderful structure carefully constructed from its component parts. The editors of the Talmud followed the system of Rabbi Jehudah in editing the *Mishnah* and not merely did they gather the material, but they also sought to integrate it into an organic unit. Rav Ashi and Ravina, the compilers of the Babylonian Talmud, sought to link the subjects treated in the Talmud in a logical sequence. For this purpose they employed a technical terminology to serve as a binding cement.

After the period of the *tannaim* the language of the talmudic literature was not preserved in its original purity. The early *amoraim* still used a language closely resembling that of the *Mishnah* and even some of the later ones sought to achieve this end. But the majority of their sayings were in Aramaic, the ordinary language of the Jews of Babylonia, interspersed with some Hebrew elements. The resulting language did not resemble the language of the *Mishnah*.

The two Talmuds, the Babylonian and the Jerusalem, differ in language and also in style. The reason for this is that the methods of interpretation in the two countries differed. This is not surprising when one considers how the interchange of ideas between the two countries occurred. The constant exchange of scholars between the two lands resulted in many errors, and quotations were frequently interpreted in a manner foreign to the author. Some scholars even ascribed their opinions to their predecessors in order to lend weight to their own words. At other times the authors of various statements were forgotten. Considerable confusion was thus engendered in establishing the authorship of numerous decisions. At times the statements quoted were in direct contradiction to the opinions of the authors. This was especially true of the opinions ascribed to Rav (Abba Arecha). For example, when Rabbi Jehudah bar Ezekiel quoted Rav, his brother Rami remarked: "You should not listen to him when he speaks in the name of Rav."[7] Another *amora* likewise said: "Whatever Rabbi Jehudah bar Ezekiel says in the name of Rav is incorrect, for Rav never said it."[8]

Even the compilers of the Talmud at times erred in this respect and they would describe a dispute between two *amoraim* in contradicting versions on different occasions. There are several instances of such contradictions.[9]

Some subjects occur both in the Jerusalem and in the Babylonian Talmud with this difference. The Jerusalem Talmud quotes conflicting opinions while the Babylonian Talmud quotes only one opinion.[10]

One should not assume that the Talmud is a unified work. The teachings of seven centuries do not readily fuse into a unit. This is particularly true since so many different men of differing tastes shared in its creation. But the Talmud does possess a homogeneous character and it constitutes an integrated work.

In the prefaces to the first two parts, an attempt was made to acquaint the reader with the ideas of the scholars concerning the various problems of life. These ideas can now be supplemented to provide a complete picture of their mode of thought. The ideas of Jewish scholars concerning God were original and differed from those accepted among the surrounding peoples. Greek culture which was then highly developed still clung to polytheism. The same was true of the Romans, the Parthians, and the Persians. One therefore marvels at the endurance of the scholars and at their success in resisting all attempts to introduce polytheism.

The representation of God in corporeal form such as the phrases "the hand of God" or "the mouth of God," the scholars interpreted as being merely a form of speech used to convey the idea of God to the common people. But they expressly warned against accepting these terms in their literal meaning.[11] They then referred to God in terms that would indicate his superhuman nature. He was called *Shekhinah*, (glory). On other occasions he was referred to as *Gevurah* (strength) and *Makom* (place), because He is omnipresent. He was also called *Shamayim* (heaven), because of the belief that God lived in heaven. The creation of the world they explained to be a process of creation out of nothing. Its aim was the creation of man who was made in the image of God, walking erect and facing heaven. Man is imbued by a soul and possesses a free will to do as he chooses. Of all men the Jews are the chosen ones; the outstanding men among the Jews are the just men.[12]

The concept of God's unity the scholars held to be of the greatest significance. They believed it to be an honor that the Jews followed the only God and that He chose them as His people. The reason why man was created last was explained by them to indicate that man did not share with God in any work of creation.[13]

God is merciful even when man does not deserve it and His very anger is an expression of His kindness.[14] It is the duty of the Jew to fear God and the life of a Jew should be based on three foundations: study of the Torah; serving God with prayers, and charitable deeds.[15]

While studying the Torah one should bear in mind that its purpose is to observe the commandments. But the worth of the observance is conditioned by the belief in God who gave the commandments. A Jew must therefore do everything for the sake of God and not merely out of a feeling of duty.[16]

Faith implies the assumption of the burden of the kingdom of heavens. This implies gratitude to God for the good as well as for the evil, and acceptance of His rule presupposes obedience to His rule and a conviction that whatever He does is for the best. God should be served with love and one should strive to make His name beloved among all. This will lead to the elevation of man's conduct to the level of God. Even as God is merciful so also should man strive to be merciful.

Before the introduction of prayer, sacrifices were offered. The purpose of sacrifices was not merely slaughter of animals but elevation of human thought. After the destruction of the Temple one could only assume the vow of a Nazarite, not to drink wine and not to cut his hair, or one could undertake fasts to torment the body with lack of food and drink.

Charitable deeds, whether by offering money or through personal effort to aid another, were considered to be the noblest deeds possible. This was based on the principle of love for one's neighbor enunciated by Hillel when he said, "Do not unto others what you would not have done unto you."

Moralizing others on their faults, the scholars held to be of great importance and they said it should be continued until the person corrected becomes angry enough to beat the moralist. Such moralizing helps people avoid gossip, hatred and envy, and encourages peace.

One must also believe that God sees all deeds of man, that He knows the needs of the world, and that He aids all Jews because of their justice and their faith in Him.

God's messengers are angels, prophets, and *tzadikim*. The piety of the *tzadik* may lead him to become inspired by the holy spirit and he would thus be capable of interceding for the Jews with his prayers. Repentance has a similar effect and protects the penitent from evil.[17]

However, the most fascinating element of the faith was the belief in reward and punishment after death. God also credits children with the good deeds of their parents. Like the individual, the group also awaits a collective compensation which takes the form of the coming of the Messiah and the resurrection. These matters the scholars discussed tersely when they spoke of the wars of Gog and Magog, the return of the House of David and "the future that is to come" which would compensate the whole nation for their present sufferings.

Throughout the years there were numerous sects among the Jews who questioned the authority of the oral law. But none of these doubted the value of the moral teachings of the scholars.

The scholars also believed that God had previously created worlds which he destroyed and when He created the present world He said: "This one finds favor in my eyes while the others did not."[18]

When God decided to create Adam, the scholars said, He realized that both just and wicked men would be descended from him. Because of the just descendants he wished to create man at once, but the prospect of wicked descendants tempted him to destroy man even before he was created. God therefore disregarded the future and proceeded to create man.

At first God considered creating man out of heavenly materials. But realizing that such a creature would incur the envy of the angels who might attempt to harm him, He created man out of a mixture of heavenly and earthly materials.[19] He then endowed man with free will to do as he chose. He implanted in him good and evil desires and He gave him the power to control his desires. The scholars were convinced that there was much heroism in subduing one's evil desires since these are with man since his birth, while his good desires manifest themselves only after he reaches the age of thirteen.[20]

But they did not consider the Torah as the only means of dealing with human passions. Piety was held to be a necessary supplement and one who possessed learning without piety was compared to the caretaker of a palace who was given the interior but not the outer keys.[21]

The scholars strongly stressed the significance of justice. One who passes just sentence they compared to a partner of God, and they interpreted the biblical verse (Deut. 12:28) to show that good fortune would attend him who practices deeds that are both good in the eyes of man and also find favor in the eyes of God.

If a poor man and a rich man come to trial, the poor man should not be given preference. He must not be declared just, if he had been unjust, on the ground that the rich man would have to support him anyway. Such judgment would be tantamount to accepting a bribe which blinds even the wisest man. It was also held that bribes could be offered in words as well as in money.[22]

Truth is the signature of God.[23] Man must therefore make sure that all his utterances are true. He who is honest is considered to have observed the whole Torah.[24]

Just as God punished the generation of the flood, He also punishes anyone who does not abide by his word. One who departs from his word may be compared to one worshipping idols.[25] For deceit with words is worse than deceit with money[26] and God abhors the man who speaks otherwise than he thinks.[27] But gossip was held to be even worse than deceit, and those guilty of it were considered fit to be fed to the dogs.[28] Slander, they said, is capable of killing all three parties concerned; the one who utters the slander, the one who heeds it, and the one who was slandered. Its power extends over long distances and the only reason that the Jews who left Egypt were condemned to perish in the desert was that they heeded slander.[29]

Four types of people do not merit feeling the *Shekhinah*: the scornful, those who ridicule others, liars, and slanderers.[30] There are also numerous types of thieves and the worst of these is the one who deceives people with words; another is the type who invites one to come to his house without really wishing him to do so; the third offers gifts when he is certain they will not be accepted; the fourth shows merchandise to a customer after the merchandise had already been sold. All of these are compared to swindlers who give false weights and measurements.[31]

The blessings of the Torah, the scholars said, can only be fulfilled when people follow in the ways of God. What are the ways of God? God is gracious to all and he feeds all creatures without exception. People should likewise be kind to each other. God grants health and life to those who believe in Him as well as to those who reject Him. People should also forgive acquaintances and strangers.[32]

All of these moral teachings originating with the explanations of the essence of God, ended by scrutinizing social relations. It grew out of the recognition that man is the flower of creation and that God wished man to act justly and kindly. As time went on these teachings expanded in depth and profundity.

Charity was also viewed by the scholars as of great importance. The entire world is provided with food because of charity.[33] One who contributes to charity is worthier than one who offers sacrifices.[34] Charity is the greatest of all commandments[35] and even the poor man who receives charity should offer some of it.[36] But the scholars also stressed that offering a loan was at times more important than giving charity, and the aid that one extends with his body may be better than financial aid.[37] Scholars were also warned against living in cities that did not have a fund for the poor to which at least two people belonged.[38]

One must also love to be preached to, for so long as there will be moralizing there will be joy and blessings in the world and evil will depart. The scholars nevertheless warned that one must improve his own ways before he begins to preach to others,[39] and just as it is a good deed to suggest something that will be obeyed, even so is it a good deed not to make a suggestion that is sure to be disobeyed.[40]

The sin of hatred equals in magnitude the commandment to love one's neighbor. One must not say: "I will love scholars but I will hate their disciples" or "I will love disciples but I will hate rude people." One may show hatred only to those who deny God and who incite to sin. Thus King David said: "Your enemies I will hate and I will contend with those who rise up against you."[41] One must also bear in mind what the consequences of hatred will be. Why was the First Temple destroyed? Because idol worshiping, immorality, and violence existed. But during the time of the Second Temple the people observed the Torah and its commandments. Why then was it destroyed? It was destroyed because hatred prevailed. We may therefore conclude that hatred is the equivalent of idol worshipping, immorality, and bloodshed.[42]

Speaking of the significance of peace, the scholars declared that blessings are of no avail if they are not accompanied by peace.[43] Even in time of war one should think of peace. It is therefore permissible to alter the words of another, when quoting him, in the interests of peace.[44] The stones of which the altar was built and whose function it was to cause peace between Jews and their Father in heaven, could not be hewn by any iron implement. It was therefore concluded that one who brings about peace between man and wife, between one city and another, between one nation and another or between one family and another, would not meet with any harm. One must therefore heed the command to preserve peace and not to engage in quarrels. Such great significance was attached to peace that it was believed that even when people worship idols they could not be harmed by enemies if they lived in peace among themselves.[45]

Marriage was held to be the most important event in the life of any man. It was considered to be the duty of every Jewish man to participate in the increase of the people. This conviction, together with the natural fertility of the Jewish women, contributed to the survival of the people throughout the period of persecution. No man even thought of avoiding this responsibility toward his people. Thus Rabbi Akiba once asked, "Who may be considered a rich man?" and he replied that a rich man is one "who has a wife noted for her good deeds."[46] Ben Sira was also quoted as saying that "a good woman is the best gift. Happy is the husband of such a woman; the days of his life are doubled."[47] The verse which declared that the days of the poor were evil, the scholars interpreted as referring to a man who has a wicked wife.[48] Man was also commanded to honor his wife for the blessing of one's house was entirely dependent upon the wife,[49] and he who honored his wife more than himself and loved her even as he loved himself would be blessed with peace and plenty.

Amicable relations between man and wife caused the *Shekhinah* to dwell in the house and when discord prevails, they are both consumed as by a fire.[50] Another scholar explained the significance of peace in a still different manner. He said: The Hebrew words *ish* and *ishah* (man and woman) contain two of the letters of the name of God and God would preserve them from all evil. But this is true only so long as they live in peace. As soon as they leave the ways of peace, these two letters are withdrawn and only the letters spelling *eish* remain. These signify fire that would consume them.[51]

The education of the children naturally occupied a prominent place under the circumstances. Study of the Torah was the central theme of this training. One of the scholars declared that as soon as a child learns to talk his father should teach him the Hebrew language and the Torah and any father who does not do so may be compared to a father who kills his child.[52] But one who obeys this commandment is credited with teaching his descendants to the end of all generations.[53]

Speaking in the same vein, the *tanna* Rabbi Jochanan declared that of the three types of people who deserve a share in the world to come one is the father who raises his children in the ways of the Torah.[54] The entire world exists because of the breath of children at study and therefore they must not be disturbed from their studies even when the Temple is to be rebuilt. Any city in which the voices of children at study is not heard will certainly be destroyed in the end.[55] It was thus related that every child who had a father would be taught by him, but fatherless children remained uneducated. It was therefore ordered that schools be established in every city and every province where children were brought at the age of 6 or 7 years. No children began their studies before they reached the age of 6.[56]

Rabbi Jose declared that every man is obligated to study and none should assume that he will inherit his learning. Another scholar therefore said that one should beware of the children of the poor for they might grow to be great students.[57] The same attitude should be maintained toward the children of the *amei aratzim* for they too might become scholars.[58] Parents were also enjoined to teach their children trades and any parent who did not do so was considered to be the same as one who taught his son to be a robber.[59]

Learning a trade was therefore of great importance. Not only did a trade provide one with a livelihood but it also brought him honor. The importance of a man who lived off the practice of a trade was held to be equal to that of a pious man.[60] In the opinion of Rabbi Gamaliel, the son of Rabbi Jehudah, knowledge of the Torah that was not accompanied by the practice of a trade was of no value and was sure to lead to sin.[61]

Both parents as well as God share in the creation of a human being. As long as one honors his father and mother God considers it as though He had been honored.[62] At one time the scholars declared that it is more important to honor one's father and mother than it is to honor God. Man is thus obligated to fulfill the commandments concerning a *sukkah*, a *shofar*, feeding the poor, and others, only if he can afford to do so; but the commandment to honor one's parents must be fulfilled under all circumstances.[63] When the question arose how one should honor his parents and whether one could do so by word of mouth only, the scholars invoked the verse "Honor God from your wealth," and they declared that one must honor his parents with all his possessions, with food, and with garments. The honor due to one's father they further explained by saying that one might not stand in his father's place nor sit in his seat, nor contradict his words, nor side with his opponents.[64]

The scholars also interpreted this biblical commandment to prove that one is obligated to honor his stepmother in the same measure as he would honor his own mother; his stepfather in the same measure as he would honor his own father and also his older brothers and his father-in-law.[65]

But not only parents were to be accorded honor. Scholars were to be granted the same respect[66] and greeting a scholar was equivalent to greeting the *Shekhinah*.[67] The honor due to the Torah was so great that a bastard who was a scholar was ranked higher than a High Priest who was an *am ha'aretz*.[68]

Modesty was also a virtue the sages praised highly and Rabbi Levitas of Jabneh said: "One should be very humble for there is no real reason for pride, considering that in the end all men will be consumed by worms."[69] One who is humble, other scholars declared, will be raised by God and one who is proud will be put to shame. It is similar to one who seeks greatness and greatness eludes him, but one who avoids it will certainly achieve greatness.[70]

Modesty is a quality of God. When He appeared to Moses the first time He did not appear in the form of a proud cedar tree, but in the form of a lowly bush. When He gave the Torah to the Jews He did so from Sinai, which is small compared to the great mountains.[71] God therefore declares that He will avoid those who are proud, and one who walks erect with pride crowds the feet of the *Shekhinah*.[72]

Satisfaction with one's lot was equal in importance to modesty. "Who is a wealthy man?" asked the *tanna* Ben Zoma, "He who is satisfied with his share."[73] For one should be content with what he has. Rabbi Akiba further clarified this idea when he said that "one should arrange his Sabbaths like weekdays in order to avoid being dependent on charity."[74] One way of attaining such contentment is by avoiding gluttony.[75] At the same time the scholars ruled that one should not deny himself the pleasures of life, and Rav (Abba Arecha) declared that any man who denies himself joys he can attain will have to account for it in the world to come.[76]

One must avoid mutilating his body.[77] There is also no action which may not be performed nor is there any food which may not be eaten in order to preserve an endangered life, with the exception of idolatry, bloodshed, and immorality for the avoidance of which one must be ready to sacrifice his life.[78] Regarding the observance of the Sabbath, Rabban Simeon ben Gamaliel said that it may be desecrated for the sake of a living day-old-child, but not for the sake of a dead King David.[79] Rabbi Menasia likewise said that the Sabbath was given to people to observe but the people were not given to the Sabbath.[80]

Shyness and chastity were likewise held in great esteem, and these qualities were considered to be the outstanding merit of the Jews.[81] It was believed that shame leads to avoidance of sin while arrogance leads to transgression. Scholars were warned to heed their behavior.[82]

Regarding faith and dependence on God, it was said that Jews deserve to have miracles performed for their sake because of their unbounded faith.[83] He who trusts in God will be protected by Him both in this and in the coming world.[84] On another occasion it was declared that a penitent is credited with making a pilgrimage to Jerusalem and offering sacrifices there. When Rabbi Eliezer ben Hyrcanus enjoined his disciples to repent one day before their death, they questioned how one could know when he would die, and Rabbi Eliezer explained that one must repent daily for fear that he would die on the morrow.[85]

Prayer ranked close upon repentance and was held to be of greater value than sacrifices. Its significance was so great that at least half of one's prayers were certain to be granted.[86] Another sage said that even were a sword to be at one's throat he should still feel confident in prayer.[87]

Some gentile pedagogues at that time declared that it was better for children to study at home, each one separately. Our scholars, on the other hand, believed that group study tended to develop the minds of children. There is no mention, however, of even gentile pedagogues questioning the efficiency of schools, for their usefulness was recognized by all. It was only a small number of wealthy gentiles who could afford to maintain a private tutor for their children. Children of the poor largely remained without any education. Education was still looked upon as a privilege of the rich.

The educational situation among the Jews was entirely different. Education was democratic and so organized that the whole people benefited from it. Classes were not always held indoors and frequently study would take place in the street. However, Rabbi Jehudah prohibited teaching in the street and when Rabbi Chiya taught his two sons outside the house, he incurred the displeasure of Rabbi Jehudah.[88] Such study as took place outside involved adult pupils mostly and usually under unusual circumstances. Otherwise all learning took place in the synagogues where prayers were also said. There were no convenient school buildings at that time. Since the people were impoverished it was said that no money should be spent even for synagogues.

At first all learning took place while the students stood. Later it became customary to sit. The teacher was seated on a rock or on a bench while his pupils sat on the ground around him. The Talmud declared that from the days of Moses until the time of Rabban Gamaliel older people studied while standing, but that after the death of Rabban Gamaliel maladies afflicted the world and people were forced to sit while studying.[89]

Special furniture for school use was not needed or thought about at that time. If the teacher sat on a couch, his pupils also reclined on couches. Teachers were also not permitted to be served by their pupils. Thus we find that Rabbi Jehudah was in the habit of carrying his own bench to the academy.

The seating of pupils was arranged so that the teacher should be able to see the faces of all and so they were seated in a semicircle. The value of facing one's teacher while at study can be seen in the remark of Rabbi Jehudah who complained that he could not always see the face of his master Rabbi Meir, and that this fact hindered his proficiency in learning.[90] Another sage instructed his pupils to seat themselves so that they could watch their teacher's mouth while he was teaching them.[91]

It was the accepted rule that children started their schooling at the age of six. One *amora* warned that study at an earlier age might adversely affect the health of the child. Others said that it would also affect his intellectual development. But the most common suggestion offered was that the physical development of each child should be considered individually.[92]

No records of the required qualifications for teachers exist, but it may be assumed that they were required to be well-acquainted with the subject of instruction. The qualities that were enumerated for scholars were probably also required of teachers.

A popular maxim of that time declared: "In my native city I am known by my name, but in a strange city I am known by my clothes."[93] It was likewise said that a scholar who wears dirty clothing deserves to forfeit his life, and that it is a shame for a scholar to wear patched shoes.[94] Scholars were also warned to heed their eating and drinking habits. It was also said that one who arranged his feasts without choosing a proper place would forget his learning, he would cause quarrels, and his words would not be heeded.[95]

Not all teachers were considered capable of teaching and not all pupils were capable of learning. But the blame was mostly ascribed to the teachers. Rava once declared: "If you see a pupil having difficulties in learning, it is a proof that his teacher does not show him friendliness."[96]

Every scholar must consider it his duty to teach others without compensation. But since teachers were required to devote their whole time to their work, some means had to be devised to provide for their needs. Thus the Talmud declares that he who studies without teaching others may be compared to a plant in the desert,[97] and he who refrains from teaching a law to his pupil is like one who robs him.[98]

According honor to one's teacher was therefore held to be of greater importance than honoring one's father.[99] Should one see his father and his teacher carrying loads, he was to help his teacher first. Likewise, if one's father and teacher are imprisoned he was to ransom his teacher first.[100] One who contradicts his teacher may be compared to one contradicting the *Shekhinah*.[101] Walking on the right side of one's teacher indicated rudeness.[102]

Respect for one's neighbor was likewise stipulated and it was to equal the respect one has for himself.[103] A man who was known to be superior even in one respect deserved to be honored.[104] One's position was entirely irrelevant in this respect, for a man brings honor to his position and not vice versa.[105]

71

RAV, ABBA ARECHA

AFTER THE PERIOD OF THE *tannaim*, the first important *amora* in the period of *amoraim* was known not by his name but by his title of *Rav*.

His name was Abba, and some called him Abba Arecha (Long Abba), because he was the tallest man of his generation.[1] It is also possible that Arecha was the name of Rav's birthplace in Babylon.

His title *Rav* was the same as that of all his successors who were allowed by the *Resh Galuta* (the ruler of the Jewish Diaspora in Babylon), to preside over their own academy. Just as Rabbi Jehudah Hanasi was called Rabbi, omitting his own name, so Abba Arecha was always called *Rav*.

It was Rav who founded the academy in the city of Sura. The ruler of Babylon at that time was the Persian king Artaban who was very friendly to the Jews and a great admirer of Rav. Rav's academy quickly attracted over 1,000 students from far and near.

Abba Arecha was born in the year 155 c.e. When he founded his academy, which existed thereafter for seven centuries, he was a man of 64. His family was of aristocratic stock and highly respected among scholars. By marriage, he was related to the family of the *Resh Galuta* of Babylon, which was an even more important lineage than that of the *Nasi* in Palestine, because that family was descended from King David through the paternal line and the Nasi was descended from David only through the maternal line.

Rabbi Jehudah Hanasi once admitted this himself when he said: "If Rav Huna, *Resh Galuta*, should ever come to Palestine, I will seat him higher than myself because he is descended from the tribe of Judah and I from the tribe of Benjamin, and in addition he is related to King David in the paternal line while I am related to King David only in the maternal line."[2]

An uncle of Rav, Rabbi Chiya Rabbah, had a genealogical record showing him as a descendent of Shefatiah, a son of King David by his wife Avital.[3] To be sure, there is a quotation to the effect that it was Rabbi Jehudah Hanasi who was descended from Shefatiah, and that Rabbi Chiya descended from Shimi, a brother of David.[4] But we have the personal statement of Rabbi Jehudah Hanasi, already given, against this source.

It should be stated, also, that Rav's family tree had wide connections and a great number of scholars were found in its branches in later generations.

Rav's father was Ibo ben Rabbi Acha Karsela of Kafri. He was only a half-brother of Rabbi Chiya Rabbah. Rabbi Chiya's mother had a daughter by a former husband named Imma and Rav's father married this daughter. Consequently Rabbi Chiya had the same father as Rav's father and the same mother as his mother.

This relationship had a great influence on the course of Rav's life, for he was always with Rabbi Chiya. He was brought up in his home, and when Rabbi Chiya went to Palestine, Rav accompanied him. And just as Rabbi Chiya was Rav's teacher in Babylon, so he continued to teach him in Palestine. On the other hand Rav supervised all of Rabbi Chiya's business and had a hand in everything he did.

Rabbi Chiya took care of Rav so devotedly because he was his sister's son. It seems that scholars at that time held it every man's duty to take an interest in his sister's son. And even though Rav was Rabbi Chiya's brother's son, which should perhaps have been more important because they were sons of the same father, Rabbi Chiya always called him "my sister's son" and other scholars did likewise.[5]

Rav and Rabbi Chiya showed great similarity in their way of living and their character, demonstrating the influence of Rabbi Chiya in Rav's life, and in his aims, and the ideals of his academy, as well as on those of his descendants and pupils.

Many of Rav's remarks and those of his pupils are preserved only in the Jerusalem Talmud, because before he founded his academy in Sura, many of his greatest pupils and their pupils left Babylon and emigrated to Palestine where they spread the wisdom of their teacher.

Out of the great respect of the scholars of that time for Rav, many would send their children to him to be blessed.[6] Since his views were often opposed to those of the *Mishnah*, people said of him: "Rav is a *tanna*, but a dissenter," that is even though he might have been counted as a *tanna* of the *Mishnah*, he nevertheless differed from them in his opinions.[7]

As we have said, Rav was related by marriage to the Exilarch. They were equals in status. After them the family branched very widely and most of the scholars until the last generations of *amoraim* were descendants of their family. When Rav once put a question concerning human conduct to Rabbi Chiya, Rabbi Chiya called him *pachati* (son of aristocrats).[8]

Once in speaking about the great leaders of the Jews, Rav said that every generation must have three such leaders, sometimes two of them in Babylon and one in Palestine and sometimes two in Palestine and one in Babylon. The Talmud relates that the scholars who heard him turned their eyes toward his grandsons, his daughter's children, Rabbana Ukba and Rabbana Nehemiah, of whom it is known only that they were the students of Rabbi Chisda, signifying that these were the two great leaders whom the Jews needed in Babylon.[9]

Rav laid great stress on matters of lineage. A student quoted him as saying that the verse about the descendants of Asher, referring to them as chosen warriors, chiefs of the captains (I Chronicles 7:40), and signifying their standing in the army and the battlefield was written so that their reputations and prestige of the ancestors might protect them in battle.[10]

This was the general attitude of Rav's family in the question of lineage. Another of Rav's students quoted him as saying that "since genealogical records have been lost, scholars have lost their ability, and the light of their eyes has been extinguished."[11]

In spite of its high position, Rav's family used to conduct themselves very modestly and they were well known for making friends among all classes of people. Rav himself did not discriminate among his friends because of position and would try to make friends with men of lower origin. It was characteristic of Rav's family to respect the dignity of women more than had been customary among Jews. This tendency is best seen in his legal decisions limiting the rights of a father with regard to his daughter and of a brother with regard to his orphaned sister.

Women were mentioned by their own names in his family, such as Judith (Rabbi Chiya's wife), Pazi and Tabi (Rabbi Chiya's daughters), Imma (Rav's mother). It is probable that this custom of calling women by their own names was the rule in the homes of the Jewish aristrocracy, the *Nasi* in Palestine or the *Resh Galuta* in Babylon, because other women who are mentioned by name in the Talmud or in the *midrashim* were also of the same family, like Yalta (wife of Rabbi Nachman of Nehardea), or Chova (the wife of Rav Huna).

This family also followed the custom of naming children after dead parents and near relations, as was the custom of aristocratic Gentiles of that time, as well as of the *N'siim* in Palestine and the *Resh Galuta* in Babylon.

Various customs of an extraordinary sort were prevalent in this family because of common ideals or the influence of ancient traditions. Such, for instance, was their love of education for the younger generations. All the members of Rav's family took a broad interest in and had a fine understanding of educational problems and devoted all their time and energy to them.

These people also had an accent different from that of other people. In general, their accent was similar to that of the Galileans and like them they slurred the gutturals in their speech and obscured the differences between them. They would pronounce an "h" where it was not written and omit it where it was needed, had difficulty in pronouncing the *ayin* and jumbled the sounds of the letters *z, s, tz,* and *sh.*

When Rabbi Chiya once told Rabbi Simeon bar Bari that if Rabbi Simeon were a "priest" it would be wrong to permit him to give the blessings from the pulpit, because he had a hoarse voice. Rabbi Simeon's father once told Rabbi Chiya that he himself should not be permitted even to read from the Bible in the synagogue because he spoke indistinctly and he could not pronounce the *chet* correctly.[12]

Rav was a strong and healthy man of a healthy family.[13] This is clear also, if one considers what he suffered during his life, how much wandering he did, and what he did for Jews by personal intercession. In spite of all his troubles, he lived a long time and reached a great age in perfect soundness of body and mind. He had a penetrating eye for people and events. He understood the central importance of every event and weighed everything accurately.

He was also a great student of nature and loved to observe the course of the stars and to investigate the behavior of all sorts of creatures. He made friends gladly with shepherds and hunters, because he saw that their company could enrich his knowledge. He used to listen to their proverbs with great curiosity because it was his way to consult everybody's opinion.

Being interested in human needs, Rav was always aware of the limits of human capacity. Thus he was interested in the character of the cities Jews inhabited at that time and tried to discover the essential differences in their nature. For this reason he was called *gever bekula,* meaning that he was great in every sort of knowledge.[14]

When teaching his students, Rav would keep close watch on all their expressions. He knew just how attentive each one was at any time. Whenever his eye caught any student behaving strangely, he would want to know whether the student was worrying about some personal difficulties at home.[15] With his deep instinct Rav could sense a student's unconscious meaning through the intonation of his words. Thus he was once incensed when he saw his pupil Rabbi Kahana combing his hair during class, because he felt that it was distracting his attention from study.[16]

Endowed with varied abilities and many-sided knowledge, he was a great statesman as well as a man of practical affairs. He spent much effort in settling Jews in Sura where he founded his academy. At the same time he managed his own large weighing business and the enterprises of his uncle Rabbi Chiya. He built toll bridges and dealt in wheat and other goods. On certain occasions he also served as judge; in addition he composed a large number of prayers for the holidays. Since his voice was good, he was also a *posek sidra* (a reader in the synagogue), as well as a *meturgaman* (a translator).[17] Only a person with a melodious voice would have been chosen for this position.[18]

In many of his ways Rav imitated his uncle Rabbi Chiya, of whom it was told that once when he hired mule-drivers to bring him some flax they brought it to him damp and he could not use it. Rabbi Chiya said to Rav, "Go out and give them their wage. But tell them I am paying them not because I must, but because I do not choose to insist on my rights.[19]

A similar event once happened to Rav. His widowed daughter-in-law came to demand that her marriage portion be returned to her. He told her, "If I were not an open-handed person I would tell you that even the small ornaments you wear on your head belong to me."[20]

Generous himself, Rav always watched other people to see who gave freely and who were stingy. His own lavish charity often seemed "wasteful" to him, and in order to have some control over his expenditure, he instructed his agent that whenever he was ordered to give a person some gift which he—the agent—did not think the recipient needed, he was to consult Rav a second time before making the payment.[21]

In spite of the accepted rule that a student must not express his opinion in the presence of his teacher, Rav gave his students full permission to decide legal cases and instruct pupils to the extent of their ability. He would often take many of his pupils to judge cases with him. He said, "A man may teach a student and at the same time have him act as an associate judge in his court."[22] In the same vein he said, "If a student is capable of teaching others and he does not do so, it is as bad as murder."[23] On another occasion, he said, "Whoever prohibits his students from practicing the commandments is as bad as one who robbed him of his inheritance."[24]

Rav wished to be kind to everybody and thought better of people than they deserved. He also loved truth and tried to speak only the truth even when it brought him personal harm. It is said that his wife used to torment him because she never would cook what he wanted to eat. When his son Chiya was grown, he used to bring his mother his father's orders for each meal. However, he changed his father's orders in repeating them to his mother, so that she gave him just what he wanted by giving him the opposite of what he had asked for. Once Rav said to his son, "It seems to me that your mother is getting better." "I am to blame for that," answered Chiya. His father understood that the son had twisted the orders to his mother, so that Rav would get what he wanted. This disturbed him and he said, "Nevertheless, you mustn't do it any longer, because you create a tangle of lies."[25]

Rav's colleagues and students sometimes caught him contradicting what he had said on another occasion. When they brought it to his attention he would be silent, not answering until he thought the matter out. In such cases the Talmud says, "Rav was silent." Even in other instances when Rav had a difference of opinion with some other scholars, he would very often be silent, and since he considered that not allowing oneself to be drawn into a dispute to be a mark of a high-born family, he said: "The silence of Babylon is its nobility."[26]

Nevertheless, he was frequently violently angry. Sometimes a matter did not seem to bother him for a long time, and all at once the same thing would make him burst into a fury of rage.

Thus he was once reading from the Bible in Rabbi Jehudah Hanasi's synagogue. While he was in the midst of his reading, his uncle Rabbi Chiya came in and he began over again for him. Later Rabbi Jehudah Hanasi's son came in and he began all over again once more. Afterwards Bar Kapara came in and he had to begin all over once more. Thus he began reading the same chapter of the Bible three times. To cap the story Rabbi Chanina entered and asked him to begin the reading again. At this he burst into anger, "How often do I have to begin reading from the beginning?"

His anger was only momentary, however, for when he had time to consider he hastened to seek out the one whom he had "insulted" and apologized to him, and—as the story goes— Rabbi Chanina refused to accept his apology. For thirteen years after that Rav went to Rabbi Chanina on Yom Kippur eve to apologize for the "insult" but it was never accepted. Another story relates that Rav had an argument with a butcher who also refused to accept his apology.[27]

A similar incident occurred when Rav acted as an interpreter for Rav Shila. In the course of the lecture Rav translated one word differently from Rav Shila's wish, even though Rav Shila had told him expressly how to translate, and in spite of the rule that "when one works for another he must even wash his wet wool."[28]

In his anger Rav would sometimes utter a curse. Once the municipal judge annoyed him with childish questions, and Rav wished that the judge might grow a horn out of his eyes. Another time Shmuel of Nehardea took him home and gave him food that spoiled his digestion, and for that Rav said that he hoped he would never have any children.[29]

The slightest reflection on his honor would often infuriate him. But even more than of his own honor, he was touchy and jealous of the honor of the Bible and of the Jewish faith. He would curse people who allowed themselves to do things other scholars had declared forbidden.[30] He once cursed a man who planted a tree during Purim.[31]

Because Rav often withdrew what he had previously said, it was an accepted rule that "sometimes he said yea and sometimes nay." Many of his opinions are related by different students in dissimilar versions not because the students introduced differences in their quotations, but because he himself changed his formulation.

In general Rav believed that any person might change his mind about a matter while dealing with it, and he stated a rule that "when a person began an action conditionally and stopped it unconditionally one may assume that he had abandoned his original intention."[32] When a merchant once complained that he had been cheated in the price of some goods that he had sold, he told the "cheated" merchant that he was probably fully aware of the fact at the time, but nevertheless he had accepted the lower price because he needed money, and therefore his present change of mind would do him no good.[33]

Rav went to Palestine from Babylonia twice. The first time was during a strong wave of migration of the Babylonian Jews. For some reason everybody there was seized with a sudden desire to wander. Economic conditions in Babylonia were normal at the time and there was no pressing need for anyone to leave the country. But the reports from Palestine were bad, and it seemed to the Jews in Babylonia that the Torah was sinking into oblivion in Palestine, and they had to go there in masses in order to revive its study. So at that time people of energy, strong will, and warm hearts came to Palestine. Their presence brought about a revival of life. The seat of the *Nasi* was occupied at the time by Rabbi Jehudah, the editor of the *Mishnah*. But still there must have been something wrong if the Talmud later said that "when the Torah had been forgotten in Palestine, Rabbi Chiya came with his children and they revived it.[34]

This Rabbi Chiya was Rav's uncle, as was already stated, and when he went to Palestine he took along with him his two sons, Hezekiah and Jehudah, his brother's son Rabbah bar Bar Chana, his colleagues Rabbi Chanina bar Chama, Rabbi Simlai, and the Rav. It seems that all these scholars were descendants of ancestors who had fled from Palestine during the persecutions of Hadrian or perhaps during later persecutions. They all kept together in Babylonia and together they returned to Palestine.

At that time everybody felt the need to continue the

systematization of the Jewish faith through the principles of the *Mishnah* and Rav, of course, took part actively in this work. He was concerned with the efforts to understand Jewish life clearly and he wanted to aid in the new systematization of the Jewish faith. The frenzied turmoil of events stirred Rav's soul to constant anxiety about the Jewish position. His whole life fluctuated between desperation and hope but his only desire was to see his people secure in its national existence.

One may see this aim in every act of his life, even while he was still a student in the academy and his abilities were just beginning to reveal their splendor—especially in his questions to the teachers under whom he studied. One may see the same qualities in his later life when he was already thinking independently and all the older scholars under whom he had studied were dead.

He came to Palestine with his uncle Rabbi Chiya and several other scholars from Babylonia. It has already been stated that the purpose of their coming was to aid in their people's spiritual rebirth. In this common aim each had his own method: one wished to restore the spiritual soundness of the masses, another was concerned with the political situation, still another was busy protecting Jews from pagans, and another one tried to set an example by his own good deeds.

The arrival of Rabbi Chiya and his family and students in Palestine was an event of great importance, because besides the effect of their teaching, they brought new life to the crushed spirits of the Palestinians, who had almost given up all hope of a free life. Since the Babylonians were in a better position at that time than the Palestinians, Rabbi Chiya's group did not have bent backs, and their free manners influenced the Jews of Palestine.

The Palestinians saw a revival of the Torah in the coming of Rabbi Chiya. At the same time the social life of the scholarly groups was revived; they began to visit each other and meet in conference.

The arrival of those scholars in Palestine was a great blessing for the people, especially the coming of Rabbi Chiya. Palestine profited doubly from his presence, economically and culturally, for in addition to his activity as a teacher he was also active in commerce. He bought land and had it cultivated at his own expense or rented it out to tenants. Then he exported many divers goods from Palestine to foreign lands. He employed many people, both relatives and strangers. He had connections in the most distant countries, and a lively trade developed between Palestine and the neighboring countries. This provided a livelihood for those who helped him and also stimulated others to follow in his footsteps.

Rabbi Chiya's chief item of trade was flax. It is related that once he did not wish to sell his flax for the prevailing price because he hoped for a better price later. The merchants offered his flax at the next *Purim's* price when flax was usually at its dearest. Rabbi Chiya asked Rabbi Jehudah Hanasi whether such a transaction was permissible. The latter said that such a profit could be called usury and was therefore illegal. Rabbi Chiya therefore, declared that such a transaction was a transgression against Jewish law.[35]

When Rabbi Chiya and his friends came to Palestine they did not settle in Sepphoris, where Rabbi Jehudah Hanasi had the seat of power, but they went to live in Tiberias. It is believed therefore that Rabbi Chiya's arrival in Palestine and his activity there was not entirely pleasing to the Nasi. He did not wish another spiritual power to grow in Palestine beside his school in Sepphoris, especially since it was headed by a person who reckoned his descent from King David.

Other historians, however, see no significance in the fact that Rabbi Chiya settled in Tiberias instead of Sepphoris. They say there were no ulterior motives for this act, but that the Babylonians who were accustomed to a warmer climate could not stand the atmosphere of Sepphoris. They believed that most people die of colds in Sepphoris.

People in Palestine used to say also, that since the arrival of Rabbi Chiya with his sons and students, hurricanes and earthquakes hardly ever occurred, the wine stopped turning sour, and the flax no longer spoiled.[36]

While Rav was in Tiberias with his uncle, he spent a great deal of time with the students of Rabbi Meir, Rabbi Simeon ben

Eleazar, Rabbi Simeon ben Chalafta, and Symachos, from whom he acquired several of Rabbi Meir's sayings, that he repeated in Rabbi Meir's name as though he had heard them directly from him.

Thus Rav always used to say: "A man must accustom himself to think that whatever the Almighty does is done for the best,"[37] or that "One should always try to teach students as briefly as possible."[38] On other occasions he would say that "One should always leave the house when the streets are light."[39]

The sayings Rav learned from Rabbi Meir's students and which he quoted in the name of Rabbi Meir usually dealt with human conduct and the aims of life. Rav loved life and did not regard it only as a passing phase of universal existence.

After Rabbi Chiya had settled in Tiberias he often took Rav with him to visit Rabbi Jehudah Hanasi in Sepphoris. The trip from Tiberias to Sepphoris and back took quite some time, and they would stop frequently during the trip because someone wished enlightenment on some subject about which the Nasi could not be consulted at that particular time. In this way a sort of traveling religious center was established, which often met in different places. When Rabbi Jehudah Hanasi died Rabbi Chiya considered himself a more competent religious authority than the later Nasi, Rabban Gamaliel (the son of Rabbi Jehudah Hanasi) or his brother Rabbi Simeon. He was therefore hurt when he was not chosen for some position of national leadership.

During his trips with Rabbi Chiya, Rav satisfied his interest in King David, and in tracing all the places where David had hidden from Saul and where he had waged war on the Philistines, Rav acquired a precise knowledge of Palestinian geography as well as of the differences in the situation of the Jews and their customs in different places.[40]

While Rav was traveling abroad with his uncle, his sharp eye studied the life and culture of different nations. He gained an understanding of the Jewish situation in various countries,[41] and learned the customs of idolatry in different places in Palestine, Babylon, and Media.[42]

It is probable that Rav stayed in Palestine no more than five or six years the first time he came there with his uncle, Rabbi Chiya and his students. Then he returned to Babylonia for a short time. It seems that this trip to Babylonia had no influence upon the later course of his life or upon the history of the Jews.

The reason for his return to Babylonia, it seems, was his desire to marry. Although not expressly stated, one can infer it from his leave-taking from Rabbi Chiya who said to him in farewell, "May the Almighty protect you from a fate worse than death!" Later Rav wondered what could be worse than death, until he remembered the verse in Ecclesiastes (7:26) "Woman is more bitter than death." One may infer therefore that his uncle wished to warn him to be very careful in picking his wife.[43]

When Rav was about to leave Palestine, Rabbi Chiya said to Rabbi Jehudah Hanasi: "My sister's son is going to Babylonia, may he teach there?" The Nasi answered, "He may." Then Rabbi Chiya asked, "May he give judgment concerning the firstborn of clean cattle?" and the answer was, "That he may not do."[44]

For almost the whole period that Rav then remained in Babylonia, he stayed in Nehardea where he continued his studies. He used to correspond with Rabbi Jehudah Hanasi and introduced certain religious problems in his letters.[45]

A short time later when Rav had returned from Babylonia, Rabbi Jehudah Hanasi died. This occurred around 190 c.e. Not long afterwards Rabbi Chiya, Rav's uncle, also died. After Rabbi Jehudah Hanasi's death, his son Rabban Gamaliel took his place and occupied the position of Nasi for about ten years. Rav continued at the Nasi's school as a student. He later quoted a great deal of what he had learned from Rabban Gamaliel. Only after Rabban Gamaliel died and Rabbi Jehudah N'siah I was chosen to take his father's place, did Rav feel that he no longer wished to remain in Palestine and he returned to Babylonia again, where he remained until the end of his life.

The deteriorating political situation of the Jews in Palestine had a great influence upon Rav's final decision to return to Babylonia permanently. Because of the political situation,

Rabbi Chiya once said the Almighty knew the Jews would not be able to stand the persecutions of Edom (the Romans) and therefore he dispersed them into Babylonia where they could live in better political circumstances.[46]

It is possible that if Rabbi Chiya had not felt too old and weak to go to Babylonia, he might also have left Palestine. Still the difficult political situation was not the only reason why Rav returned to Babylonia. Undoubtedly, the greater part in his decision was because Rabbi Jehudah N'siah had not granted him any particular position in his school; for patiently as Rav may have suffered his low position up to then, he surely did not wish to stand it any longer and therefore left Palestine.

It should be mentioned also that when Rav returned from Babylonia the first time, Rabbi Jehudah again allowed him to grant releases from vows and to give judgment in cases of feminine cleanliness. When Rabbi Jehudah Hanasi died, Rav asked his successor, Rabban Gamaliel, to allow him to make decisions about the use of firstborn cattle. Rabban Gamaliel answered, "I cannot give you more than my father gave you."[47]

Even though Rav was ordained only in a lesser degree, he was often invited to sit with the Sanhedrin, and when the opinions of the judges were asked for, since he was then the youngest of them all, his opinion was always asked first.[48]

Rabbi Jochanan used to tell a story about Rav's importance at that time. He said that when he sat in Rabbi Jehudah Hanasi's school, he sat seventeen rows behind Rav. During the discussion sparks used to fly from Rav's mouth to Rabbi Jehudah Hanasi's mouth and from Rabbi Jehudah Hanasi's mouth to Rav's mouth, and Rabbi Jochanan would listen carefully to them and not understand a word.[49]

It appears also that others of Rabbi Jehudah Hanasi's students were awed by the greatness of Rav. The story goes that Rabbi Chanina bar Chama once had a dream in which Rav was placed on a palm tree. That was counted as a sign of future greatness. Rabbi Chanina began to fear that he would be overtaken by Rav. He wished therefore to send him back to Babylonia.[50]

After the death of Rabban Gamaliel, Rabbi Jehudah

Hanasi's son, the first period in Rav's life in which he was a pupil ended and he wished to take the role of a teacher. Not having the same respect for Rabbi Jehudah N'siah as he had had for his grandfather, Rabbi Jehudah Hanasi, and his father, Rabban Gamaliel, he no longer wished to stay with him as a pupil.

When Rav returned to Babylonia, the period of mutual influence of the scholars was at its greatest height although at the same time there was great friction and sharp differences of opinion between them. Even then there were several different spiritual centers and academies. Besides the academy of the Nasi in Sepphoris, there were academies in Tiberias and Caesarea. Rabbi Jehudah Hanasi attempted to concentrate all religious authority in his own hands, and since there were many scholars who rivaled the Nasi in learning, he was very stingy in granting ordinations and such scholars as Levi ben Sisi, Shmuel of Nehardea, as well as Hezekiah and Jehudah, the two sons of Rabbi Chiya were not ordained and never entitled to be called Rabbi.

In the meantime things went from bad to worse politically. After the death of the Emperor Commodus (192 c.e.) Pescenius Niger tried to seize power in Rome. He was defeated in open warfare by Septimus Severus. It is hard to know today with whom the Jews sided in the war just as it is not known whether either of the rivals promised certain national concessions in the event of his victory.

Judging by the circumstances and the documents of that war which have remained, one may say that the Jews did not even dream of national liberation. They felt instinctively, however, that they ought to take the side opposite from the side taken by the heathen inhabitants of Palestine (Romans, Greeks, and Syrians), who supported Pescenius Niger. The Samaritans of Shechem did the same—and there is only a hint in a saying of Rav as to the side the Jews took, when he said: "I am for Sufianus."[51]

At the same time severe fighting broke out between the Jews and the Samaritans and a great deal of blood was shed. When Septimus Severus won and became Emperor of Rome, the followers of Pescenius Niger were severely punished. In the year 200 when Septimus Severus returned from the field after having laid waste the Parthian lands, he passed through Palestine and issued repressive laws against the Gentiles and Samaritans.

Concerning the Jews he said merely that "If they persist in their stupid faith, they may preserve their stupidity without interference. But if a Gentile shall allow himself to be converted to Christianity or Judaism, such an act shall be punished by death."

Still Palestine continued to be the scene of wars and slaughters. A certain Claudius, of whom nothing is known except that the Romans called him *ladro* (which means "bandit"), became the leader of guerrillas who operated in Syria and Palestine. From their lairs in the hills of Judah, they would swoop down upon passersby or upon neighboring cities and rob and murder at will.

And since many Jews were found among these guerrillas for some reason or other, the Roman government demanded that Rabbi Eleazar ben Rabbi Simeon ben Yochai and Rabbi Ishmael the son of Rabbi Jose ben Chalafta help them discover the Jewish bandits in their caves and turn them over to the government.

At this Rabbi Joshua ben Korcha sent the following message to Rabbi Eleazar ben Rabbi Simeon: "You vinegar, son of wine, how long will you hand over the people of our God to be murdered?" Rabbi Eleazar answered: "I am merely uprooting the thorns in the vineyard." To which Rabbi Joshua replied, "Let the owner of the garden come and destroy the thorns himself."[52]

As noted, Rav supported Septimus Severus. But before he left Palestine he said, "It is better to be a subject of Ishmael than of Edom."[53]

About the year 219 C.E., when Rav (Abba Arecha) was 64 years of age, he returned to Babylonia from Palestine for the second time and remained there for the rest of his life.

It is possible that he considered returning to Palestine at some time because it is said that he once told his son Chiya to build him a house in Palestine. It was in this connection that he discussed the boundaries of the land which may properly be called Eretz Israel. One may infer that Rav dreamed of leaving Babylonia and never succeeded in accomplishing his desire; and Chiya never carried out his father's wish.[54]

Before Rav arrived in Babylonia, according to legend Shmuel and Karna who were judges in Nehardea were once standing beside the King's River, the canal King Hammurabi (Amraphel, King of Shinear) had constructed to connect the Tigris and the Euphrates. The water of King's River was dark and stormy. The two scholars knew by this sign that a man was coming to Babylonia who would stir up the whole of Jewry.

No sooner had Rav arrived then there was falling-out between him and the other two scholars that ended in Rav's already-mentioned curse. Later Rav always tried to be friendly to Shmuel of Nehardea and treated him with great respect, even though Shmuel always tried to say directly the opposite of Rav. The story goes that they were both guests at a circumcision once and Rav did not wish to precede Shmuel into the house, and Shmuel wished to yield to still another scholar who accompanied them. Rav then took Samuel upon his shoulders and went into the house with him.[55]

The academy at Nehardea was called Sidra at that time, and its head was Rav Shila. When Rav came to Babylonia, Abba bar Abba, the father of Shmuel of Nehardea, was still living. And since Rav was unsuited to be the reciter (*posek sidra*) or the interpreter (*meturgaman*), he tried to make a living in another field. The Exilarch appointed him as the supervisor of the municipal market to check the weights and measures, to appraise the value of goods, determine their price, and to protect buyers from being deceived. It was his duty also to see that the wine brought to market should not be adulterated.

But Rav did not fit this position either. He felt that it was his duty only to regulate weights and measures, not the price or the quality of the goods, and he felt that if a buyer let himself be deceived concerning the price or the quality of what he bought, nobody had a right to interfere, for these were matters that concerned only the individual buyer and not the general welfare. For these views the Exilarch removed him from his post and since he had not obeyed the orders of the Exilarch precisely, he was arrested.[56]

After Rav Shila's death, Rav left the academy in Nehardea to Shmuel and went to Hutzel where Rabbi Achi bar Jashiah had been head of the academy. Since Rabbi Achi's pupils lacked a leader at that time, Rav was appointed to head their academy. Hutzel was the first landmark of Rav's independent activity in Babylonia. From then on his words were heard and his name began to be known among the scholars. And when Rav later founded his academy in Sura, the students of Hutzel were the first who came in droves to Sura.

It is hard to tell why Rav chose the valley of Sura and the city of Mata Machasia for the site of his work. The academy in Sura had a loftier title than the one at Nehardea, and was called not Sidra but Metivta, even though the area of Sura was sparsely inhabited and served as a home for a pack of suspicious characters, most of whom were robbers and thieves. Rav's academy brought culture and the security of life to the place. With the arrival of so many scholars, sources of livelihood opened for the inhabitants, who became more civilized under the influence of the academy.

Sura had a very hot climate as was natural for a valley of that sort. Palestinians used to say, "The Babylonians are fools who live in a dark country"[57] but the hot climate of Sura was not stable and the rainy season irregular. Therefore people said: "Just as the Babylonians are liars so are their rains."[58] Yet the whole area was rich in water. Besides the stormy Tigris and the quiet Euphrates, the whole countryside was covered with a network of lakes and ponds whose shores were covered with reeds from which they wove mats and many workers were employed at cutting these reeds.

Various strange creatures—worms and mosquitoes that spread all sorts of contagious diseases throughout the region— were found among those reeds. Many epidemics broke out near Sura, but it is related that none of them prevailed in Rav's vicinity.[59] The reason probably is that the Jews knew methods of warding off epidemics. They usually planted groves of date-palms that cleansed the atmosphere with their scent. The palm trees had other uses also. Various vessels were made of their wood, a beer was made of the dates, and the twigs and branches were used for weaving baskets.

Beer drinking was very prevalent in Babylonia. It was usually made of dates. Other beers were brewed from hops and the country carried on a widespread trade in these.[60] A malt beer is also mentioned.[61] Many of the Babylonian scholars made beer and grew rich. In general beer was considered a sort of wine substitute, and a problem arose whether *Kiddush* (the sanctification of the Sabbath) might be pronounced with beer. Rav said that *Kiddush* might not be pronounced with beer, but *Havdalah* (the separation of the Sabbath) might.[62]

Babylon had very little olive oil, and when Rabbi Tarphon said that Friday-night candles could be made only of olive oil, Rabbi Jochanan ben Nuri rose and asked: "What are the Babylonians to do, who have only sesame oil?"[63]

The various oils allowed by the scholars for use for Sabbath candles were all to be found in Babylonia. There were various sorts of aromatic plants also as can be inferred from the blessing Rav composed for good scents.[64]

There was also a great deal of wheat in the vicinity of Sura. Other parts of Babylonia would get wheat from there when they lacked it. The country also grew a great deal of fruit and had enough waterways to allow them to transport the fruit easily from one place to another. Thus the Talmud says: "Who brought it about that the storehouses of Babylon are full of grain?" and answers: "The country has vast water resources." And Rav added, "Babylonia is rich and fruitful even without rain."[65]

Rav as well as his students used to work in the fields and plant gardens with their own hands. For this work they would borrow money in the month of *Tishri* and pay their debts in grain in the month of *Tevet* at the price of *Tishri*.[66]

It may be assumed that Rav tried to make his students self-supporting so that they would not have to depend on the charity of kind-hearted people, who made gifts to scholars in order to share in the reward of their learning. Therefore Rav set aside only two months of the year for study—the months of *Adar* and *Elul*—and made the students work for their living the rest of the year. He probably chose those two months because in Babylonia one could not work or study during the summer because of the great heat: only in *Elul,* when the air had begun to cool off a bit could one begin to think of studying. The second month, *Adar,* always came after the harvest during *Tevet* and *Shevat.* There was an additional advantage in studying during those two months because they could review the laws of the approaching holidays.

Babylonia was a country of broad pastures and there was range for the breeding of large numbers of cattle. Rav's students did a great deal of cattle-herding. Rav himself was greatly interested in lightening the religious proscriptions about the observance of Sabbath which made it difficult to allow the men to graze cattle during the Sabbath. Thus he spoke about the problem of saving an animal that had fallen into a pond on the Sabbath[67] and about tying an animal to a stake on the Sabbath.[68]

As already stated, Rav could not or did not wish to remain in Nehardea and he chose Sura for the center of his future work. Since then Sura was called Rav's place and just as Babylonia itself was divided geographically into the upper hilly region and a lower region of valleys, the leadership of the Jews was divided between Sura and Nehardea.

The center in Sura quickly became the more important and most of the communities in the country accepted Rav's theories and regulated their lives according to them. The Nehardean scholars often tried to put their ideas over but without success.

Rav did not remain content with merely the work in his academy. He travelled from city to city throughout Babylonia trying to establish his policies. His students after him did the same, settling in over twenty cities and in spite of opposition succeeded in propagating Rav's religious views. By the revolutionary struggle and the wanderings of these people over the broad prairies and sandy wastes of Babylonia, the region of Sura became thickly populated with Jews. Overnight Jewish settlements sprang up there.

Together with the Jews a cosmopolitan mass of different peoples also came and drove out the earlier Parthians and settled in their place. In many parts of Babylonia, Jewish tribes declared themselves politically independent and set up rulers out of their midst. Elsewhere, the heathen persecuted the Jews and the Jews bent their backs under the yoke of oppression. Frequently, the Jews sowed the fields and cultivated them, only to see other peoples come and take over the fields with the aid of a new government. A new law based on the right of power developed, and whoever seized a field was its lawful owner until someone stronger came and seized it for himself.

When Rav came to Babylonia, King Artaban, his friend, ruled there. After Artaban's death, Babylonia was captured by a foreign tribe, the Sassanides, who set their own king, Ardjir Babegan, upon the throne. Under his rule the condition of the Jews quickly deteriorated. Power was in the hands of the old Aramites, who regarded themselves as descended from the ancient Babylonians who destroyed the First Temple and drove the Jews out of Palestine.

There was a strong hatred between the Jews and the Aramites and most of the anti-Gentile passages in the Talmud were directed against them.[69] Jews ordinarily regarded them as murderers and highwaymen. Jews did not even trust their doctors, as Rav said: "Whoever wishes to become blind, may have his eyes treated by an Aramite doctor."[70]

At the same time, there was a tendency among those peoples to convert to Judaism, in order to enjoy the rights of a *ger* (proselyte) among Jews. Rav, as well as other scholars of that time, protested sharply against the acceptance of prose- lytes for fear of mixture of races.

In addition to his fear of racial mixture, Rav was also afraid of the confusion of cultures. He continually issued warnings against those who followed the ways of magicians (*am gushi'im*) who occupied themselves with stargazing and grave-robbing for magical purposes. They believed, also, that the dead continue to live in another world, eat, and marry just as though they were alive. In addtion to the magicians, Rav cautioned the people against imitating the *Chabarim*, that is the Persians who later overran the whole of Babylonia.

Because of the change in the political situation in Babylonia that caused much suffering among the Jews, Rav was desperately burdened. He used to say: "A time will yet come when the Torah will be completely forgotten by the Jews."[71]

At first the customs of the magicians and the *Chabarim* struck the Jews as being very queer. A proverb concerning the magicians said that "They jabber they know not what."[72] Nevertheless Rav was afraid that the Jews might learn their ways and he waged a lively war against this. He said that when the Almighty promised a son to the Patriarch Abraham, Abraham took his horoscope and saw that he could not have any children, and the Almighty told him: "Do not stargaze, for a Jew should not believe in destiny."[73]

On another occasion Rav said: "In the next world there is no eating and drinking, no trade or commerce, no jealousy, hatred or intrigue; the good sit with crowns on their heads and partake of the glow of the Holy Spirit."[74]

When Rav saw that the people refused to heed his words, and insisted on believing in a new sort of life after death, with food and drink, as the magicians persuaded them to believe, he said; "My son, be happy in what you have now, for there is no pleasure in the pit, and when death comes, one cannot tell him to wait. Men are like the grass of the field, some sprout and others wilt."[75]

It should be noted also that when Rav arrived in Babylonia, the moral condition of the people in Nehardea and its vicinity was very low. Living mainly in the cities where luxury was rife, the people were much given to sin. A legend relates that one of the *amoraim* once met the Prophet Elijah and asked why the Messiah delayed his coming. Elijah answered him: "How can Messiah come when there is so much sin among you even on Yom Kippur?"[76]

In many places in the vicinity of Nehardea, because of the people's loose morals, men's clothing imitated women's styles so that mingling of the sexes should be unnoticeable. Promiscuity was so widespread and so uncontrollable that a rule was actually adopted stating that a witness could not be disqualified because of moral turpitude.[77]

Before Rav's arrival in Sura the people there were rather uncivilized and are described as having been bold, immodest, and obscene in their speech. It was only because they were mostly shepherds and farmers that they were not as dissolute as the Nehardeans. Rav expended much effort in teaching morals, especially regarding sexual relations. When speaking on this subject Rav always clothed his remarks in real-life allegories; he threatened the sinners with God's severest punishment saying that it was precisely because of crimes of this sort that Jerusalem was destroyed.

Religion as well as morality existed at a low level in Sura. Rav instituted a number of regulations designed to strengthen religious feeling. He was very strict in demanding that the commandments be obeyed and religious duties performed. His strict regulations are known as "Rav's prohibitions."[78]

He would curse anybody who permitted any act that should have been prohibited.[79] He was convinced that if a person was suspected of a crime, he was probably guilty, if not entirely then in part, and if he had not even partially committed the crime, then he had contemplated doing so.[80]

After Rav came to Sura the city was rebuilt in a beautiful style. Rav decreed that the synagogue should be the highest structure in the city. Rabbi Chama bar Guria, quoting Rav, says that "A city which builds the roofs of its houses higher than the roof of its synagogue is doomed to destruction."[81] It is known that Rav loved beauty in general, and it is said he always wore handsome silk robes.[82] His clothes were embroidered with jewelry[83] and his seal signature had the form of a fish.[84]

His school had a garden planted around it, just as his city and even the cemeteries were encircled by gardens. He built an anteroom all around the school that had walls built up to a balcony. He had over 2,000 students, all of whom ate at his table,[85] and he built the wall because he didn't want chance passersby to look at them and put a curse upon them. In addition he had the place where his students ate furnished with mats for them to sleep upon.[86]

It seems probable also that Rav's school was situated in a high place for the expression "they went up to Rav's house" is often used.[87] He also ordered the synagogue to be built in the center of the town, so that all the houses should be near the synagogue.[88]

By studying Rav's teachings, one soon learns that he had an individual system. The great difficulty in reconstructing this system is the fact that most of Rav's utterances were not handed down directly but only as quotations from his students. The only conclusion that can safely be drawn from all the material that exists concerning Rav, is that when Rav issued judgment on any legal problem, he tried first of all to understand the spirit of the legal rule to be applied to that problem. This method is particularly clear in cases where he tried to discover the author of a certain anonymous *Mishnah*. He would ask "From which *tanna* does this *Mishnah* derive?" and in his further analysis of the problem, Rav showed himself to be the greatest of all the previous scholars.

He knew there were certain definite rules in the system of the *Mishnah* defining the stand any *tanna* would take on a given problem. Knowing the rule defining a *tanna's* bias from the *Mishnah* where his name was mentioned, Rav could easily discover the author of any anonymous *Mishnah* which bore the unmistakable stamp of the same tendency. In the discussion of the law concerning the "vermin and reptiles" which were forbidden food for a Jew, it is stated that if a Jew caught or wounded one on the Sabbath, providing this catching or wounding was not necessary for his own use, he was innocent of a sin. Rav then asked: "On the basis of whose legal opinions has this law been constructed?"—for this was an anonymous *Mishnah*. And he answered that the *Mishnah* agreed with the opinion of Rabbi Simeon (ben Yochai) who stated, "Some work which is not necessarily for one's personal needs is not considered a sin even when it is done on the Sabbath."[89]

This method of seeking out the author of all anonymous *Mishnayot* remained the system of the academy in Sura until it ceased to exist. In Nehardea, on the other hand, there was never any interest in the authorship of any *Mishnah*. For them it was the law itself that was important without regard to its origin and authorship.

Rav also had a fine style both in Hebrew and in Aramaic. Everything he said seemed to be carved out of a single piece. Even today it is an aesthetic delight to study any of Rav's utterances, whether the contents are of interest or not.

Concerning the scope of the term "sacrilege," Rav declared that a man like himself would be guilty of that transgression "if he bought some meat from a butcher and did not pay immediately," because the butcher might think that Rav had simply stolen the meat, and that might lead him to think lightly of the crime of robbery himself.[90]

In speaking of the precise meaning of the term "idler," Rav said that "an idler means a man like Rabbi Shmuel bar Shilet who eats of his own, and drinks of his own, and sleeps like a prince in a palace, and the tax collector never comes to his door."[91]

When asked to what extent a man is obliged to preach to his fellowmen, Rav answered, "Until the hearer begins to beat the preacher." When they mentioned the rule that a person who travels a good deal ought always to put up at the same house and the question was raised, "How long should he continue to do so?" Rav answered, "Until they beat him there."[92]

In Rav's opinion a man ought to perform his religious duties consistently and not be deterred by hindrances which might bar his way. He was consequently very severe and would have anybody flogged who disobeyed him. He paid special attention to the morals and protection of women. It is said that he flogged anyone who married a woman simply through intercourse, or when a man met a woman in the street and married her without a prior agreement about the wedding contract. He did the same when a man revoked his divorce or declared that the divorce he had given to his wife was invalid. He also had a man flogged who lived with his wife in his father-in-law's house.[93]

Although Rav tried to make his words and his meaning clear, he ordinarily spoke so succinctly that his students understood very little of what he said. Yet they were afraid to ask him to repeat. The only ones who summoned up enough courage to ask him to explain his statements were Rav Kahana and Rav Asi. When he explained his meaning to them, they asked why he hadn't used those words previously. He said it was because he had not supposed that they needed an explanation."[94]

In citing the text of the *Mishnah* Rav would hardly ever say what, in his opinion, the *Mishnah* meant, or why he supported one interpretation rather than another. He would do this only when his students asked him. He never explained anything of his own accord, because he assumed that the matter was as clear to his audience as it was to him. Occasionally in study it was discovered that a certain law would have been reversed if the action to which it had referred had taken place in a different region. Rav left such apparent contradictions unexplained, and even when questioned about them he was silent.[95]

It seems that the habit of reading things into the *Mishnah* which were not there often displeased him. He said therefore that the words "all the days of the poor are evil" refer to those who deal with the *Gemara* while "the good of heart live a continual feast" refers to those who get their knowledge from the *Mishnah*.[96]

In Sura every word Rav spoke was heard in pious awe and hardly ever questioned. It was different in Nehardea. His sayings often seemed queer to the scholars there. Because of this he said, "I sometimes have to declare the reason for what I say so that the future generations may not criticize me."[97]

As already stated, Rav encouraged his students to teach others and sit in judgment without assistance. This, too, he did in opposition to other scholars who tried to limit the rights of their students and insisted that during their lifetime no student of theirs was to pass any judgment without consulting them first. Rav would say to his students: "You may advise on any legal matter that comes to your attention, because a judge can know only that which his eyes see."[98]

Before he opened class he always said the *Shema* and
when he referred to God, he experienced his greatest exaltation
of spirit. He said that a blessing without mention of God was
no blessing.[99] He said also that God's name contained the ten
attributes of God with which He created the universe: wisdom,
understanding, knowledge, power, fury, strength, justice,
law, grace, and mercy.[100] He said that an oath taken in court
was useless without mention of God's name, for he felt the
mention of God's name in an oath frightened a witness.[101]

It is said that when he stood praying, his whole body
would quiver and his soul would fill with a peculiar joy. He
always said at such a time "where there is rejoicing there must
be trembling."[102] Before he rose to pray, he would always try to
cleanse his thoughts and he set up a rule that "if one knows
that his thoughts are troubled, he should not pray."[103] Once he
proclaimed a fast for rain and it did not help. When another
person rose to pray in the synagogue and his prayer was
granted, Rav immediately tried to find out what the good deeds
of the petitioner were whose prayer the Almighty had heard
and granted rain.[104]

It is uncertain how much of his later life Rav lived in
Babylonia. According to the *Epistle of Rav Sherira Gaon* Rav
headed his academy in Sura for twenty-four years. Other
historians estimate the amount of time he spent in Babylonia
after his second remove from Palestine at twenty-eight years.
Both opinions may be correct, for it is possible that he headed
the academy for not more than twenty-four years. There were
four years between Rav's return to Babylonia and the time he
founded the academy in Sura, during which he was an
interpreter for Rabbi Shila in Nehardea and a supervisor of the
municipal market.

In any case it is certain that Rav reached a ripe old age and
had the good fortune to see many of his ambitions realized
during his life. His academy developed in a brilliant fashion
and his opinions were accepted everywhere. Large groups of
students, old and young, many of whom later became prominent scholars, always surrounded him when he walked in the
street or came into the school. Everybody paid him the greatest

respect. His academy was called a "minor holy place" and he was referred to as "Our Great Rabbi."

His opponents made peace with him and whenever he did not abandon his opinion as he was wont not to, his authority was recognized in various religious decisions. Even Shmuel of Nehardea, who always took exactly the opposite point of view from Rav, later began to submit to Rav's opinion in the interpretation of many laws.[105]

It is characteristic that Shmuel treated Rav's opinions with scorn when he heard them from one of his students. At such times he would not call him Rav, but Abba. Once Rabbi Chiya bar Joseph told him some opinion of Rav's and Shmuel replied: "If Abba said that it proves he knows nothing about the laws of the Sabbath."[106] In the same manner Shmuel said to the same student of a case on impure foods: "If Abba said that it proves that he knows nothing about the laws of impure foods."[107]

It is related that a man once came to Rav to ask what his own status was among Jews since his mother had conceived him by an Aramite. "You are a proper Jew," said Rav, because he believed that "When a heathen or a slave has sexual relations with a Jewish woman, the child of such a union is a good Jew." No sooner had Rav declared his opinion than Rabbi Chama bar Guria, a pupil of Rav, said to the man: "Get away from here as fast as you can, because as soon as Shmuel comes and hears what Rav has said, he will decide against you."[108]

Rav studied day and night. People said the same of him as had been said of King David, that he slept no longer than sixty breaths.[109] Since he was always wanted on business, he would say: "Scholars never have any rest, neither in this world nor in the next."[110]

As already mentioned, Rav had great influence with King Artaban who was his personal friend. It was through the support of this friend that Rav founded the academy in Sura. When King Artaban died, Rav said "The bond is loose," referring to their tie of friendship, just as Rabbi Jehudah N'siah had said when Emperor Antoninus died.[111] It is certain that the later rulers of the country respected the academy in Sura, and in spite of the political upheavals as well as the frequent change of rulers, the academy was not suppressed. It is certain however, that the Jews were greatly afflicted outside the academy, and Rav groaned in pain at the evil lot of the people. He said, for example: "If all the seas were ink and all the reeds in the swamps were pens, they would not suffice to describe all the evil torments a ruler can invent for his subjects."[112]

Rav believed in a comfortable and quiet life and he used to say of certain people that "their life was not worth living" as, for example "tent-dwellers and those who wander in the desert."[113] or "people who are merciful, emotional, and sensitive."[114] Food and clothing were matters of the highest importance for Rav. Therefore he always prayed that the Almighty should give him a life of peace, a secure living, so that he could straighten his bones, a life of wealth and honor, of which he need not be ashamed.[115]

What he said of food and clothing is also typical: "A man should sell even the balconies of his house so that he may wear shoes on his feet. If he has had himself bled and has nothing to eat to revive himself, let him sell his shoes and buy food."[116] It is recorded, also, that Rav ate meat like bread, salted and dried meat.[117] He used to fill out his repast with a few young doves stuffed with meal.[118] In addition he liked to eat fish. He followed the instructions given him by an old fisherman strictly as to the best time for catching fish and when they are good to eat.[119]

Just as important as food and fine clothing for Rav was a life without humiliation. He used to say "Shame shortens men's lives."

Like all other Babylonians Rav seems to have had stomach trouble. It was said that "more people die of a full pot than an empty belly,"[120] and Rav was certainly among those who suffered as one can see from his remark, "A man can stand any sickness except kidney trouble; any pain can be borne except the pain of the heart, any ache but a headache."[121]

In his later years Rav's eyes were weak. He lived at that time with his grandson, Shimi bar Chiya. He was unable to see the people who spoke to him and recognized them only by their voices. His eyes were never cured even though they were treated with a special salve.[122] His memory was poor at the same time and people said, "He has forgotten his knowledge." To a certain question he himself replied: "We had a citation for that and we have forgotten it."[123] Seeing that he sometimes forgot what he himself had said made him realize that a person might sometimes forget a commandment and would be reminded of it only if something happened to recall that commandment.[124]

Nevertheless, his reason was unclouded until his last day. He used to defend his earlier views with special stubbornness and he would say: "Anybody who feels competent to answer me, may come and do so."[125] Once he had a debate with one of his pupils concerning a law and was defeated. He said: "Even though he has defeated me, I feel that the law should be as I say."[126]

When his health was completely undermined, Rav became desperate. He would say that an old man who walks with a bent back and his eyes fixed on the ground "tries to find what he has not lost."[127] and also that "when a man's end approaches, anybody can be his ruler."[128]

When Rav died, the whole of Jewry was shocked and when the news was told to Shmuel of Nehardea he tore thirteen suits of clothing and said: "The man whom I feared is dead."[129] Thousands of scholars from all over Babylonia came to Rav's funeral. All of them tore their clothes and bewailed the great misfortune which had befallen the Jews. All the Jewish communities resolved to mourn Rav's death twelve months, and in sign of mourning they did not carry palms and myrtles to their children's weddings as they had been accustomed to do.[130]

After Rav's death his students continued to meet. Each one would repeat what he had heard from Rav, and anyone who could repeat something clever of Rav's felt proud and was honored by the other students. For a long time Sura remained without a leader, and continued to be called "Rav's house." But now the academy in Nehardea became authoritative in all religious decisions in the lives of the Jews of Babylonia, and questions too difficult for Sura were referred to Shmuel in Nehardea.

The acting head of Sura was Rav Hamnuna Saba; as the Talmud says, wherever one sees "Rav's house says," the person meant is Rav Hamnuna,[131] and Rav Hamnuna himself was known as "the old man of Rav's house."[132]

Rav's influence on later generations of Jewish people was particularly strong because of his splendid prayers which he used to compose extemporaneously while praying as representative of the congregation, or before opening his class. His faith in the power of prayer was enormous. Nevertheless he seldom prayed for any personal benefit, but always for the general welfare or on behalf of other people.[133] He would say, "Whoever can pray for his fellow man and does not do so, must be called a sinner."[134] He said also that there are three transgressions from which a man cannot be saved and one of these is the delusion "that if one has prayed earnestly the Almighty will surely be compelled to grant his prayer."[135]

Rav's prayers usually contained thanks for the grace the Almighty shows unto his people Israel, from the days of Abraham until the time when Messiah will come; and the greatest kindness of all was the fact that He chose the Jews so that they may stand before Him, thank His Blessed Name, and name Him as their only God. In his prayers Rav would ask further that the Almighty might eventually open the eyes of the heathens and make them realize their idols were of no use. Then the whole world would realize the greatness of Israel's God, who in his kindness chose the Jews from among all the nations, and who from the beginning of time had set aside for them so precious a heritage as the Torah, which was the very purpose for which the universe was created.[136]

On other occasions Rav would pray that just as He had cast His fear on all the nations when the Jews were delivered from Egypt, and when He led them for forty years in the wilderness, so may He again cast His fear upon all His creatures, so that all men together might make one bond to serve the Almighty; for if the heathens feared the Jews, they would also fear God.

Four kinds of people, said Rav, were especially obliged to thank God for His grace: one who completed an ocean voyage or crosses the desert, one who is released from prison, or arises from a sickbed.[137]

Rav was a great stylist and his prayers often rival the prophets in their simplicity. It is characteristic of Rav that he mentioned the end of the Jewish dispersion in many of his prayers. Thus he ordered that every day one should say: "Break off the yoke of the heathens from our necks and lead us in pride into our own land." He added to the Sabbath prayer these words: "Let the Almighty bring us in joy into our land and plant us in our own boundaries." Similarly for the prayer on holidays: "Gather up our scattered remnants from among the heathens and our dispersed ones from all lands of the earth."

It is typical of Rav's prayers that rather than asking for future favors, he expressed his gratitude for what the Almighty has already done. Merely the privilege of being allowed to praise God he felt, was itself a cause for thanks. He ordered, therefore, that we say, "We thank Thee our God for having led us out of Egypt, delivered us out of bondage, and because Thou hast even permitted us to render thanks unto Thy great name."[138]

If a person undertakes a fast said Rav, he must declare in his prayers the purpose of the fast. It is not sufficient that he knows the Almighty is aware of the purpose of his prayer, but he must declare it expressly.[139] Rav had the same thing in mind when he ordered that whenever there is an additional prayer (*Musaf*) the purpose of the *Musaf* must be declared in praying.[140]

In the controversy of whether the creation of the universe took place in the month of *Nissan* which is called the first month in the Bible, or in the month of *Tishri* when the Babylonians celebrated their New Year, Rav argued for *Tishri*. It is an accepted tradition also that Rav arranged the verses of the

Malkhiyot, Zikhronot, and *Shofrot* which is recited during *Musaf* on New Year, and in the Talmud they are called *Tekiyata Derav.*[141]

In the introduction to the so-called *Seder Malkhiyot* he says: "Rule Thou o God, over the universe with Thy glory, rise up in Thy splendor over the earth, and shine forth in Thy sublime strength over all those who inhabit Thy earth, so that every creature may know that Thou hast created it, and every creature that has the breath of life in its nostrils may say that the God of Israel is the only King of the universe and His majesty rules over all."

As an introduction to the so-called *Seder Zikhronot* he ordained that the following be said: "O God, Thou rememberest all the happenings on earth and the creatures of all time. To Thee are revealed all dark and hidden things, the secrets of creation, for in the seat of Thy glory there is no forgetting and nothing is hidden from Thine eyes. Thou recallest everything that has happened to every creature, everything is apparent and known to Thee, for Thou lookest and seest all unto the end of all the generations. Thou hast also set aside a time of remembering for all Thy creatures, wherein various events and infinite multitudes of creatures shall be called to mind, which Thou hast long known and already revealed. This day is the beginning of Thy work; a memorial of the first day of creation for the Jews, wherein the God of Jacob sits in judgment over man. This day the judgment of the kingdoms is set forth, which to the sword and which shall have peace, which shall have hunger and which shall have fullness. Who is not mentioned on this day? The memory of every living thing comes before Thee today, and Thou recallest every human deed, every thought of a man, every human deception. Happy is that man who forgets Thee not and holds fast to Thee, for they who pray to Thee are never deceived and they who trust in Thee are not shamed forever."

Besides all these prayers Rav also arranged the *Haftarot* to be recited from Prophets after the reading of the Pentateuch every Sabbath and holiday.[142]

It was the general opinion of scholars concerning Rav, and

nobody presumed to contradict it, that "he was worthy to have had the Holy Spirit rest upon him." This was not possible however because "he lived in Babylonia."[143]

It is related too that Rav did a great deal of traveling. He was continually visiting various cities in the interest of the Torah and its propagation, both in Palestine and later when he was in Babylonia. He therefore spoke frequently about proper behavior on a trip or when a man puts up at an inn. Wherever he travelled Rav acquainted himself with conditions and appreciated the hospitality he encountered everywhere. He frequently warned people against the dangers of journeying and he would say, "No person should go out alone at night."[144] Another time he said that "if one accompanies his friend who is setting out on a journey even so short a distance as four ells within a city, the traveller will meet with no harm."[145]

In everything that Rav ever said about human conduct his intention to protect the weak from the strong is apparent; he tried in the first instance to make women independent and equal in their rights with men so that they should not be dependent on man's caprice. At that time a man had the right to divorce his wife on the slightest pretext. The concept of "scandalous thing" (Deuteronomy 24:1) was so interpreted that the slightest cause could serve as grounds for a divorce. It was enough for a man to want a woman more beautiful than his wife for him to divorce her.[146] But the woman could never get rid of the husband whom her father or older brother had chosen for her.

The scholars introduced many changes in those laws, to enable a woman to demand a divorce under certain conditions and gave the courts the right to force her husband to grant it to her: for example if her husband was disabled, or lost an eye or a hand, or broke his leg; or if his trade gave him an unpleasant odor. There was even one opinion that even if a woman knew of her husband's disabilities or unpleasant occupation and still agreed to the match, she could declare that she did not understand at the time how much she would have to suffer and did not she perceived her error until later.[147]

All these aids for the woman getting a divorce were not

enough for Rav. He was greatly distressed when he saw a woman bound to a bad husband without any chance of release because the husband did not have any of those disabilities. He added, therefore, a number of causes for divorce, saying that "When a man takes a vow that he will no longer seek any pleasure in his wife, he must divorce her immediately and pay her the sum of her contract." In such a case one need not wait to see whether the man cannot get a release from his vow, but he must divorce her immediately.[148]

A man's duty to feed his wife and provide her with everything she needed was regarded by Rav as the most important part of the marriage contract, and he declared that if a man said to his wife: "I will no longer feed you!" one should not wait until he carried out his threat, but the court must order him to give his wife a divorce and pay her the sum of her contract.[149]

In order to prevent such unhappiness between man and wife, Rav said that "a man must not marry off his daughter when she is young and cannot tell whom she would like to marry."[150] In addition he forbade the marriage of one's daughter to an old man or the marriage of a son who had not reached maturity.[151] Married life was the most sacred thing he knew and he was always thinking of ways to preserve its sanctity. He considered it woman's duty to be devoted to her husband and to see to the rearing of their children. He said in this connection that a woman is elevated by the lofty character of her husband, but she must not allow herself to descend to his level if he degenerates.[152] He used to say also that "one should be careful not to hurt his wife, for being quick to weep, a woman feels herself aggrieved at the smallest trifle."[153]

It was Rav's greatest care to keep people from all temptations and even to prevent their putting themselves in a position where they might be tempted to sin.[154] He used to keep himself from thinking about temptation. When walking with his pupil Rabbi Jehudah once, they saw a woman walking before them, and Rav said to Rabbi Jehudah: "Let us hurry and pass this woman so that we need not continue to walk behind Gehenna."[155] For the same reason he would never debate with those of a different faith, and he would say: "Happy is he who repents while still in his full manly vigor."[156]

Rav kept himself clean not only from any sin with regard to women, but he was also very scrupulous in all his other actions. He used to say: "A man should never have a lighter and a heavier measure, so that he has never a chance to use them."[157] In the same way he would say: "if one has a coin whose metal has been lightened, he should not keep it with him, because he may have a chance to use it in a transaction and thereby swindle people."[158] Concerning a similar matter Rav said: "Whoever lends anything to another person without a witness, tempts the borrower to deny the loan, and this is equivalent to placing stumbling blocks before the blind."[159] More than anything else, however, Rav fought against corrupt manners and loose morals. He decreed the severest laws and when he saw that their effect was slight, he tried to influence people by little stories which he would weave into his lectures from time to time.

One of these stories relates: There was once an apprentice who coveted his master's wife. The master needed a certain amount of money to continue his work and the apprentice said to him: "Send me your wife and I will lend you the money you need."

The master sent his wife off to the apprentice to fetch him the money. The apprentice kept her several days. Then the master came to the apprentice and said: "Where is my wife whom I sent to you?" The apprentice answered: "I was through with her immediately and sent her home. But I have heard that a band of young men seized her on the road and misused her."

"Then what shall I do now?" asked the master.

"If you will hear my advice," answered the apprentice, "you should divorce her."

"Unfortunately I cannot divorce her," said the master, "because her marriage contract calls for a large sum of money, which I don't have."

"Then I will lend you the money to pay her contract," answered the apprentice.

The apprentice did as he had promised and lent his master

the money to pay his wife's contract. Thus the master divorced his wife, and the apprentice married her immediately afterwards.

When the time came for the master to pay his debt to the apprentice, he had no money to pay and the apprentice forced him to serve him as a slave until he had worked off his debt. Then when the apprentice and his wife sat at the table and entertained each other with food and drink, the master had to stand behind them and watch them kiss each other while he served them—and when he would bring them wine his tears would fall into their cup.

The Almighty could not allow such a crime to go unnoticed and at that moment the doom of Jerusalem was sealed, and the place where such a thing could occur was condemned to be destroyed.[160]

Rav related such another tale in a lecture of his: There was once a man who fell sick of desire for a certain woman. Doctors were consulted. They said the man could not be cured until he possessed that woman. . . . The scholars said: "Let him die, but he shall not have the woman!"

The doctors said: "If you show him the woman undressed there is a chance he may get better." The scholars replied: "Let him die, but he shall not see the woman undressed."

At last the doctors said: "Just let him speak with the woman over a screen." The scholars answered: "If his desire is so strong, he must be allowed to die, but he cannot be permitted to converse with that woman over a screen."[161]

Besides the question of women, Rav paid a great deal of attention to education. He set the age for beginning school in his remark to Rabbi Shmuel bar Shilet, who was a school teacher in Sura: "Until a child turns six, do not begin to teach him, and if you should ever want to strike a child, use only the sole of a shoe."[162] Study too was considered highly important by Rav. He would say: "A man should not willingly stay even one hour away from school."[163]

Rav was a "rationalist" in questions of religion, and he. used to say: "The Almighty gave us the commandments in order to refine the Jews, as the goldsmith takes gold in his crucible and refines it of the dross."[164]

Rav fought shameless conduct with all his strength. He inveighed in the strongest terms against those who went along false ways, and he frequently could not restrain himself from cursing them. He considered backsliding from religious faith to be a form of lax morals. But above all Rav fought for social justice, to protect the weak against the strong. He stood for the workers' right to freedom of movement when they were hired by the day and he said: "A worker may change his mind about a job he has undertaken even in the middle of the day."[165]

He attacked employers sharply when they oppressed their workers and he said: "For four reasons the property of house-holders comes to ruin: when they withhold the wages of their hired workers, or when they deceive their employees, or when they shift the burden of public service to others, and when they are proud."[166] Rav's fight against those who refused to shoulder their share of public burdens was particularly bitter. This was a consequence of his own nature, for he himself was always prepared to assume responsibility for any community interest. He wanted to see the same sort of devotion on the part of officials to their posts as to the persons whom they loved. The leaders of the people should not feel themselves superior to ordinary folk. Rav said: "Any representative of the people who creates an atmosphere of fear around him, and not for the sake of Heaven, will never have the fortune of seeing his son become a scholar."[167]

Rav was particularly angry about proud people and he said: "Whoever is proud and considers himself too good for other people, loses his learning, if he is a scholar,[168] and if someone was proud, even though he was not a scholar, Rav said: "Whoever struts about in the garb of a scholar, and is not a scholar, will never be admitted into the company of the Almighty."[169]

As much as he hated boastfulness and vanity, Rav disliked people who caused excessive fear in their own household. He said: "Whoever causes excessive fear in his own house, drives people to lax morals, shedding of blood, and desecration of the Sabbath."[170]

Speaking about the inhabitants of neighboring cities whom he considered dangerous thieves, he said: "If a citizen of Geresh ever kisses you, count your teeth to see if you have them all. If anybody from Kefar Pekud falls into step with you, it is surely because he is pleased by your cloak and wants to take it from you. If a man from Pumbedita accompanies you, change your inn, so that he will not know where you are staying."[171] When he was told of a man who came to Babylon and could not get either food or work, he said: "The rich men of Babylon are destined for hell; they are descended from the mixed multitude of Egyptians who went out with the Jews from Egypt, for only merciful people are descended from Father Abraham."[172]

As already noted Rav traveled a great deal in Palestine as well as in Babylonia, and even though he considered his voyages burdensome saying "A man's traveling is more difficult than a woman's traveling,"[173] he loved the work of spreading the Torah with which he occupied himself on his travels. It seemed to him that "The Almighty has made everyone's trade delightful in his own eyes."[174] Still it seems that he grew tired of traveling and consequently said: "Any town where the roads go up and down hills makes man and beast old too soon."[175] Rav learned the value of hospitality on the road; he would often speak about the Patriarchs and their behavior towards strangers and wanderers. He praised Barzilai the Gileadite who brought King David various utensils and foodstuffs when he was in flight before his son Absalom (II Samuel 17:28). Since the verse mentions the word *kali* twice, Rav concluded that Barzilai brought two kinds of cooked food and stewed fruits.[176]

He interpreted the fact that David sent ten of his men to Nabal the Carmelite (I Samuel: 25) saying that because Nabal gave the ten to eat (although the Bible does not mention the fact), God granted him ten more days to live in return for the meal.[177] Rav said also that if Jonathan, son of Saul, had given David two loaves of bread when he told him to flee from his father's wrath, David would not have had to take any bread from Ahimelech and the priests of Nob would not have been slain.[178]

As already noted Rav was friendly with hunters and shepherds, from whom he learned a great deal about wild and domestic animals.[179] Rav allowed his own son Chiya to shoot with a bow.[180] In general hunting was not uncommon among the Jews of Babylonia. The story goes that a certain Tabi Rishba would set out nets and snares to trap birds and animals,[181] and another named Joseph Rishba engaged in the same trade.[182]

Rav's aphorisms are very instructive:

"The curse of a scholar," he said, "even if spoken conditionally will always be realized."[183] "When a person gives a present to his friend, he should tell him about it."[184] "Even the casual conversation of a scholar demands careful analysis."[185] "The camel wanted to have horns so the ears he previously had were cut off."[186] "A prisoner cannot break out of jail himself."[187] "You need not be surprised that your offspring can sometimes teach you wisdom."[188] "One should not speak insultingly of a Gentile in a proselyte's presence."[189] "If a hound barks at you, you may enter the house, but if a bitch barks at you, do not enter the house."[190] This quotation is ordinarily explained as meaning that a person may enter his son-in-law's house even if he growls like a dog, but should not enter his son's house if his wife howls like a bitch.

"A Jew, even though he has sinned, is still a Jew."[191] On another occasion Rav advised one of his students to take to skinning carcasses in the streets rather than be dependent on charity.[192] "Whose hope lies on another person's table lives in a world of gloom."[193] "Pious people regard their money more highly than their lives, for they come by their money with difficulty since they do not practice robbery."[194]

Rav's aphorisms that speak of things found in threes are particularly interesting:

Three sorts of people should be guarded: sick men, brides, and grooms.[195] There are three sins from which one cannot guard oneself: thinking of sin, inattention during prayer, hearing or repeating gossip.[196] Three on whom God should

have mercy, so they may be not spoiled: a good king, a good
year, and a good dream.[197] Three things shorten men's lives:
when a person is offered the privilege of reading from the Bible
in the synagogue and refuses, when he is offered the privilege
of blessing the wine and refuses, and when he lives in grand
style.[198] Three things which lengthen men's lives if much time
is spent on them: prayer, eating at the table, and cleaning the
body.[199] Three sorts of persons whom God loves: one who
never gets angry, one who never gets drunk, and one who is
not stubborn.[200]

Rav dealt with hundreds of religious problems, as well as
with problems of ordinary human conduct; in addition he had
to settle hundreds of disputes concerning property, or the sale
or purchase of various objects. He even had to judge a case
once in which a thief sold his loot to the original owner.[201]

It is known that Rav had a sharp eye for people and
events. He was incomparably sympathetic and interested in all
phases of life. He always kept the limits of propriety in mind.
His dearest wish was to see the Jewish people secure in their
national existence. He overestimated people in his kindness
and yet he was very concerned for the truth. He took a deep
interest in the differences in human character and tried to learn
the true worth of all human occupations. When teaching his
students, he was very observant of their behavior and immediately detected any inattention. He was very strict in demanding religious regularity and did not recognize any obstacles in
the way of observance.

It is related that when Rav came to Babylonia, he saw how
lightly the Jews treated certain commandments; for instance,
how they would mix meat and dairy dishes as though there
were no law on the subject which forbade one to leave meat
without special care. Consequently he was "severe" on all
these questions, even though in other cases he tried to make
the legal proscriptions easier when he saw that times required
it. In these matters he was very meticulous in discovering
exactly the proper change required by the times or the case. For
instance, when a case arose concerning oaths, he ruled differ-

ently concerning the oath a person took to guard anything that was given or lent to him, and which he later loaned to another or refused to return, and concerning the oath a person took to do or not to do something."[202] Rav also ruled differently concerning "sacred property" when it was something a person had voluntarily decided to give to God, that is to the priests, and when it was the gifts a person was obliged to give to the priests.[203] Rav made the same distinction in dealing with the difference between selling and giving away an object.[204] He said also that if a man transfers his property to his wife he may no longer have its profits. But if he sells his field to his wife and she pays him with her own money, he may have the use of its fruits.[205]

Rav's ruling was also quite different in the case of an "original marriage contract," which he considered as the price a man had to pay for his wife, and an "addition to the contract," which he considered a gift. In questions concerning the transfer of property he considered it to be of the highest importance by whom and under what circumstances the property was being transferred.[206]

These laws seemed particularly important in Rav's eyes because of the difference in the rights of a priest and an ordinary Jew, as well as between a Jew and a Gentile, or when an ordinary Jew owned something which he had inherited from his mother, which his mother had from her father, who was a priest.[207]

Rav held likewise that a man might change his mind in the middle of a transaction. He therefore established a rule that "if a man begins something conditionally and then stops it unconditionally, we may assume that he has changed his mind."[208]

Since Rav felt the responsibility of a leader of his people he worried about the regulations governing all the Jewish cities and all the academies, the field work, and the draining of swamps. At the same time he enacted laws concerning Jewish life and settled disputes.

The rules tradition has handed down as those that guided Rav in his decisions are very interesting. Rav said that no man would lie about an event that had occurred in public.[209] A man does not leave an oath as an inheritance to his children, since children cannot perform an act that their father had sworn to do.[210]

He felt also that a dying man would not lie.[211]

If a person alters an object or sets it down in a place that is unsuited for it and it is later damaged by a second person, the latter is not required to pay the damages.[212]

Although a Jew is forbidden to receive interest on money loaned, he may lend his own children money at interest so that they may know the feelings of one who has to pay it.[213]

72

SHMUEL YARCHINA'AH
OF NEHARDEA

He WAS CALLED SHMUEL YARCHINA'AH,[1] although his real name was Shmuel ben Abba Hacohen. Together with Rav he was one of the first founders of the
Babylonian Talmud. Shmuel lived in Nehardea where he
conducted an academy and after the death of Rav Shila he
received the title *reish sidra* (the Head of the Academy).

Concerning the relations of Shmuel and Rav it is impossible to arrive at definite conclusions. At times it appears that
Shmuel was an intimate friend of Rav and even dependent on
him.[2] At other times Shmuel directed his questions to Rav as to
his master.[3] But sometimes he opposed the opinions of Rav
and maintained contrary ideas.[4]

Nevertheless it is related than when Rav died Shmuel rent
thirteen garments and said: "The man I needed so much has
departed."[5]

Regarding Shmuel's scholarship it was said that he was
primarily an astronomer versed in the ways of the stars, the
moon, and the planets and that he could calculate the seasons
and the months. It is also known that Shmuel once declared:
"The paths of heaven are known to me like the streets of
Nehardea."[6] Another time he said: "I could calculate the leap
years for all the Jews."[7]

In addition Shmuel was also known to be a learned doctor and acquainted with the laws of nature.[8] When Rabbi Jochanan wrote to him he addressed him as "our outstanding comrade in Babylonia."[9] Other scholars referred to him as the "lion" and allegorically called him "the lion, the king of the laws."[10]

Due to the great honor accorded to Shmuel, his father was referred to as "the Father of Shmuel," although he was a prominent man in his own right and was highly respected by the Nasi. He probably also occupied an important post among Babylonian Jewry for he addressed questions to Rabbi Jehudah Hanasi of a general religious nature such as the one concerning the order of *Havdalah* when a holiday begins on a Saturday evening.[11] On another occasion Shmuel's father visited Palestine in order to ask Rabbi Jehudah Hanasi's advice concerning a problem of money matters.[12]

It was said of Shmuel's father that he was a silk merchant and Rabbi Jehudah ben Bathyra once sent him a message that he wanted to buy some silk. When Shmuel's father arrived with the merchandise he was told that Rabbi Jehudah had no intention of buying any. But Shmuel's father said: "I have more faith in your words than in your money." To this Rabbi Jehudah replied: "Because you have believed my words, you shall have a son who shall equal the prophet Samuel."[13]

In his youth Shmuel studied with his father and later he went to Palestine. There he became the physician of Rabbi Jehudah Hanasi and cured the latter of an eye disease. It was said at that time that the Nasi regretted that he could not ordain Shmuel. No cause for the inability of the Nasi to ordain Shmuel is mentioned and it therefore may be assumed that since Rabbi Jehudah was sick he could not convoke the other scholars to grant ordination. Shmuel consoled him by saying that most likely it was foretold even before Adam that he was destined to be a wise man but not an ordained Rabbi.[14]

Although Shmuel devoted much study to medicine he declared three ailments he could not cure were: the effect of eating bitter fruit on an empty stomach; the effect of wearing a moist flax belt, and the effect of eating a meal and then not walking at least a distance of four ells.[15]

Since many of the people in the neighborhood of Shmuel suffered from eye ailments, he developed a salve that became famous. But although he had originated the salve, he nevertheless declared that a drop of cold water in the morning and washing one's hands and feet with warm water in the evening are better than any salve in the world.[16] Another time he said that he who does not wipe his face well after washing will suffer from rough skin.[17] For one who suffers from a cold it is permissible to make a fire during the Sabbath, even if the weather is as warm as in the middle of the summer.[18]

In accordance with his medical theories, he listed the foods that should be given to a person who faints from hunger.[19] He also used the order of the Hebrew alphabet to explain his medical ideas. Thus he said that the letters *nun, samekh,* and *ayim* are the initials of *nuna sama le'einaya,* which means that eating fish is good for the eyes."[20]

Among Shmuel's friends there was a gentile astrologer Ablat with whom he discussed the heavenly bodies. Shmuel proved to him that astrology did not influence the life of the Jews for by means of prayer they could change any decree that the stars might foretell for them.[21]

After the death of King Artaban and his successor Ardeshir, the throne of Persia and Babylonia was ascended by King Sapor I who was a friend of Shmuel. (In the Talmud this king is known as Shavour Malka.) He declared war against Cappadocia and conquered its capital where he slew 12,000 Jews. But Shmuel did not mourn this event for he was of the opinion that they had deserved their fate for fighting against Shavour Malka.[22]

Shmuel was courageous in his convictions and he did not fear to attend the debates at Bei Avidan and he also argued matters of faith with King Sapor.[23]

It may be assumed that upon his return from Palestine Shmuel brought the *Mishnah* of Rabbi Jehudah Hanasi which he taught to his pupils. He was also the first one who allowed himself to add matters that were not included in the *Mishnah*. He usually prefaced his additions by the words: "Something is missing and it should be studied as follows."[24]

The regulations that emanated from Shmuel's academy are usually referred to as the "teachings of the house of Shmuel." It is related that in Shmuel's academy there was a blind scholar who knew the entire *Mishnah* by heart and who arranged the *beraitot* of Shmuel.[25]

From Shmuel's teachings it is evident that he always sought to find more lenient interpretations of the laws even if they did not agree with the opinions of other scholars. Thus he ruled that in mourning regulations the law should follow the less strict interpretation.[26] On another occasion when the regulations of fast days were discussed he said that the law was as Rabbi Meir said, because he believed Rabbi Meir to be the most lenient in these matters. But when he discovered that Rabban Simeon ben Gamaliel was even more lenient in his interpretations, he ruled that the law was according to Rabban Simeon.[27]

It appears that Shmuel attempted to introduce some radical innovation in the matter of fasts when he said: "There is no public fast in Babylonia other than the ninth day of *Av*."[28] But the exact nature of the innovation is not entirely clear. It appears that he was not a believer in the merit of fasts for he said that "one who spends too much time in fasts may be called a sinner."[29]

Among Shmuel's other innovations, mention should be made of his modifications of the Sabbath regulations.[30] Thus he permitted lighting a fire for a woman in childbirth[31] and cooling red hot metal that may lie in a public thoroughfare and constitute a danger to passersby.[32]

He also ruled that in regard to Passover dishes, the law did not require the destruction of dishes used for leavened food before Passover, but such dishes could be put away before Passover and be used after the holidays. He also permitted the use of dishes that had been used for cold leavened foods to be used as Passover dishes.[33]

Shmuel's contemporaries did not think highly of his abilities as an expounder. He was in the habit of introducing fantastic interpretations into biblical verses. Although these interpretations were very interesting, they bore no relation to the text which they were supposed to explain. Thus he said that the only difference between his days and the time of Messiah was the subjection to government. This was a very novel statement but it was hardly related to the verse: "The poor shall not cease from the earth," upon which he based it.[34]

In money matters or problems pertaining to personal rights, the scholars always preferred the opinions of Shmuel to those of Rav.[35] Thus it was also said that "he who does not agree with the opinions of Shmuel does not know the laws pertaining to damages."[36]

Shmuel strove to adapt Jewish laws in money matters to those of the country. This is evident from the rule he established that "the law of the land is the law."[37] He also introduced the principle of the burden of the proof resting with the plaintiff.[38] A similar rule established by him declared that in the case of doubt concerning a debt, the doubter had to offer proof that it had not been paid.[39]

Despite the fact that Shmuel Yarchina'ah did not receive ordination from the Nasi in Palestine he is referred to in the Babylonian Talmud on numerous occasions as Mar Shmuel, and in the Jerusalem Talmud he is referred to as Rabbi on three occasions.[40]

When the scholars discussed the margin of profit allowed before the price of an article could be considered exorbitant and the transaction invalid, Shmuel set the margin of profit at one-sixth of the price of the article.[41]

From Shmuel's statements one may conclude that he was dissatisfied with the leaders of Jewish communal life of his time whose honesty he also doubted. He railed that "as soon as one becomes a representative of the community he immediately acquires riches." According to the concepts of that time, every "leader" had to come from a family bearing some taint. Shmuel explained this popular belief by saying: "Why was the rule of Saul so brief? Because his family was untainted."[42]

In accordance with his medical convictions, Shmuel believed in frequent washing and he said: "The dust which gathers on one's head will blind one if he does not wash frequently. The dust on garments which are not washed frequently leads to moodiness. The dust on one's body leads to filth."[43]

Of the friendship of King Sapor (Shavour Malka) it is interesting to relate that whenever Shmuel visited the king, he would perform acrobatic feats; thus it was told that he could raise eight beakers full of wine without spilling a drop of their contents.[44]

It is known that one of Shmuel's sons died during his father's lifetime.[45] Regarding the clash between Rav and Shmuel it is said that when they first met, Shmuel invited Rav to his house and served food that later proved indigestible. Rav thereupon cursed him and invoked the death of his children and this curse came true with the death of Shmuel's son.[46] Of his three remaining beautiful daughters, two of these were imprisoned during the wars of Rome against Babylonia and were taken to Palestine where they remained.[47] Shmuel's third daughter was captured during an attack on Nehardea and was married to a non-Jew whom she later sought to convert. The son she bore him is mentioned in the Talmud as Rav Mari bar Giora and also as Rav Mari the son of Rachel, daughter of Shmuel.[48]

Shmuel always wanted to adapt Jewish laws to the laws of the land insofar as the former were not deeply grounded in religion. He was not always successful, however, for the other scholars failed to share his point of view. Thus the Persians held that one acquired the right of possession only after a period of forty years. Jewish law called for ownership after a period of only three years. Shmuel likewise wanted to introduce a Persian law allowing a wealthy man to buy the land of a poor man by paying the outstanding taxes on the land to the government.

He questioned the principle of a majority vote when rendering a verdict in money matters.[49] He often preferred the opinions of individuals, which were not shared by the majority, when those individuals gave a strict interpretation of the law that was not in conflict with the *Mishnah*.[50] He also believed that customs accepted by the Jewish community carried more weight and could modify a law.[51]

Shmuel also invalidated forced divorces in cases where there was no compulsion at the time of the marriage, and where the man had not done anything to justify the court's forcing him to divorce his wife.[52]

Wishing to aid the oppressed and the weak, Shmuel established humanitarian laws for widows and orphans. He thus ruled that movable property inherited by orphans who depended on it for their sustenance should be sold at once.[53] He also allowed the money that was left to orphans to be lent at interest.[54]

He who registers his property in the name of his wife – Shmuel said – may afterward only manage that property. It is not to be considered that such a man deprives his children of their inheritance, but rather that he wishes them to respect their mother more highly as a result of being dependent on her.[55]

A widow – Shmuel ruled – who finds some object becomes its sole owner.[56] Also when her dowry (*ketubbah*) is about to be paid, the value of the garments she wears should not be deducted from it.[57]

At that time the custom of declaring a moratorium on all debts during the sabbatical year was practiced in Babylonia. The only exception (instituted by Hillel the Old) to this custom were cases allowing a creditor to transfer to the lender a so-called *Prozbol*, a "declaration" to a court before the sabbatical year, so that he could collect after that time. Shmuel did not approve this custom but there is no knowledge of his plans for any reform. At first he objected to the idea that any three persons could declare themselves a court and could write *Prozbols*. Later he objected to the principle of the *Prozbol* and said that if he could he would do away with it entirely.[58]

It is improbable, however, that Shmuel wished the sabbatical-year moratorium to be enforced in all its implications. More likely he wished that all debts contracted without any definite condition concerning the sabbatical year should be payable after that year. But unable to put this view into

practice, he merely warned that not all courts could write a
Prozbol. Later he more specifically declared that only the courts
of Sura and Nehardea could write *Prozbols*. All of these confusing statements make it impossible to ascertain just what
Shmuel sought to achieve. There are two contradictory statements in this matter, both quoted by his pupil Rav Jehudah in
his name. The first states that "if one lends money to his friend
for ten years, the sabbatical invalidates the debt."[59] Immediately after that there is the statement "If one loans money to his
friend for ten years, the debt remains valid."[60]

It is certain, however, that although he did not succeed in
doing away with the *Prozbol* altogether, nor did he reestablish
the old Biblical law concerning the moratorium of the sabbatical
year, at least he exerted an influence to diminish the significance of the *Prozbol*. He further ruled that orphans did not need
a *Prozbol* and that the Sabbatical year could not void debts owed
to them.[61]

Like Rav he also insisted on the observance of all the moral
regulations by all people. When the people of Nehardea
showed a certain amount of indifference toward marriage
ceremonies and divorce, Shmuel declared that "one who is not
thoroughly acquainted with marriage ceremonies and divorce
procedures must maintain no attitude toward them."[62]

Shmuel considered marriage to be the the most important
moral principle of society. When he saw that men took the
matter lightly because they could wed a woman with a ring
worth less than a penny, he ruled that if one weds a woman
even with a date (which in Babylonia is not worth very much)
the marriage is sanctified because a date is more valuable in
other lands.[63]

Shmuel put little trust in the chastity of women. He did
not easily credit the testimony of women who had been held
captive among pagans and who later declared that they had not
been defiled.[64] If a bride became pregnant while still living in
her father's house even though it was known that the bridegroom was the father of the child, Shmuel nevertheless ruled
that such a child was of doubtful parentage and could not in the

future marry a Jewish person, for a bride who could allow herself to conceive before the marriage ceremony could not be trusted as being of unquestionable conduct with other men.[65]

In the attempt to keep men and women apart he declared that one may not employ a woman servant either young or old, nor should one greet a woman in the street so that she is not forced to answer the greeting.[66] Even the voice of a woman he held to be sufficient to inspire evil thoughts in men.[67] He therefore ruled that a man may not remain alone with any of the nineteen degrees of female relatives one is forbidden to marry according to the Torah.[68]

When Rav arranged the prayers, he was sometimes aided by Shmuel. Shmuel likewise wrote a short prayer for travellers who don't have time to recite the entire *Shemoneh Esrei*.[69]

Shmuel was known for his great modesty. He believed that it was Hillel's modesty that was responsible for the fact that all of his opinions were accepted by the people and that this quality of modesty had also been passed down to Hillel's disciples.[70]

Shmuel exhibited a like measure of modesty toward his disciples. If one of them called his attention to a contradiction in his statements he never sought to justify the contradiction or to claim he had been misunderstood, as some scholars were in the habit of doing; instead he admitted the validity of the remark or he remained silent.[71] Often he opposed the opinions of Rav, but he would also concede the argument whenever Rav was correct. When a pupil once asked him whether a certain regulation pertaining to *eruvin* was to be practiced according to his opinion or Rav's, he admitted that Rav's opinion was the right one.[72]

At times he even tried to adapt his system to Rav's.[73] When Rav visited Shmuel and spent a Sabbath with him, Shmuel ordered his entire household to follow all of Rav's observances.[74]

As was related above, both Rav and Shmuel had difficulties with the Nasi in Palestine regarding ordination. Rav's objections were not so great because he did receive partial ordination. But Rav was angry because when he asked Rabban Gamaliel III to grant him a full ordination, the latter said that he could grant him no more than his own father had already.

Shmuel, on the other hand, did not even receive a limited ordination but never tried to change this state of affairs. When Rabbi Jehudah N'siah I (the grandson of Rabbi Jehudah Hanasi) permitted the use of oil bought from pagans and the news of this regulation reached Babylonia, Rav refused to abide by it. Shmuel ordered him to obey it and threatened to expose him as a "dissenting elder" (*zakein mamrei*).[75]

It is probable that Shmuel was most incensed because Babylonian Jews had to depend on messengers from Palestine to inform them of leap years as well as the dates of holidays. The Jews of Babylonia had to celebrate an additional day each holiday because of this custom, despite the fact that Shmuel had astronomically calculated the order of the leap years and the exact time of the holidays.

He even wrote a so-called *Beraita of the Secrets of the Leap Year*, from which anybody could reckon the time of a leap year. But this *Beraita* was not adopted by the scholars because Abba, the father of Rabbi Simlai, once asked Shmuel a question concerning the leap year that the latter could not answer. Abba then said to him: "If you cannot answer this question, there must be many other matters concerning which you are ignorant."[76]

73

MAR UKBA
THE EXILARCH

T HE JEWS OF BABYLONIA were isolated from the non-Jewish environment. This isolation was enhanced by the fact that they had an autonomous administration which regulated their religious and national life. In exchange for paying taxes to the central government, they were promised protection, insofar as any government could protect its citizens at that time.

The taxes levied on the community were generally not paid to the government directly. Instead there were agents, empowered to collect the taxes, who thus became a class of middlemen acting as go-betweens for the Jews and the government. Whenever one of these go-betweens had to hand over the taxes to the king or his representative, he had an opportunity to request more efficient protection or to exert his influence with the king against those regulations the Jews considered to be harmful to themselves. Since the Jews knew that these men were close to government circles, they accorded them authority as well in internal Jewish matters, and in time these men assumed the right of expressing opinions in all internal Jewish matters.

The Exilarch was such a representative of the Jews and his authority extended over the entire region of the Persian Gulf and the area between the Tigris River on the west to the Indian border on the east. The influence of the Exilarch was still further enhanced by the coincidence that he like the Nasi in Palestine was also a descendant of the royal House of David.

It may be assumed that not all those who bore the title of Exilarch were generous in their relations with the people. The Talmud refers to Exilarchs who "rule over Israel with the rod and the cane" compared with the Nasi of Palestine, the descendants of Hillel who devoted themselves to cultivating the knowledge of the Torah among the children.[1]

Unfortunately no chronological record of the Exilarchs exists. The Talmud only mentions four or five of them by name and it is difficult to determine who preceded whom. A more exhaustive list is offered in the *Epistle* of Rabbi Jose but many of the names mentioned in that work have been proved by historians to be incorrect.

According to the *Epistle of Rav Sherira Gaon*, Mar Ukba succeeded Rav Huna in the office of Exilarch. Rav Huna lived at the time of Rabbi Jehudah Hanasi. But there exists a statement in the Jerusalem Talmud to the effect that Mar Ukba once sent a letter to the Exilarch chiding him for his custom of going to sleep and waking in the morning to the sounds of musical instruments.[2] This statement is interpreted by some to indicate that Mar Ukba was not an Exilarch. However, it is possible that at the time he wrote the letter he was not the Exilarch, but later assumed that office.

It is known that when Rav came to Babylonia he was appointed by the then Exilarch to be in charge of weights and measures in the marketplace of Nehardea. While holding this office, Rav did not fulfill his duties to the satisfaction of the Exilarch who had him arrested.[3] One may assume that the Exilarch referred to in this story was not Mar Ukba for he was a kindly and pious man and would never allow a man like Rav to be arrested.

Another proof that Mar Ukba was an Exilarch is the fact that he was kept informed concerning the order of the leap years.[4] He also found two letters from the high court in Palestine that were sent to a previous Exilarch where the high court announced its decision to declare a leap year.[5]

One thing is certain, that at some time during his career Mar Ukba was only head of the court. In this capacity he conducted an academy and exerted an influence on the development of Jewish life in Babylonia.

It is possible that Mar Ukba was a son of the Exilarch Rav Huna and succeeded him to the office. The Exilarch at the time of Rav may have been a different person. But of Mar Ukba's father one only knows that he was an important man in the Jewish community. When the question arose as to how long one must wait after eating meat before he may eat cheese, Mar Ukba said: "In this respect I am as vinegar is to wine when compared with my father. Whenever he ate meat he would not eat cheese until the following day."[6]

Mar Ukba held court in the city of Kafri in Babylonia.[7] Shmuel Yarchina'ah was one of Mar Ukba's associate judges. Although he was like a pupil of Shmuel and often quoted his statements, he nevertheless presided over the court. Thus it was related that whenever the two were engaged in study, Mar Ukba would sit four ells in front of Shmuel as one does in front of his master; but when they were sitting in judgment the order was reversed and Shmuel occupied a particularly low seat.[8] Shmuel knew how to honor Mar Ukba and he told his pupil that he should consider Mar Ukba as his master's master.[9]

Mar Ukba often quoted laws in the name of Shmuel.[10] It is also probable that Shmuel imparted to him some of his medical knowledge for there is an instance of Rabbi Jannai of Palestine requesting Mar Ukba for some eye salve of Shmuel.[11] Similar instances relate that when Rav Acha bar Joseph felt a pain near his heart, he came to Mar Ukba for treatment.[12] Mar Ukba followed a custom, probably adopted from Shmuel, of not sitting in judgment on hot days.[13]

Aside from being a pupil of Shmuel, Mar Ukba apparently also studied with Shmuel's father and with Levi ben Sisi.[14]

The stories told of Mar Ukba's generosity are of great interest. As he was blessed with great wealth and his wife was also of a kind nature, he could distribute as much as he chose. Thus it was told that a poor man lived near Mar Ukba who wanted to aid him secretly lest the man refuse to take charity.

He therefore placed four silver coins on the poor man's doorstep so that he could easily notice them as he entered his house. When Mar Ukba saw that the man bought food with the money, he repeated the same procedure for many days. But the beneficiary of these gifts decided to find out who his benefactor was and he waited in his house all day until he heard a commotion at the door. As the door opened Mar Ukba fled and as he was being pursued, he jumped into a lime pit and burned his ankles.

Another story concerns a poor neighbor of Mar Ukba to whom he sent 400 silver coins every year on the eve of the Day of Atonement. Once he sent the money with his son who returned with the money and declared that those people did not need it since he saw them using expensive wines. Mar Ukba became angry with his son and said: "If that poor man is used to a luxurious life, the money will help him maintain it."

Mar Ukba's piety and kindness is also evident from his will. As he approached death, he asked that an accounting be given to him of the money he had spent for charity. Finding the sum to be not more than 7,000 dinars, he was saddened and said: "Are these all the provisions I have prepared for such a long trip?" He then ordered that half of his wealth should be distributed to the poor after his death.[15]

Mar Ukba's fame spread as far as Palestine and when the scholars of that country wrote to him they addressed him as "the one whose nobility is equal to the nobility of Moses who was like a son to Batya the daughter of Pharaoh."[16]

It is also related that when his brother-in-law's son died, Mar Ukba wished to observe thirty days of mourning out of respect for the feelings of his wife, and Rav Huna, the pupil of Rav, then came to console him.[17]

At about the same time a student named Gneiva had a dispute with Mar Ukba which greatly saddened the latter. The same Gneiva also disputed the opinions of Rav[18] although on other occasions he quoted the decisions of Rav.[19] Because of this tendency to dispute, Gneiva was called the "half-educated" by Rav Chisda and Rav Huna. Rashi interprets this nickname to signify "one who disputes."[20]

Mar Ukba then turned to Rabbi Eleazar ben Pedat in Palestine with the following question: "There are people who rise against me and I can report them to the government. What shall I do? Rabbi Eleazar replied to him with a verse from Psalms: "I have thought that I will guard my path from sinning with my tongue; I will make a lock for my mouth as long as the wicked one is confronting me." Mar Ukba replied with another verse from Psalms: "Wait for God's help and hope on Him." Rabbi Eleazar answered him by interpreting the verse to mean: "Hope to God that He will overthrow your enemies."[21]

The story ends that Gneiva finally fell into the hands of the government and was condemned to death.[22]

74

RABBAH BAR AVUHA

THROUGHOUT THE LIFETIME of Shmuel Yarchina'ah, no one dared to install another man as head of the academy of Sura outside of Rav. The academy of Nehardea therefore remained the only center of Jewish spiritual life in Babylonia. All decisions pertaining to religious conduct emanated from there, and the political representation of Jews in the Persian Empire was concentrated in that city.

After the death of Shmuel Yarchina'ah, the academy of Nehardea remained orphaned, for although a scholar of the calibre of Mar Ukba was Exilarch and the people were compelled to obey him, he never commanded the same respect as Shmuel did. Nor was Mar Ukba the only one who participated in the leadership of Babylonian Jewry. Rabbah bar Avuha, another representative of Jewry was active at that time.[1]

In his *Epistle*, Rav Sherira Gaon lays claim to being a descendant of the Exilarch Rabbah bar Avuha. Some historians doubt this statement for if it can be assumed that Mar Ukba was Exilarch, it would have been impossible for Rabbah bar Avuha to hold this office at the same time. Nevertheless, such a situation is not altogether impossible. The office of Exilarch was a political one and its holder had to collect taxes and settle internal disputes. The government of Babylonia could easily have assigned those positions to Mar Ukba and to Rabbah bar Avuha at different times.

Rabbah bar Avuha was a pupil of Rav (Abba Arecha) in whose name he quoted numerous statements. It may also be assumed that after the death of Rav many of his pupils went to Nehardea to continue their studies in the academy of Shmuel. But their devotion to the teachings of Rav was so great that even though they paid the highest respect to Shmuel, they did not quote any of his statements.

This was also true of Rabbah bar Avuha who later occupied a prominent position among the Jews of Babylonia and who probably conducted an academy of his own, assuming that he did not occupy the office of Exilarch. Aside from Rav Nachman bar Jacob, who quoted Rabbah about 100 times, none of the other *amoraim* ever mentioned his name. This situation may be explained by the fact that Rav Nachman was a son-in-law of Rabbah bar Avuha. But Rabbah bar Avuha was a friend of Rav Huna and Rav Jehudah with whom he studied at the academy of Rav.[2] When Rav Nachman and Rav Huna visited Rabbah bar Avuha during his sickness they used the opportunity to question him concerning certain decisions of Rav.[3]

Rav Nachman's father was one of the judges in the court of Shmuel Yarchina'ah. He frequently brought his son to attend the trials and later sent him to the school of Rabbah bar Avuha, who liked him so much that he gave him his daughter in marriage. The young man was beardless and some doubts were entertained as to his manhood. Rabbah bar Avuha then asked some scholars of Nehardea to investigate the matter.[4] The scholars reported favorably and soon after that, Rabbah bar Avuha gave his gifted daughter, Yalta, in marriage to Rav Nachman. The Talmud contains many stories about Yalta from which it appears that she wished to be treated as an equal and rebelled against the treatment then accorded to women. Thus it is told that Ula, a pupil of Rabbi Jochanan, once visited Rav Nachman and was invited to dinner. After the meal was eaten and grace pronounced, Ula handed the "beaker of blessing" to Rav Nachman, but the latter said: "Let us send it to my wife

Yalta." Ula refused to do so and quoted a statement of Rabbi Jochanan who held women in contempt. Yalta heard this remark and in her anger she wrecked four hundred barrels of wine (!). "Let us send her another beaker," Rav Nachman then said to Ula, but Ula replied: "Any wine that is contained in a barrel is like the wine of the beaker of blessing. If she wishes she may drink of it." To this Yalta retorted: "From such wanderers one can hear only empty words and torn rags only harbor filth."[5]

Another story is related concerning Rav Amram, the pious, who suffered much from the servants of the Exilarch. The latter were annoyed by his extreme piety. Weary of their tormenting, he left the palace of the Exilarch and spent the night in the snow. On the following day the servants asked him what he would like to eat, and he asked for lean meat and wine mixed with water. The servants then brought him fat meat and undiluted wine. Rav Amram became sick as a result of eating this food and his body was covered with a rash. When Yalta heard of this she took the man under her care, and he allowed her to cure him.[6]

On another occasion, when Rav Jehudah—a pupil of Rav and Shmuel— quoted Shmuel to the effect that one may not send greetings to a woman even through her husband, Yalta said to her husband: "Send away this person that you may not be confused with other *amei aratzim*."[7]

In addition it was said that she questioned her husband concerning the accepted rule that everything the Torah forbade had a counterpart that was permissible.[8]

It is said that Rabbah bar Avuha met the prophet Elijah twice. The description of one of these meetings has a purely allegorical significance. Elijah took him to paradise and told him to remove his mantle. Rabbah did so and squeezing the garment he sold the extracted odor for 12,000 ducats; half of this sum he gave to his sons-in-law.[9]

Shortly after Shmuel's death a great war broke out in the vicinity of Nehardea. A leader of a Roman robber band Papa ben Netzer—referred to as Odenatus by Roman historians— attacked the city of Nehardea and destroyed it. The academy was then closed for some time and Rabbah bar Avuha together with his son-in-law were forced to leave the city. They wandered from city to city until they finally settled in Mechoza on the banks of the Tigris. In that city Rabbah bar Avuha organized a court and continued to guide the life of the Jews of Babylonia.[10]

Two of Shmuel's daughters were taken captive during the war on Nehardea and led to Palestine. Despite Shmuel's rule that a woman who had been held captive should not be trusted when she declares that she had not been defiled, the scholars of Palestine did believe his daughters when they declared that they were pure.[11]

Shmuel's third daughter was also taken captive and married a non-Jew. She tried to convert her husband and the son she bore him is mentioned in the Talmud as Rav Mari bar Isur Giora or Rav Mari bar Rachel bat Shmuel.[12] Later the question of inheritance of this Giora came up, for he was conceived before his father was converted.[13]

Odenatus succeeded in vanquishing the Persians in the district of Nehardea and he also interfered with its development. He thus rose from the status of a robber chieftain which was punishable by death, and became an important supporter of Roman rule in Asia Minor. The Roman government later recognized him as an independent ruler of Palmyra, a city built 1,000 years earlier by King Solomon. With his power augmented, Odenatus declared war against the Persian Empire and forced its King Sapor to abandon his capital Ktensiphon.

For six years Odenatus maintained himself in power and Emperor Galianus had to recognize him as an equal in the rule of Rome (264 c.e.). Then he was assassinated by one of his retainers and many believed that his wife Zenobiah had a hand in the plot.

Christian historians relate that Queen Zenobiah was favorably inclined toward the Jewish faith. It was also said that in opposition to her husband's policy of aiding Rome she sought to liberate the Asian possessions of Rome. But the Jews of Palestine did not support Queen Zenobiah and when Emperor Aurelianus waged war against her, he was supported by the Jews.

75

RAV NACHMAN
BAR JACOB

THIS RAV NACHMAN IS OFTEN mentioned without
the name of his father and he was one of the younger *amoraim*
of Babylonia. He was close to ninety years old when he died,
but he lived during an age of freedom from the year 235 until
325 C.E. The Jews of Babylonia, living under conditions of
comparative political security, were characterized by a certain
self-confidence and gaiety.

As already stated, the city of Nehardea was attacked
during the time of Rabbah bar Avuha and the academy forced
into exile. This unrest seems to have lasted only a few years,
however, and it had no influence on the situation of the Jews in
general. Rabbah bar Avuha remained in Mechoza and may
have died there. But his son-in-law, Rav Nachman, returned to
Nehardea and guided his own academy which continued the
work of Shmuel Yarchina'ah and Rabbah bar Avuha.[1]

As son-in-law of the Exilarch, Rav Nachman had very
lordly manners, and the reproach Mar Ukba once directed
against another Exilarch for going to sleep and awaking to the
sound of music[2] could have been directed to Rav Nachman in
a much more severe form. Although he was only a son-in-law
of the Exilarch, he lived in a style unparalleled among Jews at
that time. Servants armed with staffs and whips always encir-

cled him when he appeared in the street or when he sat in court, ready to beat anybody who did not pay him the proper respect or refused to accept his decisions.[3] His father-in-law had appointed him to the position of Chief Justice in Nehardea, and he felt himself superior to all his colleagues, and he used to tell them that they had no right to criticize his decisions because he was the judge and not they.[4]

He never allowed for circumstances in making his decisions. A typical story tells of an old woman who came to him to complain about the servants of the Exilarch because they had stolen a few planks in order to build a religious tabernacle (*sukkah*) for the Exilarch. She screamed that the Exilarch and all his guests were feasting in a stolen tabernacle.

During the woman's testimony Rav Nachman paid no attention to her and did not even heed her cries. This made the woman angry and she asked, "Why don't you listen to my outcry? Are you too proud of your army of servants? Who do you think I am? I am a daughter of Father Abraham and in my father's house there were 318 servants, although nobody pays any attention to my cries here!" Rav Nachman answered, "She is a noisy woman and all she gets is the money for her wood."[5]

In his pride of office, Rav Nachman once asked Rav Huna, "Is the law as you say or as I think?" Rav Huna answered, "The law is certainly as you think, for you are close to the house of the Exilarch where the judges sit."[6]

Until Rav Nachman's time it was an accepted rule that civil suits were heard by three judges. Only occasionally were such cases heard by a single judge. Rav Nachman did this constantly, thus breaking a long-standing rule.[7] On another occasion when the case of a note of indebtedness was being judged, Rabbi Jehudah bar Ezekiel tore up the note because he held it to be invalid. Rav Nachman said that only a "child" would have torn up that note, and added that "they were all children compared to me."[8]

Rav Nachman was also ruthless in his treatment of his slaves. Whenever Shmuel Yarchina'ah examined a female slave who was ill, it was his custom to pay the slave four gold coins to compensate for any shame he was forced to cause her. When someone asked him why he did this, he answered, "The Bible says, to be sure, that a slave must work forever, which we must understand as meaning that a slave is our property for work but not to humiliate." Rav Nachman, on the other hand, had no regard for the shame of his female slaves. Shmuel Yarchina'ah used to marry his female slaves to his male slaves, according to their own choice. Rav Nachman would mix them up at will, and when he chose, he would take a woman from one of his slaves and give her to another, without regard to their moral sensibilities.[9]

Rav Nachman also made an innovation in trial procedure. It had been the custom until then that when one party claimed a debt and wished to be repaid by a second party who entirely denied the debt, the second party did not have to pay and did not even have to take an oath, for it was thought that when a person owed someone money, he would never have the nerve to deny it outright. In Rav Nachman's time, however, there was an increase in the number of daring swindlers who denied their debts and could not be forced to back up their denials with an oath. Rav Nachman ordained a so-called *shevuat heseit* which was an oath administered in cases where the claimant had no witnesses to substantiate his claim of debt and the accused denied the debt completely. Rav Nachman thought that a debtor would ordinarily deny his debt if he knew that he would not be forced to swear, but nobody would claim a debt where it did not exist.[10]

There is a great deal of comment concerning Rav Nachman's wealth. His wife, Yalta, once flew into a rage because a certain scholar did not wish to send her the "cup of blessing," and she broke 400 barrels of wine. It is related, also, that Rav Nachman would drive out in a golden wagon, wearing a robe of purple-dyed wool and led by slaves.[11]

It is related that once one of the Palestinian scholars Rabbi Isaac came to visit Rav Nachman. Rav Nachman welcomed him very cordially and after the guest had eaten and drunk his fill, Rav Nachman asked for his blessing. In answer Rabbi Isaac told him the following story:

Once a traveller had lost his way in a desert and was

wandering about tired, starved, and thirsty. He came upon a tree unexpectedly, with sweet fruit, pleasant shade, and watered by a stream that flowed under it. The wanderer ate the tree's fruit, sat in its shade, and drank from the spring.

When he was ready to go on, the wanderer turned to the tree and said, "With what shall I bless thee, o thou excellent tree? Shall I say may your fruit be sweet? It is sweet already. Shall I say may your shade be pleasant? It is pleasant already. Shall I ask for a stream to flow beneath you? There is such a stream already. Then I will merely wish that all the plants that are cut from you may grow up to be like you."

"It is the same with you," Rabbi Isaac added, "How shall I bless you? Shall I bless you with learning? You have learning enough already. Shall I bless you with riches? You have riches already. Shall I bless you with children? You have children already. Then I will merely wish that all of your descendants may be like you."[12]

Rav Nachman's scholarly activity dealt mainly with the regulation of practical life and money matters. His decisions in these fields were considered binding by later Babylonian judges. As they said, "In any money matter, the law is as Rav Nachman said."[13] In his decisions Rav Nachman was not bothered by the fact that very often the literal law of the *Mishnah* was opposed to his stand. Following the precedent of Shmuel Yarchina'ah who held that the law of the Gentiles was valid, he adopted certain Persian regulations as part of Jewish law. It should be remarked also that in spite of his strict principles he often tried to moderate the severity of religious custom; for instance, he said that bricks or other building materials left after a building was completed might be removed on the Sabbath because they were in the same category as vessels and utensils, no longer being considered as building materials.[14]

Concerning "claims through possession" Rav Nachman said that the household of the Exilarch could lay no claim to the property of others on the basis of possession and vice versa: If a member of the Exilarch's household occupied the fields of another person, this did not constitute a claim of possession, just as it was not a valid claim of possession if anyone held some of the Exilarch's property, because the Exilarch's household could not be denied anything, and they were allowed to do anything they chose. Similarly there could be no talk of claims of possession against the Exilarch's property, because his servants used to let strangers live in their houses and cultivate their fields and said nothing, because they did not care if other people took care of the Exilarch's houses or fertilized his fields, since they knew that they could take everything back by force whenever they wanted to.[15]

Once there was talk of the Messiah in Rav Nachman's presence, and various opinions were expressed as to who the Messiah was. Rav Nachman said that "if the Messiah were alive it might be that it was he (Rav Nachman)."[16] On another occasion one of the scholars studying with Rav Nachman quoted the *Bereita* that said that since the death of Rav Jehudah Hanasi humility and piety had vanished. Said Rav Nachman in answer: "As long as I am alive you need not say that piety has disappeared."[17]

Once Rav Nachman dared to order Rav Jehudah bar Ezekiel, the head of the academy in Pumbedita, to appear on trial before him in Nehardea. The story was as follows: A certain Nehardean came to Pumbedita to buy meat at a butcher's. He came at the same time as one of Rav Jehudah bar Ezekiel's servants. The butcher said to the Nehardean, "Wait awhile until I give Rav Jehudah bar Ezekiel's servant his meat." The man made a grimace and said, "Who is this Rav Jehudah bar Shveskal, that I should wait for him." The story was related to Rav Jehudah who was considerably annoyed, and having heard similar tales about the same fellow, had him excommunicated. The man complained about Rav Jehudah to Rav Nachman. Without hesitation Rav Nachman sent a "summons" to Rav Jehudah to appear and explain his action. Rav Jehudah would not have paid any attention to Rav Nachman's summons, had he not gone to Rav Huna first and asked him what to do. Rav Huna told him that by right he should not go because his learning was greater than Rav Nachman's. How ever, since he was the son-in-law of the Exilarch, Rav Nachman should be paid the respect of having Rav Jehudah appear before him.[18]

The scholars of Babylon were generally angry at Rav Nachman because he presumed too much upon the authority of his father-in-law, the Exilarch, and even expressed himself about earlier scholars in a manner considered sinful. For example he once swore in a discussion of a law of Rabbi Jochanan's that he would not accept it even if he heard it from Rabbi Jochanan himself.[19]

As already stated, Rav Nachman's wife was a woman of strong character and she made many decisions in the household. This may have been the reason why when Rav Nachman came to the city of Shchenziv he ordered his servants to find him a woman who would be willing to be his wife during his stay in the city and agree to a divorce thereafter.[20]

There is also a frightful story about Rav Nachman's daughters who were captured by pagans. At first they used to stir the boiling pots on the oven with their bare hands so that whoever saw it would think that because of their great virtue they did not feel their hands burning. Later, however, Rav Ilish was also a captive together with them and wanted to ransom them because they were Rav Nachman's daughters. But he once heard them in conversation saying: "What do we lack here? In Nehardea we had man and here we have them, too. Let us have them take us far away from here so that our husbands cannot come and ransom us from captivity."[21]

It is interesting that when Rabbah sat by Rav Nachman's bed as he was dying, Rav Nachman promised that he would appear to him from the next world. When Rav Nachman did appear to Rabbah, he asked him if he had felt any pain at death. Rav Nachman said that the departure of his soul was like drawing a hair out of milk. If the Almighty wanted to send him back now to whence he had come, he would not accept because he would be afraid to suffer once more the pains of life and the fear of the Angel of Death.

76

RAV HUNA,
HEAD OF THE ACADEMY
IN SURA

AT THE TIME NOW UNDER discussion the Jews of
Palestine were suffering terribly from material need and political oppression. Large sections of the country lay waste and
uninhabited. As a result any Jew who could possibly leave the
country did so, and anyone who was able to go to Babylonia
was considered lucky. All of Jerusalem was inhabited by
Gentiles, but in Babylonia on the other hand a new sort of
Jewish life began to flourish. Since the community had been
based from the beginning on the functions of prayer and study,
the Torah was held in high honor and the scholars were the real
leaders.

One of these scholars was Rav Huna of Diakora (Diokra
and Diokereth in the Talmud) who must not be confused with
Rav Huna Rabbah, the Exilarch of Babylonia, who lived at the
time of Rabbi Jehudah Hanasi. This should be carefully noted,
since the existence of several Rav Hunas has led some commentators to confuse the two men. Rav Huna of Diakora was
born about 216 C.E. He spent most of his life in the academy at
Sura where he arrived in early youth as a student of Rav (Abba
Arecha) and remained until the end of his days.

Like Rav Chisda, Rav Huna was called the pious Babylonian[1] and it was said that he was worthy to have had the Holy

Spirit rest upon him, but this was not because he lived in Babylonia.[2] Most of Rav's decrees have reached us through Rav Huna's words. In addition, many of the sayings of Rav Huna are obviously quoted from Rav although this is not declared expressly. One should also be aware that Rav often spoke to Rav Huna in a contemptuous tone.[3]

Following Rav's death Rav Huna became head of the academy in Sura. During Shmuel Yarchina'ah's lifetime however, Babylonian Jews considered the academy in Nehardea as the more important. But for some time Rav Huna was considered the spiritual heir of Rav. In addition many of the scholars of Sura left in order to continue their studies elsewhere, in the new academies that were beginning to develop. Only after the death of Shmuel Yarchina'ah and when the academy in Nehardea began to lose its former significance, and especially after the destruction of Nehardea, did Rav Huna receive the title of Head of the Academy in Sura.

Rav Huna's parents are not known. However, one learns from the *Epistle of Rav Sherira Gaon* that he was descended from the family of the Exilarch and many historians state that he was a grandson of Rav Huna Rabbah, who was Exilarch in the time of Rabbi Jehudah Hanasi. But Rav Huna does not mention his ancestors anywhere.

It is interesting to note the mention of Rav Huna's wealth. At first stories are told of his poverty then suddenly he seems to have become a wealthy man. When he was still poor it is related, he used to labor in his own field, and when people came to him for judgment he would say: "Get someone to do my work for me while I listen to your arguments and I will undertake the judgment."[4] On another occasion it is said, Rav Huna was letting his cattle graze in the pasture, when someone approached and asked him to testify for him in a certain matter, about which he seems to have been well informed. Rav Huna said to him: "If you pay me for what I will lose by leaving my work, I will bear witness for you." Similarly when two people came before him for trial while he was up in a date palm picking the fruit, he said: "If you will come up here and take my place, I will take on your case."[5]

It was from this time also that he derived his knowledge of trees which he was able to use later in deciding cases.[6] Other stories relate that when he once needed money for wine for the Sabbath, he pawned his belt and used a rope instead. When Rav saw him enter the school in this fashion, he asked what that meant. Rav Huna told him the whole story and Rav blessed him that he might eventually be girded in silk.[7]

Suddenly one learns that Rav Huna owned many fields and vineyards that he no longer cultivated himself, but rented out to tenants, and his flocks of sheep were pastured in the broad plains of southern Babylonia.[8] At this time his family, too, had grown great in sons, daughters, in-laws, and grandchildren. When Rav Huna married off his son Rabbah, he sat on a divan in a side room and, being short of stature, he remained unnoticed. Then his daughters and daughters-in-law draped their silken robes over him and covered him completely. When he was later discovered, people were reminded of the days of his poverty when he wore a rope even into the school, and Rav blessed him that he might some day be wrapped in silk.

Another story is told of the accomplishments of Rav Huna and of his wealth. Whenever there was a storm, of the sort that often uprooted trees and damaged houses in Sura, Rav Huna would walk through the streets after it was quiet, and when he saw a wall damaged by the storm and about to cave in, he would order his slaves to tear down the wall so that it might not injure passersby, and then had a new one constructed at his own expense if he knew that the owner could not afford to do so.[9]

When Rav Huna sat down to eat, he opened the doors of his house wide and invited anyone who was hungry to eat with him.[10] It is related that in the months of *Adar* and *Elul* when the students of the academy gathered, he would feed 800 students at his own expense.

In those two months Rav Huna was surrounded by thirteen scholars who acted as interpreters and whatever they heard him say was repeated to the students in a simplified form. In this connection the number of students who sat at the feet of Rav Huna was so great that "When they stood up and shook the dust from their clothes, they would becloud the sun in Palestine."[11]

He said, "Whoever devotes himself entirely to study and does not act generously towards his fellows is like a man without a God."[12] Nevertheless the scholars were never timid when Rav Huna needed ethical correction. Thus once 400 barrels of wine turned sour and he suffered a great loss in money. The scholars came to console him and said: "Now is the time you should consider your past actions, for it is inconceivable that the Almighty should punish somebody unless he deserved it. You have probably treated your tenant unjustly and have not given him his proper share of the grapes." Rav Huna listened to their words and began to better his ways.[13]

Rav Huna is supposed to have been Head of the Academy in Sura for forty years. Under his guidance, the Jews in Babylonia slowly began to liberate themselves from their dependence in religious matters upon the Palestinian scholars. Rav Huna was the first to cut off relations with Palestine in many cases saying: "We have made ourselves like unto Palestine."[14] In fact the learning of Babylon surpassed that of Palestine at that time, and it was only devotion to the old seat of Jewish faith that made the Jews continue to send their inquiries to Palestine for decisions in such cases the Babylonian scholars did not wish to decide on their own responsibility. It was an accepted rule among Babylonian scholars that "one of them (Palestinian scholars) is as good as two of us, and one of ours who goes there is as good as two of theirs."[15] As long as Rabbi Jochanan (the compiler of the Jerusalem Talmud) was alive in Palestine, Rav Huna's prestige was great only in Babylonia, but when Rabbi Jochanan died, Rav Huna's importance was recognized even in Palestine, where he was called "the head of all the chiefs."[16] Even though he was not of priestly family, he used to read the first chapter in the synagogue on Sabbath and holidays, and the Palestinian *amoraim*, Rabbi Ami and Rabbi Asi, who were both high-born priests permitted him to do so.[17]

In examining Rav Huna's sayings one finds traces of Rav's spirit, and a similarity of concise style that says everything in a few words. Only in a few places does Rav Huna seem to oppose Rav. Nevertheless, he did proclaim the rule that "The law in all religious matters is as Rav said, and in civil suits as Shmuel said."[18] In other places Rav Huna falls victim to hair-splitting which led him far from the point at issue.[19] It is characteristic of Rav Huna also that even when he disagreed with his friend and contemporary Rav Nachman bar Jacob, in a matter of law concerning money he conceded that "The law is probably on Rav Nachman's side because he is more familiar with these matters than I am."[20]

Rav Huna's statement reveals the spirit of the times when he spoke concerning the problem of the books rescued from a fire on the Sabbath. The *Mishnah* says that translations of Holy Scriptures even if they are not read in the synagogue may be rescued on the Sabbath and in any case should be hidden away and not left without care. Rav Huna, on the contrary, felt that "Holy Scriptures in Aramaic translation or in other languages should not be rescued from a fire on the Sabbath."[21]

Certain moral teachings of Rav Huna's should be mentioned, as for instance, what Rav Helbo said in his name: "Whoever sets aside a definite place for his prayer, is helped by the God of Father Abraham, for Abraham too had a definite place for his prayers." And further, said Rav Helbo, when such a person dies, he is mourned in the following manner: "Alas, what a modest and pious man he was, one of the disciples of Father Abraham." Again Rav Helbo said in the name of Rav Huna, that in leaving the synagogue one should not walk with long paces. And if a person makes a custom of praying behind the synagogue, such a man may be called an evildoer. One should be very careful to say the vesper prayers, for the prophet Elijah was aided by God in his battle against the prophets of Baal during the time of vespers. One should know also that the words of the God-fearing are heard in Heaven. On another occasion Rav Helbo said in the name of Rav Huna that "One who knows that his friend is accustomed to greet him should greet him first. If one person greets another and the latter does not respond to the greeting, he is worthy of being called a bandit."[22]

Like many other scholars of the time, Rav Huna regretted that the Jews were no longer able to offer sacrifices and whenever he came to the passage "and Abraham called the place 'God will see' (as it is said to this day) on the hill God shall be seen" (Genesis 22:14). In the course of his reading in the Bible, he would shed many tears and say "Oh how sad that a slave, whose master wishes to see him, should be forced to remain apart from his master!" It was the same way when he reached the verse "and thou shalt offer up peace-offerings and thou shalt eat there" (Deuteronomy 27:7), he would weep and say: "O! that a slave, whose master wishes him to eat at his table, should be forced to remain apart from his master!"[23]

It is probable that Rav Huna lived more than eighty years and he was never sick until the day of his death. His significance was so great that his successors used to pray that the Almighty might give them the wisdom of Rav Huna.[24]

77

RAV CHISDA THE PRIEST

W HEN RAV HUNA WAS NAMED to head the academy in Sura, Rav Chisda (called Rav Chisdai in the Jerusalem Talmud) was among Rav's prominent pupils. It is said that he was a priest.[1] When he was still a child, astrologers predicted that he would be a scholar.[2] For a long time Rav Chisda conducted his own academy in Kafri, and after Rav Huna and Rav Jehudah bar Ezekiel died, he took Rav's place in the academy of Sura.

Judging by the number of years that Rav (aba Arecha) lived in Babylon, it seems likely that Rav Chisda was about 30 years old when Rav died. From this one infers that he probably studied under Rav, although there is no mention of any personal encounter between Rav Chisda and Rav or Shmuel; for during Rav's life Rav Chisda apparently sat modestly in a corner and listened to his words with pious attention. Later, however, he repeated certain laws in the name of Rav.[3] On one occasion in mentioning a law of Rav's he called him *Rabbenu* (our Rabbi).[4] Since he considered himself the greatest expert on the laws of Rav, he once said that he would give two portions of his "perquisites of priesthood" to anyone who could tell him of some new saying of Rav's.[5]

Only after the death of Shmuel Yarchina'ah, when Rav Huna became the Head of the Academy did Rav Chisda attain recognition as a student of Rav Huna's. He was a man of forty at the time and had previously studied under a number of other of Rav's pupils, and people were beginning to pay attention to his opinions. Still it is characteristic that in all the time that Rav Chisda sat under Rav Huna as a student, he was very careful never to say anything that might appear to be a statement of a law.[6] And when someone once came to consult him on a question of law, he immediately referred him to Rav Huna.[7] Only one exception is recorded: When the Exilarch asked Rav Huna the basis of the law that forbade bride and groom to wear crowns at a wedding. Rav Huna answered: "This was an enactment of the Rabbis who relate that in the time of the war against Emperor Vespasian it was forbidden to wear bridegrooms' crowns and to celebrate engagement parties." After this statement Rav Huna left the school. Then Rav Chisda said: "It is not only an enactment of the Rabbis, but there is also a Bible text for it: 'Remove the mitre and take off the crown ' (Ezekiel 21:31). It is natural to ask what is the relation between the mitre and the crown? The following exegesis solves the problem thus: The verse means that so long as the mitre remains on the head of the High Priest, others may wear the crown, but when the mitre is removed from the head of the High Priest, the crown on the heads of others must also fall!"

In the meantime Rav Huna returned, and hearing Rav Chisda's interpretation, he was not angry that Rav Chisda had expressed an opinion in opposition to his own, but he said: "I swear to God that the prohibition of which we spoke is an enactment of the Rabbis. But concerning the words of Chisda, we can say only that just as his name is Chisda, so are his words full of *chesed* (grace).[8]

Rav Chisda and Rav Huna were usually called "the elders of Sura" by their contemporaries.[9]

The work of both served to raise the prestige of the academy in Sura, and additionally Rav Huna attained great fame in Palestine.[10] Both lived very long with Rav Chisda reaching the age of 92, and it seems that he outlived Rav Huna by more than ten years.[11]

Like Rav Huna who was a poor man and later became

rich, Rav Chisda, according to his own story, also became rich after an earlier period of poverty. Once when the importance of eating vegetables was being discussed, Rav Chisda said: "I never ate any vegetables. When I was poor I did not eat them because they arouse appetite, and I had nothing with which to satisfy my appetite. When I became rich I didn't eat them because I preferred to eat meat and fish."[12] A story of Rav Chisda's wealth says that it came to him in a natural manner. His own statement was that he became rich when he became a manufacturer of beer.[13] In proof of the immensity of his wealth it is related that his deer ate nothing but the finest meal.[14] His students, however, seem to have been treated differently, because he used to train them in frugality and would say: "Anyone who can eat rye bread and eats a wheaten loaf, is guilty of a transgression against the commandment 'Thou shalt not destroy.'"[15] In spite of the wealth that permitted him to maintain a large retinue of servants, he personally supervised all the work of his fields and kept an eye on every bit of expense.[16] It is interesting, too, that he would entrust the whole conduct of his household to his servants, but he always kept the key to the woodshed himself.[17]

It is related that Rav Chisda was the pupil of the Babylonian *amora* Avimi for a long time. This man had no title and is only known through Rav Chisda's quotations of his rules, as well as by Rav Chisda's statement that he had often been beaten by Avimi and had borne the blows patiently.[18]

When Rav Chisda grew rich he felt his pride rebel against Rav Huna. However he continued to be as modest as before in his ordinary life, and whenever he met anyone in the street, even a pagan, he greeted them in a friendly manner."[19] But since he seems to have been hurt in some way by Rav Huna, he was on the lookout for a chance to pay him back for the injury. He found his opportunity when the two of them had an argument about the respect one is obliged to pay one's teacher. Rav Chisda asked how the case stood with a student whose teacher needed his acute questions in order to sharpen his own mind by formulating answers. Rav Huna understood that Rav Chisda meant himself by the reference and intended to cast a reflection upon Rav Huna. He replied: "Chisda, Chisda, know that I need you not at all, but you *do* need me." Afterwards they parted from each other for forty long years. Rav Chisda left Sura and settled in Kafri where he established an academy of his own and taught students according to his own methods.[20] Later Rav Chisda fasted forty times in repentance for having caused his teacher pain, and Rav Huna also fasted forty times for having wrongly suspected Rav Chisda of wishing to insult him.[21]

Rav Chisda was very keen in the interpretation of law and he was also very clever in reading new meanings into things by skillful analogies. Here are two examples of his way of thinking: In explaining the reason why a man is allowed to go 2,000 ells away from his place on the Sabbath even though the Bible says, "Let no man leave his place on the seventh day" (Exodus 17:29) Rav Chisda said that inasmuch as the expression "place" was also used in the verse "and I shall set up a place for you" (Exodus 21:13), in the case of an accidental homicide the two passages were parallel and the world "place" (*makom*) should be understood to mean a city. Later the words "he will flee" is used concerning an accidental homicide, so that one must understand the word "place" used concerning the Sabbath to refer also to flight. The problem arises how far one may flee. There is another verse "the boundary of his city of refuge that he flees" (Numbers 38:26) that one must interpret "let no man leave his place" as if it used the word "boundary." The meaning of the word boundary must be inferred from its use in the verse using the expression outside "and their measures are 2,000 ells outside the city" (Numbers 35:5). Therefore the measure of a "Sabbath pale" from which a man is allowed to flee is the boundary of "2,000 ells."[22]

Rav Chisda performed a similar feat of interpretation in connection with the law of "searching out leaven." How do we know that leavened bread must be searched out before Passover with a candle? In dealing with the matter, the Bible says "rye shall not be found for seven days" (Exodus 12:19) and since in the story of Joseph's cup, the Bible says "and he searched and he found" (Genesis 44:12) it is clear that in order to find one must search. There is also a biblical verse concerning searching that states "I will search Jerusalem with candles" (Zephaniah 1:12) so that one knows that in order to search to find, one must use candles. And if one wishes to know how many candles to use there is a verse stating "The spirit of man is the candle of the Lord searching all the inward parts of the belly" (Proverbs 20:27). From this we may infer that if one searches in order to find, one should search with one candle.[23]

After Rav Chisda left Rav Huna's academy, they had frequent differences of opinion over matters of law where each one directly contradicted the other, as for instance in the question of how pure a place must be in order that *Shema* may be said there,[24] or whether one may make a hole in a barrel on the Sabbath in order to put in a tap,[25] or concerning the problem that all foods have to be salted, and whether a dish kept overnight had to have spices.[26] On another occasion they differed concerning an important problem: a man had given his messenger a divorce for his wife, and the messenger had faithfully carried out his mission and delivered the divorce. Later the man regretted his action and claimed that he had simply given the divorce papers to his messenger for safekeeping. The messenger, on the other hand, claimed that he had received the papers for delivery to the wife. Rav Huna said the man was to be believed and the divorce could not stand. Rav Chisda, on the other hand, said that the agent was to be believed and the divorce was valid.[27]

But even though Rav Huna was annoyed by Rav Chisda, he told his son Rabbah to go to Rav Chisda's academy. At first Rabbah did not want to do so, but his father insisted because Rav Chisda was very keen in his legal arguments and he could learn a great deal from him.[28] Later Rabbah bar Rav Huna became a devoted friend of Rav Chisda's. Since they used to study together they would often concur in their opinions, and the Talmud says, "Rav Chisda and Rabbah bar Rav Huna who both say. . . ."[29] Later they would often sit in judgment together.[30]

Rav Chisda was very much inclined to interpret various biblical verses in order to derive new laws or to justify accepted laws. Thus, for instance, he said that anyone who prays for another person should not mention the name of the person for whom he is praying, just as Moses prayed for his sister Miriam and said no more than "Please Lord heal her please" because the Almighty knows without being told for whom the prayer is meant.[31]

Since the Sabbath was the most important element in the Jewish religion and everybody considered it a *mitzvah* to aid in the preparation of the Sabbath, Rav Chisda said that a person should rise very early on Friday morning in order to have everything ready for the Sabbath.[32]

It is certain that Rav Chisda spent some time in Palestine, but it is not known when this occurred. Some say that Rav Chisda went to Palestine for Rav Huna's burial. But this is hard to believe since Rav Chisda was a man of 80 at the time of Rav Huna's death and the trip from Babylon to Palestine would have been too difficult for a man of that age.

Rav Chisda's friends were Rav Nachman bar Jacob, Rav Sheshet, and as already mentioned, Rabbah bar Rav Huna. It is said that when Rav Chisda once met Rav Sheshet his lips trembled with fear lest Rav Sheshet ask him some difficult questions. At the same time Rav Sheshet was trembling all over for fear that Rav Chisda start on one of his involved disputations.

Rav Chisda was accustomed to stay up all night and study. It is said that once one of his daughters suggested he get a little sleep. Rav Chisda answered that soon enough the long days of the grave would come and then he would have plenty of time for a long sleep.[33]

Rav Chisda had six learned and prominent sons. Nevertheless, he once said that daughters were preferable to sons.[34] In his anxiety for the welfare of his daughters, he once urged them to be temperate in their intimate relations with their husbands.[35] Since he lived such a long time Rav Chisda had the good fortune to attend sixty weddings of his children and his grandchildren.[36]

The Talmud relates that when the time of his death drew near, the Angel of Death could not approach him because he did not interrupt his studies for an instant. Therefore, the Angel of Death seated himself in a cedar in the garden of the Temple, and when the tree broke Rav Chisda was silenced for a moment . . . and died instantly.

78

RAV JEHUDAH BAR EZEKIEL

PARTICULARLY PROMINENT IN HIS views and be-
cause of his personal traits was Rav Jehudah bar Ezekiel, who
is usually mentioned in the Talmud without his patronymic
as Rav Jehudah. It appears from his sayings that have survived that he was very sharp-tongued in his dealings with
people, and when somebody dared to say something that did
not please him, he almost slew that person with his barbed
speech.

While Rav (Abba Arecha) was alive, Rav Jehudah bar
Ezekiel was one of his outstanding students with whose
opinions Rav was forced to reckon. Whenever Rav had to make
a trip in the interests of the community he took Rav Jehudah
along in order to have someone to talk to on the road.[1] And
when Rav sent away his son Chiya to study, he chose Rav
Jehudah as his teacher.[2]

Rav Jehudah bar Ezekiel was born in 219 C.E. on the very
same day that Rabbi Jehudah Hanasi died in Palestine,[3] and
died around 299 C.E. His father Rav Ezekiel was also a scholar.
It is said that Shmuel Yarchina'ah used to treat him respectfully
and would rise when he met him.[4] Rav Jehudah received his
first instruction from his father.[5] Later he made such progress
through his own diligence that when his father was teaching

his brother Rami, he permitted himself to tell his father that he was teaching him incorrectly.[6]

When Shmuel Yarchina'ah died, the great academy of Nehardea was transferred to Sura under Rav Huna. At that time Rav Jehudah was about 60 years of age when he founded the academy in Pumbedita. Even though Rav Jehudah was the head of that great academy, he remained under the influence of Rav Huna in Sura for a long time. As noted, Rav Jehudah was a student of Rav's and when Rav died, he studied a short time with Rav Asi in Hutzel. Later he studied with Shmuel Yarchina'ah in Nehardea. It occurred frequently, however, that when Rav Jehudah quoted some statement of Shmuel's, other scholars would deny that he had ever said it. Even Rav Jehudah's own brother, Rami bar Ezekiel, once said, "Pay no attention to what my brother says in the name of Shmuel."[7] On other occasions when Rav Jehudah said something in his own name, other scholars said: "What Rav Jehudah is now saying in his own name is really a quotation from Shmuel!"[8]

Being extremely sharp-witted and more brainy than emotional, Rav Jehudah felt that study was the essential thing and prayer merely of incidental significance; and since he never wanted to stop studying, it is said that he prayed only once every thirty days.[9] Nevertheless, he once said on the same subject that he considered it one of his merits that he observed the commandment of contemplating the prayer.[10] This saying of his was later interpreted in the sense that when he prayed only once in thirty days, he would cleanse his soul first and only then would he pray.[11]

His mind was of a logical bent and he devoted himself mainly to problems of fiscal law, where he had a broad field for the exercise of his reasoning powers. It was related also that when he came across the laws of ritual purity in the course of his study, or other matters which had no legal significance in his own time, he would say: "Such matters were of interest to Rav and Shmuel."[12]

Because of his keenness Shmuel called him Shinana which means sharp-witted.[13] At another time Shmuel said that he was not born of woman because he was simply an angel.[14]

Coming from very aristocratic stock that traced its descent straight from the prophets, he was very scrupulous in matters of racial purity, and this often involved him in very bitter disputes. He felt that the whole significance of the return of the Exiles in the time of Ezra the Scribe consisted of the fact that Ezra removed all the mixed families to Palestine and left all the pure families in Babylon.

As already noted, the scholars of Babylon worked hard to free the intellectual and spiritual life of the Babylonian Jews from the wardenship of Palestine. However, there were always many scholars in the Babylonian academies who felt impelled to go to Palestine. This displeased Rav Jehudah and he said that "anyone who lives in Babylon is as though he lived in Palestine."[15] And if a Babylonian still wanted to go to Palestine, it was no less than a sin, as the Almighty warned us through the Prophet Jeremiah, "To Babylon they shall come and there they shall be."[16] For many scholars, however, their love for Palestine was a stronger force than their teacher's opposition, and they said nothing to him about leaving the country because they knew he would not have permitted them to leave. One of these students was Rav Abba, a native of Babylon, who studied with Rav Jehudah and left without asking his permission.[17] Rabbi Zeira did the same. Even Rav Jehudah's own brother, Rami, did not heed his brother's opinion and left Babylon to settle in Palestine.[18]

As already mentioned the purity of the family was the most important element in the whole national existence of the Jewish people, according to Rav Jehudah. And since he was always examining the purity of various families, he found it difficult to find a suitable wife for his son Isaac, who had long been of marriageable age. Ula, on one of his numberless trips between Babylon and Palestine, arrived in Pumbedita and heard of Rav Jehudah's constant inquiry into the history of various families. Said he: "How do we know what our own origin is? Perhaps we, too, are descendants of those pagans who slipped into the fold during the time when the Temple was destroyed?" Because of Rav Jehudah's agitation about family purity, a number of betrothals were broken off in Jewish homes and there were even a number of divorces. The people grew angry at Rav Jehudah and a mob once formed in order to stone him. He was not the least bit frightened by the mob and threatened if they annoyed him, he would reveal that they all came from impure families. The crowd was frightened and they all threw their stones elsewhere and did not trouble Rav Jehudah any longer.[19]

Through his desire to reveal the impure families, Rav Jehudah once came into conflict with a certain political boss, Bati bar Tobia. He was a freedman who had managed to win the esteem of King Sapor. In consequence the whole world toadied to him and tried to find favor in his eyes. Only Rav Jehudah had the courage to say that since the freedman in his pride had not asked his former owner for a certificate of liberation, he was still legally a slave and no free man could marry his children.

As has already been related, a certain person from Nehardea once came to Pumbedita and went to a butcher to buy meat, at the same time that one of Rav Jehudah bar Ezekiel's servants came there. The butcher said to him: "You will have to wait while I give meat to Rav Jehudah bar Ezekiel's servant." The man made a grimace and asked: "Who is this Rav Jehudah bar Sheveskal, that I must wait for him?" The story was repeated to Rav Jehudah and he was highly annoyed. And since he was told in addition that the man boasted of an ancestry that reached back to the Hasmoneans and was accustomed to calling everyone "slave," Rav Jehudah excommunicated him according to Shmuel Yarchina'ah's long-established rule that "anyone who boasts of his descent from the Hasmoneans is certainly a slave," because King Herod had killed off all the Hasmoneans without exception. The condemned man complained to Rav Nachman bar Jacob about Rav Jehudah. Rav Nachman did not hesitate a moment but sent Rav Jehudah a summons to appear before him and explain his actions. Rav Jehudah would not have heeded Rav Nachman's summons nor appeared for trial but he went to Rav Huna first to ask his advice. Rav Huna said that by right he should not have to go, because his learning was greater than that of Rav

Nachman. But seeing that the latter was the son-in-law of the Exilarch, he should do him the honor of obeying his summons.

When Rav Jehudah arrived at Rav Nachman bar Jacob's house, he found him making a balcony for his roof, and Rav Jehudah said: "How is it that you are doing work unsuited to your social status, work that ought to be done by someone else?" And no matter what Rav Nachman answered him in the argument that followed, Rav Jehudah corrected the grammar of each sentence or attempted to prove to him that he was wrong as to the law. Yalta, Rav Nachman's wife, heard the argument and said to her husband: "Send the man away or you will get a reputation as an ignoramus."[20]

After the destruction of Nehardea, Pumbedita became a center of Jewish spiritual life in Babylonia and when people spoke of the Jews in the Diaspora at that time, they meant Pumbedita.[21] Later Pumbedita became a holy city for the Babylonian Jews. People said that whoever leaves Pumbedita in order to go somewhere else is the same as someone who leaves Palestine to live in the Diaspora."[22]

Old documents reveal that Pumbedita was a very clean city with many sanitary devices and the houses were like palaces. For a long time also there was a sort of competition between the academy in Sura, called Mata Machasia and the academy in Pumbedita. One of the scholars enjoined his children that they should rather live "in the dirt of Mata Machasia than in the palaces of Pumbedita."[23]

Whenever the academy of Pumbedita was mentioned, interesting stories were told of the manner of study there and people said that true wit flourished wherever Rav Jehudah taught. A story was told of one of Rav Jehudah's students, Rami bar Dikola, who once arrived in Pumbedita from Sura on the eve of Yom Kippur and saw them discarding the udders of their cows, for in Sura they did not eat the flesh of the udders, fearing that a lick of milk might still have remained there, while in Pumbedita they *did* eat it after having slit it in two directions. So Rami bar Dikola gathered the discarded udders and ate them. He was brought before Rav Chisda to explain his actions. Rav Chisda asked him why he had eaten cows' udders, knowing, as he did, that this was not in accordance with the custom of Sura. "I come from the city where Rav Jehudah is the head of the academy, and there it is our custom to eat the udders of cows." "You know the rule," said Rav Chisda, "that a stranger who comes to a city where there is a religious custom different from that of his own town should always follow the stricter practice of the two, and therefore you should not have eaten the udders." To this Rami answered: "I ate the udders outside the city limits." "And how did you roast them?" asked Rav Chisda. "With grape twigs," replied Rami. "What if they were the twigs of impure vines?" asked Rav Chisda. Rami replied, "The twigs were more than twelve months old and all dry so that the law of impure vines does not apply to them."

Later on they noticed that the man did not put on his phylacteries. When asked the reason for this, he replied: "I have stomach trouble and Rav Jehudah has ruled that anyone with stomach trouble is exempt from the duty of putting on phylacteries." Later on they noticed that he did not wear the ritual fringes on his garments. When he was asked the reason for this, he answered: "My garment is borrowed and Rav Jehudah has ruled that a borrowed garment need not be worn with ritual fringes."

During this conversation Rami noticed that they were bringing in a man to be flogged for disrespect to his parents. When they had bound the man to a post, he said: "Let him go. Wherever the Bible promises a reward for observing a certain commandment, as in the case of the commandment to respect one's father and mother, where the Bible promises long life for the observance of the law, the punishment for nonobservance should be left to God and the courts of man should not deal with such cases."[24]

Rav Jehudah bar Ezekiel developed a whole group who were famous as the keen minds of Pumbedita,[25] and were said to be able "to drive an elephant through the eye of a needle" by their sharp logic.[26] This sort of study was very popular with the younger students. There were others who did not care for Rav Jehudah's form of teaching, however, and they left his academy. Many of them even used the excuse that they were suddenly seized by a desire to go to Palestine. In truth however, one may assume that the sophistry of Pumbedita was a very important factor in their decision to leave. It may be assumed also that Rav Jehudah's method of study was well known in Palestine also, and nobody granted it recognition. And when one of Rav Jehudah's students, Rav Abba, decided to go to Palestine, he was afraid of being ridiculed for his ways of argument. When he came to Palestine and reasoned something, the scholars did in fact laugh at him.[27]

Two years before the death of Rav Jehudah, Rav Huna died. Almost automatically Rav Jehudah became the head of all the Jews in Babylon. Since nobody was elected to take Rav Huna's place, all his students came to study under Rav Jehudah in Pumbedita.

Many of Rav Jehudah's sayings prove that he was well versed in natural history. This is not to be wondered at since he studied under Shmuel Yarchina'ah who was always considered to be a great authority in such matters.[28] He also knew the value of trees for human health, and he said that if one were out walking in the month of *Nissan* and saw the trees covered with leaves, he must utter a special benediction.[29]

There is an interesting story about the conduct of Rav Jehudah when he was a student in Shmuel's school. Once a woman came, making an outcry about various injuries that had been done to her. Shmuel paid no attention to her nor to her outcries. Then Rav Jehudah said: "Don't you respect the biblical warning that anyone who stuffs his ears so as not to hear the outcries of the poor will someday cry out himself and no one will hear him?"[30]

It is related also that one of Rav Jehudah's neighbors died without leaving any kin to mourn him; Rav Jehudah gathered together ten people to sit and mourn for him seven days. After the seventh day that man came to Rav Jehudah in a dream and thanked him for the kindness he had done him.[31]

In teaching Rav Jehudah placed most stress upon the matter of damages and said that "Anyone who wants to pass as

pious, must devote his attention to damages."[32] In his academy, too, most of the time was devoted to studying the laws of
damages.[33]

In spite of his greatness, Rav Jehudah did not make his
learning a source of income, for it seems that he made his living
from trading in wine.[34]

Rav Jehudah was one of the tallest men of his time, but he
only reached to the shoulders of Rav.[35] He also had large eyes[36]
and when he grew old his eyesight grew dim.[37] He was also
sickly and would faint from an empty stomach.[38]

Of his regulations we need only mention that he made a
rule for the writing of a *shetar halitzah*[39] and determined the
form of the document for freeing a slave.[40]

79

RABBAH BAR NACHMANI

AFTER RAV JEHUDAH BAR EZEKIEL died, the inhabitants of Pumbedita decided unanimously that the head of their academy should be Rabbah bar Nachmani. But he was a very poor and very modest man and did not wish to accept. Since the heads of the academy in Sura were mostly wealthy men, Rabbah thought that Pumbedita should have the same distinction. So 400 scholars, apparently at the suggestion of Rabbah himself went to Rav Huna bar Chiya[1] and crowned him head of the academy in Pumbedita.

However, it became known immediately that Rav Huna bar Chiya had made his fortune as a tax collector over the Babylonian Jews for the Persian king. This occupation was considered highly dishonorable at the time, and it was a widely accepted opinion that a Jewish tax collector who served a pagan king lost his share in Heaven. The scholars therefore sent a special delegation to Rav Huna bar Chiya saying: "Choose one of the two posts, either be head of the academy or tax collector, for you cannot hold both these posts simultaneously." Rav Huna bar Chiya immediately resigned his post as tax collector. But many scholars were not content that Rav Huna bar Chiya had given up his position as tax collector, for they felt that once a man had held that position he no longer deserved the respect of the Jews.[2]

And in fact the prestige and honor of the academy in Pumbedita suffered at that time, and when Rav Huna died they had to pick a man for his position who could restore the good name of the academy with his great learning and personal virtues. There were only two suitable candidates for this post, Rabbah bar Nachmani and Rav Joseph bar Chiya.

Both were famous scholars, the greatest in their time. During the period when Rav Huna bar Chiya was head of the academy in Pumbedita, Rabbah bar Nachmani continued to grow in importance until he was called the "uprooter of mountains," meaning that he could pull up mountains and grind them to powder by the sheer force of his argumentation. Since they believed that Rabbah bar Nachmani would not accept the position, they had to have a second candidate. This was Rav Joseph bar Chiya who was called "Sinai," because all the laws of the Torah were so systematically arranged in his head that it seemed as though he had really heard them directly from the mouth of God on Mount Sinai. The Babylonian scholars did not know what to do and sent to Palestine for advice. The Palestinians replied that since "Sinai" is more important than an "uprooter of hills," they should choose the "Sinai." But Rav Joseph bar Chiya did not wish to accept the position either because an astrologer had once told him that if he became the head of an academy he would not live to officiate any longer than two years.[3] Immediately on receiving this news, the scholars forced Rabbah bar Nachmani to accept the position. He had immediate success in raising the prestige of the Pumbedita academy, where 12,000 people and sometimes more would gather in the school months of *Adar* and *Elul*.

The dates of Rabbah bar Nachmani's birth and death are obscure. The accepted opinion is that he lived no more than forty years.[4] Another source says that Rabbah's brothers told him to study with Rabbi Jochanan in Palestine,[5] and later it was said that he was head of the Pumbedita academy for twenty-two years.[6] According to the *Epistle of Rav Sherira Gaon* he died in the year 330 C.E. so that one must conclude that he lived much longer than 40 years. Otherwise Rabbah would have had to be less than 10 years old when he was a student of Rabbi Jochanan.

According to the Talmud, Rabbah bar Nachmani came from the town of Mimla (Mimalis) in Babylonia, the majority of whose inhabitants were priests and, as they then believed, all of them were descendents of the family of the High Priest Eli, upon whom there rested a curse that all the males of his family would die early. Thus every traveler who visited Mimla would wonder at the absence of elderly males.[7] It is related also that Rabbah bar Nachmani had three brothers whose names were Chailil, Rav Chanina, and Rav Oshaiah, all of whom were extremely poor. Rav Chanina and Rav Oshaiah went to Palestine where they made shoes for a living. And since they avoided sin very carefully they were known as "the holy rabbis of the land of Israel." Their virtue expressed itself in the fact that although they sat in the market of the prostitutes, and sewed their shoes, and the prostitutes cast lecherous eyes upon them, they paid no heed to those glances.[8]

From early youth Rabbah bar Nachmani was very astute. Like many other Babylonian scholars he went to Palestine as a young man to study, and when he returned to Babylonia to study with Rav Nachman bar Jacob, and with Rav Huna and Rav Chisda, his brothers would continually pound it into his head to go back to Palestine and study there. He obeyed them and returned to Palestine for a short time. However, his keen mind found no satisfaction in the simplicity of learning in Palestine and he returned again to Babylonia.

As already noted Rabbah was very poor, and additionally he was a sickly person. People used to remark on the injustice of fate, saying that Rabbah was as great a saint as Rav Chisda had been, and yet Rav Chisda lived to the age of 92 and Rabbah lived only to the age of 40. Rav Chisda lived to see sixty marriages among his children and grandchildren and Rabbah's household suffered from sixty kinds of ailment. Rav Chisda's deer disdained to eat the finest wheat and the people of Rabbah's house sought a bit of oaten meal and could not find it.[9]

As head of the academy, it was Rabbah's job to try to popularize what he had heard from his teachers. In addition he specialized in the laws of ritual purity and tried to make them intelligible to his students; though he found few auditors for this subject, because people were interested in studying the laws then in force and not the laws of the Messianic era. As Rabbah complained: "I am alone in studying the laws of blight and the laws of the impurity of a tent."[10] In his lectures Rabbah bar Nachmani would give all the relevant aspects of a matter with great understanding, and would often weave a bit of legend into his legal disquisitions. To lighten the difficulty of the law, when he was teaching his students he frequently began with a *bon mot* to capture their attention.

For all these reasons the scholars held Rabbah bar Nachmani in high honor, both because of his clear grasp of the Torah and his own virtues. Still, because he was a man of truth and very strict in the observance of the laws, and respected no sinner but punished them severely for their transgressions, the masses in Pumbedita hated him.[11] Once when there was no rain, Rabbah ordered a fast and prescribed the prayers to be said. None of this was of any avail. People said to him: "It seems that God held Rav Jehudah bar Ezekiel more dear because no prayer of his went unanswered." To this Rabbah bar Nachmani answered: "It is not through our fault that God is keeping back the rain, because in our knowledge of the Torah we are greater than Rav Jehudah's generation. But what can we do if the people today are not as good as the people of that generation?"[12]

For the greater part of his life, Rabbah was very poor. As a result he had to depend on the aid of the Exilarch. The heads of the academy in Sura were rich, and usually maintained their students at their own expense. The heads of the academy in Pumbedita, on the other hand, were poor folk and collection boxes were set up into which anyone who was able threw his contribution to support the head of the academy and his students.[13]

At that time there began a series of religious persecutions against the Jews of Babylonia, and even though they were mere child's play compared to the persecutions that broke out in Palestine at the same time, nevertheless they did undermine the political security the Jews had enjoyed up to that time. The historical accounts of these events are very meager, yet it is known that Rabbah bar Nachmani lost his life through these persecutions. They came during the reign of King Sapor II. He ruled longer than any other Persian king before him or after him, sitting on the throne for more than a full human life (309-380 C.E.). He was crowned king before he was born, for the priests placed the crown on the pregnant body of his mother, Ifra Hurmiz, as a sign that the unborn child was the king of Persia.

Between King Sapor I, who was a friend of Shmuel Yarchina'ah, and King Sapor II there was an interval of about seventy years (240-309 C.E.). In this interval six different kings ruled the Persians, and all maintained the tradition of friendship towards the Jews established by King Sapor I. King Sapor II broke this tradition. All over the Persian kingdom persecution of the Jews broke out then and because of the Jews the Christians too were persecuted.

Yet the condition of the Jews at that time was better than that of the Christians because Queen Ifra Hurmiz protected the Jews as much as she could. It is said that Queen Ifra Hurmiz had a strong leaning toward the Jewish religion and respected the Jewish scholars. When she saw how severely her son was oppressing the Jews, crushing the marrow out of their bones for taxes, she took a coffer of gold to the academy at Pumbedita and gave it to the scholars to be used as they saw fit. It was decided to use this money to help those Jews who could not pay their taxes and were in danger of being sent to jail by the king.[14]

Concerning those persecutions, the Talmud relates that when the royal army came to Pumbedita, Rabbah bar Nachmani and Rav Joseph bar Chiya fled.[15] Then the king was told that there was a certain Jew around whom 12,000 others would gather two months during the year, once during the winter and once during the summer, thus interfering with the work of the people and causing damage to the king's treasury. The king sent soldiers to catch Rabbah who fled further into the swamps around Pumbedita. He lost his way there and came to a forest and sat down under a tree. Suddenly he heard the footsteps of a man, and thinking that he had been captured died of fright.

This flight and disappearance of Rabbah bar Nachmani has been adorned with many miracles. It is related how once in the course of his flight he met the king's messenger at an inn and was miraculously delivered from his hands and how he died in a miraculous manner. In the "academy of Heaven" a difference of opinion developed concerning a certain problem in the laws of ritual purity, where God Himself had decided "pure," and the rest of the academy decided "impure." It was decided to call on Rabbah bar Nachmani for his opinion because this was his special field. But this was impossible as long as he was alive so they sent the Angel of Death to fetch Rabbah. But the Angel of Death could not approach Rabbah because he never ceased studying not even for a moment. Then the Angel of Death decided on the ruse of making Rabbah think that he was caught, and he interrupted his study for a moment. The Angel of Death used this moment to seize his soul and bring it to the "academy of Heaven." The scholars in Pumbedita did not know what had happened to Rabbah. A note fell from Heaven saying, "Rabbah bar Nachmani has been summoned to the 'academy of Heaven.'"

Then Abayei and Rava along with other scholars went to find Rabbah's corpse in order to bury it but did not know the place where his body lay. They went to the swamps where Rabbah had been hiding. They saw a flock of birds and the scholars said: "Apparently our dead is lying there." They mourned for Rabbah three days and three nights. Then another note fell from Heaven, upon which was written: "Whoever abandons the dead man now is excommunicated." The scholars mourned for Rabbah seven days longer. Then another note fell from Heaven, saying, "Go home in peace."[16]

Wherever the Talmud mentions Rabbah without a patronymic, it means Rabbah bar Nachmani. Concerning the length of his life he apparently studied with Rabbi Jochanan in his early years, for it is related that Rav Chisda once said to him what he used to say to others of Rabbi Jochanan's students:

"Who pays any attention to you and your teacher, Rabbi Jochanan?"[17] One must remember that Rabbah's brothers insisted on his going to Palestine to study and they wrote him: "Although you are a very learned person, there is no comparison between studying by oneself and studying with a teacher; and if you should say that there is no teacher in Palestine we tell you there is. And who is he? Rabbi Jochanan."[18]

Before Rabbah bar Nachmani went to Palestine, he studied with Rav Huna, the head of the academy in Sura,[19] and after Rav Huna died Rabbah went to Rav Chisda to study. His manner of study with Rav Chisda was not like that of a student and a teacher but more like that of two colleagues.[20] Not long afterwards Rabbah left Sura and went to Pumbedita to study with Rav Jehudah bar Ezekiel.[21]

80

RAV JOSEPH
BAR CHIYA

AFTER RABBAH BAR NACHMANI'S DEATH Rav
Joseph bar Chiya had to accept the position as head of the
academy in Pumbedita. For a long time they had been considered the two greatest scholars, since Rabbah was known as the
"uprooter of mountains," meaning that he could tear up hills
and grind them into dust by the power of his reasoning; and
Rav Joseph bar Chiya was called "Sinai" because all the laws of
the Torah were as systematically arranged in his head as if he
had heard them directly from the mouth of God on Mount
Sinai. When the scholars wanted to appoint him head of the
academy in Pumbedita before they chose Rabbah bar Nachmani, he went to consult an astrologer.

 Rav Joseph bar Chiya, who is always simply called Rav
Joseph without a patronymic, was born about 270 C.E. and died
333 C.E. He was a sick man, always ailing, and very irritable. He
would say, There are three kinds of people whose life is not
worth living: merciful people, angry people, and sensitive
people, and I have inherited all these qualities.[1] It is related that
later he grew sicker and even became blind. He was not pained
by the fact that he had to live in darkness, but because he was
exempt from all those commandments that require vision.[2] Still
later Rav Joseph suffered another very severe illness, through
which he lost his memory and with it his learning. Several

times some of Rav Joseph's own laws came up for study, and he said that he had never heard of them and had to be reminded that they were his own.[3] Then he said that just as the whole and the broken tablets of the Mosaic law lay side by side in the Holy Ark, so we must avow that when a scholar has forgotten his learning he must not be humiliated.[4] Concerning his blindness it is not known whether this occurred before his last illness or whether he remained blind until his end.

Unlike Rabbah bar Nachmani, Rav Joseph bar Chiya was a wealthy man, who owned gold and silver, fields and vineyards of such excellent quality that his wine could be diluted with twice as much water as could be mixed with ordinary wine.[5] It sounds somewhat strange therefore when he says that "poverty suits a Jew like a red accoutrement suits a white horse."[6]

On his sixtieth birthday, when he invited other scholars to a feast he said in a similar whimsical vein: "No matter how I misbehave I can no longer die young."[7]

Rav Joseph was different from his colleague Rabbah in every way, in his private conduct as well as in his manner of studying. Though he was modest, he said "a teacher who has no regard for his dignity, has no dignity."[8] The difference between the scholarship of Rabbah and that of Rav Joseph was manifold. Rabbah would usually depend on his own reason and never hesitated if his opinion was in the minority. When he brought proof of his contentions, they ordinarily were of a very complex sort and at first sight, subject to objections of various sorts.[9] Rav Joseph's sayings were based, on the other hand, upon simple declarations and did not require complex reasoning, because he always kept the *Mishnah* and the *Beraita* in mind, and avoided refinements and interpretations.[10]

Since it was known that Rav Joseph was acquainted with metaphysics and cosmology, he was often asked to teach these subjects to his students. He would never agree to do so, however, and when they pressed him hard he evaded them with a quotation, interpreting the verse "honey and milk under your tongue" to mean that when some subject is as good as honey and milk it should be kept under the tongue and not expressed.[11]

Rav Joseph bar Chiya also paid great attention to the

Aramaic translation of the Bible and especially to the *Haftarot*. Since the masses understood very little Hebrew, the biblical portions that were read on the Sabbath and holidays had to be read in the Babylonian tongue. Rav Joseph tried to prepare a correct translation of these synagogue readings in the Chaldean language, following the Greek translation of Aquilas (Onkelos the convert) and this became the basis of the *Targum Onkelos*.

He was very fond of using folk proverbs in his scholarly statements, as for instance: "A master who makes a spoon may still burn his tongue with it when it is full of broth,"[12] or "even if you utter curses upon a dog's tail, he will continue to do the same thing."[13]

Since Rav Joseph was very rich, he fed his students at his own table, stating their number as about 400.[14] It is said that he was very modest and was aware of it himself, and when people said that since the death of Rabbi Jehudah Hanasi modesty had died out among the Jews, he said: "Do not say that, for I am here."[15]

Along with Rabbah bar Avuha, Rav Joseph held that just as Jews should not leave Palestine to come to Babylon, so Babylonians should not leave their homes to go to another country, even not so far as from Pumbedita to Be-Kobi, the nearest city. When someone left Pumbedita for Be-Kobi, Rav Joseph excommunicated him. Another person left Pumbedita for Asthonia, located in southern Mesopotamia, and he died at once.[16]

When he was nearing his end, Rav Joseph wanted assurance that the Torah would remain in his family, and he fasted forty days until he saw in a dream the verse "My words which I have placed in thy mouth will not pass from out of thy mouth" (Isaiah 59:21). Not being satisfied with this, he fasted forty more days until he was shown the verse "They shall not pass from thy mouth and from the mouth of thy seed." When he fasted another hundred days he was shown the verse "They shall not pass from thy mouth and from the mouth of thy seed and from the mouth of the seed of thy seed." With this he was satisfied, for knowing that his grandchildren would be scholars also, he believed that the Torah would remain in his family.[17]

81

RABBAH
BAR RAV HUNA

Rav Huna, head of the academy in Sura, left a son named Rabbah who studied assiduously with his father and also inherited all his good qualities. When Rabbah bar Rav Huna died, the academy at Sura was orphaned, for it lacked a great focal personality. The greater number of its students left it, and went to Pumbedita to study. It seems that Rabbah bar Rav Huna was fortunate enough to have studied under Rav and Shmuel and he quoted many talmudic sayings in their name. Later he went to Palestine and studied a short time under Rabbi Jochanan.[1] Later he headed his own academy, even while Rav Chisda, who had succeeded Rav Huna to the position of the head of the academy in Sura, was still alive.

It is certain that Rav Huna urged his son to be friendly with Rav Chisda because once when Rabbah neglected his visits to Rav Chisda, Rav Huna punished him and Rabbah had to defend himself.[2] In addition Rabbah was a judge in Rav Chisda's court[3] and Rav Chisda regarded him so highly that in spite of the difference in age Rav Chisda would often honor him by attending his lectures.[4]

Yet the achievements of Rabbah bar Rav Huna in the development of the Talmud are virtually unknown. It is known only that he was modest and would treat inferiors respectfully

725

when dealing with them. In addition he was also quite rich with fields and forests of his own from which he made his living.[5] Even in later times, Rabbah's modesty was still a matter of comment, and many of the later *amoraim* wished that they might achieve Rabbah bar Rav Huna's modesty.[6]

Rabbah bar Rav Huna's relations with the Exilarch are highly interesting, but it is not clear how close these were. In spite of the fact that he would make "holiday visits" to the Exilarch with Rav Chisda[7] and the fact that when the *amora* Ula once came to the Exilarch on the Sabbath and found Rabbah there,[8] this is not to be taken as an unequivocal sign of loyalty and devotion, because it may be that these occurrences were limited to Rav Chisda's lifetime. Later when Rabbah bar Rav Huna became an independent leader of an academy in Sura, he quarreled with the Exilarch's men saying: "I did not get my right to teach from you, but from Rav (Abba Arecha) and Rav got it from Rav Chiya and Rav Chiya got it from Rabbi Jehudah Hanasi."[9]

Rabbah bar Rav Huna died at the same time as Rav Hamnuna and they were both brought to Palestine for burial. The two coffins were carried abreast all the way until they came to a narrow bridge where they had to be carried one behind the other. The camels that bore the coffins stopped before the bridge. A traveling merchant approached and asked why they had suddenly stopped. They told him that they were bringing two scholars to burial and each one desired his colleague to precede him. After the traveling merchant was told who the two scholars were, he decided that Rabbah bar Rav Huna should go first. They sent Rabbah's camel ahead. But this, it seems, did not please the dead scholar, because his camel kicked up his heels and knocked out the merchant's teeth.[10]

82

ABAYEI BAR CHAILIL

W HEN RABBAH BAR RAV HUNA headed the academy in Sura, the Pumbeditans could not unite on a candidate for the position of head of their academy to take the place of Rav Joseph bar Chiya. There were four men who were considered for the position: Abayei bar Chailil, Rava (Rav Abba bar Chama, the priest), Rav Zeira II, and Rabbah bar Matana. These four agreed to resolve some difficulty over a law, and the one whose answer would be the best, clearest, and indisputable would be named head of the academy of Pumbedita. Abayei won this contest, because his remarks could not be criticized.[1]

Abayei was born in the year 280 C.E. and died about 338 C.E. He is often called Nachmani after his grandfather Nachmani, the father of Rabbah, at whose house he was raised. His father (Rabbah's brother) died before he was born and his mother died in giving birth, so his uncle Rabbah took the orphaned child to raise. He acquired his great legal learning from this uncle as well as his depth and keenness of mind. Besides this he was known for nobility of character and a pure-mindedness best expressed by the following saying: "A man should always be open-hearted in his dealings with God, friendly, and careful never to anger anyone. He must always be at peace with his relations as well as with every other person, even a pagan in the street, so that he may be loved by all who are superior to him as well as all who are inferior."[2]

With a childlike respect, Abayei mentions his foster mother who took the place of his own mother and gave him various bits of practical counsel in life concerning human nature and the nature of the world. He quotes a score of her remarks with the greatest esteem, as though they had been the sayings of some prominent rabbi. He would usually preface these sayings with the words "my foster-mother said to me," and all these quotations show that she must have been an extraordinary woman with a great deal of experience and broad understanding.[3] It is probable also that she really deserved the honor that Abayei paid her, for she cared for him as if he were her own child and saw to it that he lacked nothing, and was not disturbed in his studies. He said once that had his foster mother asked him to do the smallest thing, he would have disturbed his studies.[4]

Abayei owned gardens and vineyards that he ordinarily rented out to tenants for cultivation. Yet it is uncertain whether he was wealthy, because he lived modestly, as one can see by the fact that when his widow asked the court to grant her food and wine, they answered that as far as they knew there was never any wine on Abayei's table.[5]

One can see how widespread Abayei's fame was from the fact that even the Samaritans, who normally lived on bad terms with the Jews, were admirers of his. Once they found an ass he had lost and they returned it on his claim, without asking for any further signs of identification.[6] It is therefore a puzzle why the number of students in Pumbedita decreased to 200 during the time that Abayei headed the academy in Pumbedita from the previous mass of thousands. One may assume that this decline in students in Pumbedita was not because the desire for learning grew suddenly weaker among the Jews of Babylonia, but because all the students at that time tried to go to Mechoza, drawn by the personality of Rava, the head of the academy there. Although he had the same system of study as Abayei, he was nevertheless always in conflict with him, and the students always tended more to Rava's side.

Almost all the scholars at that time had ceased to feel the need to make new interpretations of the commandments of the Torah. As everybody thought then, the laws of the Jewish religion had already been interpreted in every possible way. It was at this time that Abayei and Rava began to turn up new problems which had not yet been touched upon by others. These were problems that had developed out of the daily life of the people and therefore had not been previously noticed. Their attempts to solve these problems as best they could are known in the Talmud as *Havuyot Abayei Verava* (discussions of hypothetical cases which may sometimes arise.)

In order to explain the nature of these *havuyot* more clearly here are two examples. One question stated: When witnesses appeared and testified to a certain matter, and later others came and proved that those witnesses had lied, their credibility as witnesses was lost forever and they were no longer trusted. Now the problem was: how far back did this loss of credibility reach? Did it begin with the original false testimony or only after the proof of the lie was established? For if these witnesses had signed documents or given true testimony in other matters during the interval between their false testimony and its proof of a lie, the questions then arose whether their signatures or their later testimony should be credited or not.

The second question was whether a moneylender, getting collateral from the borrower has the right of ownership from the very first day of the loan with the possibility of disposing of it according to his own wishes or has he the right to do so only if it is clear that the borrower cannot or will not pay his debt?

There are differing opinions about the length of time that Abayei was the head of the academy in Pumbedita. Some say that it was only five years and others say that it was twelve or thirteen. Towards the end of Abayei's life, bad news began to be heard from Palestine. The Jews were being terribly oppressed by Emperor Constantine. Many refugees from Palestine arrived in Pumbedita, bringing with them the learning of Rabbi Jochanan, and they aided in the further development of the law in Babylonia.

These refugees told Abayei, citing Rabbi Jochanan as their

authority, that a woman whose two first husbands had died was allowed to wed a third time. For Rabbi Jochanan held that it could not definitely be ascertained that her husbands died because of her sins. Abayei accepted Rabbi Jochanan's opinion and immediately married the beautiful Huma, a grandchild of Rav Jehudah bar Ezekiel, who had already been widowed twice. He died soon after at the age of 58.

His name was Abayei bar Chailil the priest, and as the *Epistle of Rav Sherira Gaon* relates, this Chailil was the brother of Rabbah bar Nachmani. The meaning of neither the name Chailil nor Abayei is known. Some say that the name Abayei is an anagram of the verse *"asher bekha yeruham yatom."* Others say that it is a Syrian name meaning solace and almost equivalent to Nachmani as others called him.[7] At the time Abayei was born his uncle Rabbah bar Nachmani was still a young man, not more than 17 years old. He was a student under Rav Jehudah bar Ezekiel in Pumbedita. When Abayei was still quite young his uncle sent him to study in the same academy. And even though the work there was beyond Abayei's comprehension at the time, his uncle wished him to hear it anyway. When Abayei was mature enought to grasp what he was being taught, his teachers were Rabbah bar Nachmani and Rav Joseph bar Chiya, who had become the leaders of the academy in Pumbedita. Abayei acted towards his uncle like a pupil towards his teacher, with deep respect mixed with a certain childlike love. Rabbah bar Nachmani also continually tried to fill his young nephew with every variety of wisdom, and to sharpen his mind in every possible way.[8] For Rav Joseph bar Chiya, Abayei felt nothing but respect. It is related that when Abayei saw the ears of Rav Joseph's ass as a sign that his teacher was approaching, he would stand up in respect.[9]

Even when Abayei was still young, he was famous for the depth of his learning and headed his own academy even when his teacher Rav Joseph bar Chiya was still alive.[10] As already mentioned, Rav Joseph forgot his learning in his illness. Abayei would often remind him of his own laws. But even before this, Rav Joseph would discuss various problems with Abayei, treating him like a colleague and not like a student.

Abayei grew up with his colleague Rava.[11] Later circumstances developed so that while Abayei was studying with Rabbah bar Nachmani, Rava studied with Rav Nachman bar Jacob in Mechoza and Nehardea. This was the reason for the continuing differences of opinion between them that were always carried on in a friendly spirit. The phrase the Talmud uses "Abayei and Rava who both say" refers to the time they were studying together. In addition one frequently finds, "Abayei questioned Rava . . ." or "Abayei explained to Rava . . . ."

Abayei was very scrupulous about the cleanliness of people after they came in from the street. Since people were very careful to wash their hands and mouths before eating, Abayei said,"It is even more important to wash the hands and mouth after eating."[12] Concerning the problem of leavened bread, which must not be used on Passover or after Passover, Abayei said that if a person uses it against his will, he has not committed a sin.[13] Concerning a divorce, he said that discussion of giving a woman a divorce does not impose the obligation to do so.[14] If a man tells a woman that he weds her with a gift of a previous loan, the marriage is not valid; but, if he says that he weds her with the gift of interest on that loan, then the marriage is legal.[15]

If a witness comes to court and testifies that he saw a certain thing, and later another witness proved that the first had lied, making his testimony inadmissible forever, Abayei said that this inadmissibility begins at the moment of the false testimony.[16] Concerning the mortgaged property of a debtor, Abayei said that the property belongs to the moneylender from the moment of the loan, and he may dispose of it as if it were his own.[17]

Another important problem was when someone lost something and gave it up for lost. This gave the finder the right to keep it. But if the loser was unaware of his loss it was called "unconscious renunciation" and Abayei held that since this was not true renunciation, the finder had no right to keep it.[18]

Abayei often included proverbs in his lectures, as when he said: "Let no man open his mouth to evil, lest he give Satan a chance to do harm."[19] On another occasion he said: "A servant who angers her mistress very often gets paid for it all at once,"[20] or "When a peasant becomes a king, one can always detect the place of his origin."[21]

When Abayei studied with his uncle Rabbah bar Nachmani, he did not cease day or night, and when he was asked why he did not make an *eruv* at the entrance of his house he said: "How can I keep such things in mind, when I am always busy studying?"[22]

Abayei was afflicted with illness a long time. He suffered from so-called "watery stomach" that did not permit regular digestion of food so that he simply starved.[23] He was unable to perform the priest's duties in the synagogue because of his ailment.[24] He also suffered a great deal from bad teeth.[25] His mouth was full of dangerous sores around his teeth, for which he used various ineffectual remedies, until a traveling merchant came to Pumbedita, and gave him the right remedy.[26]

To be able to put on phylacteries, which required a clean body, was apparently considered a cause for rejoicing by the scholars of the time. It is related that Abayei was once sitting with his uncle Rabbah bar Nachmani and saw that he was very pleased about something. Abayei asked how it was that his uncle allowed himself to be over-happy when the Bible warned to "rejoice with trembling." His uncle answered: "I have just worn my phylacteries."[27]

As already noted Abayei owned gardens and vineyards that he rented out to tenants, but nevertheless he worked in the fields himself. It seems that he had an agreement with his tenants concerning this, for it is related that he sat and studied all day, and at night he irrigated his fields. When a student came to him once and asked to study with him, Abayei replied that he could not because all his time was taken up, what with his own study during the day and irrigating his fields during the night.[28]

After the death of Rav Joseph bar Chiya, they had to choose the head of the Pumbedita academy, and when Abayei emerged as the victor over three other candidates his name grew even more famous than before. This attracted large numbers of students to him and he said: "The reward for hearing the Rabbi's lecture is the crush trying to get in to hear."[29] He had great love for his students saying: "May it be remembered that whenever I saw a student had finished a tractate of the Talmud, I made a celebration for all the scholars."[30]

It is related that every Friday evening, Abayei would receive a greeting from Heaven. He then heard that the pious Abba Umna got such a greeting every day. This irked him, not because the other had such great merit, but because he himself had not such merit; so he sent a few students to investigate the merit of Abba Umna. They reported that Abba Umna was really great in his good deeds and deserved the daily greeting.[31]

Abayei was tolerant and would think the best of everybody, since he understood that it was impossible for a man to sit and study all the time.[32] Similarly he would say that the whole world could not be like Father Jacob.[33] And if a scholar did not know something that was no proof that he was not a great man.[34]

When Abayei once had to scold the people for carelessness in regard to Sabbath observance, he said that this was the very cause of the destruction of Jerusalem.[35] When Abayei saw that there were Jews who helped the government in its merciless squeezing of money from the Jews, he told a story of a Jewish royal officer who was bitten by a snake and could not be aided by any remedies. All this was a result of the fact that he had no regard for the honor of the scholars, whose bite is no worse than the bite of the snake.

Because of Abayei's descent from Eli the High Priest, he should have lived forty years like his uncle Rabbah bar Nachmani. But he spent much time in study and charitable works and therefore an exception was made for him and he lived sixty years.[36]

83

RAVA BAR JOSEPH
BAR CHAMA

THE CLOSEST FRIEND OF ABAYEI bar Chailil was Rava, the son of Rav Joseph bar Chama, who is always called simply Rava. Even though the two were always sharply divided in opinion and also lived far apart, they are nevertheless always mentioned together. They were brought together in the days of their youth, though the details of this are not known. In spite of their conflicts of opinion there are also rare instances when they were in agreement.

It is interesting that when their differences are mentioned, Abayei is usually mentioned first. One cannot deduce from this, however, that Abayei was the greater of the two. It is simply because Abayei gained fame by becoming the head of the academy of Pumbedita. In addition it should be mentioned that even though Rava headed his own academy in Mechoza, he would often go to Pumbedita to hear Abayei's opinion in matters he found somewhat difficult to decide by himself.

Rava learned most of what he knew from Rav Nachman bar Jacob, who laid the foundation for all his learning. Every one of Rav Nachman's words was carved deeply into his memory and anyone who found some difficulty with Rav Nachman's words would come to Rava for an explanation.

Before he studied with Rav Nachman bar Jacob, Rava was a student of Rabbah bar Avuha. Later he studied at length under Rav Huna and Rav Chisda, whose daughter he married after she was widowed by the death of her husband, Rami bar Chama.

Concerning this marriage, it is related that when Rav Chisda's daughter was a child and sat upon her father's knee while he was teaching, the two students who sat in the first row were Rami bar Chama and Rava, who were trying to hear exactly what their teacher said. Rav Chisda asked the child which of the two students she wished to have for her husband, and the child answered, "I want both." To this Rava answered: "First Rami will be her husband and then I." And so it happened in fact. First Rav Chisda's daughter married Rami bar Chama, and after she was widowed she married Rava.[1]

For awhile after Rav Nachman's death, Rava studied under Rav Joseph bar Chiya and also under Rav Sheshet.

It is said that Rava was blessed with riches. He had fields and vineyards that he hired out to tenants. He also engaged in trade and owned ships.[2] Because of his riches, he was able to keep the whole population of Mechoza under his control. And being blessed with wisdom, he was also accorded the greatest respect by everybody. Therefore he would say concerning himself that "I requested the Almighty to give me the wisdom of Rav Huna and the riches of Rav Chisda and He gave them to me. There is only one good thing that I have not been granted. I prayed the Lord to grant me the modesty of Rabbah bar Rav Huna and I did not receive it."[3] But it may be said with certainty that what Rava says about his modesty is not true. Some of his sayings prove that he could compare with the most prominent modest men. Only through modesty could a person in Rava's place have the insight that "When a man does not insist upon the dignity of his rank, God pardons his sins."[4] And in speaking of learning, Rava said that "the Torah was not given to angels."[5] Once he mentioned the verse "it is not in Heaven" referring to the Torah, and he said that Torah cannot be grasped by those who are as proud in their opinions as the height of Heaven.[6] At the end of his prayer every day, Rava would say: "Before I was born I did not deserve to be born, and now that I am born I am as though I had never been born. Dust am I in my life and how much more so after my death."[7]

It was characteristic of Rava also that he loved truth and hated flattery fearfully.[8] Therefore he said: "A scholar who is otherwise alone than when he appears in company cannot be considered a scholar."[9] Rava did much to increase the honor of the Torah and scholars flocked around him in thousands. He asked, however, that they should not come to him in the months of *Nissan* and *Tishri*, because in these two months people prepared their livelihood for the rest of the year. In *Nissan* the harvest was gathered from the fields, and in *Tishri* the grapes were trodden in the winepress.[10]

Rava had his school in Mechoza. He was born there and his father, Rav Joseph bar Chama, had had his own school there in the days of Rabbah bar Avuha, after Papa ben Netzer destroyed Nehardea and the scholars had had to flee. Mechoza was a large city where the Jews were a majority of the population. Most of the people were merchants[11] and some were very wealthy.[12] The happy situation of the Jews in Mechoza encouraged many pagans to convert.[13]

Nevertheless there were also poor people in Mechoza, as can be seen from the fact that when Rafram bar Papa spoke in praise of Rav Huna saying that when he broke fast he would have his gates and doors opened to every needy person to come and eat with him, Rava replied: "All this could be imitated here except the part of breaking fast with bread, for we have here too many poor people who would be glad to come if only they were invited.[14]

Rava founded a center of Jewish learning here that competed successfully with the academy in Pumbedita. In a city of such a mixed population it is easily understood that the head of the academy needed a large degree of tolerance towards the various elements. It is remarkable therefore that Rava instructed his children not to marry converts.[15] This might lead one to believe that Rava was very careful never to come in contact with pagans. Yet, he once sent a pagan, Bar-Shishach, a present, or perhaps even a "sacrifice" in honor of a pagan holiday, for he said that Bar-Shishach was not an idolater.[16]

One can see how Rava venerated the Torah from the fact that when he saw Rav Hamnuna spending a long time at his prayers, he said: "People abandon eternal life and devote themselves to their temporal interest,"[17] from which may be inferred that Rava did not consider prayer to be particularly important. The scholars who observed the commandments of the Torah were far more important in his eyes, and he would say, "How foolish are those people who stand up before a Bible scroll and do not stand up before a great man."[18]

Rava's attitude to poor people is particularly interesting. It is said that when a poor man came to Rava once and asked for food, Rava asked him: "What sort of food do you ordinarily eat?" The pauper replied: "I am accustomed to eat stuffed birds and to wash them down with old wine." To this Rava said: "Aren't you concerned about the bad times which afflict the general public?" The man countered: "Does my food belong to them then? I eat only what the Almighty has destined for me." While they were speaking Rava's sister arrived whom he had not seen for thirteen years, and she brought with her a stuffed bird and old wine. Rava turned to the poor man and said: "I have been given this because of you; come then and eat with me."[19]

It is related that thieves once dug their way into Rava's stable and stole some sheep. The sheep were later recovered and Rava refused to accept them because, since the thieves had accomplished their theft at the risk of their lives, the property belonged to them.[20] There are dozens of legends about Rava. For instance it is said that Rava would be greeted from Heaven every year on the eve of Yom Kippur. He was therefore a little disappointed that Abayei would get such greetings every Friday. When Rava inquired the reason, he was told to be satisfied that the whole city was protected by his merit.[21]

The old queen Ifra Hurmiz, the mother of King Sapor II, felt particular affection for Rava. As already noted, King Sapor II was bad to the Jews. His mother, Ifra Hurmiz, often stopped him from perpetrating some evil against the Jews because of her affection for Rava. Rava once had a Jew flogged for marrying an Aramite woman, and the victim died of his wounds. On hearing this the king wanted to punish Rava severely. The old queen said to him, "I pray you do not get into a fight with the Jews because whatever these people want, their God does for them." "What, for instance, can their God do for them?" the king asked his mother with a skeptical smile upon his lips. "For instance, he gives them rain whenever they ask for it." "Then let this Rava bring it about that now, suddenly in the month of *Tammuz,* there be rainfall, and I will remit his punishment," said the king. So Rava prayed for rain and after a short pleading with the Lord, there was a violent rainfall extending from Mechoza to the Tigris.[22] On another occasion it is related that Queen Ifra Hurmiz sent 400 golden armlets to Rav Ami who did not wish to accept her gift. Rava accepted this donation and divided it among the poor Gentiles.[23] It is related that the queen once sent Rava a sacrifice to be offered up in the name of the Jewish God.[24]

The question of how long and when Rava lived is very complicated. According to Rashi, Rava lived only forty years.[25] There is a place in the Talmud that says that Rava was born on the day Rav Jehudah bar Ezekiel died. But the *Epistle of Rav Sherira Gaon* says that Rava was born in the year 352 C.E. which contradicts the time cited in the Talmud. For if it is true, then Rava would have been born not on the day of Rav Jehudah bar Ezekiel's death but thirteen years later. Another theory is that of Maimonides who amends the talmudical source to read that Rava was born *before* the death of Rav Jehudah. The Talmud also once mentions that Rava said something to Rav Jehudah.[26] On another occasion he quoted something in Rav Jehudah's name.[27] Since Rava was head of the academy in Mechoza for fourteen years, there are some who estimate his lifespan at seventy-four years.

It should be noted that during the time of Rava's life the greatest worry of the Babylonian scholars was to determine the beginning of a new month and the holidays, since they always had to wait for the decision of the High Court in Palestine. Then Hillel II, the Nasi of Palestine, wanted to introduce a radical change in the manner of determining the Jewish calendar. Times were such as made it a life risk to send messengers with news of the observation of the new moon and ratification of the new month by the High Court, even within Palestine itself. One can imagine the dangers involved in sending messengers to Babylonia. At that time Rav Huna bar Abin gave Rava the system of the leap years. The scholars also had the system of leap years introduced by Shmuel Yarchina'ah. Later Hillel II set up the Jewish calendar in such a way that anyone could figure out the beginnings of the months and the dates of the holidays by himself. It was provided, however, that even though the Babylonians would be able to determine the months by themselves they should nevertheless continue to observe the second day of the holidays as they did before they had correct calendars. Rava was very strict with himself in this matter, more even than with others and he used to observe Yom Kippur two days, for he thought that perhaps the High Court in Palestine had set the day of Yom Kippur one day later than he had done himself.[28]

84

RAV NACHMAN
BAR ISAAC

TOWARDS THE END OF THE THIRD century of the Christian era, the persecution of the Jews in Palestine assumed a terrible form and the academies disappeared entirely. Learning continued to flourish in Babylonia, however, although it lost its former intensity. After Rava died, nobody could be found who was learned enough to fill his place. The academy in Mechoza, which he had headed, disintegrated and the fame of Pumbedita grew again. But even Pumbedita was not as brilliant as formerly. At the same time a new center of Jewish life and learning was established in the city of Narash (Nares). Then Rav Nachman bar Isaac was chosen to head the academy in Pumbedita.[1]

Rav Nachman bar Isaac was born about 280 C.E. and died 356 C.E. This was the time when the Babylonian *amoraim* began to record their Talmudic teachings. The *Mishnayot* of Rabbi Jehudah Hanasi as well as the *beraitot* of Rabbi Chiya and Rabbi Oshaiah had long been written down. Similarly the Jerusalem Talmud circulated among the scholars in written form even if not in final form. Since they were afraid that the teachings of the Babylonian *amoraim* might be lost, every scholar wrote down for his own use what he remembered of what his predecessors had taught. Rav Nachman bar Isaac had a great part in the written composition of these teachings. Therefore he used to say: "I am not learned nor skilled in interpretation, so that I might express my own opinion. I never say anything on the authority of one man either, because whatever I say I heard in studying in the academy, and I always constructed what I heard to meet the approval of my teachers."[2]

Rav Nachman was held in high esteem by his contemporaries for his far-renowned piety, and because he was a man of courage and did not fear even the Exilarch. It is related that when he was sitting with Rava, a member of the Exilarch's family wrapped in a green mantle was carried by in a golden sedan chair. Rava hastened to greet the person and Rav Nachman bar Isaac did not stir from his place saying: "Rava may need him, but I do not need him."[3]

As a young man Rav Nachman bar Isaac studied with Rav Nachman bar Jacob. When Rava was in school, Rav Nachman bar Isaac sat one row behind him.[4] Later Rav Nachman bar Isaac studied under Rav Chisda.[5] And while Rav Joseph bar Chiya was still alive and Rava conducted his own school in Mechoza, Rav Nachman bar Isaac was his *rosh kallah* (the chief of the lecturers).[6] Even at that time he was famous for his piety. Abayei said he was very scrupulous in his religious conduct.[7]

Even though Rav Nachman bar Isaac was Rava's *rosh kallah* Rava did not treat him with much respect when he asked a question that displeased him. On such an occasion Rava said: "We will have to wait for the prophet Elijah to settle that question for us."[8] On another occasion Rav Nachman tried to reply to some ruling of Rava by changing the interpretation of a *beraita*, and Rava grew very angry with him.[9]

Rav Nachman used to call himself "a whole man, son of a half." Rashi explains that this was because his father was not an ordained scholar. Other commentators say that this was because Rav Nachman was a wealthy man and his father was not.[10] It is said that Rav Nachman's mother always tried to lead her son in the paths of the righteous and when astrologers once told her that her son was destined to become a thief, she never allowed him to go into the street with a bare head, saying, "Cover your head so that you may fear God. You should also pray for his mercy so that evil impulses may not overcome you."[11]

85

RAV PAPA

RAV PAPA WAS ABOUT TWENTY years younger than Rav Nachman bar Isaac, but a more prominent figure. He was a student of Abayei in Pumbedita and he remained there studying with Rava until the latter died.[1] Rav Papa was born about 300 c.e. and died 375 c.e. In his youth it appears that Rav Papa was a poor man. Later he began to make beer out of dates and became very rich.[2] He also dealt in poppyseeds.[3]

Rav Papa carried on his business affairs in partnership with Rav Huna, the son of Rav Joshua, and the friendship of these two scholars was so great that they never parted from each other all their life, neither at home nor on journeys.[4] And when Rav Papa later became head of the academy, Rav Huna was his is *rosh kallah*.[5]

After Rava died, Rav Nachman bar Isaac became the head of the academy in Pumbedita and Rav Papa conducted his own school in Nares. Almost all the scholars in Mechoza went there and their number was more than 200.[6]

It is said that Rav Papa was more scrupulous than the law required in his everyday conduct. Once he bought a field from a man who needed the money to buy an ox. Later this seller no longer needed the money and he regretted the sale. Rav Papa returned his field without making difficulties even though legally he did not have to do so.[7] For such acts Rav Papa's good name was known to all the people, even to Samaritans who did not ordinarily have any confidence in Jewish scholars also came to visit him.[8] Very different was Rav Papa's attitude to the pagans, whom he did not trust. It is said that he once went to collect a debt from an Aramite woman. She invited him to sit down on the bed. He would not sit down until he had examined the bed to see whether there was not something about it that would enable her to falsely charge him, and as the story goes he did indeed find a dead child in the bed.[9]

One should add that Rav Papa was a warden of charity in his city and because of the conditions of that time, it was impossible to act to everybody's satisfaction.[10] It is related that Rav Papa once slipped on his step and almost fell. He said: "If I had fallen I should have suffered the punishment prescribed for a profaner of the Sabbath without having deserved it." Said Chiya bar Rav Medafti of this: "It may be that you deserved it because a poor man came to you and you did not provide for him."[11]

Rav Papa was also known as a great eater, who consumed at least four times as much as an ordinary man.[12] Although Rav Papa was the head of an academy and a very prominent scholar, he had a pupil named Rav Shimi bar Ashi who used to catch Rav Papa with questions that humiliated him because he was unable to answer them. He therefore prayed to God to be delivered from Shimi's questions.[13] Rav Papa and his friend, Rav Huna, the son of Rav Joshua, once came to trial with several merchants who complained about them to Rava. And when Rava decided in favor of those merchants, Rav Papa said: "White geese try to pull the clothes off a man."[14]

The laws and proverbs of Rav Papa number in the hundreds. As a merchant with a wide experience in life, he said things that still have value today: "At the door of a foodshop there are many brothers and friends, but at hunger's door there are no brothers and no friends."[15] "When you set out on a journey settle your accounts with your enemies first, so that they may fear you."[16] "In a house of sorrow it is well to be silent."[17] "Whoever has a short wife, should bend down to speak with her."[18] "If you let a quarrel stand overnight, it disappears by itself."[19] "Anybody who takes vengeance in the midst of his wrath destroys his own house."[20] "In the presence of a convert, even after the tenth generation, one should never refer to a Gentile in any derogatory manner."[21] "Sow your wheat so that you need not buy, because no matter what you realize out of it it will still be a blessing."[22] "Even wool-washing is an honest occupation and one should not be ashamed to call one out to the gate and sit down near him."[23] "If somebody tells you that your friend is dead, don't believe it."[24] "A dog and a cat sometimes make a meal together in peace, when they get rid of a common enemy."[25] "When the grain runs out of the jar, conflict comes into the house."[26] "Go down a degree to take a wife; go up a degree to choose your relations."[27] "Many old camels carry the skin of young ones upon them."[28] "Be quick in buying a field and slow in taking a wife."[29] "Go put silk on a pig, when he wallows in the mud."[30] "Anybody who can drink beer and insists on drinking wine, transgresses against the commandment 'Thou shalt not destroy.'"[31]

86

RAV HUNA,
THE SON OF
RAV JOSHUA

AS ALREADY WRITTEN, Rav Huna, son of Rav Joshua, was a friend of Rav Papa. They were in business together and they were so friendly that they were never apart whether at home or on a journey. When they were young they both studied under Abayei and Rava, and when Rava was still alive they both conducted a school in Nares, where they were both judges. Even though Rav Huna is always mentioned with his father's name and his father is given the title of Rav, we do not know who and what Rav Huna's father was.

It is related that when Rav Papa and Rav Huna, the son of Rav Joshua, once went somewhere with Abayei, Rav Papa walked on his right side and Rav Huna walked on his left side. Suddenly there sprang up a violent wind from the left side and Abayei commanded Rav Papa to walk on his left side and Rav Huna on the right.[1]

Rav Nachman bar Isaac was the head of the academy in Nares and his friend, Rav Huna, the son of Rav Joshua, became the *rosh kallah* (chief of the lectures); but even though Rav Papa was the head of the academy and Rav Huna only held the title *rosh kallah*, they were both equal in their dignity. They also made all decisions on religious and social affairs jointly, because what one of them said the other always agreed to. It seems that Rav Huna did not have any students of his own. All the students in the academy of Nares were considered the students of Rav Papa. Whenever they quoted a saying, it was quoted in Rav Papa's name and yet nowhere is there any evidence that Rav Huna, the son of Rav Joshua, was jealous about this. Only one student named Rav Jacob from Nehar Pekud once quoted a law in the name of Rav Huna, the son of Rav Joshua.[2]

As dependent as they were on each other, their friendship nevertheless was without sentimentality. It is related that once when Rav Huna was sick, Rav Papa came to see him and thought he was near death. Without a sign of grief he ordered them to prepare shrouds. And later when Rav Huna recovered, confounding their expectations, Rav Papa did not show the least sign of pleasure that his friend had lived but simply wanted to know what Rav Huna had heard and seen when he lay so near death.[3]

It is clear from Rav Huna's talmudic sayings that he was a medical expert.[4] Of his remarks only this has remained: "May I be aided by the fact that I never went four paces with a bare head."[5]

87

RAV CHAMA
OF NEHARDEA

THIS RAV CHAMA OF NEHARDEA, who is usually called just Rav Chama, was fortunate enough to have been a student of Rav Chisda.[1] But it may be that he was named so simply because he was born there, although his academy was probably in Pumbedita. It is possible that after Rav Chisda's death he studied under Rava.[2] However, that is not known either and it may have been actually in Nehardea. The only thing that is certain is that he headed the academy for twenty-one years, from 356 to 377 C.E.

It is said that when Rav Papa was the head of the academy in Nares and there was no academy in the whole of Palestine, King Sapor II of Persia once asked Rav Chama whether the burial of the dead was simply a folk custom among the Jews or a commandment of the Bible. The reason for this question was that the Persians, who worshipped fire, used to cremate their dead. King Sapor was not pleased with the Jewish custom of burial for he wished the Jews to burn their dead as the Persians did. Rav Chama of Nehardea was silent and did not answer the king's question. At that moment, it seems he did not know what to answer. Rav Acha bar Jacob heard of this and said: "The world has been handed over into the hands of fools who do not know that burial of the dead is a commandment of the

Bible and when they are asked, they forget the verse which says expressly, 'for thou shalt bury him on that day.' "[3]

In Rav Chama's times a great change in the government of the Roman Empire took place, which greatly influenced the history of the Jews in Babylonia. Emperor Flavius Claudius Julianus, or as history calls him, Julian the Apostate, (because he denied the Christian religion), was educated in Greek philosophy and his teachers inculcated in him a love for the Greek idols. He abjured the Christian faith, already the state religion of the Roman Empire and attempted to reestablish ancient Greek idolatry in its place.

For a long time Emperor Constantine suspected that he had his eye on the position of Roman emperor. At first he drove him into exile, but later he made him his assistant in ruling. After a successful attack on the Germans who had attacked the northern districts of the Roman Empire, Julian had himself proclaimed emperor by his soldiers. Hearing this Emperor Constantine went out with a great army to attack the usurper. But he died on the way. With his death there was no longer any obstacle to Julian's climb to the throne. He immediately recognized the old Greek religion and had himself named *Pontifex maximus.*

He did not persecute the Christians but simply took away those privileges that earlier emperors had given them. In addition it is said that he lived simply, without luxury or superfluity. His philosophy taught him that the only task of a ruler was to extend his protection to all his subjects without regard to religion, and he wished to apply his maxims to the rule of his land. Julian always manifested a particular interest in the condition of the Jews in the Roman Empire. Since Emperor Alexander Severus, the friend of Rabbi Jehudah N'siah II, there had been no emperor of the Romans who took as much interest in the Jews as Julian. In his youth he read the Bible and learned to respect the wisdom of the Jews; and after he became the emperor of the Romans, he declared publicly that he regretted all the evil his predecessors had done to the Jews. And since he undertook to revive the ancient Greek idolatry, he thought a great deal about sacrifices. He was much taken therefore with the idea of rebuilding the Jewish Temple in Jerusalem, where God would be served with sacrifices.

Many believe that Julian's kindness was only politically motivated. They think that since he intended to end Persian control over Babylonia and he began to war against King Sapor, he wished to win over the Jews, for he knew that the Jews of Babylonia had great influence in politics, and therefore he announced that he wished to rebuild the Temple in Jerusalem.

Julian did not content himself with a simple promise to build a Temple in Jerusalem, for in spite of being fully occupied preparing the war against the Persians, he set about rebuilding the Temple in full earnest and appointed a special official, Alifius of Antioch, who had previously been the Roman governor of Britain. He instructed him not to spare any money in building the Temple but to finish it quickly. At the same time he sent an imperial command to the governors of Syria and Palestine to support Alifius in his work and supply him with all necessaries.

All the materials were ready in Jerusalem. Great camps of workers were clearing away the debris that had accumulated on the site of the Temple in the three centuries since its destruction. When they had cleared away the wreckage, accumulated underground gases suddenly exploded and many workers were killed. This was regarded as a sign from Heaven that God did not wish the Temple to be rebuilt. Thus, the history of Emperor Hadrian's times repeated itself, for Hadrian too, had wanted to have the Temple rebuilt and the work was interrupted by an explosion of gases while the debris was being removed. It was said then that the Almighty did not wish His Temple to be rebuilt by the same people who had destroyed it.

It is noteworthy that the Jews were not enthusiastic about the project for in contemporary Jewish books it is not even mentioned. Only Christian chronicles relate that Jews sent gold and silver from all corners of the earth for the construction of their Temple. It is possible that the previous failed revolutions against the Romans discouraged the Jews from any new undertaking with them, lest it fail and they have to pay dearly for its failure. In any case, before the Jews could study the matter it was too late, because Julian after twenty months of rule died in the war against the Persians in 363 c.e. at the age of 32.

In his war against the Persians, Julian had planned to break King Sapor's might in Babylonia. His dream was for the Roman eagle to spread his wings over the Tigris. King Sapor not only wanted to maintain his rule over Babylonia but to drive the Romans completely out of Asia. Between these two giants the small people of Israel stood as between two fires. The end of this conflict of the titans was not good for the Jews, both as to the attitude of King Sapor and as to the attitude of Julian's successors.

88

RAV SHESHET

WHEN PAPA BEN NETZER destroyed Nehardea, famous scholars such as Rav Nachman bar Jacob, Rabbah bar Avuha, and Rav Joseph bar Chama had to flee. Among those who fled was also Rav Sheshet who did not become the head of the academy in his new residence nor even the judge, even though he conducted his own school and many of the most prominent *amoraim* of that time were his students. All the scholars who fled from Nehardea dwelt in Mechoza, in Pumbedita, or in some other city near the Tigris, where new centers of Jewish life were springing up at the time. Rav Sheshet settled in Shilhi (Fhoum al Selhi).

In his youth Rav Sheshet was among the pupils of Rav Huna, when he occupied the seat of Rav (Abba Arecha) in Sura.[1] Later Rav Sheshet sat in Rav Chisda's school and often disagreed with him about various problems of law. His diligence in study was so great that even in the midst of prayer he did not cease studying.[2] He was blind but his memory was so strong that he knew not only the whole *Mishnah* by heart, but all the *Beraitot* and *Tosefot*. Many of the scholars said that he was a man as hard as iron.[3]

Rav Sheshet was also a pupil of Rav Jeremiah bar Abba, who was a student and a friend of Rav.[4] But he did not always show the proper respect for Rav's opinions and when he did not agree with them, he dared to say: "Rav could have said such a thing only when he was sleepy or snoring."[5] On another occasion he said, "Rav's words on this matter are like those of a Kutite (meaning an ignoramus).[6]

If there was any difficulty in anything studied, all one had to do was to ask Rav Sheshet. When Rav Chisda met Rav Sheshet he was afraid to speak to him of matters of scholarship, lest he be overwhelmed.[7] In addition he was very keen-witted. Rav Chama of Nehardea said that the verse "Wisdom is good with inheritance" referred to Rav Sheshet and meant that it is good to have wisdom and acuteness together with the inheritance of the *Mishnah*.[8]

Nevertheless it sometimes happened that in spite of his great keenness and prodigious memory, Rav Sheshet forgot something. Once when this happened he asked his students: "Should you ever catch me forgetting something, do not tell anyone about it."[9]

It is evident that Rav Sheshet did not care for logic-chopping in contriving new laws or in deriving them from old ones in a hair-splitting fashion. Once when there was a debate about the question of whether a prisoner should be considered as dead and his children permitted to receive their inheritance even though it was not certain that he had died, an attempt was made to derive this law from the verse "and I shall kill you and your children will be orphans and your wives widows." It was remarked that if God wanted to kill anyone there was no need to add that his children would be orphans and his wives widows, since this was self-evident. Then what was the purpose of these words in the verse? One must infer therefore that the verse intimates that the widow of the dead man would desire to remarry and would not be allowed to do so, and his children would desire to inherit his property and they would not be allowed to do so. This interpretation was given to Rav Sheshet by one of his students as an answer to the problem, and Rav Sheshet said to him: "I see that you are one of those people from Pumbedita who can drive an elephant through the eye of a needle."[10]

Rav Sheshet always supported his own views by a quotation from the *Mishnah*.[11] When he studied he was interested in finding the origin of every law, whether it came from the *Mishnah* or from the *Beraita*.[12] He also had an assistant who was engaged in composing the *Beraitot*.[13]

Here it may be mentioned that just as Rav Nachman bar Jacob's decisions in matters of money were considered authoritative, so were Rav Sheshet's decisions in matters of permitted and prohibited actions.

It is not known who and what Rav Sheshet's father was. And since he said of himself: "I am no scholar and I am not the son of a scholar," many historians believe that Rav Sheshet's father was not a scholar. But this may not be accurate either, since he said that he too was not a scholar.[14]

A story is related about Rav Sheshet's blindness. Once the people of his town went to welcome the king and Rav Sheshet went along. A certain wag wanted to fool him, and whenever one of the king's company went by the wag said to Rav Sheshet: "Here comes the king!" But Rav Sheshet was not fooled. When at last it grew quiet and the wag said nothing, Rav Sheshet understood that the king had really come. And when the wag later asked him how he had known when the king was approaching even though he was blind, Rav Sheshet explained that it was in the same way that the prophet Elijah recognized the presence of God's Majesty, when He came to him in the cave where he was hiding from the wrath of Ahab and Jezebel.[15]

It is assumed that Rav Sheshet was not born blind. How he went blind is rationalized in the interpretations of the elderly talmudists who apparently had it from earlier generations. It seems that Rav (Abba Arecha) never lifted his eyes from the ground so that he would not see any impure thing. Rav Sheshet and Rav Joseph bar Chama wanted to imitate him, and they strained their eyesight by not lifting their glances from the earth until they grew blind.

There are many who seek to prove that Rav Sheshet was not born blind by the fact that he is said once to have seen a snake in a dream and killed it.[16] For if he had been blind from birth, he would not have had any conception of the appearance of a snake and he would not have been able to dream about it. On another occasion it is related that his mother came into his school once to pray for a student of his named Ahadboy bar Ami who had been stricken dumb because he had mocked Rav Sheshet. When Rav Sheshet refused to listen to his mother's pleas, she cried out: "See the breast which you suckled." And if he had been born blind, she would not have used the word "see."[17]

Rav Sheshet did not make his living from scholarship but from trade. It is related that he sold clothing on credit.[18] He also worked as a porter carrying packs on his shoulder and he would say: "Work is a great thing because it warms people up."[19]

Rav Sheshet was a delicate soul who ate meagerly and had a weak stomach. If he ate something in the morning, he could not eat at night. Therefore he fasted on the eve of Passover so that he could eat the matzot with appetite at night.[20] Nevertheless his spirit was as hard as steel.[21] It is related that Rav Sheshet had continual conflicts with the Exilarch and his household. It seems that the people of the Exilarch's house would treat the scholars with contempt, and they were also careless in the observance of the commandments. When Rav Sheshet once sent one of his people, Rav Gada, to set up the *eruv* at the Exilarch's house he was arrested there.[22]

The Exilarch often invited Rav Sheshet to eat with him, but Rav Sheshet always excused himself with one reason or another. Once he claimed that the servants of the Exilarch served meat torn from living flesh.[23] On another occasion Rav Nachman bar Jacob and Rav Chisda were at the Exilarch's table on the second day of the holiday, and they were served a stag that had been caught on the first day of the holiday and slaughtered on the second. Rav Nachman and Rav Chisda ate the meat but Rav Sheshet refused.[24]

The cause of Rav Sheshet's conflict with the Exilarch is not known. It may be that Rav Sheshet was insulted when the

Exilarch once told him: "Although you are all very famous and venerable rabbis, the Persians have better manners at the table."[25]

Rav Sheshet was not fortunate enough to have any sons to benefit from his learning. When he became a widower and was asked why he didn't marry a second time and have a son, he answered that his daughter's children were as dear to him as though they were his own.[26]

When Rav Sheshet was about to die, it is said that the Angel of Death met him on the street and tried to take his soul there. So Rav Sheshet said: "You want to kill me on the street like a steer? If you want to take my soul, come into my house."[27]

89

RAV ASHI,
COMPILER OF THE
BABYLONIAN TALMUD

AFTER THE DEATH OF KING Sapor II, the condition of the Jews in Babylonia greatly improved. The successors of this king were just to all the peoples of their realm and they treated the Jews with particular kindness. They held Jewish learning in great esteem and if the Jews paid their royal taxes on time, they were allowed to maintain their academies and practice their religion.

Then there arose a man who collected all the lore of the *Mishnah* and the interpretations made by the scholars of Babylonia and Palestine up to that time. He was Rav Ashi and the people of his time gave him the title *Rabbana* (our Rabbi), meaning that he was not only a teacher with his own pupils, but that he was really the teacher of the whole generation. Others would say that he was a "Sinai and uprooter of hills," filled with Torah like the mountain of Sinai, but at the same time a subtle thinker who tore up the hills with his dialectic.

Rav Ashi was born about 352 and died in the year 427 C.E. The year of his birth is not certain for it is possible that he was born earlier and lived longer than is generally supposed. When he was still very young—some say he was hardly 14 years of age—he had already distinguished himself by his keen mind, deep insight, and personal virtues. He was then chosen to head the academy at Mata Machasia near Sura[1] which had been laid waste and deserted for a long time.

The magnetic personality of Rav Ashi raised the prestige of his academy. All the scholars of his time were as respectful of his words, as had not been paralleled since the death of Rava. People would say that "since the time of Rabbi Jehudah Hanasi no one had so united wealth with Torah."[2] Raised in wealth, Rav Ashi continued wealthy all his life and owned many fields and forests. He would allow his wool to be sold for use in idol worship without regard to the prohibition which forbade this.[3] But this cannot be considered as evidence of his tolerance of pagan customs, for his expressed opinions were that the pagans in his neighborhood were a worthless group. Thus he could never understand that the pagans in Mata Machasia did not recognize the worth of the Torah and convert to Judaism even though they had the opportunity of seeing the splendor with which it endows its scholars twice a year.[4]

No details of Rav Ashi's youth, nor the name of his father are known. It seems that he studied under the most prominent students of Abayei and Rava. It is also likely that he was born in Mata Machasia and tried to aid his city in every way he could. In earlier days there had been a synagogue there which now lay in ruins because of its great age. Rav Ashi had it rebuilt and stood there each day to see that the workmen kept to their work. He even had a bed set up for himself there until the building was finished.[5] Then he built a splendid school so that there would be room for his students as well as the auditors who came to hear him during the "lecture months" of *Adar* and *Elul* of every year. He never allowed the people of Mata Machasia to build their houses higher than the synagogue or the academy, because he believed in an old saying of Rav's (Abba Arecha) that a city whose dwellings are taller than its synagogues or its academies was doomed to destruction. He said, therefore, that this rule of his saved Mata Machasia from destruction.[6]

According to many historians Rav Ashi remained head of the academy in Mata Machasia for sixty years. At the same time the academy at Nehardea regained some of its former splendor under its head, Amemar. The same thing took place at Pumbedita. There were eight leaders there during Rav Ashi's days. But not a single *amora* reached the heights of Rav Ashi who was listened to by everyone and supported in his efforts to regulate religious life. Even the two Exilarchs of that time (Rav Kahana and Mar Zutra) who were recognized scholars and also rulers of the country always looked up to Rav Ashi and followed his words.

It was the custom in those days for the Exilarch to visit once a year those cities with the best academies in order to receive the greetings of the Jewish communities. Even though there were several academies of importance in Rav Ashi's time, the Exilarch came only to Sura which was near Mata Machasia. Usually this would take place on the Sabbath morning when the chapter *Lekh-le'kha* was read, in the beginning of the month *Marheshvan*. This was a festival Sabbath in honor of the Exilarch who would then give a feast to honor the head of the academy. In Sura or in Mata Machasia the assemblies would also convene at which the Exilarch made his reports concerning the political situation. Although the Exilarch lived in another city, he used to call these assemblies in Sura during Rav Ashi's time. Mata Machasia, therefore, became the capital of Jewish life in Babylonia and almost all the Jews of the land would assemble there during the lecture months (*Elul* and *Adar*) when the head of the academy lectured about the laws of the holidays, as well as on a holiday sabbath when the people came to greet the Exilarch, or when they gathered for a general assembly.

Since Rav Ashi united all the virtues, surpassing all the men of his times, he also had the ability to undertake the great task of compiling and arranging all the legal decisions and religious interpretations of the *Mishnayot*, as well as the *Beraitot* and *Tosefot*, in one great work from which the Babylonian Talmud later developed. One reason for the collection of this work was probably the desire to facilitate the preservation of all this religious and legal material that kept on growing from generation to generation as a living work and to maintain it for coming generations. After many of those interpretations and decisions had been forgotten, as Rav Ashi complained, and the memory of people seemed to be growing weaker, he said "If hearts of former generations were as wide as the gates of a palace, our hearts are as narrow and insignificant as the eye of a needle."[7] Since the time of Rav (Abba Arecha) the material of scholarship had increased so much that it overwhelmed the capacity of human memory. Rav Ashi collected all this material and had it written down so that it would not be forgotten.

It seems that Rav Ashi was head of the academy in Mata Machasia for sixty years, and he spent all of this time in collecting all the interpretations of the Talmud that had accumulated in the various academies. He was very careful and wrote things into his collection only after long scrutiny. In the lecture months of each year when all of Rav Ashi's students would assemble from all corners of Babylonia, he would assign a topic for study or a section of that topic to be discussed by the scholars and the students. In this way the whole of the *Mishnah* and the Talmud were divided into sixty parts (*masekhtot*). Thus Rav Ashi completed the division of the *Mishnah*, the great work of Rabbi Jehudah Hanasi 200 years before. This was a very difficult task, not to be compared with the editing of the *Mishnah*, which contained short, simple statements of the laws of the Torah, as they were interpreted at that time. Incidental matters and details were collected separately in the *Beraitot*. The *Gemara*, however, contains everything and excludes nothing with even the slightest connection to the topic under discussion.

The Babylonian Talmud became the cornerstone of the further development of the Jewish people. Rav Ashi did not finish this immense work but began to assemble all the material. Each academy had had its own system of interpreting the *Mishnah*, which was taught at that academy. The urge to find new interpretations of the commandments was still alive. Rav Ashi could not restrain himself to merely collecting and arranging the matter, because he was called upon to decide all sorts of differences of opinion at the same time and to resolve doubts and supply explanations where they were needed.

For almost the entire period that Rav Ashi headed the

academy in Mata Machasia, the Persian King Yezdigerd II ruled the land. His religious conduct was displeasing to the Persian priests and they called him "the sinner." He was criticized particularly for his behavior towards the Jews, whom he protected from harm as long as he ruled. The three Babylonian academies flourished under his protection. Jews were invited to all the court celebrations, and the heads of the three academies, Rav Ashi of Mata Machasia and Sura, Mar Zutra of Pumbedita, and Amemar of Nehardea, had to represent the Jews among the prominent leaders of the realm who were present at all the feasts in the king's house.

King Yezdigerd lavished special honors upon the Exilarch of the time, Rav Huna bar Nathan. It is related that the Exilarch once appeared before the king wearing a belt under his sleeves after the fashion of ordinary people. The king lowered this belt to his loins and said: "You Jews are the priests of God Almighty and should wear your belts after the fashion of our priests."[8]

The closing days of the Roman Empire were approaching. On all sides Rome was pounded by different enemies. Internal conflict and outer war united for the same purpose, and anyone with clear vision could see that the days of the Roman Empire were numbered. There were many Jews who saw these political complications as signs of the advent of the Messiah. At the same time, the *Book of the Jubilees* from the Apocrypha in which all the historic occurrences of the world were reckoned according to the count of the jubilee years, became known to the people. The book stated that the world had only eighty-five jubilee years for its entire existence. They calculated that this meant that the year 439 C.E. would mark the end of the world, and since this year was rapidly approaching, they expected the imminent arrival of Messiah.

All these fantasies inflamed the imaginations of the people and they fell easy prey to all sorts of cranks. The Jews in Crete in Rav Ashi's day were deluded into following such a demagogue. He was a madman who called himself Moses and promised his followers to perform miracles such as Moses performed in leading the Jews out of Egypt. He would lead them through the Mediterranean Sea to Palestine and the sea would dry up under their feet. The Jews of Crete believed him and abandoned their work and their property and followed their Messiah. At last the day came when the new Moses had promised the great miracle to occur. He went ahead and all the Jews of Crete with their wives and their children followed him to the shore of the sea. There the new Messiah stood at the crest of a cliff and ordered his followers to jump into the sea and it would part immediately. Following the precedent of Moses, for whom Nachshon ben Aminadav sprang into the sea to have it open when he was standing neck deep, all the followers of the new Moses jumped from the cliff into the sea. All but a small remnant were drowned. Sailors who were out on the sea in small boats managed to save a few.

Meanwhile the Roman Empire came nearer to its doom with every passing day. The Romans were fanatical Christians at the time, full of hatred for the Jews. One after another the academies in Palestine were shut down, and the love of learning had almost died. At the same time the power of the Jewish Nasi whose position had previously been the most brilliant light in the darkness of the Exile was destroyed. After the Nasi Rabbi Hillel II, who introduced the regular calendar, there were three N'siim: Rabban Gamaliel V, Rabbi Jehudah N'siah III, and Rabban Gamaliel VI. But the position of Nasi was without practical importance because the government no longer supported the Nasi. It merely demanded that he squeeze the last penny out of the Jews for taxes, and in order to cover the expenses of his establishment, the Nasi had to send agents to all the communities of the Jewish Diaspora to collect charity.

Theodosius the Great was emperor then and he always protected the Jews, even though the Christian priests agitated against them and threatened that Theodosius's soul would burn in Hell because he did not assist in the persecution of the Jews. Theodosius paid no attention but he issued a decree to permit the Nasi to continue to excommunicate anyone whom he considered harmful to the Jewish community. He forbade anyone to interfere with the inner government of the Jewish community and in their internal quarrels. Theodosius's evenhandedness toward the Jews was best proven when the Nasi Rabban Gamaliel V complained that the Roman Consul Hesichius had robbed him of many valuable documents. Calling the consul for a hearing, the Emperor found him guilty and sentenced him to death. Theodosius was hard put to soothe the fanatical hatred of the priests for the Jews. They continually tried to disturb the Jews with regard to their worship. Whenever the Jews erected a synagogue, they were subjected to all sort of harassment, their synagogues were pilfered, sacred objects were stolen, and the building would be set to the torch.

The outstanding figures in this continuing destruction were John Chrysostom of Antioch and Ambrosius of Milan in Italy. Chrysostom was enraged when he saw that many of the Christians were sympathetic to the Jews. Every Saturday and holiday certain Christians came to the synagogues for religious inspiration. Aristocratic women were known to visit the synagogue regularly, fast on Yom Kippur, and sit in a *sukkah*. When Christians fell out between themselves they would often choose to go before a Jewish court, because they knew that they would get justice there. This was something Chrysostom could not bear and he fought against with all his strength.

Meanwhile other occurrences enraged Chrysostom still further. In Rome the Christians burned a Jewish synagogue. The emperor ordered the senate to rebuild the synagogue at the expense of the Roman Christians. On another occasion the bishop of Kalinikat in northern Mesopotamia ordered his priests to tear down the Jewish synagogue. Theodosius not only ordered him to rebuild the synagogue at his own expense, but made him punish all those who took part in the destruction. On hearing this Chrysostom was fearfully angry and threatened the emperor with the fiercest pains of Hell until he was forced to rescind the bishop's punishment.

In order to end all these attacks on the Jews Theodosius issued a proclamation declaring that the Jewish religion had always been allowed in Rome and the Jews had always been recognized as citizens. Then the emperor ordered all his consuls to punish anyone who disturbed the Jewish community or destroyed their synagogues.

Wishing to secure the safety of his successors' empire, Emperor Theodosius divided it into two parts: the western part with the city of Rome as the capital was separated from the eastern part with its capital in Byzantium. This arrangement did not secure peace, however, and the Jews had to suffer in both parts of the empire. They knew, however, how to soften the wrath of their rulers by the use of coin. And so it came about that the emperor issued a proclamation protecting the Jews from attack just as the Jewish Nasi was protected from insult. The emperor's proclamation ordered the rulers not to allow mobs to attack Jewish synagogues. He also renewed the rule exempting Jewish N'siim as well as Christian priests from taxes in each country. In addition he ordered that disputes between Jews be settled in the Jewish court, and the Roman officials were ordered to support the Jewish courts in the execution of those decisions.

In the time of Emperor Theodosius II (in Byzantium) Jewish gifts could accomplish very little. The emperor prohibited the building of new synagogues and denied the Jewish courts the right to judge disputes between Jews and Christians. During this emperor's rule the office of Nasi was abolished. The last Nasi of the Jews was Rabbi Gamaliel VI, the son of Rabbi Jehudah N'siah III. He was more honored by the royal court than all his predecessors. In all this esteem however, there was not the least hint of power. It is related that he received some honors for his great learning in medicine, and especially for having found a remedy for a sick spleen.

He was wrong, however, if he thought that he could accomplish anything for the good of his people. Thinking that he was not required to obey the letter of all the imperial commands, he built new synagogues and judged disputes between Jews and Christians. The result was that Theodosius II revoked all his titles in 415 c.e. and took away all his power as Nasi. He was left only with the title of Nasi without any power. With no children to follow him the line of N'siim in Palestine was broken after five centuries and fifteen generations, when he died in 426 c.e.

And these are the names of all the N'siim: Rabban Gamaliel the Old, Rabban Simeon ben Gamaliel, Rabban

Gamaliel of Jabneh, Rabban Simeon ben Gamaliel II, Rabbi Jehudah Hanasi, Rabban Simeon ben Rabbi Jehudah Hanasi. Rabbi Jehudah N'siah, Rabbi Gamaliel ben Rabbi Jehudah N'siah, Rabbi Jehudah N'siah II, Rabbi Gamaliel V, Rabbi Jehudah N'siah III, Rabbi Hillel II, Rabbi Gamaliel ben Rabbi Hillel, Rabbi Jehudah N'siah IV, and Rabbi Gamaliel VI.

90

TAVYOMI MAR
BAR RAV ASHI

FOR HUNDREDS OF YEARS THE JEWS of Babylonia
lived in peace and quiet and knew nothing of persecution.
They made their living from agriculture and trade. And since
they lacked for nothing and the government protected their
lives, they were able to devote themselves to learning and to
observe the commandments of the Torah. The Jews were
especially well off under the rule of the Parthians who defeated
the Chaldeans and conquered their land. But even later under
the Persians, only the early years were bad when the Persians
were still religious fanatics and had not learned to be tolerant of
other faiths. Later the situation changed, and the Jews entrenched themselves in complete security as a "nation within a
nation." The cities with their great academies were purely
Jewish cities and the Jews governed themselves. The Jews lived
in Babylonia as though in their own state; they had only to pay
taxes to the central government and received protection from
outside enemies in return.

Those good times suddenly changed, and the former
difficulties with King Sapor II were made to seem like mere
sport by the troubles the Jews suffered later. Since the scholars
decided that the government had resolved to destroy the
Jewish people and their religion, they felt that the time had

come to finally collect all the documents of Jewish tradition and save them from oblivion and all mischances. The Babylonian Talmud was created to contain all the creations of the Jewish spirit and everything the Jews had thought about from the last prophets to Rav Ashi and Ravina.

It is a revealing fact that about thirty years after the death of Rav Ashi, the leaders of the academy in Mata Machasia near Sura were merely nominal leaders, for their work had no influence on the life of the Jews, and in Pumbedita conditions were still worse. Among the most prominent of those heads of the academy was Rav Nachman bar Huna, a student of Rav Ashi's. After his death they were ready to choose as his successor Tavyomi, a son of Rav Ashi, who had long deserved to occupy that position. This son is known in the Talmud as Mar bar Rav Ashi. Various elements intrigued against the choice of Tavyomi. Another *amora*, Rav Acha Midifto, who was related to the Exilarch, was chosen to head the academy in Mata Machasia. While this was happening Mar bar Rav Ashi was away on a trip to Mechoza. The news hurt him very much for he had set his heart on filling his father's post.

When Mar bar Rav Ashi returned from his trip, the scholars in Mata Machasia realized they should have asked his opinion about the man they had chosen to fill the post that should rightly have been his. They sent two scholars to meet him and tell him whom they had chosen as head of the academy. Tavyomi kept the two scholars and would not let them depart. They sent two other scholars. Tavyomi kept them also. The same thing was repeated until Tavyomi had ten scholars with him. Then he answered their report of the election of a new head of the academy with a lecture that so enthralled them that they ended by begging him to become the head of their academy, and he accepted the post.

This happened in the year 456 C.E. That same year terrible persecutions of the Jews broke out that were unparalleled in the previous history of Babylonia. A concerted campaign of slaughter and murder that aimed at the total extinction of the Jews now began.

Mar bar Rav Ashi was the greatest of the later *amoraim* and his contemporaries were fully aware of his importance so that his opinions were law. Nevertheless, he was unable to restore the academy in Sura to its former importance. He continued the work of his father in the compilation of the Talmud, gathering all his legal rulings and clearing up some obscure points in his father's teachings. Beyond this very little is known of him. Because of the troubles of that time there is no record of the accomplishments of a whole series of important scholars who lived then.

The Jews suffered particularly at that time at the hand of King Yezdigerd (Harmizdas) III who was a very evil person and bore a special hatred to the Jews. His first step was to prohibit the observance of the Sabbath, and at the same time he shut down the academies.

There are various legends which purport to explain the reasons for this sudden wrath of the Persian kings against the Jews who had always been loyal and true to them. The true reason is simply religious fanaticism. Since the Persian priests had a strong desire to convert the Jews to their faith, they sought every opportunity for religious debates; in these contests the Jews did not spare the religious beliefs of the Persians and insulted them together with their idols. The priests were terribly enraged and began to persecute the Jews as enemies of their faith.

In one such debate between a Persian priest and Amemar, the head of the academy of Nehardea, the priest was determined to prove that the universe was ruled by two divinities, Ormuzd, who was the god of light and life, and Ahriman who was the god of darkness and destruction. Seeing that Amemar would not be convinced, he tried to argue on the analogy of the human body, the upper half of which belonged to Ormuzd because it is the seat of understanding and all good sensations, and the lower half which belonged to Ahriman, because the beastly part lies there. Amemar answered that the analogy with the human body would not hold, because a god like Ahriman should not have allowed the whole of human filth to be borne through the canals of his kingdom. Amemar said further that in the universe, too, there was no boundary between good and evil for they were both derived from the same God.[1]

The first law of King Yezdigerd III against the Jews forbade the observance of the Sabbath. Whoever refused to profane the Sabbath had to pay with his life. There is no report, however, of the measures the Jews took to avoid this law, or how many Jews were killed for disobedience. The law did not last long because the king was killed after ruling for one year, and his two sons, Hodor Varda and Piruz, could not agree about the succession to the throne. They fought each other for a year and had no time to cause trouble for the Jews.

Concerning the death of King Yezdigerd the chronicles say merely that he was slain. Rav Sherira Gaon says in his *Epistle*: "We have heard elders relate what is also written in the chronicles that the Jews prayed to God to have mercy upon them, and a snake came and killed King Yezdigerd in his bedroom and the hostile laws fell into disuse."

After a year of fighting over the Persian throne King Piruz (Pherases) took his father's place and ruled about thirty years. The situation for the Jews in Babylonia went from bad to worse. Yezdigerd III occasionally had a Jew killed for refusing to profane the Sabbath, but his son Piruz had Jews killed as a sport. The mere existence of a Jew so enraged the king and his soldiers that they felt forced to kill him.

It was alleged that the cause of these continuing murders was that Jews had killed two Persian priests and skinned them, and this caused the king to take revenge on all the Jews in the borders of his kingdom. He decreed the slaughter of half the Jews in Ispahan and then ordered all the Jewish children to be taken away from their parents and educated in the Persian faith.

One of the first Jews to be slain at that time was the Exilarch Huna Mari bar Mar Zutra. The king had demanded that he collect a large sum of money from the Jews and bring it to him. The Exilarch refused and gave up his life. The king demanded that two other scholars, Amemar bar Yanka and Mesharshia bar Pekud, publicly declare that the Jewish

Sabbath was abrogated. When they refused, he jailed and later killed them. This happened in the year 471 C.E. Later the persecution grew worse and around 473 C.E. all the Jewish schools in Babylonia were closed; the cities of Sura, Pumbedita, and Nehardea were burned; there was no Jewish court and all Jewish children under the age of ten had been taken from their parents and sent to be educated in the Persian faith.

In his malevolence against the Jews, King Piruz reminds one of the Roman Emperor Hadrian. Like him Piruz wanted to destroy the Jews with their Torah, and just as the Talmud always adds the expression "may his bones be crushed" to the name of Hadrian, so to the name of Piruz there is always added the title *reshiya* (the wicked).[2]

RAVINA, THE FINAL COMPILER OF THE BABYLONIAN TALMUD

AFTER THE DEATH OF KING PIRUZ (495 C.E.) the persecutions against the Jews ceased for a while, and normal times such as Babylonia had previously enjoyed returned. The academies were reopened in Sura and Pumbedita and new heads of these two rebuilt academies were appointed. The head of Sura was Ravina (Rav Avina) and Rav Joseph, of whom very little is known, was chosen head of Pumbedita.

It should be noted that a generation later another Ravina, who was this Ravina's nephew, was active as an *amora*, and according to the *Epistle of Rav Sherira Gaon* his name was Rav Avina, the son of Rav Huna. In order to make a distinction between them the scholars called him Ravina, the younger.

It seems that Ravina was head of the academy in Sura for only one year, from 499 to 500 C.E. In those days the Babylonian *amoraim* saw only one purpose for their work and this was to finish the great work begun by Rav Ashi in compiling the Talmud. The contemporary persecutions were the cause for the decrease in the numbers of the students and the decline of the influence of the Torah on the life of the Jews. In Palestine there had long ceased to be any academies and in Babylonia evil monarchs sought to bring about the same condition in their own land. The *amoraim* understood that in order to save the spiritual treasures of the Jewish people, created by its scholars in the course of so many centuries, they would have to hasten the completion of the Talmud begun by Rav Ashi.

Rav Ashi and Ravina were the last to leave their stamp on the development of the Jewish law.[1] With these two, the work of the *amoraim* in Babylonia was finished. There were, to be sure, still two generations of *amoraim* but these were simply people who had no original contribution to make to the development of the law and simply echoed the teachings of their predecessors.

When Ravina is mentioned, he is usually coupled as a second after Rav Ashi. Even though it seems that Ravina was the older of the two, he outlived Rav Ashi by a long time. Like all the scholars of his time he was a student of Rav Ashi, and he would listen to his words without ever contradicting him.[2] It should therefore be mentioned that Rav Ashi treated Ravina not like a student but like a colleague and a friend.[3]

He was born in Mata Machasia near Sura and was an owner of fields and forests, and even though it was a time when one could easily grow rich from speculation, it was said of Ravina that he renounced any sort of profit that was not in harmony with his religious and moral principles. As an outstanding student of Rav's, Ravina would often go from Mata Machasia to Mechoza where Rava had his academy to listen to his interpretation of the Torah, or to ask some question concerning a matter of law. Ravina grew in learning before the eyes of Rava. And when the people of Mechoza once addressed an inquiry to Ravina, Rava permitted him to instruct them and to answer their questions according to his understanding. He did not wish to do this in Mechoza, however, for Rava was active there. Not being the head of any academy at the time, he would travel through the large cities of Babylonia and wherever he stopped, he would set up a tent for the Torah and he would teach there even while Rava was still alive. There are laws therefore that are quoted in the names of both Rava and Ravina.[4]

Ravina would study day and night. The verses of the Bible served him as foundations of the law. Sacred and not to be tampered with was the text of the *Mishnah*. It was only with a *beraita* or a saying of some *amora* that he would permit himself to make an emendation, even if it changed the meaning of the quotation.[5] On another occasion he said: "Since the beginning of that *Beraita* contradicts the end, it is clear that there is a mistake somewhere, and it has not been quoted in the form it had the first time the teacher said it."[6]

Ravina always tried to make the commandments easier to observe, whenever possible. He believed that the dignity of man was more important than the dignity of the commandments.[7] And the law almost always followed Ravina's decision.[8]

Justice is the main thread through all of Ravina's work, and the people called him "the Just."[9] Like other righteous men he was active in charitable works and begged money from the rich to care for the needs of the poor. Rich women used to take off their jewelry and give it to him for the poor.[10]

When Rav Ashi was head of the academy at Mata Machasia near Sura, prominent Babylonian Jews approached him with the idea that the time was ripe for the Babylonian Jews to set up a *Babylonian Talmud* just as the Palestinian Jews at a similar time had set up the Jerusalem Talmud. The government, they argued, was no longer as favorable to the Jews as before, study was suppressed and almost entirely prohibited. The behavior of the last two kings towards the Jews had proved how little the favors of monarchs could be depended upon, and how uncertain was Jewish existence. There was a danger therefore that if everything that had been created by the scholars after Rabbi Jehudah Hanasi was not written down, the learning of the Jews might be forgotten. They desired to collect everything that had been said since the edition of the *Mishnah*, to select and arrange it critically. All the scholars naturally proposed the inclusion of their own words or what they had gleaned from their teachers, and whatever met the approval of Rav Ashi was included in the canon of the *Gemara*.

Of the scholars who assisted Rav Ashi in his work, Ravina was most important, and in addition the following scholars: Rav Acha bar Rava, Rav Mordecai, Rav Hillel, Rav Acha bar

Ivia, Rava Mibarnish, Rav Yemar, Rav Gevihah from Bei Kesil, Rabbah Zuti, Rav Asi, and Rav Abba from Palestine who told Rav Ashi all the Palestinian customs in the observance of the law.[11]

It should be noted that the Palestinian scholars who came to Babylonia at that time were of great assistance in the collation of the *Babylonian Talmud*, contributing the finest and the best of the *Jerusalem Talmud*. Just as the *amoraim* of Palestine had formerly included the sayings of the Babylonian scholars in their Talmud, so the Babylonians now included the wisdom of Palestine.

There was no system of arranging the sayings in the *Jerusalem Talmud*. The Babylonian Jews, living in relatively secure circumstances, had a better chance to meet and debate, and agree on the order of the work. Because of the unceasing persecutions, the Palestinian scholars never had the chance to arrange their Talmud in tranquillity as it should have been arranged. Therefore the *Jerusalem Talmud* remained a fragmentary work unsuited to be a "national work," for much of it was certainly lost and what was lost may have been the finest and the best. Only a small part of the *Jerusalem Talmud* was saved from oblivion by those Palestinian scholars who succeeded in escaping to Babylonia. Those scholars who edited the *Babylonian Talmud* deserve great praise for preserving all the conjectures in law that were in the Jerusalem Talmud. Further it must be noted that a great part of the Babylonian Talmud, even a majority of the included sayings, came from Palestinian scholars.

It may be assumed also that the Jerusalem Talmud was well known in Babylonia and everything in it that agreed with Babylonian laws was included in the Babylonian Talmud. Thus the Jew and the Talmud are twin-born, and even if certain periods of Jewish history saw less time spent in the study of Talmud, its ruling spirit was handed down to every period of Jewish history and has always remained a strong influence. For various historical reasons, the Babylonian Talmud and not the Jerusalem Talmud became the unchallenged guide for Jewish life, and formed its every detail so that any who wish to renounce it, renounce also God's covenant with His people.

Notes

PART I: MISHNAH

1. Introduction

1. *Yoma* 69b.
2. *Yadayim* 4:3.
3. *Eruvin* 6b.
4. *Bereshit Rabbah* 19:4.
5. Jerusalem Talmud *Shabbat* 1:2.
6. Jerusalem Talmud *Shabbat* 7:2.
7. *Berakhot* 4b, *Sanhedrin* 88b.
8. *Kiddushin* 80b.
9. *Yevamot* 21a, Jerusalem Talmud *Yevamot* 2:3.
10. *Shabbat* 73a.
11. *Betzah* 36b.
12. *Berakhot* 33a.
13. *Shabbat* 35b, 114a, *Sukkah* 57b, *Hullin* 26b.
14. *Gittin* 3a, 19b.
15. *Gittin* 8b.
16. Jerusalem Talmud *Sotah* 8:2.
17. *Berakhot* 28b.
18. *Bava Batra* 60b, *Avodah Zarah* 30a.
19. *Eruvin* 13b.
20. *Bava Metzia* 30b.

21. *Sukkah* 49b.
22. *Yevamot* 109b.
23. *Yevamot* 62b.
24. *Bava Batra* 133b.
25. *Yoma* 23a.
26. *Bava Kamma* 93a.
27. *Shabbat* 114b.
28. *Eikhah Rabbati* 1:4.
29. *Derekh Eretz Zuta* 4–5.
30. *Yoma* 25b.
31. *Sanhedrin* 4b, *Zevahim* 37b, *Menahot* 34b.
32. *Yoma* 33b.
33. *Eruvin* 96a.
34. *Berakhot* 20b.
35. *Kiddushin* 29a.
36. *Kiddushin* 34a.
37. *Eruvin* 96a.
38. *Bekhorot* 30b.
39. *Mekhilta Parshat Bo.*
40. *Mekhilta Parshat Yitro.*
41. *Yoma* 38b.
42. *Berakhot* 6a.
43. *Gittin* 56b.
44. *Sanhedrin* 38b.
45. *Shemot Rabbah* 29:4.
46. *Shemot Rabbah* 6:6.
47. *Midrash Tanhuma Parshat Shmini.*
48. *Arakhin* 16b.
49. Jerusalem Talmud *Pe'ah* 1:1.
50. *Sanhedrin* 99b.
51. *Arakhin* 8b.
52. *Rosh Hashanah* 16b.
53. *Yevamot* 121b.
54. *Avot* 3:14.
55. *Shir Hashirim Rabbah* 1:20.
56. *Shabbat* 31a.
57. *Kiddushin* 40a, *Yevamot* 79b.
58. *Shabbat* 31b.

2. The Three Main Parties of the Talmudic Period

1. *Berakhot* 47b.
2. *Sotah* 22b.

3. The Samaritans

1. *Yoma* 69a.
2. *Shevi'it* 8:10.
3. Jerusalem Talmud *Avodah Zarah* 5:4.

4. Simon the Just

1. *Avot* 1:2.
2. *Yoma* 39a.
3. According to Josephus, the name of this High Priest was Jaddua, but we will accept the opinion of the Talmud that it was Simon the Just, the grandson of Jaddua.

5. Antigonos of Socho

1. *Avot* 1:3.

6. Jose ben Joezer and Jose ben Jochanan

1. *Pe'ah* 2:10.
2. *Avot* 1:4.
3. *Avot* 1:5.
4. Jerusalem Talmud *Sotah* 9:4.
5. *Bava Batra* 133b.

7. Jochanan the High Priest

1. This version of the manner in which Jochanan forsook the Pharisees to join the Sadducees is told by Josephus. In the Talmud it is stated that it happened during the reign of King Jannai. However, the reference could not be to Alexander Jannai, the son of Jochanan Hyrcanus, for on another occasion the Talmud states "Jannai and Jochanan are the same person."

8. Joshua ben Perachiah and Nittai of Arbela

1. *Tosefta Makhshirin* 3.
2. *Megillah* 10a.
3. *Avot* 1:6.

9. Jehudah ben Tabbai and Simeon ben Shetach

1. *Hagigah* 16b.
2. *Sotah* 22b.
3. *Hagigah* 16a.
4. *Avot Derabi Natan* 10.
5. Jerusalem Talmud *Hagigah* 2:2.
6. *Sanhedrin* 46a.
7. Jerusalem Talmud *Sanhedrin* 6:6.
8. *Sanhedrin* 37b.
9. *Sanhedrin* 19a.
10. *Sanhedrin* 19b.
11. *Shabbat* 12b.
12. Jerusalem Talmud *Ketubbot* 8:11.
13. Jerusalem Talmud *Bava Metzia* 2:5.

10. Shemaiah and Abtalion

1. The names of the princes of the Hasmonean family were constantly repeated. This must be borne in mind when one comes across similar names.
2. *Yoma* 71b.

12. Choni the Circle Drawer

1. *Ta'anit* 23a.

13. Hillel

1. Jerusalem Talmud *Pesahim* 6:1.
2. *Yoma* 35b.
3. *Pesahim* 66a, Jerusalem Talmud *Pesahim* 6:1.
4. *Shabbat* 31a.
5. *Ketubbot* 67a.
6. *Shabbat* 30b.
7. *Sukkah* 28a.
8. *Berakhot* 60a.
9. *Vayikra Rabbah* 34:3.
10. *Sukkah* 53a.
11. *Berakhot* 63a.
12. Of the traditional reverence in which these rules were held we learn from a statement in the Talmud which says: Thus spoke God. And if one says all the Torah is from heaven except this

minutia or this argument from minor to major or this argument by analogy, he has not accepted the Torah (*Sanhedrin* 99). Our scholars therefore believed that all interpretations of the Torah that were derived from its exposition, including those innovations that ranking scholars of the future will introduce, are as law handed down to Moses from Mount Sinai.

13. *Bava Kamma* 84a.

14. Shammai—Hillel's Colleague

1. *Hagigah* 16a.
2. *Eruvin* 13b.

15. Akabia ben Mahalalel

1. *Eduyyot* 5:6.
2. This story of the Sotah who was a freed woman is also related in *Berakhot*, 19. In commenting on it, Rashi states that when Akabia said *dugma hishkuha* he referred to the fact that Shemaiah and Abtalion were proselytes and they therefore considered the freed servant equal to a Jewish woman and did give her the prescribed water.
3. Jerusalem Talmud *Sotah* 9:9.
4. *Sanhedrin* 88a.

16. Rabban Gamaliel the Elder

1. *Sotah* 41a.
2. *Gittin* 61a.
3. *Pesahim* 64a, *Tosefta Pesahim* 4.
4. *Rosh Hashanah* 23b.
5. *Yevamot* 122a.
6. *Shekalim* 3, 6.
7. *Megillah* 21a.
8. *Mo'ed Katan* 27b, *Ketubbot* 8b.
9. *Sanhedrin* 11b, Jerusalem Talmud *Ma'aserot* 5:4.

17. Rabban Simeon ben Gamaliel

1. *Avodah Zarah* 20a.
2. *Avot* 1:17.

3. Jerusalem Talmud *Yoma* 1:1.
4. *Pesahim* 57a.

18. Rabbi Chanina and His Contemporaries

1. Rashi, *Yoma* 39a.
2. *Avot* 3:2.
3. *Sifri Parshat Naso.*
4. *Avot Derabi Natan* 20.
5. *Pesahim* 14a, *Gittin* 20b, *Zevahim* 84a.
6. *Midrash Tanhuma Parshat Tetzaveh* 3.
7. Jerusalem Talmud *Betzah* 2:6.
8. *Ketubbot* 105b.
9. *Yoma* 18a, *Yevamot* 61a.
10. *Yoma* 37a.
11. The story of the manner in which Joshua ben Gamala became High Priest is related by Josephus and is verified on two occasions by the Talmud. But the Talmud states that Martha gave the bribe to Jannai instead of to Agrippa. This is due to the fact that aside from Agrippa I all the kings who ruled during the Second Temple are referred to in the Talmud as Jannai. Tosefot remark that it could not have been Alexander Jannai, the brother-in-law of Simeon ben Shetach, because the latter was High Priest himself and would never consent to give this office to another. There still remains some doubt as to the identity of Joshua ben Gamala because of the inconsistency that the man who "saved the Torah from being forgotten among Jews" should stoop to buy the high priesthood for money. It is for this reason that many historians claim that we are dealing with two different personalities. Rashi and Tosefot (*Bava Batra* 21) maintain that it is one and the same person.

19. The Time of the Destruction of the Temple

1. *Gittin* 57b.
2. *Shabbat* 17a.
3. Jerusalem Talmud *Shabbat* 1:4.
4. Jerusalem Talmud *Berakhot* 4.
5. Opinions vary regarding the exact nature of a *bat kol*. Some declare it to be a natural phenomenon, while others say it is an expression of the will of God. According to the first it is a reflection of popular opinion, a voice from among the people,

while the latter say it is a voice from heaven. When the Talmud states that after the death of the last prophets (Haggai, Zachariah, and Malachi) the Holy Spirit (*Ruach Hakodesh*) appeared no more and the *bat kol* took its place, Tosefot remark that "some say they did not hear a voice coming from heaven but only an echo such as one hears reflected." (*Sanhedrin* 11.)

6. Jerusalem Talmud *Berakhot* 1:4.

20. Rabban Jochanan ben Zakkai

1. *Gittin* 56.
2. *Eikhah Rabbati* 1:31.
3. Jerusalem Talmud *Shabbat* 15:8.
4. *Avot Derabi Natan* 4:5.

21. The Colleagues of Rabban Jochanan ben Zakkai

1. *Eduyyot* 7.
2. *Eikhah Rabbati* 1:31.
3. *Ketubbot* 27:a,b.
4. *Mishnah Eduyyot* 8.
5. *Ta'anit* 16a.
6. *Pesahim* 29a.
7. Jerusalem Talmud *Yevamot* 1.
8. *Hagigah* 12a.
9. *Ta'anit* 21a.

22. Rabbi Chanina ben Dosa

1. *Berakhot* 17b, *Ta'anit* 24b.
2. *Avot* 3:9.
3. *Shir Hashirim Rabbah* and *Kohelet Rabbah*.
4. *Bava Batra* 74a.
5. *Yevamot* 121b.
6. *Berakhot* 34b.
7. *Ta'anit* 24b.
8. Jerusalem Talmud *Demai* 1:3.
9. *Avot Derabi Natan* 8.
10. *Midrash Mishlei* 11.

23. Rabban Gamaliel the Second of Jabneh

1. *Yadayim* 3:5.
2. *Sanhedrin* 104b.

3. *Bava Kamma* 74b.
4. *Berakhot* 27b.
5. Jerusalem Talmud *Sanhedrin* 7:13, *Devarim Rabbah* 2:24.
6. Our scholars held varying opinions relative to the significance of some of the books of the Scriptures. Particular doubt was expressed regarding the books of Ezekiel, Proverbs, Song of Songs, and Ecclesiastes, and these were almost excluded from the Scriptures. The causes of these disputes are mentioned in numerous places in the Talmud, but nowhere are they described in detail. From these it seems that the book of Ezekiel was objected to because of the description of the Divine Chariot whose mysteries must not be discussed before the uninitiated. The Talmud relates that a child *(yenuka)* once pondered the subject of the light of the Divine Chariot, and a fire descended from heaven and consumed the child. When the scholars discovered in Ezekiel contradictions to the Torah, one of them, Chananiah ben Hiskia, pondered these contradictions so long that he used up three hundred jars of oil before he succeeded in explaining them. Of Proverbs and Ecclesiastes it was said that they contradicted themselves, and several verses in Ecclesiastes were held to be deviations in the direction of heresy.
7. Jerusalem Talmud *Bava Kamma* 4:3.
8. *Demai* are grains or fruits bought from an *am ha'aretz* concerning which there is doubt whether the tithe has been offered.

24. Rabbi Eliezer ben Hyrcanus

1. I have previously commented on the *bat kol*. Regarding the leaning of the walls of the academy in support of Rabbi Eliezer's view, it is held by some that this was but an imaginative description of what took place. When, in desperation, Rabbi Eliezer turned to the pupils of the academy for support of his views, Rabbi Joshua scolded them saying that it was not for them to interfere in the dispute.
2. *Bava Metzia* 59b.
3. *Sukkah* 28a, *Yoma* 66b, *Nega'im* 9:3.
4. *Berakhot* 27b.
5. *Avot Derabi Natan* 6, *Bereshit Rabbah* 42.
6. *Avot Derabi Natan* 6:3, *Midrash Tanhuma Parshat Lekh Lekha*.
7. *Eruvin* 63a.
8. *Ta'anit* 25b.

9. *Avot* 2:10.
10. In his will to his pupils Rabbi Eliezer used the words "prevent your children from reasoning" *(min hahigayon)*. Rashi interprets these words to mean that children should not be permitted to study the prophets. Other commentators agree with the interpretation that it is meant as a warning against penetrating analysis of the logic of events.
11. *Berakhot* 28b.
12. *Shir Hashirim Rabbah* 1:2.

25. Rabbi Joshua ben Chananiah

1. Jerusalem Talmud *Yevamot* 1:6.
2. *Sukkah* 53a.
3. *Ta'anit* 7a.
4. *Hagigah* 14b.
5. *Bava Batra* 60b.
6. *Berakhot* 56a.
7. *Shabbat* 119a.
8. *Shabbat* 127a.
9. *Tana Devei Eliyahu Zuta* 23.
10. *Kohelet Rabbah* 2:8.
11. The place of disputes between Jews and their opponents that was named Bei Avidan is mentioned in the Talmud a number of times (*Shabbat* 116, *Avodah Zarah* 17, etc.). The meaning of the name is not clear and it is also uncertain who the opponents were. Some would have it that Avidan is an erroneous form of Eviyoni and that the disputes were with the Christians who were then called Ebionim. Others say it is the name of a Persian sect and the disputes were held with Persians.
12. *Kiddushin* 39b, *Hullin* 142a.
13. *Zevahim* 113a.
14. *Hullin* 59b.
15. *Pe'ah* was set aside from the food eaten from plates as well as from the grain in the fields. When eating, everyone was supposed to leave some of the food, which was later given to the cook or to poor people.
16. *Hagigah* 5b.

26. Rabbi Eliezer of Modiin

1. *Bava Batra* 10b.
2. Jerusalem Talmud *Ta'anit* 4:5, *Midrash Eikhah Rabbati* 2:4.

3. *Shabbat* 55b.
4. *Tosefta Sanhedrin* 4.
5. *Yoma* 76a.
6. *Zevahim* 116a.

27. Onkelos the Proselyte

1. The name Aquilas closely resembles Onkelos in the Palestinian pronunciation. The *ayin* is pronounced as a nasal sound and resembles a *nun*. The stories related in the Talmud and *Midrashim* regarding Onkelos are substantially the same as those told in other places regarding Aquilas. The main difference is in that the Babylonian Talmud relates Onkelos to Titus and Rabban Gamaliel the elder, which would indicate that he lived at the time of the destruction of the Temple, while Aquilas is connected with Hadrian and Rabban Gamaliel of Jabneh, which would indicate that he lived after the destruction. Some historians are therefore of the opinion that Onkelos and Aquilas are two different persons. But the Gaon of Vilna believed that they were the same person, and he corrected (*Gittin* 56) to read "the son of the sister of Hadrian" instead of "the son of the sister of Titus."
2. *Midrash Tanhuma Parshat Mishpatim.*
3. *Avodah Zarah* 11a.
4. *Gittin* 56b.
5. *Bereshit Rabbah* 70:5.
6. Jerusalem Talmud *Hagigah* 2:1.
7. *Tosefta Mikva'ot* 6.
8. *Tosefta Demai* 6.

28. Rabbi Eleazar ben Azariah

1. *Tosefta Sotah* 7.
2. *Rosh Hashanah* 31b.
3. *Shir Hashirim Rabbah* 2.

29. Rabbi Ishmael ben Elisha

1. *Gittin* 58a, Jerusalem Talmud *Horayot* 3:4.
2. *Tosefta Hallah* 1.
3. *Tosefta Bava Kamma* 8:14.
4. *Berakhot* 7a.

5. *Berakhot* 51a.
6. "Phabi" was a Greek name and signified "light," the same as Meir and Nehorai. Since many Jews of that time possessed two names, one Greek and one Hebrew, it is possible that the High Priest Ishmael ben Phabi was called in Hebrew Ishmael ben Elisha.
7. *Mekhilta Parshat Mishpatim.*
8. *Avot Derabi Natan* 38:3.
9. *Mekhilta Parshat Mishpatim.*
10. *Berakhot* 57b.
11. *Avot* 3:12.
12. *Gittin* 58a.
13. *Avodah Zarah* 11b, *Hullin* 123a.
14. *Arakhin* 16b.
15. *Shabbat* 31a.
16. *Yevamot* 122b.
17. *Arakhin* 15b.
18. *Berakhot* 19a.
19. *Yoma* 39a.
20. *Berakhot* 32a.
21. *Shabbat* 88b.
22. *Pesahim* 3a.
23. *Rosh Hashanah* 16a.
24. *Yoma* 43b.
25. *Berakhot* 60a.
26. *Sukkah* 52b.
27. *Bava Batra* 25a.
28. *Shabbat* 114a.
29. *Shabbat* 151b.
30. *Ketubbot* 5b.
31. *Gittin* 7a.
32. *Bava Metzia* 111b.
33. *Pesahim* 43a.
34. *Shabbat* 35b.

30. Rabbi Tarphon

1. The *Shem Hameforash*, the express name of God, is the name JHVH, which was forbidden to be pronounced. Only the High Priest could pronounce it on the Day of Atonement, and even then he melodiously whispered it so that others might not hear it. In later years the *Mishnah* ruled that whoever pronounces the

name of God according to the manner in which it is written loses his share in the world to come. Before that time the scholars taught the Name to their pupils only once in seven years (*Kiddushin* 71.) Later it was entirely forbidden. The Talmud says that Rabbi Chananiah ben Teradion was punished because he taught his pupils the *Shem Hameforash* (*Avodah Zarah* 17.) In passing it is worth mentioning that the form in which Gentile Bible critics read the *Shem Hameforash* is certainly incorrect. In ancient times the Name probably combined the vowel dots of *Adonai* and *Elohim,* but the correct form has been forgotten.
2. Jerusalem Talmud *Yoma* 1:1.
3. Jerusalem Talmud *Yevamot* 4:12.
4. *Gittin* 67a.
5. *Avot Derabi Natan* 18.
6. *Bekhorot* 51b.
7. *Tosefta Ketubbot* 5:1, Jerusalem Talmud *Yevamot* 4:12.
8. *Masekhet Kalah Rabbati* 2.
9. *Vayikra Rabbah* 34:16.
10. *Avot* 2:16.
11. *Midrash Eikhah Rabbati* 2.

31. Rabbi Jose of Galilee

1. *Zevahim* 57a.
2. *Zevahim* 82a.
3. *Hagigah* 14a.
4. *Avot Derabi Natan* 18.
5. *Sanhedrin* 90a.
6. Jerusalem Talmud *Ketubbot* 11:3, *Bereshit Rabbah* 17:3.
7. *Sanhedrin* 72a.
8. *Tosefta Shabbat* 16.
9. *Bikkurim* 1:10.
10. *Sukkah* 26a.
11. *Kiddushin* 32b.
12. *Pesahim* 23a, 32a.
13. *Shabbat* 130a, *Hullin* 113a.
14. *Sotah* 30b, *Mekhilta Parshat Beshalah.*

32. Rabbi Akiba ben Joseph

1. *Ketubbot* 62b.
2. *Avot Derabi Natan* 6.

3. Jerusalem Talmud *Shabbat* 6:1.
4. Jerusalem Talmud *Pesahim* 6:3.
5. *Ketubbot* 62b.
6. Jerusalem Talmud *Shabbat* 6:1, *Sotah* 9:15.
7. *Menahot* 29b.
8. *Avodah Zarah* 8a, *Sanhedrin* 38b.
9. *Avot Derabi Natan* 18.
10. Jerusalem Talmud *Ta'anit* 4:6.
11. Jerusalem Talmud *Ta'anit* 4:5.
12. *Avot* 3:15, *Avot Derabi Natan* 39.
13. *Pesahim* 112a.
14. *Midrash Kohelet Rabbah* 10:9.
15. *Avot Derabi Natan* 26.
16. *Berakhot* 8b.
17. *Pesahim* 112a.
18. It would seem that Yochai, the father of Rabbi Simeon, was an official of the Roman government and that it was his duty to prevent the Jews from studying the Torah. Those who engaged in such study were sentenced to death. But the political role of Yochai is not entirely clear. The entire conversation between Rabbi Simeon and Rabbi Akiba is illogical. Since Rabbi Akiba was already imprisoned for teaching the Torah, it was no longer necessary to report him to the authorities, and since he refused to teach Rabbi Simeon, there was nothing to report.
19. *Avot Derabi Natan* 3.
20. *Tosefta Bava Metzia* 6.
21. *Vayikra Rabbah* 11:8, *Bava Kamma* 90b.
22. *Berakhot* 61b.
23. *Bava Batra* 10a.
24. *Kohelet Rabbah* 8:7.
25. *Avot Derabi Natan* 11.
26. *Mo'ed Katan* 21b.
27. *Yadayim* 3:5.
28. *Tosefta Sanhedrin* 12.
29. Jerusalem Talmud *Yevamot* 9:5.
30. *Yevamot* 108b.
31. *Sanhedrin* 12a, *Tosefta Sanhedrin* 2.
32. *Eruvin* 21b.
33. *Midrash Eikhah Rabbati* 3:35.
34. *Berakhot* 61b.
35. Jerusalem Talmud *Berakhot* 9:5.

36. *Menahot* 29b.
37. *Nedarim* 50b.
38. *Avot Derabi Natan* 39.
39. *Mekhilta* 15.
40. *Pesahim* 69a.

33. The Ten Martyrs

1. *Pesahim* 50a, *Bava Batra* 10b.
2. *Masekhet Semahot* 8, *Mekhilta Parshat Mishpatim.*
3. *Tosefta Sotah* 13.
4. *Bava Kamma* 103b.
5. Jerusalem Talmud *Sotah* 9:10.
6. *Sanhedrin* 14a.
7. Jerusalem Talmud *Pe'ah* 1:1.
8. *Ketubbot* 50a.
9. *Arakhin* 28a.
10. *Mishnah Shevi'it* 10. *Prozbol* was a legal contract formula intro-
    duced by Hillel the Old for the benefit of people who loan
    money that they should suffer no losses on a Sabbatical year
    when all debts were cancelled.
11. Pappus ben Jehudah was a contemporary *tanna* of Rabbi Akiba,
    and the Talmud said of him that he was a just man.
12. *Kiddushin* 39a.
13. *Sifra Parshat Emor.*
14. *Berakhot* 61b.
15. *Avot* 3:2.
16. *Semahot* 8.
17. *Avodah Zarah* 17b.
18. I have previously remarked that Bei Avidan was a place where
    public disputes between Jews and their opponents took place.
    The exact meaning of the name has not been clarified to this day.
    Some claim that it should be read Bei Ebion and that it indicates
    that the disputes were with the early Christians who were then
    referred to as Ebionim, while others maintain that it was the
    name of a Persian sect and the disputes were with Persians.
    Since Rabbi Eleazar was accused of not coming to the gathering
    at Bei Avidan, it would seem to indicate that the disputes were
    not with Christians or with Persians.
19. *Semahot* 12.

20. *Sanhedrin* 98a.
21. *Avot* 3:9.
22. *Ta'anit* 19b.
23. *Arakhin* 15a, *Tosefta Arakhin* 2.
24. *Kilayim* 4:8, *Makkot* 3:9.
25. *Sanhedrin* 17b.
26. *Sotah* 34a.
27. *Avot* 3:4.
28. *Tosefta Shevu'ot* 3.
29. *Hagigah* 14b.
30. *Niddah* 52b.
31. *Ketubbot* 62b, *Vayikra Rabbah* 21:6.
32. Jerusalem Talmud *Rosh Hashanah* 1:5.
33. *Hagigah* 2:1.
34. *Yoma* 9:1.

34. Simeon ben Azai and Simeon ben Zoma

1. The literal meaning of Pardes is a grove. The entrance of the four into the Pardes is explained by some commentators to show that by the power of sacred names they ascended heaven and were punished for looking at the *Shekhinah*. Later commentators explained the word Pardes according to its letters as symbolizing a four-branched system of expounding the Torah—*Peshat*, simple explanation; *Remez*, hidden hints; *Derash*, exposition; *Sod*, mystical interpretation. Describing what they saw in the Pardes, the Talmud states that Rabbi Akiba warned his colleagues that when they come to the place of the "pure marble" they should not shout, "Water." Rashi comments on this that the marble resembled water and Rabbi Akiba intended that they should not become discouraged and say: "Here is a body of water; how can we cross it?"
2. *Kiddushin* 49b, *Sanhedrin* 17b.
3. *Horayot* 2b.
4. *Yevamot* 4:13, *Yadayim* 3:5.
5. *Kohelet Rabbah* 10:1.
6. *Tosefta Shevi'it* 2.
7. *Tosefta Bava Metzia* 3.
8. *Tosefta Berakhot* 4.
9. *Bava Batra* 158b.
10. *Yoma* 25a, *Yevamot* 49a.

11. *Bekhorot* 58a.
12. *Avot* 4:3.
13. *Sotah* 49a.
14. *Sotah* 4b.
15. *Ketubbot* 63a.
16. *Yevamot* 63b.
17. *Berakhot* 57b.
18. *Yadayim* 3:5.
19. *Sotah* 2a.
20. *Bekhorot* 9:5.
21. *Tosefta Berakhot* 3.
22. *Avot* 4:2.
23. *Bereshit Rabbah* 62, *Tanhuma Parshat Pekudei*.
24. *Avot Derabi Natan* 25.
25. *Bereshit Rabbah* 1, *Avot Derabi Natan* 11.
26. *Avot Derabi Natan* 25.
27. *Eikhah Rabbati* 1.
28. *Shir Hashirim Rabbah* 1:10.
29. *Avot Derabi Natan* 25.
30. *Tosefta Berakhot* 6.
31. *Arakhin* 16b.
32. *Berakhot* 6b, *Hullin* 83a.
33. *Sanhedrin* 17b.
34. *Sotah* 49a.
35. *Berakhot* 57b.
36. *Bereshit Rabbah* 4:7.
37. *Berakhot* 41b, *Hagigah* 14b.
38. *Nazir* 59b.
39. *Berakhot* 12b, *Tosefta Berakhot* 1, *Mekhilta Parshat Bo* 16.
40. *Avot* 5:1.
41. *Hagigah* 15a. The biblical verse "Let there be a sky within the water and let it separate between water and water" was interpreted by the scholars to indicate that there exists water in heaven just as on earth. But on this occasion Ben Zoma's words are unintelligible, as is the subsequent remark of Rabbi Joshua.

    It is characteristic of the four who entered the Pardes that they all spoke of the upper waters. Before entering the Pardes, Rabbi Akiba warned them not to exclaim "Water, water" when they see the clear marble stones.
42. *Tosefta Hagigah* 2.
43. *Berakhot* 58a, *Tosefta Berakhot* 7.

35. Elisha ben Avuyah—"Acher"

1. *Mo'ed Katan* 20a.
2. *Avot* 4:19.

36. Rabban Simeon ben Gamaliel the Second

1. The ruling people of Babylonia were called Parthians after the river Euphrates, which formed the boundary of their domain. They are not to be confused with the Persians, who later conquered their country.
2. *Bereshit Rabbah* 65:12.
3. *Horayot* 13b, *Tosefta Sanhedrin* 7, Jerusalem Talmud *Bikkurim* 3:3.
4. Jerusalem Talmud *Mo'ed Katan* 3:1.
5. Jerusalem Talmud *Kilayim* 9:3.
6. *Megillah* 5b.
7. Jerusalem Talmud *Megillah* 1:9.
8. *Pesahim* 53a.
9. *Gittin* 37b.
10. *Makkot* 7a.
11. *Sifri* 18.
12. *Kiddushin* 15b.
13. *Avot* 1:18.
14. Jerusalem Talmud *Pe'ah* l, *Vayikra Rabbah* 9:9.
15. *Avot Derabi Natan* 28.
16. *Shemot Rabbah* 38:5.
17. *Tosefta Sotah* 15.
18. *Ta'anit* 26b, *Bava Batra* 121a.
19. *Avot Derabi Natan* 38.
20. *Arakhin* 10b.
21. *Ta'anit* 30b.
22. *Eikhah Rabbati* 8:10.
23. *Shabbat* 13b.
24. *Mekhilta* 14.
25. *Bava Metzia* 84b.
26. *Shabbat* 130a.
27. *Shabbat* 151b.
28. *Megillah* 27a.
29. *Shekalim* 7a.
30. *Horayot* 3b, *Tosefta Sotah* 15.
31. *Nedarim* 54b.
32. *Avot Derabi Natan* 23.
33. *Kohelet Rabbah* 1.

37. Rabbi Nathan of Babylonia

1. The story of this mission is described in *Berakhot,* 66 as well as in Jerusalem Talmud *Nedarim* 6:5 and *Sanhedrin* 1:5. The names of the messengers that are given in the Babylonian Talmud are different from those listed in the Jerusalem Talmud. The Jerusalem Talmud also omits the name of Rabban Simeon ben Gamaliel and only mentions "Rabbi," which might indicate that this event occurred during the days of the Nasi Rabbi Jehudah. But such an assumption is hardly probable since the office of the Nasi in Palestine during the time of Rabbi Jehudah was secure and it was unlikely that anyone in Babylonia would have tried to compete with the Palestinian leadership at that time.
2. *Sifri Parshat Re'eh.*
3. A *beraita* is an opinion on law that was not included in the *Mishnah,* when it was compiled by Rabbi Jehudah, the Nasi. The *beraitot* are scattered throughout the Babylonian and Jerusalem Talmuds as well as in *Mekhilta, Sifra,* and *Sifri* and usually are prefaced by the words "our teachers have taught us" *(tannu rabbanan, tanna, tannina, tanya).*
4. *Horayot* 13b.
5. *Mekhilta Parshat Shemot* 20.
6. *Ketubbot* 92b, *Temurah* 16a.
7. *Bava Metzia* 86a.
8. *Bava Kamma* 53a.
9. *Bava Batra* 131a.
10. *Bava Metzia* 59b, *Masekhet Gerim* 4.
11. *Menahot* 98b.
12. *Shabbat* 32b.
13. *Nedarim* 22a.
14. *Mekhilta Shemot* 26.
15. *Sanhedrin* 47a.
16. *Kiddushin* 49b, *Ester Rabbah* 1.
17. *Avot Derabi Natan* 25.
18. *Pesahim* 94b.

38. Rabbi Meir

1. *Eruvin* 13b.
2. *Sanhedrin* 99a.
3. *Bereshit Rabbah* 65:15, *Yalkut Parshat Toldot* 115.

4. *Midrash Rut* 1.
5. *Bereshit Rabbah* 36:1.
6. *Sanhedrin* 38b.
7. *Sotah* 49a.
8. Jerusalem Talmud *Hagigah* 3:1.
9. *Bava Kamma* 38a.
10. *Kiddushin* 36a.
11. *Avot* 6:1.
12. Jerusalem Talmud *Berakhot* 2:7.
13. *Sanhedrin* 24a, Jerusalem Talmud *Nedarim* 9:1.
14. Jerusalem Talmud *Shabbat* 1:5.
15. *Eruvin* 13b.
16. *Hagigah* 15b.
17. *Ketubbot* 48b.
18. *Gittin* 5b.
19. *Kiddushin* 64b.
20. *Bava Kamma* 39a.
21. *Hullin* 82a.
22. *Kiddushin* 52b.
23. *Berakhot* 17a.
24. It may be assumed that Rabbi Meir possessed a Bible that substituted the words *tov me'ot* instead of *tov me'od* as well as *kitnot or (alef)* instead of *kitnot or (ayin)*. Some commentators cannot imagine that Rabbi Meir should have used a faulty text, and they maintain that the text was correct and these differing versions must have been inscribed in the margin. Others say that Rabbi Meir's Bible contained these changes in the text but that for purposes of exposition he used a standard text.
25. Jerusalem Talmud *Bikkurim* 3:3.
26. *Pesahim* 49b.
27. *Tohorot* 7:2.
28. *Bava Kamma* 7b, *Bava Batra* 72a.
29. *Bekhorot* 31a.
30. *Avot Derabi Natan* 8. The text of *Avot Derabi Natan* states the exact opposite, that it is better to learn from one master. But this version is obviously erroneous, although none of the commentators ever called attention to it. Since we know that Rabbi Meir was a disciple of three scholars, he could not have said that a man who learns from several masters will see no blessing in his efforts.
31. *Kohelet Rabbah* 2:22.

32. *Eruvin* 49a, *Bekhorot* 30a.
33. *Sanhedrin* 27a.
34. *Kiddushin* 82a.
35. Jerusalem Talmud *Kiddushin* 4:11.
36. *Berakhot* 61b.
37. *Berakhot* 48b.
38. *Yoma* 86b.
39. *Sanhedrin* 39b.
40. *Bereshit Rabbah* 15:8.
41. *Bereshit Rabbah* 48:16.
42. *Gittin* 90a, *Tosefta Sotah* 5.
43. *Kohelet Rabbah* 4:14.
44. *Niddah* 24b.
45. *Tosefta Berakhot* 2.
46. *Kiddushin* 81a.
47. *Pesahim* 62b.
48. *Eruvin* 53b.
49. *Berakhot* 10a.
50. *Avodah Zarah* 18a,b.
51. *Bereshit Rabbah* 92:6.
52. *Midrash Mishlei* 31.
53. Jerusalem Talmud *Sotah* 1:4.

39. Rabbi Jehudah bar Elai

1. *Eruvin* 23a, 64b.
2. *Menahot* 18a, *Pesahim* 39a, *Sukkah* 27b.
3. *Gittin* 6b.
4. *Kiddushin* 52b.
5. *Avot* 4:13.
6. *Bava Metzia* 33b.
7. *Avot Derabi Natan* 28, *Tosefta Hagigah* 2.
8. *Nedarim* 49b.
9. *Kiddushin* 29a, *Tosefta Kiddushin* 1.
10. *Berakhot* 35b.
11. *Ketubbot* 17a, Jerusalem Talmud *Hagigah* 1:7.
12. *Megillah* 20a.
13. *Shabbat* 29b, Jerusalem Talmud *Sotah* 2:2.
14. *Shabbat* 33b.
15. *Sanhedrin* 20a.
16. *Nedarim* 49b.

17. *Ketubbot* 17a, *Bava Kamma* 103b.
18. *Pesahim* 114a.
19. *Megillah* 16a.
20. *Nedarim* 66b.
21. *Ta'anit* 16a.
22. *Shabbat* 33b.
23. *Bava Batra* 10a.

40. Rabbi Jose ben Chalafta

1. Jerusalem Talmud *Ta'anit* 4:2.
2. *Kiddushin* 71a.
3. *Ta'anit* 16b.
4. *Kilayim* 26:6, *Bava Kamma* 70a, *Bekhorot* 26a.
5. *Shabbat* 115a.
6. *Kilyaim* 7:5, *Terumot* 4:13, *Tosefta Parah* 4.
7. *Eruvin* 36a.
8. *Bava Batra* 75b.
9. Jerusalem Talmud *Gittin* 6:7.
10. *Gittin* 67a.
11. *Terumot* 10:3, *Eruvin* 86b.
12. Jerusalem Talmud *Berakhot* 3:4.
13. *Berakhot* 3b, *Yevamot* 63a, *Sanhedrin* 113a.
14. *Sukkah* 5a, *Mekhilta Parshat Yitro*.
15. *Rosh Hashanah* 15a.
16. *Shabbat* 51a.
17. *Gittin* 9a, *Tosefta Pe'ah* 8.
18. *Shabbat* 118a.
19. Jerusalem Talmud *Shabbat* 4:2.
20. *Yoma* 66a.
21. *Rosh Hashanah* 22a.
22. *Hagigah* 16b.
23. *Hagigah* 12b.
24. *Sanhedrin* 27b.
25. *Bava Metzia* 71a.
26. *Bereshit Rabbah* 68:4.
27. *Shabbat* 118b.
28. *Ta'anit* 22b.
29. Jerusalem Talmud *Avodah Zarah* 3:1.
30. *Mo'ed Katan* 28b.
31. Jerusalem Talmud, end of *Sotah*.

41. Rabbi Simeon ben Yochai

1. *Pesahim* 112a.
2. *Shabbat* 33b, *Bereshit Rabbah* 79:6.
3. The two above mentioned quotations from the Talmud use the name Parsim (Persians) but it is obvious that the Parthians and not the Persians were referred to.
4. Jerusalem Talmud *Sanhedrin* 8:3.
5. *Me'ilah* 17b.
6. Jerusalem Talmud *Sanhedrin* 1:2.
7. *Rosh Hashanah* 18b, *Tosefta Sotah* 6.
8. *Gittin* 67a.
9. *Bava Metzia* 115a.
10. *Shabbat* 22a.
11. *Shabbat* 95a, 106b.
12. *Sukkah* 45b.
13. *Nedarim* 26b.
14. *Shir Hashirim Rabbah* 1:31.
15. *Mekhilta Parshat Beshalah.*
16. *Yevamot* 61a.
17. *Berakhot* 31a.
18. *Pesahim* 87b.
19. *Avot* 3:3.
20. *Pesahim* 49a.
21. *Shabbat* 33b.
22. *Berakhot* 5a.
23. Jerusalem Talmud *Berakhot* 1:2.
24. *Berakhot* 7b.
25. *Horayot* 10b.
26. *Bava Metzia* 58b.
27. Jerusalem Talmud *Berakhot* 9:2.
28. *Ketubbot* 77b.

42. Rabbi Eleazar ben Shamua and Rabbi Jochanan the Sandalmaker

1. *Bereshit Rabbah* 61:3.
2. Rashi, *Shabbat* 19b.
3. *Yevamot* 84a.
4. *Eruvin* 53a.
5. *Menahot* 18a.
6. *Avot* 4:12.

7. *Sifri Parshat Re'eh.*
8. *Avot Derabi Natan* 28.
9. *Kohelet Rabbah* 11:2.
10. *Yevamot* 104b.
11. *Avot* 4:11.

43. Rabbi Nehemiah and Other Disciples of Rabbi Akiba

1. *Bereshit Rabbah* 61:3.
2. *Berakhot* 63b.
3. *Ketubbot* 26b, Jerusalem Talmud *Bava Metzia* 6:6.
4. *Pesahim* 54a.
5. *Sanhedrin* 86a.
6. Jerusalem Talmud *Ta'anit* 4:2.
7. *Shabbat* 147b.
8. *Eruvin* 13b.
9. *Sanhedrin* 92a, *Devarim Rabbah* 3:10.
10. *Mekhilta* 20.
11. *Shabbat* 32b.
12. *Mekhilta* 14:31.
13. *Sanhedrin* 97a.
14. Jerusalem Talmud *Rosh Hashanah* 3:5.
15. *Shabbat* 34b.
16. *Bekhorot* 58a.
17. *Megillah* 28a.
18. *Ketubbot* 26b.
19. *Kiddushin* 41b.
20. *Avodah Zarah* 7a.
21. *Sanhedrin* 99a.
22. *Ketubbot* 68a.
23. *Bava Metzia* 83b.
24. *Megillah* 28a.
25. *Berakhot* 63b.
26. *Hullin* 89b.
27. *Bereshit Rabbah* 5:3.

44. Rabbi Jehudah Hanasi

1. *Kiddushin* 72b.
2. Jerusalem Talmud *Shabbat* 10:5.

3. *Bava Kamma* 83a.
4. *Rosh Hashanah* 26b, *Megillah* 18a, Jerusalem Talmud *Shevi'it* 9:1.
5. *Pesahim* 95b, *Yevamot* 80b.
6. *Bava Metzia* 83b.
7. *Ketubbot* 104a.
8. *Bava Batra* 8a.
9. *Bava Metzia* 84b.
10. *Makkot* 6a.
11. Jerusalem Talmud *Ta'anit* 1:1.
12. Jerusalem Talmud *Demai* 1:3.
13. Jerusalem Talmud *Demai* 2:1.
14. *Ta'anit* 14b.
15. *Sanhedrin* 37a, *Gittin* 59b.
16. Jerusalem Talmud *Sanhedrin* 1:2.
17. Jerusalem Talmud *Rosh Hashanah* 2:1.
18. *Hullin* 6a, Jerusalem Talmud *Avodah Zarah* 5:3.
19. *Hullin* 6b, Jerusalem Talmud *Demai* 2:1.
20. *Eruvin* 61a, Jerusalem Talmud *Eruvin* 5:7.
21. *Yevamot* 60b, Jerusalem Talmud *Yevamot* 5:2.
22. *Megillah* 5b, Jerusalem Talmud *Megillah* 1:4.
23. *Sanhedrin* 5b.
24. *Ketubbot* 103b.
25. Jerusalem Talmud *Kilayim* 1:4.
26. Jerusalem Talmud *Mo'ed Katan* 3:1.
27. *Bava Metzia* 86a.
28. *Sanhedrin* 38a.
29. *Avot* 6:8–9, Jerusalem Talmud *Sanhedrin* 11:3.
30. *Berakhot* 57b.
31. *Shevu'ot* 7a.
32. *Bava Metzia* 85b.
33. *Avot* 2:1.
34. *Sifri* 15.
35. *Avot Derabi Natan* 16.
36. *Avot Derabi Natan* 28.
37. *Avot* 4:17.
38. *Kohelet Rabbah* 2.
39. *Mo'ed Katan* 16b.
40. *Pesahim* 49b.
41. *Bava Batra* 5a.
42. *Bereshit Rabbah* 38.
43. *Avot Derabi Natan* 21.

44. *Berakhot* 16b.
45. Jerusalem Talmud *Hagigah* 2:1.
46. *Bava Metzia* 88a, *Bereshit Rabbah* 33:3.
47. *Ketubbot* 104a.
48. *Bereshit Rabbah* 67:6.
49. Jerusalem Talmud *Shevi'it* 6:1.
50. Jerusalem Talmud *Megillah* 3:2.
51. *Bereshit Rabbah* 11:2.
52. *Sanhedrin* 91b.
53. *Pesahim* 4:1, *Megillah* 1:1.
54. Jerusalem Talmud *Shevi'it* 1:1.
55. *Shabbat* 139a.
56. Jerusalem Talmud *Hagigah* 1:8.
57. *Eruvin* 13b.
58. Jerusalem Talmud *Yevamot* 12:1.
59. Jerusalem Talmud *Pesahim* 4:3.
60. *Sukkah* 28a.
61. Jerusalem Talmud *Nazir* 1:1.
62. *Sifri Parshat Ki Tetze.*
63. *Yevamot* 9a, 10a.
64. Jerusalem Talmud *Ma'aser Sheni* 8:1.
65. *Menahot* 104b.

45. Contemporaries of Rabbi Jehudah Hanasi

1. *Kohelet Rabbah* 9:7.
2. *Ketubbot* 14b, *Bava Metzia* 106b.
3. *Avot* 6:8.
4. *Betzah* 26a.
5. Jerusalem Talmud *Sanhedrin* 11:3.
6. *Sanhedrin* 6b, *Tosefta Sanhedrin* 1.
7. *Yoma* 85b.
8. *Sanhedrin* 59b, *Avot Derabi Natan* 1.
9. *Shabbat* 33b.
10. *Tosefta Oholot* 18.
11. Jerusalem Talmud *Demai* 1:3.
12. Jerusalem Talmud *Shekalim* 5:1. Similar stories concerning an ass that refused to eat grain that had not been tithed have been related about the ass of R. Chanina ben Dosa.
13. *Avodah Zarah* 20b, Jerusalem Talmud *Shekalim* 3:3.
14. *Sotah* 49a.

15. *Hullin* 7a.
16. Jerusalem Talmud *Demai* 1:3.
17. *Hullin* 7b.
18. *Avot* 4:21–22.
19. *Avot Derabi Natan* 26.
20. *Shabbat* 135a, *Hullin* 84b.
21. *Shabbat* 151b.
22. *Megillah* 29a.
23. *Sifri Parshat Naso* 142.
24. *Mekhilta Parshat Bo* 4.
25. *Hullin* 27b.
26. *Kohelet Rabbah* 1:4.
27. *Bava Batra* 154b, Jerusalem Talmud *Horayot* 3:5.
28. *Sanhedrin* 94a.
29. *Kohelet Rabbah* 9:6.
30. *Derekh Eretz Zuta* 9.
31. *Avot Derabi Natan* 29.
32. *Ketubbot* 5a.
33. *Kiddushin* 41a.
34. *Nedarim* 50b.
35. *Berakhot* 57a.
36. *Kohelet Rabbah* 11:1. A similar story of a shipwrecked noble who was saved by a *tanna* is told concerning Rabbi Eleazar ben Shamua.
37. *Berakhot* 39a.

46. Rabbi Chiya Rabbah bar Abba

1. *Shabbat* 38b.
2. Jerusalem Talmud *Ta'anit* 4:2.
3. *Ketubbot* 62b.
4. *Sukkah* 20a.
5. *Ketubbot* 34a.
6. *Shabbat* 111b, *Sanhedrin* 8a.
7. *Ketubbot* 103b, *Bava Metzia* 88b.
8. *Eruvin* 73a.
9. *Menahot* 88b.
10. Jerusalem Talmud *Kilayim* 9:3.
11. *Avodah Zarah* 36b.
12. *Nedarim* 41a.
13. *Bava Metzia* 62b.
14. *Shabbat* 10b, *Sukkah* 52b, *Bava Metzia* 92a.

15. *Hullin* 141b.
16. *Hagigah* 5b, *Tanhuma Parshat Vayeshev.*
17. *Mo'ed Katan* 16b.
18. *Sanhedrin* 11b.
19. *Rosh Hashanah* 23a.
20. *Rut Rabbah* 1.
21. Jerusalem Talmud *Bava Metzia* 5:6.
22. *Bava Kamma* 99b.
23. *Shabbat* 151b.
24. *Yevamot* 65b.
25. *Berakhot* 16b.
26. *Berakhot* 17a.
27. *Sanhedrin* 11a.
28. *Hullin* 86a.
29. *Bava Metzia* 88b.
30. *Mo'ed Katan* 28a.
31. *Mo'ed Katan* 25b.

47. Rabbi Simeon ben Chalafta

1. *Shabbat* 118b, Jerusalem Talmud *Yevamot* 1:1.
2. *Mo'ed Katan* 9b.
3. *Shabbat* 152a, *Vayikra Rabbah* 18.
4. *Bereshit Rabbah* 79:8.
5. *Uktzin* 3:12.
6. *Rut Rabbah* 5.
7. *Midrash Tanhuma Parshat Pekudei.*
8. *Rut Rabbah* 3:4.
9. *Sanhedrin* 59b.
10. Jerusalem Talmud *Yoma* 8:3.
11. *Berakhot* 4b, Jerusalem Talmud *Berakhot* 1.
12. *Sotah* 41b.
13. Jerusalem Talmud *Ta'anit* 2:1.
14. *Devarim Rabbah* 7:4.
15. *Kohelet Rabbah* 3.
16. *Hullin* 57b.
17. *Kohelet Rabbah* 5.

48. Levi ben Sisi

1. *Shabbat* 59b, *Sukkah* 53a.
2. Jerusalem Talmud *Berakhot* 1:5, *Rosh Hashanah* 1:5, *Sukkah* 2:4.
3. *Avodah Zarah* 19a.

4. *Ketubbot* 103b.
5. *Zevahim* 30b.
6. *Sanhedrin* 17b.
7. *Yevamot* 9a, *Menahot* 80b.
8. *Ketubbot* 8b.
9. *Yevamot* 105a, Jerusalem Talmud *Yevamot* 12:6, *Bereshit Rabbah* 81.
10. *Sukkah* 53a, *Ta'anit* 25a, *Megillah* 22b.
11. Jerusalem Talmud *Avodah Zarah* 2:2.
12. *Shabbat* 156a.
13. *Kiddushin* 76b, *Bava Batra* 52a.
14. Jerusalem Talmud *Bava Batra* 6:5.
15. *Ketubbot* 53b.
16. *Rosh Hashanah* 21a, *Kiddushin* 72a.
17. *Pesahim* 107a.
18. Jerusalem Talmud *Sukkah* 4:3.
19. Jerusalem Talmud *Ta'anit* 3:8.
20. *Ta'anit* 28a.
21. *Menahot* 38a.
22. *Bereshit Rabbah* 80.
23. *Shabbat* 59b.
24. Jerusalem Talmud *Berakhot* 2:8.

PART II. JERUSALEM TALMUD

49. Introduction

1. For a better enlightenment of the subject, we have to repeat that a teacher of the *Mishnah* was called *tanna* (plural: *tannaim*) and a teacher of the *Gemara* was called *amora* (plural: *amoraim*).
2. *Niddah* 61b, *Midrash Tehillim* 56.
3. *Sanhedrin* 56b.
4. *Hullin* 92a.
5. *Sanhedrin* 108b.
6. *Shabbat* 125b.
7. *Berakhot* 47b, *Sukkah* 30a, *Bava Kamma* 94a.
8. *Menahot* 99b.
9. *Yoma* 82a.
10. *Pesahim* 25a.
11. *Yoma* 83a.
12. *Mekhilta Masekhta Deshabbata* 14.
13. *Mekhilta Parshat Ki Tisa* 47.

14. *Sanhedrin* 74a.
15. *Sanhedrin* 37a.
16. *Bava Kamma* 91b.
17. *Makkot* 22a, *Sifri Parshat Devarim* 23.
18. *Hullin* 6a, *Ta'anit* 11a, *Vayikra Rabbah* 32:3.
19. *Berakhot* 19b, *Shabbat* 21b, *Eruvin* 41b, *Menahot* 37b.
20. *Bava Kamma* 79b.
21. *Sanhedrin* 91b.
22. *Ta'anit* 11a, *Sotah* 15a, *Keritot* 26a.
23. *Ta'anit* 22b.
24. *Ketubbot* 1:1.

50. Life in Palestine During the Creation of the Jerusalem Talmud

1. *Ketubbot* 111b.
2. *Demai* 3:1.
3. *Bava Metzia* 8:8.
4. *Megillah* 3b.
5. *Bava Batra* 75b.
6. *Shekalim* 3:4.
7. *Hagigah* 25a.
8. *Shabbat* 103b.
9. *Berakhot* 60a.
10. *Tosefta Avodah Zarah* 1.
11. *Sanhedrin* 102b.
12. *Eikhah Rabbati* 1:2.
13. The law concerning the transportation of objects from one place to another on Sabbath.
14. *Eruvin* 53a.
15. Jerusalem Talmud *Shabbat* 6:1.
16. Jerusalem Talmud *Pesahim* 8:1, *Ketubbot* 7:4.
17. *Terumot* 11:10, *Pesahim* 50b.
18. *Pesahim* 40a.
19. *Berakhot* 37b.
20. *Eruvin* 82b.
21. *Shabbat* 11a.
22. *Hagigah* 13b.
23. *Betzah* 32a.
24. Jerusalem Talmud *Berakhot* 1:1.
25. *Eruvin* 55b.
26. *Sanhedrin* 17b.
27. *Bava Kamma* 83a.

51. Rabbi Jehudah N'siah the I and His Successors

1. *Bava Batra* 83b.
2. Jerusalem Talmud *Pe'ah* 1:5, 2:5.
3. Jerusalem Talmud *Betzah* 1:11.
4. *Avodah Zarah* 35b.
5. *Avodah Zarah* 37a.
6. Jerusalem Talmud *Avodah Zarah* 2:9, *Tosefta Avodah Zarah* 4.
7. *Pesahim* 51a, *Tosefta Mo'ed Katan* 2.
8. Jerusalem Talmud *Shabbat* 6:5.
9. *Megillah* 5b, Jerusalem Talmud *Megillah* 1:4.
10. Jerusalem Talmud *Sanhedrin* 1:2.
11. Jerusalem Talmud *Sanhedrin* 2:1, *Horayot* 3:2.
12. Jerusalem Talmud *Sanhedrin* 2:6.
13. Jerusalem Talmud *Berakhot* 3:1, *Tosafot, Avodah Zarah* 33b.
14. Jerusalem Talmud *Avodah Zarah* 1:1.
15. *Ta'anit* 14b.
16. *Rosh Hashanah* 20a, Jerusalem Talmud *Avodah Zarah* 2:4.
17. *Niddah* 52a.
18. *Rosh Hashanah* 20a.
19. *Shabbat* 119b, Jerusalem Talmud *Hagigah* 1:7.
20. Jerusalem Talmud *Avodah Zarah* 5:2.
21. Jerusalem Talmud *Terumot* 8:4.
22. Jerusalem Talmud *Berakhot* 6:1.
23. Jerusalem Talmud *Megillah* 3:2.
24. Jerusalem Talmud *Avodah Zarah* 5:15.
25. *Shir Hashirim Rabbah* 2:12.
26. *Avodah Zarah* 4a.
27. *Bereshit Rabbah* 16:7.
28. Jerusalem Talmud *Nedarim* 6:16.
29. Jerusalem Talmud *Mo'ed Katan* 3:1.
30. *Sotah* 40a.
31. *Bava Batra* 127b.
32. *Bava Batra* 158b.
33. *Shabbat* 115a, *Bava Batra* 41b, *Sanhedrin* 29a.
34. *Rosh Hashanah* 20a, Jerusalem Talmud *Eruvin* 3:9.
35. *Sanhedrin* 12a.
36. Jerusalem Talmud *Yevamot* 16:1, *Sotah* 9:4.

52. The Aggadah and Its Authors

1. *Bereshit Rabbah* 8:7.
2. *Makkot* 23b, 24a.

3. *Devarim Rabbah* 2:12.
4. *Shabbat* 56a.
5. *Sanhedrin* 29a.
6. Jerusalem Talmud *Ta'anit* 2:1.
7. Jerusalem Talmud *Sukkah* 5:1, *Bereshit Rabbah* 98:16.
8. Jerusalem Talmud *Rosh Hashanah* 4:1, *Sanhedrin* 2:3.
9. *Bereshit Rabbah* 20:30.
10. Jerusalem Talmud *Berakhot* 1:5.
11. *Bereshit Rabbah* 66:3.
12. *Bereshit Rabbah* 20:1.
13. *Bereshit Rabbah* 48:1.
14. *Midrash Shoher Tov* 7:15.
15. *Bereshit Rabbah* 24:5, *Kohelet Rabbah* 3:14.
16. *Kohelet Rabbah* 3:17.
17. *Bereshit Rabbah* 2:4.
18. *Bereshit Rabbah* 53:12.
19. *Bereshit Rabbah* 48:8.
20. *Midrash Shoher Tov* 8.
21. *Devarim Rabbah* 2:24.
22. *Vayikra Rabbah* 23:3, *Shir Hashirim Rabbah* 2:6.
23. *Vayikra Rabbah* 25:50.
24. *Bereshit Rabbah* 79:7.
25. *Shabbat* 118b.
26. *Berakhot* 31b.
27. *Midrash Shoher Tov* 90:1.
28. Jerusalem Talmud *Sanhedrin* 7:13.
29. *Vayikra Rabbah* 27:5.
30. *Berakhot* 7a.
31. *Berakhot* 10b.
32. *Yoma* 23b.
33. *Yevamot* 97a, *Sanhedrin* 90a.
34. *Yevamot* 79a.
35. *Bereshit Rabbah* 8:4.
36. *Bereshit Rabbah* 22:11.

53. Rabbi Jochanan, Compiler of the Jerusalem Talmud

1. *Kiddushin* 31b.
2. *Berakhot* 5b.
3. *Ketubbot* 25b, *Bava Metzia* 85b, *Sanhedrin* 96a, Jerusalem Talmud *Rosh Hashanah* 2:5.

4. Jerusalem Talmud *Ma'aserot* 1:2.
5. Jerusalem Talmud *Avodah Zarah* 3:1.
6. *Ta'anit* 21a.
7. *Hullin* 137b.
8. *Bava Metzia* 88b, *Bava Batra* 154a.
9. *Niddah* 26b, Jerusalem Talmud *Horayot* 2:8.
10. Jerusalem Talmud *Bava Metzia* 2:11.
11. Jerusalem Talmud *Eruvin* 5:1, *Sanhedrin* 11:6.
12. Jerusalem Talmud *Terumot* 2:3, *Kiddushin* 1:2.
13. Jerusalem Talmud *Nazir* 1:1.
14. *Eruvin* 53a.
15. *Yoma* 9b.
16. Jerusalem Talmud *Pe'ah* 2:6.
17. *Yoma* 5a, Jerusalem Talmud *Pe'ah* 1:1.
18. Jerusalem Talmud *Shevi'it* 1:6.
19. Jerusalem Talmud *Orlah* 3:8.
20. *Pesahim* 50b.
21. Jerusalem Talmud *Berakhot* 1:4.
22. Jerusalem Talmud *Bava Kamma* 8:4.
23. Jerusalem Talmud *Yoma* 8:8.
24. Jerusalem Talmud *Avodah Zarah* 3:3.
25. *Avodah Zarah* 26b.
26. *Hullin* 5b.
27. Jerusalem Talmud *Demai* 2:3.
28. *Megillah* 16a.
29. *Shabbat* 114a.
30. *Pesahim* 87a.
31. Jerusalem Talmud *Mo'ed Katan* 3:7.
32. *Hagigah* 15b.
33. *Eruvin* 55a.
34. *Rosh Hashanah* 23a.
35. *Horayot* 17a.
36. Jerusalem Talmud *Shabbat* 2:3.
37. Jerusalem Talmud *Shevi'it* 9:11.
38. Jerusalem Talmud *Berakhot* 2:1.
39. Jerusalem Talmud *Yevamot* 3:10.
40. Jerusalem Talmud *Yevamot* 3:7.
41. *Ketubbot* 54b.
42. *Shabbat* 115a.
43. *Berakhot* 24b.
44. *Pesahim* 33b, *Nedarim* 59a.

45. *Hullin* 95b.
46. *Sotah* 21a.
47. *Berakhot* 15a.
48. Jerusalem Talmud *Berakhot* 5:1.
49. *Berakhot* 5a.
50. Jerusalem Talmud *Berakhot* 4:4.
51. Jerusalem Talmud *Betzah* 5:2.
52. *Yoma* 82b. In the Jerusalem Talmud (*Yoma* 8:4) this story is related as concerning two women, one of whom completed her fast while the other remained unaffected by the reminder; it is there said to have occurred during the time of Rabbi Tarphon.
53. *Pesahim* 3b.
54. Jerusalem Talmud *Berakhot* 5:1.
55. *Berakhot* 13b.
56. *Ketubbot* 62a.
57. *Berakhot* 20a.
58. *Bava Metzia* 84a.
59. Jerusalem Talmud *Berakhot* 2:3.
60. *Berakhot* 17a.
61. *Berakhot* 6b.
62. *Berakhot* 16b.
63. *Kiddushin* 33a.
64. *Shir Hashirim Rabbah* 5:1.
65. *Bava Batra* 107b.
66. *Nedarim* 22a, *Shir Hashirim Rabbah* 8:10.
67. *Shabbat* 145b.
68. *Pesahim* 87b.
69. *Sanhedrin* 97a.
70. *Bereshit Rabbah* 76:5.
71. *Berakhot* 31a.
72. *Sotah* 21b.
73. *Shemot Rabbah* 40:1.
74. *Shabbat* 114a.
75. Jerusalem Talmud *Berakhot* 5:1.
76. *Berakhot* 5b.
77. *Bava Batra* 116a.
78. *Sanhedrin* 37b.
79. Jerusalem Talmud *Berakhot* 5:1.
80. *Temurah* 14b.
81. We have already remarked that the Talmud often confused the name of the Parthians, who originated in the lands about the

Euphrates, with the Persians, who ruled Babylonia at a later date.

82. *Yevamot* 63b.
83. *Rosh Hashanah* 31b.
84. *Ta'anit* 5a.
85. *Ketubbot* 111a.
86. *Sanhedrin* 102b.
87. Jerusalem Talmud *Megillah* 1:10.
88. Jerusalem Talmud *Kilayim* 9:3, *Bereshit Rabbah* 96:9.
89. *Hullin* 155b.
90. Jerusalem Talmud *Rosh Hashanah* 1:3.
91. *Pesahim* 118a.
92. *Shabbat* 114a.
93. *Pesahim* 114a.
94. *Berakhot* 5b.
95. *Shir Hashirim Rabbah* 2:35.
96. *Sanhedrin* 101a, *Shevu'ot* 47b.
97. *Hullin* 84a.
98. *Ketubbot* 96a.
99. *Berakhot* 7b.
100. *Avodah Zarah* 8a.
101. *Shir Hashirim Rabbah* 7:8.
102. *Pesahim* 113a.
103. *Sotah* 47a.
104. *Sanhedrin* 103a.
105. *Pesahim* 88a.
106. *Bava Metzia* 58a.
107. *Sanhedrin* 103a.
108. *Shabbat* 127a.
109. *Mo'ed Katan* 25b.

54. Rabbi Simeon ben Lakish

1. Resh Lakish is an abbreviation of Rabbi Simeon ben Lakish. The mark indicating the abbreviation was in time transformed into a *yud*. We may also remark that his appellation ben Lakish does not prove that Lakish was the name of his father but might indicate that he was a native of a city called Lakish, possibly the biblical "Lachish." One of the last *tannaim* was also called Rabbi Jehudah ben Lakish, and in this case also the appellation may indicate the city of origin rather than the name of the father.

2. *Bava Metzia* 84a.
3. Jerusalem Talmud *Betzah* 5:2.
4. *Eruvin* 65b.
5. *Yevamot* 57a.
6. Jerusalem Talmud *Sanhedrin* 1:2.
7. Jerusalem Talmud *Yevamot* 16:5.
8. Jerusalem Talmud *Bava Kamma* 4:7.
9. Jerusalem Talmud *Berakhot* 8:7.
10. *Sanhedrin* 24a.
11. Jerusalem Talmud *Sanhedrin* 2:1.
12. *Bava Metzia* 84a.
13. Jerusalem Talmud *Yoma* 1:1.
14. Jerusalem Talmud *Eruvin* 1:1.
15. Jerusalem Talmud *Gittin* 3:2.
16. *Yoma* 9b.
17. Jerusalem Talmud *Terumot,* end of 10.
18. *Ta'anit* 5a.
19. Jerusalem Talmud *Ketubbot* 12:3.
20. *Yevamot* 37a.
21. *Kiddushin* 44a.
22. *Ketubbot* 9b.
23. Jerusalem Talmud *Sotah* 2:6.
24. Jerusalem Talmud *Eruvin* 1:7.
25. Jerusalem Talmud *Kilayim* 1:6, *Bava Kamma* 5:8.
26. *Sanhedrin* 27a.
27. Jerusalem Talmud *Sotah* 5:6, *Bereshit Rabbah* 56:3. This passage from the Jerusalem Talmud attempts to explain a contradiction, for Resh Lakish is first quoted as saying that Job lived during the days of Abraham and later he declared that there was no Job. The Talmud explains this contradiction by saying that Resh Lakish did believe in the existence of Job, but he did not believe that Job, who was a just man, would have sinned because of his suffering.
28. Jerusalem Talmud *Rosh Hashanah* 1:2.
29. *Shabbat* 119b, *Gittin* 47a. The Talmud says that "he sold himself to the Luddites" and some commentators said that the Luddites were a people of cannibals. Actually it implied a group of people who trained man-eating animals.
30. *Mo'ed Katan* 47a, Jerusalem Talmud *Mo'ed Katan* 3:1.
31. Jerusalem Talmud *Sanhedrin* 10:1.
32. *Yoma* 9b.

33. *Sukkah* 20a.
34. Jerusalem Talmud *Kilayim* 9:4, *Ketubbot* 12:3.
35. *Bava Metzia* 85b.
36. *Yoma* 9b.
37. *Kohelet Rabbah* 9:16.
38. Jerusalem Talmud *Terumot* 5:3.
39. *Bava Metzia* 84a.
40. *Avodah Zarah* 18b.
41. *Pesahim* 63b.
42. *Bereshit Rabbah* 75:12.
43. *Arakhin* 15b.
44. *Sanhedrin* 58b.
45. *Shabbat* 97a.
46. *Yoma* 86b.
47. *Pirkei Derabi Eliezer* 43.
48. *Eruvin* 19a.
49. *Bava Metzia* 106b, *Bava Batra* 60b.
50. *Kohelet Rabbah* 1:4.
51. *Sanhedrin* 7b, *Avodah Zarah* 52a.
52. *Sanhedrin* 8a.
53. *Kohelet Rabbah* 7:16.
54. *Shabbat* 63a.
55. *Shabbat* 104a, *Yoma* 38b.
56. *Vayikra Rabbah* 23:12.
57. Jerusalem Talmud *Berakhot* 9:5.
58. *Ta'anit* 11b.
59. *Shir Hashirim Rabbah* 2:11.
60. *Shabbat* 63a.
61. *Tanhuma Parshat Terumah.*
62. *Shabbat* 119b.
63. *Eruvin* 99a.
64. *Mo'ed Katan* 17a.
65. *Menahot* 91a.
66. *Eikhah Rabbati* 2:3.
67. *Tanhuma Parshat Lekh Lekha.*
68. *Hagigah* 5a.
69. *Eruvin* 65a.
70. Jerusalem Talmud *Berakhot* 1:1.

55. Jehudah and Hezekiah, the Sons of Rabbi Chiya

1. *Sanhedrin* 38a.
2. *Bava Batra* 75a.

3. *Yevamot* 65b.
4. *Sukkah* 20a.
5. *Hullin* 86a, Jerusalem Talmud *Ma'aser Sheni* 5:5.
6. *Bava Metzia* 85b.
7. *Betzah* 9b.
8. *Berakhot* 18b.
9. *Ketubbot* 62b.
10. Jerusalem Talmud *Bikkurim* 3:3.
11. *Vayikra Rabbah* 10:8.
12. *Sanhedrin* 37b.
13. *Sotah* 49a.
14. *Eruvin* 54a.
15. *Vayikra Rabbah* 12:3.
16. *Vayikra Rabbah* 9:9.
17. *Midrash Shoher Tov* 1:4.
18. *Sanhedrin* 29a.
19. *Shemot Rabbah* 44:8.
20. *Megillah* 5b.
21. *Tosafot, Gittin* 84b.
22. *Mo'ed Katan* 29a.

56. Rabbi Jannai Rabbah

1. Jerusalem Talmud *Eruvin* 8:4.
2. Jerusalem Talmud *Ta'anit* 4:2.
3. *Bava Batra* 14a.
4. *Mo'ed Katan* 12a.
5. *Kiddushin* 11a.
6. *Yevamot* 93a, Jerusalem Talmud *Demai* 7:1.
7. *Ketubbot* 62b, Jerusalem Talmud *Bikkurim* 3:3.
8. Jerusalem Talmud *Berakhot* 3:1, *Nazir* 7:1.
9. *Bava Batra* 111a.
10. *Avot* 4:15.
11. *Sanhedrin* 26a, Jerusalem Talmud *Shevi'it* 4:1.
12. *Shir Hashirim Rabbah* 5:11.
13. *Shir Hashirim Rabbah* 4:8.
14. *Avodah Zarah* 19a.
15. *Sotah* 22a.
16. *Tanhuma Parshat Terumah.*
17. *Shabbat* 31b.
18. *Vayikra Rabbah* 16:2.
19. *Arakhin* 6b.

20. *Hagigah* 5a.
21. Jerusalem Talmud *Nedarim* 1:6.
22. *Shabbat* 32a.
23. *Ta'anit* 20b.
24. Jerusalem Talmud *Berakhot* 4:4.
25. *Zevahim* 102a.
26. *Bava Batra* 145b.
27. Jerusalem Talmud *Pesahim* 1:5, *Yoma* 4:2.
28. Jerusalem Talmud *Berakhot* 4:2.
29. *Shabbat* 114a.

57. Rabbi Jonathan ben Eleazar

1. *Shabbat* 49a, b.
2. *Midrash Shoher Tov* 12:2.
3. *Tanhuma Parshat Behukotai* 50.
4. *Yoma* 9b, *Sanhedrin* 103a.
5. Jerusalem Talmud *Pesahim* 5:3.
6. *Yevamot* 109b.
7. *Sanhedrin* 7a.
8. Jerusalem Talmud *Bava Batra* 2:11.
9. *Sotah* 3b, *Avodah Zarah* 5a.
10. *Arakhin* 16a.
11. *Bava Kamma* 9a.
12. *Bava Metzia* 85a.
13. *Tamid* 28a.
14. Jerusalem Talmud *Pe'ah* 1:1.
15. *Ta'anit* 20a.
16. *Agadat Bereshit* 8.
17. *Berakhot* 59a.
18. *Bereshit Rabbah* 8:7.
19. *Bereshit Rabbah* 9:4.

58. Rabbi Oshaiah Rabbah

1. *Hullin* 141a.
2. Jerusalem Talmud *Bava Kamma* 4:6.
3. Jerusalem Talmud *Horayot* 3:5.
4. *Niddah* 14b.
5. Jerusalem Talmud *Shabbat* 3:1.
6. Jerusalem Talmud *Betzah* 1:11, *Bava Kamma* 2:1.
7. Jerusalem Talmud *Nedarim* 6:8.

8. *Ketubbot* 62b.
9. *Mo'ed Katan* 22a.
10. Jerusalem Talmud *Mo'ed Katan* 3:5, *Niddah* 2:1.
11. *Bava Batra* 59b.
12. Jerusalem Talmud *Gittin* 4:2.
13. Jerusalem Talmud *Terumot* 10:2.
14. The question of Rabbi Oshaiah was in accord with the oriental custom of allowing the beard to grow, which was also followed by Origines. It could not have applied to the Romans, who shaved their beards but allowed the hair on their heads to grow.
15. *Bereshit Rabbah* 11:7.
16. *Eruvin* 53a.
17. *Megillah* 7a, Jerusalem Talmud *Megillah* 1:4.
18. *Avodah Zarah* 18a.
19. *Ta'anit* 7a.
20. *Pesahim* 86b.
21. *Bereshit Rabbah* 76:3.
22. *Devarim Rabbah* 1:8.
23. *Sanhedrin* 22a.

59. Rabbi Chanina bar Chama

1. *Ta'anit* 27b, *Yevamot* 43a, Jerusalem Talmud *Yevamot* 2:1.
2. *Bekhorot* 51b.
3. *Yoma* 49a, Jerusalem Talmud *Terumot* 8:3.
4. Jerusalem Talmud *Ta'anit* 3:4.
5. *Ketubbot* 103b.
6. *Hullin* 24b.
7. Jerusalem Talmud *Berakhot* 5:1.
8. *Yoma* 49a.
9. *Hullin* 7b.
10. *Bava Metzia* 107b, *Bava Batra* 144b.
11. Jerusalem Talmud *Shabbat* 14:3.
12. *Ketubbot* 77b.
13. *Ketubbot* 103b.
14. *Yoma* 87b.
15. Jerusalem Talmud *Betzah* 1:1.
16. *Vayikra Rabbah* 21:7.
17. Jerusalem Talmud *Bava Metzia* 2:11.
18. *Mo'ed Katan* 24a.
19. Jerusalem Talmud *Niddah* 2:7.

20. Jerusalem Talmud *Horayot* 3:4.
21. Jerusalem Talmud *Pe'ah* 7:3.
22. Jerusalem Talmud *Mo'ed Katan* 3:1.
23. *Bava Kamma* 50a.
24. *Kiddushin* 40a.
25. *Berakhot* 33b.
26. *Sanhedrin* 58b.
27. *Kohelet Rabbah* 9:13.
28. *Sanhedrin* 7b.
29. *Bava Batra* 9b.
30. *Sanhedrin* 99a.
31. *Bava Batra* 75a.
32. *Shabbat* 173a.
33. *Eikhah Rabbati* 1:38.
34. *Nedarim* 32b.
35. *Shabbat* 156b.
36. Jerusalem Talmud *Pe'ah* 8:8.
37. *Shabbat* 119a.
38. *Eruvin* 65a.
39. *Shabbat* 151b.
40. *Bava Kamma* 91b, *Bava Batra* 26a.
41. Jerusalem Talmud *Ta'anit* 3:2.
42. Jerusalem Talmud *Ta'anit* 4:2.

60. Rabbi Joshua ben Levi

1. *Bereshit Rabbah* 35:2.
2. *Ketubbot* 77b.
3. *Yevamot* 45a.
4. *Eikhah Rabbati* 3:7.
5. Jerusalem Talmud *Berakhot* 8:1.
6. Jerusalem Talmud *Hagigah* 1:8.
7. Jerusalem Talmud *Mo'ed Katan* 3:1.
8. *Kiddushin* 33b.
9. *Masekhet Sofrim* 16:2.
10. *Berakhot* 8b, 19a.
11. *Berakhot* 21b.
12. *Eruvin* 54a.
13. *Ketubbot* 28a.
14. Jerusalem Talmud *Pe'ah* 2:7.
15. *Berakhot* 8a.

16. *Berakhot* 47b.
17. *Berakhot* 8b.
18. *Shabbat* 119a.
19. Jerusalem Talmud *Berakhot* 8:8.
20. *Avodah Zarah* 4b.
21. *Berakhot* 7a.
22. *Vayikra Rabbah* 16:7.
23. *Zevahim* 88b.
24. *Pesahim* 3a.
25. *Kiddushin* 71a, b.
26. Jerusalem Talmud *Yoma* 5:1.
27. Jerusalem Talmud *Ta'anit* 4:7.
28. *Sanhedrin* 98a.
29. *Makkot* 11a.
30. This proof of Rabbi Joshua is contained in *Tosefta* (*Terumot* 7:23) and not in the *Mishnah*.
31. Jerusalem Talmud *Terumot* 8:4.
32. *Ketubbot* 77b.
33. *Berakhot* 51a.
34. *Sanhedrin* 14a.
35. *Kiddushin* 30a, Jerusalem Talmud *Shabbat* 1:1.
36. *Berakhot* 10a.
37. *Bava Kamma* 54a.
38. *Bava Batra* 145b.
39. *Sotah* 35b.
40. *Devarim Rabbah* 1:16.
41. *Eikhah Rabbati* 1:1.
42. *Masekhet Derekh Eretz Perek Hashalom*.
43. *Tanhuma Parshat Behukotai*.
44. *Shemot Rabbah* 42:7.

61. Rabbi Shmuel bar Nachmani

1. The name Bar-Nachmani is used throughout the Babylonian Talmud (with one exception). The Jerusalem Talmud uses the name Bar-Nachman throughout, except on four occasions, where Bar-Nachmani is employed.
2. *Vayikra Rabbah* 31:1, *Eikhah Rabbati* 1:43.
3. Jerusalem Talmud *Berakhot* 1:1.
4. *Bereshit Rabbah* 12:9.
5. *Ta'anit* 8b.

6. *Eikhah Rabbati* 1:30.
7. *Mo'ed Katan* 17a.
8. *Pesikta Rabbati* 24.
9. *Bereshit Rabbah* 5:9, *Kohelet Rabbah* 3:16.
10. Jerusalem Talmud *Berakhot* 4:1, *Bereshit Rabbah* 65:11. As long as the Jewish calendar was not definitely determined, it was the duty of the High Court to determine the holidays as they saw fit and even the Day of Atonement could be postponed, it has proved, as when Rabbi Simeon b. Gamaliel the First commanded Rabbi Joshua ben Chananiah to appear before him bearing his cane and his wallet on the day that he considered to be the Day of Atonement.
11. *Bereshit Rabbah* 11:9.
12. *Pesahim* 68b.
13. Jerusalem Talmud *Shabbat* 15:3.
14. *Bamidbar Rabbah* 2:16.

62. Rabbi Simlai bar Abba

1. *Pe'ah* 5:5.
2. *Rosh Hashanah* 20b.
3. *Avodah Zarah* 37a.
4. Jerusalem Talmud *Avodah Zarah* 2:9.
5. *Bava Batra* 111a.
6. *Bekhorot* 36b.
7. *Makkot* 23b.
8. *Sotah* 14a.
9. *Midrash Tanhuma Parshat Vayera*.
10. *Pesikta Rabbati* 23.
11. Jerusalem Talmud *Pe'ah* 5:5.
12. *Avodah Zarah* 2, 3.

63. Rabbi Eleazar ben Pedat

1. *Ketubbot* 112a.
2. *Shabbat* 153a, *Eruvin* 65b, Jerusalem Talmud *Pesahim* 4:3.
3. *Megillah* 15a.
4. Jerusalem Talmud *Berakhot* 2:1.
5. *Makkot* 5b.
6. Jerusalem Talmud *Shekalim* 2:5.
7. *Hagigah* 13a.

8. *Yevamot* 72b.
9. *Bava Kamma* 100a.
10. *Berakhot* 16b.
11. *Sanhedrin* 14a.
12. *Bava Batra* 128b.
13. *Eruvin* 54b.
14. Jerusalem Talmud *Berakhot* 9:5.
15. *Megillah* 25a.
16. *Sukkah* 49b.
17. *Bava Batra* 9b.
18. *Ketubbot* 68a, Jerusalem Talmud *Pe'ah* 5:8.
19. *Bava Batra* 7b.
20. *Sanhedrin* 108b.
21. Jerusalem Talmud *Bava Metzia* 2:3.
22. *Yoma* 2b, *Gittin* 19b, *Niddah* 20b.
23. *Betzah* 4b, *Gittin* 73a, Jerusalem Talmud *Kiddushin* 1:4.
24. Jerusalem Talmud *Terumot* 1:2, *Shekalim* 1:4.
25. Jerusalem Talmud *Shevi'it* 2:6.
26. Jerusalem Talmud *Terumot* 5:3.
27. Jerusalem Talmud *Yevamot* 1:1.
28. Jerusalem Talmud *Yevamot* 2:3.
29. Jerusalem Talmud *Kiddushin* 1:4.
30. *Sanhedrin* 32a.
31. *Midrash Mishlei* 17.
32. *Betzah* 4b.
33. *Nedarim* 81a.
34. *Eruvin* 65a.
35. *Berakhot* 31a.
36. *Sanhedrin* 58b.
37. *Bava Batra* 9a.
38. *Ketubbot* 5a.
39. Jerusalem Talmud *Pe'ah* 8:9.
40. *Ketubbot* 5b.
41. *Yoma* 86b.
42. *Avodah Zarah* 18b.
43. *Sotah* 5a.
44. *Sotah* 41b.
45. *Sotah* 42a.
46. *Sanhedrin* 96a.
47. *Bava Metzia* 58a.

48. *Yevamot* 63a.
49. *Bereshit Rabbah* 2:22.
50. *Yevamot* 63a.
51. *Sanhedrin* 92a.

64. Rabbi Avahu of Caesarea

1. *Berakhot* 60a.
2. Jerusalem Talmud *Bava Metzia* 4:7.
3. *Shabbat* 119a.
4. *Ketubbot* 17a.
5. *Hagigah* 14a.
6. *Sukkah* 48b, *Sanhedrin* 39a.
7. *Avodah Zarah* 28a.
8. Jerusalem Talmud *Pesahim* 2:2.
9. *Gittin* 44b.
10. *Shir Hashirim Rabbah* 1:39.
11. *Sotah* 40a.
12. Jerusalem Talmud *Ta'anit* 1:4.
13. *Sanhedrin* 110a.
14. Jerusalem Talmud *Mo'ed Katan* 3:3.
15. *Berakhot* 34b.
16. *Bava Kamma* 93a.
17. *Gittin* 7a.
18. *Bereshit Rabbah* 3:9.
19. Introduction to *Eikhah Rabbati* 17.
20. *Bereshit Rabbah* 2:2.
21. *Sotah* 40a.
22. Jerusalem Talmud *Berakhot* 3:1, *Sanhedrin* 1:1.
23. Jerusalem Talmud *Berakhot* 2:3.
24. *Shir Hashirim Rabbah* 1:52.
25. Jerusalem Talmud *Avodah Zarah* 3:1.
26. *Bava Metzia* 59a.
27. *Shabbat* 119a.
28. Jerusalem Talmud *Pesahim* 3:7.
29. *Sotah* 49a.
30. *Yoma* 38b.
31. *Vayikra Rabbah* 29:3.
32. *Rosh Hashanah* 32b.
33. *Tanhuma Parshat Acharei* 12.

34. Jerusalem Talmud *Pe'ah* 1:1.
35. *Midrash Shmuel* 7.
36. *Shemot Rabbah* 29:4.
37. *Berakhot* 55a.
38. Jerusalem Talmud *Sanhedrin* 6:10.

65. Rabbi Chiya bar Abba Hacohen

1. Jerusalem Talmud *Avodah Zarah* 2:8.
2. *Berakhot* 5b.
3. Jerusalem Talmud *Hagigah* 1:7.
4. Jerusalem Talmud *Shevi'it* 3:1.
5. Jerusalem Talmud *Hagigah* 1:8.
6. *Yevamot* 46a.
7. Jerusalem Talmud *Ma'aser Sheni* 4:1.
8. *Bereshit Rabbah* 52:2.
9. *Bereshit Rabbah* 11:4.
10. This well-known *midrash* does not name the animal and merely refers to it as *gora*, a young beast. This was assumed to be a *re'eim*, concerning the nature of which commentators differed. According to a *midrash* the *re'eim* was a gigantic animal that Noah could not take into the Ark because of its size, and he therefore tied it to the Ark that it might swim along with it. The Septuagint (Greek translation of the Bible) identified the *re'eim* as a unicorn. Others gave differing descriptions. It nevertheless appears that the animal referred to in the *midrash* was a young elephant that uprooted trees and fled when it heard the call of its mother.
11. Jerusalem Talmud *Berakhot* 3:1.
12. *Bereshit Rabbah* 31:18.
13. Jerusalem Talmud *Shabbat* 16:1.
14. *Tosafot, Bava Batra* 113a.
15. *Bava Kamma* 55a.
16. *Vayikra Rabbah* 3:1.
17. *Shemot Rabbah* 21:4.
18. *Midrash Pesikta Hadata Lehag Hashavu'ot.*
19. *Kiddushin* 30b.
20. *Shir Hashirim Rabbah* 2:18.
21. *Shemot Rabbah* 51:4.
22. Jerusalem Talmud *Berakhot* 4:2.

66. Rabbi Ami and Rabbi Asi

1. *Yevamot* 16b, Jerusalem Talmud *Ta'anit* 4:5.
2. Jerusalem Talmud *Terumot* 5:10.
3. Jerusalem Talmud *Hagigah* 1:7.
4. *Hullin* 7a.
5. *Mo'ed Katan* 25a.
6. *Shabbat* 145b.
7. *Ketubbot* 17a.
8. *Shevu'ot* 47a.
9. *Kiddushin* 31b.
10. *Sanhedrin* 17b.
11. *Gittin* 59b.
12. *Yevamot* 21b.
13. *Hullin* 103b.
14. *Berakhot* 5a, 30b.
15. *Shabbat* 10a.
16. Jerusalem Talmud *Megillah* 3:4.
17. Jerusalem Talmud *Kilayim* 6:1.
18. *Bava Kamma* 60b.
19. Jerusalem Talmud *Terumot* 8:3.
20. *Menahot* 29b.
21. *Ta'anit* 14b.
22. *Hullin* 107b.
23. *Bava Metzia* 28b.
24. *Gittin* 44a.
25. Jerusalem Talmud *Pesahim* 4:1.
26. Jerusalem Talmud *Demai* 4:3.
27. Jerusalem Talmud *Gittin* 2:6.
28. *Gittin* 54b.
29. *Berakhot* 62a.
30. Jerusalem Talmud *Pesahim* 4:9.
31. *Ta'anit* 5a.
32. This story was poetically rewritten in Hebrew by Moshe Laski under the name *Ne'emanei Aretz* (1840), by Eliyahu Mordechai Werbel under the name of *Chuldah Vabur* (1852), and by Alexander Langbank under the name of *Ha'eidim Ha'ilmim*. In Yiddish it was dramatized by Abraham Goldfaden in the well-known operetta, *Shulamis*.
33. Jerusalem Talmud *Terumot* 8:3.
34. *Horayot* 12a, *Keritot* 5b.

35. *Shemot Rabbah* 42:9.
36. *Hagigah* 13a.
37. *Bereshit Rabbah* 8:3.
38. Jerusalem Talmud *Pe'ah* 8:6, *Shekalim* 5:2.
39. *Yoma* 74b, 75a.
40. *Vayikra Rabbah* 7:3.
41. *Kohelet Rabbah* 9:5.
42. Jerusalem Talmud *Avodah Zarah* 3:1.
43. *Mo'ed Katan* 25b.

67. Rabbi Yitzchak the Blacksmith

1. *Tosefta Eruvin* 7.
2. *Bereshit Rabbah* 20:24.
3. *Shir Hashirim Rabbah* 2:14.
4. *Yevamot* 48b, *Avodah Zarah* 24a, *Mo'ed Katan* 20a.
5. *Hullin* 48b.
6. *Nedarim* 57b.
7. *Betzah* 27a.
8. *Bava Kamma* 117b, *Bava Batra* 170a.
9. *Mo'ed Katan* 24b.
10. *Gittin* 60a.
11. *Megillah* 6a.
12. *Kohelet Rabbah* 1:4.
13. *Sukkah* 52a, *Kiddushin* 30b.
14. *Kiddushin* 80b.
15. *Bereshit Rabbah* 22:11.
16. *Yoma* 87a.
17. *Bava Batra* 9b.
18. *Midrash Shmuel* 1.
19. *Yevamot* 64a.
20. Jerusalem Talmud *Nedarim* 9:1.
21. *Kohelet Rabbah* 1:13.
22. *Sanhedrin* 24a.
23. *Devarim Rabbah* 11:2, *Midrash Tanhuma Parshat Berakhah* 2.
24. *Midrash Ester Rabbah* 7.

68. Rabbi Abba bar Kahana and Rabbi Chanina bar Papa

1. Jerusalem Talmud *Sotah* 9:13, *Bereshit Rabbah* 4:9, *Vayikra Rabbah* 35:9.
2. Jerusalem Talmud *Berakhot* 6:6, *Shabbat* 3:4, 6:5, *Yevamot* 4:6.

3. *Shabbat* 121b.
4. Jerusalem Talmud *Pesahim* 4:9.
5. *Bereshit Rabbah* 65:12.
6. *Bereshit Rabbah* 58b, *Kohelet Rabbah* 1:10.
7. *Kohelet Rabbah* 10:14.
8. *Vayikra Rabbah* 6:1.
9. Jerusalem Talmud *Pe'ah* 1:1.
10. *Midrash Shoher Tov* 18.
11. *Shir Hashirim Rabbah* 5:11, *Eikhah Rabbati* 1:43.
12. *Bereshit Rabbah* 37:8.
13. Jerusalem Talmud *Shevi'it* 4:3.
14. *Berakhot* 5a.
15. *Mo'ed Katan* 28b.
16. *Kiddushin* 39b.
17. Jerusalem Talmud *Pe'ah* 8:8.
18. *Ketubbot* 77b.
19. *Sukkah* 49b.
20. *Berakhot* 35a, *Sanhedrin* 102a.
21. *Sanhedrin* 110a.
22. *Midrash Shoher Tov* 104.
23. *Bereshit Rabbah* 52:7.

69. Rabbi Zeira

1. Jerusalem Talmud *Kiddushin* 1:7.
2. *Berakhot* 39a, *Yevamot* 78b.
3. *Bava Kamma* 9a, Jerusalem Talmud *Shabbat* 7:2.
4. *Betzah* 33b, *Ketubbot* 95a, Jerusalem Talmud *Shevi'it* 10:2, *Eruvin* 1:1.
5. Jerusalem Talmud *Berakhot* 8:5.
6. *Bava Metzia* 85a.
7. *Berakhot* 57a.
8. *Shabbat* 41a.
9. *Ketubbot* 112a.
10. *Kiddushin* 52a.
11. *Avodah Zarah* 16b.
12. *Bava Metzia* 85a.
13. *Sanhedrin* 37a.
14. *Niddah* 48a.
15. Jerusalem Talmud *Terumot* 11:3.
16. *Bava Metzia* 85a.

17. *Hullin* 49b, 107a.
18. *Bava Batra* 84b.
19. *Shabbat* 130b.
20. *Berakhot* 33b.
21. Jerusalem Talmud *Shabbat* 1:2, *Kiddushin* 1:7.
22. *Nedarim* 36a, Jerusalem Talmud *Berakhot* 8:2.
23. *Berakhot* 46a.
24. *Berakhot* 28a, *Eruvin* 28b.
25. *Sanhedrin* 14a.
26. *Megillah* 28a.
27. Jerusalem Talmud *Bava Metzia* 4:7.
28. *Ta'anit* 16a.
29. *Hullin* 122a.
30. *Yoma* 87a.
31. *Sanhedrin* 25b.
32. *Ta'anit* 26b.
33. Jerusalem Talmud *Berakhot* 3:5.
34. *Shabbat* 112b, Jerusalem Talmud *Shekalim* 5:1.
35. *Sotah* 4a.
36. *Berakhot* 6b.
37. *Avodah Zarah* 36b.
38. *Sukkah* 46b.
39. *Ketubbot* 17a.
40. Jerusalem Talmud *Ma'aserot* 3:4.
41. *Bava Kamma* 9b.
42. *Berakhot* 28a, *Eruvin* 28b.
43. *Megillah* 7b.
44. *Megillah* 28a, *Ta'anit* 20b.
45. *Mo'ed Katan* 25b.

PART III: BABYLONIAN TALMUD

70. Introduction

1. *Yevamot* 21a, Jerusalem Talmud *Yevamot* 2:3.
2. *Shabbat* 73a.
3. *Betzah* 36b.
4. *Berakhot* 33a.
5. *Shabbat* 35b, 114a, *Sukkah* 57b.
6. *Mekhilta Debahodesh* 6, *Yalkut Parshat Yitro* 292.

7. *Ketubbot* 21a, *Hullin* 44a.
8. *Hullin* 74a.
9. *Tosafot, Menahot* 28b.
10. *Bava Kamma* 6b, Jerusalem Talmud *Gittin* 5:1.
11. *Mekhilta Parshat Yitro.*
12. *Yoma* 38b.
13. *Sanhedrin* 38b.
14. *Pesahim* 86b.
15. *Avot* 1:2.
16. *Yevamot* 109b.
17. Jerusalem Talmud *Pe'ah* 1:2.
18. *Bereshit Rabbah* 9:2.
19. *Bereshit Rabbah* 12:7.
20. *Sanhedrin* 91b.
21. *Shabbat* 31b.
22. *Ketubbot* 105b.
23. *Shabbat* 55a.
24. *Mekhilta Masekhta Devayasa* 1:27.
25. *Sanhedrin* 92a.
26. *Bava Metzia* 58b.
27. *Pesahim* 113b.
28. *Pesahim* 118a.
29. *Arakhin* 16a.
30. *Sotah* 42a.
31. *Mekhilta Masekhta Nezikin* 13:3.
32. *Tana Devei Eliyahu* 26.
33. *Berakhot* 17b.
34. *Sukkah* 49b.
35. *Bava Batra* 9b.
36. *Gittin* 7b.
37. *Shabbat* 63a.
38. *Sanhedrin* 17b.
39. *Bava Metzia* 107b.
40. *Hagigah* 4b.
41. *Avot Derabi Natan* 16:5.
42. *Yoma* 60b.
43. *Bamidbar Rabbah* 11:16.
44. *Yevamot* 65b.
45. *Sifri Parshat Naso* 42.
46. *Shabbat* 25b.
47. *Yevamot* 63b.

48. *Bava Batra* 148b.
49. *Bava Metzia* 59a.
50. *Sotah* 17a.
51. *Pirkei Derabi Eliezer* 12.
52. *Sifri Parshat Eikev* 46.
53. *Kiddushin* 30b.
54. *Pesahim* 113a.
55. *Shabbat* 119b.
56. *Bava Batra* 21b.
57. *Nedarim* 81a.
58. *Sanhedrin* 96b.
59. *Kiddushin* 29a.
60. *Berakhot* 8a.
61. *Avot* 2:2.
62. *Kiddushin* 30b.
63. Jerusalem Talmud *Pe'ah* 1:1.
64. *Kiddushin* 31b.
65. *Mekhilta Masekhta Devayishma Yitro* 40:7.
66. *Pesahim* 22b.
67. *Mekhilta Parshat Yitro* 1:12.
68. *Horayot* 13b.
69. *Avot* 4:4.
70. *Eruvin* 13b.
71. *Sotah* 5a.
72. *Berakhot* 43b.
73. *Avot* 4:1.
74. *Shabbat* 118b.
75. *Bava Metzia* 92a.
76. Jerusalem Talmud *Kiddushin* 4:12.
77. *Bava Kamma* 91b.
78. *Yoma* 82a.
79. *Shabbat* 151b.
80. *Mekhilta Masekhta Deshabbat* 1.
81. *Nedarim* 20a.
82. *Masekhet Derekh Eretz Zuta* 6.
83. *Mekhilta Masekhta Debeshalah* 3.
84. *Menahot* 29b.
85. *Shabbat* 153a.
86. *Devarim Rabbah* 5:1.
87. *Berakhot* 10a.
88. *Mo'ed Katan* 16b.

89. *Megillah* 21a.
90. *Eruvin* 13b.
91. *Horayot* 13a.
92. *Ketubbot* 50a.
93. *Shabbat* 145b.
94. *Shabbat* 114a.
95. *Pesahim* 49a.
96. *Ta'anit* 5a.
97. *Rosh Hashanah* 23a.
98. *Sanhedrin* 91b.
99. *Horayot* 13a.
100. *Bava Metzia* 33a.
101. *Sanhedrin* 110a.
102. *Yoma* 37a.
103. *Avot* 2:13.
104. *Pesahim* 103b.
105. *Ta'anit* 21b.

71. Rav—Abba Arecha

1. *Niddah* 24b.
2. Jerusalem Talmud *Ketubbot* 12:3, *Bereshit Rabbah* 33:3.
3. *Ta'anit* 4b, *Bereshit Rabbah* 98:13.
4. *Ketubbot* 62b.
5. *Sanhedrin* 5a, *Bereshit Rabbah* 33:3.
6. *Mo'ed Katan* 9b.
7. *Eruvin* 50b, *Ketubbot* 8a, *Gittin* 38b, *Bava Batra* 42a.
8. *Berakhot* 13b, *Shabbat* 3b.
9. *Hullin* 92b.
10. *Kiddushin* 76b.
11. *Pesahim* 62b.
12. *Megillah* 22b.
13. *Hullin* 84a.
14. *Hullin* 54a.
15. Jerusalem Talmud *Niddah* 1:3, *Bereshit Rabbah* 2:14.
16. *Sanhedrin* 111a.
17. *Yoma* 20b.
18. *Kohelet Rabbah* 7:12.
19. Jerusalem Talmud *Bava Metzia* 6:1.
20. Jerusalem Talmud *Gittin* 4:3.
21. Jerusalem Talmud *Bava Metzia* 4:2.

22. *Sanhedrin* 36a.
23. *Sotah* 22a.
24. *Sanhedrin* 91b.
25. *Yevamot* 63a.
26. *Kiddushin* 71b.
27. *Yoma* 87a.
28. *Yoma* 20b.
29. *Shabbat* 108a.
30. *Shabbat* 120b.
31. *Megillah* 5b.
32. *Ketubbot* 72b.
33. *Bava Metzia* 51a.
34. *Sukkah* 2a.
35. Jerusalem Talmud *Bava Metzia* 8:6.
36. *Hullin* 86a.
37. *Berakhot* 60b.
38. *Pesahim* 3b.
39. *Pesahim* 2a.
40. Jerusalem Talmud *Ketubbot* 9:9.
41. *Kiddushin* 71b.
42. *Avodah Zarah* 11b, Jerusalem Talmud *Avodah Zarah* 1:2.
43. *Yevamot* 63a.
44. *Sanhedrin* 5a. The question concerning the firstborn of pure cattle was this: After the Temple was destroyed Jews could not slaughter the firstborn of pure cattle unless it had suffered some injury. The extent of such an injury necessary to enable it to be slaughtered had to be certified by a court. Rabbi Jehudah Hanasi permitted Rav to give judgment on all sorts of matters except in this case.
45. Jerusalem Talmud *Gittin* 5:3.
46. *Pesahim* 87b.
47. *Hagigah* 5a.
48. *Gittin* 59a.
49. *Hullin* 137b.
50. *Yoma* 87b.
51. Jerusalem Talmud *Berakhot* 9:1.
52. *Bava Metzia* 82b.
53. *Shabbat* 11a. The text of this remark, which is quoted by Raba bar Machasia in the name of Rab Chama bar Gurya, who heard it from Rav, is certainly incorrect. It says, "It is better to be subject to Ishmael than to Edom, to Edom than to a *chabar*, to a *chabar*

than to a scholar, to a scholar than to a widow and an orphan." The part which says "to Edom than to a *chabar*" is of a later period than Rav's referring to a time when the Babylonian fire-worshippers, the *chabarim*, persecuted the Jews, and the Jews preferred the sufferings inflicted by the Romans to those of the Persians. But the following passages are simply meaningless in the context. Since the whole quotation comes to us third hand, and the hand of the censor also did its share of damage, we may state with assurance that the end is an apocryphal addition, and God knows who its author is.

54. *Bereshit Rabbah* 16:5.
55. *Bava Kamma* 80b.
56. Jerusalem Talmud *Bava Batra* 8:5.
57. *Pesahim* 34b, *Yoma* 57a.
58. *Ta'anit* 9b.
59. *Ta'anit* 21b.
60. *Bava Metzia* 92b.
61. *Pesahim* 107a.
62. *Pesahim* 107b.
63. *Shabbat* 26a.
64. *Berakhot* 43a, Jerusalem Talmud *Berakhot* 6:6.
65. *Ta'anit* 10a.
66. *Bava Metzia* 72b.
67. *Shabbat* 125b.
68. *Shabbat* 113a.
69. It should be noted that most of the censors who supervised the printing of the Talmud did a great deal of destruction in erasing the word *arami* (Aramite), and substituting idolator, as one may see in the texts printed by R. N. Rabinowitz in his book *Dikdukei Sofrim*, for which he used a Talmud manuscript of the year 1502.
70. *Niddah* 35b, Jerusalem Talmud *Avodah Zarah* 2:2.
71. *Shabbat* 138b.
72. *Sotah* 22a.
73. *Shabbat* 156a, *Nedarim* 32a.
74. *Berakhot* 17a.
75. *Eruvin* 54a.
76. *Yoma* 19b.
77. *Sanhedrin* 26b.
78. Jerusalem Talmud *Shekalim* 7:2, *Avodah Zarah* 2:5.
79. *Megillah* 5b.
80. *Mo'ed Katan* 18b.

81. *Shabbat* 11a.
82. *Sanhedrin* 4a.
83. Jerusalem Talmud *Berakhot* 4:1.
84. *Bava Batra* 161b.
85. *Ketubbot* 106a.
86. *Berakhot* 25a.
87. Jerusalem Talmud *Berakhot* 6:6, *Mo'ed Katan* 3:6.
88. *Bava Metzia* 107b.
89. *Shabbat* 107b.
90. *Yoma* 83a.
91. *Ketubbot* 62a. It is somewhat strange, to be sure, that Rav should have chosen a person like Rabbi Shmuel bar Shilet to illustrate the meaning of the word *idler*, because it is believed that this Rabbi Shmuel bar Shilet was neither a rich man nor an idler, but a teacher of children who lived on what his pupils paid him. Rav probably meant that a man like Rabbi Shmuel bar Shilet had all his needs provided for him in his house and did not need to work in the fields to get his food, as the other scholars in Babylonia had to do, and therefore he could sleep quietly in his bed as though it were a palace and the tax collector knew him not.
92. *Arakhin* 16b.
93. *Yevamot* 52a, *Kiddushin* 12b.
94. *Megillah* 27a, *Nazir* 19a, *Sotah* 12b, *Sanhedrin* 10b.
95. *Betzah* 6a.
96. *Bava Batra* 148b.
97. *Shabbat* 75b.
98. Jerusalem Talmud *Niddah* 2:7.
99. *Berakhot* 40b.
100. *Hagigah* 12a.
101. *Shevu'ot* 38b.
102. *Berakhot* 20b, *Yoma* 4b.
103. *Eruvin* 68b.
104. *Ta'anit* 24a.
105. *Bava Metzia* 107a.
106. *Shabbat* 53a.
107. *Hullin* 45b.
108. Jerusalem Talmud *Kiddushin* 3:12.
109. *Sukkah* 27a.
110. *Berakhot* 64a.
111. *Avodah Zarah* 10b, 11a.
112. *Shabbat* 11a.

113. *Eruvin* 55b.
114. *Pesahim* 113b.
115. *Berakhot* 16b.
116. *Shabbat* 129a.
117. *Shabbat* 140b.
118. *Pesahim* 119b.
119. *Mo'ed Katan* 11a.
120. *Shabbat* 33a.
121. *Shabbat* 11a.
122. *Hullin* 111b.
123. *Zevahim* 59a.
124. *Pesahim* 66a, *Sanhedrin* 82a.
125. Jerusalem Talmud *Ketubbot* 9:9.
126. Jerusalem Talmud *Sanhedrin* 7:11.
127. *Shabbat* 152a.
128. *Nedarim* 41a.
129. *Mo'ed Katan* 24a.
130. *Shabbat* 110a.
131. *Sanhedrin* 17a.
132. *Bava Kamma* 75a.
133. Jerusalem Talmud *Nedarim* 9:3.
134. *Berakhot* 12b.
135. *Bava Batra* 164b.
136. *Sanhedrin* 91b.
137. *Berakhot* 54b.
138. Jerusalem Talmud *Berakhot* 1:6.
139. Jerusalem Talmud *Berakhot* 2:3.
140. Jerusalem Talmud *Berakhot* 4:6, 9:2.
141. *Rosh Hashanah* 27a, Jerusalem Talmud *Rosh Hashanah* 1:3, *Avodah Zarah* 1:2, *Vayikra Rabbah* 29:1.
142. *Megillah* 31b.
143. *Mo'ed Katan* 25a.
144. *Berakhot* 43b.
145. *Sotah* 46b.
146. *Gittin* 90a.
147. *Ketubbot* 77a.
148. *Ketubbot* 61b.
149. *Ketubbot* 63a, 77a.
150. *Kiddushin* 41a.
151. *Sanhedrin* 77b.
152. *Ketubbot* 61b.

153. *Bava Metzia* 59a.
154. *Sanhedrin* 107a.
155. *Kiddushin* 81a.
156. *Avodah Zarah* 19a.
157. *Bava Batra* 89b.
158. *Bava Metzia* 52a.
159. *Bava Metzia* 75b.
160. *Gittin* 55a.
161. *Sanhedrin* 75b.
162. *Bava Batra* 21a.
163. *Shabbat* 83b.
164. *Midrash Shmuel* 4.
165. *Bava Kamma* 116b, *Bava Metzia* 10a.
166. *Sukkah* 29b.
167. *Rosh Hashanah* 17a.
168. *Pesahim* 15b.
169. *Bava Batra* 95a.
170. *Gittin* 6b.
171. *Hullin* 127a.
172. *Betzah* 32b.
173. *Ketubbot* 25a, *Sanhedrin* 26a.
174. *Berakhot* 43b.
175. *Eruvin* 56a.
176. *Avodah Zarah* 35b.
177. *Rosh Hashanah* 18a.
178. *Sanhedrin* 104a.
179. *Mo'ed Katan* 11a, *Sanhedrin* 5b.
180. *Nedarim* 76b.
181. *Shabbat* 17b.
182. *Shabbat* 130a.
183. *Makkot* 11a.
184. *Shabbat* 10b.
185. *Sukkah* 21b, *Avodah Zarah* 19a.
186. *Sanhedrin* 106a.
187. *Berakhot* 5a, *Sanhedrin* 95a.
188. *Yevamot* 63a.
189. *Sanhedrin* 94a.
190. *Eruvin* 87a.
191. *Sanhedrin* 44b.
192. *Bava Kamma* 110a.
193. *Betzah* 32b.

194. *Sotah* 12a.
195. *Berakhot* 54b.
196. *Bava Batra* 164b.
197. *Berakhot* 55b.
198. *Berakhot* 55b.
199. *Berakhot* 54b.
200. *Pesahim* 113a.
201. *Bava Metzia* 16b.
202. Jerusalem Talmud *Shevu'ot* 8:2.
203. Jerusalem Talmud *Demai* 7:6.
204. *Bava Batra* 53a.
205. Jerusalem Talmud *Ketubbot* 9:1.
206. *Ketubbot* 86a.
207. *Arakhin* 33a.
208. *Ketubbot* 72b.
209. *Bekhorot* 36a.
210. *Shevu'ot* 48a, Jerusalem Talmud *Shevu'ot* 7:7.
211. Jerusalem Talmud *Bava Kamma* 9:7.
212. *Bava Kamma* 20a.
213. *Bava Metzia* 75a.

72. Shmuel Yarchina'ah of Nehardea

1. *Bava Metzia* 85b.
2. *Megillah* 22a.
3. *Ketubbot* 22a, Jerusalem Talmud *Shabbat* 3:1.
4. *Shabbat* 53a, *Hullin* 48b.
5. *Mo'ed Katan* 24a.
6. *Berakhot* 58a.
7. *Rosh Hashanah* 20b.
8. *Niddah* 25b.
9. *Hullin* 95b.
10. *Kiddushin* 39a, *Menahot* 38b.
11. *Pesahim* 103a.
12. Jerusalem Talmud *Bava Metzia* 4:1.
13. *Midrash Shmuel* 10.
14. *Bava Metzia* 85b.
15. *Bava Metzia* 113b.
16. *Shabbat* 108b.
17. *Shabbat* 133b.
18. *Shabbat* 129a.

19. *Yoma* 83b.
20. *Nedarim* 54b.
21. *Shabbat* 157b.
22. *Mo'ed Katan* 26a.
23. *Sanhedrin* 88a.
24. *Shabbat* 34b, *Betzah* 31b, *Kiddushin* 39a.
25. *Betzah* 16b.
26. *Eruvin* 46b.
27. *Ta'anit* 18a.
28. *Pesahim* 54b.
29. *Ta'anit* 11a.
30. *Shabbat* 19b, 22a, 51a.
31. *Shabbat* 129a.
32. *Shabbat* 42a, *Zevahim* 91b.
33. *Pesahim* 30a,b.
34. *Berakhot* 34b, *Shabbat* 63a.
35. *Bekhorot* 49b.
36. Jerusalem Talmud *Kiddushin* 1:6.
37. *Gittin* 10b.
38. *Bava Kamma* 46a.
39. *Ketubbot* 76b.
40. *Pe'ah* 4:5, *Shekalim* 4:4, *Nedarim* 2:2.
41. *Bava Metzia* 40b, *Bava Batra* 90b.
42. *Yoma* 22b.
43. *Nedarim* 81a.
44. *Sukkah* 53a.
45. *Mo'ed Katan* 18a.
46. *Shabbat* 108a.
47. *Ketubbot* 23a.
48. *Yevamot* 45b.
49. *Bava Batra* 92b.
50. *Megillah* 18b, *Yevamot* 83a.
51. *Bava Metzia* 112b, *Shevu'ot* 45a.
52. *Gittin* 88b.
53. *Ketubbot* 100b.
54. *Bava Metzia* 70a.
55. *Bava Batra* 144a.
56. *Ketubbot* 96a.
57. *Ketubbot* 54a.
58. *Gittin* 36b.
59. *Makkot* 3a.

60. *Makkot* 3b.
61. *Bava Kamma* 37a.
62. *Kiddushin* 6a.
63. *Kiddushin* 12a.
64. *Ketubbot* 23a.
65. *Yevamot* 69b.
66. *Kiddushin* 70a.
67. *Berakhot* 24a.
68. *Kiddushin* 81b.
69. *Berakhot* 29a.
70. *Eruvin* 13b.
71. *Eruvin* 74a.
72. *Eruvin* 90b.
73. *Bava Metzia* 107a.
74. *Eruvin* 94a.
75. Jerusalem Talmud *Avodah Zarah* 2:9.
76. *Rosh Hashanah* 20b.

73. Mar Ukba, the Exilarch

1. *Sanhedrin* 5a, *Horayot* 11b.
2. Jerusalem Talmud *Megillah* 3:3.
3. Jerusalem Talmud *Bava Batra* 5:5.
4. *Rosh Hashanah* 19b.
5. Jerusalem Talmud *Megillah* 1:5.
6. *Hullin* 105a.
7. *Kiddushin* 44b.
8. *Mo'ed Katan* 16b.
9. *Shabbat* 55a.
10. *Eruvin* 81a, *Bava Kamma* 112b.
11. *Shabbat* 108b.
12. *Shabbat* 140a.
13. *Eruvin* 68a.
14. *Shabbat* 108b, *Mo'ed Katan* 26b.
15. *Ketubbot* 67b.
16. *Sanhedrin* 31b.
17. *Mo'ed Katan* 2b.
18. Jerusalem Talmud *Avodah Zarah* 2:8.
19. *Berakhot* 25a, *Avodah Zarah* 36b.
20. *Gittin* 31b.
21. *Gittin* 7a.
22. Jerusalem Talmud *Gittin* 6:5.

74. Rabbah bar Avuha

1. The name Rabbah is a contraction of Rab Abba.
2. *Shabbat* 134b.
3. *Gittin* 72a, *Bava Batra* 136a.
4. *Yevamot* 80b.
5. *Berakhot* 51b.
6. *Gittin* 67b.
7. *Kiddushin* 70b.
8. *Hullin* 109b.
9. *Bava Metzia* 114b.
10. *Shabbat* 59b, *Eruvin* 26a, *Yevamot* 115b.
11. *Ketubbot* 23b.
12. *Yevamot* 48b.
13. *Bava Batra* 149a.

75. Rav Nachman bar Jacob

1. *Bava Batra* 153a.
2. Jerusalem Talmud *Megillah* 3:3.
3. *Kiddushin* 33a.
4. *Ketubbot* 94b.
5. *Sukkah* 31a.
6. *Bava Batra* 65a.
7. *Sanhedrin* 5a.
8. *Bava Metzia* 66a.
9. *Niddah* 47a.
10. *Bava Metzia* 5a, *Shevu'ot* 40b.
11. *Gittin* 31b.
12. *Ta'anit* 5b, 6a.
13. *Ketubbot* 13a, *Kiddushin* 59b, *Bava Metzia* 10a.
14. *Betzah* 31b.
15. *Bava Batra* 36a.
16. *Sanhedrin* 98a.
17. *Sotah* 49b.
18. *Kiddushin* 70a.
19. *Hullin* 124a.
20. *Yoma* 18b, *Yevamot* 37b.
21. *Gittin* 45a.

76. Rav Huna, Head of the Academy in Sura

1. *Ta'anit* 23b.
2. *Mo'ed Katan* 25a.

3. *Eruvin* 16a, *Hullin* 95a.
4. *Ketubbot* 105a.
5. Jerusalem Talmud *Sanhedrin* 1:1.
6. *Shabbat* 54b.
7. *Megillah* 27a.
8. *Berakhot* 5a, *Bava Kamma* 80b.
9. *Megillah* 27a, b.
10. *Ta'anit* 20b.
11. *Ketubbot* 106a.
12. *Avodah Zarah* 17b.
13. *Berakhot* 5b.
14. *Gittin* 6a, *Bava Kamma* 80a.
15. *Ketubbot* 75a.
16. Jerusalem Talmud *Hagigah* 1:8.
17. *Megillah* 22a, *Gittin* 59b.
18. *Berakhot* 49b.
19. *Bava Batra* 47b, *Hullin* 49b, *Arakhin* 14a.
20. *Bava Batra* 65a.
21. *Shabbat* 115a.
22. *Berakhot* 6b.
23. *Hagigah* 4b.
24. *Mo'ed Katan* 28a.

77. Rav Chisda the Priest

1. *Berakhot* 44a, *Hullin* 44b.
2. *Yevamot* 21b.
3. *Berakhot* 43a, *Pesahim* 107a.
4. *Berakhot* 38b.
5. *Shabbat* 10b.
6. *Eruvin* 62b.
7. *Bava Metzia* 7a.
8. *Gittin* 7a. This story is related in a different form in the Jerusalem Talmud (*Sotah* 9:15). There it seems that the Exilarch sent to Rav Chisda to inquire the meaning of the verse "Remove the miter and take off the crown." Rav Chisda interpreted the verse and when Rabbi Jochanan heard it he said, "His name is *Chisda* and his words are full of *chesed.*"
9. *Sanhedrin* 17b.
10. *Gittin* 59b.
11. *Mo'ed Katan* 21a.

12. *Shabbat* 140b.
13. *Pesahim* 113b.
14. *Mo'ed Katan* 28b.
15. *Shabbat* 140b.
16. *Bava Kamma* 91b.
17. *Gittin* 57a.
18. *Menahot* 7a.
19. *Gittin* 62a.
20. *Eruvin* 62b.
21. *Bava Metzia* 33a.
22. *Eruvin* 51a.
23. *Pesahim* 7b.
24. *Berakhot* 28a.
25. *Shabbat* 147a.
26. *Betzah* 14a.
27. *Gittin* 64a.
28. *Shabbat* 82a.
29. *Shabbat* 89a, *Pesahim* 10b, *Ketubbot* 89b.
30. *Shabbat* 10b.
31. *Berakhot* 34a.
32. *Shabbat* 117b.
33. *Eruvin* 65a.
34. *Bava Batra* 111a.
35. *Shabbat* 140b.
36. *Mo'ed Katan* 28a.

78. Rav Jehudah bar Ezekiel

1. *Kiddushin* 81a, *Avodah Zarah* 71a.
2. *Eruvin* 2b, 11a.
3. *Kiddushin* 72b.
4. *Kiddushin* 33b.
5. Jerusalem Talmud *Berakhot* 9:2, *Ta'anit* 1:3.
6. *Kiddushin* 32a.
7. *Ketubbot* 21a, *Hullin* 44a.
8. *Eruvin* 7a, *Yevamot* 18a, *Ketubbot* 12a.
9. *Rosh Hashanah* 38a.
10. *Shabbat* 118b.
11. *Berakhot* 30a.
12. *Berakhot* 20a, *Ta'anit* 24a, *Sanhedrin* 106b.
13. *Berakhot* 36a, *Rosh Hashanah* 24b. The expression *shenana* is found

always where Rav Jehudah differed from his teacher, Shmuel
Yarchina'ah. From the context of the speeches it would seem
that the words were used in a complimentary sense. It may be,
however, that this title was used ironically.

14. *Niddah* 13a.
15. *Ketubbot* 111a.
16. *Berakhot* 22b, *Shabbat* 41a.
17. *Berakhot* 24b.
18. *Ketubbot* 111b.
19. *Kiddushin* 70a, b.
20. *Kiddushin* 70a.
21. *Rosh Hashanah* 23b.
22. *Ketubbot* 111a.
23. *Horayot* 12a.
24. *Hullin* 110a, b.
25. *Sanhedrin* 17b.
26. *Bava Metzia* 38b.
27. *Betzah* 38b.
28. *Shabbat* 77b.
29. *Berakhot* 43b, *Rosh Hashanah* 11a.
30. *Shabbat* 55a.
31. *Shabbat* 152b.
32. *Bava Kamma* 30a.
33. *Ta'anit* 24b.
34. *Bava Metzia* 40a, *Hullin* 94a.
35. *Niddah* 22b.
36. *Bekhorot* 44a.
37. *Gittin* 19b.
38. *Shabbat* 37b.
39. *Yevamot* 39b.
40. *Gittin* 86a.

79. Rabbah bar Nachmani

1. Not to be confused with Rav Huna, the head of the academy in
   Sura, or Rav Huna Rabbah, the contemporary of Rabbi Jehudah
   Hanasi.
2. *Bekhorot* 31a.
3. *Berakhot* 64a, *Horayot* 14a.
4. *Mo'ed Katan* 28a.
5. *Ketubbot* 111a.

6. *Berakhot* 64a.
7. *Bereshit Rabbah* 59:1.
8. *Pesahim* 110b.
9. *Mo'ed Katan* 28a.
10. *Bava Metzia* 86a.
11. *Shabbat* 153a.
12. *Ta'anit* 24b.
13. *Gittin* 60b.
14. *Bava Batra* 8a.
15. *Hullin* 46a.
16. *Bava Metzia* 86a.
17. *Nedarim* 59a.
18. *Ketubbot* 111a.
19. *Gittin* 27a, *Bava Metzia* 18b.
20. *Eruvin* 38b, *Betzah* 28a.
21. *Eruvin* 40b.

80. Rav Joseph bar Chiya

1. *Pesahim* 113b.
2. *Bava Kamma* 87a.
3. *Eruvin* 10a, *Nedarim* 41a.
4. *Menahot* 99a.
5. *Menahot* 87a.
6. *Hagigah* 9b.
7. *Mo'ed Katan* 28a.
8. *Kiddushin* 32b.
9. *Shabbat* 23b, *Eruvin* 19b, *Bava Batra* 31a, *Avodah Zarah* 41a.
10. *Shabbat* 18a, *Eruvin* 29b, *Ketubbot* 81b, *Menahot* 75b.
11. *Hagigah* 13a.
12. *Pesahim* 28a.
13. *Mo'ed Katan* 17a.
14. *Ketubbot* 106a.
15. *Sotah* 49b.
16. *Ketubbot* 111a.
17. *Bava Metzia* 85a.

81. Rabbah bar Rav Huna

1. *Pesahim* 90a, *Bava Batra* 135b.
2. *Shabbat* 82a.
3. *Shabbat* 10a.

4. *Gittin* 46a.
5. *Bava Metzia* 108a.
6. *Mo'ed Katan* 28a.
7. *Sukkah* 10b.
8. *Shabbat* 157b.
9. *Sanhedrin* 5a.
10. *Mo'ed Katan* 25b.

82. Abayei bar Chailil

1. *Horayot* 14a.
2. *Berakhot* 17a.
3. *Shabbat* 134a, *Eruvin* 29b, *Yoma* 75b, *Mo'ed Katan* 12a, *Ketubbot* 10b.
4. *Eruvin* 65a.
5. *Ketubbot* 65a.
6. *Gittin* 45a.
7. *Shabbat* 33a, *Nedarim* 54b.
8. *Berakhot* 33a.
9. *Kiddushin* 33a.
10. *Bava Batra* 22a.
11. *Berakhot* 42a.
12. *Eruvin* 17b.
13. *Pesahim* 25b.
14. *Gittin* 34a.
15. *Kiddushin* 6b.
16. *Bava Kamma* 73a.
17. *Gittin* 34a.
18. *Bava Metzia* 21b.
19. *Berakhot* 19a.
20. *Shabbat* 32a.
21. *Megillah* 7b.
22. *Eruvin* 68b. The law forbidding the carrying of objects from one place to another on the Sabbath was overcome by an *Eruv*. This created an artificial boundary, by wiring the outskirts of the city or town, and thus they were allowed to transport objects from one place to another.
23. *Shabbat* 33a.
24. *Hullin* 133a.
25. *Yoma* 84a.
26. *Avodah Zarah* 28a.

27. *Berakhot* 30b.
28. *Gittin* 60b.
29. *Berakhot* 6b.
30. *Shabbat* 118b.
31. *Ta'anit* 21b.
32. *Kiddushin* 33a.
33. *Yevamot* 76a.
34. *Gittin* 6b.
35. *Shabbat* 119a.
36. *Rosh Hashanah* 18a.

83. Rava bar Joseph bar Chama

1. *Bava Batra* 12b.
2. *Bava Batra* 153a.
3. *Mo'ed Katan* 28a.
4. *Yoma* 23a.
5. *Berakhot* 25b.
6. *Eruvin* 55a.
7. *Berakhot* 17a, *Yoma* 87b.
8. *Ketubbot* 105b.
9. *Yoma* 72b.
10. *Berakhot* 35b. These are not the same as the "lecture months," *Elul* and *Adar,* when the scholars did gather to study the laws of the oncoming holidays.
11. *Gittin* 6a.
12. *Bava Kamma* 119a.
13. *Kiddushin* 73a.
14. *Ta'anit* 20b.
15. *Berakhot* 5b.
16. *Avodah Zarah* 65a.
17. *Shabbat* 10a.
18. *Makkot* 22b.
19. *Ketubbot* 67b.
20. *Sanhedrin* 72a.
21. *Ta'anit* 22a.
22. *Ta'anit* 22b.
23. *Bava Batra* 10b.
24. *Zevahim* 116b.
25. *Avodah Zarah* 19b.
26. *Bava Batra* 97a.

27. *Shabbat* 129a.
28. *Rosh Hashanah* 21a.

84. Rav Nachman bar Isaac

1. We must note here that occasionally sayings have been quoted in the Talmud in the name of Rav Nachman bar Isaac, and these have been confused with those of Rav Nachman bar Jacob.
2. *Pesahim* 105b.
3. *Gittin* 31b.
4. *Eruvin* 43b.
5. *Avodah Zarah* 63a.
6. *Bava Batra* 22a.
7. *Shabbat* 37b.
8. *Berakhot* 35b.
9. *Bava Batra* 87a.
10. *Ta'anit* 21b.
11. *Shabbat* 157b.

85. Rav Papa

1. *Eruvin* 51a, *Pesahim* 111b.
2. *Berakhot* 44b, *Menahot* 71a.
3. *Gittin* 73a.
4. *Berakhot* 58a, *Shabbat* 136a, *Yevamot* 85a.
5. *Berakhot* 56a.
6. *Ketubbot* 106a.
7. *Ketubbot* 97a.
8. *Bava Metzia* 69a.
9. *Berakhot* 8b.
10. *Bava Batra* 9a.
11. *Bava Batra* 10a.
12. *Pesahim* 89b.
13. *Ta'anit* 9b.
14. *Gittin* 73a.
15. *Shabbat* 32a.
16. *Sanhedrin* 95b.
17. *Berakhot* 6a.
18. *Bava Metzia* 59a.
19. *Sanhedrin* 95a.
20. *Sanhedrin* 102b.
21. *Sanhedrin* 94a.

22. *Yevamot* 62a.
23. *Yevamot* 118b.
24. *Gittin* 30b.
25. *Sanhedrin* 105a.
26. *Bava Metzia* 59a.
27. *Yevamot* 63a.
28. *Sanhedrin* 52a.
29. *Yevamot* 63a.
30. *Berakhot* 43a.
31. *Shabbat* 140b.

86. Rav Huna, the Son of Rav Joshua

1. *Pesahim* 111b.
2. *Sanhedrin* 69a.
3. *Rosh Hashanah* 17a.
4. *Avodah Zarah* 12b.
5. *Shabbat* 118b.

87. Rav Chama of Nehardea

1. *Nazir* 20a.
2. *Ketubbot* 86a.
3. *Sanhedrin* 46b.

88. Rav Sheshet

1. *Ketubbot* 69a.
2. *Berakhot* 5a.
3. *Menahot* 95b.
4. *Eruvin* 12a, *Menahot* 39a.
5. *Yevamot* 24b.
6. *Niddah* 69a.
7. *Eruvin* 67a.
8. *Bekhorot* 52b.
9. *Eruvin* 11b, 39b.
10. *Bava Metzia* 35b.
11. *Yevamot* 35a, *Zevahim* 96b.
12. *Ketubbot* 68a.
13. *Sanhedrin* 86a, *Horayot* 9a.
14. *Avodah Zarah* 2b.
15. *Berakhot* 58a.

16. *Berakhot* 57b.
17. *Bava Batra* 9b.
18. *Gittin* 14b.
19. *Gittin* 67b.
20. *Pesahim* 108a.
21. *Menahot* 95b.
22. *Eruvin* 11b.
23. *Gittin* 68a.
24. *Eruvin* 39b.
25. *Berakhot* 46b.
26. *Yevamot* 62b.
27. *Mo'ed Katan* 28a.

89. Rav Ashi, Compiler of the Babylonian Talmud

1. Rav Sherira Gaon, who lived in Babylonia all his life and who wrote the history of its academies, says that Sura is the same as Mata Machasia, although other historians cite proof that they were two separate places. They remark, however, that the two cities were close together. Today of course it is hard to decide this question. Neither of the cities exists any longer and their sites are not even known. It is notable, however, that wherever the name of Rav Ashi is mentioned in the Talmud, it is always in connection with the name of Mata Machasia instead of Sura.
2. *Gittin* 59a, *Sanhedrin* 36a.
3. *Nedarim* 62b.
4. *Berakhot* 17b.
5. *Bava Batra* 3b.
6. *Shabbat* 11a.
7. *Eruvin* 59a.
8. *Zevahim* 19a.

90. Tavyomi Mar bar Rav Ashi

1. *Sanhedrin* 39a.
2. *Hullin* 62b.

91. Ravina, the Final Compiler of the Babylonian Talmud

1. *Bava Metzia* 86a.
2. *Berakhot* 24b.
3. *Eruvin* 63a.

4. *Kiddushin* 9b.
5. *Shabbat* 114a, 119b.
6. *Gittin* 73a.
7. *Menahot* 37b.
8. *Pesahim* 74b, *Hullin* 93b.
9. *Mo'ed Katan* 25b.
10. *Bava Kamma* 119a.
11. *Shabbat* 150b, *Gittin* 34b.

INDEX

Aaron, 67, 84, 200, 240, 424, 425, 467, 497, 599

Abayei bar Chailil, 391, 720, 727–733, 733, 737, 741, 746

Abba. *See* Chiya bar Abba; Kapara, Bar; Simlai bar Abba

Abba (father of R. Simlai), 678

Abba, Rav (disciple of Jehudah Hanasi), 709, 713, 774

Abba Arecha. *See* Rav

Abba bar Abba, 417, 642

Abba bar Kahana, Rabbi, 592, 594

Abba of Acco, Rabbi, 568, 583

Abba Sikra, 152–153

Abba Umna, 733

Abel, 423, 477

Abel, Pales., 539

Abimelech, 425

Abiyah, king of Israel, 595

Abnimos Hagardi, 329, 330

Abraham, 13, 14, 160, 166, 173, 219, 257, 272, 412, 422, 424, 425, 455, 474, 477, 479, 497, 506, 513, 550–551, 558, 589, 647, 664, 698, 699

Absalom, 543, 664

Abstinence, vows of, 19

Abtalion (Jewish leader), 53, 79, 82–84, 85, 86, 95, 96, 97, 100, 108, 111, 118, 120, 779*n*

Abtilas, Rabbi (son of Jose ben Chalafta), 351

Abtolemos (Tanna Rabbi), 348

Academies
 in Palestine, 285–286, 348, 363, 402. *See also* Caesarea; Jabneh; Lud; Shefarom; Usha
 in Babylonia, 404–405, 458, 486–487, 489–491, 554, 580, 592, 597, 598, 611, 612, 642, 695, 757, 761. *See also* Mata Machasia; Mechoza; Nares; Nehardea; Pumbedita; Sura

Acco, Pales., 145, 183

Acha bar Chanina, Rabbi, 595

Acha bar Ivia, Rav, 764

Acha bar Jacob, Rav, 748–749

Acha bar Joseph, Rav, 681

Acha bar Rava, Rav, 764

Achbara (Achbaria), Pales., 514

Acher, 296, 303, 305. *See also* Elisha ben Avuyah

Achi bar Jashiah, Rabbi, 643

Achijah of Shiloh, 522

Adam, 261–262, 301–302, 335, 395, 423, 472, 473, 477, 478, 525–526, 555, 556, 616

Adiabene, kingdom of, 141

Admon ben Gadai (judge), 136–137

Adultery, 11, 423, 507, 590, 609
Aelia Capitolina, 225. *See also*
   Jerusalem
Aggadah, aggadot, 9–10, 126, 219, 230,
   341, 364, 462–463, 469–480, 519,
   520, 536, 537, 540–541, 546, 554,
   563, 571, 576, 581, 586, 592, 602
   authors of ("men of"), 471, 473–479
   definition and purpose of, 469–470
Agriculture
   in Babylonia, 644, 645, 736
   in Egypt, 68–69
   in Palestine, 23, 31, 69, 244, 422,
     430–433, 435
Agrippa. *See* Herod Agrippa
Agunah, 243
Ahab, king of Israel, 172, 347, 544
Ahasuerus, 590
Ahava River, Pales., 563
Akabia ben Mahalalel, 116–120, 171,
   797*n*
Akiba ben Joseph, Rabbi, 172, 188,
   189, 190, 218, 226, 230, 237, 238,
   240, 252, 255, 257–264, 269–279,
   283, 284, 292, 293, 295, 296, 299,
   321–322, 389, 545
   academy of, disciples in, 296, 300,
     305, 328, 329, 330, 334, 336, 342,
     347, 348, 357–358, 367–370
   death of, 261, 262, 269, 277–279, 282,
     296, 333, 336, 372, 593
   education of, 258–259
   and Eliezer ben Hyrcanus, 194–200,
     258–260, 274, 281
   Jewish revolt and, 257, 262–265, 285,
     286
   maxims of, 281, 307–308, 619–620,
     622, 789*n*
   Mishnah and, 15–16, 389, 390
   in prison, 271, 275, 276, 352, 362, 366
   rules of, 270–272, 281
   and Tarphon, R., 246, 247, 248–249
   Torah of, interpretation of, 261–262
   wife of, 258–260
Alexander, as Jewish name, 47, 49
Alexander (son of Aristobolus II), 81,
   87
Alexander Jannai, 71, 72, 73, 74, 77,
   78, 87, 445, 780*n*
Alexander Severus, emperor of Rome,
   455, 469, 493, 749

Alexander the Great, king of
   Macedonia, 7, 37–38, 47–48, 51
Alexandri, Rabbi, 596
Alexandria, Egy., 74, 207, 326, 455, 568
   Greek massacre of Jews in, 145–146
   Jewish community in, 48, 129, 322,
     400
   Jewish revolt in, 441–442
   wheat shipment restrictions from,
     68–69
"Alexandrians," 330, 366
Alfius of Antioch, 750
Alkimos (High Priest), 54, 57
Altars, 8, 159, 424, 619. *See also* Sacri-
   fices
Amalek, 51, 62, 221
Amalekites, 51, 507
Amariah (High Priest), 54
Ambrosius of Milan, 767
Amei aratzim (people of the soil), 23,
   65, 139, 192, 251, 333–334, 342,
   373, 380, 449–451, 521–522, 621,
   782*n*
Amemar (head of Nehardea academy),
   759, 761, 768–769, 770
Ami, Rabbi, 457, 458–459, 461, 488,
   567, 574, 578–585, 587, 593, 594,
   599, 698, 738
Ammonites, 190–191
Amoraim, 10, 393, 394, 403, 404, 417,
   421, 469, 474, 480, 481, 488, 510,
   528, 530, 549, 559, 574, 586, 592,
   802*n*
   of Babylonia, 421, 559, 597, 626, 628,
     771, 772
Amos, 473
Amram, sons of, 552
Amram the Pious, Rav, 686
Anan (High Priest), 137
Angel of Death, 398, 408, 412–413, 535,
   539–540, 542, 589, 595–596, 693,
   706, 720, 756
Angels, 19, 166, 180, 214, 244, 281–282,
   304, 335, 395, 401, 495, 541, 576,
   616
   functions of, 306, 472
   in Gehenna, 543–544
   naming of, 42, 502
Animal husbandry, 422, 423, 433
Animals, 465, 567, 577, 819*n*. *See also*
   Sacrifices; Slaughter

clean vs. unclean, 425
creation of, 472
Antigonos (son of Aristobolus II),
81–82
Antigonos of Socho, 26, 49–51, 53, 71
Antioch, Pales., 338–339, 455, 524, 538
Antiochus III (the Great), king of Syr-
ia, 7
Antiochus IV (Epiphanes), king of
Syria, 39, 51
Antiochus VII (Sidetes), king of Syria,
63, 70
Antipater, procurator of Judea, 80, 81
Antoninus Pius, emperor of Rome,
311, 320, 323, 324, 328–329, 353,
354, 355, 359
and circumcision, allowing of, 442
converted to Judaism, 378, 384
death of, 371, 385
Jehudah Hanasi and, 378, 381–385,
455
Apitropsim (overseers), 435
Aquilas the Proselyte, 222, 784n. *See
also* Onkelos
Arabic language, 475
Arabs, 326
Aramaic language, 52, 112, 202, 226,
391, 443, 613, 698, 724
Aramites, 647, 653, 744, 828n
Arav, Pales., 156, 175, 176
Arbel, valley of, 411
Arbela. *See* Nittai of Arbela
Ardjir, king of Persia, 646
Aristobolus (grandson of Aristobolus
II), 87
Aristobolus I, king of Judea, 71, 72
Aristobolus II, king of Judea, 70, 80,
81, 91–92
Arsikanus (Roman commander), 468
Artaban, king of Parthia, 493, 626, 646,
654, 671
Artaxerxes I, king of Persia, 7
Artaxerxes III, king of Persia, 43–44
Artisans, 434–435, 436, 437, 438, 564
Arukh, 401, 584
Asher, descendents of, 628–629
Ashi, Rav (compiler of Babylonian Tal-
mud), 612, 757–761, 767, 772,
773–774
Ashkelon, Pales., 145, 226, 396
Ashkolot, 57–58

Asi, Rabbi, 459, 488, 567, 574, 578–585,
599, 602, 651, 698, 708, 774
Ass, eating grain, 396–397, 800n
Assembly of the Pious, 58–59
Assyria, 35, 36
Assyrian alphabet, 37, 220
Astrology, 222, 533, 647, 671, 716
Astronomy, 184–185, 372
Atachshaster (Ardeshir), king of
Babylonia, 493
Athens, Elders of, 214, 215
Athletics, 58
Atidius Cornelianus, governor of Pal-
estine, 357
Atirei nekhesin (men of property), 435
Aurelian (Aurelianus), emperor of
Rome, 687
Av, month of, 467, 538
fifteenth day of, 316
ninth day of, 376, 440, 454, 538, 547,
672
Av Beit Din (father of the court), 53,
375
Avahu of Caesarea, Rabbi, 458, 462,
463, 464, 566–573, 576, 581, 587,
594, 600
Avimi (*amora* in Babylonia), 702
Avot Derabi Natan, 120, 154–156, 298,
301, 308–309, 325, 793n
Avuha, Rabbah bar. *See* Rabbah bar
Avuha
Avuyah. *See* Elisha ben Avuyah
Azai. *See* Simeon ben Azai
Azalea, 45, 159
Azariah. *See* Eleazar ben Azariah
Azariah, 285, 558
Azariah, Rabbi, 16, 252
Aziz, Pales., 237–238

Baal Habayit (peasants), 435
Baba. *See* Jehudah ben Baba
Baba ben Buta, Rabbi, 112, 333
Babylonia, 5, 34, 65, 87, 290, 502, 587,
594
geographical description, 643–645
Jewish communities, 45, 87, 95, 112,
160, 323, 347, 400, 520, 601,
610–612, 642–646, 694, 697. *See also*
Academies; Calendar; Courts;
Scholars)

administration of, 679–680
in time of *amoriam*, 421, 559, 597, 626, 628, 771, 772
feast days of, 562
and migrations to and from Palestine, 580, 592, 594, 611, 634–638, 694, 709
safe from Roman persecution, 311–312, 320–323, 329, 362–363, 611
Sassanid persecutions in, 718–720, 767–770
and scholarship in Christian era, 463–464, 466, 554, 592, 697
Simeon ben Gamaliel II's mission to, 321–322, 792n
Parthian rule in, 354, 492, 766
Persian rule in, 43–44, 607, 626, 647, 766
and revolt against Romans (*ca.* 130 C.E.), 441–442
Sassanid rule in, 493–494, 646, 670, 674, 718–720, 737–738, 748, 751, 757, 761
Babylonian exile, 9, 42, 51–52, 92, 93, 158, 160, 490, 503–504, 607, 608, 610, 709
Babylonian Talmud, 4, 136, 490, 511, 554, 567, 582, 583, 612–625, 669, 729, 792n
compilers of, 612, 740–741, 759–761, 767, 768, 771–774
vs. Jerusalem Talmud, 392, 393, 774
language of, 613
teachings of, 614–625
Bagases (Persian official), 43–44
Balaam ben Beor (prophet), 221, 522, 596
Bamah, bamot, 69–70, 325
Bana'ah, Rabbi, 482
Bar Kapara. *See* Kapara
Bar Kochba, Simeon. *See* Kochba
Barnezer Odenate. *See* Odenatus.
Barur Chail, Pales., 163
Barzilai the Gileadite, 664–665
Bat kol (divine voice), 113, 150, 194, 204, 388, 401–410, 504, 536, 540, 543, 552, 780n–781n, 782n
Baths, 48, 426, 448, 454
Bathyra. *See* Jehudah b. Bathyra

Bathyra, Men of, 86–87, 94, 103, 104, 105, 150, 376
Bati bar Tobia, 710
Batiach, Ben, 154
Beards, 473, 526, 813n
Beer, beer making, 646
Bei Avidan, 210–211, 289, 671, 783n, 788n
Benjamin, tribe of, 627
Benjamin of Tudela, 586
Berachiah, Rabbi, 480
Beraita, beraitot, 323, 362, 387, 400, 401, 406, 416, 502, 517, 536, 692, 759, 763, 792n
of Hezekiah, 511
Oshaiah Rabbah and, 524
Beraita of the Secrets of the Leap Year (Shmuel Yarchina'ah), 678
Berakhot, 386
Berenice (Idumean princess), 144, 148, 149, 160, 440
Beruriah (wife of R. Meir), 328, 337–338, 339–340
Betar, Pales., 267, 269, 439, 444
siege of, 39, 263, 268, 275, 280, 328, 370
Bet Din, 61
Beth El, 35, 36
Beth Yazek, 125
Bible, 4–5, 7, 15, 63, 494, 698, 699. *See also* Torah
books excluded from, 191, 782n
Hebrew language in, 389, 724
New Testament, 25, 471
Onkelos' Greek translation of, 225–226, 724
Pharisaic customs regarding, 29
study of, in Christian era, 462, 463, 472–474, 478
Bikkurim (food offerings), 255
Birds, 212, 413, 594
Biri, Pales., 454
Birkat haminim (prayer against disbelievers), 150
Bisa, Rabbi, 525
Bitter herbs, 192
Blacksmith. *See* Yitzchak the Blacksmith
Bnei Brak, Pales., 262, 265, 292
Boetus, 26, 50, 137
Boetusians, 50. *See also* Sadducees

Brides, dancing before, 113
Burial customs, 50–51, 126, 748–749
Byzantium, 764

Caesarea, Pales., 123, 124–125, 145, 278, 287, 382, 462, 482, 529, 536, 538, 583
  academy in, 525, 567, 568, 569, 571, 587–588, 640
Cain, 423, 477
Calendar, 8, 350, 455, 458–459, 466, 468, 592. *See also* Feast days
  in Babylonia, 464, 466–467, 547, 562, 678, 742–743
  Hillel II's reforms of, 739
  Jabneh codifications of, 150, 151, 186
  Jehudah Hanasi's reforms of, 375
  Judea, determination in, 405–407, 455, 525
  leap years, 276, 318, 321, 322, 330, 458, 464, 466, 467, 547, 549, 572, 678, 739
  new month and, 125, 150, 375
    new moon and, 458, 466–467, 495, 525
    testimony on beginning, 125
  permanent, 468
  thirteen-month, 126, 263
Caligula, emperor of Rome, 122, 123
Cappadocia, 671
Capital punishment, 232, 250, 315, 428, 437–438
Caracalla, emperor of Rome, 515
Castration, 423, 442
Cattle breeding, herding, 645
Chabar, 828n
Chailil. *See* Abayei bar Chailil
Chalafta. *See* Jose ben Chalafta; Simeon ben Chalafta
Chalafta, Rabbi, 347–348
Chaldean language, 391, 724
Chaldeans, 326, 492, 766
Chama bar Abba, Rabbi, 496
Chama bar Bisa, Rabbi, 524, 525
Chama bar Chanina, Rabbi, 595
Chama bar Guria, Rabbi, 648, 653, 827n
Chama of Nehardea, Rav, 748–751, 753
Chamor, sons of, 422, 479
Chanamel (High Priest), 87

Chanan ben Avi Shalom (judge), 136, 137
Chananiah, 285, 558
Chananiah. *See* Joshua ben Chananiah
Chananiah, Rabbi (nephew of R. Joshua ben Chananiah), 320–323
Chananiah ben Hezekiah, 115, 128
Chananiah ben Hiskia, Rabbi, 782n
Chanina, Rabbi, Deputy to the High Priest, 134–136, 171
Chanina bar Chama, Rabbi, 383, 416–417, 464, 482, 485, 497, 500, 519, 528–534, 559, 574, 593, 633, 634, 640
Chanina bar Papa, Rabbi, 594–596
Chanina ben Chachinai, 291–293
Chanina ben Dosa, Rabbi, 175–181, 781n
Chanina ben Teradion, Rabbi, 282, 286, 287–288, 289, 290, 328, 333, 334, 336, 337, 786n
Chanukah, origin of, 61
Chanut, Pales., Sanhedrin moved to, 122
Charity, 19, 124, 138, 161, 174, 181, 229, 239, 244–245, 249, 271–272, 346, 451, 495, 516–517, 532, 589, 595, 631, 666, 682, 696, 744, 773
  Hillel's rule of, 19
  as Jews' duty, 615, 618
  Usha regulations regarding, 234–235
Chassidim, 30
Chastity, 623. *See also* Women
Cherubim, 8
Children, 16. *See also* Education; Schools
  fasting on Day of Atonement, 108–109, 411
  fathers' responsibility toward, 234, 235, 342, 620–621
  favoritism toward, 13
  illegitimate, 332, 485
  naming of, 629
  Persian capture of, 769
  punishment of, 235
  reasoning abilities of, 783n
  of slaves, 438, 653
  sons
    disobedient, law of, 254
    firstborn, 424
Chisda, Rav, 486, 598, 628, 683,

694–695, 700–706, 711, 717, 721,
      725, 726, 735, 741, 748, 752, 753,
      755, 837n
Chiya. See also Huna bar Chiya; Joseph
      bar Chiya
Chiya (son of Rav), 632, 642, 665, 707
Chiya bar Abba I (Chiya Rabbah the
      Great, disciple of Jehudah
      Hanasi), Rabbi, 10, 376–378,
      404–408, 410, 411, 412, 501, 504,
      510, 511, 530, 536, 562, 571, 611,
      624
   academy at Tiberias, 406, 636–637
   ancestry, 404, 627
   beraitot of, 524
   death of, 408, 638
   family of, 407, 627, 629
   and Jehudah Hanasi, 405–406, 408,
      636, 638, 726
   laws and rulings of, 406
   legends about, 407–408
   occupation of, 407, 621, 625–626
   in Palestine, 627, 635–638
   pupils and disciples of, 453, 514, 519
   and Rav (Abba Arecha), 627–628,
      631, 633, 634
Chiya bar Abba II, Rabbi, 404, 459,
      490, 574–577, 581, 583, 599–600
Chiya bar Ashi, Rabbi, 593
Chiya bar Joseph, Rabbi, 653
Chiya bar Rav Medafti, 744
Choni the Circle Drawer, 89–93
Chovlim, 527
Christianity, 122, 225, 382, 566
   and Bible, interpretation of, 462,
      471–473, 478
   as Jewish sect, 250, 455, 462, 471
   and Sabbath, postponement of, 548
   spread of, in Palestine, 566
   as state religion, 462, 762–764
Christians, 17, 250, 455, 580, 788n
   circumcision and, 471, 473
   Diocletian's persecution of, 459
   Essenes and, 30
   Jewish. See Minim
   persecution of Jews, 468
   and Samaritans, 580
   Sassanide persecutions of, 493
Chronicles, Book of, 628
Cilicia (Asia Minor), 468
Circumcision, 25, 58, 142, 298, 304,

324, 351, 384, 412, 465, 525–526
   Christian repudiation of, 471, 473
   origin of law of, 424, 425
   Roman prohibition of, 295, 356, 371,
      372, 442
Cities, 442–449, 451, 459
Claudius, emperor of Rome, 123, 131
Claudius (guerrilla leader), 641
Cleanliness. See Purity, laws of
Cloth making, 422, 433
Clothing, apparel, 448. See also Gar-
      ments
Coins, 267
Commodus, emperor of Rome, 640
Compensation. See also "Eye for an
      eye"
   after death, 19–20, 50
   monetary, 8–9, 51, 104
Constantine I (the Great), emperor of
      Rome, 462, 465, 467, 582
Constantine II, emperor of Rome, 462,
      468
Constantinople, 466
Constantius, emperor of Rome, 730,
      749
Court of the Hasmoneans, 60–62
Courts, 138–141, 355, 423, 445, 447,
      507, 573, 763, 764. See also False
      witnesses; Sanhedrin
   in Babylonia, 592, 689
   fair judgment in, 520–521
   Gentiles in, 315
   Jewish revolt and, 440–441
   judges, conduct of, 8, 136, 395, 507,
      689–690, 695–696
   oaths in, 140–141
Creation of world and man, 18, 212,
      299, 307, 327, 330, 350, 360,
      472–473, 478, 522–523, 548, 555,
      564, 565, 569, 570–571, 585, 614,
      616, 658
Crete, 762
Ctesiphon (Ktensiphon), Persia, 687
Customs (minhagim), 388–389
Cyprus, 441
Cyrenaica, 441
Cyrus, king of Persia, 36, 42

Dama ben Nathina, 204
Daniel, 453, 558

Darius III (the Mede), king of Persia, 47, 558

David, House of, 35, 84, 182, 233, 344, 371, 374, 376, 460, 610, 611, 616, 627, 680
  restoration of, 20, 99

David, king of Judah and Israel, 17, 240, 318, 401, 404, 473, 474, 479, 480, 539, 570, 619, 627, 637, 654, 664–665

Day of Atonement (Yom Kippur), 28, 45, 48, 134, 156, 231, 244, 281, 349, 477, 488, 572, 739, 785n
  children fasting on, 108–109, 411
  girls' parade on, 316
  postponement of, 549, 816n
  Sabbath observance of, 495
  violations of, 170–171, 711–712

Day of Judgment, 24, 212–213, 385, 399

Dead, uncleanliness of, 50–51, 55–56. See also Resurrection of the dead

Dead Sea, 433, 434

Death. See also Angel of Death; Burial customs; Mourning customs
  life after, 647. See also Gehenna; Paradise
  omens accompanying, 298
  Roman persecutions and view of, 332–333
  Torah's protection from, 157
  witnesses to, 125, 140

Death sentence, 254, 277, 281, 295. See also Capital punishment

Decapolis, Pales., 444

Deceit, 617–618. See also Falsehood

Demai, 66, 192, 782n

Demetrius Soter, king of Macedonia, 54

Deputy of High Priest, office of, 134

Derash (exposition of Torah), 789n

Derashah, derashot, 388, 391

Deuteronomy, Book of, 124, 212, 240, 241, 245, 484, 551, 576, 617, 659, 699

Diakora, Babyl., 694

Diaspora, 527, 562, 626, 657, 711, 767

Dietary laws, 138, 159, 231, 255, 318, 319, 372, 681, 711–712
  Essene, 31, 32–33
  meat, eating of, 423, 432
  Mishnaic law, 390

Pharisaic, 23

Dinah, 25

Dio Cassius, 263, 264, 266, 445

Diocletian, emperor of Rome, 459–460, 465, 575, 582

Disciples, R. Gamaliel's types of, 126

Diseases, 451, 527, 547, 644. See also Medicine

Disobedient sons, law on, 254

Disputing ground. See Bei Avidan

Dissenting elder, law of the, 75, 120, 678

Divine Chariot, 161–162, 183, 206, 299, 560, 782n

Divorce, 78, 125, 192, 242–243, 253, 254, 331–332, 358, 438, 448, 651, 675, 704, 731
  of deaf women, 169
  grounds for, 659
  Hillel's vs. Shammai's rulings on, 113–114

Divorce certificates, 29, 583

Documents, 135, 141, 315

Doeg the Edomite, 543

Dogs, 450, 665

Domitian, emperor of Rome, 202, 442

Dosa. See Chanina ben Dosa

Dosa ben Harkinas, Rabbi, 171–172, 269

Dowries, dower rights (ketubbah), 253, 315, 331, 425, 675

Drawing of water, festival of, 205–206

Dybbuks, 356

Eber, academy of, 497

Ebionim, 788n

Ecclesiastes, Book of, 191, 297, 307, 466, 638, 782n

Eden, garden of, 472, 478

Edom, 557, 641, 828n. See also Rome

Edomites, 365

Education, 78, 101–102, 308–309, 439, 620–621, 623–625, 664. See also Academies; Schools

Eduyot (Mishnah tractate), 389

Egypt, 326, 327, 432, 433, 441. See also Alexandria
  agriculture, 70–71
  Jewish communities in, 45, 317, 422–423
  Jewish enslavement in, exodus from,

15, 16, 62, 231, 255–256, 265–266,
300–301, 365, 368, 400, 422, 506,
517, 664
Persian invasion of, 43
Pharisees' refuge in, 73–74, 76, 82
Syria, wars with, 51, 58
ten plagues in, 203, 267
Ein T'enah, Pales., 409
Ein Tuv, Judea, 406, 525
Elai. See Jehudah bar Elai
Elai, Rabbi, 341–342
Elam, land of, 327
Elasha, Ben, Rabbi, 377, 411–412
Elders
  ordination of, 121
  regulations of the, 387
Elders of Athens, 214, 215
Eleazar. See also Jonathan ben Eleazar
Eleazar, Rabbi (son of Jose ben
  Chalafta), 351, 356
Eleazar, Rabbi (son of Simeon ben
  Yochai), 353, 358, 360, 369
Eleazar ben Arach, Rabbi, 161–162,
  183, 328, 368
Eleazar ben Azariah, Rabbi, 188, 189,
  199, 228–235, 236, 238, 252, 253,
  300
Eleazar ben Parta, Rabbi, 287, 288–289,
  788n
Eleazar ben Pedat, Rabbi, 485,
  496–497, 505, 559–565, 575, 580,
  587, 599, 683
  aggadic statements of, 563
  charity of, 561, 563–564
  and Jochanan, R., 559–560
  legal interpretations, 561–562
  maxims, 563–565
  pupils, 567
Eleazar ben Poirah, 66, 67
Eleazar ben Shamua, Rabbi, 362–365,
  372
Eleazar ben R. Simeon ben Yochai, 641
Eleazar ben Simeon, Rabbi, 318
Eleazar ben Zadok, Rabbi, 167
Eleazar Chisma, Rabbi, 189
Eleazar Hakapar, Rabbi, 399–400, 401
Eleazar Harsina, Rabbi, 293–294
Elephants, 577, 819n
Eli (High Priest), 564, 593
  descendents of, 157, 474, 514, 717,
  733

Eliezer, Rabbi, 23, 41
Eliezer, Rabbi (son of R. Jose of
  Galilee), 103, 370
Eliezer ben Hyrcanus, Rabbi, 152, 162,
  165, 185, 188, 192, 193–204,
  206–207, 212, 213, 223, 224, 225,
  237, 240, 304–305, 623, 777n
  and Akiba ben Joseph, 194–200,
  258–260, 274, 279
  character of, 197
  disciples of, 193–197, 324, 341
  maxims of, 198, 204
  on prayer, 201
Eliezer of Modiin, Rabbi, 217–221,
  230–231, 291
  death of, 268
Elijah (prophet), 173, 278, 289, 331,
  339, 349, 353, 379, 408, 590–591,
  648, 686, 698–699, 754
  and Joshua ben Levi, 535, 538–539,
  540, 542
Elisha. See Ishmael ben Elisha
Elisha ben Avuyah ("Acher"), 200–201,
  295–296, 303–310, 329, 330, 331,
  334, 544
Elohim (God), 555–558
Encyclopedists, 56–57
Enosh, generation of, 477
Ephes, Rabbi, 417, 500, 524, 529, 534
Ephraim, tribe of, 35, 36
Epiphanos (church-father), 461
Epistle of Rav Sherira Gaon, 680, 684,
  695
Erroneous, books of the, 303–304
Eruv, eruvin, 14, 501, 732, 755,
  840n
Esaradon, 36
Esau, 477, 491, 526–527
  children of, 364
Essenes, 21, 30–33, 107
Esther, Book of, 450–451
Euphrates River, 611, 642, 643–644,
  791n, 807n
Eusebius of Caesarea (church-father),
  459, 465
Eve, 395, 474, 513, 555, 556
Evil nature and desires, 19, 379, 380,
  480, 548, 564, 588, 615, 616–617.
  See also Suffering
Excommunication, 548
Exilarch of Babylonia, 320, 323, 376,

378, 510, 562, 611, 626, 627,
679–680, 684–685, 692, 759
Exodus, Book of, 241, 281, 612, 703,
704. *See also* Egypt, Jewish
enslavement in
"Eye for an eye" commandment, 8–9,
28, 51, 104
Ezekiel. *See* Jehudah bar Ezekiel
Ezekiel (prophet), 161, 450
Ezekiel, Book of, 457, 701, 782*n*
Ezra the Scribe, 7, 11, 37, 54, 65, 220,
229, 405, 504, 563, 608, 610, 709

Fairs, 449
Faith, 615, 616, 623
Falsehood, 488
False witnesses, 28, 75, 76–77, 140,
335, 350, 729, 731
Families, racial purity of, 708–710
Famines, 145, 147–148, 373, 547
Farm workers, 435, 437. *See also Amei
aratzim*
Farmers, farming, 110, 192, 430–431,
434, 435, 564. *See also* Agriculture
contract, 436
tithes and, 65–66
Fasting, fast days, 19, 164–165, 351,
376, 428, 454, 457, 458, 474, 507,
527, 599, 657–658, 672
by children, on Day of Atonement,
108–109
Roman prohibition, 600
Sabbath prohibition, 579
Fathers
grandfathers called, 237
honoring of, 204, 312. *See also* Parents
responsibilities of, toward children,
234, 235, 342, 620–621
Feast days, 9, 321–322, 468, 495, 572.
See also Fasting
Babylonian Jews and, 562
Hasmonean innovations, 62
Jehudah Hanasi's reforms, 376
Mishnah on, 390
postponement of, 549, 816*n*
prohibited activities on, 583
sacrifices on, 54–55
two-day duration, 562
Feast of Lights. *See* Chanukah
Feast of Tabernacles. *See* Sukkot

Feast of Weeks. *See Shavuot*
Firstborn sons, 424
Fishing, 434
Flattery, 564
Flood, the, 41, 221, 423–424, 477
Flowers, correspondence of, 383
Food. *See also Bikkurim;* Dietary laws;
Passover; *Pe'ah*
blessings over, 48, 191
in cities vs. villages, 449
Hasmonean restrictions on, 65
Rav's pronouncements on, 654
renouncing of, after destruction of
Jerusalem, 206–207
Fortified cities, 443–444, 447
Fowl, raising of, 433
Frankincense, 27–28
Free will, 18, 24, 27, 269, 614, 617
Friends of the Greeks, 58
Fruit trees, 92, 244, 427, 432–433, 438,
478, 483, 644

Gabala, Pales., 575
Gabiha ben Pasisa, 48
Gabriel (angel), 42, 472
Galianus, emperor of Rome, 578, 687
Galilean fools, 251
Galilee. *See* Jose of Galilee
Galilee, 156, 363, 458, 525, 555
agriculture of, 431, 432, 433, 435
anti-Samaritan revolt in, 131, 132
inhabitants of, 251
Jewish revolt in, 147, 266, 267
refugees in, 252, 363
speech accent of, 629–630
Galilee, Sea of, 434
Gallus, emperor of Rome, 462
Galus (Roman commander), 146
Galuta, Resh, Exilarch in Babylonia,
626–627, 628, 629
Gamaliel. *See* Simeon ben Gamaliel
Gamaliel I of Jabneh (the Elder),
Rabban, 112–113, 121, 124–127,
153, 165–166, 178, 182, 236, 348,
624
Gamaliel II of Jabneh, Rabban, 163,
182–192, 195, 198–199, 201, 207,
211, 219, 226–230, 233, 247–248,
260, 262, 284, 293, 312, 316, 341,
348, 374
as astronomer, 184–185

impeachment of, 187–189, 236
innovations of, 190–191, 315–316
vs. Joshua ben Chananiah, 185–189
land management of, 435–436
money lending and, 184
slaves and, 184, 438
Gamaliel III (son of Jehudah Hanasi),
Rabbi, 376, 416, 452, 453, 529, 542,
621, 637, 638, 639, 640, 678
Gamaliel IV, Rabbi, 457–458, 569
Gamaliel V, Rabbi, 461, 464, 465–466,
762, 763
Gamaliel VI, Rabbi, 464, 466, 762,
764–765
Gaon of Vilna, 224, 784n
Garments
in cities vs. villages, 449
for Sabbath, 557
for sacrifices, 244
of scholars, 625
Gates, to cities, 446, 447
Gedaliah ben Achikam, 36
Gehenna, 244, 273, 307, 475–476, 506,
518, 526, 537
Joshua ben Levi in, 542–543
Gemara, 394, 410, 651, 760, 774. *See also*
Mishnah
Genealogies, Book of *(Yuhasin)*, 282,
366, 367
Genesis, Book of, 477, 526, 699, 704
Gennesaret. *See* Galilee, Sea of
Gentiles, 213, 436, 454, 484, 555, 567,
577
converts to Judaism. *See* Judaism;
Proselytes
and education of children, 623–624
in Jewish courts, 315
and natural science, 372–373
robbing of, 191–192
scholars among, 161
Geresh, Babyl., 664
Gerizim, Mount, Samaritan temple on,
36–39, 40, 45, 47–48, 49, 64–65, 375
Germans, Germanic tribes, 355, 588,
749
Gershom Meor Hagolah, Rabenu, 368
Gevurah (name of God), 17, 614
Gilead, 433
Gilgal, Pales., 291
Gimso, Pales., 172
Ginai River, Pales., 397–398

Gira (daughter of Antoninus Pius), 383
Glass vessels, purification of, 55–56
Gneiva (student), 682–683
Gnostics, Gnosticism, 304
Goats, keeping of, 283
God, 17–20, 141, 171, 215, 225, 243,
299, 399, 412, 478, 572. *See also*
Creation of world and man;
Shekhinah
anger of, 522
attitudes toward, 302
attributes of, 652
Babylonian Talmud on, 615–615, 618,
622
as builder of Jerusalem, 191
corporeal forms of, 17, 614
duties toward, 615
fear and love of, 13–14
Gnostic view of, 304
and the Jewish nation, 51
names of, 17, 472, 555–556, 614, 652,
803n–804n. *See also* Shem
Hameforash
omniscience of, 19
Patriarchs' intercession with, 550–553
Pharisaic beliefs about, 24
Sadducean beliefs about, 27
and suffering, cause of, 208–209
unity of, 18
Gog and Magog, wars of, 19, 401, 616
Golden calf, 109, 513, 537
Goldfaden, Abraham, 821n
Good deeds, 13, 24, 231, 309, 310,
379–380, 521, 532, 568–569, 617
of parents, 616
recording of, 306
Graetz (historian), 455, 515
Grandfathers, 237, 453
Great Academy (Jerusalem), 126
Great Court. *See* Sanhedrin
Great Mishnayot, 524
Great Synagogue (Jerusalem), 5, 6–9,
10, 37, 45, 61
Greek culture, 17, 429, 614
Greek customs, 58
Greek language, 52, 372, 391, 400, 454,
487
Greek names, 49–50, 785n
Greek philosophy, 303, 309, 329, 749
Greek religion, 28, 56, 329, 614,
749–750

Greek translations of Scripture, 202, 225–226, 314, 348, 724
Greeks, 455, 594
  in Alexandria, 145–146, 441
  and the Jewish revolt, 145–146
  and Palestine, occupation of, 21, 26, 39, 51, 55–56, 59–65, 640
  Sassanid persecution of, 493
  Syrian, 30, 52, 59, 63–64, 607
Guerrilla warfare, 289–290. *See also* Robber bands
Guests, receiving of, 316
Guphia, 293
Gevihah, Rav, 774

Hadrian, emperor of Rome, 341, 462, 634, 770
  and circumcision, prohibition of, 442
  death of, 348, 367
  decrees of, 211, 212, 218, 280, 295, 372, 382
  Jewish revolts under, 267–269, 280, 311, 320, 329, 352, 441. *See also* Kochba, Simeon bar
  and Joshua ben Chananiah, 210–215, 217–218, 222–226
  and Onkelos the Proselyte, 222, 223, 224, 225, 226, 784*n*
  successors to, 355, 356
  and Temple, rebuilding of, 210, 211, 213, 217–218, 442, 750
Haftarot, 659
Haggadah, Passover, 272
Haggai (prophet), 7, 263, 781*n*
Haifa, Pales., 145
Hair cutting, 46, 428, 473, 615
Hakanah. *See* Nechunia ben Hakanah
Hakapar. *See* Eleazar Hakapar
Hakatan. *See* Shmuel Hakatan
Hakham, title of, 312, 313, 375, 608
Halakhah, halakhot, 9, 10, 126, 341, 364, 401, 479, 486, 492, 508, 519, 571, 581, 587
  codification of, 171, 388, 390–391
  decline of scholarship in, 463, 464, 469
  of Jannai Rabbah, 514
  origin of customs in, 388
Halitzah, 113, 159, 232, 275–276, 365–366, 415, 501. *See also* Marriage, levirate

Hallel (prayer), 572
Haman, 590
Hammurabi, king of Babylonia, 642
Hamnuna the Scribe, Rav, 529, 656, 695, 726, 737
Hanan the Egyptian, Rabbi, 291
Hannah, 564
Hanukka. *See* Chanukah
Hapharaim, 432
Harkinas. *See* Dosa ben Harkinas
Hasmoneans, 52, 59, 100, 431. *See also* Maccabees
  Court of the, 60–61
  under Herod I, 83–84, 85, 87, 88, 710
  religious innovations, 64–67
  revolt against Greeks, 21, 26, 30, 60–62, 146, 610
Hatred, sin of, 619
Havdalah, 12, 48, 345, 460, 644
Hazakah. See Posession, laws of
Healing, 167, 178–179, 244, 353–354, 413, 496–497, 528. *See also* Medicine
  Essene customs of, 30, 31, 32
Hebrew language, 51–52, 331, 400, 620
  Jehudah Hanasi's attempts to establish, 372
  and the *Mishnah*, 391
  script form of, 37, 219–220, 671
  and vowel signs in Bible, 389
Hebrew names, 785*n*
Helbo, Rav, 698, 699
Helene, queen of Adiabene, 141–142
Heliogabalus (Elagabalus), emperor of Rome, 515
Hellenist movement, 27, 49–50
Herbs, 192, 413, 519. *See also* Sabbath
Heretics, books of, 303–304
Herod I (the Great), king of Judea, 82–88, 94, 99–100, 101, 107, 110, 123, 710
  persecutions of Hasmoneans by, 87, 88
  and the Sanhedrin, 85, 86, 87–88, 94, 112
Herod Agrippa I, king of Judea, 115, 123–125, 127
Herod Agrippa II, king of Judea, 131, 137, 143–144, 146, 148, 149, 160, 238, 780*n*

Herod Antipas, tetrarch of Galilee, 71, 354

Hesichius (Roman consul), 763

Hezekiah (guerrilla leader), 83

Hezekiah (son of R. Chiya), 378, 510–513, 634, 640

Hezekiah, king of Judah, 401, 480

Hieronymus (church-father), 226, 382, 466

High Priest, office of, 6–7, 8, 26, 28, 43, 131–132, 237, 238–239, 294, 785n–786n. *See also* Nasi, office of
deputy of, 134
trials of, 456, 457
selling of, 131

Hillel (brother of Jehudah N'siah I), 453, 454

Hillel, dynasty of, 155, 182, 452, 460, 466, 546

Hillel, school of, 10, 13, 108, 109, 112–115, 146, 150, 190, 193, 211, 489
and *Mishnah*, compiling of, 387
and Roman rule, 114–115

Hillel I of Babylon (the Old), 53, 86, 94–106, 116, 121, 127, 229, 237, 284, 374, 389, 405, 504, 556, 675, 677, 774
ancestry of, 99
and charity, 97
on learning, 101–102
maxims of, 19, 97, 100–101, 455, 615
on oral vs. written law, 102
patience of, 97–99
pupils of, 99, 100, 109, 111, 155–157, 312
on religious questions, 86, 95, 105–106
rules of logic of, 103–106, 778n–779n
vs. Shammai's teachings, 107–113
and Torah, renewal of, 100, 102, 103
and unjust suffering, 101

Hillel II, Rabbi, 464, 465, 467, 468, 779
calendrical reforms of, 739

Holidays. *See* Feast days; individual days

Holy Ark, 381, 474

Holy Congregation, 394

Holy of Holies, 28, 44, 238

Holy Spirit, 781n

Honesty, 617

Honorius, emperor of Rome, 466

Hosea, Book of, 457, 473–474, 490

Huma (wife of Abayei bar Chailil), 730

Human bones, profaning the Temple, 40–41, 213

Humility, 622

Huna (son of Rav Joshua), Rav, 743, 744, 756–757

Huna bar Abin, Rav, 739

Huna bar Chiya, Rav, 715–716

Huna bar Nathan, Rav, exilarch of Babylonia, 761

Huna Mari bar Mar Zutra, 769–770

Huna of Diakora, Rav (head of academy in Sura), 689, 693, 694, 699, 700, 701, 708, 710, 713, 717, 721, 725, 735, 736

Huna Rabbah, Rav, exilarch of Babylonia, 376–377, 598, 611–612, 627, 629, 680, 681, 682, 683, 685, 694, 695

Hunting, 433–434, 480, 665

Hutzel, Babyl., 643

Hutzpit the Interpreter, Rabbi, 284, 293, 309

Hypnotism, healing by, 496

Hyrcanus. *See* Eliezer ben Hyrcanus; Jochanan the High Priest; Jochanan Hyrcanus II

Ibo ben R. Acha Karsela, 627

Ibur (thirteen-month year), 263

Idol worship, 7–8, 40, 55, 56, 199, 427, 563, 564, 619, 638

Idumea, Idumeans, 64, 79, 80, 85, 129, 137, 142, 335, 434

Ifra Hurmiz, queen of Persia, 719, 737–738

Igeret bat Machlat (queen of evil spirits), 180

Ikonomusin (managers), 435

Ima Salim (wife of Eliezer ben Hyrcanus), 195

Inheritance laws, 13, 234, 435, 485, 753
and Nasi, office of, 316
origin of, 425
Sadducean, 28
for widows and orphans, 675

Iron, in altar construction, 159, 619

Isaac (patriarch), 255–256, 272, 474, 477, 497, 513, 589

Isaac (son of Jehudah bar Ezekiel), 709
Isaiah (prophet), 307, 450, 472, 473,
477, 479
Isaiah, Book of, 236–237, 307, 401, 406,
520, 550, 724
Ishmael, Rabbi (son of Jose ben
Chalafta), 349, 351, 375, 641
Ishmael, descendents of, 425, 641,
838*n*
Ishmael ben Elisha (High Priest), 103,
132, 136, 171, 236–245, 252, 324,
325, 329, 389
academy of, disciples of, 242, 342,
348
death of, 281, 282
laws and moral teachings of, 103,
242–245
ransom of, 236–237
Ishmael ben Phabi (High Priest), 131,
238, 785*n*
Ishmaelites, 78, 326
Ishmael the High Priest (grandfather
of Ishmael ben Elisha), 236, 238,
241–242
Israel, 238, 267, 273, 326, 327, 331, 347,
549
Israelites, 32, 35, 478, 512
Izates II, king of Adiabene, 142

Jabneh, Pales., 112–113, 126, 219, 230,
236, 247, 251, 252, 342, 343, 359,
439
academy in, 158–159, 162, 164, 232
pilgrimages to, 158
as sanctuary during Roman revolt,
143, 148–152, 162, 164, 370
Sanhedrin at, 149, 151, 182–183, 189,
193, 262, 284, 285, 343
Sanhedrin leaves, 232–233
Jacob. *See* Nachman bar Jacob, Rav
Jacob (patriarch), 272, 281, 375, 422,
424, 425, 477, 479, 491, 497, 513,
527, 558, 566
Jacob ben Dostai, Rabbi, 433
Jacob Minaa, 580
Jacob the Miller, Rabbi, 547
Jaddua, 777*n*
Jannai, 780*n*. *See also* Alexander Jannai
Jannai Rabbah (the Old), Rabbi, 461,
482, 502, 511, 514–518, 555, 681
Jehonadab ben Recheb, 347

Jehoshaphat, king of Judea, 54
Jehoyachin, king of Judea, 42
Jehu, king of Israel, 347
Jehudah (son of R. Chiya), 378,
510–513, 634, 640
Jehudah, Rav (pupil of Rav and
Shmuel Yarchina'ah), 685, 686
Jehudah bar Chanina, Rabbi, 508
Jehudah bar Elai, Rabbi, 234, 283, 332,
341–346, 367, 372, 586, 792*n*
education of, 343
maxims of, 342–343
modesty and piety of, 344–345
and Rome, attitude toward, 343–344
Jehudah bar Ezekiel, Rabbi, 548,
598–600, 613, 689, 692–693, 700,
707–714, 716, 721, 730, 738, 838*n*
Jehudah bar Simeon (ben Pazi),
476–479
Jehudah ben Baba, Rabbi, 282,
283–284, 289, 328, 347, 352
Jehudah ben Bathyra I, Rabbi, 118, 120
Jehudah ben Bathyra II, Rabbi, 320,
322, 323, 324, 362, 670
Jehudah ben Gadidiah, 66–67, 68
Jehudah ben Gerim, Rabbi, 343, 344,
353
Jehudah ben Nehemiah, Rabbi, 247
Jehudah ben Tabbai, 53, 72–76, 79
Jehudah Hanasi, Rabbi, 308, 316, 336,
349, 350, 369, 370, 391–393, 415,
469–470, 488, 506, 515, 517, 525,
546–547, 548, 593, 611–612, 624,
627, 636, 637, 638, 670, 726, 773,
792*n*
ancestry of, 371, 374, 376, 404
and anger, outbursts of, 376–378, 408
and animals, kindness toward, 381
and Antoninus Pius, 378, 381–385,
455
appointed Nasi, 371
birth of, 371–372
and Chiya, sons of, 378, 510
contemporaries of, 394–417
on Day of Judgment, 385
death of, 381, 530, 638, 692, 707
education of, 363, 372
maxims of, 373, 379–380
and *Mishnah*, compiling of, 385–393,
524, 612, 671
ordinations of, 640

pupils and disciples of, 373, 376,
    409, 414, 452–453, 482, 487, 499,
    500, 514, 528–531, 535–536
and Rav (Abba Arecha), 633, 638,
    827n
religious reforms of, 375–376
rulings of, 373–374
on Sabbath food, 384–385
and Shmuel Yarchina'ah, 377, 670,
    671
successors to, 452, 457
on the Torah, 380
wealth of, 373
will of, 416–417
woman servant of, 372, 391, 548
Jehudah N'siah I, Rabbi, 452–457, 461,
    463, 473, 487, 525, 555, 638, 639,
    640, 678
Jehudah N'siah II, Rabbi, 468–472, 473,
    504, 515, 517, 518, 547, 555, 569,
    574, 575, 587
Jehudah N'siah III, Rabbi, 461–462,
    464, 579–580, 582, 762
Jehudah N'siah IV, Rabbi, 464, 466
Jehudah the Ammonite proselyte, Rab-
    bi, 190–191
Jehudah the Baker, Rabbi, 293, 309
Jeremiah (prophet), 243, 307, 437, 549,
    550, 552
Jeremiah, Rabbi, 461
Jeremiah bar Abba, Rav, 752
Jericho, 87, 183, 432, 433, 447
Jeroboam, 35
Jeroboam ben Nebat, 544
Jerusalem, 13, 40, 220, 225, 316, 317,
    327, 542, 588, 694
    Alexander's march on, 38, 47
    in ancient times, 443–444, 445, 446
    expulsion of Jews from, 440
    God as builder of, 191
    Greek occupation of, 59, 63–64
    Hadrian's decrees on, 225
    Hasmonean work restrictions in, 66
    Jochanan Hyrcanus II's siege of,
        80–81, 91–92
    Passover massacre in, 130
    pilgrimages to, 64, 158, 176, 364,
        375, 623
    Roman siege and destruction of,
        145–149, 153, 154, 158, 206, 257,
        439, 571

and Samaritans, relationship with,
    35–36, 37–38
water supply, 48
Jerusalem Talmud, 4, 5, 93, 104, 136,
    226, 263, 387, 421–429, 498, 511,
    567, 582, 583, 586, 740, 792n
    vs. Babylonian Talmud, 392, 393, 774
    language of, 613
Jeshu (disciple of Joshua ben
    Perachiah), 71
Jeshua ben Jozadak, 54
Jesus Christ, 71, 122, 455
Jewish revolt (66–73 C.E.), 143–149,
    151–154, 158, 192, 218, 232–233,
    252, 262–269, 438, 440–441. See also
    Betar; Kochba, Simeon bar; Ten
    Martyrs
    in Galilee, 147, 266, 267
    guerrilla warfare, 289–290
    Parthian aid to, 354–355
    peace movement, 288, 289, 290
    traitors to, 309, 310
Jewish revolt (351 C.E.), 467–468
Jews, 326, 327, 345
    annihilation of, 590–591, 594
    arrogance of, 584–585
    as chosen people, 18, 20, 51, 232,
        299, 468, 614, 657
    Christian. See Minim
    Christian persecutions of, 468
    in exile, 272. See also Babylonia;
        Babylonian Exile; individual Jew-
        ish communities
    Greek persecutions of, 55–57
    languages and scripts of, 219–220,
        372, 400
    occupations of, 434
    racial purity of, 723–725
    redemption on Day of Judgment of,
        212
    wealth of, 129, 134
Joab, 539
Job, Book of, 13, 333, 348, 489, 502,
    809n
Jochanan. See also Jose ben Jochanan
Jochanan, Rabbi (editor of Jerusalem
    Talmud), 392, 414, 445, 456, 457,
    458, 459, 463, 474–475, 481–498,
    513, 526, 530, 531, 574, 585, 586,
    595, 599, 600, 620, 670, 693, 697,
    846n

academy and disciples of, 490–500, 559–560, 567, 569, 580, 581, 716, 721, 725
and Babylonian scholars, 486–487, 489–491, 639
beauty of, 481, 478–479, 496–497, 490–500, 544
biblical interpretations of, 494
birth of, 481, 487–488
childhood and youth of, 481–482, 487, 488
death of, 494, 568
on *Halakhah*, 492
healing powers of, 496–497
and the Jerusalem Talmud, 498
legal opinions of, 483–484, 730
maxims of, 497–498
and *Mishnah*, 482–483, 498
moral qualities of, 483
old age of, 492, 494
and political conditions, 491, 492
poverty of, 495–496
on prayer, 487, 489, 492
robbery of, 503
and Simeon ben Lakish, 486, 499–503, 504–505
sons of, 481, 483, 492
studies of, diligence in, 483, 488, 489
on talmudic legends, 492
on the Torah, 484–485, 491–492, 497–498
Jochanan ben Gudgada, Rabbi. *See* Nechunia
Jochanan ben Nuri, Rabbi, 348, 644
Jochanan ben Toratha, Rabbi, 263–264
Jochanan ben Zakkai, Rabban, 111, 149, 150, 152–163, 164, 175, 178, 179, 182, 184, 187, 391, 545
at Arav, 155, 175
colleagues of, 164–174
and Vespasian, 153–154, 155, 164–165
death of, 163
destruction of Temple and, 155
escape from Jerusalem of, 152–155
and laws, interpretation of, 159–160
origin and descent of, 155–156
pupils and disciples of, 161–162, 175, 183, 194, 195–196, 199, 205, 206, 393
Jochanan Hyrcanus II, king of Judea,

63, 70, 80–82, 83, 87, 91–92
Jochanan of Hauran, Rabbi, 112
Jochanan the High Priest (John Hyrcanus I), 40, 60, 63–67, 68, 71, 72, 777*n*
Jochanan the Sandalmaker (Hasandlar), Rabbi, 275, 330, 362, 363, 365–366
Joezer. *See* Jose ben Joezer
John Chrysostom of Antioch, 753–754
John Hyrcanus I. *See* Jochanan the High Priest
John Hyrcanus II. *See* Jochanan Hyrcanus II
Jojada ben Eliashiv, 36–37, 44
Jojariv (priest), 59
Jonah (prophet), 171, 412
Jonathan (son of Saul), 665
Jonathan, Rabbi, 323, 472, 547
Jonathan ben Amram, Rabbi, 373
Jonathan ben Eleazar, 519–523
Jonathan ben Uziel, 100, 108
Jordan River, 291
Jose ben Chalafta, Rabbi, 313, 331, 343, 344, 347–352, 428, 451, 479, 621
Jose ben Jochanan, 53, 54, 55, 56, 57–58, 68
Jose ben Joezer, 52, 53, 55, 56–58, 68
Jose ben Kisma, Rabbi, 286–287, 288, 290
Jose Hacohen, Rabbi, 162, 206
Jose of Galilee, Rabbi, 203, 238, 251–256, 293, 337, 362, 389
son of, 370
wife of, 253
Jose the Maonite, 455
Joseph (son of Jacob), 104, 428, 558, 719
grave of, 479
Joseph, Rav (son of Joshua ben Levi), 536
Joseph bar Chama, Rav, 736, 737, 752, 754
Joseph bar Chiya, Rav, 716, 720, 722–724, 727, 730–731, 733, 737, 741
Joseph of Tiberias, 468
Josephus (Joseph ben Gurion Hacohen), 132
Josephus, Flavius (historian), 30, 36, 37, 39, 57, 70, 107, 294, 430, 434,

438, 443, 445, 461, 610–611

Jewish revolt, on the, 144, 147, 148, 149, 780*n*

Joshua (High Priest), 44, 291

Joshua, Rabbi, 23

Joshua ben Chananiah, Rabbi, 153, 157, 162, 166, 168, 171, 205–216, 218, 220, 223, 225, 301, 304–305, 816*n*

and Eliezer ben Hyrcanus, 194, 198, 199, 200, 202, 258, 259

vs. Gamaliel II, 185–189

pupils and disciples of, 296, 300, 323, 348, 362

and ransom of Ishmael ben Elisha, 236–237

Joshua ben Gamala (High Priest), 137, 780*n*

Joshua ben Korcha, Rabbi, 368–370, 641

Joshua ben Levi, Rabbi, 360, 417, 500, 529, 535–545, 574

and the Angel of Death, 535, 539–540, 542

education of, 535–536

and Elijah, 535, 538–539, 540, 542

in Gehenna, 542–544

and *Aggadah*, 536, 537, 540–541

maxims of, 538, 541–542

in Paradise, 439–540, 542, 544–545, 586

on prayer, 537

pupils and disciples of, 541

on scholars, 536–537

Joshua ben Nehemiah, Rabbi, 292–293

Joshua ben Nun, 100, 442–443, 593, 611

Joshua ben Perachiah, 53, 68–71, 73, 74

Joshua Hagarsi, Rabbi, 276–278

Josiah, king of Judah, 36

Jozadak. *See* Simeon ben Jozadak

Jubilee years, 8, 437, 761–762

Judah, tribe and kingdom of, 35, 36, 326, 627

Judaism

Constantine I's prohibitions of, 465

converts to, 141–142, 202–203, 378, 384, 642, 646. *See also* Proselytes

and Egyptian-Syrian wars in Palestine, 50, 51, 58

Roman suppression of, 242, 295, 303,

309, 310, 311, 320–321, 336. *See also* individual emperors

Theodosius I's protection of, 763–764

Judea, kingdom of, 36, 202, 251, 264, 266

agriculture in, 432, 433

calendar determination in, 406–407, 455, 525

Judges. *See* Courts

Julian the Apostate, emperor of Rome, 465, 749–751

Julianus ben Jehudah, 285

Julius Severus (Roman commander), 267–268

Just men, 19

Justice, 617

Justin Martyr (church-father), 250, 473

Kabul, Pales., 454

Kadosh, 478

Kafri, Babyl., 681, 700, 703

Kahana. *See* Abba bar Kahana

Kahana, Rav, exilarch of Babylonia, 631, 651, 759

Kalba Savua, 145, 257–260

Kalinikat, Mesop., 754

Kapara, Bar, Rabbi, 377, 381, 400–403, 524, 525, 530, 633

Karaites, 30

Karna (judge in Nehardea), 642

Kefar Chitaa, Pales., 593

Kefar Pekud, Babyl., 664

Kerachim (fortified cities), 443–444, 447

Ketubbah (marriage contract), 78, 253, 315, 331, 425, 651, 660, 667, 675

Keturah, sons of, 425

Kezib, Pales., 183, 218

Kiddush, 12, 48, 345, 644

King's River, Babyl., 642

Kings, book of, 579

Kisma. *See* Jose b. Kisma

Knowledge, Garden of (Pardes), 295, 296, 303, 306, 789*n*, 790*n*

Kochba, Simeon bar, 41, 217, 218, 220, 257, 262–269, 289, 312, 440, 442, 445

Korach, 543–544

Korah, Pales., 213

Korcha. *See* Joshua ben Korcha

Kuta, Kutim, 34, 35. *See also* Samaritans

Laban, 375, 425, 558
Laborers, 249–250, 435–436. *See also*
  amei aratzim
  farm, 435, 437
  rights, 663
  wages, payment of, 245
Lacedemonians (Spartans), 60
Lakish, 808*n*. *See also* Simeon ben
  Lakish
Lamentations, 298–299
Laments, 281
Land purchases, 12, 64
Landowners, landownership, 435
Langbank, Alexander, 821*n*
Laski, Moshe, 820*n*
Latin language, 226, 391
Laws. *See also Beraita; Halakhah;*
  Mishnah; Oral law; individual
  scholars
  Aggadic interpretation of, 474
  in Babylonia and Persia, 691
  codification of, 9
  destruction of Second Temple and,
    149–151
  of the Hasmonean Court, 60–61,
    64–65
  Pharisaic, 24–25
  "some say" vs. "others say" before,
    313–314
  at variance with Torah, 240
  at Usha, enacted by Sanhedrin,
    234–235
  written, 27, 151
Lawsuits, 139–141
Lebanon Mountains, 434
Lecture months, 758, 759, 760, 841*n*
Levi, Rabbi, 464, 474–475, 476
Levi, books of, 416
Levi ben Sisi, Rabbi, 392–393, 414–417,
  535, 640, 681
Levitas of Jabneh, Rabbi, 622
Levites, 23, 65, 66, 168, 205, 246, 375,
  386, 424, 478
Leviticus, Book of, 9, 11, 69
Lineage, Book of *(Yuhasin)*, 282, 366,
  367
"Lions' Converts," 35
Locusts, as food, 56
Lodacea (Lodakia), Pales., 285, 575
Logic, Hillel's rules of, 103–106,
  778*n*–779*n*

Lot, 173
Lucilla (daughter of Marcus Aurelius),
  356
Lucius Varus, emperor of Rome, 355,
  356, 371
Lud, Judea, 326, 433, 468, 536, 555,
  809*n*
  academy at, 193, 199, 247, 249
Lulav, 324, 612

Maariv (evening prayer), 187
Maccabee, Jonathan, 60
Maccabee, Judah, 30, 60
Maccabee, Simeon, 60, 62–63
Maccabees, 27, 30, 39, 57. *See also*
  Hasmoneans
Machasia, Rabbah bar, 828*n*
Machpelah, cave of, 422, 479
Magdiel, king of Edom, 582
Magic, 647. *See also* Witchcraft
Mahalalel. *See* Akabia ben Mahalalel
Maimonides, 738
Makom (name of God), 17, 472, 614
Makrinus, emperor of Rome, 515
Malachi (prophet), 7, 781*n*
Melakhah (work) 11
Malchi-Zedek, 424
M'anenet, 276
Marcus Aurelius, emperor of Rome,
  355, 356, 371, 579
Mardutha (academy at Caesarea), 571
Mari bar Giora, Rav, 674, 687
Market places, market days, 446, 447,
  448, 449
Marriage, 47, 271, 276, 565, 619–620,
  631, 676, 731. *See also* Divorce;
  Ketubbah
  Essene beliefs about, 31
  Hillel vs. Shammai on, 109–110,
    113–114
  levirate, 28, 113, 159, 232, 389
  and love between husband and wife,
    13
  mixed, 7, 8, 11, 23, 37, 594, 709
  Pharisaic rules on, 32
  priests' prerogatives in, 248
  of slaves, 351, 438, 653, 690
  weddings, 283, 701
Marriage contracts, 78, 253, 315, 331,
  425, 651, 660, 667, 675
Martha (daughter of Boetus), 137, 780*n*

Masekhet Gan Eden (Joshua ben Levi), 542

Mata Machasia, Babyl., 643, 758, 759, 760, 761, 767, 772, 773, 844n

Matana, Rabbah bar, 727

Matia ben Harash, Rabbi, 323

Mattathias ben Jochanan, 59–60, 61, 217

Matzot, 95, 106, 192

Mechoza, Babyl., 687, 688, 728–729, 734, 735, 736, 738, 740, 752

Media, Medians, 34, 271, 326, 594

Medicine, 433, 434, 529, 670–671, 673–674, 681, 765

Megillah, 343

Megillat Bet Chashmonai, 146

Megillat Esther, 220

Megillat Setarim (scroll of secrecy), 406

Megillat Taanit, 146

Meir, Rabbi, 289, 328–340, 342, 356, 358, 536, 624, 672
  at Antioch, 338–339
  children of, 334, 340
  daily benedictions of, 329
  death of, 332, 336
  excommunication and exile of, 314, 330
  legal opinions of, 331–332
  maxims of, 332–334
  modesty of, 340
  pupils and disciples of, 395, 409, 636, 637
  and Simeon ben Gamaliel II, dispute with, 312–314, 330
  studies of, 305–308, 329–331, 334, 793n
  wife of. *See* Beruriah

Mekhilta, 9, 325, 341, 810n

Men of the Great Synagogue, 6, 45

Menachem (head of court), 107

Menahem, Rabbi (son of Jose ben Chalafta), 351

Menasheh, 37

Menasheh (High Priest), 45

Menasheh, king of Judah, 498

Menasia. *See* Simeon ben Menasia

Menorah, 45–46, 135, 325, 384

Menstruation, 426

Merchants, 435, 564, 571

Meron, Pales., 360

Mesharshia bar Pekud, 770

Messiah, 19, 20, 50, 263, 264, 290, 355, 368, 378, 384, 475, 491, 506, 510, 535, 538–539, 542, 557, 610, 616, 761–762

Metateron (angel), 281–282, 306

Metivta (academy at Sura), 643

Mezuzot, 8, 23, 224

Mibarnish, Rav, 774

Micah, 473, 544

Michael (angel), 42, 472

Michal (daughter of Kushi), 16

Michal (daughter of Saul), 16–17

Midat Hadin (emanation of justice), 401

Midrash, 9, 153–154, 224, 263, 280, 470, 550

Mimla, Babyl., 717

Minaa, Jacob, 567

Minchah offering, 206

Mines, mining, 149, 434

Minim (Jewish Christians), 326, 462, 463, 467, 473, 537, 555–556

Miriam (sister of Moses), 705

Miriam the Hasmonean (wife of Herod I), 63, 87, 88, 123

Mishael, 285, 558

Mishnah, mishnayot, 10, 50, 261, 341, 348, 360, 362, 394, 405, 463, 482–483, 490, 498, 524, 531, 612, 628, 635, 649–652, 671, 760
  anonymous authors of, 649–650
  classification of, 388. *See also Derashah; Halakhah*
  compiled into books or tractates, 324–325, 367, 385–393, 498
  customs in, 388–389, 483
  interpretive method in, 386–387
  Jerusalem vs. Babylonian versions of, 392, 393, 421
  language of, 391
  laws in, 386, 388–389, 423–429
  orders (subject groups) of, 387, 390, 415–416, 508
  Roman persecutions and, 386
  text changes in, 392–393

Mishnah of Bar Kapara, 401

Moabites, 190–191, 365

Modesty, 622

Modiin. *See* Eliezer of Modiin

Modiin, Pales., 59, 217

Money changing, 449

Money, lending and disputes, 139,

184, 272, 314, 350, 435, 507, 661–662, 673, 674, 788n
collateral disputes and, 729, 731–732
compensation and, 8–9, 51, 104
debt moratoria and, 675–676
and debtors' oaths, 690
and documents of indebtedness, 135, 315
interest on, 272, 334, 474, 668, 675
profit margins on, 673
Moralizing, as Jews' duty, 299, 615, 618
Mordechai, 590, 591
Mordechai, Rav, 774
Moriah, Mount, 255–256
Moses (leader in Crete), 762
Moses (prophet), 7, 18, 29, 51, 53, 54, 57, 100, 104, 171, 200, 201, 204, 210, 240, 243, 291, 299, 335, 349, 424, 428, 442, 480, 483, 497, 506, 508, 513, 517, 522, 542, 556, 560, 591, 593, 599, 600, 622, 705
death of, 589–590
intercessions with God of, 472–473, 551–553
letters of Torah and, 261
Mountain tops
cities built on, 445
fires on, and calendar setting, 376
Mourning customs, 428, 713
Murder, 105, 165, 427, 541
Musaf (prayer), 658
Mutilation, 622

Nabal the Carmelite, 665
Nachman bar Huna, Rav, 767
Nachman bar Isaac, Rav, 740–742, 743, 746, 842n
Nachman bar Jacob, Rav, 629, 685, 688–693, 698, 705, 710–711, 717, 731, 737–738, 741, 752, 754, 755, 842n
Nachmani. *See* Rabbah bar Nachmani; Shmuel ben Nachmani
Nachmani (father of Rabbah), 727
Nachum Halavlar (the Scribe), 53–54
Nachum of Gimso, Rabbi, 172–174, 258
Nakdimon ben Gurion, 145, 154
Napcha, Pales., 586
Nares (Narash), Babyl., 740, 743, 746–747, 748

Nasi, office of, 53, 121, 125, 182, 184, 186, 229, 232–233, 461–462, 680, 762–763, 764–765, 792n. *See also* High Priest
augmented under Jehudah Hanasi, 374
decline of and rise of Christianity, 464, 466, 467, 488, 546
dynastic succession to, 316, 344
Simeon ben Gamaliel II's regulations and, 312–314, 316
Nathan (son of Joseph), Rabbi, 23
Nathan of Babylonia, Rabbi, 23, 324–327, 427, 612. *See also Avot Derabi Natan*
maxims of, 325–326
vs. Simeon ben Gamaliel II, 312–314, 321–322
travels of, remarks on, 326–327
Natural sciences, 350, 372–373, 413
Nazarite (vow of abstinence), 19, 46, 62, 390, 615
Nebo, Mount, 556
Nebuchadnezzar II, king of Babylon, 8, 41, 160, 213, 558
Nechunia ben Gudgada, Rabbi, 168–169, 189
Nechunia ben Hakanah, Rabbi, 12, 169–171, 237
Nehardea, Babyl., 320, 554, 611, 638, 647–648, 676, 770
academies at, 416, 417, 554, 642, 643, 650–652, 656, 669, 671–672, 684, 685, 687, 693, 695, 708, 759
Roman war on, 686–687, 736, 752
Nehemiah (leader of Jews), 7, 11, 29, 36–37, 45, 54, 608, 610
Nehemiah, Rabbi (disciple of R. Akiba), 367–368
Nehemiah, Rabbana, 628
Nehemiah ben Chachaliah, 7
Nehemiah the Thirshata, 367
Nehorai, Rabbi, 328, 367–368
Nero, emperor of Rome, 131
Netsivin, Babyl., 320, 362
New Testament, 25, 471
New Year, 8, 467, 495, 572, 584
Nezikin, 508
Nicea, Council of, 462
Nikhsei malug (property of wives), 234
Nimrod, 558

Nimukim (arguments), 349
Nineveh, Babyl., 171, 412
Nittai of Arbela, 53, 68, 70
Noah, 221, 424, 425, 472, 476, 577, 837*n*
  sons of, 423, 558
Noam, 527
Nob, Pales., 507
Numbers, Book of, 243, 245, 443, 703

Oaths, 652, 667, 668. *See also* Vows
  in courts, 140–141
  of debtors, 690
  Essene customs, 31
  false, 594
Obadiah (prophet), 335
Occupations, 192, 335, 342–343, 350, 380, 394, 422, 432, 609, 621
Odenatus (Barnezer Odenate, Papa ben Netzer), 578, 686–687, 737, 752
Oil, 20, 433, 453–454, 529, 534, 555, 570, 644, 678
Omer (first ripened sheaf), 81, 106
Omri, king of Israel, 445, 494
Onias (son of Simon the Just), 48, 69, 70, 87
  temple of, at Alexandria, 48, 69–70, 81, 319
Onkelos the Proselyte, 202, 222–227, 724, 784*n*
Ono, Pales., 433
Oral law, 20, 22, 27, 102, 138–139, 151, 260, 261, 286, 360, 386
Ordinations, 242, 283–284, 640
  in Babylonia, 540, 600, 670, 677–678
  of Elders, 121
Organ, in the Temple, 317
Original sin, 395
Origines (church-father), 441, 455, 472, 525, 813*n*
Orphans, property inherited by, 675
Oshaiah Rabbah, Rabbi (pupil of Chiya bar Abba I), 405, 473, 482, 485, 486, 500, 524–527, 571

"Pairs," time of the, 53–59, 68, 72, 79
Palestine (Eretz Israel), 5, 7, 319, 531–532, 562, 642
  cities in, 442–449
  Egyptian-Syrian wars in, 51, 58

Greek administration of, 21, 26, 30, 39–40, 51, 55–56, 59–64
Greek-Persian wars in, 43–44
Hasmonean extensions of, 64
Jews' return to, from Babylonian Exile, 9, 42–43, 44, 51–52, 610
and "Pairs," time of the, 53–59, 68, 72, 79
as Roman province, 81–82, 114–115, 122–124, 124, 129–137, 211–212, 228, 291, 512, 549–550
  agriculture in, 431–432
  census of Herod Agrippa I in, 124
  Christianity in, spread of, 463–465, 568
  civic works in, 343–344
  improvements under Antoninus Pius, 311–312, 323
  Jewish revolts in. *See* main entry
  persecutions in, 324, 612, 634, 629, 747–746, 740. *See also* Ten Martyrs
  religion in, suppression of, 242
  villages of, 443, 449–450
Palmyra, Syr., 578–579, 687
Papa ben Netzer. *See* Odenatus
Papa. *See* Chanina bar Papa
Papa, Rav, 743–745, 746, 747, 748
Pappus ben Jehudah, 285, 788*n*
Paradise, 177, 307, 360, 518, 595
  Joshua ben Levi in, 539–540, 542, 543–544, 596
Pardes (Garden of Knowledge), 295, 296, 303, 306, 789*n*, 790*n*
Parents. *See also* Children; Fathers
  good deeds of, 616
  honoring of, 597–598, 621–622, 712
  sins of, 304
Parta. *See* Eleazar ben Parta
Parthians, 17, 64, 311, 354–356, 492, 493, 515, 614, 641, 766, 791*n*, 796*n*, 807*n*
Paschal offerings, 240
  census of Palestine and, 124
  Hillel's question on, 95, 106
  on Sabbath, 86–87, 96–97, 104, 105, 384, 610
Passover, 62, 86, 104, 156, 244, 255, 345, 389, 397–398, 458, 609–610
  leavened food during, 255, 672, 704, 731
  ovens on, 90

Passover massacre (Jerusalem), 130
Patriarchs, intercession with God, 550–553
Patriots, party of, 114–115, 127, 129, 132, 133, 134, 137
Paul (Saul of Tarsus), Apostle, 122
Paul, bishop of Byzantium, 465
Pazi. *See* Jehudah bar Simeon
Peace, 512–513, 619, 620
Peah (food offering), 215, 783*n*
Pedat. *See* Eleazar ben Pedat
Pekiin, academy at, 211
Pentateuch, 4, 551, 588
Perachiah. *See* Joshua ben Perachiah
Persia, 42–44. *See also* Babylonia
  Jewish communities in, 45
  wars between Rome and, 441–443, 578, 674, 687, 750–751
Persian culture, 429
Persian laws, 691
Persian religion, 478, 768–769
Persians, 17, 41, 207, 290, 326, 327, 557–558, 607, 614, 626, 647, 766, 788*n*, 791*n*, 796*n*, 808*n*
Pesach, 192
Pescenius Niger, 640–641
Peshat (explanation of Torah), 789*n*
Pharaoh, 62, 171, 266, 424, 517
Pharisees, 21–26, 68, 86, 88, 111, 354
  Christian derogation of, 25
  Jochanan's forsaking of, 66–67, 68
  laws, rituals and customs of, 22–23, 28, 29, 32
  membership in group of, 24
  plague of, 213
  religious beliefs of, 24, 27
  and Sadducees, conflict with, 26, 27, 29, 72–74, 79
  seven types of, 25–26
Philistines, 172, 637
Philo of Alexandria, 388
Phoenicia, Phoenicians, 47, 431
Phoenician script, 37, 220
Phylacteries *(tefillin)*, 8, 14–17, 487, 489, 712, 732
Piety, 617
Pilpul, 331, 393, 530
Pinchas, reward of, 74
Pinchas ben Yair, Rabbi, 353–354, 374, 396–399, 526
Pious fools, 30, 213

Pirkei Avot, 128
Piruz, king of Persia, 769–770, 771
Plagues, 203, 213, 265–266
Pleasures of life, denial of, 622
Pliny the Elder, 430, 433
Plowing, prohibitions on, 110, 387
Polemos Quietus revolt, 441
Polytheism, 17, 614. *See also* Greek religion; Idol worship
Pompey (the Great), 40, 81
Possession, laws of. *See also* Property rights
  Jewish *(hazakah)*, 235, 646, 674, 692, 732
  Roman, 582
Potiphar's wife, 558
Poverty, 617
Prayers, 8, 9, 169, 178, 201, 335, 517, 537, 548, 576, 589, 631, 652, 654, 656–659, 705
  aggadic interpretation of, 480
  cities, on entering and leaving, 454
  daily benedictions of R. Meir, 329
  against disbelievers, 150
  Hasmonean regulations on, 61
  Jochanan, editor of Talmud, on, 487, 489, 492
  order of, 191
  origin of, 610
  for the sick, 178–179
  significance of, 623
Preaching, 19
Pride, 428, 622, 663–664
Priests, priesthood, 23, 375, 478, 515, 585, 630, 657. *See also* High Priest; Nasi; Ordinations; Rabbi
  marriage and, 248
  origin of, 424
Prisons, 428
Profit, margin of, 673
Promiscuity, 648
Property rights, 425, 438, 667, 675, 729, 731–732. *See also* Possession, laws of
Prophets, 19, 596, 616
Proselytes, 79, 85, 142, 188, 201–203, 222, 224–225, 376, 384, 426, 509
Prostitution, 326, 335, 338, 339, 590, 717
Proverbs, Book of, 516, 520, 704, 800*n*

Prozbols (legal contract formulas), 284,
675–676, 788*n*
Psalms, 48, 66, 307, 480, 516, 547, 569,
683
Ptolemy, king of Egypt, 16
Ptolemy ben Chabub, 62–63
Pumbedita, Babyl., 664, 711, 752
academy at, 580, 598, 692, 708–716,
722, 725, 727–730, 733, 740, 744,
748, 761, 767, 770, 771
Punishment, 11, 235
after death, 19, 20, 24, 325–326
origin of, 426–427
redemption from, 240–241
Purim, 450–451, 603, 611, 633, 636
Purity, laws of, 12–13, 40, 138, 139,
243, 411, 718, 720, 731
animals, clean and unclean, 425
and the dead, 50–51, 55–56
Egyptian wheat restrictions, 68–69
Essene, 31, 32
Hasmonean, 61, 64–65
Hillel's question on, 95, 105–106
Mishnah on, 390
origins of, 426
Pharisaic, 22–23, 29
Sadducean, 28

Quietus, Lucius, governor of Palestine,
441
Quorum *(minyan)*, 489

Ra'atan (skin ailment), 529
Ra'atan (teachers of Hagada), 471
Rabbah (colleague of R. Zeira), 603
Rabbah bar Avuha, 666–687, 688, 693,
724, 735, 752
Rabbah bar Nachmani, 715–721, 722,
723, 730, 731, 732, 733
Rabbah bar Rav Huna, 696, 704–705,
725–726, 727, 735
Rabbah ben Shilah, 331
Rabban, title of, 121
Rabbi, title of, 121. *See also* Ordination;
Priests
Rabinowitz, R. N., 828*n*
Rachel (daughter of Kalba Savua),
258–260
Rachel (wife of Jacob), 550, 553

Rafram bar Papa, 736
Rahab, 447
Rami bar Dikola, 711
Rami bar Ezekiel, 613, 707, 708, 709,
711–712
Rape, 105
Raphael (angel), 42, 472
Rashbam (Samuel ben Meir), 368, 423
Rashi, 232, 243, 290, 368, 416, 473, 524,
584, 738, 741, 780*n*, 783*n*, 789*n*
Rav (Abba Arecha), 392, 409, 414, 453,
482, 486, 492, 530, 613, 622,
626–668, 694, 695, 696, 698, 726,
754
academy at Sura of, 626, 631, 643,
645, 648, 649, 652–654
ancestry of, 626–627, 628, 629
in Babylonia, 638–640, 642, 652–653
birth of, 626
and Chiya bar Abba I, 627–628, 631,
633, 634
death of, 655–656
education of, 638, 639–640
influence of, 656
and Jehudah Hanasi, 633, 638, 827*n*
legal opinions of, 631, 633–634, 639,
649–650, 653, 667–668, 682–683
on magic and astrology, 647
maxims of, 636, 637, 647, 661,
665–666, 758
and *Mishnah*, 628, 635, 649–652
occupations of, 631, 642–645, 653,
680
old age of, 653–655
ordination of, 677–678
in Palestine, 634, 635–638, 640–642
personal qualities of, 629–633,
648–649, 653–654, 666
prayers of, 631, 653, 654, 656–659
pupils and disciples of, 559, 592–593,
628, 631, 644–645, 646, 653, 685,
700, 707, 725, 752–753, 772
religious and moral teachings of,
648, 649, 650–652, 659, 661–664,
829*n*
and Shmuel Yarchina'ah of
Nehardea, 633, 640, 642, 643, 653,
655, 669, 674, 687
as teacher, 630–632, 640, 645,
651–652, 666

travels of, 659, 664–665
wife of, 632
and women, rulings on, 629, 639, 651, 659–662
Rava bar Joseph bar Chama, 391, 625, 720, 727, 729, 731, 734–739, 741, 746, 748, 772, 773
Ravina (compiler of Babylonian Talmud), 612, 771–774
Ravina (student of R. Meir), 331
Red Heifer, sacrifice of, 28, 46–47, 159, 297
Remez (hidden meanings of Torah), 807n
Repentance, 19, 335, 379–380, 499, 506–507, 512, 537, 569, 616, 623
Resh Lakish. *See* Simeon ben Lakish
Resurrection of the dead, 24, 27, 51, 212, 213, 408, 603, 616
Reuben (son of Jacob), 474
River of Fire, 214
Road clearance, Hasmonean laws on, 61–62
Robber bands, 130, 288, 339, 369, 449, 641, 686–687
Robbery, 136, 140, 156, 191–192, 423, 437
of Gentiles, 191–192
punishments for, 427–428
Roma, Pales., 575
Roman Empire, 17, 217, 373, 431–432, 594, 640, 761–765. *See also* Palestine, Roman province
Christianity as state religion in, 462, 762–765
cities of, 446, 447
culture in, 429
decrees against Jews of, 515. *See also* individual emperors
divided into East and West, 466, 764
and Persia and Babylonia, wars against, 441–443, 578, 674, 687, 750–751
revolts, 354–355, 468, 640. *See also* Jewish revolts
treaty with Jews, 63
Romans, 39, 41, 557, 614, 813n
Rome (Edom), 208, 270, 326, 327, 356, 557, 641, 763–764, 828n
Rosh Hashanah, 135, 151, 244

Rufus (Tyranos Rufus, Roman commander), 262, 264, 266, 273, 277–278, 280, 285
wife of, 278–279

Saadiah Gaon, 424
Sabbath, 9, 11–12, 39, 95, 203, 204, 208, 219, 231, 270, 315, 318, 447, 479, 533, 556, 576, 705
beginning of, 245
Christian repudiation of, 471, 548–549
Day of Atonement and, 495
duration of, 12, 609
Essene rules regarding, 32
Hasmonean Court laws regarding, 61
Holy Scriptures rescued on, 698
labors performed on, 11–12, 255, 303, 387, 609
Mishnah on, 9, 390
Persian proscription of, 768, 769, 770
Pharisaic rules of, 32
phylacteries on, wearing of, 16
prohibitions of, 11–12, 170, 303, 306, 357, 371, 384–385, 395, 427, 509, 623, 645, 672, 691–692, 703, 704, 732, 840n
walking limits on, 306, 447
women wearing jewelry on, 417
sacrifices on, 54, 86–87, 96–97, 104, 105
Shammai's advice about, 108
testimony on, 125
Sabbath (herb), 208, 385
Sabbatical year, 140, 373–376, 788n
debt moratoria in, 675–676
eating food harvested during, 587
plowing fields during, 110, 191, 470, 515
Sacrifices 8, 9, 18–19, 59, 81, 135, 138, 139, 160, 381, 423, 433, 479–480, 699. *See also* Paschal offerings; *Peah*; Red Heifer
animals for, 160, 381, 423, 433
choice of, 479–480
first born of, 117, 587, 639, 827n
pity on, 160, 381
placing of hands on *(semikhah)*, 54–55, 110–111

on feast days, 54–55
first ripened sheaf and, 81, 106
and garments worn, 244
Hasmonean rules, 66
from Jews outside Palestine, 55–56
Mishnah on, 390
origin and purpose of, 423–424, 615
reassessed after destruction of Temple, 143, 150, 439
on Sabbath, 54, 86–87, 96–97, 104, 105
Sadducean beliefs about, 27
at Temple of Onias, 69–70
Sadducees, 21, 26–29, 50, 88, 102–103, 111, 128, 161, 389
customs of, 28–29, 50–51
Jochanan joins, 66–67, 68
laws and rituals of, 27–28, 55
and Pharisees, conflicts with, 26, 27, 29, 72–74, 79
Safra, 9, 341, 792n
St. John's bread, 353
Saints, 544, 545, 616
Salome, queen of Judea (wife of Aristobolus I), 71
Salome Alexandra, queen of Judea (wife of Alexander Jannai), 74, 78, 80
Samaria (city), 40, 41, 64, 445, 494
Samaria (district), 34, 35, 266
Samaritans, 34–41, 211, 220, 315, 728, 744. *See also* Gerizim, Mt.
and Alexander the Great, 47–48
calendar sabotage of, 375
with Christians, friendship of, 580
Diocletian's persecutions of, 459
during exile of Ten Tribes, 34–36
Hasmonean laws against, 64–65
and the Jewish revolt, 192, 264, 267, 268
vs. Jews, 39–40, 129, 131, 142, 641
and opposition to restoration of Temple, 442
origins of, 34–35
and slaughter of animals, 486
wine of, 459
Samuel (prophet, hero), 593
Books of, 17, 563, 570, 665
Sanbalat the Horonite (Samaritan), 37, 39, 45
Sancherib, king of Assyria, 82, 401

Sandalmaker. *See* Jochanan the Sandalmaker
Sanhedrin, 50, 67, 68, 79, 95, 121, 451, 461, 592. *See also* Nasi, office of
and calendar, determination of, 466, 478, 605, 828n
and Chanut, move to, 122
function and activities of, 608–609
Herod I and, 85, 86, 87–88, 94
at Jabneh, 149, 151, 182–183, 189, 193, 262, 284, 285, 343
Mishnah on, 390
reorganized under Simeon ben Gamaliel II, 312–316, 320
under the Romans, 82, 83, 129, 344
Sadducees and, 68, 73–74, 77
at Usha, 232–238, 242, 284, 285, 312, 320, 324, 341, 343, 359, 367, 370
wanderings of, 232–233, 237–238, 251, 343, 359
Sapor I (Shavour Malka), king of Persia, 671, 674, 687, 710, 719
Sapor II, king of Persia, 719–720, 737, 738, 748, 750, 751, 757, 766
Sar ha'olam (angel), 401
Sarah, 477
Sargon, king of Assyria, 34, 35
Sassanide dynasty, 493, 646, 718–720, 767–770
Satisfaction with one's lot, 622
Saul, king of Israel, 240, 507, 543, 570, 637
Scapegoat, 159, 350
Scholars, scholarship, 14, 133–134, 270, 274, 480, 482, 507–508, 536–537, 589, 608. *See also* Academies
in Babylonia, 463–464, 486–491, 527, 533, 612, 613, 640, 729, 766–767, 773–774
decline of
under Herod, 85, 86
in Christian era, 462–463, 546, 551, 634
disputes over interpretations of Torah, 230
Eleazar's types of, 363–364
Gentile, 161
habits of, clothing, 625
Herod I's persecution of, 85, 94, 112
honor due to, 622
at Jabneh, 143, 149–150

and Jewish revolts, 265, 430
migrations of, to Palestine, 635–638,
   709
sins of, and repentance, 243
supported by cities, 496, 503
and trade prohibitions, 229
Schools, for children, 459, 621, 623–625
Schuerer (Christian historian), 442
Scorpions, 180
Scribes *(Sofrim)*, 6, 7, 43, 161, 448, 451,
   483, 608
Sects, 303–304, 616
Seder, 48, 263, 265–266
Seder Hadorot, 515
"Seder Haolam" (Jose ben Chalafta),
   350
Self-incrimination, laws against, 140
Semikhah (placing hands on sacrifice),
   110–111, 242
Semikhat zekeinim (ordination of
   Elders), 121
Sepphoris, Pales., 232, 268, 284, 331,
   344, 381, 406, 409, 462, 479, 485,
   519, 575
   academy at, 416–417, 455, 525, 528,
      531, 569, 636, 640
   court in, 348, 536
   Hadrian's destruction of, 348
   uprising (351 C.E.), 468
Septimus Severus, emperor of Rome,
   41, 640, 641
Septuagint, 202, 225, 389, 577, 819*n*
Seraphim, 472
Severus. *See* Alexander Severus; Julius
   Severus; Septimus Severus
Sexual offenses, 427. *See also* Rape
Sexual relations, laws governing, 423
Shamayim (name of God), 614
Shammai (sage), 53, 107–115, 116, 120
Shammai, school of, 10, 108, 111–115,
   146, 150, 185, 188, 190, 191, 193,
   211, 479
   Mishnah, compiling of, 387
   revolutionary patriots and, 114–115
Shamua. *See* Eleazar ben Shamua
Shatnes, 159
Shavuot (Feast of Weeks), 27, 29, 191,
   246
Shchenziv, Babyl., 693
Shechem, Pales., 36, 38–39, 62, 375,
   426

Shechem, son of Chamor, 25
Shekhinah (majesty of God), 17, 111,
   206, 246, 250, 252, 272, 349, 490,
   508, 520–521, 541, 571, 614, 617,
   789*n*
Shefarom, Pales., academy at, 232,
   371
Shefatiah (son of King David), 99, 404,
   627
Shekalim, 95
Shem, academy of, 497
Shema (prayer), 23, 71, 109, 277, 336,
   386, 487, 547, 571, 576, 652
Shemaiah (Jewish leader), 53, 79,
   82–84, 85, 86, 95, 96, 97, 100, 108,
   111, 118, 120, 779*n*
Shem Hameforash (express name of
   God), 279, 281, 289, 785*n*–786*n*
Shemoneh Esrei (prayer), 99, 191, 201,
   400
Shenana, 838*n*
Shepherds, 140
Sherira Gaon, Epistle of, 494, 652, 680,
   684, 695, 716, 730, 738, 769, 771,
   844*n*
Sheshet, Rav, 587, 705, 735, 752–756
Shetach. *See* Simeon ben Shetach
Sheva ben Bichri, 539
Shila, Rav, 633, 642, 643, 669
Shilhi, Babyl., 752
Shiloah River, water from, 28–29,
   316–317
Shiloh, Pales., 36, 589
Shimei (brother of King David), 404
Shimei (son of Simon the Just), 48
Shimi bar Ashi, Rav, 744
Shimi bar Chiya (grandson of Rav),
   655
Shishach, Bar, 737
Shmuel bar Shilet, 650, 663, 829*n*
Shmuel bar Yitzchak, Rav, 602
Shmuel ben Nachmani, Rabbi,
   472–473, 474, 520, 522, 546–553,
   588, 595, 599, 815*n*
Shmuel Hakatan, Rabbi, 150, 191, 283
Shmuel Yarchina'ah of Nehardea,
   377–378, 414, 417, 556, 669–678,
   684, 688, 695, 700, 701, 707, 710,
   713, 725, 739, 838*n*
   children of, 674, 687
   death of, 708

father of, 670, 681
and Jehudah Hanasi, 377, 670, 671
and Jochanan, editor of Talmud,
    486–487, 670
legal opinions of, 672–675, 691
medical practice of, 670–671,
    673–674, 681, 690
modesty of, 677
moral and religious teachings of,
    676–677
and ordination, 377, 670, 677–678
and Rav, 633, 640, 642, 643, 653, 655,
    669, 674, 677
Shofar (ram's horn), 12, 151, 221, 245,
    445–446, 609, 621
Sicarii (patriotic band), 130
Sidon, Pales., 358, 359, 362, 433, 438
Sidra (academy at Nehardea), 642
Sifri, 9, 341, 792*n*
Sikra, Abba, 152–153
Silone family, 575
Simchat Beit Hashoeva, 128
Simeon. *See* Jehudah bar Simeon
Simeon (brother of Chiya bar Abba II),
    574, 575
Simeon (son of Hillel of Babylon), 121
Simeon, Rabbi (son of Jehudah
    Hanasi), 407, 410, 414, 415, 416
Simeon bar Abba, 464, 532, 561
Simeon bar Bari, Rabbi, 630
Simeon ben Azai, Rabbi, 23, 291,
    295–300, 368–369
Simeon ben Chalafta, Rabbi, 351,
    409–413, 534, 636
Simeon ben Eleazar, Rabbi, 481, 636
Simeon ben Gamaliel I, Rabban, 41,
    127–128, 132, 134–136, 163, 182,
    239, 282, 316, 623, 816*n*
Simeon ben Gamaliel II, Rabban,
    312–319, 324, 325, 330, 349, 356,
    363, 371, 372, 672
  mission of, to Babylonia, 321–322,
    792*n*
Simeon ben Jozadak, Rabbi, 480
Simeon ben Lakish (Resh Lakish),
    Rabbi, 414, 456–457, 486, 499–509,
    531, 559, 560, 574, 579, 809n
  on the Babylonians, 503–504
  and *beraitot*, 502
  death of, 474, 503, 507
  leaves academy, 502–503

and logic, use of, 500–501
maxims of, 505–509
moral qualities of, 501
pupils of, 567–568
and Rabbi Jochanan, 486, 499–503,
    504–505
and robbers, 499, 502–503, 504–505,
    507
Simeon ben Menasia, Rabbi, 378,
    394–395, 427, 623
Simeon ben Nathanel, 162
Simeon ben Shetach, 53, 71, 72, 73,
    76–78, 79, 91, 102–103, 128
Simeon ben Yochai, Rabbi, 271, 292,
    352–361, 365–366, 395, 396, 535,
    540, 650, 787*n*
  hiding in cave, 353–354, 360–361, 538
  on marriage, rulings of, 358
  and Romans, attitude toward,
    343–344, 352–353, 359
  and Torah, interpretation of,
    356–357, 359–360
Simeon ben Zoma, Rabbi, 291, 295,
    296, 299–302, 622, 790*n*
Simeon of Pakula, Rabbi, 191
Simlai bar Abba, Rabbi, 453, 473–474,
    515, 520, 554–558, 595, 634
Simon the Just, 5, 7, 44–49, 386, 429,
    777*n*
  and Alexander the Great, 37–38, 47
  customs introduced under, 48
  disciples of, 49
  wonders in Temple of, 45–46
Simunia, Pales., 415
"Sinai." *See* Joseph bar Chiya
Sinai, Mount, 7, 39, 204, 220–221,
    252, 483, 509, 511, 512–513, 542,
    622
Singers, in the Temple, 246
Sins, 349, 379, 380, 475, 476, 532, 542,
    623, 648, 666
  Jonathan ben Eleazar's seven, 521
  observance of Torah commandments
    and, 426–427
  original, 395. *See also* Tree of Knowl-
    edge
  of parents, 304
  of scholars, 243
  of women, punishment of, 245
Sira, Ben, 39, 620
Sisi. *See* Levi ben Sisi

Slander, 66–67, 291, 506, 521, 522, 538, 617
Slaughter, regulations governing, 97, 160, 332, 401, 425, 434, 484
Slaveowners, 437–439, 690
Slaves, 12, 77, 184, 382, 458, 537, 699
children of, 438, 653
freeing of, 159, 241, 315, 465, 710, 714
Jewish, 8, 159, 241, 437–438
and marriage, 351, 438, 653, 690
rights of, 437, 438, 583
women as, 438–439, 690
Slavery, 427, 568
Essene beliefs about, 31
prohibition against, 8
Sadducean laws on, 28
Snakes, 395, 474, 505, 593
Socrates, 329
Sod (interpretation of Torah), 789n
Sodom, Pales., 213, 434
Sofrim. See Scribes
Solomon, king of Israel, 35, 516, 541, 579
Song of Songs, 191, 274–275, 279, 297, 549, 782n
Sophistry, 463, 471, 712–713
Sotah (unfaithful wife), 117–119, 120, 160, 779n
Soul, 18, 27, 214, 589–590, 614, 693
Stealing, 169
Strabo, 430
Suburbs, 446
Suffering, 101, 208–209, 239, 277–278, 287, 295, 317, 368, 470, 496, 512
Hillel of Babylon on, 101
Jews' blame for, 475–476
sins of parents and, 304
Sukkot (Feast of Tabernacles), 9, 28, 29, 73, 109, 205–206, 244, 483, 621
"Sulamith" (Goldfaden), 821n
Supreme Court, 68, 79, 321. *See also* Courts; Sanhedrin
Sura, Babyl., 580, 626, 631, 643–649, 652–653, 654, 676
academy at, 626, 631, 643, 645, 648, 649, 652–654, 684, 694, 696–699, 700, 701, 708, 711, 715, 718, 725, 759, 761, 768, 770, 771, 844n
Suriel (angel), 238
Sylvester, bishop of Rome, 465

Symachos, 636
Synagogues, 445, 451, 489, 624, 648, 649, 758, 763–764
Syria, 47, 433, 640, 641, 750
Egyptian wars on, 51, 58
Hasmonean annexations in, 64
Parthian invasion of, 355
Roman rule in, 578
Syrian Greeks, 30, 52, 59, 63–64, 619

Tabbai (slave), 17, 439
Tabbai. *See* Jehudah ben Tabbai
Tacitus (Roman historian), 202
Tadmor, Syr. *See* Palmyra
Talmidei hakhamim, 14
Talmud, 463, 470, 492. *See also* Babylonian Talmud; Jerusalem Talmud
censorship of, 828n
laws in, codification of, 9–10
Pharisee authors of, 21
Tamalion, Bar, 356
Tamar, trial of, 581
Tanchum ben Chanilai, 541
Tannaim, 10, 89, 94, 391, 392, 394, 417, 421, 612–613, 628, 649, 802n
Targum Onkelos, 202, 226, 724
Tarphon, Rabbi, 109, 199, 238, 246–250, 252, 267, 292, 296, 336, 597, 644, 807n
disciples of, 342, 343, 344–345, 348, 362
Tavyomi Mar bar Rav Ashi, 767–770
Taxation, 140, 158, 451, 456, 462, 467, 470, 504, 561, 674, 679, 719, 763
Tax collectors, 140, 451, 461, 491, 575, 585, 601, 679, 715–716
Teachers, 70, 78, 624, 625
Tefillin. See Phylacteries
Temple, in Jerusalem, 55, 56, 69
First, 7, 8, 549, 594, 619
dead bones profaning, 40–41
destruction of, 8, 19, 35, 36, 41, 492
purchased by David, 479
Second, 7, 34, 316–317
Caligula's decree and, 122–123
destruction of, 36, 39, 41, 112, 133, 135–136, 148–151, 152, 155–158, 164, 166, 201, 241, 264, 273, 432,

439–440, 492, 541–542, 549–550,
594, 611, 619
Greek desecration of, 59
Julian the Apostate's promise to
restore, 750–751
restored by Hadrian, 210, 211, 213,
217–218, 442, 750
and Simon the Just, 45–46, 48
Ten Commandments, 215, 231, 249,
250, 551, 576, 594, 615
Ten Martyrs, 238, 250, 280–294, 363
Ten Tribes of Israel, 34, 35, 347
Tenant farmers, 436
Teradion. *See* Chanina ben Teradion
Theatre, Jews ridiculed in, 569–570
Theodosius I (the Great), emperor of
Rome, 466, 467, 763–764
Theodosius II, emperor of Rome, 466,
764–765
Theophil of Antioch (church-father),
472
Tiberias, Pales., 131, 268, 290, 296,
383, 384, 409, 455, 456, 462, 467,
479, 485, 513, 530, 569, 585, 587
academy at, 406, 411, 486, 494, 495,
561, 563, 580–581, 582, 583, 587,
600, 636–637, 640
Jews permitted to reside in, 354
uprising in (351 C.E.), 468
Tiberius, emperor of Rome, 123
Tiberius Alexander (Greek leader), 146
Tigris River, 611, 642, 643–644
Tishah b'av, fast of, 136, 317
Tithes, 23, 179–180, 192, 247–248,
284, 290–291, 396–397, 599, 782n
Hasmonean innovations, 64, 65–66
and Jehudah Hanasi's reforms, 374,
375–376
origin of laws regarding, 424
Titus, emperor of Rome, 144, 147, 148,
149, 158, 224, 269, 440–441, 550,
784n
Torah, 3, 10–20, 66, 167, 200, 203,
380, 405, 412, 474, 480, 515–516,
589, 590, 694. *See also Aggadah;
Halakhah; Midrash; Mishnah*
age of students of, 308–309, 319
books missing from, 588
crowns on letters of, 261
disputes over interpretations of, 230.

See also Bei Avidan
"fence around," 10–11, 608
four-branched system of expounding, 789n
Gentile interest in, 161
giving of, 20, 29, 220–221, 255, 261,
299, 359, 477, 509, 513, 551, 622
Greek translation of, 202, 314, 348
Hillel's renewal of, 100, 102, 103,
778n–779n
Hillel vs. Shammai on, 111, 114
and intercession with God, 550–551
Jewish rvolt and, 142, 143, 149–151,
262, 272–273, 295, 309, 318, 329,
787n
Jochanan, editor of Talmud, on,
484–485, 491–492, 497–498
laws at variance with, 240
and *Mishnah*, laws of, 389
number of commandments in, 556
Pharisees and the, 21–22
priests' monopoly of, 49
reading of, 8
Samaritan claims about, 39
study of, in Roman times, 129,
133–134
superfluous words of, hidden meanings in, 237, 255, 260–261,
298–299, 368, 386–387
teaching of
to *amei aratzim*, 521
in street, 515, 520, 624
to women, 203, 297, 337
Torture, self-inflicted, 428
Tosefta, Tosefot, 9, 341, 364, 367, 387,
405, 517, 569, 584, 759, 780n
Totafot, 15–16
Tov (good), 576
Trade prohibitions, 228–229
Trajan, emperor of Rome, 211, 441
Trans-Jordania, 434
Travelers, 451
Tree of Knowledge, 335, 395, 477, 513
Tree of Life, 545
Trinity, 17, 478
Truth, 617
Turba, Marcius, 441–442
Tyre, Pales., 37, 438, 575
Tzitzit, 300, 467
Tzitzit Hakeset, Ben, 145

Ukba the Exilarch, Mar, 628, 680–683, 684, 688, 693, 726, 741, 755
Ula (pupil of R. Jochanan), Rabbi, 500–501, 685–686, 726
Ula ben Kushab, 539
Unicorns, 577
Urim and *tummim*, 8, 610
Usha, Pales., Sanhedrin at, 232–234, 237–238, 242, 284, 285, 312, 324, 341, 343, 359, 367, 370
  regulations adopted at, 234–235
  seat of reorganized Sanhedrin, 320
Usury, 350, 636. *See also* Money, lending

Valagesia, king of Parthians, 355
Varus, emperor. *See* Lucius Varus
Vespasian, emperor of Rome, 147–148, 149, 153–154, 155, 164–165, 701
Viliages, 443, 449–451
Vineyard of Jabneh, 150
Virginity, 28
Vows, 325, 425, 589. *See also* Oaths

Wages, payment of, 245
Wanderer's Stone, 91
Wanderers to Usha, 234
Weasel and well, story of, 583–584, 821*n*
Werbel, Eliyahu Mordechai, 821*n*
White mules, 398–399
Widows
  garments of, taken in pawn, 357
  property of, 675
  remarriage of, 125, 140, 730, 753. *See also* Marriage, levirate
Wild beasts, 203
Winding oven (*tanur shel achnai*), 193, 207
Wine, 32, 48, 210, 350, 422, 428, 432, 433, 442, 453, 615, 736
  on Passover, 610
  on Sabbath, 609
  of Samaritans, 459
Witchcraft, 76–77, 326, 327, 423
Wives, 13, 56, 240, 253–254, 292–293, 619–620. *See also* widows

  of cohanim, and entitlement to tithes, 290–291
  deserted, 12
  duties of, 660
  non-Jewish, expelling of, 36–37
  as property of husbands, 16
  property rights of, 78, 235, 667, 675
  Roman violations of, 335–336
  unfaithful (*sotah*), 117–119, 120, 160, 779*n*
Women, 56, 337–338, 350. *See also* Divorce; Marriage; Wives; Widows
  age at marriage of, and rejection of husbands, 113, 276
  chastity of, 28, 335–336, 623, 676–677, 687
  and childbearing, 407
  Gentile, beauty of, 128
  and jewelry, wearing on Sabbath, 417
  morality of, during Roman times, 160, 167–168, 335–336
  names of, 629
  and phylacteries, wearing of, 16–17
  as proselytes, 142
  punishment of, 245
  purification of, 29, 426
  responsibilities of, 407–408
  rights of, 629, 659–660
  as slaves, 438–439, 690
  testimony by, 139, 140
  Torah, learning, 203, 297, 337

Yair. *See* Pinchas ben Yair
Yalta (wife of Nachman bar Jacob), 629, 685–686, 690, 693, 711
Yarchina'ah. *See* Shmuel Yarchina'ah
Yemar, Rav, 774
Yeshebab the Scribe, Rabbi, 284
Yetzer hara (evil desire), 244
Yezdigerd II, king of Persia, 761
Yezdigerd III, king of Persia, 768, 769
Yibum, 113, 232. *See also* Marriage, levirate
Yitzchak bar Tavlai, Rabbi, 586
Yitzchak ben Eleazar, Rabbi, 498
Yitzchak the Blacksmith (Napcha), Rabbi, 581, 586–591, 594
Yochai. *See* Simeon ben Yochai

Yochai (father of R. Simeon), 271, 352, 369, 787*n*

Yom Kippur. *See* Day of Atonement

Yuhasin (Book of Genealogies), 282, 366, 367, 401

Zachariah (prophet), 7, 478, 527, 589, 781*n*

Zachariah ben Ishmael, 54

Zadok (pupil of Antigonos of Socho), 26, 50

Zadok ben Eleazar, Rabbi, 153, 164–167

Zakkai. *See* Jochanan ben Zakkai

Zealots, 127, 145, 147, 152, 154, 440

Zechariah ben Hakatzav, Rabbi, 167–168

Zedekiah, king of Judah, 437

Zeira, Rabbi (Babylonian Amora), 393, 475, 575, 595, 597–603, 709, 727

Zeira bar Chanina, 579

Zenobiah, queen of Palmyra, 547, 578–579, 697

Zephaniah, Book of, 704

Zeraim, 508

Zerubabel, 36, 54, 610

Zeus, 40, 59

Zimri, 74, 546–547

Zion, 322, 592

Zivtai (scholar), 334

Zohar, Book of, 361, 396

Zoma. *See* Simeon ben Zoma

Zoroastrians, Zoroastrianism, 493–494, 768–769

Zuti, Rav, 774

Zutra, Mar, exilarch of Babylonia, 759, 761